Africa, with its mix of statute, custom and religion, is at the centre of the debate about law and its impact on gender relations. This is because of the centrality of the gender question and its impact on the cultural relativism debate within human rights. It is therefore important to examine critically the role of law, broadly constructed, in African societies. This book focuses on women's experiences in the family. This is because the lives of women continue to be lived out largely in the private domain, where the right to privacy is used to conceal unequal treatment of women, which is justified by invoking 'custom' and 'tradition'. The book shows how law and its interpretation is used to disenfranchise women, resulting in their being deprived of land and other property that they may have helped to accumulate. It also considers issues of violence within the home and examines the issue of female genital cutting. Moreover, the book considers African women's reproductive rights, as well as participation in development and decision making. A major theme of the book is a consideration of the linkages of constitutional and international human rights norms with local values. This is done using feminist tools of analysis. The book considers the provisions of the Protocol to the African Charter on Human and Peoples' Rights on the Rights of Women, which was adopted by the African Union in July 2003.

Women, Law and Human Rights

An African Perspective

Fareda Banda

·HART·
PUBLISHING
OXFORD – PORTLAND OREGON
2005

Hart Publishing
Oxford and Portland, Oregon

Published in North America (US and Canada) by
Hart Publishing
c/o International Specialized Book Services
920 NE 58th Avenue, Suite 300
Portland, OR 97213-3786
USA
Tel: +1 503-287-3093 or toll-free: (1) 800-944-6190
Fax: +1 503 280 8832
E-mail: orders@isbs.com
Website: www.isbs.com

Hart Publishing, Salters Boatyard, Folly Bridge,
Abingdon Rd, Oxford, OX1 4LB
Telephone: +44 (0)1865 245533 Fax: +44 (0)1865 794882
email: mail@hartpub.co.uk
Website: http//:www.hartpub.co.uk

British Library Cataloguing in Publication Data
Data Available

ISBN-13: 978-1-84113-128-3 (hardback)
ISBN-10: 1-84113-128-8 (hardback)

Typeset by Hope Services, Abingdon in Minion 10/12 pt
Printed and bound in Great Britain by
Biddles Ltd, King's Lynn

We read about other people, reflect on them and never think that we ourselves, the readers, could be our own book to read and reflect upon; that we could become the subject of a book we could write about ourselves and watch ourselves become somehow more important in our own eyes because we have become a subject of reflection.

Njabulo Ndebele *The Cry of Winnie Mandela: A Novel*

If I don't fight my battles now, who would fight them for me, and when?

Ama Ata Aidoo *The Girl Who Can*

FOR MY MOTHER AND FATHER—WITH MY LOVE
AND THANKS ALWAYS

Fari

PREFACE

My father is a great raconteur. Growing up, he regaled me with stories of life as a migrant. He had moved from Nyasaland (now Malawi) to Southern Rhodesia (now Zimbabwe) to find work. Having matriculated and graduated standard six (high school) he considered himself to be an educated man, hampered only by a lack of money to undergo the necessary training to enable him to pursue a career as a teacher, and also by the lack of educational opportunities available to African people in Nyasaland and later Rhodesia. All too soon he came to learn that his education did not count for anything. His blackness precluded any notions that he too had human dignity. Although told with humour, his stories are poignant tales of discrimination and dispossession, but also dignity and strength. They show an indomitable spirit and finally the stubbornness that is sometimes said to characterise his daughter.

Of the many stories that he has told me, two come to mind. I will call them the bicycle story and the shirt story. First the bicycle story. Tired of walking from his job as a clerk for a bakery in the city centre to his home in the 'African township', my father decided that it was time that he bought a bicycle. He went to a bicycle shop in the capital city Harare, then Salisbury, and attempted to gain entry to the shop to examine the bicycles on display more closely. Before he could cross the threshold the owner (sometimes called the white man, or with a laugh the British man) denied him entry. My father explained his mission. Still the white man did not budge. There was a policy that Africans were not allowed into the shop. But how, my father asked was he to acquire a bicycle? He was pointed to a stable door at the side of the shop. 'From there,' said the white man. That is where Africans could go to look at the bicycles in the shop. My father proceeded to the stable door and from the limited selection of bicycles, pointed to his chosen one. He was told the price and duly handed over the money. At that point the owner of the shop beckoned him into the shop. 'But Africans are not allowed into the shop,' he said. 'Oh no, you can come in,' said the owner. My father persisted, 'But you said that Africans were not allowed into the shop.' Patiently, the owner said that he could come in. 'How can I break the rule?' my father asked. Frustrated the owner told him that it was acceptable for him to enter the shop because he had given him permission to come in. At this point, my father came out with a novel solution. 'Well,' he said, 'you sold me the bicycle through the window (stable door), so you give me the bicycle through the window.' By this time the owner was exasperated by this obduracy, but still keen to make his sale; 'It is all right for you to come in and pick up your bicycle,' he reiterated, 'I have given you permission.' My father was having none of this. He saw that his humanity was only worth recognising when he had something that the white man wanted—his money. The rest of the time he could be denigrated and excluded—treated as a second-class citizen. This was not for him. He refused to go into the shop, and eventually had his money returned.

Switch to a different continent and a different era: twenty-first-century Britain and, to be precise, 55 years after the first bicycle encounter. Formally colonialism is at an end, as is apartheid. This time the bicycle story is told from my perspective, an academic lawyer teaching in an institution that claims for itself the title 'world leading centre in the study of Asia and Africa'.[1] Like my father before me, I am considered to be educated, having been the first black African woman from my country to graduate with a doctorate in law from the University of Oxford. Six years after I joined the educational institution, I made an alarming discovery. Through a process of detective work, I discovered that I had been getting paid less than white colleagues whose academic qualifications do not match my own, whose teaching loads were lighter and whose research profiles were not as good. Like my father before me, I came to the realisation that that while my labour was worthy of use and exploitation, my humanity and dignity was not worth honouring or validating. This disregard was shown by paying me less than white colleagues. I could not enter the 'bicycle shop' that is equal pay for all, because I was not constructed as an equal, but an inferior.[2] Despite appearances, it turns out, that like my father before me, I had been conversing with my colleagues from the stable door. However, unlike my father, I had never been made aware (explicitly) that there was a policy of exclusion operating. Egged on by my mother, who had long grown weary of the seemingly endless examples/experiences of discrimination that I had hitherto endured, I sued. I obtained a legal acknowledgement of discrimination and, specifically, two declarations that the institution (bicycle shop) had violated race relations legislation and legislation on equal pay by paying me less than a white man. Compensation for injury to feelings was made a part of the award for restitution of back pay.[3]

The point of the bicycle story is this: often those who claim for themselves the mantle of 'civilisation, fair play and justice' can only ever see those qualities from a perspective that ensures that the beneficiaries are people like themselves. This is what has lead to the African-American aphorism that says when white people

---

[1] See http://www.soas.ac.uk

[2] On entry/exclusion policies see P Williams *The Alchemy of Race and Rights* (Cambridge, Harvard University Press, 1991) 41.

[3] *Dr F Banda v School of Oriental and African Studies* Unreported Employment Tribunal Case No. 2206025/03. R Verkaik 'A Lesson in Racism' *Independent* (London, 17 May 2004), also available at http://www.africaspeaks.com/weblog/archives/00000201.htm; 'UK's Shameful Lesson in Racism' *Daily Mirror* (Harare, 28 May 2004). See also A Sivaramakrishnan 'An Under-Caste in Britain?' *Hindu* (24 May 2004); S Soundararajan 'Adequately Addressed' *Hindu* (27 May 2004); T Sewell 'It Takes a Race Case for Firms to Listen' *Voice* (London, 4 June 2004).

speak of justice, they mean just us.[4] As a teacher of human rights of women, my father's bicycle story has often struck me as a perfect metaphor for the exclusion of women from participation in norm making and the full enjoyment of their human rights. Like the limited rights of entry offered to my father on production of the acceptable entrée (money), so too women[5] find themselves excluded unless they are prepared to accept the often derisory and second-rate benefits offered them. Surrendering their humanity is the price of entry. Only then are they 'permitted' some benefits—but only as befits their status as not fully human. For powerful men and elites—justice really does mean 'just us'.

Now on to the shirt story. My father walks past the leading department store in the city and sees a shirt that he likes in the window. Again he tries to enter the shop. The policy of exclusion is again in force. The 'helpful' salesman asks him to point out the shirt that has caught his eye. My father does so. It is brought to him at the door of the shop. He is told how much it costs. Ever the 'difficult' African, another adjective used to describe his daughter, he asks if it is possible for him to try the shirt. He is told that he cannot—black people are not permitted into the shop. 'But what if it does not fit?' he asks. 'Well, just take it and try it at home.' Liking the shirt and no doubt reasoning that he cannot exit every retail transaction, he pays for the shirt and takes it home where he finds that it does not fit. If they do not let black people into the shop he thinks they are hardly likely to accept the return of 'soiled' shirts from Africans, so he keeps it.

Again from the perspective of human rights of women, the shirt story reminds me that often women, and, in international relations, Africa, are asked to don (accept) shirts (norms) that do not fit them. We are told that law is neutral and that it treats everyone the same, but we know that it does not. We know this because, unlike the men who are allowed to factor in their needs in the making of the shirt, and indeed who get to try before they buy, we come to a finished product and are told to take it or leave it. We take it, but it does not fit us or our needs. However, unlike my father, we do not have the choice of exercising the exit option and deciding to go shirtless, or buying our shirts from a more inclusive supplier. It is often either use the law as constructed, even if it is discriminatory, or 'lump it'.

My father first told me the shirt story when I was 14 and in high school. The uniform for my school was held exclusively by the store that had sold my father a shirt at the door all those years ago. We went to replenish my uniform together. 'You know, Fareda,' he said, 'I have not been in this shop since 1948 after they sold me a shirt from the door that did not fit. But for you, and this uniform, I would never have come in here again.' There is a twist to the tale. I was at the same high school as the two granddaughters of the proprietor of the store. I am not sure that the

---

[4] C Mills *The Racial Contract* (Ithaca, Cornell University Press, 1997).
[5] Not all women.

shirt will ever properly fit, but the fact that people like me, who had previously been barred, were allowed entry not only to the shop but to formerly whites-only schools, without any negative effects on either the store, the school or their patrons and pupils, shows that the inclusion of (Africans) women in the conversation that is norm making and the enjoyment of human rights does not have to lead to a loss of rights for existing rights holders. It just means that our collective humanity is honoured—surely a win-win situation for all.

This book explores both the bicycle and shirt stories from within the framework of law and human rights. It substitutes the voices of women of the African continent for that of my father, and hopes that their stories will engage, challenge and stimulate you as his stories have done me over the years. With any luck, they may also raise the occasional chuckle.

ACKNOWLEDGEMENTS

I sometimes feel as if I have lived many lives. There have been so many people who have helped me and carried me along life's journey. These are just some of them—and apologies in advance if I leave you out. If this acknowledgement reads like the sleeve notes to an R&B album, then sorry, but I do not intend to repeat this experience in a hurry.

The first person I need to thank is my beloved grandmother with whom I spent my formative years. My purest and happiest memories always have you in them. For my brother Adam—one of the most optimistic people I know. The person who always manages to pick me up when I am low, and who reminds me of how far we have travelled—not least on the trips *kumusha* (to the village) in the fourth-class carriages of Rhodesia Railways—sleeping sitting up and listening to Ngwaru Mapundo twanging that stupid banjo all night. As you sometimes tell me, if we survived that, then we can survive anything! With you in my life, I know that to be true. And for my niece Naomi, don't let anyone tell you that you cannot be a doctor and a fashion designer at the same time. They may not be able to, but you certainly can.

For Dorothy Twiss, who taught 'her girls' that anything boys can do, girls can do too—well, better actually. Alice Armstrong kept up on that theme, saying to me 'when you go to grad school'. Until you said it, the thought had not entered my mind. Thank you. For the wonderful Mavis Maclean, co-supervisor for my doctoral thesis. Thanks for seeing 'A:suffer.doc' through to the end with me. Writing this book (not based on the thesis) I have tried to remember your injunction—'It's only words on a page.' Probably, like this acknowledgement, way too many words on a page. Alan Milner, the other co-supervisor—who still tells it like it is, and who manages to crack me up every time we speak—which, by the way, is not often enough.

I have often thought that if integrity had a face, it would look like John Eekelaar, the best and most supportive mentor anyone could ever wish for. Together with Pia, Gran, Catherine and Louise, you have cared for me, supported me and embraced me within your family, and I thank you.

The beginning of 2004 was quite challenging for me. That I am still standing is in no small part thanks to Robin Lewis of Bindman and Partners. For the many kindnesses, the lessons learnt and, most importantly, for the laughter, thank you. You returned me to myself stronger, more positive and peaceful than I had been for a long time, and for that I shall be always be grateful to you.

For Christine Chinkin, icon, mentor and now best of all, friend—you have taught me so much about human rights of women; your spirit and enthusiasm are inspirational. I hope that we continue to work together for many years to come—not least because Prêt à Manger and all the cake shops in London would fold if we stopped. Thank you.

I should like to acknowledge the kindness and intellectual companionship of Lynn Welchman. For my 'sister', or more accurately sistren, Juliet Ssentongo, for always being such an enormous support, I thank you. I should also like to thank Malen Gordoa, Susana Arrese, and all at the Institute for the Sociology of Law in Onati, Spain for the wonderful times spent 'working' at the Institute. Special thanks to all at Antonn's. I am grateful to Bart Rwezaura for the encouraging emails from across the miles and for reading part of this manuscript. Theresa Piconto Novales and Manolo Calvo, my generous and constant friends in Spain—thank you. My two PhD students Tina Akoto and Thoko Kaime—who keep me updated—OK, I acknowledge that without you I would be ignorance central—thanks. Many people helped with materials and encouragement. They include Ulrike Wanitzek, Sylvia Tamale, Anne Hellum, Rachel Murray, Chaloka Beyani, Craig Liddle, Patricia Daley, Chuma Himonga, Ahmed Motala, Simukai Utete, Rumbi Mabuwa, Gina Torrey, Patrick Smith, Enid Tyler and Ibrahima Kane. I thank them all and apologise to those I have not mentioned by name.

Other friends I would like to acknowledge include Patrick and Marina Milmo, for your generosity of spirit (and food!) and support over the years. Ted and Margaret Thomas, have been the warmest and kindest of friends—thank you. For Sowon Park and my godson Theo Suh, who have always been there for me—Theo making me laugh and Sowon—for being my best pal and helping me keep British Telecom in profit. Thanks to Nancy Naro for friendship and cheesecake, and Eileen Wood—where do I begin?

Richard Hart and the team at Hart Publishing deserve my thanks for seeing the project through to completion—love the cover of my beautiful mother! I would like to pay special tribute to Sarah Newton who edited the book with skill and diplomacy—not once did she ask if I had ever been introduced to grammar or a spell-checker! I enjoyed working with her and am grateful to her for kindness and support throughout the editorial process.

And finally—my parents.

For my father, the man who can make me laugh like no other, the person who told me that my humanity was never to be the subject of compromise or negotiation, and who, with my mother, taught me the importance of standing up to discrimination. The price has sometimes been high and the consequences painful. Nevertheless your support, humour and courage (who else would dare to call me picanini missis?) have sustained me.

To the woman who has known me for longer than I have known myself, who understands me better than I understand myself, and who has carried me and supported me through some of my darkest moments and cheered me on at the happiest times—my mother. I know just how much (of your life and dreams) you gave up so that I could achieve my dreams. Not once have you complained. How do I begin to tell you what your love has meant to me over the years and how grateful I am to have you, the kindest and most generous woman, as my mother?

This book is for my parents with my love.

.

CONTENTS

TABLE OF CASES

NATIONAL JURISDICTIONS

Namibia

Nigeria

South Africa

EUROPEAN CASE LAW

INTER AMERICAN SYSTEM CASE LAW

UNITED NATIONS

INTERNATIONAL CRIMINAL TRIBUNAL FOR RWANDA

HUMAN RIGHTS COMMITTEE CASE LAW

STATUTES AND LEGAL MATERIALS

AFRICA

ICCPR

ICESCR

Optional Protocol to CEDAW

CRC

DEVAW

INTERNATIONAL LAW—AFRICA

ACRWC

African Protocol on Women's Rights

REGIONAL TREATIES

Arab States

EAC

SADC Addendum on Violence 1998

INTERNATIONAL LAW—AMERICAN STATES

INTERNATIONAL LAW—EUROPE

1

Introduction

'The World's Most Popular Man Reaches 80 and Ponders Buying a Wife in Exchange for 60 Cows.' This was the headline that announced Nelson Mandela's marriage to Graca Machel in July 1998.[1] The first line of the article warned 'The world's feminists had better brace themselves'. Those two lines were loaded with cultural assumptions. The use of the verb 'to buy' to describe the custom of *lobolo*,[2] common to many patrilineal societies in Africa and an essential element of the customary marriage contract of those societies, was associated with purchase. The analogy was not dissimilar to the purchase of human beings associated with slavery. In engaging in such questionable practices, Mandela had evidently disappointed his liberal admirers in the west. The opening sentence warning feminists to brace themselves assumed that Mandela had fallen short of the feminist standard and would incur the wrath of said people. Although not defined, the *Guardian*'s 'feminism' was evidently of the western variety. As an African feminist, I wondered what Graca Machel would make of this construction of her marriage. I could see how difficult it would have been for Mandela not to give *lobolo* for his wife. To have failed to respect the local custom in this way would have been tantamount to him rejecting the 'ways of our people' and by extension our people. Mandela's fall from grace did not last long, for in another newspaper piece[3] written to mark the fiftieth anniversary of the Universal Declaration of Human Rights 1948 (UDHR), Mandela was said to be the embodiment of the principles of the UDHR. However, unlike the earlier article that had concentrated on his private life, this article focused on his fight for civil and political rights for his people. Clearly then there were two distinct Mandelas. One was the disappointing African patriarch who bought wives, whereas the other was the example of everything that was decent, principled and good about humankind and highlighted the best of his public persona.

The juxtaposition of the views presented in these two articles started me thinking. Was the representation of Mandela as a buyer of wives any more than the

---

[1] *Guardian* (17 July 1998). The *Guardian* is a left of centre newspaper published in London.
[2] Loosely translated here as bridewealth.
[3] *Independent* (6 December 1998).

vaguely essentialist ramblings of the western media, examples of which abound daily? How was one to square this 'particularisation' with the universalising of Mandela's prison experience and political life as evoking values to which all societies should aspire? It soon became clear that the representations of Mandela themselves offered a commentary on the perennial debates over the universality of human rights.[4] Mandela as the embodiment of civil and political rights was the 'universal', but Mandela in private sphere mode was more problematic. Arguably this juxtaposition is reflected in international debates over human rights. There are human rights over which there is universal consensus. These include the right to life, the right to be free from degrading and inhuman treatment and torture, and the right not to be enslaved. Less clear, and often the subject of intense debate, are rights more closely associated, though not exclusively, with 'private sphere' violations. These would include the right to choose a spouse, to be free from interference in one's personal life and, for women, the right to be treated the same as men in their societies. It is the last right to be free from discrimination based on sex and gender that has proved to be one of the most contentious at both international and national levels. The equitable resolution of that problem has been the raison d'être of feminist movements across the ages and across continents. Although the naming of the problem may have varied from group to group and the strategies for challenging women's inequality may also have differed, the goal has always been the same—or has it? Although the *Guardian* article assumed a common position amongst women who call themselves feminists, the vast feminist literature clearly shows that such commonalities cannot be taken for granted. What one finds then, is that the universal/local debate in human rights is mirrored by the 'we', us and them debates that occur amongst women the world over.[5]

This book seeks to explore both those issues. It does so by examining the position of women[6] in Africa and seeing what, if any, role law can play in their empowerment efforts. 'Law' is at the best of times a loaded concept.[7] In the African context law is plural and complex.[8] What does one understand by the term law, who does it protect, whose interests does it serve, how and why?[9] It will be shown

---

[4] Examples abound: M Jacobsen and O Bruun (eds) *Human Rights and Asian Values: Contesting National Identities and Cultural Representations in Asia* (London, Curzon Press, 2000); A An Na'im *Human Rights in Cross-Cultural Perspectives* (Philadelphia, University of Pennsylvania Press, 1992).

[5] The Mandela analogy was first used in F Banda 'Global Standards: Local Values' (2003) 17 *International Journal of Law, Policy and the Family* 1 at 1.

[6] This is not a book about all women in Africa—clearly that would be an impossible task for even the most assiduous of researchers. It makes no claims to speak for or indeed represent the experiences of all the women of the continent.

[7] T Dahl *Women's Law: An Introduction to Feminist Jurisprudence* (Oslo, Norwegian University Press, 1987).

[8] C Bowman and A Kuenyehia (eds) *Women and Law in Sub-Saharan Africa* (Accra, SEDCO Publishing, 2003).

[9] A Manji 'Imagining Women's "Legal World": Towards a Feminist Theory of Legal Pluralism in Africa' (1994) 8 *Social and Legal Studies* 434; M Maboreke 'Understanding Law in Zimbabwe' in A Stewart (ed) *Gender, Law and Social Justice* (Oxford, Blackstone, 2000) 101.

how the interpretation of law, particularly that related to issues of custom and sometimes religion, is used to disentitle women from, amongst other things, acquiring or managing property. A major theme of the book is a consideration of the linkages between constitutional and international law, human rights norms and local personal laws.

The emergence of human rights as one of the dominant discourses means that the book also explores the impact and use of human rights norms to challenge gender ascriptions within the African continent. Although presented here as a given, the human rights movement is not without its critics and sceptics.[10] Debates about the suitability of transplanting human rights from their western Enlightenment origins to other societies have jostled with counter claims that human rights norms can be found in all societies. More recently still, the contestations over the uses and misuses of the human rights discourse have shifted to a critique of globalisation and the international political field that has the dominant north using the language of rights, good governance and democracy to impose upon southern states northern economic and political ideologies.[11] The argument is that northern imperialism continues to reign, albeit wearing a different guise. Non-western societies are constructed as backward and needing salvation that only the north can provide.[12] The fact that northern states are themselves complicit in human rights violations, and that they ignore or minimise human rights abuses within their own societies, reinforces the sense of injustice felt by those in the south who hear a message of 'do as I say and not as I do'. The powerlessness of southern states to challenge these double standards leaves some with a view of the world that is analogous to that of the hierarchical structure envisioned by Roman family law, with the north as the all powerful paterfamilias (head of the household) while the south comprises the women and children of the family—voiceless and subject to the whims of the omnipotent father.

Women's rights in Africa are explored by looking at various human rights instruments, including the African Charter on Human and Peoples' Rights 1981 (the African Charter)[13] the Convention on the Elimination of all Forms of Discrimination against Women 1979 (CEDAW)[14] and the African Charter on the

---

[10] D Kennedy 'The International Human Rights Movement: Part of the Problem?' (2002) 15 *Harvard Human Rights Journal* 101. See too rejoinder by H Charlesworth 'Author! Author! A Response to David Kennedy' (2002) 15 *Harvard Human Rights Journal* 127.

[11] Here it must be noted that this ideology now appears to have been voluntarily embraced by African states. This can most clearly be seen in the Constitutive Act of the African Union 2000 available at http://www.africa-union.org: see the preamble, the objectives in arts 3(g) and 3(h), the principles in art 4(m).

[12] M Mutua 'Savages, Victims, and Saviors: The Metaphor of Human Rights' (2001) 42 *Harvard International Law Journal* 201.

[13] African Charter on Human and Peoples' Rights (26 June 1981) OAU Doc CAB/LEG/67/3REV 5, reprinted in (1982) 21 *International Legal Materials* 59. See also Constitutive Act of the African Union 2000 art 3(h).

[14] Convention on the Elimination of All Forms of Discrimination against Women 1979 1249 UNTS 13.

Rights and Welfare of the Child 1990 (ACRWC).[15] The book also focuses on the Protocol to the African Charter on Human and Peoples' Rights on the Rights of Women in Africa 2003[16] (hereafter African Protocol on Women's Rights). What do we learn about the universality or otherwise of human rights, particularly as they relate to their implementation on the African continent?

The issue of gender is particularly important to the discussion. As opposed to sex, which focuses on biological and physical differences between men and women,[17] the concept of gender[18] is more complex:

> The term 'gender' refers to the socially constructed roles of men and women that are ascribed to them on the basis of their sex, in public and private life . . . Gender roles are contingent on a particular socio-economic, political and cultural context, and are affected by other factors, including age, race, class or ethnicity. Gender roles are learned, and vary widely within and between cultures. As social constructs they can change.[19]

The Catholic Church, amongst other (religious) groups, has long argued for a narrow construction of gender. The Vatican rejects the definition of gender as encompassing socio-structural and historical constructions of the roles of masculinity and femininity within any given society, in favour of a more biologically deterministic sex model.[20] This is an attempt to avoid engaging with issues of sexuality, which in fairness is not a problem unique to the Catholic Church.[21]

---

[15] African Charter on the Rights and Welfare of the Child 1990 available from www.africa-union.org.

[16] Protocol to the African Charter on Human and Peoples' Rights on the Rights of Women in Africa 2003. Assembly/AU/Dec 14(II), Decision on the Draft Protocol to the African Charter on Human and Peoples' Rights Relating to the Rights of Women available at http://www.africa.union.org. See Appendix A in this book. Gender equality is promoted in the Constitutive Act of the African Union in the preamble, and art 4(l).

[17] This is put very simply and does not tell whole story. Sex is not necessarily fixed for all time. It is possible for a person to change sex. *Goodwin v The United Kingdom* (2002) 35 EHRR 18. It is also important to acknowledge the existence of inter-sex people who are born with both sets of genital organs. V Baird *Sex, Love and Homophobia* (London, Amnesty International, 2004) 53–59. Finally it is as well to acknowledge the linkage between sex and gender, not least that sex is the underpinning of gender discrimination.

[18] See J Davison *Gender, Lineage, and Ethnicity in Southern Africa* (Oxford, Westview, 1997) 31–41, especially 32 for gender, and 234–38; S Tamale *When Hens Begin to Crow: Gender and Parliamentary Politics in Uganda* (Boulder, Westview Press, 1999) 28–30.

[19] Trends Regarding the Integration of a Gender Perspective into the Work of the United Nations Human Rights Treaty Bodies, Report by the Secretary-General, submitted to the 10th Meeting of Persons Chairing Human Rights Treaty Bodies (3 September 1998) UN Doc HRI/MC/1998/6 at para 16. See also United Nations *1999 World Survey on the Role of Women in Development: Globalization, Gender and* Work (New York, United Nations, 1999) ix.

[20] D Buss 'Robes, Relics and Rights: The Vatican and the Beijing Conference on Women' (1998) 7 *Social and Legal Studies* 339 at 345. See also definition of gender in the Rome Statute of the International Criminal Court 1998 UN Doc CONF.183/9 art 7(3).

[21] A Lorde *Sister Outsider: Essays and Speeches* (New York, Crossing Press, 1984); I Amadiume *Male Daughters, Female Husbands: Gender and Sex in an African Society* (London, Zed Press, 1987) 9. Cf O Nnaemeka 'Introduction: Reading the Rainbow' in O Nnaemeka (ed) *Sisterhood: Feminisms and Power from Africa to the Diaspora* (Asmara, Africa World Press, 1998) 1 at 7. But see P McFadden 'Sexual Pleasure as Feminist Choice' in (2004) *Feminist Africa* at http://www.feministafrica.org/ 2level.html; M Hames 'The Women's Movement and Lesbian and Gay Struggles in South Africa' (2004) *Feminist Africa* at http://www.feministafrica.org/2level.html.

A topic which takes up a great deal of time and space in both feminist and human rights discourse is that of 'culture',[22] here broadly defined to include social practices, customs, laws, morals, dress, music and arts.[23] For the present purposes discussions of 'culture' are confined to the first three issues identified. 'Cultures' (for all societies are composites of plural cultures, some indigenous, some absorbed through contact with other cultures) can be both positively and negatively construed. Although often presented as fixed, timeless and immutable sets of norms, cultures are contested, contingent and historically located.

Central as it is to the construction of gender, culture is particularly important to women, who are often seen as the embodiment of cultural identity. Entrusted with the upkeep of culture and tradition, women are often left with little choice but to acquiesce in the group or collective definitions thereof. However, there are examples in this book of women contesting negative and outdated cultural constructions of gender in their societies. There are examples too of enormous resistance to these contestations by both 'status quo cultural rights holders' and cultural interpreters, not least courts. In navigating the minefield that is 'culture', I am guided by Rao's four point 'questionnaire':

> First, what is the status of the speaker? Second, in whose name is the argument from culture advanced? Third, what is the degree of participation in culture formation of the social groups primarily affected by the cultural practices in question? Fourth, what is culture anyway?[24]

A proper understanding of gender requires not only the interrogation of 'cultural frameworks' but also the impact of religion, which sometimes interacts with 'culture' to produce its own cultural-religious hybrid.[25] By their very nature religions are based on doctrinal beliefs grounded in faith. These doctrinal beliefs are therefore hard to challenge, and indeed to challenge them is in itself often constructed as a betrayal of faith.[26] For Chekir the answer lies in secularism:

---

[22] U Narayan *Dislocating Cultures: Identities, Traditions, and Third-World Feminism* (New York, Routledge, 1997).

[23] T Bennett *Customary Law in South Africa* (Cape Town, Juta, 2004) 78–80.

[24] A Rao 'The Politics of Gender and Culture in International Human Rights Discourse' in J Peters and A Wolper (eds) *Women's Rights, Human Rights: International Feminist Perspectives* (New York, Routledge, 1995) 167 at 168. See also A An Na'im 'Cultural Transformation and Normative Consensus on the Best Interests of the Child' (1994) 8 *International Journal of Law, Policy and the Family* 62 at 76–77.

[25] Davison above n 18 at 40.

[26] See generally S Bruce *Politics and Religion* (Cambridge, Polity Press, 2003); A An Na'im (ed) *Islamic Family Law in a Changing World: A Global Resource Book* (London, Zed Press, 2002) xii; S Ali 'Development of the International Norm of Non-Discrimination on the Basis of Sex: An Evaluation of Women's Human Rights in Islam and International Law' in A Stewart (ed) *Gender, Law and Social Justice* (Oxford, Blackstone, 2000) 45 at 47; J Kerr 'From "Opposing" to "Proposing": Finding Proactive Global Strategies for Feminist Futures' in J Kerr, E Sprenger and A Symington (eds) *The Future of Women's Rights* (London, Zed Press, 2004) 14 at 20–22.

There needs to be a clear distinction made between religion and politics, since as long as the patriarchal order continues to be connected in people's minds with religion and politics, attempts to combat it are hampered by the fear of attacking people's faith and religious freedom.[27]

However, there are feminist scholars who argue for an engagement with religion from within the faith.[28] They argue that religions such as Islam do not discriminate against women. Quite the contrary. Women's equality is guaranteed within the tenets of the religion. In states where religious law is the national law or casts a shadow over national policy making, legal reform becomes a fraught exercise.[29] Sometimes religion is put forward as the reason for the non-implementation of human rights.[30] However, the 'religion and human rights' issue is rendered complex by the different interpretations of the tenets of religion within various faith groups. The gendered interpretation of most of the world's religions creates particular problems for women. This raises the question whether it is religion or cultural interpretations thereof that inform the construct of gender relations in the society?[31] My discussions of women, law, human rights, culture and religion are informed by an analytical model based on the typology of hierarchies of power advanced by Wanzala:

> [T]here are at least three broad dimensions of power that do not occur in isolation from each other, but which are in a complex dialectical relationship, often reinforcing each other. Firstly, patriarchal relations which subordinate women legally, politically, socially and economically. Secondly, hierarchical social relations based on class, racial, ethnic, religious and other social boundaries . . . Thirdly, unequal relations among women which reflect socio-historical reality, related social stratifiers, and multiple factors aside from gender ideologies and positionality that shape the socialization of individuals.[32]

The work of Crenshaw has also been influential.[33] Crenshaw has alerted us to the fact that for too long we have seen discrimination as existing in discrete

---

[27] H Chekir 'Women, the Law and the Family in Tunisia' (1996) 4 *Gender and Development* 43 at 46.

[28] See discussions on feminist positions in H Afshar *Islam and Feminisms: An Iranian Case Study* (Basingstoke, Palgrave, 1998) 8–9.

[29] H Abdullah 'Religious Revivalism, Human Rights Activism and the Struggle for Women's Rights in Nigeria' in A An Na'im (ed) *Cultural Transformation and Human Rights in Africa* (London, Zed Press, 2002) 151; A Iwobi 'Tiptoeing through a Constitutional Minefield: The Great Sharia Controversy in Nigeria' (2004) 48 *Journal of African Law* 111; M Kukah 'Shariah, Justice and Constitutionalism in Nigeria' in J Murison, A Griffiths and K King (eds) *Remaking Law in Africa: Transnationalism, Persons and Rights* (Edinburgh, Centre of African Studies, 2004) 173; F Mernissi *Beyond the Veil: Male Female Dynamics in Muslim Society* (London, Saqi Books, 2003) 17.

[30] Ali above n 26 at 63.

[31] Ali above n 26 at 53–55, 57.

[32] W Wanzala 'Towards an Epistemological and Methodological Framework of Development' in P McFadden (ed) *Southern Africa in Transition: A Gendered Perspective* (Harare, SAPES, 1998) 1 at 1. See also M Nussbaum 'Women and Human Development: The Capabilities Approach' in M Molyneaux and S Razavi (eds) *Gender, Justice, Development and Rights* (Oxford, Clarendon Press, 2003) 45.

[33] K Crenshaw 'Mapping the Margins: Intersectionality, Identity Politics and Violence against Women of Colour' (1991) 43 *Stanford Law Journal* 1241. See also Report of the World Conference

categories, for example, sex or race or religion. She asserts that it is more than likely that a person may experience many forms of discrimination simultaneously. She calls this intersectional discrimination. Crenshaw's analysis is particularly helpful when considering the lives of African women, not least because more often than not, they suffer multiple and intersecting discrimination.[34]

Given the book's focus on the rights of women, one cannot get away from the issue of feminism as an analytic tool. Feminism is here loosely defined as a political movement that has as its central aim the improvement of women's lives, their emancipation from discrimination and their empowerment to enable them to live their lives fully and with real choices. Now a global movement, feminist voices have grown more plentiful, and the understandings and strategies about how to achieve the aims of the movement more diverse. There have been vigorous debates about the various standpoints of feminist scholars. These debates have yielded a rich and stimulating literature.

Feminist debates

The northern (western) literature on the topic is enormous. Women from the south have questioned the dominant northern feminisms, which, they contend, do not adequately reflect their experiences and whose strategies for change cannot be applied in the southern context. Not surprisingly, the work produced by non-western feminists (or from a non-western perspective) has also grown in volume.[35] The main criticism made of 'northern feminism'[36] has been that it is insular or essentialist and reflects the world as viewed through the eyes of white

---

against Racism, Racial Discrimination and Related Intolerance (2001) UN Doc A/CONF.189/12, Declaration, para 2; UN Division for the Advancement of Women, Office of the High Commissioner for Human Rights and United Nations Development Fund for Women, *Report of the Expert Group Meeting, Gender and Racial Discrimination* (Croatia, 2000) available at http://www.un.org/women-watch/daw/csw/genrac/report.htm.

[34] See also S Msimang 'Caution! Women Moving: Strategies for Organizing Feminist Visions of the Future' in J Kerr, E Sprenger and A Symington (eds) *The Future of Women's Rights* (London, Zed Press, 2004) 170 at 170, 174; J Kerr 'From "Opposing" to "Proposing" ' above n 26 at 29–30.

[35] K Bhavanani *Feminism and Race* (Oxford, Oxford University Press, 2001); M Mohanty a Russo and L Torres (eds) *Third World Women and the Politics of Feminism* (Indianapolis, Indiana University Press, 1991); E Spelman *Inessential Woman: Problems of Exclusion in Feminist Thought* (London, Women's Press, 1990); R Meena (ed) *Gender in Southern Africa: Conceptual and Theoretical Issues* (Harare, SAPES,1992); G Mikell (ed) *African Feminism: The Politics of Survival in Sub-Saharan Africa* (Philadelphia, University of Pennsylvania Press, 1997).

[36] Of which there are many types—cf H Charlesworth and C Chinkin *Boundaries of International Law* (Manchester, Manchester University Press, 2000) 38–46. See also J Conaghan 'Reassessing the Feminist Theoretical Project in Law' (2000) 27 *Journal of Law and Society* 351.

middle class women.[37] Black/Diaspora feminists have introduced race and class as important factors in understanding their situation.[38] Muslim women have long engaged in feminist debates, some from within the umbrella of Islam and others from without.[39]

Southern feminists have also criticised northern feminism for not taking on board the impact of colonialism on the lives of women in the south. They have challenged the silence as a refusal to acknowledge the benefits enjoyed by white women of the privileges associated with whiteness.[40] On a different note, Amadiume has excoriated white women for what she sees as victim imperialism, that is using the experiences of black women to highlight gender discrimination.[41] More recently the feminist debate has also taken on a socio-economic dimension with a challenge by southern feminists to northern feminists to interrogate globalisation and the negative impact of northern economic dominance on the lives of women in the south.[42]

It is important to acknowledge that the use of feminist analyses in the African context is not without difficulty, not least because of feminism's roots in western gender politics.[43] The issue of what constitutes 'African feminism(s)' is itself the subject of increasing debate and contestation.[44] Nnaemeka links the existence of African feminism to its resistance of the northern feminist agenda.[45] She identifies several areas of disagreement that frame the African resistance to northern feminisms. These include 'radical feminism, motherhood, language, sexuality, priorities (gender) separatism'.[46] Despite some of the identified shortcomings of northern

---

[37] b hooks *Feminist Theory: From Margin to Centre* (Boston, Southend Press, 1984). See generally K Bhavanani above n 35; O Oyewumi 'Ties That Bind: Feminism, Sisterhood and Other Foreign Relations' (2001) *Jenda: A Journal of Culture and African Women Studies* at http://www.jendajournal.com/jenda/vol1.1/oyewumi.html 1–12; O Oyewumi *The Invention of Women: Making an African Sense of Western Gender Discourse* (Minneapolis, University of Minnesota Press, 1997).

[38] Crenshaw above n 33; hooks above n 37.

[39] H Moghissi *Feminism and Islamic Fundamentalism* (London, Zed Press, 1999) 125–48; P Reynolds 'Transitional Perspectives in Women's Rights' (2004) 14 *Interights Bulletin* 143 at 146.

[40] Nnaemeka (ed) *Sisterhood* above n 21 and Bhavanani above n 35.

[41] Amadiume above n 21 at 8. See also B Adeleye Fayemi 'Creating a New World with New Visions: African Feminism and Trends in the Global Women's Movement' in J Kerr, E Sprenger and A Symington (eds) *The Future of Women's Rights* (London, Zed Press, 2004) 38 at 49.

[42] J Oloka-Onyango and S Tamale 'The Personal is Political, or Why Women's Rights are Indeed Human Rights: An African Perspective on International Feminism' (1995) 17 *Human Rights Quarterly* 691 at 725–30; A Illumoka 'African Women's Economic, Social and Cultural Rights: Toward a Relevant Theory and Practice' in R Cook (ed) *Human Rights of Women: National and International Perspectives* (Philadelphia, University of Pennsylvania Press, 1994) 307; Msimang above n 34 at 171–75.

[43] Oyewumi *Invention of Women* above n 37 at ix.

[44] Mikell (ed) above n 35; S Arnfred (ed) *Rethinking Sexualities in Africa* (Lund, Nordic Africa Institute, 2004). All the papers in this volume are challenging and stimulating examinations of contemporary gender debates within the African context. See in particular S Arnfred 'Re-thinking Sexualities in Africa: Introduction' 7 and M Kowalowol 'Re-Conceptualizing African Gender Theory: Feminism, Womanism and the *Arere* Metaphor' 251.

[45] Nnaemeka *Sisterhood* above n 21 at 6.

[46] *Ibid.*

analyses of women's situation, Tamale would argue that western gender discourse can be used as 'scaffolding' for the discussion of African societies, not least because of the post-colonial legacy that bequeathed on Africa western based social and legal structures.[47]

Oyewumi questions the suitability of transposing western critiques of patriarchy on to non-western societies.[48] She identifies language and the difficulty of cross-cultural translation as leading to misinterpretations and distortions of concepts rooted in African societies that are not familiar to northerners. Picking up on this theme, Nzegwu notes that the western discourse on gender ignores differences in the structuring of non-western societies.[49] Using the Igbo of Nigeria as an example,[50] she argues that this group operated along a dual sex model that saw men and women as inhabiting different spheres, which spheres were not overlaid with the negative gender constructs that are part of western feminist discourse. Specifically she notes that women had real and meaningful power and were respected. While Nzegwu's analyses are challenging and stimulating, it is noteworthy that her discussions of the society under consideration are in the past tense, suggesting that the situation has changed and that the complementary gender relations that she identifies no longer pertain.[51] Indeed she acknowledges as much herself.[52] Hellum has noted that much of the analysis of African societies is based on a consideration of patrilineal groups, which may manifest greater gender disparities. She contends that greater attention should be paid to matrilineal societies.[53] It is, however, debateable whether these societies are, in modern times, any more egalitarian than patrilineal groups.

Other African feminists caution against an over-romanticisation of a (mythical) African past where gender relations were based on mutual co-operation.[54] In this vein, Nnaemeka has expressed a general concern that sometimes the highlighting of Queens and monarchs to show that women were powerful in centuries past obscures a proper study of gender relations on the continent, not least because these women were not, and cannot be seen as, representative of African womanhood.[55]

---

[47] Tamale above n 18 at 30–31.

[48] Oyewumi *Invention of Women* above n 37.

[49] N Nzegwu 'Gender Equality in Dual-Sex System: The Case of Onitsha' (2001) 1 *Jenda: A Journal of Culture and African Women's Studies* at http://www.jendajournal.com/jenda/vol1.1/nzegwu.html 1.

[50] Reference is also made to the Yoruba.

[51] See for example her views on women's rights within marriage in Nzegwu above n 49 at 16.

[52] *Ibid* at 19.

[53] A Hellum 'Gender and Legal Change in Zimbabwe: Childless Women and Divorce from a Socio-Cultural and Historic Perspective' in S Adelman and A Paliwala (eds) *Law and Crisis in the Third World* (London, Zell, 1993) 243.

[54] Wanzala above n 32 at 7. See too H Becker 'The Least Sexist Society? Perspectives on Gender, Change and Violence among the Southern African San' (2003) 29 *Journal of Southern African Studies* 1; H Chigudu 'Introduction' in H Chigudu (ed) *Composing a New Song: Stories of Empowerment from Africa* (London, Commonwealth Secretariat, 2003) xiii at xix.

[55] O Nnaemeka 'Development, Cultural Forces, and Women's Achievement in Africa' (1996) 18 *Law and Policy* 251 at 262–64.

Given these differences one might wonder what the constituent parts of African feminism are. Nnaemeka argues that for African women, strategies for challenging existing gender inequality are an important part of finding the African voice:

> [T]he majority of African women are not hung up on articulating their feminism, they just do it. In my view, it is *what* they do and *how* they do it that provide the 'framework'; the 'framework' is not carried to the theatre of action as a definitional tool. It is the dynamism of the theatre of action with its shifting patterns that makes the feminist spirit/engagement effervescent and exciting but also intractable and difficult to name.[56]

The scheme of this book

This introductory chapter has looked at some of the concepts to be used in the book. The next chapter considers the evolution of legal systems in Africa, focusing on the development of customary law norms from the time of colonisation to the present day. It engages with the different constructions of customary law as well as the problems and opportunities thrown up by plural legal systems. It then moves on to consider different theoretical models of equality before considering how three African constitutions deal with conflicts between discriminatory inheritance laws and the constitutional guarantees of equality and non-discrimination. A consideration of human rights on the African continent follows. It must be noted from the outset that due to time and resource constraints, this book does not look closely at the evolving mechanisms of the newly constituted African Union.[57]

Chapter 3 starts with a consideration of Charlesworth, Chinkin and Wright's feminist analysis of international law,[58] which has been adapted by Murray[59] for the African context. Specifically, while Charlesworth *et al* argue that women's interests have been left out of the construction and interpretation of international law, so too Murray argues that the continent's interests are similarly excluded. Africa appears to be the 'woman' in the global world order. Mutua's 'Africanist' critique of the international human rights framework is then examined.[60] Thereafter the chapter considers the provisions of the African Charter and other sub-regional initiatives. It also considers briefly the African Union institutional framework on human rights, particularly as it applies to issues of gender. This is

---

[56] Nnaemeka *Sisterhood* above n 21 at 5. See also G Mikell 'Introduction' in G Mikell (ed) above n 35 at 1. But see Adeleye Fayemi above n 41 at 50.

[57] For this see R Murray *Human Rights in Africa* (Cambridge, Cambridge University Press, 2004).

[58] H Charlesworth, C Chinkin and S Wright 'Feminist Approaches to International Law' (1991) 85 *American Journal of International Law* 613.

[59] R Murray *The African Commission on Human Rights and International Law* (Oxford, Hart Publishing, 2000).

[60] Mutua above n 12.

interspersed with a consideration of the provisions of CEDAW, which was used as the template for the African Protocol on African Women's Rights adopted in Maputo in 2003. It has yet to come into force.[61] The chapter explores the drafting history of this Protocol. The key areas of contestation are explored. This, the 'African CEDAW', represents the framework for women's rights on the continent in the twenty-first century. Reference is made to it throughout the book. What does it provide, and what are the prospects for delivery of the rights contained therein?

Chapter 4 is the family law chapter. Much of the discrimination that African women face is linked to personal status laws. The chapter combines a considera-tion of family laws in various African states with a consideration of state reports to the Committee on the Elimination of All Forms of Discrimination and the concluding observations of the Committee. It is telling that both states and the Committee identify issues of culture and gender as being central to understanding the disenfranchisement of women from family decision making and, more importantly, accessing resources.

Thereafter Chapter 5 is a consideration of the topical issue of violence against women and reproductive rights. This chapter starts with a consideration of the increased recognition of issues pertaining to gender-based violence at the inter-national level, before looking at domestic laws and societal norms that encourage or facilitate the continuation of violence against women and the girl child. The sec-ond part is on reproductive rights. These incorporate a gamut of human rights. The life-cycle model is used to show how issues of reproduction impact on girls and women throughout their lives, and in some cases even before. Given the impact of the AIDS crisis on the continent, the chapter also considers issues per-taining to patents and the difficulty of poor states accessing cheap anti-retroviral drugs to give to people who are HIV positive. It is by considering the reasons for women's higher infection rates that issues of gender and violence are most clearly thrown into relief.

This is followed by a chapter on an issue that directly affects the rights of the girl child, female genital cutting. One of the most contentious issues between north-ern and southern women, and indeed between southern women themselves, has been over the practice of female genital cutting.[62] This is a topic that impacts upon discussions of women, law and culture. Already much explored,[63] the chapter

---

[61] It needs 15 ratifications to bring it into force (art 29). As of October 2004 it had been ratified by five states: Comoros, Lesotho, Libya, Namibia and Rwanda.

[62] Names for the practice vary from circumcision, to 'circumcision', to clitoridectomy, to excision, to infibulation, to female genital mutilation and, more recently, female genital cutting emerging out of female genital surgeries.

[63] There is a huge literature on female genital cutting in all genres including: autobiography—N El Sadaawi *The Hidden Face of Eve: Women in the Arab World* (London, Zed Press, 1997), F Kassindja and L Bashir *Do They Hear You When You Cry?* (London, Bantam Press, 1998), W Dirie and C Miller *Desert Flower* (London, Virago Press, 1998); literature—Alice Walker *Possessing the Secret of Joy* (New

focuses on female genital cutting (FGC) because of what it reveals about developments in feminist discourse and its recognition as a human rights issue. It also considers the efficacy of adopting a legal approach to deal with what is generally seen as a cultural problem.

Chapter 7 brings together discussions of culture, development and participation of women in public life. It also considers the role of non-governmental organisations (NGOs). The discussion on culture leads. An examination of the work of the UN committees, and indeed the African Commission, shows clearly that 'culture' is seen as an impediment to the enjoyment by women of their human rights. The debate about how to reconcile culture and human rights norms is a long-running one. A brief examination of various arguments is undertaken before moving on to consider issues of development. This section considers the evolution of theories pertaining to women's participation in the development process, otherwise known as WID, WAD, GAD and now GLAD.[64] The current thinking is that there should be a rights-based approach to development. Women's participation in political and public life is considered in section three. Although there is much rhetoric on the importance of including women in decision-making processes, this is seldom done consistently. The use of temporary special measures as a tool to ensure women's participation is addressed. The final part considers the role of NGOs in the promotion of women's rights. Although NGOs are increasingly replacing states in service delivery, questions should still be asked about the agendas, ideologies and staffing of these organisations. The Conclusion follows.

York, Pocket Books, 1992); film—K Longinotto *The Day I will Never Forget* (New York, Women Make Movies, 2002); politics—J Kenyatta *Facing Mount Kenya: The Tribal Life of the Gikuyu* (New York, Vintage Books, 1965); anthropology—E Babatunde *Women's Rights versus Women's Rites* (Eritrea, Africa World Press, 1998), E Gruenbaum *The Female Circumcision Controversy: An Anthropological Perspective* (Philadelphia, University of Pennsylvania Press, 2001); law—A Rahman and N Toubia *Female Genital Mutilation: A Guide to Laws and Practices Worldwide* (London, Zed Press, 2000); children's rights—A Renteln 'Is the Cultural Defense Detrimental to the Health of Children?' (1994) 7 *Law and Anthropology International Yearbook for Legal Anthropology* 27, A Renteln *The Cultural Defense* (Oxford, Oxford University Press, 2004); and refugee studies—H Crawley *Refugees and Gender: Law and Process* (Bristol, Jordan Publishing, 2001).

[64] Women in Development (WID), Women and Development (WAD), Gender and Development (GAD), Gender, Law and Development (GLAD).

2

Law in Africa

Of law and its usefulness to women, much has been written. 'Law' in Africa is a multi-faceted concept. In addition to the 'received' or, more accurately, imposed general or common law, there exist laws based on the various customs and practices of the many groups that inhabit the continent, as well as religious norms including Christianity (the norms of which are often constructed as forming part of the general law) and Judaism, Hindu Law and Islamic laws.[1] At the top of national legal hierarchies are national constitutions. Contained within national constitutions are bills of rights, which are, more often than not, derived from international human rights law. International law forms the very top of the legal pyramid with varying degrees of influence at the national level. This chapter examines the development of 'local laws', starting with the evolution of customary law during colonialism before looking at the concept of equality. It then considers national constitutions and how they deal with the existence of personal laws that may conflict with the principle of non-discrimination based on sex or gender.[2]

Describing the evolution of norms enshrining the human rights of women, Hevener divided the process into three phases.[3] These were the protective, corrective and non-discrimination or equality phases. Interestingly, her typology seems to be mirrored in the development of laws in 'Anglophone' Africa. During the colonial period and in some limited cases thereafter, laws were constructed and interpreted in a way which was framed as being for the 'protection' of African women, although in reality this merely served to mask their enforced disenfranchisement. An example of the protective approach can be seen in the attitude of the Rhodesian government of Ian Smith, which in 1969 rejected a proposal that African women be given legal capacity for the first time since colonisation. The Minister of Internal Affairs argued:

---

[1] Some North African states proclaim Islam as the national religion. These include Algeria, Egypt, Libya and Tunisia. J Allain and A O'Shea 'African Disunity: Comparing Human Rights Law and Practice of North and South African States' 24 (2002) 2 *Human Rights Quarterly* 86 at 100.

[2] T Bennett *Customary Law in South Africa* (Cape Town, Juta, 2004) 76–100.

[3] N Hevener 'An Analysis of Gender-Based Treaty Law: Contemporary Developments in Historical Perspective' (1986) 8 *Human Rights Quarterly* 70.

> The present position is that ninety nine percent of African women would find legal emancipation of that nature quite intolerable. It would be disastrous to do anything too quickly.[4]

The post-independence period saw states trying to correct past gender discrimination by way of legislative change. This is most clearly seen in changes made to family and other personal laws. This 'corrective' phase of law making has often merged with the non-discrimination or equality phase, which has seen states enacting or amending constitutions to include provisions prohibiting discrimination on the basis of sex or gender. The Hevener typology is adapted here for discussion of the evolution of gender-based laws on the African continent.

This chapter starts with a brief history of the development of law and legal institutions in colonial Africa. Here it is important to note that we start at the time of colonisation because one has to start somewhere; it is in no way reflective of a view that until the white man came Africans were without law or institutional structures.[5] The difficulty of discussing pre-colonial social and political systems is, as Read has noted, partly because of the unreliability of the recording of oral histories and also because of the readiness of colonial administrators to dismiss pre-colonial polities.[6] A consideration of customary law, its sources, content and current standing in the African legal system follows.

Creating law(s) and legal systems

Common to most African countries is a history of colonialism, not only European but, in some cases, Arab as well.[7] A conference of European states was held in Berlin in 1884 to formalise 'right to territory staked' and thus the carving up of Africa. The colonisation process itself was a process of first come first served, so that Britain and France had the larger portions, though Belgium, having the geographically massive Congo, did not do too badly.[8] In addition to Cameroon,

---

[4] Rhodesian Legislative Assembly Debates 1969, Minster of Internal Affairs, col 629.

[5] Chanock would take a different approach. M Chanock *Law, Custom and Social Order: The Colonial Experience in Malawi and Zambia* (Cambridge, Cambridge University Press, 1985) 10.

[6] Read in J Read and HF Morris *Indirect Rule and the Search for Justice* (Oxford, Clarendon Press, 1972) 169, 174. But see A Cheater 'The Role and Position of Women in Pre-Colonial and Colonial Zimbabwe' (1986) XIII *Zambezia*. See also F Oyekanmi 'Women and the Law: Historical and Contemporary Perspectives in Nigeria' in A Obilade (ed) *Women in Law* (Lagos, Southern University Law Centre and Faculty of Law, 1993) 28 at 31; N Bhebe and T Ranger (eds) *The Historical Dimensions of Democracy and Human Rights in Zimbabwe* (Harare, Zimbabwe Publishing House, 2001).

[7] This cannibalised history is not meant to be definitive. Indeed there was movement and 'colonisation' between ethnic groups on the continent.

[8] Other European colonial powers included Spain in the north and Portugal in Angola, Mozambique and São Tomé amongst others.

Rwanda and Tanganyika, Germany had Deutsche Sud Ouest Africa, now Namibia, all of which she lost at the end of the First World War. In the terms of the Treaty of Versailles 1919, German colonies became mandated territories of the League of Nations. They were parcelled out amongst the victorious powers to govern, so that Cameroon was divided between Britain and France, Rwanda-Burundi was given to the Belgians, Tanganyika (Tanzania) went to the British and South Africa was to administer South West Africa.

The significance of this brief colonial history is that one of the results of the new political dispensation was the imposition of a legal system on the colonised country. There were of course regional variations. Moreover, there were differences in the approaches of the different colonisers, not least because they had different legal traditions.[9] This would explain why to this day, most of the former British colonies have legal systems that reflect the English common law tradition, while the former French colonies follow the civil law tradition. The exception to this general rule can be found in Southern Africa, where some of the countries operated (and continue to operate) under the Roman-Dutch legal system. Basically this is because the Dutch had beaten the English in being the first Europeans to colonise South Africa, thus imposing their legal system. In allowing Roman-Dutch to be used in both the English-speaking parts of South Africa and subsequently in other colonies,[10] the English were merely bowing to the need for administrative efficiency. It must also be remembered that a country like Southern Rhodesia, now Zimbabwe, was run initially by the British South African Company, which was a mainly commercial venture. The Company Administrator made a proclamation that the laws of the Cape Colony were to be applied to the Company's territory.[11] The focus of this section is on the British approach in selected territories.

The law, generally the public law provisions applying in the conquering country, was to be imposed on the colonised country hence the public law was to apply to all persons, unless otherwise provided.

If the foreign law became the general law governing public law issues, what was to be the personal law? An initial attempt, by Britain at least, at direct rule had to be abandoned in favour of a policy, refined by the British governor in Nigeria, Lord Lugard, called indirect rule.[12] The policy of direct rule had called for a

---

[9] See K Mann and S Roberts *Law in Colonial Africa* (London, James Currey, 1991); F Snyder 'Colonialism and the Legal Form: The Creation of Customary Law in Senegal' (1981) 19 *Journal of Legal Pluralism* 49.

[10] M Mamashela 'Legal Dualism in Lesotho (with Particular Reference to Marriage and Succession)' (1989) 4 *Law and Anthropology* 59; T Nhlapo *Marriage and Divorce in Swazi Law and Custom* (Mbabane, Websters, 1992).

[11] Administrator's Proclamation No 1, 28 September 1890 (BSAC Proc (1890)). This was repeated in subsequent Proclamations and Orders in Council. See W Ncube *Family Law in Zimbabwe* (Harare, Legal Resources Foundation, 1989) 5.

[12] F Lugard *The Dual Mandate in British Tropical Africa* (London, William Blackwood and Son, 1922).

takeover of the governed populations, politically, legally[13] and administratively. However, due to a shortage of staff and the resistance of the indigenous people to a change in their personal laws or ways of doing things, it was decided to allow the customs of the people to continue to operate in the private law sphere.[14] This was subject to the proviso that the law be not 'repugnant to natural justice and morality'—the repugnance, it is assumed, referring to British Victorian sensibilities. The Chief Justice of Southern Rhodesia defined it thus:

> The words 'repugnant to natural justice and morality' should only apply to such customs as inherently impress us with some abhorrence or are obviously immoral in their incidence.[15]

'Repugnance' was also heavily influenced by Christian doctrine and missionary influence, so that in Ghana, 'the wrong African approach to marriage was seen in such practices as betrothals, "forced marriages" and the "inheritance of wives."'[16] It has to be said that the missionaries were not always sensitive to the effects of their proselytising on the lives of African women. Banning polygyny and asking men already in polygynous marriages to choose one wife and to discard the others was singularly un-Christian. This was not the only un-Christian act. There is a saying amongst Africans that highlights the unlawful expropriation of land. It goes:

> When the white man came to Africa . . . he held the Bible in his hand, and Africans held the land. The white man said to the Africans 'Let us bow our heads in prayer.' When the Africans raised their heads, the white man had the land and the Africans had the Bible.[17]

Although clearly asserting the superiority of the British worldview, Palley contends that the instances where custom was found to be repugnant for the most part related to the status of women, particularly if the woman was a party to a Christian marriage, the grounds of divorce and the welfare of children.[18]

Although under indirect rule Africans were to be allowed to keep their personal laws, subject to the repugnance proviso, the judicial tasks were to be carried out by Native Commissioners Courts who were to apply 'native law'—to use a colonial turn of phrase. Sometimes local chiefs were permitted to run local courts admin-

---

[13] However, again in Southern Rhodesia, the Royal Charter of 1890, which gave the British South Africa Company governorship rights over the territory, specified that in dealing with Africans 'careful regard shall always be had to the customs or laws of the class or tribe or nation to which the parties respectively belong': cited in Ncube above n 11 at 5.

[14] Cf T Bennett 'Conflict of Laws: The Application of Customary Law in Zimbabwe' (1981) 30 *International and Comparative Law Quarterly* 59.

[15] *Chiduku v Chidano* 1922 SR 55, 58. Cf J Read in Read and Morris above n 6 at 162.

[16] K Adinkrah 'Ghana's Marriage Ordinance: An Inquiry into a Legal Transplant for Social Change' (1980)18 *African Law Studies* 1 at 9.

[17] In M Engelke 'The Book, the Church and the "Incomprehensible Paradox": Christianity in African History' (2003) 29 *Journal of Southern African Studies* 297 at 297.

[18] C Palley *The Constitutional History and Law of Southern Rhodesia 1888–1965* (London, Oxford University Press, 1966) 511.

istering 'native law'. Skard notes that, after the women's war in 1929 in Nigeria, women were permitted to sit on these courts.[19] In East Africa, Read has noted that:

> The native courts were to administer such laws, the magistrates and superior courts were to be guided by such laws in cases involving natives; and legislators, in enacting new laws, were enjoined to respect customary laws.[20]

Bennett identifies three phases in the customary law story in South Africa. Initially the British administration in the Cape Colony refused to recognise 'native law', regarding it as 'pre-legal custom'. In phase two it gained 'grudging recognition' in Natal, Transvaal and Transkei in the middle of the nineteenth century. Finally, by the twentieth century and the formalisation of apartheid it had been renamed 'Bantu law'. Bennett contends that at no point was customary law in pre-independence South Africa ever treated as the equal of Roman-Dutch law.[21]

The difficulty faced by those colonial administrators tasked with administering local laws was in ascertaining the content of 'native law'. Unlike the French with their civil code and the English with a common law tradition and statutes, the African law was not, to the European mind at least, in any recognisable and easily ascertainable form. There were no written statutes, and precedents did not exist. What were they to make of it?[22]

Creating customary law

In looking at theories of the genesis of various legal systems, one is struck by the similarities of certain theorists. Mackinnon's assertion, that in northern states the law is a masculinist construct reflective of a masculinist state and protecting male interests,[23] is similar to that put forward by Chanock on the construction of 'African' customary law. He sees customary law as being no more than the sum parts of a selective presentation of claims by African male elites/elders and a selective understanding of said claims by male colonial officials.[24] Specifically, Chanock

---

[19] T Skard *Continent of Mothers: Understanding and Promoting Development in Africa Today* (London, Zed Press, 2003) 178.

[20] Read in Read and Morris above n 6 at 167.

[21] T Bennett 'The Equality Clause and Customary Law' (1994) 10 *South African Journal on Human Rights* 122 at 122. See also H Simons *African Women: Their Legal Status in South Africa* (London, Hurst and Co, 1968); M Chanock *The Making of the South African Legal Culture 1902–1936* (Cambridge, Cambridge University Press, 2001); E Bonthuys 'Accommodating Gender, Race, Culture and Religion: outside Legal Subjectivity' (2002) 18 *South African Journal on Human Rights* 41 at 42, 51–53.

[22] J Harrington and A Manji 'The Emergence of African Law as an Academic Discipline in Britain' (2003) 102 *African Affairs* 109 at 112–13.

[23] C Mackinnon *Towards a Feminist Theory of the State* (Cambridge, Harvard University Press, 1989) 282–84.

[24] M Chanock 'Neither Customary nor Legal: African Customary Law in an Era of Family Law Reform' (1989) 3 *International Journal of Law and Family* 72.

notes that African men, fearful of losing power and control over women, restated a version of customary law rooted less in the fluidity of daily practice but more in an assertion of a draconian version of custom that kept women in their place.[25] In excluding women from norm construction, a desire to control women and to prevent them 'becoming too independent' was also clearly an aim, so that in Malawi:

> This reaction among Malawian men was shared by the colonial courts. District courts grew impatient with the number of marriage cases and came to believe that the men were right, that women were getting out of control, that the authority of parents and husbands was being dangerously undermined, and that this threatened the moral standards and well being of the community as a whole.[26]

It is here worth noting that the construction of African women as not enjoying the same rights as men would have made sense to colonial officials, not least because in the nineteenth century, when most of the colonisation of Africa took place, 'their (white colonial) women' were not considered to be the bearers of rights.[27] It would therefore have been inconceivable that the 'inferior native race' could grant women rights which were denied to white women.

Chanock's thesis on the creation of customary law accords with that put forward by An Na'im and some feminist Muslim scholars on the construction and interpretation of Islamic law.[28] They contend that the mullahs who recorded the words of the Prophet (Peace be upon Him) reflected the understanding and perspectives of male religious leaders at the time. Similarly Quassem notes that: 'The Quaran was revealed at a time when Arabs disdained women and considered them inferior.'[29] He then goes on to say that it was Islam that 'resurrected women'.[30] Chanock and An Na'im are united in their view that Islamic legal principles and what is now known as 'customary law' should be read and understood within the historical contexts in which they were articulated and formulated. In its concluding observations to the Moroccan report to CEDAW, the Committee said: 'The cultural conditions of 13 centuries ago no longer existed. There was nothing in Islam that would stand in the way of the universal rights of all women.'[31]

---

[25] M Chanock 'Neo-Traditionalism and the Customary Law in Malawi' in M Hay and M Wright (eds) *African Women and the Law: Historical Perspectives* (Boston, Boston University Press, 1980) 80 at 88.

[26] *Ibid.* See also N Bhebe and T Ranger 'Introduction to Volume 1' in N Bhebe and T Ranger (eds) *The Historical Dimensions of Democracy and Human Rights in Zimbabwe* (Harare, Zimbabwe Publishing House, 2001) xxi at xxxii.

[27] A Fraser 'Becoming Human: The Origins and Development of Women's Human Rights (1999) 21 *Human Rights Quarterly* 853.

[28] A An Na'im (ed) *Islamic Family Law in A Changing World: A Global Resource Book* (London, Zed Press, 2002) xi–xii, 2–21, see in particular 3–4; A Mayer *Islam and Human Rights* (Boulder, Westview, 1999) 98.

[29] Y Quassem, 'Law of the Family (Personal Status Law)' in N Bernard-Maugiron and B Dupret (eds) *Egypt and Its Laws* (The Hague, Kluwer Law International, 2002) 19 at 29 fn 35.

[30] *Ibid.*

[31] UN 'CEDAW Concludes Consideration of Morocco's Report' (20 January 1997) Press Release WOM/937, downloaded from http://www.un.org/News/press/docs/1997/19970102.wom937.html at p 5.

An Na'im and Chanock see law as politically charged, manipulable and dynamic. They also identify quite clearly that the sometimes sexist constructions put on the various laws can be attributed to the absence of women in their formulation.[32] With regard to customary law, Ranger would go further and argue that those excluded, included young men who found themselves disenfranchised by the 'invented' tradition which arose in colonial Africa.[33]

However, it must be acknowledged that Ranger has been criticised for overstating the case for an 'invented tradition'. Indeed, looking at theories on the genesis of customary law, one can plot a continuum along which one finds the views of Ranger at the one end and the more sceptical Roberts at the other. Roberts challenges the 'invention of tradition' theory, noting:

> The idea of the invention of tradition seems to me to imply an impoverished and grossly simplistic understanding of the operation of ideology. It calls up a version of the manufacture, transmission and assimilation, intact, of some new world view, and the corresponding destruction of existing cognitive and normative foundations of the life world. Much more persuasive is an account of ideology as working with what is already to hand, covertly upon and within an existing life world, transforming without eradicating.[34]

Whichever theory one subscribes to, it seems clear that women were not well served by the version of customary law that took root after colonialism.

Customary law in post-colonial states

The coming of independence to African countries, from Ghana in 1957 to South Africa in 1994, brought about its own dilemmas. Having fought against colonial oppression, there was the much romanticised notion of restoring 'customary law' and 'African culture' to their former glory. An example of this is the preamble to the OAU Cultural Charter for Africa 1976, which provides in part:

> [C]ultural domination led to the depersonalization of part of the African peoples, falsified their history, systematically disparaged and combated African values, and tried to replace progressively and officially, their languages by that of the colonizer.[35]

---

[32] See also Oyekanmi above n 6 at 32.

[33] T Ranger 'The Invention of Tradition' in T Ranger and E Hobsbawm (eds) *The Invention of Tradition* (Cambridge, Cambridge University Press, 1983) 211 at 254.

[34] S Roberts 'Some Notes on "African Customary Law"' (1984) 28 *Journal of African Law* 1 at 4–5. Roberts is supported in this view by M Mutua 'Banjul Charter: The Case for an African Cultural Fingerprint' in A An Na'im (ed) *Cultural Transformation and Human Rights in Africa* (London, Zed Press, 2002) 67 at 83. For other perspectives see generally (1984) 28 *Journal of African Law*.

[35] OAU Cultural Charter for Africa 1976 arts 1(b) and 1(c) available at http://www.africa-union.org. See too J Sachs in *S v Makwanyane and Mchunu* 1995 (3) SA 391 paras 364–71.

The first problem that needed to be addressed was the removal of the racial criteria that had been used to determine both choice of law as well as the courts which could be used by the different racial groups. During the colonial era Africans did not have access to High Courts to resolve interpersonal disputes. Occasionally exceptions were made for those Africans who were said to have adopted a 'Europeanised' lifestyle. An example of this is the Rhodesian case of *Jirira v Jirira.*[36] This was a divorce case involving two black Africans. The wife, a nurse, sought to override the application of customary law to the distribution of the marital property in preference for the general law, the application of which would give her a larger portion of the matrimonial property. Holding in her favour, the court relied partly on the fact that at their wedding, the couple had had a white bridesmaid, as proof that theirs was no 'ordinary' union between Africans.[37] In Francophone Africa, educated Africans were given a different status to other Africans by a process known as *association.*[38] These Africans were said to have *statut civil français.*[39]

In attempting to deal with the parallel legal system inherited at independence, three models were mooted. The first was to keep things as they were, thus retaining the parallel system. The second involved getting rid of the customary courts and only retaining the general law courts, which would then administer both systems of law. The third option was to integrate the court system.[40] Malawi was one country that opted for a completely different approach—the setting up of Traditional Courts to deal with both customary and criminal law matters. Similarly in Swaziland, chiefs appear to enjoy powers that cannot be challenged by general law courts.[41] Many states appear to have gone for option three, the integrated model, with the primary or lower courts handling customary law claims and provision being made for appeal to higher courts.[42]

This has resulted in customary law being put on a par with the imported general law.[43] However, in the former French colony of Côte d'Ivoire the state prefer-

---

[36] *Jirira v Jirira* 1976 RLR 7.

[37] Cf A Armstrong *et al* 'Uncovering Reality: Excavating Women's Rights in the African Family' (1993) 7 *International Journal of Law, Policy and the Family* 314 at 322.

[38] J Toungara 'Changing the Meaning of Marriage: Women and Family Law in Cote d'Ivoire' in Royal Tropical Institute (KIT) and OXFAM *Gender Perspectives on Property and Inheritance* (Amsterdam, KIT; Oxford, OXFAM, 2001) 33 at 34.

[39] J Toungara 'Changing the Meaning of Marriage: Women and Family Law in Cote d'Ivoire' in G Mikell (ed) *African Feminism of the Politics of Survival in Sub-Saharan Africa* (Philadelphia, University of Pennsylvania Press, 1997) 53 at 55.

[40] Cf Chanock above n 5 at 22–23.

[41] Swaziland Administrative Order No 6 of 1998.

[42] M Nzunda 'Criminal Law in Internal Conflict of Laws in Malawi' (1985) 29 *Journal of African Law* 129.

[43] See Constitution of the Republic of Namibia 1990. Both systems of law are made 'subject to the Constitution or any other statutory law': Art 66(1). Constitution of Zimbabwe 1979 as amended ss 23(3)(b), 89, reproduced in C Heyns (ed) *Human Rights Law in Africa 1996* (The Hague, Kluwer, 1996).

ence was to abandon customary law in favour of a French-style civil code. This preference was linked to a desire to develop the economy in the capitalist mode. Monogamous nuclear family units were the preferred model as this family unit was seen as freeing people from obligations to the wider family and thus improving the chances of acceleration towards a modern capitalist economy—not unlike France itself.[44] In the countries formerly under Portuguese rule there was an attempt to absorb customary law into the general law, while Ethiopia, which successfully fought off Italian attempts at colonisation, and Tunisia 'abolished' some aspects of customary law.[45]

Choice of law dilemmas

Across Africa, after independence, the racial criteria in the choice of law process were removed, so that in Tanzania, the Magistrates Court Act 1963 abolished the dual court system replacing it with an integrated system.[46] This approach, followed in many countries, created the potential for an internal conflict of laws problem to arise.[47] New criteria for determining which system of law should be applied were put into place, so that in Zimbabwe the Customary Law and Local Courts Act provides:[48]

Subject to this Act and any other enactment, unless the justice of the case otherwise requires—

(a) customary law shall apply in civil cases where—
   (i) the parties have expressly agreed that it should apply; or
   (ii) regard being had to the nature of the case and the surrounding circumstances, it appears just and proper that it should apply;

(b) the general law shall apply in all other cases.

'Surrounding circumstances' are defined as including:

(a) the mode of life of the parties;
(b) the subject matter of the case;

---

[44] Toungara above n 38 at 36–37.

[45] UNDP *Human Development Report: Cultural Liberty in Today's Diverse World* (New York, United Nations, 2004) 58.

[46] SF Moore *Social Facts and Fabrications: 'Customary' Law on Kilimanjaro, 1880–1980* (New York, Cambridge University Press, 1986) 156–59. She later (at 160 ff) notes administrative changes brought in by the ruling party which included the introduction of tribunals run by local party personnel.

[47] Bennett 'Equality Clause' above n 21 at 129.

[48] Customary Law and Local Courts Act 1990 [Cap 7:05] s 3(1). For the Ghanaian choice of law rules see G Woodman 'Family Law in Ghana under the Constitution 1992' in A Bainham (ed) *International Survey of Family Law 2003* (Bristol, Jordan Publishing, 2003) 195 at 197.

(c) the understanding by the parties of the provisions of customary law or the general law of Zimbabwe as the case may be which apply to the case;

(d) the relative closeness of the case and the parties to customary law or the general law of Zimbabwe as the case may be.

Using the above criteria, a white farmer in Zimbabwe tried to get out of being tried by the Community Court for seducing one of his workers.[49] As a white man, he said that he should be tried under the general law. On appeal to the Supreme Court, Chief Justice Dumbutshena held that the colour of a person's skin did not automatically indicate which system of law was to govern. In the case of the farmer, he was found to be familiar with customary practices, and had therefore to submit to the jurisdiction of the Community Court applying customary law.

While the provisions listed above resolve the conflict of law issues that arise between general and customary law, it is not clear what would happen if there were two or more competing systems of custom. Arguably the state version of customary law is ethnocentric, reflecting the practices and viewpoint of the dominant group within the society.[50] This can be traced back to the colonial era when diverse groups were forcibly merged and bound together in what the Europeans called 'nation states', in effect no more than an arbitrary drawing of boundaries.[51] Although each group has its own 'customs', often state and judicial customary law reflects the practices of the dominant group or an amalgamation of customs and practices.

What starts to emerge is the fact that after independence, there was a transformation of court structures and a retention of the state version of customary law. Even the much maligned repugnance clause was retained by some states post independence,[52] although the interpretation of it may have varied to that adopted in colonial times.[53] In the Kenyan case of *Otieno v Joash Ougo* the court held that Luo customary law, which determined that a man must be buried at his family homestead irrespective of the lifestyle he had chosen or indeed the wishes of his wife, was not repugnant to natural justice and morality.[54]

The customary law invoked in post-independent states was not the flexible, dynamic custom of pre-colonial years, but rather the court/state/man manufactured hand-me-down of the colonial era. This was helped in part by misplaced initiatives such as the Restatement of Customary Law Project based at the School of Oriental and African Studies in London.[55] The aims of the project were to record

---

[49] *Lopez v Nxumalo* SC-H 115/85, discussed in Ncube above n 11 at 20.

[50] Mutua above n 34 at 84–85.

[51] This arbitrary merging of groups has been the source of much tension and the reason for many of the civil wars which have flared up in post-colonial African states.

[52] Kenya Judicature Act cap 8 art 3.

[53] A Kolajo *Customary Law in Nigeria through the Cases* (Ibadan, Spectrum Books, 2000) 13–14.

[54] *Otieno v Joash Ougo* (1982–88) KAR 1049 (CA).

[55] A Costa 'The Myth of Customary Law' (1998) 14 *South African Journal on Human Rights* 525 at 528. Tanzania also had a unification of customary law project. See Moore above n 46 at 159.

customary law in written and 'ordered' form. It goes without saying that 'restating' or 'unifying' a fluid system is likely to lead to the ossification of customary law. Ironically, even in those countries lucky enough to have escaped the 'Restatement Project', the old method of determining customary law principles has been retained.[56]

Botswana appears to hold to the principle that customary law should be applied where customary marriage or its ancillaries are being considered. Although the High Court has inherent jurisdiction to hear all cases brought before it, practical considerations, including time, cost, accessibility and local knowledge, may warrant preferring customary cases to be heard before customary courts.[57]

In common with other African legal systems, South Africa recognises customary law.[58] However, the Constitution provides:

> When interpreting any legislation, and when developing the common law or customary law, every court, tribunal or forum must promote the spirit purport and objects of the bill of rights.[59]

This suggests an interpretive process that will lead to respect for the bill of rights, and which in turn may lead to the abandonment or modification of those aspects of customary law that are not in keeping with principles of non-discrimination and equality. Similarly, the Namibian Constitution recognises the possibility of an evolving customary law:

> Subject to the terms of this Constitution, it shall be competent by Act of Parliament for any part of such common or customary law to be repealed or modified, or for the application thereof to be confined to particular parts of Namibia or for particular periods.[60]

Although the state-sanctioned version of customary law has continued in use by the courts, other versions exist, thus highlighting the point made by Sally Falk Moore that 'state law' represents but one dimension of the entire legal field.[61] She

---

[56] See Zimbabwe Customary Law and Local Courts Act [Cap 7:05] s 9.

[57] S Morolong 'Overview of Recent Developments in the Law of Marriage in Botswana' in A Bainham (ed) *International Survey of Family Law 2002* (Bristol, Jordan Publishing, 2002) 67 at 73. However, the gender bias of customary courts has been extensively discussed. See A Griffiths *In the Shadow of Marriage: Gender and Justice in an African Community* (Chicago, University of Chicago Press, 1997).

[58] Constitution of the Republic of South Africa, Act No l08 of 1996 s 211(3). Bennett *Customary Law* above n 2 at 78 notes that customary law is taken to be included in the constitutional provisions on culture in ss 30 and 31; M Pieterse 'The Promotion of Equality and Prevention of Unfair Discrimination Act 4 of 2000: Final Nail in the Customary Law Coffin?' (2000) 117 *South Africa Law Journal* 627 at 627.

[59] Constitution of South Africa s 39(2). J Sinclair 'Embracing New Family Forms, Entrenching Outmoded Stereotypes' in P Lodrup and E Modvar (eds) *Family Life and Human Rights* (Oslo, Gyldendal Akademisk, 2004) 801 at 822.

[60] Constitution of the Republic of Namibia 1990 Art 66(2).

[61] SF Moore *Law as Process* (Oxford, James Currey, 1978); J Griffiths 'What is Legal Pluralism?' (1986) 24 *Journal of Legal Pluralism* 24. See also F Butegwa 'Mediating Culture and Human Rights in Favour of Land Rights for Women in Africa: A Framework for Community Level Action' in A An

identifies other normative orders, which she terms autonomous social fields. These are other 'systems' of regulating behaviour, adhered to by people belonging to different communities.[62] The 'community' in Moore's example can be as diverse as small kin groups in Tanzania to garment workers in New York. All are subject to, and respect, the normative orders or autonomous social fields within which they operate. This can best be seen in the Egyptian report to CEDAW, in which the government noted: 'In Egypt, family matters belong to the sphere of personal status and they and the disputes in their regard are subject to the internal laws of the community to which the family member belongs.'[63]

The Moore thesis is reinforced by Chiba, who has also criticised the legal centralist approach to ordering.[64] Bennett contends that an authentic customary law is one which exists outside the formal state structure. This 'extra-judicial' system is sometimes known as the 'living law', which is described by Rwezaura as:

[T]he unwritten, irregular i.e. flexible and highly negotiable representing the law governing the actual social life of the people in their day to day lives often changing in response to changing conditions.[65]

It is noteworthy that courts have started to recognise that state customary law may differ from people's day to day practices or living law, so that in the Tanzanian case of *Chiku Lidah v Adam Omari*[66] Mwalusanya J noted: 'Our customary law is a living law capable of adaptation and development. It is not immutable.'[67] He then went on to say:

The judicial role of recognising customary law that has by evaluation been modified by the society itself is very important. In the past the High Court has not been instrumental in spearheading this crusade. The courts should be courageous enough to recognise and give effect to such a change.[68]

Na'im (ed) *Cultural Transformation and Human Rights in Africa* (London, Zed Press, 2002) 108 at 109. See also Costa above n 55.

[62] SF Moore 'Law and Change: The Semi-Autonomous Social Field as an Appropriate Area of Study' (1973) 7 *Law and Society Review* 719. See also M d'Engelbronner-Kolf *A Web of Legal Cultures: Dispute Resolution Processes amongst the Sambyu of Northern Namibia* (Maastricht, Shaker Publishing, 2001) 14–18.

[63] Combined Fourth and Fifth Periodic Report of States Parties: Egypt (30 March 2000) CEDAW/C/EGY4–5 at 29.

[64] M Chiba (ed) *Asian Indigenous Laws in Interaction with Received Laws* (New York, KPI, 1986). See also A Manji 'Imagining Women's "Legal World": Towards a Feminist Theory of Legal Pluralism in Africa' (1994) 8 *Social and Legal Studies* 434.

[65] B Rwezaura as quoted in A Armstrong above n 37 at 327. See also C Himonga and C Bosch 'The Application of Customary Law under the Constitution of South Africa: Problem Solved or Just Beginning?' (2000) 17 *South Africa Law Journal* 306 at 319ff.

[66] *Chiku Lidah v Adam Omari* at Singida (PC) Civil Appeal No 34 of 1991 (Unreported), reproduced in C Peter *Human Rights in Tanzania: Selected Cases and Materials* (Cologne, Rudiger Koppe Verlag, 1997) 66–67.

[67] *Ibid* at 70.

[68] *Ibid* at 70. See too the South African case of *Mabena v Letsoalo* 1998 (2) SA 1068 at 1074H and the Zimbabwean case of *Jengwa v Jengwa* 1999(2) ZLR 120 at 128.

For Wanitzek, the good thing about the approach of the Tanzanian court is that it not only broadens the definition and understanding of customary law, but it also 'directs the attention of the agents of the legal system to adopt a more critical attitude towards concepts such as customary law'.[69] She sees this as a positive development that helps to bridge the gap between state customary law and social reality.

The very existence of 'living law' creates opportunities for challenging the staid versions of custom and customary law, providing avenues and opportunities for fashioning a more egalitarian community world view.[70] A counter point to this is to note that even in informal normative ordering, women's power to influence events is limited. Maboreke contends that while law grants women rights and legal capacity, it does not address the issue of women's social dependency.[71] It has also been noted that pluralism poses a problem to those who prefer a more 'unified system' and those who fear that allowing pluralism will result in the promotion of traditional practices that are contrary to democracy and human rights.[72]

Moving towards guaranteeing women's rights: the impact of liberation struggles

In countries that gained independence as a result of liberation struggles, there was an official recognition of the contribution of women towards the liberation of their countries.[73] In one volume of her autobiography, Maya Angelou recounts meeting the wives of South Africa's African National Congress and other liberation veterans in London. They appear to have been well aware of their own contributions and were eager to do more:

> Ruth Thompson, a West Indian journalist, led the conversation as soon as lunch was finished. 'What are we here for? Why are African women sitting, eating, trying to act cute while African men are discussing serious questions and African children are starving? Have we come to London just to convenience our husbands? Have we been brought here as portable pussy?' The Luo woman laughed. 'Sister, you have asked completely, my

---

[69] U Wanitzek 'The Power of Language in the Discourse on Women's Rights: Some Examples from Tanzania' (2002) 49 *Africa Today* 3 at 12.

[70] C Nyamu-Musembi 'Are Local Norms and Practices Fences or Pathways? The Example of Women's Property Rights' in A An Na'im (ed) above n 61 at 126; J Stewart 'Why I Can't Teach Customary Law' in J Eekelaar and T Nhlapo (eds) *The Changing Family* (Oxford, Hart Publishing, 1998) 217.

[71] M Maboreke 'Understanding Law in Zimbabwe' in A Stewart (ed) *Gender, Law and Social Justice* (Oxford, Blackstone, 2000) 116.

[72] UNDP above n 45 at 8.

[73] 'Initial Report of States Party: Algeria' (1998) CEDAW/C/DZA/1 at 11.

question. We, in Kenya, are women, not just wombs. We have shown during the Mau Mau that we have ideas as well as babies.' Mrs Okala agreed and added, 'At home we fight. Some women have died in the struggle.' A tall wiry lawyer from Sierra Leone stood. 'In all of Africa women have suffered . . . I have been jailed and beaten. Because I would not tell the whereabouts of my friends, they also shot me . . . Because I fought against imperialism.'[74]

The recognition of women's contribution to the liberation of their countries was to lead to the removal of legal disabilities affecting African women.[75] In the case of Zimbabwe the principle of sexual equality was one of the cornerstones of the Marxist Leninist rhetoric, which was such a prominent feature of politics in the early years of independence. Indeed in 1986 the Zimbabwean government refused to accede to a demand made by the Iranian delegation on a state visit to Zimbabwe to the effect that women should not be allowed to sit at the top table at the formal state dinner. The Iranian delegation asked that in addition to not serving wine, women should be placed at the table farthest from the top table.[76] The government said that the women had been a part of the liberation struggle which had freed the country and could not therefore be discriminated against by barring them from participating in public life.[77] In Eritrea, the contribution of women during the liberation struggle has been acknowledged in the preamble of the Constitution, which reads in part:

> The Eritrean women's heroic participation in the struggle for independence, human rights and solidarity, based on equality and mutual respect generated by such struggle, will serve as an unshakeable foundation for our commitment to create a society in which women and men shall interact on the basis of mutual respect, solidarity and equality.[78]

The Constitution reflects the ideology of equality that formed the directives of the Eritrean Peoples Liberation Front during the struggle.[79] It has, however, to be acknowledged that this recognition of women's role in the liberation struggle has

---

[74] M Angelou *The Heart of a Woman* (London, Virago, 1986) 135–36.

[75] C Walker 'Women, Tradition and Reconstruction' (1994) *Review of African Political Economy* 347 at 351. See also C Walker *Women and Resistance in South Africa* (London, Onyx Press, 1982); S Hassim 'Nationalism, Feminism and Autonomy: The ANC in Exile and the Question of Women' (2004) 30 *Journal of Southern African Studies* 433–55. See also N Mandela 'Special Contribution' in UNDP above n 45 at 43.

[76] Mayer above n 28 at 116.

[77] *Ibid.* See also N Bhebe and T Ranger 'Introduction' in Bhebe and Ranger (eds) above n 56 at xlii.

[78] The Constitution of Eritrea 1997 reproduced in C Heyns (ed) *Human Rights Law in Africa* (The Hague, Martinus Nijhoff, 2004) vol 2 1066 at 1066. The Constitution of Mozambique 1990 Art 57(2) also acknowledges the contribution of women to the liberation struggle. On the importance of the liberation struggle generally see preamble and Art 7, reproduced in C Heyns (ed) *Human Rights Law in Africa* (The Hague, Kluwer International, 1996) 251 at 255 (Art 57(2)), 251 (preamble), 252 (Art 7).

[79] L Favali and R Pateman *Blood, Land and Sex: Legal and Political Pluralism in Eritrea* (Indianapolis, Indiana University Press, 2003) 129, 190.

not always resulted in the practical delivery of rights, or even changes to discriminatory laws.[80]

One of the ways in which post-colonial states have sought to guarantee the human rights of their citizens is through their constitutions, which provide for guarantees of equality before the law and non-discrimination on many grounds, including sex.[81] This would be phase three, the equality or non-discrimination phase in Hevener's typology.

What, then, is the basis of equality or non-discrimination in these constitutions? A brief diversion here to look at equality.

Equality

In many legal systems, the liberal model of equality is used.[82] With regard to sex discrimination, Mackinnon notes that the law requires one to 'reverse the sexes and compare. To see if a woman was discriminated against on the basis of sex, ask whether a similarly situated man would be or was so treated.'[83] If one sex is treated less favourably than the other, then that constitutes discrimination. Although that seems simple enough, this model is not without its problems.[84] The first and most obvious one is that the sexes cannot always be compared, for example pregnancy only happens to women. If a woman who is pregnant is fired from her job, or indeed has a job offer withdrawn because she is pregnant, what is the equivalent male comparator to use as the yardstick to ascertain whether discrimination has indeed occurred?[85] Unsatisfactorily, this difficulty has sometimes been resolved by equating pregnancy with illness.

---

[80]   *Ibid* at 190–93. Cf K Jayawardena *Feminism and Nationalism in the Third World* (London, Zed Press, 1986) 14; M Arthur 'Mozambique: Women in the Armed Struggle' in P McFadden (ed) *Southern Africa in Transition: A Gendered Perspective* (Harare, SAPES, 1998) 67; R Gaidzanwa 'Bourgeois Theories of Gender and Feminism and Their Shortcomings with Reference to Southern African Countries' in R Meena (ed) *Gender in South Africa: Conceptual and Theoretical Issues* (Harare, SAPES, 1992) 92 at 101–13; T Skard above n 19 at 180.

[81]   S Chiriga 'Perspectives on the Post-Beijing Policy Progress in the SADC Region' in P McFadden (ed) above n 80, 103 at 107; B Ibahwoh 'Between Culture and Constitution: Evaluating the Cultural Legitimacy of Human Rights in the African State' (2000) 22 *Human Rights Quarterly* 836. In 2004 Nigeria was commended by the Committee on the Elimination of Discrimination against Women for including sex as a ground for non-discrimination in its 1999 Constitution. CEDAW Concluding Comments Nigeria CEDAW/C/2004/1/CRP.3/Add.2/Rev.1 para 14.

[82]   N Lacey 'Feminist Legal Theory and the Rights of Women' in K Knop (ed) *Gender and Human Rights* (Oxford, Oxford University Press, 2003) 13 at 19–22. Gaidzanwa above n 80 at 99.

[83]   Mackinnon above n 23 at 217.

[84]   See generally Mackinnon above n 23 at 215–34.

[85]   Mubangizi, 'Too Pregnant to Work: The Dilemma of Economic Rationality versus Equality *Woolworths (Pty) Ltd v Whitehead*' (2000) 16 *South African Journal on Human Rights* 691.

The difficulty of using the liberal model of equality to deal with pregnancy was highlighted in the Zimbabwean case of *Mandizvidza v Morgenster College*.[86] The defendant institution, a teacher training institute, had a rule that said if a student fell pregnant or caused the pregnancy of another student, then that student would be withdrawn from the course.[87] The plaintiff, a married woman, became pregnant and the rule was invoked to exclude her. She challenged her exclusion, arguing that it constituted gender discrimination in violation of section 23(1) of the Constitution, as it only affected women and not men. The High Court judge who heard the case found for the plaintiff. She noted that the rule was specifically targeted at women, not least because a man who made a fellow student (or indeed students) pregnant while he was studying was not likely to be expelled, because it would be difficult to prove that he was responsible for the pregnancy or pregnancies. For women, pregnancy was not a state that could be hidden. The judge further noted that the rule was absurd, because if a male student impregnated his wife and she was not studying at the College then his position would be secure and he would not be asked to leave. Gwaunza J noted: 'The discriminatory effect, not to mention unreasonableness, of the clause needs no emphasis.'[88]

Despite its pretensions at equality, Gwaunza J held that the offending clause constituted gender discrimination in that 'such equality is in almost all respects not feasible'.[89] Moreover, the respondents' argument that the purpose of the rule was to discourage immorality in a Christian institution was dismissed as discriminatory in that it was targeted against female students.[90] The contention of the respondent institution, that it did not have the necessary facilities to have mothers and babies on campus, was also dismissed as discrimination against women, not least because 'it negates the right by women to combine their roles as mothers and productive members of society, when at the same time the father of the child is free to pursue his productive activities unencumbered by such responsibilities.'[91] In summary Gwaunza pointed out that both government and society were moving

---

[86] *Mandizvidza v Chaduka NO, and Morgenster College and The Minister of Higher Education* Unreported HH–236–99. For the reported Judgment see *Mandizvidza v Chaduka NO & Ors* 1999(2) ZLR 375 (H). Confirmed on appeal to the Supreme Court SC 114/2001. References here are to the unreported High Court judgment.

[87] This was clause 7(a) of the contract signed when a student joined the college. *Ibid* (unreported/cyclostyled judgment) at 2.

[88] *Ibid* at 10.

[89] *Ibid.*

[90] *Ibid.* See too the case of *Mofolo and Others v Minister of Education and Another* 1992 (3) SA181, cited with approval in *Mandizvidza* at 16–17 and also in Mubangizi above n 85 at 697. *Student Representative Council of Molepole College of Education v Attorney-General* Civil Appeal No 13 of 1994, discussed by E Quansah 'Is the Right to Get Pregnant a Fundamental Human Right in Botswana?' (1995) 39 *Journal of African Law* 97.

[91] *Mandizvidza v Chadukua & Ors* HH–236–99 at 11, 14. See also CEDAW art 5(b).

towards a society based on the idea that women should enjoy equality with men both in law and practice.[92]

The pregnancy example highlights the main criticism of the liberal model of equality—that it uses men as the norm for non-discrimination.[93] If men are the standard then women become the 'other', who have to be measured by their distance from the 'norm'.[94] The way that pregnancy has been dealt with appears to confirm Mackinnon's analysis of the inequity created by the liberal model of equality to the effect that when differences between men and women are acknowledged, then such a difference is treated as a condition deserving of 'special exemptions'.[95]

But why is a process that keeps the human race in business, the burden of which is borne by one half of humanity, albeit with some major contributions at the beginning of the process by the other half, classified as 'abnormal' or as outside the (male) norm? In its General Recommendation No 25 on temporary special measures, the Committee overseeing CEDAW notes that the interpretation of article 4(2) of CEDAW, which provides that measures taken by states parties that protect maternity shall not be considered discriminatory, illustrates that there is a need for 'the non-identical treatment of men and women due to their biological differences'.[96]

For cultural feminists it is important that differences between men and women be acknowledged. This requires us to see the roles and place of women in the world as separate and *different* from men's, but as having equal value and as being equally valued.[97] Indeed this is the argument sometimes made for understanding difference in the treatment of women in Islamic law. It is argued that men and women inhabit different spheres, and their roles should thus be seen as being 'complementary.'[98] During the drafting of CEDAW for example, the Moroccan representative argued for a change in the wording of the provision requiring that men and women should have 'the same rights and responsibilities during and after dissolution of marriage' because, as drafted, the provision:

---

[92] *Mandizvidza v Chadukua & Ors* HH–236–99 at 14.

[93] S Fredman 'A Difference with Distinction: Pregnancy and Parenthood Reassessed' (1994) 110 *Law Quarterly Review* 106 at 110. S Fredman 'Less Equal Than Others—Equality and Women's Rights' in C Gearty and A Tomkins (eds) *Understanding Human Rights* (London, Pinter, 1999) 197 at 199–200.

[94] Mackinnon above n 23 at 225–30, especially 226.

[95] Mackinnon above n 23 at 228.

[96] CEDAW General Recommendation No 25 CEDAW/C/2004/WP.1/Rev.1 paras 11 and 31(a) on 'placing a *gender* perspective at the centre of all policies and programmes affecting women's health'.

[97] Gilligan's seminal work on child development is often cited in this regard. C Gilligan *In a Different Voice: Psychological Theory and Women's Development* (Cambridge, Harvard University Press, 1982).

[98] World Bank *MENA Development Report: Gender and Development in the Middle East and North Africa* (Washington DC, World Bank, 2004) (hereafter referred to and cited as MENA Development Report (2004)) 10, 94.

[F]ailed to take into account a fact which was a matter of common sense, namely, that men and women, in order to be truly equal, did not need to be treated as being the same, which would be contrary to nature.[99]

It is also the argument made by Nzegwu in her robust critique of western feminism and in particular the liberal model of equality:

In a dual-sex context where individuals are valued for the skills they bring to community building and the role they play in developing the culture, gender identity is differently constructed. Identity is not abstractly constructed in terms of sameness, but concretely defined in terms of the worth of social duties and responsibilities. Because gender equality implies comparable worth, women and men are complements, whose duties, though different, are socially comparable.[100]

It here is worth noting that if we lived in a world where the work (reproductive, home and public sphere work) done by women was equally valued, the 'different by equal complementarity model' would be an admirable one. Sadly, this is not the world inhabited by the majority of the world's women. Indeed the operation of the 'different spheres/complementarity' model is one of the explanations given for the low participation of women in the public sphere in the Middle East and North Africa.[101] For these reasons cultural feminists have been described as out of touch with reality and as reinforcing gender stereotypes grounded in biological determinism.[102]

An older model of equality is based on the Aristotelian framework of treating 'likes alike and unalikes unalike'. Of this Chinkin notes:

The problem lies in determining what characteristics determine likeness. Equal treatment of men and women assumes commonality based upon human dignity. The standard of equality therefore works best where women are most like men, for example in public fields of employment. But equality also assumes meanings that have been constructed by patriarchy and uses men as the yardstick for comparison (for example in workplace practices). Women are either the same as men or different from men, and it is men who have determined the standard and who devalue the difference.[103]

However, not all men are alike; similarly not all women are alike. The model creates a pyramid of hierarchies, so that one can only complain of discrimination if

[99] L Rehof *Guide to the Travaux Préparatoires of the United Nations Convention on the Elimination of all Forms of Discrimination against Women* (Dordrecht, Martinus Nijhoff, 1993) 147.

[100] N Nzegwu 'Gender Equality in Dual-Sex System: The Case of Onitsha' (2001) 1 *Jenda: A Journal of Culture and African Women's Studies* at http://www.jendajournal.com/jenda/vol1.1/nzegwu.html at 11, see also 6, 7, 13, 17.

[101] MENA Development Report (2004) above n 98 at 13, 21, 93–127.

[102] C Smart *Feminism and the Power of Law* (London, Routledge, 1989) 75.

[103] C Chinkin 'Gender Inequality and Human Rights Law' in A Hurrell and N Woods (eds) *Inequality, Globalization and World Politics* (Oxford, Oxford University Press, 1999) 95 at 107. See also Fredman, 'Less Equal than Others' above n 93 at 201–2; Mackinon above n 23 at 225.

one is being treated less favourably than a person in one's status group.[104] Research done on the Twa of the Great Lakes showed that Twa women were paid up to 50 per cent less than women from other ethnic groups, thus showing that although both groups comprised women (technically 'alikes'), the two groups were in reality treated as 'unalikes'.[105] This example illustrates a common occurrence, namely that it is possible for minority and indigenous women to be paid less than majority women, who may in turn be paid less than majority men but more than minority men. Interestingly, both Twa men and women were paid less than other ethnic groups but the same as each other, meaning that in the public labour sphere Twa men and women are constructed as 'alike', but not necessarily in the private sphere.[106]

Mayer contends that some Islamic states operate using the Aristotelian principle of equality, holding women and non-Muslims as not having the same entitlements as Muslim men. She says that the 'prevalent approach' is to see these two groups as subordinate.[107] Arguably women on the continent continue to be treated as deserving a different status from men, which status is always inferior.

During the 'corrective' phase of law reform, there have been many legal changes that 'remove discrimination' and then expect women to 'get on with it'. To take such an approach is to ignore the long history of discrimination against women and the *effects* of the past discriminatory policies and practices on women. The playing field may appear to be level but it is not. It is like asking a group of people to run a 400 metre race when one section of the group (men) is given a 200 metre head start. It could not be claimed that this is a fair race.[108] Yet by ignoring that in many societies women's life chances are hampered by poverty and lack of resources, voice and education, especially when compared to men and boys, the liberal model of equality fails women.[109] For Kennedy: 'Treating people as equal who are not equal only creates further injustice.'[110] These are the main arguments against liberalism put forward by radical feminists.

Law and human rights have tried to deal with the inequities created by a formal application of the liberal model of equality by making provision for temporary special measures that permit derogation from a strict application of the liberal model of equality. These temporary special measures are to remain in place until

[104] Cf Gaidzanwa above n 80 at 100; Nzegwu above n 100 at 12.

[105] D Jackson *Twa Women, Twa Rights in the Great Lakes Region of Africa* (London, Minority Rights Group, 2003) 9.

[106] *Ibid* at 9, 26.

[107] Mayer above n 28 at 84.

[108] N Lacey 'Legislation against Sex Discrimination: Questions from a Feminist Perspective' (1987) 14 *Journal of Law and Society* 411.

[109] Chinkin above n 103 at 115; C Mannathoko 'Feminist Theories and the Study of Gender Issues in Southern Africa' in P McFadden (ed) *Southern Africa in Transition: A Gendered Perspective* (Harare, SAPES, 1998) 71 at 73–74.

[110] H Kennedy *Just Law* (London, Chatto & Windus, 2004) 196. CERD General Comment No 14 on Definition of Discrimination HRI/GEN/1Rev 3 para 2.

'their desired results have been achieved and sustained for a period of time'.[111] With this in mind, the Constitution of South Africa provides in part:

> Equality includes the full and equal enjoyment of all rights and freedoms. To promote the achievement of equality, legislative and other measures designed to protect or advance persons or categories of persons, disadvantaged by unfair discrimination may be taken.[112]

It is noteworthy that both Namibia[113] and South Africa have acknowledged the importance of addressing the historical inequities of apartheid.[114] Additionally, the Namibian Constitution lists as its first principle of state policy, the need to enact 'legislation to ensure equality of opportunity for women, to enable them to participate fully in all spheres of Namibian society'.[115] It goes without saying that the use of temporary special measures is controversial.[116]

A different criticism of the (liberal) equality model used in bills of rights is its individualism. Here it is argued that the individual nature of rights-based claims is at odds with cultures that see group identity as being more important than personal autonomy.[117] The criticism hones in on the construction of people as disconnected and not in any way linked to their wider communities. It is said that Africans and women understand 'a concept of self as dependent on others, as defined through relationships to others, as perceiving self-interest to lie in the welfare of the relational complex'.[118] The issue may thus not be about equality but

---

[111] See for example CEDAW art 4(1). See also CEDAW General Recommendation No 25 paras 20, 22.

[112] Constitution of South Africa 1996 s 9(2).

[113] Constitution of Namibia 1990 Art 63(2)(i).

[114] Bonthuys above n 21 at 53. South Africa has passed legislation seeking to address past discrimination. This includes The Employment Equity Act No 55 of 1998, The Promotion of Equality and Prevention of Unfair Discrimination Act 4 of 2000 (hereafter Equality Act 2000). See in particular the preamble; Pieterse above n 58; B Pityana 'The Challenge of Culture for Human Rights in Africa: The African Charter in Comparative Context' in M Evans and R Murray (eds) *The African Charter on Human and Peoples' Rights: The System in Practice, 1986–2000* (Cambridge, Cambridge University Press, 2002) 219 at 240. UNDP (2004) above n 45 at 69–72. See also Constitution of Uganda 1995 ss 32, 33(5), reproduced in Heyns (ed) (1996) above n 43, 371 at 384.

[115] Constitution of Namibia 1990 Art 95(a). However, it is noteworthy that principles of state policy are not justiciable, although courts can have regard to them when interpreting any laws based on them. *Ibid* Art 101. See also Constitution of Malawi 1994 Principles of State Policy s 13(a) on gender equality reproduced in Heyns, (ed) (1996) above 43, 216 at 217.

[116] K Henrard 'From the Constitutional Drawing Board to the Challenges of Implementation: Equality and Population Diversity' in J Murison *et al* (eds) *Remaking Law in Africa: Transnationalism, Persons and Rights* (Edinburgh, Centre of African Studies, 2004) 71 at 83–88; Kennedy above n 110 at 141.

[117] Sinclair above n 59 at 819–20. While she cautions against an over-reliance on northern-inspired equality jurisprudence, Sinclair does not indicate what she sees as being the key components of an African standard of equality or alternative to the northern model.

[118] S Harding *The Science Question in Feminism* (Milton Keynes, Open University Press, 1986) 170, as cited in H Charlesworth, C Chinkin and S Wright 'Feminist Approaches to International Law' (1991) 85 *American Journal of International Law* 613 at 617; A Armstrong 'Rethinking Culture and Tradition in Southern Africa: Research from WLSA' in A Stewart (ed) *Gender, Law and Social Justice* (Oxford, Blackstone, 2000) 87 at 96; Nzegwu above n 100 at 2, 7, 10. But see Maboreke above n 71 at 109, 113, and 114.

about a 'clash of normative orders'. It is of course clear that in the context of women's rights, the claim for entitlement by one woman may be resisted by the group because it 'upsets' the social order and also because it challenges existing power relations. However, it is as well here to acknowledge the changes in community and family obligations brought about by AIDS and collapsing economies.

The third phase of law reform on the continent, constitution making, is linked to the coming of independence to African states. In many ex-British colonies independence was granted on the understanding that the black government would accept the Westminster-type constitution. This constitutional model focused on providing for that which had not existed during colonialism, namely 'democracy' evidenced by universal suffrage and multi-party politics, and also on ensuring that the rights of the remaining white minority were secured, for example in Zimbabwe.[119] In the British derived constitutions the rights of African women were not prioritised. This can be seen by the omission of sex as a ground on which discrimination was proscribed, and also the uncritical exemption of customary law from the non-discrimination and equality provisions. This constitutional model has been retained in some states, including Botswana, Zambia and Zimbabwe. The constitutions of states that arose out of internal discussions with opposing parties were more progressive and attended to the needs of women, albeit with some hard lobbying from women to ensure that this was the case.

I shall now consider the effect of these different constitutional models on the rights of women. Specifically I look at how African states have dealt with the thorny issue of reconciling principles of non-discrimination on the basis of sex found in national constitutions and the demands of 'custom, culture and tradition', which sometimes appear to be in conflict.[120]

Constitutional protection of women's rights

A cursory examination of the constitutions of different Anglophone African states highlights the fact that the responses to the existence of plural laws and their interaction with each other and with human rights norms, as found in constitutional bills of rights, vary. Common to the constitutions of many Anglophone African states is a recognition of customary law as being part of the formal legal system in the territory. Linked to this is the issue of whether constitutional guarantees of freedom from discrimination include sex and (latterly) gender, and whether

---

[119] S Adelman 'Constitutionalism, Pluralism and Democracy in Africa' (1998) 42 *Journal of Legal Pluralism* 73 at 79.
[120] A broader discussion of how to reconcile cultural considerations with human rights norms is found in Chapter 7.

customary law is made subject to such non-discrimination provisions or given special dispensation? Some systems see customary law and 'culture' as being subject to non-discrimination provisions contained within the bill of rights.[121] Yet others grant customary law immunity from non-discrimination provisions.[122] In general it seems that the newer (post-1990) constitutions are the more progressive. They embody human rights principles of equality and non-discrimination, the third phase of the Hevener typology. In so doing, these constitutions fulfil the first state obligation of CEDAW, requiring states to 'embody the principle of the equality of men and women in their national constitutions'.[123] As already noted, some of the newer constitutions acknowledge that some people have been subject to multiple forms of discrimination, including race and gender, and therefore provide that special attention should be paid to redressing the effects of the intersectional discrimination.[124]

In summary, one can identify three basic constitutional models, which are labelled for convenience: (i) strong cultural relativism, which allows customary law to exist unfettered by considerations of non-discrimination or equality before the law provisions; (ii) weak cultural relativism, which recognises customary law and also provides for equality before the law without making explicit the hierarchy between the formal recognition of equality provisions and the continued existence of customary law; and (iii) the 'universalist' position, which, whilst recognising customary law and a right to culture, makes both subject to the test of non-discrimination and equality before the law.

It must be acknowledged from the outset that these categories are merely abstractions and are not scientific. They are used as hooks on to which to hang the analysis of cases that follows. In creating this typology I do not mean to suggest that there are 'fixed' positions that can be plotted accurately, but rather that the question of cultural relativism and universality are not two parallel lines but are part of a continuum. Seen in this way, one can plot 'relativisms' depending on context/historical position and other chosen variables.

Santos questions the whole universal/relativist dichotomy, arguing that universalism is no more than a western hegemonic world view that constructs different cultures as somehow deviant from the norm.[125] Viewed from this perspective, my

---

[121] The constitutions of Ghana 1992 Art 27(4)(d); Ethiopia 1994 Arts 9(1), 25; Malawi 1994 ss 20(1), 24(2); Mozambique 1990 Arts 66, 67, 162 and Uganda 1995 s 21(2), 33(5) and Principle of State Policy XXIV(a) amongst others. All reproduced in Heyns (ed) (1996) above n 43 and Heyns (ed) (2004) vol 2 above n 78.

[122] The constitutions of Sierra Leone 1991 s 27(4)(d); Zambia 1991 s 23(4)(c) and Botswana 1966 Art 15(4)(c), reproduced in Heyns (ed) (1996) above n 43 and Heyns (ed) (2004) vol 2 above n 78.

[123] CEDAW art 2(a).

[124] Constitution of Ghana 1992 Art 17(4)(a); Constitution of Uganda 1995 ss 32, 33(5) and Principles of State Policy VI.

[125] B Sousa Santos 'Towards a Multicultural Conception of Human Rights' (1997) XXIV *Sociologia del Diritto* 27.

own categorisation of constitutions that uphold 'cultural norms' as relative, leaves me open to criticism and the assertion that I am myself suffering from what Nzegwu calls an idolisation of the western value system, that is constructing what is closest to a supposedly northern or Eurocentric model of human rights as 'universal', and what is more in tune with a supposedly 'African worldview' as culturally relative. To which or whose culture is it relative, and why should the 'northern inspired model' be the standard?[126] In my defence, I reiterate my earlier assertion that the categories are merely hangers on which to place concepts in advance of discussing them.

The three broadly drawn categories are explored in Table 1, which examines the constitutions of Zimbabwe (strong cultural relativism), Tanzania (weak cultural relativism) and South Africa (universal) as representations of the categories as described.

Table 1. *Basic constitutional models*

	Zimbabwe (strong cultural relativism)	Tanzania (weak cultural relativism)	South Africa (universal)
Recognise customary law	X	X	X
Sex/gender non-discrimination	X		X
Customary law subject to non-discrimination provision			X
Customary law not subject to non-discrimination provision	X		
Equality before the law provision		X	X

It seems, therefore, that three strands can be isolated:

(1) Whether local law, in this case customary law, is recognised in the constitution?
(2) Whether human rights norms in the form of non sex/gender discrimination provisions and equality before the law provisions are included in the Constitution?

---

[126] Nzegwu above n 100 at 15.

(3) Assuming that the answer to both is yes, whether provision is made for reconciling any conflicts/contradictions between the customary/local law provisions with human rights norms?[127]

Arguably (3) is made easier where (2) is clearly part of a legal system that holds
equality before the law and a prohibition against discrimination on the grounds of
sex as being non-derogable. This would require that customary law be put through
the non-discrimination filter. It therefore becomes important to see how customary norms or traditional African values have been dealt with in domestic case law,
focusing on inheritance law cases. Although issues of succession and inheritance
are canvassed more fully in Chapter 4 on family law, it is here worth noting that
the state version of customary law in patrilineal societies, provides that the inheritance rights of men and boys (male relatives) are to take precedence over those of
women and girls (wives and daughters). The cases discussed in this section consider this presumption.

The Zimbabwean Constitution is a strongly relativist one. It recognises customary law as being on a par with general law. The non-discrimination provision
in section 23(2) covers race, tribe and religion, but not sex. Although amended in
1996 to include gender as a ground on which discrimination is forbidden,[128] the
Constitution ring fences customary law from the non-discrimination provision
providing:

> 23(3) Nothing contained in any law shall be held to be in contravention of subsection
> 1(a) to the extent that the law in question relates to any of the following matters—
> (a) adoption, marriage, divorce, burial, devolution of property on death or other mat-
> ters of personal law.

The effect of this provision was seen in the Supreme Court case of *Magaya v
Magaya*,[129] where it was argued successfully that a woman did not have a right to
inherit under the customary law of her group. Venia Magaya had wanted to inherit
the property of her deceased father, which property she had helped to acquire. The
Supreme Court held that the principle of non-discrimination did not operate
because customary law was shielded from the non-discrimination provision in the
Constitution by virtue of section 23(3). Ignoring Zimbabwe's ratification of the
African Charter on Human and Peoples' Rights,[130] the court, whilst acknowledg-

---

[127] This analysis may be construed as suggesting a particular fixed version of customary law that is
inherently discriminatory towards women—a position challenged by T Nhlapo 'African Family Law
under an Undecided Constitution—The Challenge for Law Reform in South Africa' in J Eekelaar and
T Nhlapo (eds) *Changing Family* (Oxford, Hart Publishing, 1998) 617, 627. This is not my intention.

[128] Constitutional Amendment Act No 14.

[129] *Magaya v Magaya* 1999 (1) ZLR 100.

[130] Zimbabwe has also acceded to CEDAW but has yet to incorporate it into domestic law as
required by the country's Constitution. F Banda 'Inheritance and Marital Rape' in A Bainham (ed)
International Survey of Family Law 2001 (Bristol, Jordan Publishing, 2001) 475.

ing the importance of advancing gender equality, adopted a static view of customary law that reinforced male privilege, and noted:

> [G]reat care must be taken when African customary law is under consideration. In the first instance, it must be recognized that customary law has long directed the way African people conducted their lives . . . In the circumstances, it will not be readily be abandoned, especially by those such as senior males who stand to lose their positions of privilege.[131]

In *Ephraim v Pastory*,[132] Tanzanian courts were presented with a claim by the nephew of a woman, arguing that, as a woman, his aunt did not, under the patrilineal customary law of the Haya group, have the right to sell the clan land that she had inherited. His contention was supported by the law on customary inheritance, which provided:

> [W]omen can inherit, except for clan land, which they may receive in usufruct but may not sell. However, if there is not the male of that clan, women may inherit such land in full ownership.[133]

Although the non-discrimination provision of the Constitution did not include sex as one of the grounds on which discrimination was prohibited,[134] the Court of Appeal used the equality before the law provision in the Constitution[135] to hold that customary law had to accord with human rights norms of equality and nondiscrimination, thus women had to be given the same rights at customary law as men. Although the Constitution was silent on the issue of the hierarchy of customary law and the equality provision, the Tanzanian courts pointed to Tanzania's international obligations[136] as showing that women's rights were to be respected and that customary law had to evolve to reflect this new order. The law on the rules of inheritance was taken to have been modified and qualified, and any law banning women from alienating land was void and of no effect.[137]

In obiter dicta, the court noted that the case had been brought by a 'simple, old rural woman', and not by 'the elite women in town who chant jejune slogans years on end on women's lib but without delivering the goods'.[138] Although clearly a dig at professional women, the judge's observation also helps to challenge the myth that it is only urban women without cultural moorings who seek a different interpretation of 'African cultural values'. It also illustrates that there is often a

[131] *Magaya v Magaya* 1999 (1) 100, 113. Cf *Nawaki v Attorney-General of Zambia* [1993] 3 LRC 231.
[132] *Ephraim v Pastory* [1990] LRC 757. See Banda above n 130 at 482.
[133] Laws of Inheritance of the Declaration of Customary Law, GN No 436 of 1963, para 20. *Ephraim v Pastory* above n 132 at 761.
[134] Constitution of Tanzania 1988 s 13(5) in Heyns (ed) (1996) above n 43 at 355.
[135] Constitution of Tanzania 1988 s 13(1)(2) in Heyns (ed) (1996) above n 43 at 355.
[136] It was noted that Tanzania had ratified the International Covenant on Civil and Political Rights 1996 (ICCPR) and CEDAW. It had also ratified the African Charter. It was noted that the bill of rights reflected the norms found in the UDHR. *Ephraim v Pastory* at 763.
[137] *Ibid* at 770.
[138] *Ibid.*

construction of feminism as a peculiarly urban and middle class 'disease' that is 'rooted in an adoption of Western ways and values', meaning that the efforts of other women engaged in challenging discriminatory cultural practices are ignored.[139]

The third case is from South Africa. In *Bhe*,[140] the courts were again faced with an African woman challenging the patriarchal construction of customary law, which favoured the rights of inheritance of men over women. The action was brought by the mother of two minor female children (in her capacity as their guardian), whose father had died intestate, requesting that the children be named their father's heirs, which would result in them being given rights to the father's property. The grandfather challenged this, noting that customary law operated on the principle of primogeniture, which gave the closest surviving male relative the right to inherit.[141] The plaintiff's counsel addressed this rule and noted that it was unconstitutional, discriminatory and irrational. The plaintiff thus sought a declaration of invalidity of the offending provisions of the Black Administration Act 1927 and the Intestate Succession Act 1987.

The High Court held in favour of the daughters, noting that the Constitution guaranteed equal rights to women and was premised upon the principle of non-discrimination including sex. The primogeniture principle was in violation of the non-discrimination provisions of the Constitution and could not be upheld:

> We should make it clear in this judgment that a situation whereby a male person will be preferred to a female person for purposes of inheritance can no longer withstand constitutional scrutiny. That constitutes discrimination before the law. To put it plainly, African females, irrespective of age or social status, are entitled to inherit from their parents' intestate estate like any male person.[142]

The rule also violated section 28 of the Constitution on the rights of children to be free from discrimination. Issuing a declaration of invalidity, the High Court ordered that until such time as the offending legislation was amended, intestate succession of black Africans was to be governed by section 1 of the Intestate Succession Act 81 of 1987, which governed the legal regimes of other population groups and did not adhere to the primogeniture principle. Ngwenya J recognised the impact of intersectional discrimination in the way that the law had hitherto been framed and operated:

[139] U Narayan *Dislocating Cultures: Identities, Traditions, and Third-World Feminism* (New York, Routledge, 1997) 20. See also Bonthuys above n 21 at 58.

[140] *Bhe and Others v The Magistrate, Khayelitsha and Others* High Court South Africa, Cape Provincial Division Case No 9489/02, unreported.

[141] *Ibid* at 13.

[142] *Ibid* at 19. See also C Himonga 'Legislative and Judicial Approaches to the Reform of the Customary Law of Marriage and Succession in South Africa: Implications for the Advancement of Women's Rights' (paper presented at the Conference on Advancing Women's Rights Hosted by the Women's Legal Centre, Cape Town, 30–31 October 2003) available at http://www.wlce.co.za/conference2003/2003conference_himonga.php 1–17 at 6.

The underlying imperative of the Black Administration Act is that of male preference as against equality of genders and that of African discrimination as against other races.[143]

In the *Bhe* case the 'universalist' construction of the Constitution won out.[144] The case went before the Constitutional Court for confirmation of the invalidity of the legislation in question. The case was heard, with two others, by the Constitutional Court. The judgment, handed down on 15 October 2004, confirmed the High Court decision.[145]

It is of course questionable whether universalism means that in all places the rights framework has to be applied in the same way. Can human rights norms not be constructed as permeable and able to be influenced by values emanating from other 'semi-autonomous fields'/normative fields?[146] Surveying the legislative and judicial interventions in South Africa, Himonga urges caution, noting that all that may be achieved by a raft of legal change is paper gains rather than substantive change on the ground.[147]

However, if one sees national constitutions as reflecting a national understanding and commitment to human rights norms, then both the framing and interpretation of those norms by governments and courts can tell us a great deal about the institutional commitment to human rights and, in this instance, the rights of women.[148] This interpretation is in line with state obligations in CEDAW and the African Protocol on Women's Rights, which provides that states should:

[I]nclude in their national constitutions and other legislative instruments, if not already done, the principle of equality between women and men and ensure its effective application.[149]

It may well be, as Himonga notes, that that problem is not with rights per se but with their packaging and presentation. With this in mind, she suggests that rejection of reform of laws and practices could be mitigated if states took greater care in forward planning by anticipating problems likely to occur before the law was

---

[143] *Bhe v Magistrate Khayelitsha* above n 140 at 18.

[144] This decision was anticipated by Pieterse who noted that s 8(c) of the Equality Act 2000 removing gender discrimination in matters of succession and inheritance made the primogeniture rule untenable: Pieterse above n 58 at 630.

[145] *Bhe v Magistrate Khayelitsha and Others* CCT-49-03.

[146] C Albertyn and B Goldblaat 'Facing the Challenge of Transformation: Difficulties in the Development of an Indigenous Jurisprudence of Equality' (1998) 14 *South African Journal on Human Rights* 248; Bonthuys above n 21 at 41–58; Pieterse above n 58 at 628.

[147] Himonga above n 142.

[148] Cf Ibahwoh above n 81 at 838, 844.

[149] African Protocol on Women's Rights art 2(1)(a), which is similar to CEDAW art 2(a). See also Victoria Falls Declaration of Principles for Promoting the Human Rights of Women as Agreed by Senior Judges at the African Regional Judicial Colloquium Zimbabwe, 19–20 August 1994, in A Byrnes et al (eds) *Advancing the Human Rights of Women: Using International Human Rights Standards in Domestic Litigation* (London, Commonwealth Secretariat, 1994) 3–5 paras 7, 9, 11. See too UNDP (2004) above n 45 at 58.

passed, rather than retrospectively as is often the case. To aid in this process, there should be greater consultation, public education and research. Moreover, lawyers and NGOs could assist by giving free legal representation and filing amicus briefs on behalf of those in need.[150]

Conclusion

This chapter began with a consideration of the development of customary laws on the continent starting from the time of colonisation until independence. After a brief look at the notion of equality, constitutional provisions were examined to see how different states have dealt with the conundrum of guarantees of non-discrimination on grounds of sex or gender, co-existing with notions of right to culture and personal laws that may discriminate against a particular group, usually women.

In addition to domestic law making, states have also had to engage with international law. The status of international law in the domestic or municipal forum is determined by reference to constitutional provisions and sometimes by way of judicial interpretation.[151] The next chapter is an examination of the adoption, at the institutional level, of human rights principles on the continent.

---

[150] Himonga above n 142 at 11–12. This is echoed in the Victoria Falls Declaration (1994) above n 149 at paras 16–21.

[151] Most of the countries formerly under British colonial rule demand parliamentary approval and sometimes a statute of incorporation before human rights instruments are used in domestic law. J Dugard 'The Role of Human Rights Treaty Standards in Domestic Law: the Southern African Experience' in P Alston and J Crawford (eds) *The Future of UN Human Rights Treaty Monitoring* (Cambridge, Cambridge University Press, 2000) 269; J Allain and A O'Shea 'African Disunity: Comparing Human Rights Law and Practices of North and South African States' (2002) 24 *Human Rights Quarterly* 86 at 98–100, 104–106; Heyns (ed) (2004) vol 2 above n 78.

3

Human Rights in Africa

Human rights have come to be seen as one of the dominant global discourses. Their power is said to lie in the common language that reflects if not shared values then certainly commonly understood, if not always enforced, minimum standards.[1] However, for as long as modern human rights have existed, so too have challenges to their legitimacy, and in particular to the universality of the norms espoused in human rights instruments. The challenges have come from a variety of sources: southern states have argued that the focus on civil and political rights has created a hierarchy of human rights that prioritises civil and political rights over more pressing concerns such as the right to food,[2] and therefore as less relevant to the vast majority of persons in the south who suffer from poverty and underdevelopment.[3] Similarly, some states have challenged human rights as being ethnocentric and not reflective of the different religious and 'cultural' diversities of the world.[4] This has resulted in ongoing challenges to the notion of the universality of human rights, questioning the shared values on which modern human rights are said to be founded.

It is fair to say that in recent times the cultural relativism debate has centred on the content, interpretation and application of personal laws, and in particular on the rights of women within these personal laws, be they based on customary or religious principles. Feminist challenges to the construct of 'universalism' as

---

[1] R Higgins *Problems and Process: International Law and How We Use It* (Oxford, Clarendon Press, 1994).

[2] C Chinkin 'The United Nations Decade for the Elimination of Poverty: What Role for International Law?' in M Freeman (ed) *Current Legal Problems* (Oxford, Oxford University Press, 2001) 553.

[3] There has been a shift from both sides so that increasingly both sets of rights are regarded as being of equal importance. See United Nations World Conference on Human Rights: Vienna Declaration and Programme of Action reproduced in 32 ILM 1661 (1993) (I) para 5; Grand Bay (Mauritius) Declaration and Plan of Action (12–16 April 1999) Grand Bay, Mauritius, CONF/HRA/DECL (1).

[4] Cf S Samuels 'Hong-Kong on Women, Asian Values and the Law' (1999) *Human Rights Quarterly* 707; A Mayer *Islam and Human Rights* (Boulder, Westview Press, 1999) 1–17; M Jacobsen and O Bruun (eds) *Human Rights and Asian Values* (London, Curzon, 2000); A An Na'im and F Deng (eds) *Human Rights in Africa: Cross-Cultural Perspectives* (Washington DC, The Brookings Institution, 1990); A An Na'im (ed) *Human Rights in Cross-Cultural Perspectives* (Philadelphia, University of Pennsylvania Press, 1992).

universalising only an idealised (northern) male perspective[5] have gone hand in hand with critiques of the defence of static 'patriarchal cultures' by male elites from southern states.[6]

This chapter starts with a consideration of the feminist critique of international law before moving on to examine the African perspective put forward by Murray and Mutua, amongst others.[7] The African framework of rights is then considered. Thereafter sub-regional initiatives on women's rights are examined before moving on to explore the provisions of the Convention on the Elimination of All Forms of Discrimination against Women 1979 (CEDAW). The final part examines the history of the drafting of the African Protocol on Women's Rights 2003.

Feminist analysis of international law

The feminist analysis of international law makes the following claims. On its face, international law is gender-neutral, being concerned primarily with state issues of sovereignty, territory or the use of force.[8] However, it is when one looks at the application of international law in its relation to individuals, and in particular to women within states, that questions of bias emerge.[9] Specifically, it is contended:

> A feminist account of international law suggests that we inhabit a world in which men of all nations have used the statist system to establish economic and nationalist priorities to serve male elites while basic human, social and economic needs are not met. International institutions currently echo these same priorities.[10]

The authors argue that in this regard, international law as currently constructed is international men's law.[11] It is thus described because its gaze or focus is on the

---

[5] H Charlesworth, C Chinkin and S Wright 'Feminist Approaches to International Law' (1991) 85 *American Journal of International Law* 613 at 644; H Charlesworth 'Human Rights as Men's Rights' in J Peters and A (eds) *Women's Rights, Human Rights: International Feminist Perspectives* (New York, Routledge, 1995) 103; H Charlesworth and C Chinkin *Boundaries of International Law* (Manchester, Manchester University Press, 2000).

[6] Cf A Mayer 'A Benign Apartheid: How Gender Apartheid has been Rationalized' (2000) 5 *UCLA Journal of International Law and Foreign Affairs* 237 at 240, 268–70, 272–73; G Mikell 'Introduction' in G Mikell (ed) *African Feminism: The Politics of Survival in Sub-Saharan Africa* (Philadelphia, University of Pennsylvania Press, 1997) 28.

[7] R Murray *The African Commission on Human Rights and International Law* (Oxford, Hart Publishing, 2000); M Mutua 'Savages, Victims, and Saviors: The Metaphor of Human Rights' (2001) 42 *Harvard International Law Journal* 201.

[8] Charlesworth *et al* above n 5 at 614.

[9] *Ibid* at 625. Fellmeth is sceptical about this claim pointing out that 'there are now about two dozen significant international instruments purporting to protect the rights of women or remedy gender-based inequalities.' A Fellmeth, 'Feminism and International Law: Theory, Methodology, and Substantive Reform' (2000) 22 *Human Rights Quarterly* 658 at 727.

[10] Charlesworth *et al* above n 5 at 615. Fellmeth questions this particular view of the state: Fellmeth above n 9 at 674.

[11] Charlesworth *et al* above n 5 at 644. See too Charlesworth and Chinkin above n 5 at 218ff.

violations perpetrated by the state or its organs and agents and that occur in the public sphere, which violations largely affect men. The lives of women are lived out largely in the private sphere, where violations against women are more likely than not to be committed by non-state actors.[12] Until fairly recently the responsibility of states for violations of rights by non-state actors had not been clearly elaborated.[13] That this is changing is acknowledged by Charlesworth and Chinkin in a later offering.[14]

Another consideration of international law's male exclusivity is the exclusion of women from norm making and also participation in international organisations.[15] The participation of women in public life is limited in many countries—if not by law then as a result of socio-structural inequalities and the demands of wifehood and motherhood which keep women out of the public arena. This lack of participation in turn means that the rights or issues that are considered important are those so considered by the largely male participants in the political process.[16] However, Fellmeth questions this assertion and argues that there is nothing in international human rights law per se that excludes women from participating.[17]

Murray has adapted Charlesworth, Chinkin and Wright's feminist analysis of international law to describe the place of Africa in international law.[18] Murray takes that part of feminist analysis which focuses on the exclusion of different voices in the construction of norms to argue that African states, like women, have been largely ignored by the international community.[19] She does, however, qualify the public-private distinction, noting that the state in Africa has evolved in such a way that the dichotomy between public and private is not as clear cut as it appears to be in the north.[20]

---

[12] Charlesworth *et al* above n 5 at 62ff. But see Fellmeth above n 9 at 676–77.

[13] See also Murray above n 7 at 37–38.

[14] Charlesworth and Chinkin above n 5 at 148–51; B Pityana 'The Challenge of Culture for Human Rights in Africa: the African Charter in Comparative Context' in M Evans and R Murray (eds) *The African Charter on Human and Peoples' Rights: The System in Practice, 1986–2000* (Cambridge, Cambridge University Press, 2002) 219 at 230.

[15] Charlesworth *et al* above n 5 at 622–25.

[16] *Ibid* at 638ff; C Mackinnon *Towards a Feminist Theory of the State* (Cambridge, Harvard University Press, 1989) 282–84.

[17] Fellmeth (above n 9) at 729.

[18] Murray above n 7 at 1–4.

[19] Murray above n 7 at 4. It is here worth noting that Charlesworth, Chinkin and Wright themselves acknowledge that the 'the sustained Third World critique of international law and insistence on diversity may well have prepared the philosophical ground for feminist critiques'. Charlesworth *et al* above n 5 at 644. But see also at 618, where they say:

> the challenge to the European origins of international law and many of its assumptions may have had an adverse effect on the development of a gender-based international law precisely because of the further level of confrontation it is assumed such an analysis would cause.

[20] Murray above n 7 at 38.

The African perspective

In much the same ways as feminists have questioned the silence and invisibility of women in both national and international law, so too Mutua asks why the dominant western model of human rights rejects the input of non-western cultures, insisting instead that they conform to the western ideal or model.[21] Mutua notes that the construction of the north and 'its' human rights as normative results in a process of '"othering" that imagines the creation of inferior clones, in effect dumb copies of the original'.[22] On issues of gender, he points to a link between Eurocentric human rights and their construction of African societies as 'savage' and the women as 'victims' needing rescuing from 'barbaric practices' such as female genital cutting, using the language of the protection of rights.[23] The construction of rights as being value-neutral is also critiqued by him.

In this regard, coming under Mutua's critical gaze are Donnelly and Howard, whose views he argues are essentialist.[24] He contends that the two hide behind human rights norms as 'neutral' when in fact they are merely reflections of a preference for the western liberal model of state.[25] A consideration of Donnelly and Howard's criteria for determining which states are 'human rights compliant' and which are not, or cannot be, shows that Mutua's concerns are not without foundation. Donnelly and Howard draw up a table with different types of socio-political regimes, whose 'human rights compliance capabilities' and social definition of human dignity are examined using selected criteria.[26] These criteria are whether the society is one based on autonomy or role fulfilment, conflict or consensus, repression of outsiders, valuation of privacy and equality or hierarchy. Liberal societies or states are autonomy based, are conflict oriented, do not repress outsiders, value privacy highly and believe in equality. In contrast 'traditional' societies, by which one assumes is meant non-western societies, believe in role fulfilment over autonomy; consensus over conflict; are said to repress outsiders; score very low on valuation of privacy and prefer hierarchy to equality. Put in this way, one can see the evident superiority of the 'liberal' over the 'traditional' society.[27] However, those who live in

---

[21] Mutua above n 7 at 205; see also Pityana above n 14 at 227.

[22] Mutua above n 7 at 205; M Mutua 'The Banjul Charter: The Case for an African Cultural Fingerprint' in A An Na'im (ed) *Cultural Transformation and Human Rights in Africa* (London, Zed Press, 2002) 68 at 78.

[23] Mutua above n 7 at 205, 226–27 and 245.

[24] Mutua 'Banjul Charter' (2002) above n 22 at 77–80.

[25] Mutua above n 22 at 78.

[26] R Howard and J Donnelly 'Human Dignity, Human Rights and Political Regimes' in J Donnelly (ed) *Universal Human Rights in Theory and Practice* (Ithaca, Cornell University Press, 1989) 66, 85–86.

[27] Howard and Donnelly note: 'only in a liberal regime can there be fundamental political commitment to the full range of internationally recognized human rights.' *Ibid* at 87; Mutua 'Banjul Charter' (2002) above n 22 at 71 fn 15.

so-called traditional societies may have a different perspective on the functioning of their societies.[28] The construction of liberal societies as believing in equality and not repressing outsiders is clearly contradicted by the overwhelming evidence of discrimination faced by outsiders within those communities.[29] In fairness to Donnelly, it is important to acknowledge that in a postscript elsewhere he is at pains to point out that:

> The label 'Western' does *not* imply that the West has necessarily made more progress in implementing internationally recognized human rights, that the West is not or has not been the source of many human rights problems and violations throughout the world, that cultural 'Westernisation' is essential or even necessarily helpful to realizing human rights, or that the West deserves special praise or should feel pride for 'discovering' (or inventing or creating) human rights.[30]

Engaging with international human rights on the African continent

Although left out of the early drafting of human rights instruments,[31] African states have been keen participants in ratifying human rights instruments thereafter, so that 48 states on the continent are parties to the International Covenant on Civil and Political Rights 1966 (ICCPR)[32] and 45 to the International Covenant on Economic Social and Cultural Rights 1966 (ICESCR).[33] Both of these instru-

---

[28] Mutua 'Banjul Charter' (2002) above n 22 at 78.

[29] An examination of the reports of states parties to the Committee on the Elimination of Race Discrimination (CERD) and of its concluding comments show that discrimination against 'outsiders' exists in liberal societies. Similarly one need only look at the demonisation of asylum seekers, non-western migrants and (increasingly) Muslims in the western media to understand that repression of outsiders is not the sole preserve of 'traditional' or southern societies. Article 19 *'What's the Story? Results from Research into Media Coverage of Refugees and Asylum Seekers in the UK'* (London, Article 19, 2003) available at http://www.article19.org; F Banda and C Chinkin *Gender, Minorities and Indigenous Peoples* (London, Minority Rights Group, 2004) 11, 24–25.

[30] J Donnelly *Universal Human Rights in Theory and Practice* (Ithaca, Cornell University Press, 1989) 64.

[31] Only four countries on the continent took part in the drafting of the Universal Declaration of Human Rights. The rest were under colonial government. The four participants were Egypt, Ethiopia, Liberia and South Africa. Seemingly without irony, South Africa formalised the policy of apartheid in 1948, the same year in which the UDHR was adopted. South Africa abstained in the vote for the adoption of the UDHR.

[32] International Covenant on Civil and Political Rights. Adopted by General Assembly Resolution 2200A (XXI) of 16 December 1966. Entered into force 23 March 1976. 48 of the 53 African states have ratified ICCPR and 3 have signed it. From http://web.amnesty.org/web/web/nsf/print/treaty-countries-ratification-eng.

[33] International Covenant on Economic, Social and Cultural Rights (ICESCR). Adopted by General Assembly Resolution 2200A (XXI) of 16 December 1966. Entered into force on 3 January 1976. 45 states have ratified the ICESCR and 2 have signed it. *Ibid.*

ments contain provisions that proscribe discrimination on the basis of sex and guarantee equality before the law.[34] In line with initiatives to mainstream gender into the work of the United Nations, the Human Rights Committee that oversees the ICCPR has also issued general comments on issues pertaining to the right of women to enjoy their human rights on a basis of equality with men.[35]

CEDAW has also been eagerly received on the continent, being ratified by all states with the exception of Somalia and Sudan.[36] Similarly all but Somalia are parties to the United Nations Convention on the Rights of the Child 1979 (CRC).[37] The main regional instrument, the African Charter on Human and Peoples' Rights 1981 (African Charter) is ratified by all Member States of the African Union.[38] The African Charter on the Rights and Welfare of the Child 1990 (ACRWC) has been ratified by 35 states.[39] The promotion and protection of human and peoples' rights is central to the African Union.[40]

African states have also participated in and hosted international human rights conferences. The Nairobi conference in 1985[41] both consolidated gains made during the UN Decade for Women and set the agenda for future conferences. Similarly the International Conference on Population and Development[42] (the Cairo population conference) marked a milestone in the re-conceptualisation of reproductive rights. The 1995 Beijing Conference[43] was well attended by African states, as was the regional preparatory conference. From the foregoing it becomes

---

[34] ICCPR arts 2, 2(1), 3 and 26; ICESCR arts 2, 2(2), 3. The UDHR also contains provisions outlawing discrimination on the ground of sex, art 2, and guaranteeing equality before the law, art 7.

[35] Human Rights Committee General Comment No 18 Non-Discrimination (21 November 1989) CCPR/C/21/Rev.1.Add.1; Human Right Committee General Comment on Equality of Rights between Men and Women (art 3) (29 March 2000); CCPR/C/21/Rev.1Add.10; CCPR General Comment 28; CERD General Comment No 14. A general comment on art 3 of the ICESCR on equality between men and women is expected to be adopted by the Committee on Economic Social and Cultural Rights (CESCR) in November 2004. ECOSOC Specific Human Rights Issues: Note by the Secretary-General (22 June 2004) E/CN.4/Sub.2/2004/33 para 9. See too Montreal Principles on Women's Economic Social and Cultural Rights 2004 *Human Rights Quarterly* 760, also available from http://cescr.org/node/view/ 697.

[36] From http://www.un.org/womenwatch/daw/cedaw/states.htm.

[37] United Nations Convention on the Rights of the Child. Adopted by General Assembly Resolution 44/25 of 20 November 1989. Entered into force 2 September 1990.

[38] Ratifications of the African Charter on http://www.africa-union.org.

[39] List available at http://www.africa-union.org/home/welcome/htm.

[40] Constitutive Act of the African Union 2002, preamble. This also has universal ratification.

[41] Report of the World Conference to Review and Appraise the Achievements of the United Nations Decade for Women: Equality, Development and Peace, held in Nairobi from 15 to 26 July 1985; including the Agenda of the Nairobi Forward-Looking Strategies for the Advancement of Women (1986) A/CONF.116/28/Rev.1 (hereafter Forward Looking Strategies for the Advancement of Women to the Year 2000 (1985) UN Doc A/CONF.116).

[42] International Conference on Population and Development, Cairo (18 October 1994) UN Doc A/CONF. 171/13 (hereafter ICPD).

[43] Beijing Declaration and Platform for Action (15 September 1995) (hereafter Beijing Platform for Action 1995) reproduced in (1996) 35 *International Legal Materials* 404.

clear that, on paper, the majority of African states are formally committed to principles of human rights as enunciated in international human rights instruments.[44]

Human rights in the African system

Attempts to mitigate criticism of human rights as being 'western' and to reflect particular continental perspectives can be found in the regional human rights instruments.[45] The African Charter starts by asserting the importance of 'the virtues of African civilization which should inspire and characterize their reflection on the concept of human and peoples' rights'.[46] It contains traditional civil and political rights as well as socio-economic and cultural rights.[47] The Charter also provides that individuals have duties as well as rights.[48] Both the preamble and article 2, the non-discrimination provision,[49] specifically include sex as a ground upon which discrimination is prohibited. Similarly, differential treatment between the sexes is proscribed by the requirement that there be equality before the law and that all should enjoy the equal protection of the law.[50]

The principles of non-discrimination and equality before the law found in articles 2 and 3 of the African Charter were considered by the African Commission in the case of *Legal Resources Foundation v Zambia*.[51] The case was brought by a non-governmental organisation challenging an amendment to the Constitution of Zambia, which provided that before a person could contest for the country's presidency, she or he had to prove that both her or his parents were of Zambian descent. It was well known that the amendment had been passed to prevent the former president of Zambia, Kenneth Kaunda, from running for office, it being alleged that his father had not been born in Zambia. Specifically, the complainant

---

[44] Grand Bay (Maurtius) Declaration and Plan of Action 1999 preamble and paras 13, 14.

[45] See F Ouguergouz *The African Charter on Human and Peoples' Rights* (Leiden, Brill Publishers, 2003).

[46] African Charter, preamble

[47] The Charter also contains third generation rights, including the right to development.

[48] African Charter arts 27–29; Wa Mutua 'The Banjul Charter and the African Cultural Fingerprint: An Evaluation of the Language of Duties' (1995) 35 *Virginia Journal of International Law* 339. A further elaboration of human rights on the continent can be found in Grand Bay Declaration and Plan of Action 1999; G Naldi 'Future Trends in Human Rights in Africa: The Increased Role of the OAU' in M Evans and R Murray (eds) *The African Charter on Human and Peoples' Rights: The System in Practice, 1986–2000* (Cambridge, Cambridge University Press, 2002) 1.

[49] For a consideration of the nature of state obligations under this provision see C Heyns 'Civil and Political Rights in the African Charter' in M Evans and R Murray (eds) *The African Charter on Human and Peoples' Rights: The System in Practice, 1986–2000* (Cambridge, Cambridge University Press, 2002) 137 at 144–46.

[50] African Charter art 3.

[51] *Legal Resources Foundation v Zambia*, Communication 211/98, Decision of the AfCmHPR, 29th Ordinary Session, April/May 2001 [2001] IIHRL 1 (1 May 2001).

contended that the amendment violated article 2 of the African Charter as it discriminated on the basis of 'birth, social origin or other status'; article 3, which guaranteed equality before the law; article 13 on the right to participate freely in government; and article 19, which provides for equality of all peoples, irrespective of place of origin. Finding for the complainant, the Commission noted that:

> The right to equality is very important. It means that citizens should expect to be treated fairly and justly within the legal system and be assured of equal treatment before the law and equal enjoyment of the rights available to all other citizens. The right to equality is important for a second reason. Equality or lack of it, affects the capacity of one to enjoy many other rights.[52]

Just as important as articles 2 and 3 of the Charter is Article 18, which, in tackling family matters,[53] makes specific provision for the protection of women, children and the disabled. Worthy of note is article 18(3):

> The State shall ensure the elimination of every discrimination against women and also ensure the protection of the rights of the woman and the child as stipulated in international declarations and conventions.

The inclusion within article 18(3) and article 60 of the requirement that international Declarations and Conventions be considered in the interpretation of the Charter makes clear that whilst wanting a continent specific document, states parties recognise that human rights operate within an international framework that demands the enjoyment of Charter/treaty-based provisions by all human beings without reference to, amongst other things, sex.[54] Egypt is the only state to have entered a reservation to article 18(3) of the African Charter, making it subject to the provisions of the Shari'a.[55]

The *Unity Dow* case[56] is an important example of the usefulness of the African Charter in vindicating women's rights. The case was brought by Unity Dow against the government of Botswana. The government had passed a Citizenship Act 1984, which provided that children born in wedlock acquired the nationality of their father but not that of their mother. Dow was married to an American citizen. Two of her three children were born after the marriage and were therefore not Tswana citizens. The Act also provided that whilst a Tswana man could pass on his nationality to his alien wife, a Tswana woman could not pass on her nationality to an alien husband. Dow challenged these provisions as being discriminatory

---

[52] *Ibid* para 63. The African Commission cited the Human Rights Committee General Comment No 18 as providing a fuller understanding of discrimination.

[53] African Charter art 18(1).

[54] F Viljoen 'The African Commission on Human and Peoples' Rights: Introduction to the African Commission and the Regional Human Rights System' in C Heyns (ed) *Human Rights Law in Africa* (The Hague, Martinus Nijhoff, 2004) vol 1 385 at 497.

[55] Egypt's reservation to art 18(3) of the African Charter, see http://sim.law.uu.nl/SIM/Library/RATIF.nsf/0/f785e93e824c92e641256c0600382f60?OpenDocument.

[56] *Unity Dow v Attorney General of Botswana* [1991] LRC 574.

on the grounds of sex and in contravention of international human rights standards. The government conceded that the Act was discriminatory, but argued that
Botswana was a patrilineal society whereby women were expected to follow their
husbands and children were held to 'belong' to the father's line. At the time the
case was heard, Botswana had not ratified CEDAW. However, she had participated
in the drafting of the 1967 Declaration, which preceded CEDAW, and had been a
signatory thereto.[57] Botswana had also ratified the African Charter. The High
Court, relying on the African Charter, was able to point to this engagement with
human rights as indicating a commitment to the principles of equal protection
before the law and non-discrimination on the basis of sex. The court held in favour
of Dow, which decision was upheld on appeal.[58]

African states' commitment to human rights was reinforced by the adoption of
the Grand Bay (Mauritius) Declaration and Plan of Action 1999, the first sentence
of which notes that 'the promotion and protection of human rights is a priority for
Africa'.[59] Linked to the prioritisation of human rights in the Grand Bay
Declaration was an acknowledgement of democracy, good governance and the
rule of law, development and the principle of non-discrimination.[60] The rights of
women and children were highlighted as a central concern.[61] The Grand Bay
Declaration then went on to welcome the decision to elaborate on a protocol on
women's rights while calling for the elimination of discrimination against women
and the 'abolition of cultural practices which dehumanize or demean women and
children'.[62] In time, the Organisation of African Unity (OAU) became the African
Union (AU), and with that accelerated its engagement with human rights issues.

From its founding document, the Constitutive Act 2000, it is clear that the AU
wishes to be seen to be taking seriously not only human rights[63] but also women.[64]
Gender mainstreaming is a key plank in the AU policy and is evident in the call for
equal representation of women in all AU organs.[65] It is noteworthy that the

---

[57] General Assembly Resolution Adopting the Declaration on the Elimination of All Forms of
Discrimination against Women (7 November 1967) A/RES/2263 (XXII) (DEDAW).

[58] *Attorney-General of Botswana v Unity Dow* 1992 LRC (Const) 623.

[59] Grand Bay (Mauritius) Declaration and Plan of Action 1999 preamble.

[60] Grand Bay (Mauritius) Declaration and Plan of Action 1999 at 3. See also para 1 on the universality and indivisibility of rights. And the Preamble, which notes in part:

[T]he expressed desires of African peoples to live in a state of law which secures the full enjoyment
of human rights and fundamental freedoms for all peoples, regardless of their gender, race, place
of origin, religion, social status, ethnic background, political opinions and language.

[61] *Ibid* 6. It is worth reflecting on the joining of women with children as if their interests always coin-
cide and reinforcing the notion that women are primarily responsible for children.

[62] *Ibid*

[63] AU Constitutive Act 2000, preamble, art 3(g) 3(h) and art 4(m).

[64] *Ibid* preamble, art 4(l).

[65] Durban Declaration on Mainstreaming Gender and Women's Effective Participation in the
African Union 2002 available at http//www.africa-union.org. See also Assembly of Heads of State and
Government, Third Ordinary Session, 6–8 July 2004, Addis Ababa, Solemn Declaration on Gender
Equality in Africa, Assembly/AU/Decl.12 (III) Rev.1 preamble. (Hereafter AU Solemn Declaration

President of the Pan-African Parliament is a woman. Commendable as these formal commitments are, it is important that these initiatives be more than paper
exercises and that all the people in the AU organs, not just the women appointed
in the 'gender quotas', be actively engaged in trying to ensure the development of
an equitable, transparent, accountable and (above all) democratic institutional
framework, in the hope that these principles will in turn find their way to the
national level.[66]

The first AU ministerial conference on human rights was held in Kigali in
2003.[67] It produced a Declaration that recalled and reaffirmed the principles
enshrined in the Grand Bay (Mauritius) Declaration and Plan for Action 1999.[68]
The Kigali Declaration calls for 'a rights-based approach to policy, programme
planning, implementation and evaluation'.[69] Importantly states parties are urged
to incorporate the provisions of the African Charter and its Protocols into their
domestic legislation if they have not already done so.[70] They are also asked to
incorporate international humanitarian law, including the four Geneva
Conventions and Protocols.[71] Of direct interest are the provisions pertaining to
the human rights of women.

Discrimination experienced by women and girls is acknowledged in the preamble, which hones in on 'harmful traditional practices in some parts of Africa that
endanger the life or health of women and children'. It is further noted that 'the
rights of women and children in spite of progress achieved remain insufficiently
protected in many African countries'.[72] The Kigali Declaration 2003 'welcomes
the progress made towards the adoption of the Draft Protocol on the Rights of
Women in Africa'.[73]

One year after the adoption of said Protocol, the Assembly of Heads of State and
Government adopted a Declaration on Gender, which expressed

on Gender Equality in Africa.) See also Maputo Declaration on Mainstreaming and the Effective
Participation of Women in the African Union, 24 June 2003. This civil society initiative calls on states
to accelerate the mainstreaming process and is available at http://www.wildaf-ao.org. Protocol to the
African Charter on Human and Peoples' Rights on the Establishment of an African Court on Human
Rights 1998 OAU/LEG/AFCHPR/PROT (III), adopted by the Assembly of Heads of State and
Government, 34th Session, Burkina Faso, 8–10 June 1998. The Protocol provides that when nominat-
ing candidates to sit on the court as judges, states should give 'due consideration . . . to adequate
gender representation' (Art12(2)); see too A Lloyd and R Murray 'Institutions with Responsibility for
Human Rights Protection under the African Union' (2004) 48 *Journal of African Law* 165.

[66] For a comprehensive discussion of AU institutions see R Murray *Human Rights in Africa*
(Cambridge, Cambridge University Press, 2004).
[67] The First AU Ministerial Conference on Human Rights in Africa, 8 May 2003, Kigali, Rwanda,
Kigali Declaration, MIN/CONF/HRA/Decl.1(I).
[68] *Ibid* preamble and art 33.
[69] *Ibid* art 4
[70] *Ibid* art 25
[71] *Ibid.*
[72] *Ibid* art 16
[73] *Ibid.* The Protocol was duly adopted two months later in July 2003 in Maputo.

[C]oncern about the status of women and the negative impacts on women of issues such as the high incidence of HIV/AIDS among girls and women, conflict, poverty, harmful traditional practices, high population of refugee women and internally displaced women, violence against women, women's exclusion from politics and decision making.[74]

Many initiatives were put forward to tackle these problems.[75] It is noteworthy that the Declaration identifies women's lack of capacity as an impediment to the exercise and enjoyment by them of their human rights, hence the suggestion that there be established 'An African Trust Fund for Women for the purpose of building the capacity of African Women'.[76] It is anticipated that both urban and rural women will access the fund.[77] In addition to states committing themselves to give annual progress reports on gender mainstreaming initiatives and gains made in ensuring that the difficulties identified as impeding women's enjoyment of their rights are overcome,[78] the Chairperson of the African Union Commission is enjoined to submit an annual report to the Assembly of Heads of State and Government doing the same.[79]

Without a doubt, the clearest manifestation of the AU's commitment to securing the human rights of women has been the completion of the process of elaborating an instrument on women's rights started under the aegis of the OAU. The process of drafting that Protocol is considered in the last part of this chapter.

In addition to the African Charter there have been other sub-regional initiatives focusing on human rights on the continent. These will now be considered.

Sub-regional initiatives

In 1990, Arab foreign ministers meeting in Cairo adopted the Cairo Declaration on Human Rights in Islam 1990 (hereafter Cairo Declaration).[80] The Declaration is premised on obedience to God.[81] It contains a non-discrimination provision:

All men are equal in terms of basic human dignity and basic obligations and responsibilities, without any discrimination on the grounds of race, colour, language, *sex*, religious belief, political affiliation, social status or other considerations. (emphasis added)

---

[74] AU Solemn Declaration on Gender Equality in Africa 2004 preamble.

[75] *Ibid* see parts 1–10, 12.

[76] *Ibid* art 11.

[77] *Ibid.*

[78] *Ibid* art 12.

[79] *Ibid* art 13.

[80] Cairo Declaration on Human Rights in Islam (5 August 1990) UN GAOR, World Conference on Human Rights, 4th Session, Agenda Item 5 (1993) UN Doc A/CONF.157/PC/62/Add.18 (English translation).

[81] *Ibid* art 1(a).

A person with a keen eye for language would note the irony of a sentence that starts with men being equal in dignity before going into grounds on which discrimination is proscribed. The inclusion of sex means that discrimination against women is not allowed.[82] Although all are said to be equal in human dignity, it is unclear whether dignity means the same thing for women as it does for men. This is dealt with in article 6(a), which provides:

> Woman is equal to man in human dignity, and has her own rights to enjoy as well as duties to perform; and has her own civil entity and financial independence, and the right to retain her name and lineage.

Dignity is nowhere defined. Although the concept of dignity is an important part of African jurisprudence,[83] it is unclear whether it is understood in the same way throughout the continent. For some dignity is seen as important in understanding and interpreting rights to equality.[84] Viewed from this perspective, 'dignity' can thus be seen as enhancing existing rights, rather than limiting or prescribing different treatment for men and women. It is doubtful that this interpretation can be said to fit the Cairo Declaration, not least because in article 6(a) there is a suggestion that a woman's rights and duties are in some respects different from those of a man.[85] Significantly there does not appear to be room for negotiation or choice on the rights and duties front.[86]

Articles 24 and 25 of the Cairo Declaration make clear that the rights in the Declaration are subject to the Shari'a, and also that the Shari'a shall be the only interpretive source for the rights contained within the Declaration. There appears to be little room for manoeuvre, or for alternative or historically situated interpretations.[87] However, the Cairo Declaration needs to be filtered through the Rao 'questionnaire',[88] which requires us to ask who speaks for or on behalf of the

---

[82] It is common in legal drafting to see 'all men' being used to mean all of humanity including women.

[83] S Cowen 'Can "Dignity" Guide South Africa's Equality Jurisprudence?' (2001) 17 *South African Journal on Human Rights* 34; J Allain and A O'Shea 'African Disunity: Comparing Human Rights Law and Practice of North and South African States' 24 (2002) 2 *Human Rights Quarterly* 86 at 107. See also the Constitution of Malawi 1994, Constitutional Principles s 12(iv); Constitution of Uganda 1995, Principles of State Policy XXIV(a).

[84] *Dawood v Minister of Home Affairs* 2000(3) SA 936 para 35.

[85] World Bank *MENA Development Report: Gender and Development in the Middle East and North Africa* (Washington DC, World Bank, 2004) (hereafter MENA Development Report) 94–98.

[86] However, in some respects a woman's rights are here more generous than those enjoyed by her non-Islamic sisters. She has the right to financial independence with no reciprocal obligations of support and also the right to retain her name.

[87] F Mernissi 'Muslim Women and Fundamentalism' in S Sabbagh (ed) *Arab Women: Between Defiance and Restraint* (New York, Olive Branch Press, 1996)162 at 163; Cairo Institute for Human Rights Studies 'In the Name of Shariah' (1996) *Sawasiah* 12.

[88] A Rao 'The Politics of Gender and Culture in International Human Rights Discourse' in J Peters and A Wolper (eds) *Women's Rights, Human Rights: International Feminist Perspectives* (New York, Routledge, 1995) 167 at 168. See too L Welchman 'Introduction' in L Welchman (ed) *Women's Rights and Islamic Family Law* (London, Zed Press, 2004) 1 at 5.

group, or here Islam? Presenting the document to the Vienna Conference on Human Rights, the Saudi foreign minister is said to have 'asserted that it embodied the *consensus* of the world's Muslims on rights issues' (emphasis added).[89] That there is no consensus on the interpretation of Islam and its relationship to human rights is evident from the different positions taken on reservations to human rights treaties by states that have Islam as the dominant religion.

The Arab Charter on Human Rights 1994 (hereafter Arab Charter)[90] reaffirms in its preamble a commitment to the ICCPR, ICESCR and the Cairo Declaration. It seems less equivocal than the Cairo Declaration in its construction of the rights of women, providing that:

> Each state party to the present Charter undertakes to ensure to all individuals within its territory and subject to its jurisdiction the right to enjoy all the rights and freedoms recognised herein, without any distinction on grounds of race, colour, sex, language, religion, political opinion, national or social origin, property, birth or other status and without any discrimination between men and women.[91]

Additionally, article 9 of the Arab Charter guarantees equality before the law and the right to a legal remedy, while article 18 provides that 'everyone shall have the inherent right to recognition as a person before the law'. Although these provisions suggest that the principles of non-discrimination and equality before the law are recognised without limitation and distinction being made between men and women, it is worth noting the reservations made to CEDAW by many of the African states that are states parties to the Arab Charter, to see that the interpretation of women's rights is understood as that endorsed by a conservative interpretation of the Shari'a.[92] In this regard it is noteworthy that the Arab Charter 'seals off' the private sphere of the family from scrutiny, providing in article 17 that:

> Privacy shall be inviolable and any infringement thereof shall constitute an offence. This privacy includes private family affairs, the inviolability of the home and the confidentiality of correspondence and other private means of communication.

Since it is the family and private sphere that is most likely to define and determine the scope of women's ability to enjoy rights to equality and to participate in the public sphere, shielding the family and home from investigation and accountability is likely to mean that discrimination against women continues unchecked.

The Southern African Development Community (SADC) is a regional bloc of 14 states.[93] In addition to the founding treaty, which proscribes discrimination on

---

[89] Mayer above n 4 at 22.

[90] Arab Charter on Human Rights 1994. Reprinted in (1997) 18 *Human Rights Law Journal* 151, also available from: http://www1.umn.edu/humanrts/instree/arabhrcharter.html.

[91] Arab Charter 1994 art 2.

[92] These are considered in more detail in the discussion on CEDAW which follows the consideration of sub-regional initiatives.

[93] These include Angola, Botswana, Democratic Republic of Congo, Lesotho, Malawi, Mozambique, Mauritius, Namibia, Seychelles, South Africa, Swaziland, Tanzania, Zambia and Zimbabwe.

the basis of sex,[94] Member States of SADC have also ratified the SADC Gender and Development Declaration 1997 and its Addendum on Violence 1998.[95] The first, the Declaration on Gender and Development, is a synthesis of the Nairobi Forward-Looking Strategies, CEDAW and the Beijing Declaration and Platform for Action. It provides that gender equality is a fundamental right[96] and that SADC Member States, by virtue of the non-discrimination provision in the founding treaty of SADC, undertook not to discriminate, amongst other things, on the basis of gender. To this end the Declaration makes provision for mainstreaming gender concerns within the work of SADC.[97] SADC countries then pledge to focus on women's interests in the socio-economic, cultural and civil, and political fields.

The SADC governments also undertake to promote women's access to productive resources such as land[98] and formal employment as a way of reducing poverty,[99] and to enhance women's access to education and health facilities. The gains made by women in Cairo are reflected in the list of state obligations to recognise, protect and promote not only the reproductive rights of women and girls, but also their sexual rights.[100] Picking up on article 18(2) of the African Charter, the SADC Gender and Development Declaration enjoins states to promote the human rights of women and children. In order to facilitate this, the mass media are to 'disseminate information and materials in respect of the human rights of women and children'.[101] Acknowledging the importance of law in social change and the impact of custom in resisting that change, the Declaration provides that states undertake to engage in:

> Repealing and reforming all laws, amending constitutions and changing social practices which still subject women to discrimination, and enacting empowering gender-sensitive laws.[102]

Although the Declaration does touch on the issue of violence against women, providing that states should deal urgently with the increased levels of violence

---

[94] Treaty of the Southern African Development Community (SADC), 17 July 1992, art 6(2), available from: http://www.iss.co.za/AF/RegOrg/unity_to_union/pdfs/sadc/8SADC_Treaty.pdf.

[95] Gender and Development: A Declaration by Heads of State or Government of the Southern African Development Community (SADC) 1997; The Prevention and Eradication of Violence against Women and Children, An Addendum to the 1997 Declaration on Gender and Development by SADC Heads of State or Government, 1998. SADC *Gender Monitor* (1999) 1 at 33 and 37.

[96] SADC Gender and Development Declaration 1997 B(i).

[97] *Ibid* F(ii).

[98] F Butegwa 'Using the African Charter on Human and Peoples' Rights to Secure Women's Access to Land in Africa' in R Cook (ed) *Human Rights of Women: National and International Perspectives* (Philadelphia, University of Pennsylvania Press, 2004) 495. See also A Ngwala 'The New Land Acts in Tanzania and Women's Access to Land Rights' (paper presented at WLSA Colloquium, Kariba, Zimbabwe, 1999; on file with the author).

[99] SADC Gender and Development Declaration 1997 H(iii).

[100] *Ibid* H(viii).

[101] *Ibid* H(x).

[102] *Ibid* H(iv). Cf CEDAW arts 2(f), 5.

against women,[103] it was felt that the issue merited particular attention, thus the SADC Gender Unit drafted an Addendum to the 1997 Declaration focusing on the issue of violence against women. Using the Vienna Declaration and Programme of Action 1993 as the starting point for international recognition of violence against women as being a serious violation of fundamental rights,[104] the SADC document identifies violence as including physical, emotional, economic, sexual and psychological violence.[105] Specific forms of violence identified include economic deprivation, sexual abuse of children, marital rape, trafficking and forced prostitution, and female genital mutilation.[106] The Addendum notes that existing measures have proved inadequate in dealing with the issue, and indeed in some instances have been biased against the victims.[107]

Other regions have also engaged with the issue of women's rights. The Union Economique et Monétaire Ouest Africaine (Economic Union of West Africa) (UEMOA)[108] passed a resolution on gender in 1999.[109] The preamble to the resolution recognises the importance of people in the integration process, and the particular role of women in the social and economic development of the Union. It notes that in social, economic, legal and economic spheres women face many constraints and obstacles. There is thus a need for Member States to prioritise the role of women. With this in mind the Recommendation provides that states parties should commit themselves to a timetabled plan of action broadly covering social, health, education and economic constraints facing women.[110] Specific issues identified as particularly problematic for women include the inferior status of women in society, the precarious health situation of women and the insufficient resources for maternity provision.

To redress these problems it is suggested that women be educated about their rights, and that campaigns be run addressing AIDS and violence against women, and covering issues such as female genital cutting. Moreover states should promote research into indigenous and traditional medicine.[111] A strategic plan is annexed to the Recommendation. On education the strategic plan identifies girls' lack of access to education, specifically at the higher levels. To redress the sex

---

[103] *Ibid* H(ix).

[104] The Prevention and Eradication of Violence against Women and Children: An Addendum to the 1997 Declaration on Gender and Development by SADC Heads of State or Government 1998 art 4.

[105] *Ibid* art 5.

[106] *Ibid* art 5(a), 5(b).

[107] *Ibid* art 7.

[108] This regional bloc includes Benin, Burkina Faso, Côte d'Ivoire, Guinea-Bissau, Mali, Niger, Senegal and Togo.

[109] Recommendation No 03/00/CM/UEMOA Relative à la mise en oeuvre d'actions communes en matière de promotion et de renforcement du rôle de la femme dans l'UEMOA, Dakar, 21 December 1999 available from http://www.izf.net/isf/Documentation/JournalOfficiel/AfriqueOuest/dec99/REC_03_99.htmI.

[110] *Ibid* art 1 and Annexe à la Recommendation No 03/99/cm/UEMOA Orientations Stratégiques.

[111] Orientations Stratégiques 1—sur le plan and 1:1 Santé (health).

imbalance, it provides that states should consider taking temporary special measures to improve the access of girls to educational establishments, including those at the higher and technical levels.[112] Finally the plan of action identifies women's poverty and under-representation in the public sector, which is contrasted with the important contribution made by women to the informal sector. In addition to expanding women's participation in the public sector, it is recommended that women's work in the informal sector be counted in national economic assessments. Moreover, women's money and finance literacy should be improved upon. There should be regional co-operation and discussions about how better to integrate women into development and the work of the Union.[113] States that have not already done so are further encouraged to ratify CEDAW and the Optional Protocol thereto.[114] States are required to report to the Commission on what they have done to meet the obligations specified.[115]

Some of the states parties belonging to UEMOA are also members of the Economic Community of West African States (ECOWAS), a regional body set up in 1975.[116] One of the fundamental principles of the Treaty[117] is the 'recognition, promotion and protection' of human rights as enunciated in the African Charter.[118] Echoing article 18 of the African Charter, women, children and youth are lumped together in the ECOWAS Protocol on Democracy and Good Governance. The development and promotion of women's welfare (but not rights) is seen as essential to development and peace. States are therefore obliged to 'eliminate all forms of discrimination and harmful and degrading practices against women'.[119] Member States are also committed to putting into place the necessary structures to ensure that women, youth and children's education and welfare promotion are enabled.[120]

ECOWAS has set up a Gender Division within the ECOWAS Secretariat. Representatives from ECOWAS states' Women's Ministries and other experts met in 2002 to work out a programme for gender mainstreaming issues in the ECOWAS Secretariat. This was based on the recognition that gender issues were impacting upon men and women in the region differently, and that this necessitated the development of a 'gender-responsive framework'. Key issues identified as

---

[112] *Ibid* 1:2 Education.
[113] *Ibid* 2—Economic Plan.
[114] Art 1.
[115] *Ibid* art 2.
[116] It has 15 member states including Benin, Burkina Faso, Cape Verde, Côte d'Ivoire, Gambia, Ghana, Guinea, Guinea Bissau, Liberia, Mali, Niger, Nigeria, Senegal, Sierra Leone and Togo. See http://www.ecowas.int/.
[117] Treaty of the Economic Community of West African States (ECOWAS) (Revised) 1993, at http://www.ecowas.int.
[118] *Ibid* art 4(g). See also Protocol to the ECOWAS Treaty on Democracy and Good Governance. Protocol A/SPI/12/01 arts 33, 34, 35.
[119] *Ibid* art 40.
[120] *Ibid* art 43.

needing attention included enhancing gender monitoring, 'the promotion of women and the girl-child through affirmative action; the promotion of women in peacekeeping, trade and finance; strategic partnerships and resource mobilisation'.[121]

The founding treaty establishing the East African Community (EAC),[122] comprising Kenya, Tanzania and Uganda, contains within it chapter 22 on enhancing the role of women in socio-economic development. In addition to seeking to mainstream women's interest into the development process and improve their participation in decision making,[123] the Treaty echoes articles 2(f) and 5(a) of CEDAW in its requirement that states should 'abolish legislation and discourage customs that are discriminatory against women'[124] and its requirement that states should 'take such other measures that shall eliminate prejudices against women and promote the equality of the female gender with that of the male gender in every respect'.[125]

CEDAW in Africa

There are many similarities between the African Charter and CEDAW, not least the recognition in both instruments of the importance of both civil and political and socio-economic and cultural rights, and their interdependence. The content of some of the rights protected by the Charter, for example on family,[126] have been fleshed out in CEDAW[127] to which African states have shown formal commitment, even if this commitment has not always translated into domestic implementation of the rights contained therein.

CEDAW has 30 articles and is divided into six parts.[128] Part 1 contains the first six articles which include the definition of discrimination, the list of state obligations,[129] a provision on temporary special measures and a provision on the suppression of trafficking and the exploitation of prostitution of women. Part 2 has provisions on women's participation in public and international life as well

---

[121] ECOWAS Gender Policy on http://www.thecommonwealth.org. Go to the Gender section.
[122] Treaty Establishing the East African Community 1999, reproduced in part in Heyns (2004) above n 54 vol 1 at 634–39.
[123] *Ibid* art 121(a).
[124] *Ibid* art 121(b).
[125] *Ibid* art 121(e).
[126] African Charter art 18(1).
[127] CEDAW art 16.
[128] N Burrows 'The 1979 Convention on the Elimination of All Forms of Discrimination against Women' (1985) 32 *Netherlands International Law Review* 419.
[129] CEDAW art 2. See also CEDAW General Recommendation No 25 on Temporary Special Measures 7.

as nationality rights. Part 3 contains a list of socio-economic rights including education, employment, health and specific development-oriented provisions pertaining to rural women. Part 4 contains the provisions on equality of men and women before the law, and article 16 on marriage and family relations. Part 5 covers the setting up and composition of the Committee which oversees CEDAW,[130] and reporting obligations of states under the Convention. The Committee, which like the Convention is also called CEDAW, comprises 23 members who are independent of states although nominated by states. In selecting members of the Committee, there is a requirement that all the regions of the world, as well as the 'different forms of civilisation' and legal systems, be represented.[131]

Of all the United Nations Committees, the CEDAW is unique in having a majority of women.[132] Members sit for four years but can be put up for nomination more than once. The CEDAW generally meets twice a year, in New York, in January and June. Occasionally a third session is convened during the year due to backlog of work. With the coming into force of the Optional Protocol to CEDAW 1999, the Committee's functions have been expanded to include receiving communications and making inquiries into violations of rights.[133] Under the reporting mechanism states are expected to send in their initial reports one year after ratification of the Convention and thereafter every four years.[134] In reality states parties do not always manage to meet this obligation and it is not unusual for states to present compound (for example second, third and even fourth reports) at the same CEDAW session. As of July 2004, at least 18 African states were identified as being more than five years late in submitting reports to CEDAW.[135] In common with other treaty bodies, the Committee encourages NGOs to submit what are called 'shadow reports' which can supplement, or indeed challenge, some of the claims made in the state reports.

Finally Part 6 of the Convention contains the 'housekeeping' provisions including provisions for ratifications, reservations, objections thereto and invocation of the International Court of Justice in case of inter-state disputes on the interpretation or application of the Convention.

Worthy of note is article 1 on discrimination, which is based on article 1 of the Race Convention and provides:

---

[130] CEDAW art 17; UN, IWRAW, Commonwealth Secretariat *Assessing the Status of Women: A Guide to Reporting Under the Convention on the Elimination of All Forms of Discrimination against Women* (London, Commonwealth Secretariat, 2000).

[131] CEDAW art 17(1).

[132] Currently 22 of the 23 members are women. The man, Professor Flinterman, is from the Netherlands.

[133] Optional Protocol to the Convention on the Elimination of All Forms of Discrimination against Women, adopted and opened for signature, ratification and accession by GA Res 54/4, 6 October 1999 (herafter Optional Protocol to CEDAW 1999). See too United Nations *The Optional Protocol: Texts and Materials* (New York, United Nations, 2000).

[134] CEDAW art 18.

[135] http://web.amnesty.org/pages/treaty-countries-reporting-eng.

For the purposes of the present Convention, the term 'discrimination against women' shall mean any distinction, exclusion or restriction made on the basis of sex which has the effect or purpose of impairing or nullifying the recognition, enjoyment and exercise by women, irrespective of their marital status, on a basis of equality of men and women, of human rights and fundamental freedoms in the political, economic, social, cultural, civil or any other field.

The provision does a number of things. It makes clear that all discrimination is prohibited, and that it is irrelevant where that discrimination occurs—that is whether it is done by a state actor, or a private individual or private organisation.[136] It prohibits both direct and indirect discrimination and makes clear that there should be equality of opportunity and result so that formal pledges of equality may not in themselves be sufficient. The state may need to do more than simply change the law to ensure both *de jure* and *de facto* equality.[137] However, the standard of equality, 'on a basis of equality of men and women', arguably retains the liberal 'reverse the sexes and compare model', albeit with exceptions made for 'special circumstances' such as pregnancy.[138]

As we have seen in the discussion on equality in Chapter 2, CEDAW, in its General Recommendation 25 on Temporary Special Measures, has challenged the formal model of equality. Noting that 'the Convention is a dynamic instrument',[139] the Committee calls for substantive rather than formal equality:

In the Committee's view, a purely formal legal or programmatic approach is not sufficient to achieve women's *de facto* equality with men . . . In addition, the Convention requires that women be given an equal start and that they be empowered by an enabling environment to achieve equality of results. It is not enough to guarantee women treatment that is identical to that of men. Rather, biological as well as socially and culturally constructed differences between women and men must be taken into account. Under certain circumstances, non-identical treatment of women and men will be required in order to address such differences. Pursuit of the goal of substantive equality also calls for an effective strategy aimed at overcoming under-representation of women and a redistribution of resources and power between men and women.[140]

This opens the door for a more aggressive use of temporary special measures to speed up the process of ensuring *de facto* equality for women. However, the case of *EFTA Surveillance Authority v The Kingdom of Norway*[141] suggests that the matter may not be so straightforward. In 1995 Norway had passed a law relating to universities and colleges which provided in part:

---

[136] See too CEDAW art 2(e).
[137] See also CEDAW art 3.
[138] CEDAW arts 4(2), 11(1)(f), 11(2)(a)(b), 12(2).
[139] CEDAW General Recommendation No 25 para 3.
[140] *Ibid* para 8. See also paras 4–7, 9–10. See also CERD General Comment No 14.
[141] *EFTA Surveillance Authority v The Kingdom of Norway* Case E-1/02, 24 January 2003.

> If one sex is clearly under represented in the category of post in the subject area in question, applications from members of that sex shall be specifically invited. Importance shall be attached to considerations of equality when appointment is made. The Board can decide that a post shall be advertised as only open to members of the under represented sex.[142]

On the basis of this legislation, the University of Oslo earmarked a number of doctoral fellowships for women (29 out of 179 positions in the period 1998–2001). Similarly it earmarked 4 permanent academic positions for women, out of a total of 227 academic appointments during the same time period.[143] Moreover, under the University's Plan for Equal Treatment 2000–2004, a further 10 postdoctoral fellowships and 12 permanent academic posts were earmarked for women.[144] The case was brought by the European Free Trade Surveillance Authority alleging that Norway's policy of reserving employment places for women academics was in violation of equality legislation.[145] Specifically, it was contended that Norway was in breach of article 2(1) of the Directive which provided:

> For the purpose of the following provisions, the principle of equal treatment shall mean that there shall be no discrimination whatsoever on grounds of sex either directly or indirectly by reference in particular to marital or family status.

Moreover article 3(1) of the Directive provided:

> Application of the principle of equal treatment means that there shall be no discrimination whatsoever on grounds of sex in the conditions, including selection criteria, for access to all jobs or posts, whatever the sector or branch of activity, and to all levels of the occupational hierarchy.

In its defence, Norway cited article 4(1) of CEDAW as authority for the recognition of affirmative action (temporary special measures) being permitted.[146] It also cited article 141(4) of the EC Treaty as permitting states to maintain or adopt measures 'providing for specific advantages in order to make it easier for the under-represented sex to pursue a vocational activity or to prevent or compensate for disadvantages in professional careers'.[147] Finally, the Norwegian government cited article 2(4) of the Directive as permitting derogation from the equality provisions in that it provided:

---

[142] Norwegian Act No 22 of 12 May 1995 relating to Universities and Colleges, art 30(3). *Ibid* para 2.

[143] *Ibid* para 3.

[144] *Ibid* para 4.

[145] EEA Agreement, Arts 7 and 70 and Council Directive 76/207/EEC of 9 February 1976, arts 2(1), 2(4) and 3(1).

[146] *EFTA Surveillance Authority v Norway* para 16.

[147] *Ibid* paras 16 and 56. This was dismissed because 'the measures in question would not be lawful under that provision, which, in any event, is not part of EEA law' (para 23).

This Directive shall be without prejudice to measures to promote equal opportunity for men and women, in particular by removing existing inequalities which affect women's opportunities.[148]

As justification for its law it noted the social reality, which was that:

The modest number of women in academia stands in glaring contrast to the percentage of women in the student body. The defendant points to the fact that women tend to leave academic careers before they are qualified for higher academic positions. The aim of the disputed legislation is to achieve long-term equality between men and women as groups.[149]

In acting as it had, the government argued that it was in compliance with the Directive. The Norwegian government further argued that 'formal equality in treatment is not sufficient to achieve substantive equality'.[150]

These laudable goals notwithstanding, Norway was held to have failed to fulfil its obligations under the EEA (European Economic Area) Agreement. Specifically the Court agreed with the contention of the applicant that:

[T]he Norwegian legislation in question must be regarded as going beyond the scope of Article 2(4) of the Directive, in so far as it permits earmarking of certain positions for persons of the under-represented gender. The last sentence of Article 30(3) of the University Act as applied by the University of Oslo gives absolute and unconditional priority to female candidates. There is no provision for flexibility, and the outcome is determined automatically in favour of a female candidate.[151]

Although Norway had tried to argue that the measures were temporary and therefore the provisions proportionate to the aim sought to be achieved, the reasoning was not accepted, not least because of the inflexibility of the rule bringing about the situation in the first place.[152] On CEDAW article 4(1) it was noted:

[T]he provisions of international conventions dealing with affirmative action measures in various circumstances are clearly permissive rather than mandatory. Therefore they cannot be relied on for derogations from obligations under EEA law.[153]

Returning to consider the other provisions in the Convention we find that in article 2 on state obligations CEDAW specifically addresses the issue of 'local values', requiring as it does that states undertake:

---

[148] *Ibid* paras 11and 16. Norway also cited art 14 of the European Convention 1950 on non-discrimination, Protocol 12 to the Convention for the Protection of Human Rights and Fundamental Freedoms, Rome, 4 November 2000, European Treaty Series—No 177; Arts 2 and 5 of the ILO Convention 111 Concerning Discrimination in Respect of Employment and Occupation, and Recommendation No R(85)2 from the Council of Europe. *EFTA Surveillance Authority v Norway* para 27.

[149] *EFTA Surveillance Authority v Norway* para 26.

[150] *Ibid.*

[151] *Ibid* 54. See applicant's contention para 22.

[152] *Ibid* paras 50 and 53.

[153] *Ibid* para 58.

> To take all appropriate measures, including legislation, to modify or abolish existing laws, regulations, customs and practices which constitute discrimination against women.[154]

CEDAW also demands that states parties tackle gender stereotyping. This requires that states parties take all appropriate measures:

> To modify the social and cultural patterns of conduct of men and women, with a view to achieving the elimination of prejudices and customary and all other practices which are based on the idea of the inferiority or the superiority of either of the sexes or on stereo-typed roles for men and women.[155]

The obligations imposed by these last two provisions are radical and far-reaching as they aim for a total transformation of society. They are also the subject of a reservation made by Niger:

> The Government of the Republic of Niger declares that the provisions of article 2, paragraphs (d) and (f), article 5, paragraphs (a) and (b), article 15, paragraph 4, and article 16, paragraph 1(c), (e) and (g), concerning family relations, cannot be applied immediately as they are contrary to existing customs and practices which, by their nature, can be modified only with the passage of time and the evolution of society and cannot, therefore, be abolished by an act of authority.[156]

Much of the resistance that has resulted in CEDAW having the highest number of reservations of all of the human rights instruments rests on article 9(2) on nationality of children and article 16 on family relations, together with other provisions of article 2.[157] Article 28(2) of CEDAW provides that reservations are permitted provided they are not 'incompatible with the object and purpose' of the Convention. Cook sees the object and purpose of CEDAW as constituting an undertaking by states parties that they 'shall move progressively towards the elimination of all forms of discrimination against women and ensure equality between men and women'.[158] In Africa, it is predominantly, although not exclusively, states which have Islam as the main religion that have entered reservations. Algeria has agreed to implement article 2 of the Convention 'on condition that they (the provisions thereof) do not conflict with the provisions of the Algerian Family Code'. Similarly Egypt has a reservation to parts of article 16 of

---

[154] Art 2(f) CEDAW.

[155] Art 5(a) CEDAW. R Holtmaat *Towards Different Law and Public Policy: The Significance of Article 5(a) CEDAW for the Elimination of Structural Gender Discrimination* (The Hague, Ministry of Social Affairs and Employment, 2004).

[156] Reservation of Niger to CEDAW available at http://www.un.org/womenwatch/daw/cedaw/reservations-country.htm.

[157] http://www.un.org/womenwatch/daw/cedaw/reservations-country.htm.

[158] R Cook 'Reservations to the Convention on the Elimination of All Forms of Discrimination against Women' (1990) 30 *Virginia Journal of International Law* 643 at 648.

CEDAW, as does Libya.[159] Mauritania makes a general reservation subjecting CEDAW to constitutional and Shari'a law. Interestingly, Islamic states reserve different provisions of the same treaty and give different interpretations and justifications for doing so, leading Mayer to contend:

> In entering their Islamic reservations, Muslim states treat Islamic law as if it were a supranational religious law that binds them, whereas in reality, where Islamic law survives, it does so in the form of very dissimilar national laws enacted by local governments and changed by them at will.[160]

Support for this assertion can be seen by looking at Morocco, which made several objections during the drafting of CEDAW, and in particular to the family law provisions in article 16, which it contended were not in line with Islamic principles. In 2003, the Moroccan King and Parliament changed the Moroccan Family Code, thereby qualifying some of the objections that had been put forward by Morocco to the aforementioned provisions of CEDAW.[161]

Non-Islamic states that have entered reservations to CEDAW include Lesotho, whose reservation provides that 'it shall not take any legislative measures under the Convention where those measures would be incompatible with the Constitution of Lesotho.'[162] The generality of the reservation notwithstanding, it is worth noting that the Lesotho Constitution is one that is 'strongly culturally relativist', meaning that it exempts customary law from the operation of principles of non-discrimination.[163] This being so, one is left to wonder why the government of Lesotho saw fit to ratify CEDAW at all?[164] It is interesting to note that Lesotho is one of the first five African states to ratify the African Protocol on Women's Rights as well as the seventh African state to ratify the Optional Protocol to CEDAW,[165] albeit with an opt out of the inquiry procedure. It is difficult to reconcile this outward manifestation of commitment to the human rights of women with the reservation to CEDAW.

---

[159] *Ibid.* Cf J Connors 'The Women's Convention in the Muslim World' in J Gardner (ed) *Human Rights as General Norms and a State's Right to Opt Out* (London, British Institute of International and Comparative Law, 1997) 85; R Holtmaat above n 155 at 29; MENA Development Report (2004) above n 85.

[160] Mayer above n 4 at 125. Cairo Institute for Human Rights Studies 'Reservation is Not a Justification (1996) *Sawasiah* 8–9.

[161] http://www.bayefsky.com/./pdf/morocco_t2_cedaw.pdf. L Rehof *Guide to the Travaux Préparatoires of the United Nations Convention on the Elimination of All Forms of Discrimination against Women* (Dordrecht, Martinus Nijhoff, 1993); G Tremlett 'Morocco Boosts Women's Rights' *Guardian* (21 January 2004).

[162] At http://www.bayefsky.com/docs.php/area/reservations/state/97/node/3/treaty/cedaw/opt/0. See also Allain and O'Shea above n 83 at 97–98 fn 71.

[163] Constitution of Lesotho 1993 s 18(4)(b), reproduced in C Heyns (ed) *Human Rights Law in Africa* (The Hague, Kluwer International, 1996) 186 at 188.

[164] E Linzaad *Reservations to UN Human Rights Treaties* (Dordrecht, Martinus Nijhoff, 1995) 363–64; B Clark 'The Vienna Convention Reservations Regime and the Convention on Discrimination against Women' (1991) 85 *American Journal of International Law* 281.

[165] Optional Protocol to CEDAW 1999 above n 133.

Opting out of state obligations also calls into question a state's commitment to improving the conditions of women and arguably violates the integrity of the treaty.[166] Finally, making a treaty subject to national law is technically problematic, not least because national law can change at any time, so that by attempting to subject international law to municipal law, it becomes difficult to ascertain a state's obligations.[167]

Given the frequency with which states reserve CEDAW, the Women's Committee has made two general recommendations tackling the issue of reservations.[168] The Committee requests that states keep any reservations made under review and, if appropriate, uplift them. Moreover, the guidelines for reporting given to states ask states to address their reservations. Finally the Committee marked the fiftieth anniversary of the UDHR by issuing a statement on reservations.[169] The statement noted that: 'Neither traditional, religious nor cultural practice nor incompatible domestic laws and policies can justify violations of the Convention.'[170]

In its statement on reservations the Committee also went on to note that experience had shown that reservations made to state obligations under article 2 and to article 16 were seldom uplifted.[171]

By way of contrast, CERD, on which CEDAW is based and which has widespread support in Africa, has a tightly framed reservation provision which provides that a reservation is not acceptable if two-thirds of states parties object to it.[172] One could argue that when the discrimination affects men, for example race, then they are prepared to be tough and not allow any derogation to the application of the relevant Convention. Gender discrimination, particularly that justified by 'culture' or religion and occurring in the family, tends to be a 'woman's issue' and is therefore seen as less important. Both the ICCPR and the African Charter are silent on reservations, although both have been reserved in part by some states

---

[166] Cook above n 158 at 649.

[167] Clark above n 164 at 317. *Specific Human Rights Issues Reservations to Human Rights Treaties Final Working Paper Submitted by Françoise Hampson* (19 July 2004) 4 E/CN.4/Sub.2/2004/42 at para 56.

[168] General Recommendation No 4, Reservations, UN Doc A/42/38 and General Recommendation No 20, Reservations to the Convention, UN Doc A/47/38. CEDAW General Recommendation No 21 also tackles reservations—see paras 41–47. See also Human Rights Committee General Comment No 24 on Issues Relating to Reservations Made upon Ratification or Accession to the Covenant or the Optional Protocols Thereto, or in Relation to Declarations under Article 41 of the Covenant (2 Nov 1994) CCPR/C/21/Rev 1/Add 6. Controversially, the Human Rights Committee claims for itself the right to strike down reservations that it deems in violation of the objects and purpose of the ICCPR: see para 11. *Belilos v Switzerland* (1988) ECHR Series A, vol 132, 4. But see R Baratta 'Should Invalid Reservations to Human Rights Treaties be Disregarded?' (2000) 11 *European Journal of International Law* 413.

[169] CEDAW 'Statement on Reservations to the Convention on the Elimination of All Forms of Discrimination against Women Adopted by the Committee on the Elimination of Discrimination against Women' reproduced in UN IWRAW, Commonwealth (2000) above n 130 at 90.

[170] *Ibid* para 17 at 92.

[171] *Ibid* para 19 at 92. Some states have uplifted reservations. These include Malawi and Mauritius.

[172] CERD art 20(2).

parties.[173] This suggests that states parties are permitted to enter reservations provided they do not violate the objects and purpose of the treaty.[174]

The issue of reservations is significant, for it impacts disproportionately on women's rights, particularly those in the family.[175] Challenging reservations made, particularly those justified using religious precepts, is difficult and rarely done. Chinkin speculates that objecting to another state's reservation may in itself be seen as a hostile act, and few states are prepared to take such actions.[176] The subject of the reservations, namely the enjoyment by women of their rights, may also not be seen as a subject worth entering into hostile debate. Although there were states that objected to the making of reservations to key provisions of CEDAW, it is significant that the majority of these were European.[177] This regional imbalance increases the likelihood of charges of cultural imperialism.

All this notwithstanding, the fact that the majority of African states have ratified CEDAW without entering reservations to articles 2, 5, 15 and 16 would seem to suggest that they are in agreement with the norms enunciated therein, or at least do not seek to detract from them. However, the lack of domestic implementation and the controversy surrounding women's rights at the domestic level, would suggest that such an analysis is simplistic and fails to take into account the grounded reality.

There is clearly a lack of consistency on the part of states in general and African states in particular when ratifying and making reservations to human rights treaties. As an example, although CEDAW is heavily reserved, the ICCPR—which, as we have noted, has a non-discrimination provision, a provision protecting the right to family life and a free-standing equality before the law provision—is not so reserved, thus suggesting that states will accept the obligations imposed upon them by one human rights instrument but not by another. Interestingly the Human Rights Committee has in General Comment No 18 adopted the definition of discrimination found in article 1 of CEDAW. The African Commission has in turn adopted the Human Rights Committee's interpretation of discrimination.[178] This means that states such as Sudan, which have acceded to the ICCPR without

---

[173] Egypt has a general reservation to the ICCPR, ICESCR and the CRC in which it cites the provisions of the Shari'a as determining the extent of its obligations: Heyns (2004) above n 54 vol 1 at 52, 53, 58–59.

[174] Murray above n 7 at 146–48.

[175] This is an issue that affects women in other parts of the world. See S Hossain 'Equality in the Home: Women's Rights and Personal Laws in South Asia' in R Cook (ed) *Human Rights of Women: National and International Perspectives* (Philadelphia, University of Pennsylvania Press, 2004) 466 at 473ff.

[176] C Chinkin 'Reservations and Objections to the Convention on the Elimination of All Forms of Discrimination against Women' in J Gardner (ed) *Human Rights as General Norms and a State's Right to Opt Out* (London, British Institute of International and Comparative Law, 1997) 64.

[177] Interestingly European states do not appear to object to reservations made by other European states. Mexico is also another state that has made objections.

[178] In *LRF v Zambia* above n 51.

making any reservations but not to CEDAW, can be said to have the same obligations to women as CEDAW-ratifying states. Arguably this argument is strengthened when one factors in articles 2, 3, 18(3) and 60 of the African Charter.

Although leading to uncertainty as to the extent of a state's commitment to
upholding the human rights of women, these inconsistencies can of course be
exploited by human rights advocates who can forum shop for the best deal for
women. This is particularly important when one considers that few[179] African
states have ratified the Optional Protocol to CEDAW 1999, which permits individuals or organisations acting on their behalf to bring complaints to the
Committee.[180] The Optional Protocol also allows the Committee to launch an
inquiry if it has reason to believe that grave or systematic violations of women's
rights are going on within a state.[181] The inquiry procedure cannot be invoked if a
state has opted out.[182] If the state has not ratified the Optional Protocol to
CEDAW, then human rights advocates should consider using the African
Commission.[183] Alternatively, assuming that the state where the violation has
occurred has ratified both the ICCPR and the First Optional Protocol[184] thereto,
a complaint could be brought before the Human Rights Committee.[185] There is as
yet no provision for complaints to be brought before the Committee on Economic
Social and Cultural Rights.

Following the CEDAW framework is the Protocol to the African Charter on
Human and People's Rights on the Rights of Women (African Protocol on
Women's Rights). The next part considers the drafting history of this instrument.

Protocol to the African Charter on Human and People's Rights on the Rights of Women—history and drafting

Despite the existence of the African Charter and the extensive ratification of
CEDAW by African states, it had over time been clear that the issue of gender was
not being seriously considered at the institutional level, with little being done by

---

[179] As of September 2004 only seven African states had ratified the Optional Protocol to CEDAW
1999. http://www.un.org/womenwatch/daw/cedaw/protocol/sigop.htm.

[180] Optional Protocol to CEDAW 1999 art 2. United Nations *CEDAW: The Optional Protocol* (New
York, UN, 2000) 110–13.

[181] *Ibid* arts 8, 9, 10. United Nations *CEDAW: The Optional Protocol* above n 180 at 113–14.

[182] *Ibid* art 10.

[183] African Charter arts 55–59 and in particular art 56. A Carbert, J Stanchieri and R Cook
*A Handbook for Advocacy in the African Human Rights System Advancing Reproductive and Sexual
Health* (Nairobi, IPAS, 2002) 35–42.

[184] Optional Protocol to the International Covenant on Civil and Political Rights, 999 UNTS 171,
reprinted in (1967) 6 *International Legal Materials* 383.

[185] For a comparative chart of individual communications and inquiry procedures see United
Nations *CEDAW: The Optional Protocol* above n 180 at 120–31 and 154–56.

the African Commission, which is responsible for monitoring the Charter, to make states parties accountable for gender-based discrimination occurring within their boundaries. However, it is true to say that in recent years the Commission has begun to interrogate states parties on gender-related issues, asking them to account for developments in women's rights within their jurisdictions.[186] States are supposed to use the CEDAW reporting guidelines in preparing reports for the Commission.[187] There are no reports of gender-related communications (complaints)[188] being brought before the Commission. This may reflect the fact that in many societies women cannot access the national legal system, thus it is virtually impossible for them to access the complaint mechanism of the African Commission.[189]

The apparent lack of commitment to upholding the human rights of women was highlighted at a joint seminar organised by a leading non-governmental organisation in collaboration with the African Commission.[190] Attended by 44 participants from 17 countries, the seminar agreed on the need for an instrument that would specifically address the needs of women.[191] In an introductory note on the Draft Protocol to the African Charter on Human and People's Rights on the Rights of Women in Africa it was noted:

> To date, no African instrument relating to human rights proclaimed or stated in a precise way what are the fundamental rights of women in Africa. There is thus a vacuum in the African Charter as regard [sic] real taking care of women [sic] current preoccupations in Africa.[192]

The contention was that there had until then been little interest in women's rights within the African Commission.[193] In deciding what form the new instrument should take, suggestions put forward included amending or revising the African Charter, which would be difficult and meet with a great deal of resistance, or

---

[186] Murray above n 7 at 44–45. It seems, however, that few questions are asked on gender. M Evans, T Ige and R Murray 'The Reporting Mechanism of the African Charter on Human and Peoples' Rights' in M Evans and R Murray (eds) *The African Charter on Human and Peoples' Rights: The System in Practice, 1986–2000* (Cambridge, Cambridge University Press, 2002) 36 at 53–56.

[187] Viljoen above n 54 at 497.

[188] Communications provided for in arts 55–56 of the African Charter.

[189] F Banda 'The Protection of Women's Rights in Africa' (2004) 14 *Interights Bulletin* 147 at 147.

[190] The African Commission and WILDAF seminar on the African Charter on Human and Peoples' Rights and the Human Rights of Women in Africa, Lome, Togo, March 1995, in 'The African Charter on Human and People's Rights and the Additional Protocol on Women's Rights' (1999) *WILDAF News* 18, 19; R Murray 'A Feminist Perspective on Reform of the African Human Rights System' (2001) 1 *African Human Rights Law Journal* 205.

[191] V Dankwa 'The Promotional Role of the African Commission' in M Evans and R Murray (eds) *The African Charter on Human and Peoples' Rights: The System in Practice, 1986–2000* (Cambridge, Cambridge University Press, 2002) 335 at 341.

[192] Drafting Process of the Draft Protocol on the Rights of Women in Africa (Item 8(e)) DOC/OS/(XXVII)/159b at 1.

[193] Viljoen above n 54 at 497; Banda above n 189 at 148.

preparing an additional protocol to the African Charter. It was decided that an additional protocol would be the best way forward.[194]

In 1996, at the 19th session of the African Commission, it was decided to appoint a Special Rapporteur on the Rights of Women in Africa, which decision was finally endorsed at the 23rd session[195] of the OAU.[196] Part of her remit includes assisting African governments 'in the development and enactment of policies that promote and protect the human rights of women in Africa'.[197] The African Commission mandated the Special Rapporteur and two other Commissioners to convene a working group to draft an additional protocol on women's rights.[198] The decision was endorsed at the 31st Ordinary Session of the OAU.[199] In addition to the work of the Special Rapporteur and her group on drafting the Protocol, contributions to the drafting process also came from within the OAU Women's Unit and civil society. Government experts first worked on the draft in November 2001.[200] Subsequent meetings were held, including a Meeting of Ministers in March 2003.[201] The Protocol was finally adopted at the African Union meeting hosted by Mozambique in Maputo in July 2003.

This section is not an exhaustive consideration of the drafting process. It starts by looking at the draft of the Special Rapporteur's working group, which received some assistance from civil society. The first draft comprised 21 articles[202] and was a skeletal document on to which much has been added. The preamble began by noting that despite the existence of articles 2 and 18 in the African Charter, and the existence of other human rights instruments, including the international bill of rights, the provisions of various conference documents and platforms for action, all of which spoke of the importance of women's human rights, still:

> [M]any people in Africa continue to perceive human and peoples' rights as being the exclusive preserve of men despite the fact that women play a fundamental role in all spheres.

[194] Viljoen above n 54 at 497.

[195] Draft Terms of Reference for the Special Rapporteur on the Rights of Women in Africa DOC/OS/34c (XXIII) Annex 11, 1996. See too M Evans and R Murray 'The Special Rapporteurs in the African System' in M Evans and R Murray (eds) *The African Charter on Human and Peoples' Rights: The System in Practice, 1986–2000* (Cambridge, Cambridge University Press, 2002) 280 at 295–98, 303.

[196] Evans and Murray above n 195 at 298.

[197] 'Who is the Special Rapporteur on the Rights of Women?' (1999) *WILDAF News* 5.

[198] Evans and Murray above n 195 at 296, 299.

[199] Resolution of the OAU Assembly of Heads of State and Government, 31st Ordinary Session, Addis Ababa, June 1995, AHG/Res 240(XXXI).

[200] Draft Protocol to the African Charter on Human and Peoples' Rights on the Rights of Women in Africa (as adopted by the Meeting of Government Experts in Addis Ababa on 16 November 2001), 22 November 2001, CAB/LEG/66/6/Rev 1 (hereafter Government Experts Draft (2001)).

[201] Draft Protocol to the African Charter on Human and Peoples' Rights on the Rights of Women in Africa (as adopted by the Meeting of Ministers, Addis Ababa, Ethiopia on 28 March 2003). MIN/WOM.RTS/DRAFT.PROT.(II)Rev 5 (hereafter Government Ministers Draft (2003)).

[202] Draft Protocol to the African Charter on Human and Peoples' Rights on the Rights of Women in Africa DOC/OS/34c(XXIII) (hereafter Draft Protocol).

This justification for the need to draft a separate instrument for women, mirrors the justification found in the preamble to CEDAW, which also begins with an acknowledgement of the existence of human rights instruments such as the UDHR which cover issues of discrimination against women, and yet:

> despite these various instruments extensive discrimination against women continues to exist.[203]

Like CEDAW, and indeed the African Charter itself, the draft incorporated civil and political and social, economic and cultural rights. The Draft Protocol followed CEDAW in many respects, not least the definition of discrimination:

> For the purposes of this present Additional Protocol, and in conformity with Articles 2 and 18 of the African Charter on Human and Peoples' Rights discrimination against women means any distinction, exclusion or restriction based on sex whose effects compromise or destroy the recognition, enjoyment or the exercise by women—regardless of their matrimonial status on an equal basis with men, of the human rights and fundamental freedoms in all aspects.[204]

The Draft Protocol also added rights not found in CEDAW, such as specific articles proscribing violence against women, so that article 11(2) provided that states parties undertook to take all appropriate measures to:

> prohibit all forms of violence against women—physical, mental, verbal or sexual, domestic and family—whether they take place in the private sphere or in society and public life including sexual harassment, sexual abuse or exploitation, rape etc;

Reflecting the growing international concern over the issue of harmful practices, it also tackled the issue of female genital cutting, which it said states should work towards eradicating.

Recognising that much of the controversy about the human rights of African women is the issue of 'African cultural values' and their interpretation, the Draft Protocol acknowledged the importance of African culture, but made a plea for the inclusion of African women in the formulation of cultural values which it argued should not discriminate on the basis of sex:

> Women shall have the right to live their life [sic] in a positive cultural environment and to participate at all levels in the determination of cultural policies.[205]

African cultural values were put through a filter in article 2, which provided:

> Women shall enjoy on the basis of equality with men, the same rights and respect for their dignity and contribute to the preservation of those African cultural values

---

[203] CEDAW preamble para 6.
[204] Art 1—there are slight differences in the two versions—CEDAW and the Draft Protocol.
[205] Art 17(1).

that are positive and are based on the principles of equality, dignity, justice and democracy.[206]

Not only did article 2 give some meaning to the concept of African values missing from the African Charter, but it made it clear that in invoking these values, the issue of complementarity, or the according of different entitlements to men and women because they had different roles and responsibilities within their societies, was not to be permitted. This was because there was provision for women enjoying rights '*on a basis of equality with men*' and therefore entitlements of men and women could not be held to differ. Moreover there was recognition within article 2 that unequal relations at the domestic level are often a reflection of unequal power relations at the national level.

Given the centrality of culture in the construction of women's entitlement to enjoy their human rights in Africa, article 5(a) of CEDAW was echoed in article 4(b), which provided that states parties undertook to:

> modify the social and cultural patterns of conduct of men and women, with a view to achieving the elimination of prejudices and customary and all other practices which are based on the idea of the inferiority or the superiority of either of the sexes or on stereotyped roles for men and women.

Like CEDAW, the original Draft Protocol considered women's rights within the family in some detail, with article 6 of the Draft Protocol mirroring many of the provisions found in article 16 of CEDAW. These included the injunction that marriage should be entered into with the consent of both parties, that women and men should have the same rights in marriage, that the spouses should have the same rights and responsibilities towards their children and that 'during her marriage the wife shall have the right to acquire her own property and to administer and manage it freely: and in the case of joint ownership of property the husband and wife shall have the same rights'. The standard of equality and in particular the use of the words 'equal', 'same' and 'jointly' were to prove controversial when government experts and ministers considered the draft in 2001 and 2003 respectively.

Article 6 of the Draft made the registration of marriage a pre-condition to making it legally valid. Although this was in keeping with CEDAW[207] and its General Recommendation on Marriage and Family Relations,[208] and the Convention on the Consent to Marriage, Minimum Age of Marriage and Registration of Marriage 1962,[209] it does not reflect the reality of many states which recognise the validity of

---

[206] In the version of the Protocol that was finally adopted this provision was amended and moved to the preamble.

[207] CEDAW art 16(2).

[208] CEDAW General Recommendation No 21 para 39.

[209] Convention on Consent to Marriage, Minimum Age of Marriage and Registration of Marriage. Opened for Signature and Ratification by General Assembly Resolution 1763A (XVIII) of 7 November 1962. Entered into force 9 December 1964.

marriages that have not been registered. Not surprisingly this was also objected to at the ministerial stage in 2003. More controversially article 6 provided for the prohibition of polygyny, which is referred to as polygamy in both the Draft and final Protocol.[210]

> Polygamy shall be prohibited except (where) otherwise consented (to) by both parties; and in any country where polygamy exists, the law shall strive to work towards its elimination.[211]

Polygyny was one of the most controversial issues during the drafting process. Although according with the injunction in CEDAW General Recommendation Number 21 that polygyny should be abolished,[212] the issue of polygyny is controversial, not least because so many customary and religious systems recognise and sanction it. All this reflects the difficulties inherent in trying to impose uniform standards on a continent where most countries have plural legal systems covering different cultural, ethnic and religious groupings.

The Draft Protocol in article 6 also drew inspiration from article 9 of CEDAW providing that a married woman had the right to retain her own nationality and also to pass it on to her husband and children. In much the same way that the related provision in CEDAW[213] on nationality of children had proved controversial during the drafting process, so too the injunction that both parents could pass on their nationality to their children generated debate at the government experts meeting in 2001. Article 7 of the Draft Protocol provided that divorce could only be by judicial order and that men and women would have the same rights to end a marriage. Given that this provision in CEDAW[214] is one of the most heavily reserved provisions by Islamic countries, not least because some legal systems provided different grounds for divorce for men and for women, it is not surprising that this was one of the more contentious points of discussion when government ministers considered the draft.[215]

Recognising the difficulties experienced by African women on the deaths of their spouses, the Draft Protocol went further than CEDAW in that it had specific provisions dealing with the rights of widows to be free from inhuman, humiliating and degrading treatment;[216] the right to retain guardianship of their children;[217] to

---

[210] Polygamy denotes the ability of a person (gender neutral) to marry more than one spouse. Polygyny is the ability of a man to marry more than one wife, whereas polyandry is the ability of a woman to marry more than one husband. However, it would appear that most references to polygamy actually mean polygyny.

[211] Draft Protocol art 6(2)(a).

[212] General Recommendation No 21 para 14.

[213] CEDAW art 9(2).

[214] CEDAW art 16(1)(c).

[215] It was objected to by Egypt, Libya and Sudan. Government Ministers Draft (2003) (above n 200).

[216] Draft Protocol art 7(2).

[217] *Ibid* art 7(4).

remarry if they wished and the right to inherit their husbands' property; and to continue living in the matrimonial home.[218]

Although drawing its main inspiration from CEDAW, the Draft did not appear to take all the provisions of CEDAW on board. Whilst recognising that women continue to be excluded from participating in public life[219] and to have limited access to education, the Draft Protocol did not, like article 4 of CEDAW, make provision for temporary special measures to redress this situation. Surprisingly, the first draft was silent on the issue of reservations which have blighted CEDAW.[220] This may be because the African Charter is also silent on reservations.

The Draft Protocol was similarly silent on the issue of the monitoring of the Protocol—which can be seen as either recognising the competence of the African Commission in this regard, or indeed forgetting that it is precisely because of the Commission's apparent lack of interest in women's rights that the Draft Protocol had become necessary, thus highlighting the need for a separate monitoring body to the Commission. A separate monitoring body would also be in keeping with the African Charter on the Rights and Welfare of the Child 1990 (ACRWC) which has a Committee of 11 members.[221] A major criticism of the first attempt at an additional protocol to the African Charter was the way in which it was drafted. It was weak on 'rights language' and seemed more programmatic. As drafted, the justiciability of its provisions was questionable.

It would seem that the best way to look at the original draft is as a wish list that tried to tackle all the practices which are considered irritants and barriers to women's enjoyment of their human rights on the African continent. These include the continued existence of polygyny, inequitable property division on divorce, the ill treatment and dispossession of widows, early and forced marriage, as well as harmful practices such as female genital cutting. Although focusing on family and 'private sphere' issues, the Draft also recognised that if states were to be made responsible for ensuring adequate social and economic provision for their societies and women in particular, then they would have to spend less on defence and more on welfare provision for their citizens.[222] An integrated model of development[223] was anticipated in article 3, which provided:

---

[218] *Ibid* art 7(4) art 7(3). Provisions in favour of widows reflect the growing concern about their plight, which is manifest in countries passing laws at the domestic level to protect widows' rights. See for example the Constitution of Ghana 1979 s 32(2) and the Intestate Succession Law (PNDC 111) 1985. See also the Zimbabwean Administration of Estates Amendment Act 1997 as well as the Zambian Intestate Succession Law 1989. Inheritance is specifically addressed in CEDAW General Recommendation No 21 paras 34 and 35.

[219] Draft Protocol art 9.

[220] With 177 ratifications as of July 2004, CEDAW is second only to the UN Convention on the Rights of the Child in the number of ratifications received. However, it is the human rights treaty with the most reservations: see http://www.un/daw/cedaw.

[221] ACRWC art 33.

[222] Art 10(3).

[223] Cf E Rathgeber 'WID, WAD, GAD: Trends and Research in Practice' (1990) 24 *Journal of*

In order to eliminate effectively all forms of discrimination against women, States Parties to this Protocol shall take all necessary measures to integrate a gender perspective in their policy decisions, legislation, development plans and all spheres of life.

Given the detailed manner in which the Draft Protocol considered aspects of personal laws such as polygyny and inheritance, one cannot help but conclude that the Special Rapporteur and her working group were firmly in the 'universalist' camp. They can be seen either as over-playing their collective hand and rendering the whole document irrelevant by laying it open to the charge that it did not have cultural legitimacy, or as showing foresight in setting standards to which states could aspire and courts could point as guiding principles when interpreting national laws. Realistically it is difficult to see how a different document could have been drafted. Much of what is in the Draft Protocol has already been accepted at the international level, for example the CEDAW General Recommendation 21 already calls for states to move towards the abolition of polygyny. Indeed, many of the Draft Protocol rights are already in other human rights instruments such as the ICESCR, CRC, ICCPR, ACRWC and the African Charter itself.

Moreover, the 1993 General Assembly Declaration on Elimination of Violence against Women also considers violence against women, including female genital cutting, as being gender-based violence which needs to be eradicated.[224] To have omitted any of these provisions, or to have tried to ring fence personal laws based on custom or religion, would have brought contradictions within the whole body of human rights, particularly as they relate to women.

This Draft was forwarded to the African Commission for consideration. The Draft Protocol to the African Charter on Human and Peoples' Rights on the Rights of Women, now comprising 23 articles, was adopted by the African Commission in November 1999 at its 26th Ordinary Session held in Kigali, Rwanda.[225] The version adopted by the Commission contained a few amendments to the original. Of note was the introduction of the rights of the girl child, so in places where the original draft had only spoken of the rights of women, the Kigali draft included (but not consistently) references to the rights of girls as well. For example, on inheritance the first draft merely provided in article 7(5) that 'A widow shall have the right to inherit her husband's property' whereas article 9(5) of the Kigali draft noted 'Women and girls shall have equal rights to inherit their parents' properties as men and boys'. Reflecting article 18(4) of the African Charter, new provision was made for the protection of elderly and disabled women. Specifically:

Developing Areas 489. UN Division for the Advancement of Women in United Nations *1999 World Survey on the Role of Women in Development: Globalization, Gender and* Work (New York, United Nations, 1999) vii–xii.

[224] General Assembly Declaration on the Elimination of All Forms of Discrimination against Women (20 December 1993) GA Res 48/104.

[225] Draft Protocol to the African Charter on the Rights of Women in Africa (Kigali, 15 November 1999) DOC/OS (XXVII)/159b.

> In conformity with the provision of article 18 of the African Charter, elderly women and women with disability have the right to specific measures of protection in relation with [sic] their physical and moral needs.

This became the new article 6. The marriage provision became article 7. Controversially, there was a reversal of the position on polygyny, so that whereas the original draft had suggested the prohibition of polygyny but had left open the possibility of its continuation 'where consented to by both parties',[226] the draft put to the African Commission for adoption in Kigali, Rwanda in 1999 provided simply: 'Polygamy shall be prohibited.'[227]

The African Commission forwarded the Draft Protocol adopted in Kigali to the OAU, which was to convene a meeting of government officials to consider the Draft.[228] In a letter to the Chairman of the African Commission, the OAU Legal Counsel noted that whilst the Secretariat was grateful for the work that had gone into the Kigali draft, it could benefit from the input of government experts and NGOs.[229] Comments were received from many sources, including the OAU Women's Unit.[230]

The input of the OAU Women's Unit to the Kigali draft factored in many suggestions for change not only to the wording of the draft, but also by highlighting existing OAU platforms/declarations which had been omitted by the original drafters. It began by suggesting that the preamble be amended to include the Addis Ababa Declaration on Violence against Women and its action points, which it described as 'a very important OAU document which should not be omitted from this listing/enumeration'.[231] There appear to be many such conferences and initiatives known to the Women's Unit, but evidently not to the Special Rapporteur and her working group. Other articles picked out for improvement by the addition of OAU initiatives included the articles on education, economic and social welfare rights, and the article on health and reproductive rights.

The OAU Gender Unit also forwarded a Draft Convention on the Elimination of Harmful Practices that it had been drafting in collaboration with the Inter Africa Committee on Harmful Traditional Practices Affecting the Health of

---

[226] Art 6(2)(a).

[227] Kigali draft art 7(3).

[228] Professor V Dankwa, Chairman of the African Commission to Dr S Salim, Secretary General of the OAU (15 November 1999) ACHPR/OS/26.

[229] Professor T Maluwa, OAU Legal Counsel to Professor Dankwa, Chairman of the African Commission on Human and Peoples' Rights (7 March 2000) CAB/LEG/72.20/27/Vol II.

[230] Suggestions of the Women's Unit to Improve the Existing Text of the Draft Protocol as Presented to the OAU. Attachment to letter from Professor T Maluwa, OAU Legal Counsel to Professor Dankwa (7 March 2000) CAB/LEG/72.20/27/Vol II. See also letter from Professor L Johnson, Director, Education, Science, Culture and Social Affairs Department, to Professor V Dankwa, Chairman of the African Commission (25 February 2000) File No ES/WU/RW/51.00.

[231] *Ibid.*

Women and Children. The Draft Convention on Harmful Traditional Practices[232] was subsumed into the main draft. Most of the amendments suggested by the Women's Unit were incorporated into the draft produced in 2000.[233]

Although the Special Rapporteur's remit required her to consult with NGOs,[234] there were complaints from civil society, and in particular those from outside West Africa, that they had not been consulted.[235] At a meeting held in Bamako, Mali, it was claimed that the drafts produced by the Special Rapporteur's working group comprised the input of only 7 out of 53 states. There was therefore a call for the expansion of the steering committee.[236] The Bamako meeting, attended by 29 participants, was an attempt to broaden the base of consultation[237] and to strengthen the provisions of the Draft Protocol 'which were not comprehensive enough to guarantee the protection of the rights of women in Africa'.[238] It was argued that as drafted, the Draft Protocol left many loopholes for governments to try to evade their obligations. Instead, it was noted that both CEDAW and the SADC regional instruments had 'stronger and comprehensive and obligatory pronouncements, which guaranteed the rights of women more effectively than the ones in the Draft Protocol'.[239]

The SADC and East Africa group duly submitted its suggestions, which not surprisingly were based on the two SADC Declarations discussed in this chapter.[240] These included a strengthening of the provisions on violence, a provision on temporary special measures, especially as related to women in political

---

[232] The OAU Draft Convention on the Elimination of All Forms of Harmful Practices Affecting the Fundamental Human Rights of Women and Girls 2000.

[233] Draft Protocol to the African Charter on Human and Peoples' Rights on the Rights of African Women in Africa (13 September 2000) CAB/LEG/66.6.

[234] See Draft Terms of Reference for the Special Rapporteur on the Rights of Women in Africa DOC/OS/34c (XXIII) Annex II, paras 1(e) and 1(f).

[235] At a colloquium organised by the Women and Law in Southern Africa Research Trust (WLSA), a seven nation regional NGO group, I presented a paper outlining the shortcomings of the Kigali draft, which I gave to the participants, none of whom had even heard of the Draft Protocol. The lack of knowledge about the Draft Protocol was surprising to me, not least because the WLSA group has a reputation as a strong lobby and advocacy group on the rights of women. It also comprises members from states that form half of the SADC bloc. Attending this colloquium was the woman who eventually represented SADC at the continental NGO meetings held to discuss the draft. Some other participants from non-WLSA countries had also not heard of it.

[236] C Warioba (Programme Officer, Gender from SADC) 'Mission Report on Draft Protocol to the African Charter on The Human and Peoples' Rights on the Rights of Women in Africa', held in Bamako, Mali, 12–16 February 2001 (unpublished—on file with the author) at 3.

[237] *Ibid* at 3. The regional breakdown of the 29 participants comprising 27 women and 2 men was as follows: North Africa (1), Southern Africa (4), East Africa (1), Central Africa (3), West Africa (18), regional/institutional level (2) including someone from the African Commission.

[238] *Ibid.*

[239] *Ibid* at 3–4. It was stated that there needed to be greater consultation and dissemination of the Protocol at the national level.

[240] Comments on the Draft Protocol to the African Charter on (the) Human and Peoples' Rights on the Rights of Women in Africa Submitted by Participants from the Eastern and Southern Sub-Regions 2001 (hereafter East Africa and SADC group 2001), on file with author.

participation, and a ban on the making of reservations. The group also suggested that there be a separate monitoring body to oversee the Protocol.[241]

The Draft Protocol with the input of civil society came before government experts in November 2001. As already noted, the issue of polygyny was problematic. The NGO sponsored draft said simply that polygyny should be abolished. The government experts objected to the proposal on three counts. The first was that the practice was recognised in both customary and religious law (Islamic) as a right of men.[242] The second was that the abolition of polygyny would leave women already in polygynous unions unprotected, and the last point was that polygyny should be permitted if consented to by both parties.[243] Emphasis was put on the need to protect the rights of women and children, and suggestions were made that states parties should work progressively towards the elimination of polygynous marriages. The three options put forward were:

Option 1—[polygamy shall be prohibited.]

Option 2—[they adopt the appropriate measures in order to recognize monogamy as the sole legal form of marriage. However, in existing polygamous situations, States Parties shall commit themselves to guarantee and protect the rights and welfare of women.]

Option 3—[polygamy must be the subject of mutual consent between the parties. The States Parties shall commit themselves to guarantee and protect the rights and welfare of women. However, the Sate Parties shall ensure and encourage monogamy as the preferred form of marriage.]

No consensus was reached and for the first time in the proceedings, text was bracketed, that is left open for further discussion. Interestingly the final version of the Protocol has a provision on polygyny which most closely approximates to Option 3.[244]

Echoing many of the debates around issues of equality and cultural-religious understandings of the roles of men and women, there were debates over whether women could be said to have the 'same, equal or joint' rights with men as regards the ability to pass on nationality to children, grounds for divorce and entitlement to property on the termination of marriage.[245]

The government experts made numerous positive suggestions, including the addition of a new article on the rights of women refugees, asylum seekers, the

---

[241] *Ibid* at 6.

[242] Gaye and Njie note that in Gambia in West Africa, which has a predominantly Muslim population, 'the polygamous privilege is regarded as an absolute, entrenched and fundamental right of every Muslim man'. A Gaye and M Njie 'Family Law in the Gambia' in A Kuenyehia (ed) *Women and Law in West Africa* (Accra, Women and Law in West Africa, 1998) 2 at 6.

[243] Government Experts Draft (2001) art 7. F Banda 'Global Standards: Local Values' (2003) 17 *International Journal of Law, Policy and the Family* 1 at 18–19.

[244] See African Protocol on Women's Rights art 6(c).

[245] These issues are further explored in Chapter 4 on family law.

internally displaced and returnees.[246] The provision in the Kigali draft on disabled and elderly women was divided into two separate articles, it being felt that the needs of these two groups were different.[247] A new article was also added on the 'special protection of women in distress'. A provision similar to article 4(1) of CEDAW on temporary special measures was strengthened, thus article 2(d) on state obligations was amended to read that states were under an obligation 'to take *corrective* and positive action in those areas where discrimination against women in law and in fact continues to exist'. Also suggested was the amendment of the definition of discrimination to incorporate the words highlighted below:

> 'Discrimination against women' shall mean any distinction, exclusion or restriction based on sex, *gender and sexual orientation*, or any differential treatment whose objective or effects compromise or destroy the recognition, enjoyment or the exercise by women, regardless of their marital status, or human rights and fundamental freedoms in all spheres of life.[248]

The inclusion of gender is in keeping with an expanded view of discrimination against women. The inclusion of sexual orientation is more controversial. Until this draft it would appear that there had been at the earlier stages of the drafting process a deafening silence on the issue of sexuality. The Special Rapporteur and her group did not raise it, nor was it ever raised by the East Africa and SADC group. The SADC bloc might have been expected to raise it because of the South African Constitution, which includes sexual orientation as one of the grounds on which discrimination is prohibited.[249] This omission may be seen as reflecting a view that to have included sexuality would have been to have taken rights discourse on the continent too far, or an indication of the fact that even where gender issues are concerned, the dominant group will put its agenda forward and not want to engage with those whose claims are deemed illegitimate or not of the moment. The issue of sexuality, and specifically homosexuality, is controversial and seen as 'Un-African'.[250] This can be seen in the refusal of the Egyptian Organization for Human Rights to intervene in the trial of 52 men who were being tried on charges of immoral behaviour and contempt of religion after police raided a Nile boat and accused them of taking part in a gay-sex party. The refusal of the Human Rights Organization was twofold. First it said that it had no mandate from the people to engage with issues of homosexual rights, and second it said

---

[246] Eventually merged into existing articles.

[247] The separation has been maintained in the final Protocol with elderly women in art 22 and women with disabilities in art 23.

[248] Art 1(d).

[249] Constitution of the Republic of South Africa 1996 s 9(3).

[250] See D Constantine-Sims *The Greatest Taboo: Homosexuality and the Black Community* (Los Angeles, Alyson Press, 2000); J Suzman *Minorities in Independent Namibia* (London, Minority Rights Group, 2002) 18.

that to have engaged with the issue would have undermined its work. The Director of the Egyptian Organization for Human Rights was quoted as saying:

> What could we do? Nothing. If we were to uphold this issue, this would have been the end of what remains of the concept of human rights in Egypt . . . We let them (gays) down, but I don't have a mandate from the people, and I don't want the West to set the pace for the human rights movement in Egypt.[251]

For those working to advance women's rights, the question becomes one of strategy. Any attempt at direct confrontation with baldly asserted 'cultural norms' may result in charges of 'westoxification',[252] inauthenticity, unrepresentativeness and illegitimacy. These charges are more likely than not to be laid at the feet of the professional women who front non-governmental organisations in Africa and who participated in the drafting of the Protocol. These women are said to represent the interests of a narrow elite and not the views of the majority of African women who are poor rural dwellers.[253] In any event, sexual orientation did not make it into the draft that was finally adopted.

By the time of the ministerial meeting in March 2003, the Draft Protocol was almost in its final form. The conflicts over issues of polygyny had been resolved and the matter of which institution was to be held responsible for interpreting and monitoring the Protocol had been decided. Once more key sticking points related to 'private sphere issues' of family and reproductive rights.[254] Objections were noted by Tunisia and Sudan to the provision that the minimum age of marriage would be 18. Other objections noted at the 2003 ministerial meeting included those of South Africa and Botswana to the provision that, where the death penalty still existed, states undertook 'not to carry out the death penalty on pregnant or nursing women'.[255] The South African objection is because South Africa no longer has the death penalty.

Following the example of the United States of America in refusing to be bound by the International Criminal Court established under the Rome Treaty,[256] Libya objected to article 11(3) on the Protection of Women in Armed Conflict, no doubt because it did not want to bring itself within the jurisdiction of a competent criminal jurisdiction if its soldiers or personnel are found to have engaged in 'such acts (as) are considered war crimes, genocide and/or crimes against humanity'.

---

[251] From http://www.washblade.com/pics/020215-kassemhisham.jpg.

[252] U Narayan *Dislocating Cultures: Identities, Traditions, and Third-World Feminism* (New York, Routledge, 1997) 1–39.

[253] M Machera 'Opening a Can of Worms: A Debate on Female Sexuality in the Lecture Theatre' in S Arnfred (ed) *Rethinking Sexualities in Africa* (Lund, Nordic Africa Institute, 2004)157 at 163–65.

[254] Objections were noted by Burundi, Libya, Senegal and Sudan to provisions contained within art 14 on health and reproductive rights.

[255] Draft Protocol to the African Charter on Human and Peoples' Rights on the Rights of Women in Africa (as adopted by the Meeting of Ministers, Addis Ababa, Ethiopia on 28 March 2003). MIN/WOM.RTS/DRAFT.PROT.(II)Rev.5.(Ministerial Draft 2003) art 4(2)(j).

[256] Rome Statute of the International Criminal Court 1998.

Given that the Draft Protocol seems to be so closely modelled on CEDAW and its subsequent General Recommendations, it seems somewhat surprising that it did not take a more robust view of reservations. As already noted, this may be because the African Charter permits reservations and therefore reservations to the Protocol are taken to be allowed. Realistically, a ban on the making of reservations would probably have resulted in the vast majority of states refusing to ratify the Protocol. As it is, ratification has not been as rapid as one might have expected.[257] Challenging reservations made, particularly those justified using religious precepts, is difficult and rarely done. Attempts to highlight the inconsistency of objections such as those made to the Draft Protocol can lead to charges of cultural insensitivity and religious intolerance.

The final version of the Protocol was adopted by the 2nd Ordinary Session of the Assembly of the Union, in Maputo on 11 July 2003.[258]

Protocol to the African Charter on Human and Peoples' Rights on the Rights of Women in Africa 2003—overview

The preamble starts with a history of the draft and notes that the process was kick started by the African Commission recommending the elaboration of a Protocol on the Rights of Women in Africa. It then goes on to consider provisions in the African Charter including articles 2, 18, 60 and 61, which provide for the protection of women and the guarantee to all people of fundamental freedoms found in international human rights instruments. International and regional conferences and Declarations are then cited before it is noted that, despite all these initiatives, 'women in Africa still continue to be victims of discrimination and harmful practices', hence the need for the Protocol. Also noted is a determination 'to ensure that the rights of women are promoted, realised and protected in order to enable them to enjoy fully all their human rights'.

In common with CEDAW, the Protocol has both civil and political and socio-economic and cultural rights. All human rights instruments are historical documents which reflect the preoccupations and debates of their time. The Protocol on Women's Rights highlights the fact that the understanding of the

---

[257] Amnesty International 'The Protocol on the Rights of Women in Africa: Strengthening the Promotion and Protection of Women's Human Rights in Africa' (June 2004) AI-Index: IOR 63/005/2004 (London, Amnesty International, 2004) 9.
[258] *Ibid.*

nature of women's oppression has become more textured. There are several provisions worthy of note, not least the definition section, which provides that:

> 'Discrimination against women' means any distinction, exclusion or restriction or any
> differential treatment based on sex whose objectives or effects compromise or destroy
> the recognition, enjoyment or exercise by women, regardless of their marital status, of
> human rights and fundamental freedoms in all spheres of life.[259]

The similarity of this definition of discrimination to that found in article 1 of
CEDAW has already been noted. However, there are minor points of difference;
for example, the Protocol definition does not have the phrase found in CEDAW
that the enjoyment of rights is to be 'on a basis of equality of men and women'.
Also, instead of itemising all the contexts in which discrimination can occur, as in
CEDAW's 'political, economic, social, cultural, civil or any other field', the African
Protocol settles on the catch-all 'in all spheres of life'.

Also worthy of note in the definition section is the inclusion of girls in the
understanding of women,[260] and most importantly the comprehensive definition
of violence against women.[261] Reflecting on our discussion of constitutional provisions on equality in Chapter 2, it is noteworthy that the first state obligation is
listed as:

> include in their national constitutions and other legislative instruments, if not already
> done, the principle of equality between women and men and ensure its effective appli-
> cation.[262]

The use of temporary special measures to address ongoing gender-based inequalities is anticipated by the injunction that states parties should:

> take corrective and positive action in those areas where discrimination against women in
> law and in fact continues to exist.[263]

Some of the controversies surrounding the drafting of the family provisions
have already been considered and will be further explored in Chapter 4 on family
law. It is worth highlighting some of the innovations of the Protocol. It is the first
human rights instrument to have substantive provisions on reproductive rights[264]
and to make (limited) provision for the right to abortion.[265] It prohibits harmful
cultural practices and confronts the controversial issue of female genital cutting

---

[259] African Protocol on Women's Rights art 1(f).
[260] *Ibid* art 1(k).
[261] *Ibid* art 1(j).
[262] *Ibid* art 2(1)(a). Cf CEDAW art 2(a).
[263] African Protocol on Women's Rights art 2(1)(d).
[264] *Ibid* art 14.
[265] *Ibid* art 14(2)(c).

(mutilation in the Protocol)[266] head on, and provides that the practice is proscribed even if performed in a medical establishment.[267]

That the Protocol is a document of the twenty-first century is manifest in its provision that the (negative) effects of globalisation, and in particular trade practices, should not affect women disproportionately.[268] Issues of sustainable development,[269] health,[270] housing[271] and other socio-economic and welfare rights are covered.[272] Given the number of civil wars on the continent, it is important that the impact of war on women's lives is addressed.[273] Moreover, given that Africa is largely responsible for managing its own refugee problem, it is significant that provisions are made for the protection of refugee women.[274] The proscribing of all forms of violence,[275] including sexual harassment in schools and the workplace, is to be welcomed.[276] On the issue of culture, the document is firm in its injunction that culture is to be rooted in principles of equality and democracy, and that women are to be consulted about the content of the cultural norms that are to operate within their societies.[277] The Protocol also recognises that one of the major impediments to accessing rights is the issue of adequate financial and institutional resources.[278] There are throughout the document demands that states parties commit themselves to implementing and enforcing the rights found within the Protocol.

However, despite this more nuanced view of the nature of women's oppression, the fact that there is a need for a separate instrument addressing women's rights goes to the question of how seriously violations of women's rights are taken on the continent, and also to (the lack of) mainstreaming within African countries.[279] Still, that this is a radical document is not in doubt. It is hoped that two things will happen. The first is that states will ratify the Protocol and bring its provisions to fruition within their borders. The fact that more than one year after its adoption

[266] *Ibid* art 5.
[267] *Ibid* art 5(b).
[268] *Ibid* art 19(f).
[269] *Ibid* art 18.
[270] *Ibid* art 14. Crucially the explicit recognition of the impact of HIV and the need to protect women by providing them with greater reproductive choice and information is a positive development.
[271] *Ibid* art 16.
[272] *Ibid* art 13.
[273] As well as art 10 on the Right to Peace and art 11 on the Protection of Women in Armed Conflict, the preamble makes reference to the 'United Nations Security Council Resolution 1325 (2000) on the Role of Women in Promoting Peace and Security'.
[274] African Protocol on Women's Rights art 4(2)(k), arts 10(2)(c), 10(2)(d).
[275] *Ibid* art 4.
[276] *Ibid* arts 3(4), art 12(1)(d). See also art 4(2)(g) on trafficking.
[277] *Ibid* preamble and art 17.
[278] See art 4(l) which provides 'make adequate budgetary allocations for the implementation and monitoring of actions aimed at preventing and eradicating violence against women'.
[279] Viljoen above n 54 at 497–98.

only five states have ratified the Protocol is a cause for concern. The African Union Solemn Declaration on Gender Equality in Africa 2004 encouraged states parties to ratify the Protocol by the end of 2004.[280] States were also encouraged to support campaigns on the Protocol with the aim of ensuring that it would enter into force in 2005.[281] It is hoped that this will in turn 'usher in an era of domesticating and implementing the Protocol as well as other national, regional and international instruments on gender equality.'[282] The second aspiration is that the African Court,[283] and with it the African Commission, will be robust in the way in which they tackle gender-based discrimination.

Conclusion

The chapter began with a consideration of the long-standing debate about a north/south split in the construction of human rights. It also considered the feminist analysis of international law which posits that, as with domestic law, international law excludes women's voices and experiences in the construction of norms. Similar in outlook, if not in tone, is Mutua's critique of northern ethno-centricity in the construction of human rights norms, and also northern imposi-tion of its perspectives and ideologies on the south. Mutua's biting analysis is captured in this observation by Ndebele:

> Every interaction with white people begins with the imposition of rules, *their* rules, of norms, *their* norms. They assume by some process of natural law, their natural law, that *their* rules and norms are universally applicable.[284]

Given feminism's acknowledged debt to the 'third world analysis' of international law, one could just as easily substitute men for white people, and the alienation and exclusion of women would also be laid bare. The feminist and 'Africanist' cri-tique of international law show that for black African women there is a double bind, or more accurately multiple intersecting issues of exclusion.

---

[280] AU Solemn Declaration on Gender Equality in Africa 2004 at 9.
[281] *Ibid.*
[282] *Ibid.*
[283] The future of the African Court is in doubt. See Amnesty International 'Open Letter to the Chairman of the African Union (AU) Seeking Clarification and Assurances that the Establishment of an Effective Court on Human and Peoples' Rights Will Not be Delayed or Undermined' (9 August 2004) AI-Index: IOR 63/008/2004, downloaded from http://web.amnesty.org/library/index/engior630082004. On the possible ramifications of this see S Gutto 'Legal Status and Implications of the Decision by the Assembly of Heads of States and Government to Integrate the African Court of Justice and the African Court of Human and Peoples' Rights into One Court,' Centre for African Renaissance Studies, University of South Africa, Pretoria (8 August 2004). On file with author.
[284] N Ndebele *The Cry of Winnie Mandela: A Novel* (London, Ayebia Clarke Publishing, 2003).

The chapter then examined the African engagement with principles of human rights by looking at the international bill of rights and the African Charter. In much the same way as CEDAW owes its existence in part to the initial non-gendered workings of the committees overseeing the two Covenants (ICCPR and ICESCR), so too the genesis of instruments targeting the human rights of women on the African continent can be directly linked to the silence of the African Commission and states parties on issues pertaining to women's disadvantage.

Also considered have been sub-regional initiatives on human rights. The SADC group has adopted two declarations, both influenced by the Beijing principles as well as CEDAW. Universalist in outlook, the two documents reflect the current emphasis on mainstreaming and the need for an integrated approach in tackling the impediments to women's rights as well as ensuring their effective enforcement. The same observations can be made about the Resolution on the role of women of the Economic Union of West African states.[285] That there are other perspectives on the issue of the interpretation of human rights norms is clear from the Cairo Declaration on Human Rights in Islam 1990, which locates human rights within a religious and specifically Islamic context. The position of women within this framework is made subject to interpretation of religious precepts. These interpretations may not be in keeping with the views of commentators who argue that only a purposive interpretation of religious principles will lead to a full recognition of the human rights of women.

That African women are determined to have their full human rights vindicated is clear from the lobbying that finally led to the agreement to draft a separate instrument to protect their rights.

The drafting process of the Protocol on African Women's Rights showed that the key 'sticking points' were over issues pertaining to 'private sphere' rights and specifically personal laws. Still, the recognition of women's rights at the institutional level is an important gain upon which women need to build by holding states accountable for the violations of their rights. The active engagement of the African Union with issues of gender gives one hope for the future. This is not to suggest that formal acceptance of women's rights as being human rights is an end in itself, but rather an important step towards achieving social and political justice for African women. In examining the position of African women within the regional human rights framework, I contend that whatever the motivations of states,[286] this new-found gender consciousness is to be welcomed and used by women to press for real change within their own communities.

---

[285] UEMOA Recommendation No 03/99.

[286] It has been suggested that with international aid being increasingly made conditional on principles of good governance, human rights and democracy, states parties cynically adopted international human rights instruments as a means of accessing that international aid. The fact that gender mainstreaming is now in vogue would mean that southern countries now feel pressured into adopting gendered language to fulfil donors' conditions for the granting of aid.

4

Family Law, Gender Equality and Human Rights

The concept of 'family' has, within the African context, always been complex.[1] Arguably it is increasingly contested and contingent upon a variety of factors that will be discussed in this chapter. Coomaraswamy has noted that family law is:

> [T]he litmus test in any society with regard to legal norms and the status of women. It is also the area where the law, ethnicity and ideology with regard to the rights of women merge to become a powerful ideological force.[2]

Part of the complexity of family law in Africa arises from the fact that in most, if not all, African countries one finds a plurality of laws that co-exist, sometimes easily, but often with the potential for an internal conflict of laws situation to arise. Included in this diversity are civil laws, common law, statutory law, customary laws and practices, and religious laws. The application/choice of law may depend on race, religion, ethnicity, whether the group is patrilineal or matrilineal, or in some instances a combination of the two, and on constitutional provisions.[3] Each group is likely to have its own family or personal status law that may exist:

---

[1] G Woodman 'Family Law in Ghana under the Constitution 1992' in A Bainham (ed) *International Survey of Family Law 2003* (Bristol, Jordan Publishing, 2003) 195; B Rwezaura, 'Parting the Long Grass: Revealing and Reconceptualising the African Family' (1995) 35 *Journal of Legal Pluralism and Unofficial Law* 25.

[2] R Coomaraswamy 'To Bellow Like a Cow: Women, Ethnicity and the Discourse of Rights' in R Cook (ed) *Human Rights of Women: National and International Perspectives* (Philadelphia, University of Pennsylvania Press, 1994) 39 at 48; C Sweetman 'Editorial' (1996) 4 *Gender and Development* 2; A Arroba 'A Voice of Alarm: A Historian's View of the Family' (1996) 4 *Gender and Development* 8. Cf R Louw 'Gay and Lesbian Partner Immigration and the Redefining of Family: *National Coalition for Gay and Lesbian Equality v Minister of Home Affairs (National Coalition)*' (2000) 16 *South Africa Journal on Human Rights* 313.

[3] On the South African experience see J Sinclair 'Ebb and Flow: The Retreat of the Legislature and the Development of a Constitutional Jurisprudence to Reshape Family' in A Bainham (ed) *International Survey of Family Law* (Bristol, Jordan Publishing, 2002) 393; J Sinclair 'Embracing New Family Forms, Entrenching Outmoded Stereotypes' in P Lodrup and E Modvar (eds) *Family Life and Human Rights* (Oslo, Gyldendal Akademisk, 2004) 801; E Bonthuys 'Accommodating Gender, Race, Culture and Religion: Outside Legal Subjectivity' (2002) 18 *South African Journal on Human Rights* 41.

(a) as part of the official state legal system,[4]
(b) outside of the state legal system,[5]
(c) in the shadow of state law,[6]
(d) as an amalgam of state law and local practice,[7]
(e) as a version modified by state law or human rights norms.[8]

How states elect to deal with this vast array of personal laws also varies. Federal systems such as Ethiopia may have separate codes.[9] Some countries operate on a unitary code system, having a civil or family code. The jurisdictions with an integrated system, that is one statute, include Algeria,[10] Burkina Faso[11] and the Côte d'Ivoire.[12] Indeed most former French colonies appear to operate on the code-based system, which is part of the civilian tradition of their former colonisers.[13] There are, however, differences between them as to whether they recognise customary and religious marriages. Mali and Senegal do; the Côte d'Ivoire does not.[14] Yet others operate a system in which multiple statutes cover different aspects such as provision for marriage and succession.[15] Although operating within one

[4] For example the Tanzania Law of Marriage Act 1971 (No 5 of 1971).

[5] Many co-habiting or 'irregular unions', that is relationships which receive no civil, customary or religious sanction but which are common in many parts.

[6] For example 'affidavit marriages' in Kenya, which are sworn affidavits used by couples to obtain housing and other social services. There is no official provision for the recognition of affidavit marriages in Kenyan law and yet they appear to have quasi-judicial effect. See J Kabeberi-Machaira and C Nyamu 'Marriage by Affidavit: Developing Alternative Laws on Cohabitation in Kenya' in J Eekelaar and T Nhlapo (eds) *Changing Family* (Oxford, Hart Publishing, 1998) 197.

[7] For example unregistered customary law unions in Zimbabwe which, although valid according to customary law, are not recognised as marriages by the State. However, they have consequences which receive legal sanction, such as the custody, guardianship and inheritance rights of the 'wife' and children.

[8] Ethiopia is one such example. T Teshome 'Reflections on the Revised Family Code of 2000' in A Bainham (ed) *International Survey of Family Law 2002* (Bristol, Jordan Publishing, 2002) 153 at 158. See also C Himonga and C Bosch 'The Application of Customary Law under the Constitution of South Africa: Problem Solved or Just Beginning?' (2000) 17 *South Africa Law Journal* 306; Bonthuys above n 3; M Hinz 'Family Law in Namibia: The Challenge of Customary and Constitutional Law' in J Eekelaar and T Nhlapo (eds) above n 6 at 139.

[9] T Teshome above n 8 at 155–56.

[10] It has a Family Code 1984 A An Na'im (ed) *Islamic Family Law in a Changing World: A Global Resource Book* (London, Zed Press, 2002) (hereafter An Na'im (ed) *Islamic Family Law*) at 165–67.

[11] Individual and Family Code enacted by *Zatu* AN VII–0013/FP/PRES of 16 November 1989— entered into force 4 August 1990. Combined Second and Third Periodic Reports of States Parties: Burkina Faso CEDAW/C/BFA//2–3 (hereafter Government of Burkina Faso (1998)) at 4, see also appendix at 29.

[12] J Toungara 'Changing the Meaning of Marriage: Women and Family Law in Cote d'Ivoire' in Royal Tropical Institute (KIT) and OXFAM (eds) *Gender Perspectives on Property and Inheritance* (Amsterdam, KIT and Oxford, OXFAM, 2001) 33; J Toungara 'Changing the Meaning of Marriage: Women and Family Law in Cote d'Ivoire' in G Mikell (ed) *African Feminism: The Politics of Survival in Sub-Saharan Africa* (Philadelphia, University of Pennsylvania Press, 1997) 53 at 54ff.

[13] An Na'im (ed) *Islamic Family Law* above n 10 at 152–53.

[14] Toungara 'Changing the Meaning of Marriage' (2001) above n 12 at 44.

[15] Kenya is one such country. See Center for Reproductive Law and Policy (CRLP) and FIDA Kenya *Women of the World Report: Anglophone Africa* (New York, CRLP, 1997) 47–48.

jurisdiction, these plural systems often make different demands of people[16] and have different formalities and consequences in their implementation.

The chapter starts with an examination of the impact of human rights on the family before examining feminist debates on the family. It then moves on to a consideration of the content of family laws on the African continent. It considers marriage, divorce, property settlement on death and divorce, and, of course, children.

Impact of human rights

Further complicating the already crowded picture of the nature of family law in Africa is the overlay of human rights principles introduced into domestic law by ratification and incorporation of international human rights instruments. The International Bill of Human Rights contains provisions declaring that the family is the fundamental base unit of society and requiring the protection of family life.[17] Regional human rights instruments similarly call for recognition and protection of the family.[18] Family in the African Charter is covered in article 18:

> The family shall be the natural unit and basis of society. It shall be protected by the State which shall take care of its physical and moral health.[19]

Although all calling for the protection of the family, which is seen as a group, the instruments considered do not throw light on the obligations and duties of family members towards each other within the family unit.[20] However, the African Charter provides in article 18:

---

[16] For example in some countries 'personal law' is still race specific, so that in Namibia and Zimbabwe, white people are recognised as only able to contract civil marriages which are monogamous. There is no recognition of either Hindu or Islamic marriage.

[17] UDHR art 16(3), ICCPR art 23(1), ICESCR art 10(1). See too Human Rights Committee General Comment No 19 on Protection of the Family, the Right to Marriage and Equality of the Spouses (Art 23) (27 July 1990) (Thirty-ninth session 1990) HRI/GEN/1/Rev.7. Cf Constitution of the Arab Republic of Egypt, 11 September 1971, as amended, Art 9, reproduced in C Heyns (ed) *Human Rights Law in Africa* (The Hague, Martinus Nijhoff, 2004) vol 2 at 1045. See also Constitution of Namibia 1990 Art 14(3); Constitution of the Republic of Seychelles, 18 June 1993, Art 32(1)—reproduced in C Heyns (ed) *Human Rights Law in Africa* (The Hague, Kluwer International, 1996) 305–18. Finally see Constitution of Ethiopia 1994 Art 34(3) in C Heyns (ed) (2004) vol 2 at 1083.

[18] European Convention on Human Rights 1950, 213 UNTS 221, art 8; American Convention on Human Rights 1969, 1114 UNTS 123, art 17(1). The Arab Charter on Human Rights 1994 art 38(a); G Van Bueren 'The International Protection of Family Members' Rights as the 21st Century Approaches' (1995) 17 *Human Rights Quarterly* 732.

[19] African Charter art 18(1). Cf Constitution of the Republic of Senegal, 7 January 2001, Art 17, reproduced in C Heyns (ed) (2004) above n 17, vol 2 at 1452. See also Constitution of the Central African Republic, 14 January 1995, Art 6, reproduced in C Heyns (ed) (1996) above n 17 at 981.

[20] Mutua contends that in Africa, the family is considered 'sacred'. He also contends that the primacy attached to the family in the African Charter places the family above the state. M Mutua 'Banjul Charter: The Case for an African Cultural Fingerprint' in A An Na'im (ed) *Cultural Transformation and Human Rights* (London, Zed Press, 2002) 67 at 89.

> The State shall have the duty to assist the family which is the custodian of morals and traditional values recognized by the community.[21]

Under the African system the individual also has duties, which include:

> To preserve the harmonious development of the family and to work for the cohesion and respect of the family; to respect his parents at all times, to maintain them in case of need.[22]

Mindful of the potential conflict between the state obligation to protect the family and women's rights, the Convention on the Elimination of All Forms of Discrimination against Women 1979 (CEDAW) provides a detailed consideration of the content of rights and responsibilities within the family.[23] The provisions of CEDAW, and in particular the requirement that states parties modify or amend customary laws that constitute discrimination against women,[24] provide a radical challenge to laws regulating family life in many African countries. In its general recommendation on marriage and family relations, CEDAW makes clear that:

> The form and concept of the family can vary from State to State and even between regions within a State. Whatever form it takes, and whatever the legal system, religion, custom or tradition within the country, the treatment of women in the family both at law and in private must accord with the principles of equality and justice for all people, as article 2 of the Convention requires.[25]

The recent adoption by the African Union of the Protocol to the African Charter on Human and Peoples' Right on the Human Rights of Women 2003 (African Protocol on Women's Rights) has brought the debates about the content and gender dimensions of law on the continent under greater scrutiny. Specifically the Protocol has provisions on family relations, including marriage,[26] divorce and separation,[27] inheritance[28] and issues of violence,[29] that closely mirror those found in CEDAW.

Seeing how countries go about reconciling the tensions that arise between the application of international human rights norms and domestic provisions, broadly defined to include normative orders outside the purview of state systems,

---

[21] African Charter art 18(2).

[22] Art 29(1).

[23] D Sullivan 'The Public/Private Distinction in International Human Rights Law' in J Peters and A Wolpe (eds) *Women's Rights, Human Rights: International Feminist Perspectives* (New York, Routledge, 1995) 126 at 127. Art 16 of CEDAW on marriage and family relations, read together with arts 2(f), 5 and 15 of CEDAW, are also relevant, as is CEDAW General Recommendation No 21 on Marriage and Family Relations.

[24] CEDAW art 2(f).

[25] CEDAW General Recommendation No 21 para 13. This is repeated in Human Rights Committee General Comment No 19 para 2.

[26] African Protocol on Women's Rights art 6.

[27] *Ibid* art 7.

[28] *Ibid* art 21. See also art 20 on the rights of widows.

[29] *Ibid* arts 4 and 5.

forms the basis of much of the literature on cultural pluralism/relativism.[30] Indeed it is sometimes said that these contradictions also exist within the human rights system. For example, does the right to culture under article 27 of the International Covenant on Civil and Political Rights 1966 (ICCPR) mean that minority communities should be able to determine, without external influence, the content of that culture or personal law, even if it violates other human rights norms such as the demand for equality before the law and the prohibition of discrimination based on, amongst other things, sex? Technically the answer would be that article 2, the non-discrimination provision, and article 26, the free-standing equality/equal protection before the law provision, would prevail because the rights in the Covenant are to be enjoyed by all without discrimination. In the *Lovelace* case, a woman belonging to the Maliseet Indian group challenged her exclusion from the reserve after she married (and later divorced) a white man. A man from her group who married outside the group would not have been so excluded. The Human Rights Committee, which found that there had been a violation of her rights, decided the case by reference to her identity as a minority indigenous woman entitled to enjoy her culture under article 27. The Committee did not address directly the sex-discrimination issue.[31]

As noted in Chapter 3, the many reservations to CEDAW, most of which are based on cultural and religious interpretations of gender relations in the private sphere, highlight the fact that finding a common consensus on what constitutes equality will be difficult. The reservations make clear that the family is the site of struggle over symbols, entitlement to property, resources and decision making. It is worth noting that these debates are not new and have existed throughout the life of the United Nations, and indeed constituted the bulk of the work undertaken by the Commission on the Status of Women for decades.[32] It is therefore not surprising that Chanock argues that the human rights paradigm is unsuitable for resolving issues pertaining to family law:

> The complex legal questions about the enduring nature of marriage and disputes over separation; of rights and duties in relation to children; about division of property and access to inheritance; about the duties between generations and kin in regard to mutual support—are not soluble by the invocation of a rights paradigm.[33]

---

[30] Cf Coomaraswamy above n 2 at 39, 48. SF Moore 'Law and Change: The Semi-Autonomous Social Field as an Appropriate Area of Study' (1973) 7 *Law and Society Review* 719 at 721, 723.

[31] See the case of *Lovelace v Canada* Communication No R.6/24/1977; Human Rights Committee Views of Committee (30 July 1981) UN Doc A/36/40, Supp 40. K Knop *Diversity and Self Determination in International Law* (Cambridge, Cambridge University Press, 2002) 360–72.

[32] United Nations *The United Nations and the Advancement of Women 1945–1996* (New York, United Nations, 1996) 22–24.

[33] M Chanock 'Human Rights and Cultural Branding: Who Speaks and How?' in A An Na'im (ed) *Cultural Transformation and Human Rights in Africa* (London, Zed Press, 2002) (hereafter An Na'im (ed) *Cultural Transformation*) 38 at 63.

Before moving on to consider the content of family law in selected African legal systems, it is as well to briefly consider debates in feminist circles about women's place within the family.[34]

Feminist perspectives on family

One finds differences in perspective about gender relations and the family between some northern-based feminists and those from the south, some of whom live in the diaspora. However, Chinkin notes that regardless of the type of society, the 'location of women within a devalued private sphere is general'.[35] Northern-based feminists such as O'Donovan[36] and Delphy[37] construct family, especially that regulated by the marriage institution, as the primary site of women's oppression. Delphy argues:

> The valuelessness of domestic work performed by married women derives institutionally from the marriage contract which is in fact a work contract. . . . it is a contract by which the head of the family—the husband—appropriates all the work done in the family by his children, his younger siblings and especially by his wife, since he can sell it on the market. . . . Conversely, the wife's labour has no value because it cannot be put on the market because of the contract by which her labour is appropriated by the husband. . . . It has therefore become limited to producing things which are intended for the family's internal use: domestic services and the raising of children.[38]

However, Delphy also notes that marriage provides women with economic security. She argues that the limitations it places on women's employability outside of the home, or, if employed outside the home, the limitations it places on women's promotion prospects, makes marriage a self-perpetuating state.[39]

For many women in Africa, marriage is made central to their lives whether or not they are married.[40] Irrespective of the legal provisions for capacity, marriage is

---

[34] 'Family' and women's place within it has received a great deal of attention and has been discussed from many standpoints. C Sweetman (ed) *Women and the Family* (Oxford, OXFAM, 1996); A Diduck and F Kaganas *Family Law Gender and the State* (Oxford, Hart Publishing, 1999); J Chandler *Women without Husbands: An Exploration of the Margins of Marriage* (London, Macmillan, 1991); S Maushart *Wifework: What Marriage Really Means for Women* (London, Bloomsbury Publishing, 2002); S Mvududu and P McFadden (eds) *Reconceptualizing the Family* (Harare, WLSA, 2001).

[35] C Chinkin 'Gender Inequality and Human Rights Law' in A Hurrell and N Woods (eds) *Inequality, Globalization and World Politics* (Oxford, Oxford University Press, 1999) 95 at 105.

[36] K O'Donovan *Sexual Divisions in Law* (London, Weidenfeld & Nicholson, 1985).

[37] C Delphy *Close to Home: A Materialist Analysis of Women's Oppression* (London, Hutchinson, 1984).

[38] *Ibid* at 95.

[39] *Ibid* at 98.

[40] An Na'im (ed) *Islamic Family Law* above n 10 at 157.

seen to give women both adult status and social respectability.[41] Those most pathologised are single women,[42] followed closely in some societies by unmarried mothers, although this is changing.[43] Nevertheless there are still some contexts in which 'unwed motherhood' is frowned upon.[44]

In some northern feminist writing, motherhood, and the disproportionate burden borne by women in the caring and nurturing of children, is seen as a major cause of their disempowerment.[45] Furthermore, society's view of women as caring and nurturing means that women who leave their children or forfeit custody of their children, are demonised and described as acting 'unnaturally'. Similarly, the motherhood ideology can be used to pathologise women who elect not to have children.[46] The framing of some human rights instruments, with their protection of women as mothers, presents another dimension of seeing women only in their reproductive roles.[47] On post-divorce care of children, Delphy has noted that women are often given custody of very young children who are labour intensive, whereas fathers are more likely to be awarded custody of older and thus self-sufficient children.[48] Interestingly, Fraser traces the improvement in the legal position of women within these societies to their being given greater access to their children on divorce, including the ability to claim custody.[49]

It has been argued that from the 'African' perspective, far from seeing family life or motherhood as the sites of women's oppression, motherhood is central to the identity of women. Nnaemeka argues:

> African feminism neither demotes/abandons motherhood nor dismisses maternal politics as non-feminist or unfeminist politics.[50]

Later she asserts:

> African feminism's valorization of motherhood and respect for maternal politics should not be pitted against the demotion of motherhood/maternal politics by radical feminism

---

[41] Marriage levels are particularly high in North Africa, with a 1997 study showing that only 1 per cent of Egyptian women remained unmarried. An Na'im (ed) *Islamic Family Law* above n 10 at 157.

[42] Cf S Tamale 'Gender Trauma in Africa: Enhancing Women's Access to Resources' (2004) 48 *Journal of African Law* 50 at 52. See also D Narayan and P Petesch *Voices of the Poor from Many Lands* (Washington DC, World Bank, 2002) 105.

[43] S Arnfred (ed) *Rethinking Sexualities in Africa* (Lund, Nordic Africa Institute, 2004) at 23, 24, 25.

[44] An Na'im (ed) *Islamic Family Law* above n 10 at 157.

[45] For a discussion of feminist perspectives (north and south) on the issue see H Lim and J Roche 'Feminism and Children's Rights: The Politics of Voice' in D Cottrell (ed) *Revisiting Children's Rights* (Leiden, Kluwer, 2001) 51.

[46] J Smith 'Ignore the Fertility Industry's Zealots: You can be Childless and a *Real* Woman' *The Times* (London, 27 August 2003) 16.

[47] CEDAW arts 4(2), 11 especially 11(2)(d); ICESCR art 10(2).

[48] Delphy above n 37 at 99. Cf Sinclair 'Embracing New Family Forms' above n 3 at 4.

[49] A Fraser 'Becoming Human: The Origins and Development of Women's Human Rights' (1999) 21 *Human Rights Quarterly* 853 at 866–68.

[50] O Nnaemeka (ed) *Sisterhood Feminisms and Power* (Asmara, Africa World Press, 1998) at 6. See also T Skard *Continent of Mothers: Understanding and Promoting Development in Africa Today* (London, Zed Press, 2003) at 174, 193; Arnfred above n 43 at 24.

in the West; rather these traits should be investigated in the context of their place and importance in the African environment.[51]

Being a mother is as important as being a wife; and if the latter does not come about, then it is considered preferable that the woman have a child which she will bring up on her own, rather than remain childless.[52] It has been said that Islam views the two roles of motherhood and wifehood as being the most sacred and essential roles for women.[53] Tamale notes that 'the domestic roles of mother, wife and homemaker become the key constructions of women's identity in Africa'.[54] Mutua contends that in pre-colonial African societies the burden of looking after the home and the children fell on women.[55] Arguably little has changed, making Mutua's subsequent statement that 'child care and rearing have always been community affairs in Africa'[56] gender blind, unless of course he sees community as being comprised primarily of women.

The importance of motherhood to some African women is highlighted in Hellum's study of infertility in Zimbabwe.[57] An empirical study, the book demonstrates the extraordinary lengths to which infertile women go to have children. Arguably, however, this is not uniquely African. The increase in reproductive technologies and infertility treatments in the north suggests that there is a strong demand for motherhood.[58]

From a jurisprudential perspective, law's role in the promotion or curtailment of women's rights in the family is the subject of many treatises.[59] Over time it has become clear that the operation of family law, and specifically customary law, has been seen as a major impediment to the enjoyment by African women of their

---

[51] *Ibid* at 9. N Nzegwu 'Questions of Agency: Development, Donors, and Women of the South' in (2002) *Jenda: A Journal of Culture and African Women's Studies* at http://www.jendajournal.com/jenda/vol2.1/nzegwu.html at 13.

[52] W Kioko 'Reforming Family Law in Kenya: The Place of the Repealed Affiliation Act' in K Kibwana (ed) *Law and the Status of Women in Kenya* (Nairobi, Women and Law in East Africa, 1995) 182 at 194.

[53] R El-Nimr 'Women in Islamic Law' in M Yamani and A Allen (eds) *Feminism and Islam: Legal and Literary Perspectives* (New York, New York University Press, 1996) 87.

[54] Tamale above n 42 at 52.

[55] Mutua above n 20 at 71 fn 35.

[56] *Ibid* at 93.

[57] A Hellum *Women's Human Rights and Legal Pluralism in Africa: Mixed Norms and Identities in Infertility Management in Zimbabwe* (Oslo, Mond Books, 1999).

[58] Indeed Hellum has also done a study of birth law in her own country, Norway. A Hellum *Birth Law* (Oslo, Scandinavian University Press, 1993). Cf M Warnock *Making Babies: Is There A Right to Have Children?* (Oxford, OUP, 2002). One of the most widely discussed books in North America in 2002 was S Hewlett *Baby Hunger: The New Battle for Motherhood* (Charleston, Atlantic Books, 2002). In this book Hewlett warned women about putting career before motherhood, arguing that some women were leaving it too late to have children and finding that when they did decide to try to have children, they were no longer able to due to infertility. It created a media frenzy.

[59] Sinclair provides an excellent synthesis of the debates around equality/difference, feminism, jurisprudence and women's place in the family. See J Sinclair and J Heaton *The Law of Marriage* vol 1 (Cape Town, Juta, 1996) 5ff.

human rights.[60] That family law is seen as the cause of much of the discrimination that women experience is clear from the Malawian Constitution 1994, which has a provision on women's rights that covers mainly family law related issues.[61] Nhlapo acknowledges that: 'Most of the sex inequalities in traditional society stemmed from the African conception of marriage.'[62]

Marriage being an almost universal starting point in discussions on family law seems a good place to begin the consideration of the content of family law systems on the continent. From the outset one has to be alive to the problem of over generalising, so that in their survey on Marriage Laws in Africa, Phillips and Morris noted:

> Any attempt to sketch in a few pages the outlines of African customary marriage must inevitably illustrate the dangers of generalization on a subject so great in its range and variety. Not only is there a vast diversity in matters of detail between the customs of different tribes and localities, but it is not even possible, save to a very limited extent, to trace any broad uniformity of basic principles. As warrant for this statement, it is sufficient to refer to the contrast between patrilineal and matrilineal societies.[63]

The chapter now moves on to look at marriage laws in various regions on the continent.

North Africa[64]

In states defining themselves as Islamic, such as Egypt,[65] one finds recognition of the personal laws of people from other religions. The Egyptian Personal Status Law

---

[60] J Akande 'Women and the Law' in A Obilade (ed) *Women in Law* (Lagos, Southern University Law Centre and Faculty of Law, 1993) 6 at 8. See also A Armstrong and J Stewart (eds) *The Legal Situation of Women in Southern Africa* (Harare, University of Zimbabwe Publications, 1990); C Bowman and A Kuenyehia (eds) *Women and Law in Sub-Saharan Africa* (Accra, SEDCO Publishing, 2003).

[61] Constitution of Malawi 1994 s 24.

[62] T Nhlapo 'International Protection of Human Rights and the Family: African Variations on a Common Theme' (1989) 3 *International Journal of Law, Policy and the Family* 1 at 10. Combined Second and Third Periodic Reports of States Parties: Nigeria (1997) CEDAW/C/NGA/2–3 (hereafter Government of Nigeria (1997)) at 63.

[63] A Phillips and H Morris *Marriage Laws in Africa* (London, Oxford University Press, 1971) 5. See also D Parkin and D Nyamwaya 'Introduction. Transformations of African Marriage: Change and Choice' in D Parkin and D Nyamwaya (eds) *Transformations of African Marriage* (Manchester, Manchester University Press, 1987) 1.

[64] For a concise overview see E Aouij 'Marriage and Family Relations' in United Nations (ed) *Bringing International Human Rights Law Home* (New York, United Nations, 2002) 39.

[65] Arts 2 of the Egyptian Constitution 1971 provide that Islam is the official religion in Egypt and that 'principles of Islamic law are the principal source of legislation'.

recognises marriage by Islamic rites, Christian, Coptic Christian and Jewish law.[66] Each type of marriage may have different formalities and consequences, so that while divorce is possible under Islamic law, it is forbidden by the Copts.[67] In Tunisia, by way of contrast, the Personal Status Code applies across the board and embraces all citizens.[68] In common with Tunisia, which specifies the age of 17 for girls and 20 for men,[69] both Egypt and Algeria have different ages of marriage for men and women. Egypt specifies the age of 18 for men and 16 for girls,[70] while Algeria specifies the ages of 21 for men and 18 for women respectively.[71] Although consent is seen as a vital component of marriage in the Egyptian system, it seems that issues of poverty and a lack of education impinge upon women's ability to give their full and free consent to marriage. The Egyptian government acknowledges that:

> [W]omen face a number of difficulties and problems, such as early marriage below the legal age, illiteracy and a low standard of living, which prevent them from freely expressing their frank opinion on their prospective spouse.[72]

Algeria requires the consent of both the woman and her father if it is her first marriage.[73] Her father or guardian is also responsible for concluding the marriage.[74] In Tunisia the consent of both parents is required under article 6 of the Personal Status Code.[75]

The continued reliance and dependence on fathers and male guardians belie the impression given in the respective state reports to CEDAW that women's status in the family in both Egypt and Algeria is in accordance with the principles of the Convention.[76] Both Algeria and Egypt are agreed that after marriage a woman retains her legal capacity and that any property which she owns or acquires is hers.[77] There is a requirement that the marriage be registered to be

---

[66] Y Quassem 'Law of the Family (Personal Status Law)' in N Bernard-Maugiron and B Dupret (eds) *Egypt and Its Laws* (The Hague, Kluwer Law International, 2002) 19.

[67] The 'rule' that there could be no divorce between Copts, was challenged in 1986 and the Court of Cassation ruled that alienation of affection was a ground for divorce which had been previously recognised by religious councils and which therefore stood. See Quassem above n 66 at 31.

[68] An Na'im (ed) *Islamic Family Law* above n 10 at 154, 182.

[69] A Na'im (ed) *Islamic Family* Law above n 10 at 183.

[70] Combined Fourth and Fifth Periodic Report of States Parties: Egypt (2000) CEDAW/C/EGY4–5 (hereafter Government of Egypt (2000)) at 16.

[71] Art 40 Algerian Family Code 1984; An Na'im (ed) *Islamic Family* Law above n 10 at 157.

[72] Government of Egypt (2000) above n 70 at 90.

[73] Algerian Family Code 1984 arts 9 and 11; Initial Report of States Party: Algeria (1998) CEDAW/C/DZA/1 (hereafter Government of Algeria (1998)) at 10, 40.

[74] Algerian Family Code 1984 art 12.

[75] Combined Second and Third Report of States Parties: Tunisia (2000) CEDAW/C/TUN 3–4 (hereafter Government of Tunisia (2000)) at para 49.

[76] Algeria does highlight that its Family Code 1984 is not wholly consistent with the understanding of equality found in the civil law. Government of Algeria (1998) above n 73 at 9, 10.

[77] Government of Algeria (1998) above n 73 at 9, 39 and 43; Government of Egypt (2000) above n 70 at 87.

valid.[78] Similarly in both systems Islamic law is said to recognise polygyny. This recognition is identified in the Algerian report to CEDAW as one of the most hotly contested provisions by human rights associations—not least because it directly contravenes article 1 of CEDAW on discrimination.[79]

By way of contrast, Tunisia, while still seeing the man as the head of the household, tries to work towards a model of marriage based on partnership and reciprocity of the spouses, hence the abolition of the wife's duty of submission.[80] Although the husband is to maintain the family, the wife can contribute if she has means.[81] In its report to CEDAW the government of Tunisia notes that 24 per cent of women are economically active.[82] As a result of its declared policy of secularism, Tunisia is the only state with Islam as the dominant religion to have outlawed polygyny, making it a criminal offence punishable by a year in prison and/or a fine.[83] However, in common with other countries, difficulties still remain in that attitudes and behaviour have not kept up with legal change, so that Tunisian women are said to complain about the law/social relations lag. Moreover, research undertaken in Tunisia appears to show that there is resistance to the economic advancement of women, which is manifested by wealthy men seeking 'brides from poor villages, since city women are "too independent". And the incidence of wife beating remains high.'[84]

It must be noted here that even when countries follow the same school of Islam,[85] the results/interpretations may vary. Similarly expert opinion on a rule and judicial interpretation thereof may also vary.[86] Indeed Quassem notes that 'When promulgating a law related to the family, the Egyptian legislature seeks the

---

[78] Government of Algeria (1998) above n 73 at 40. An Na'im notes that there is provision for marriages that have not been registered to be recognised by courts ex post facto. This is on the basis that all other formalities have been complied with. Marriages so recognised will then be registered. An Na'im (ed) *Islamic Family Law* above n 10 at 166.

[79] Government of Algeria (1998) above n 73 at 9. Cf A Gaye and M Njie 'Family Law in the Gambia' in A Kuenyehia (ed) *Women and Law in West Africa* (Accra, Women and Law in West Africa, 1998) 2 at 6–8.

[80] Government of Tunisia (2000) above n 75 paras 42–45, 1042–45.

[81] An Na'im (ed) *Islamic Family Law* above n 10 at 183.

[82] Government of Tunisia (2000) above n 75 para 44; see also para 1046 on mutual right of restitution of pre-marital gifts.

[83] *Ibid* paras 26, 1042. An Na'im (ed) *Islamic Family Law* above n 10 at 154, 183. The new Family Code in Morocco tries to curtail the practice of polygyny: G Tremlett 'Morocco Boosts Women's Rights' *Guardian* (London, 21 January 2004).

[84] 'Out of the Shadows, into the World' *Economist* (London, 19 June 2004) 29 at 29.

[85] There are four recognised schools of Islam amongst the Sunnis. These are the Abu Hanafi, Maliki, Hanbali and Shafi'i. The Shia have the Itha 'ashari (or Ja'afari) while the Ibadi and Zaidis are considered to fall between the Sunni and the Shi'i. See also W Hallaq *The Origins and Evolution of Islamic Law* (Cambridge, Cambridge University Press, 2004) 150–77.

[86] See for example the different opinions on a Muslim woman's entitlement to property on divorce under Islamic law in the South African case of *Rylands v Edros* 1997 (1) BCLR 77. L Fishbayn 'Litigating the Right to Culture: Family Law in the New South Africa' (1999) 13 *International Journal of Law, Policy and the Family* 147 at 160–63.

provisions of the Islamic law, without confining himself [sic] to the Hanafi School'.[87] Quassem then goes on to say that the aim of the law in Egypt is to serve the public interests and those of women, and when the Abu Hanafi school fails to fulfil this function, then the legislature will seek a rule under the Ibn Malik school or indeed another school of jurisprudence, again 'with a view to improving the status of women in Egypt'.[88]

However, the state reports of Algeria and Egypt to CEDAW try to argue that the reservations made to key provisions of the Convention (and justified by reference to the Shari'a and 'custom'), including 9 on nationality, 15 on equality before the law, and 16 on marriage and family relations, are compatible with the Convention.[89] Not surprisingly, the Committee does not share this perspective.[90] Indeed the Women's Committee is becoming increasingly intolerant of what it perceives as state excuses for the non-implementation of the Convention.[91] In response to the Moroccan government representative presenting the state report to CEDAW, it was observed:

> The Koran could not be used a pretext for not implementing the Convention, one expert said, noting that other Muslim countries had moved forward more than Morocco in achieving equality between men and women. Another expert said that, coming from a Muslim country, she was well aware that there was nothing in Islamic teaching which stood in the way of fully implementing women's human rights or limiting their full cultural participation in society.[92]

The initial Algerian report to CEDAW goes out of its way to emphasise the attempts of the state to move towards a more secular legal system. Commenting on the place and role of Islamic law in the Algerian system, it is noted:

> It may be said that this place and role is not only extremely limited, but that it is steadily diminishing, in light of the sophistication of present day problems, inter-cultural influences, and the secularizing trends that are under way in Algerian society. Since Algerian independence, the only juridical instrument that makes reference to the Shariah is the Family Code which, despite its literal adherence to certain provisions of the

---

[87] Quassem above n 66 at 19.
[88] *Ibid* at 20.
[89] Government of Algeria (1998) above n 73 at 1. Government of Egypt (2000) above n 70 at 3.
[90] General Assembly Meetings Coverage 'Women's Anti-Discrimination Committee Considers Report of Algeria. Committee Members Call for Further Action by Government to Achieve Gender Equality' Press Release WOM/1475, at 1, 6, 7, 8 and 9.
[91] General Assembly Meetings Coverage 'Women's Anti-Discrimination Committee Considers Situation of Women in Gabon.' Press Release WOM/1476 at 12, 13.
[92] CEDAW Concludes Consideration of Morocco's Report (20 January 1997) United Nations Press Release WOM/937, downloaded from http://www.un.org/News/Press/docs/19970120.wom937.html. See also S Ali 'Development of the International Norm of Non-Discrimination on the Basis of Sex: An Evaluation of Women's Human Rights in Islam and International Law' in A Stewart (ed) *Gender, Law and Social Justice* (Oxford, Blackstone, 2000) 45. The African Commission has also asked about the interpretation of the Shari'a in Sudan. R Murray *The African Commission on Human Rights and International Law* (Oxford, Hart Publishing, 2000) 45 n 46.

Shariah, can be seen, both in its form and in certain rulings that have been based on it, as an attempt to restrict the role of Islamic law.[93]

Algeria undertook to amend its Family Code and uplift some of its reservations.[94] Although the reservations have remained, in its second report to CEDAW Algeria reported that in 2003 the Ministry of Justice had been instructed by the country's President to examine the possibility of amending the Family Code to enable women to enjoy their rights unfettered by discriminatory social and other constraints.[95]

The increasing controversy over the application of Shari'a law in northern Nigeria is probably the clearest example of the divergence of opinion on the interpretation of principles of Shari'a. This is clearly seen in the 2003 Nigerian report to CEDAW.[96]

West Africa[97]

With the richness and diversity of its religious and ethnic groupings, Nigeria operates a federal system recognising the various customary marriage systems,[98] religious marriages and of course civil marriage.[99] The age of marriage varies depending on the region, so that in the southern parts of the country the average age of marriage is between 18 and 21 years, and in the north it is between 12 and 15 years. The government notes that in the north girls are sometimes given in marriage on reaching puberty and that it has been known for girls as young as 9 to be married. To deal with this problem it is proposed to pass a law outlawing marriage for females below the age of 18.[100]

---

[93] Government of Algeria (1998) above n 73 at 10. Quite how true this is in practice remains contested.

[94] An Na'im (ed) *Islamic Family Law* above n 10 at 167.

[95] CEDAW Concluding Observations Algeria Report above n 90 at 4.

[96] Combined Fourth and Fifth Periodic Report to CEDAW: Nigeria (2003) CEDAW/C/NGA/4–5 (hereafter Government of Nigeria (2003)) at 14. See also M Kukah 'Shariah, Justice and Constitutionalism in Nigeria' in J Murison *et al* (eds) *Remaking Law in Africa: Transnationalism Persons and Rights* (Edinburgh, Centre of African Studies, 2004) 173 at 181–86. Kukah's discussion about the class aspects of the application of Sharia and its politicisation is fascinating: see 186–92. See also A Iwobi 'Tiptoeing through a Constitutional Minefield: The Great Sharia Controversy in Nigeria' (2004) 48 *Journal of African Law* 111.

[97] See generally A Kuenyehia (ed) *Women and Law in West Africa* (Accra, Women and Law in West Africa, 1998).

[98] Government of Nigeria (2003) above n 96 at 55.

[99] Matrimonial Causes Act (Cap 220 Laws of the Federation of Nigeria 1990); Marriage Act (Cap 218 Laws of the Federation of Nigeria 1990): Government of Nigeria (2003) above n 96 at 54–55. A Rahmatian 'Termination of Marriage in Nigerian Family Laws: The Need for Reform and the Relevance of the Tanzanian Experience' (1996) 10 *International Journal of Law, Policy and the Family* 281.

[100] Government of Nigeria (2003) above n 96 at 55.

The consequences of marriage under the various systems vary. In its report to CEDAW in 2003, the Nigerian government described a wife in a customary marriage as being regarded as 'the man's property and she is generally not expected to entertain any measure of equality in whatever form'.[101] Although marriage under the Marriage Act, 1990 is technically monogamous, the reality is that men still 'marry' other women. The Constitutional Rights Project notes that since independence in 1960, there has been only one recorded case of bigamy. The Project attributes women's reluctance to have their husbands prosecuted for bigamy to 'cultural and traditional attitudes, along with patterns of socialization'.[102] As already noted, the rise of Islam in the north of the country has been seen by some as a threat to the nation state and, indeed, human rights principles enshrined in the Nigerian constitution. However, others see it as merely reflecting the diversity that is Nigeria, and the recognition of Islam as a part of the legal landscape as according with respect for constitutional principles of freedom of religion.[103] As with customary marriages, Islamic marriages are potentially polygynous.[104]

Ghana recognises customary (registered[105] and unregistered[106]), civil or Christian[107] and Islamic[108] marriages in the north of the country. However, the Children's Act provides that regardless of the type of marriage entered into, the minimum age of marriage is 18.[109] Moreover the statute provides that there should be no coercion to marry.[110] Furthermore, no child should be made the subject of a 'dowry transaction'.[111] Realistically it is difficult for this law to be enforced, not least because not all parties register their marriages, making it difficult for the state to check on both age and consent. For example, Muslim marriages are required to be registered under the Marriage of Mohammedans Ordinance 1907 but rarely are. This non-registration has been attributed to igno-

---

[101] Government of Nigeria (2003) above n 96 at 55. See also 53.

[102] Constitutional Rights Project *Unequal Rights: Discriminatory Laws and Practices against Women in Nigeria* (Lagos, Constitutional Rights Project, 1995) 13.

[103] 'Saving Amina Lawal: Human Rights Symbolism and the Dangers of Colonialism' (2004) 117 (7) *Harvard Law Review* 2365; H Abdullah 'Religious Revivalism, Human Rights Activism and the Struggle for Women's Rights in Nigeria' in A An Na'im (ed) *Cultural Transformation and Human Rights in Africa* (London, Zed Press, 2002) 151 at 157–61.

[104] Government of Nigeria (2003) above n 96 at 54.

[105] Customary Marriage and Divorce (Registration) Law 1985 (PNDCL 112); Woodman above n 1 at 199–200. See generally A Kuenyehia and E Ofei-Aboagye 'Family Law in Ghana and its Implications for Women' in A Kuenyehia (ed) *Women and Law in West Africa* (Accra, Women and Law in West Africa, 1998) 23.

[106] Customary Marriage and Divorce (Registration) (Amendment) Law 1991 (PNDCL 253); Woodman above n 1 at 200.

[107] Marriage Ordinance 1884 (Cap 127).

[108] Marriage of Mohammedans Ordinance 1907 (Cap 129).

[109] Ghana, The Children's Act 1998 (Act 560 1998) s 14(2) reproduced in Bowman and Kuenyehia above n 60 at 31–32. Woodman above n 1 at 196–97, 199–202.

[110] Woodman above n 1 at 298.

[111] Ghana, The Children's Act 1998 s 14(1).

rance of the law on the part of the affected population.[112] In truth it is also worth noting that if the 'normative field' ordering the lives of the affected people does not recognise the non-registration of a marriage as fatal to that marriage, then they will not trouble themselves with registering the marriage.

Polygny is permitted under the customary and Islamic marriage systems, whilst the civil marriage is legally meant to be monogamous. Woodman notes that although there is a technical breach between the continued existence of polygyny and the non-discrimination provisions of the Constitution, which outlaw discrimination based on gender, there have not, to date, been any cases challenging the inconsistency.[113] He also notes that the overwhelming evidence garnered from case law and social activity points to a preference amongst ordinary Ghanaians for marrying and conducting their family lives according to customary principles. This observation is supported by Kuenyehia and Ofei-Aboagye, who indicate that research undertaken in Ghana in 1988 showed that 80 per cent of Ghanaian women were married under the customary law.[114]

As already noted, Francophone countries appear to operate on a code-based system. In Burkina Faso, family relations are governed by the Individual and Family Code.[115] Under this law, freedom to choose one's spouse is recognised, consent to the marriage is necessary and there is an obligation to register the marriage.[116] The law provides different ages for marriage of men (20 years) and women (17 years).[117] There is a presumption that the marriage will be monogamous, although the parties can agree before the marriage that the husband may marry further wives. Technically this gives a woman in a monogamous marriage the right to apply to have any second or subsequent marriage that her husband purports to enter into declared null and void.[118] However, the economic dependence of women probably means that few women would actually activate the law. Indeed the government readily concedes that practice does not accord with the law due mainly to the non-implementation of the law:

> [T]here is a shortfall in the production of documents, enabling certain unscrupulous individuals to contract several marriages after opting for the monogamous regime. Civil registry officials, frequently through ignorance and occasionally by complicity, solemnize marriages without trying to carry out checks before hand.[119]

---

[112] D Dzidzornu 'Human Rights and Widow's Material Security: The Case of the "Intestate" Ghanaian Widow' (1995) 4 *Law and Politics in Asia, Africa, Asia and Latin America* 489 at 520.

[113] Woodman above n 1 at 198.

[114] A Kuenyehia and E Ofei-Aboagye 'Family Law in Ghana and its Implications for Women' in A Kuenyehia (ed) *Women and Law in West Africa* (Accra, Women and Law in West Africa, 1998) 23 at 25.

[115] The Individual and Family Code 1989. Government of Burkina Faso (1998) above n 11 at 4, see also appendix at 29.

[116] *Ibid* at 26.

[117] Government of Burkina Faso (1998) above n 11 at 26.

[118] *Ibid* at 4.

[119] *Ibid* at 26.

East Africa

It is the East African region that presents us with one of the most colourful tapestries on the marriage front. Most jurisdictions deal with the plurality of marriage forms by having multiple systems operating simultaneously. Kenya operates a system recognising marriage according to custom, religion and civil law.[120] Formalities and consequences are governed by the various statutes. A marriage under the Hindu Marriage and Divorce Act[121] is substantially similar to a marriage under the Marriage Act,[122] that is it is monogamous. Christian marriages may also be registered under the African Christian Marriage and Divorce Act.[123] By way of contrast, the Mohammedan Marriage and Divorce Act[124] recognises marriages contracted under Islamic law. Customary marriages are also recognised.

The Kenyan law tries to avoid normative order 'mix ups' by providing that a person cannot contract an Islamic marriage while married according to Christian rites or the customary law of any group.[125] This no doubt seeks to prevent the confusion that occurs in some systems when people start marrying different women under different laws, thus causing a great deal of uncertainty as to their marital status.[126] As already noted, Moore has shown that the state-recognised law is not the only system of law operating within a country. As was noted in the introduction, in the Kenyan context, there has been recognition of what became known as 'affidavit marriages', that is unions registered with the local authority to enable a couple to obtain state housing. Not recognised as legal by the formal state system, they were, however, given recognition in the administrative field, and for many of the couples involved, the affidavits are taken to have the same significance as that provided by a 'state' marriage certificate.[127]

---

[120] Human Rights Watch *Double Standards: Women's Property Right Violations in Kenya* (London, Human Rights Watch, 2003). See generally K Kibwana (ed) *Law and the Status of Women in Kenya* (Nairobi, Women and Law in East Africa, 1995); C Nyamu-Musembi ' "Sitting on her Husband's Back with her Hands in his Pockets": Commentary on Judicial Decision Making in Marital Property Cases in Kenya' in A Bainham (ed) *International Survey of Family Law 2002* (Bristol, Jordan Publishing, 2002) 229 at 231.

[121] Hindu Marriage and Divorce Act (Cap 157).

[122] Marriage Act (Cap 150).

[123] African Christian Marriage and Divorce Act (Cap 151).

[124] Mohammedan Marriage and Divorce Act (Cap 156).

[125] Center for Reproductive Law and Policy *Women of the World Report: Anglophone Africa* (New York, CRLP, 1997) 48.

[126] See for example, F Banda 'Between a Rock and a Hard Place: Courts and Customary Law in Zimbabwe' in A Bainham (ed) *International Survey of Family Law 2002* (Bristol, Jordan Publishing, 2002) 471.

[127] Kabeberi-Machaira and Nyamu above n 6 at 206.

Although it is in the process of revising its family law, currently Uganda,[128] like Kenya, recognises Hindu,[129] Muslim,[130] Christian/civil[131] and customary[132] marriages.[133] In much the same way that they have different formalities, the age at which parties are allowed to marry appears to vary. For marriage under the Hindu statute and the Customary Decree the age is 16 for girls and 18 for boys. However, there is no age limit specified for Muslim marriages, so that Naggita notes that it has been known for girls as young as 9 to be given in marriage by their father or guardian.[134] Moreover, although the Marriage Act prescribes the age of 21 for both parties to the marriage, Naggita notes that in practice priests will not marry the couple without proof that the father of the woman has consented to the marriage.[135] She then goes on to note that often the consent of the father/guardian will be conditional upon his receiving his bridewealth.[136] Echoing the position of women marrying for the first time in Algeria, she notes: 'In practice therefore, a woman's consent is insufficient unless it is shored up by that of a male relative.'[137] Polygyny is recognised in both the customary and Islamic systems.[138] Should the Domestic Relations Bill become law, then some of these inconsistencies will be removed. The Bill aims to consolidate all the marriage laws. The basis of the reform is to bring family law in line with the Constitution and its provisions on non-discrimination.[139] However, the government identifies that there is resistance to some of the proposals, and notes that the process of changing the law and attitudes and behaviour will take time.[140]

Tanzania recognises within its Marriage Act 1971 marriages contracted in terms of custom, religion (Christian, Hindu and Islamic) and of course registered civil marriages.[141] Again, the formalities of the marriage are left to the different systems

---

[128] The Domestic Relations Bill 2003. Bill No 21 2003. Bills Supplement No 9, 3 December 2003.
[129] Hindu Marriage and Divorce Act (Cap 214), Laws of Uganda 1964.
[130] Mohammedan Marriage and Divorce Act (Cap 213), Laws of Uganda 1964.
[131] Marriage Act (Cap 211), Laws of Uganda 1964.
[132] Customary Marriages (Registration) Decree, Decree No 16 of 1973.
[133] Third Periodic Report of States Parties: Uganda (2000) CEDAW/C/UGA/3 (hereafter Government of Uganda (2000)) at 66.
[134] E Naggita 'Why Men Come Out Ahead: The Legal Regime and the Protection and Realization of Women's Rights in Uganda' (2000) 6 *East African Journal of Peace and Human Rights* 34 at 44.
[135] *Ibid* at 43.
[136] *Ibid.*
[137] *Ibid.*
[138] In light of the constitutional provision covering sex and an equality before the law provision, Tibatemwa-Ekirikubinza notes that the continued recognition of polygyny 'is a clear indication that the fangs of patriarchy are still so deeply embedded in Ugandan society that those in power are not ready to put into operation the equality provision found in the fundamental law of the land.' L Tibatemwa-Ekirikubinza 'Family Relations and the Law in Uganda: Insights into Current Issues' in A Bainham (ed) *International Survey of Family Law 2002* (Bristol, Jordan Publishing, 2002) 433 at 437.
[139] Government of Uganda (2000) above n 133 at 17, 67. Domestic Relations Bill 2003 Memorandum, paras 5 and 6.
[140] Government of Uganda (2000) above n 133 at 17, 61.
[141] B Rwezaura and U Wanitzek 'Family Law Reform in Tanzania: A Socio-Legal Report' (1988) 2 *International Journal of Law, Policy and the Family* 1 at 8ff.

under which they are contracted, with the one requirement that validity is based on registration.[142] Unlike the Ethiopian Code of 2000, which demands monogamy, the Tanzanian statute recognises and allows polygyny for customary marriages and Islamic marriages. The others are presumed to be monogamous.[143] In common with many other African countries, the Tanzanian law also provides for different ages of marriage between the sexes and, in setting the minimum age for marriage for girls at 15, appears to condone child marriages. The age of marriage for males is 18. Of course some would argue that it is better for the girls to receive the protection of marriage, including access to property and the right to be maintained, than to allow them to be used and discarded because of an arbitrarily high minimum age of marriage. Whatever the reasoning, it is clear that the provision violates article 21(2) of the African Charter on the Rights and Welfare of the Child 1990.[144] With registration a requirement of marriage, it appears that judicial divorce is also a necessity. This constitutes a modification for some systems, not least the customary system, where divorce is usually the preserve of the family council comprising representatives from the respective families.

The Ethiopian Revised Family Code 2000[145] is clear and simple. It provides that marriages contracted according to custom, religion or civil law are recognised. Formalities are left to the respective custom or religion. However, the Code specifies that regardless of the religious or customary system chosen by the parties, there are minimum requirements as regards formalities. These include age (18 years),[146] the necessity of the consent of both parties to the marriage[147] and the requirement of monogamy.[148] It of course goes without saying that legal requirements do not necessarily translate into practice on the ground. One only need look at the fact that in Ethiopia most girls are married by their eighteenth birthdays.[149] Indeed the Committee on the Elimination of All Forms of Discrimination against

---

[142] Despite this, the Tanzanian system has recognised de facto marriages for a long time. See B Rwezaura 'The Proposed Abolition of *De Facto* Unions in Tanzania: A Case of Sailing against the Social Current' in J Eekelaar and T Nhlapo (eds) *Changing Family* (Oxford, Hart Publishing, 1998) 175.

[143] Rwezaura and Wanitzek above n 141 at 8.

[144] Tanzania proposes to change the law to make 18 the minimum age for both sexes. This has not yet happened. Personal Correspondence with Professor Bart Rwezaura, May 2003.

[145] Teshome notes that the 2000 Code only applies in 2 areas, Addis Ababa and the city of Dire Dawa. However, he notes that it is hoped that the 2000 Code will act as the model for forthcoming family codes. Until then many of the states appear still to be applying the 1960 Civil Code, whilst one state has passed a family code of its own, the Family Code of the National State of Tigrai, *Negrait Gazetta of Tigrai*, November 1998, 7th Year No 33. Teshome above n 8 at 155–56.

[146] Revised Family Code 2000 art 7(1). Art 7(2) provides for special Ministerial dispensation if the parties are aged between 16–18.

[147] *Ibid* art 6.

[148] *Ibid* art 11 on bigamy.

[149] Forum on Marriage and the Rights of Women and Girls *Early Marriage: Whose Right to Choose?* (London, Forum on Marriage and the Rights of Women and Girls, 2000) 24–26. Toungara notes that in Côte d'Ivoire, 'Nearly 48% of women were married by the time they reached 20 years of age' (Toungara 'Changing the Meaning of Marriage' (2001) above n 8 at 42).

Women has noted in its concluding observations to the Ethiopian report that early marriage is an issue of concern which should be addressed by the government.[150]

This regional overview of marriage laws concludes with a look at the Southern African region.

Southern Africa

In Southern African countries one also finds plural marriage systems recognising civil and customary marriages, both registered and unregistered.[151] However, unlike the countries just discussed, the only religious forms of marriage recognised in countries such as Namibia and Zimbabwe are those according to Christian or Jewish rites. This has meant that Hindus or Muslims[152] have been forced to marry under the civil law system, which bars polygyny. It has also meant that even when they had religious rites attached to their marriage (usually by way of a religious marriage performed in 'private', meaning outside the purview of the state), the religious aspect was not recognised by the formal state system. By definition, then, consequences of the marriage followed not Islamic or Hindu principles, but those of the civil (statutory) system. Wives from these two groups would therefore be entitled to whatever other women with civil marriages were entitled to on divorce and on death. However, this non-recognition has started to be challenged.

Botswana has enacted a Marriage Act 2000 that formally recognises civil, customary, Hindu, Muslim and other religious marriages.[153] The Act raises the age of marriage from 16 for boys and 14 for girls to the uniform age of 18 for everyone. This serves a dual purpose: it removes the sex discrimination inherent in having different age requirements for men and women; and it also discourages child marriage, which affects girls disproportionately. Importantly the Act provides that parties to the marriage are under a responsibility to register the marriage within two months of the completion of the respective formalities demanded by the parties' respective normative orders. On satisfying herself of the successful completion of the respective formalities, which may be recorded, the Registrar of

---

[150] CEDAW Concluding Observations Ethiopia CEDAW A/51/38 (1996) para 149, downloaded from http://www.bayefsky.com./html/ethiopia_t4_cedaw.php. By 2004, CEDAW was congratulating the Ethiopian government for setting the age of marriage at 18. However, concern was still noted about the 'persistence of the practice (of early marriage) . . . which may be perpetuated by the non-registration of births'. CEDAW Concluding Observations Ethiopia CEDAW A/59/38 (2004) para 253.

[151] Initial Report of States Parties: Namibia (1997) CEDAW/C/Nam/1 (hereafter Government of Namibia (1997)) at 170–74. See also discussion under art 15 on legal capacity and domicile at 164–69.

[152] However, sometimes black African Muslims mix their normative orders so that they move between customary and religious laws.

[153] S Morolong 'Overview of Recent Developments in the Law of Marriage in Botswana' in A Bainham (ed) *International Survey of Family Law 2002* (Bristol, Jordan Publishing, 2002) 67.

Marriages issues a certificate that is proof of marriage. Unlike other countries where non-registration is not fatal, the Botswana statute makes it a criminal offence not to register the marriage.[154] Again it is questionable whether this law has the 'cultural legitimacy' needed for people to abandon the practice of marrying under the customary system without registering their unions.

The Zimbabwean law recognises marriage contracted in terms of the Marriage Act.[155] This marriage type is monogamous. The law also recognises customary marriages registered under the Customary Marriages Act.[156] This type of marriage is potentially polygynous. However, if the man has not married a second wife and wishes to 'upgrade' his marriage into a monogamous one under the Marriage Act then he may do so. The Zimbabwean Customary Marriages Act still provides that the customary marriage officer has, before solemnising the marriage, to satisfy himself [sic] that 'the guardian of the woman and the intended husband have agreed on the marriage consideration and the form thereof'.[157] This is despite the Legal Age of Majority Act 1982, which provide that majority is reached at the age of 18.[158] It also flies in the face of decision of the Supreme Court in *Katekwe v Muchabaiwa*,[159] which held that a woman who reaches the age of 18 no longer requires her guardian's consent to marry. In obiter dicta, the Chief Justice noted that a woman could marry without bridewealth being given for her, if she so wished.

The third type of union found in Zimbabwe is the unregistered customary law union. This is private arrangement made between families by way of payment of bridewealth by the man for the woman. Technically, due to its non-registration, this type of union is not recognised as a valid marriage under the law. This is because of the Customary Marriages Act, which provides in section 3(1) that to be valid the marriage must be solemnised in terms of the Act. However, the statute does recognise that a marriage valid at customary law but not solemnised in accordance with the statute, remains valid for 'purposes of customary law and custom relating to the status, guardianship, custody and rights of succession of the children of such marriage'.[160]

The technical non-recognition of unregistered customary law unions in Zimbabwe means that if a man does contract a subsequent marriage with a different woman under the Marriage Act, it is the second marriage that trumps the first and is recognised by the law.[161] However, in the case of *Gwatidzo v Gwatidzo*[162] a

---

[154] *Ibid* at 69–71.
[155] Marriage Act (Cap 5:11).
[156] Customary Marriages Act (Cap 5:07) s 3(1).
[157] *Ibid* s 7(1)(a).
[158] Legal Age of Majority Act [General Laws Amendment Act Cap 8:07].
[159] *Katekwe v Muchabaiwa* 1984 (2) ZLR 112 (SC).
[160] Customary Marriages Act s 3(5).
[161] *Mujawo v Chogugudza* 1992 (2) ZLR 421 (SC).
[162] *Gwatidzo v Gwatidzo* Unreported Judgment HH–232–2000.

man had an unregistered customary law union with one woman before going on to enter into a Marriage Act marriage with a second. He did not divorce the first wife, who was sued for adultery by the Marriage Act wife. The judge noted that for many Zimbabweans customary law was the law with which they were most familiar, and which law was recognised in the Constitution. Although holding the defendant technically liable for adultery, he said that he did not think that the law of marriage should be used to validate one marriage form over another.[163]

As part of its post-apartheid attempt to recognise all the colours of the 'rainbow nation', the government of South Africa has sought to broaden recognition of marriages to encompass customary marriages and marriages contracted according to other systems.[164] Civil marriage, incorporating marriage by Christian and Jewish rites, has long been recognised.[165] Customary marriages have enjoyed uneven recognition in the country. The position on customary marriages was clarified by the passing of the Recognition of Customary Marriages Act 1998.[166] The statute can sometimes be confusing. It provides on one hand that the parties to the marriage have a duty to register it,[167] but then says that non-registration does not invalidate the marriage.[168] Although contracting a second marriage with a different spouse is permitted according to custom, a man cannot marry a second wife under the Marriage Act. He can, however, marry the same woman according to customary law and later register the marriage in terms of the Marriage Act, thus creating a double-decker monogamous marriage.

The recognition accorded to customary marriages emboldened Muslims in South Africa to demand recognition of their constitutional right to religion and, flowing from that, the recognition of Islamic personal law. Although an Islamic Marriage Bill was published in 2003, it is still being debated. It has been argued that the recognition of Islamic marriages has already begun, largely by way of judicial intervention followed by statutory enactment.[169]

In both the 1998 Recognition of Customary Marriages Act and the 2003 Islamic Marriage Bill, polygyny is recognised as being consonant with customary and Islamic marriage.[170] In much the same way that customary law has been said to be

---

[163] Discussed in Banda above n 126 at 476–77.

[164] Bonthuys above n 3 at 42. Sinclair 'Embracing New Family Forms' above n 3; *Juleiga Daniels v Campbell NO* CCT-40/03 paras 25–37, 54, 56, 57, 58. But see Moseneke J in *Daniels* at paras 68, 79, 90, 97–107.

[165] Marriage Act 1961 (Act No 25 of 1961).

[166] C Himonga 'Legislative and Judicial Approaches to the Reform of the Customary Law of Marriage and Succession in South Africa: Implications for the Advancement of Women's Rights' (paper presented at the Conference on Advancing Women's Rights Hosted by the Women's Legal Centre, Cape Town, 30–31 October 2003) available at http://www.wlce.co.za/conference2003/2003conference_himonga.php at 2, 5, 16; Sinclair 'Embracing New Family Forms' above n 3 at 819–22.

[167] Recognition of Customary Marriages Act 1998 (Act 120 of 1998) s 4(1).

[168] Recognition of Customary Marriages Act 1998 s 4(9).

[169] *Juleiga Daniels v Campbell and Others* 2003 (9) BCLR 969 (HC). See also the Constitutional Court judgment *Juleiga Daniels v Campbell NO* CCT 40/03 para 107.

[170] Bonthuys above n 3 at 48.

'undecided' because of its potential incompatibility with the Bill of Rights in South Africa, it is arguable that the recognition of Islamic law will throw up the same challenges (particularly as regards the consequences of marriage and the different grounds for divorce as between men and women).[171] Given the 2000 Equality Act and its stated goal to work towards the guarantee of the dignity of women and the eradication of inequality in South African society, not least that brought about by patriarchy, it is unclear how much latitude will be given to personal law systems that may contain discriminatory elements.[172]

South Africa being, in the words of one of my undergraduate students, 'too trendy for its own good', has also had to confront the issue of same sex marriage.[173] This is because of the non-discrimination provision in its Constitution, which includes in the proscribed category discrimination based on sexual orientation.[174] This provision has been used to challenge an immigration rule that only allowed family reunion of married couples, so that the partner of a South African in a same sex union was allowed to join him.[175] There have also been some statutory amendments made to take into account the prohibition of discrimination based on sexual orientation.[176] Although in the *National Coalition* case the court said that same sex relationships could not be equated with marriage as commonly understood,[177] there has been a marked change in judicial attitudes towards same sex couples. This is most clearly marked in the recognition in 2004 of same sex marriages.[178]

---

[171]   Sinclair 'Embracing New Family Forms' above n 3 at 826–33.

[172]   M Pieterse 'The Promotion of Equality and Prevention of Unfair Discrimination Act 4 of 2000: Final Nail in the Customary Law Coffin?'(2000) 117 *South Africa Law Journal* 627 at 628–29; *Daniels v Campbell NO* CCT 40/03 at para 108; Sinclair 'Embracing New Family Forms' above n 3 at 823–25. The decision in *Bhe* in the Constitutional Court is a case in point.

[173]   Cf M Machera 'Opening a Can of Worms: A Debate on Female Sexuality in the Lecture Theatre' in S Arnfred (ed) *Rethinking Sexualities in Africa* (Lund, Nordic Africa Institute, 2004) 157 at 163.

[174]   Constitution of the Republic of South Africa 1996 s 9(3).

[175]   *National Coalition for Gay and Lesbian Equality v Minister of Home Affairs* 2000 (2) SA 1. See also *Satchwell v The President of South Africa and the Minister of Justice* 2002 (6) SA 1. On custody of children see *Ex Parte Critchfield* 1999 (3) SA 132. Sinclair 'Ebb and Flow' above n 3 at 408–9. See also Human Rights Watch and International Gay and Lesbian Human Rights Commission (IGLHRC) *More Than a Name: State Sponsored Homophobia and Its Consequences in Southern Africa* (New York, Human Rights Watch, 2003) 182–83.

[176]   One such statute is the Taxation Laws Amendment Act 5 of 2001, which in s 1(d) inserted a definition of spouse into s 1 of the Transfer Duty Act 40 of 1949 to include: 'c) in a same sex or heterosexual union which the Commissioner is satisfied is intended to be permanent.' Human Rights Watch and International Gay and Lesbian Human Rights Commission (IGLHRC) *More Than a Name: State Sponsored Homophobia and Its Consequences in Southern Africa* (New York, Human Rights Watch, 2003) 179–86.

[177]   See Louw above n 2; *National Coalition for Gay and Lesbian Equality v Minister of Home Affairs* 2000 (2) SA 1 para 37; *Satchwell v The President of SA and the Minister of Justice* (2002) (6) SA1 para 9. See also *Daniels v Campbell NO* CCT 40/03 paras 58–60, 91, 92.

[178]   See 'Gay Marriage Heads to South African Appeals Court' in www.365gay.com. Judgment was delivered on 30 November 2004 and upheld the right of people in same sex relationships to marry. However, there will need to be legislative changes before the judgment can take effect. 'Lesbian Marriage Gets the Nod' at http://www.news24.com/News24/South_Africa/News,,2–7-1442_1628956, 000.html. See also Louw above n 2.

This legal recognition of same sex marriages has the potential to raise private international law problems. Validity of a marriage is said to be determined by the *lex loci celebrationis* (or the law of the place where the marriage was celebrated) and the *lex domicilii*, so that capacity to marry is governed by the ante-nuptial domicile of the spouses. Now, what would happen to a married same sex South African couple who decided to move to a different country on the continent? Zimbabwe would never recognise the marriage/union, homosexuality being a criminal offence. Similarly the Ethiopian Code of 2000 provides for the recognition of marriage contracted abroad, 'so long as it does not contravene public morals'.[179] The Code then goes on to provide that marriage contracted as a result of 'fundamental error' shall be invalid.[180] One of these errors is 'error on [sic] the behaviour of the spouse who has the habit of performing sexual acts with (a) person of the same sex',[181] thus suggesting that Ethiopia does not approve of same sex relationships and so is unlikely to welcome people who are in such a relationship, regardless of its status in the place where it was contracted. The Constitution of The Seychelles explicitly outlaws homosexuality.[182]

The Supreme Court of Namibia rejected the claim of a German lesbian woman for permission to continue living with her partner and child in Namibia. The court said that the refusal did not constitute a violation of her right to family life.[183] The court noted that it understood the concept 'family' to refer to 'a formal relationship between male and female, where sexual intercourse between them in the family context is the method to procreate offspring'.[184]

No doubt if ever confronted with a same sex South African couple seeking the right to live together as a married couple, the countries cited would argue that one cannot found one's claim on an illegal act—despite the fact that the union is legal in its place of origin.[185] Indeed the wording in article 6 of the African Protocol on Women's Rights suggests that marriage is seen in heterosexual terms, so that the first paragraph reads in part 'States Parties shall ensure that women and men enjoy equal rights and are regarded as equal partners in marriage.'[186] However, in light

[179] Revised Family Code Ethiopia 2000 art 5.
[180] *Ibid* art 13.
[181] *Ibid* art 13 13(3)(d)(3)(d).
[182] Constitution of The Seychelles 1993, Art 32(2) in C Heyns (ed)(1996) above n 17 at 305.
[183] *Chairperson of the Immigration Selection Board v Frank and Another* Unreported Sup Ct Case No SA 8/99 (5 March 2001) discussed in D Hubbard and E Cassidy 'Family Law Reform in Namibia: Work in Progress' in A Bainham (ed) *International Survey of Family Law 2002* (Bristol, Jordan Publishing, 2002) 255 at 262–63. F Viljoen 'The African Commission on Human and Peoples' Rights: Introduction to the African Commission and the Regional Human Rights System' in C Heyns (ed) *Human Rights Law in Africa* (The Hague, Martinus Nijhoff, 2004) vol 1 385 at 416.
[184] Hubbard and Cassidy note that the definition may not reflect the realities of Namibian society, which has many types of family the members of whom are not married or in a sexual relationship.
[185] See the hostile response to efforts by Professor Sylvia Tamale to get sexual orientation listed as a ground on the basis of which discrimination should be prohibited in Uganda, and her response at: www.gwsafrica.org/news/tamale2.htm.
[186] African Protocol on Women's Rights art 6; see also art 6(e).

of the African Charter articles 18(3) and 60, and the ratification by most African states of the ICCPR without reservations, it is worth noting that the Human Rights Committee has interpreted sex discrimination to include discrimination based on sexual orientation.[187]

The above listing of systems and requirements for state-recognised marriage does not tell the full story. It does not tell us about the gender dimensions of these laws. The issue of bridewealth is worth exploring a little further.

Bridewealth

The practice known amongst the Ndebele as *lobolo*, and by a myriad of other names in the many African tongues,[188] has been understood as the transfer of cattle or livestock and/or money by a prospective bridegroom, or his family, to the family of the woman whom he intends to take as his wife.[189] In some cultures the groom would perform bride service, going to live with his future in-laws and working for them until they were satisfied with his contribution, whereafter he would be allowed to live with his wife.[190] Although bridewealth was traditionally given to the father of the bride, it appears that there are now cases (living law) where the mother of a woman, who may have raised her daughter on her own, will receive the bridewealth for her. This is what happened in the South African case of *Mthembu v Letsela*,[191] an inheritance case where, amongst other things, the father-in-law of a woman whose husband had died questioned whether it could be said that the woman had a customary marriage with his son, the bridewealth having been paid to her mother. The court replied in the affirmative.

The payment of bridewealth is said to have multiple functions, including friendship and the binding together of two families. In patrilineal societies, the giving of bridewealth is also said to transfer the labour value of the woman from her family

---

[187] *Toonen v Australia* Communication No 488/1992, Human Rights Committee Views of the Committee (31 March 1994) UN Doc CCPR/C/50/D/488/1992. The Committee noted that the reference to sex in arts 2(1) and 26 of the ICCPR was to be 'taken as including sexual orientation' (para 8.7).

[188] The translation of the concept into English is not without its problems, with people taking exception to it being called 'bride price' because that connotes sale of women. Others translate it as consideration but this also has connotations of English contract law where the purchaser gives consideration, to the buyer. For this reason, some people think that the indigenous word should be used. However, as this study is not about one particular country, the term 'bridewealth' will be used. No ideological positioning should be assumed on my part.

[189] D Jeater *Marriage, Perversion and Power: The Construction of Moral Discourse in Southern Rhodesia 1894–1930* (Oxford, Oxford University Press, 1993); E Schmidt *Peasants, Traders and Wives: Shona Women in the History of Zimbabwe 1870–1939* (Oxford, James Currey, 1992) 113–15.

[190] J Davison *Gender, Lineage, and Ethnicity in Southern Africa* (Oxford, Westview, 1997) at 52–53; R Moser 'Transformation of Southern Tanzania Marriages' in D Parkin and D Nyamwaya (eds) *Transformation of African Marriage* (Manchester, Manchester University Press, 1987) 323.

[191] *Mthembu v Letsela* 1997 (2) SA 936. Upheld on appeal 2000 (3) SA 867.

of origin to her husband's family. The payment of bridewealth also transfers genetrical and uxorial rights from the family of the woman to that of the man. Uxorial 'rights' include the man's expectation that he will enjoy exclusive sexual rights to the woman. Should she commit adultery or bear a child by another man, he may sue the adulterer for damages and even claim the adulterine child as his own. Genetrical rights highlight the group nature of many marriage forms in patrilineal societies in Africa, whereby the children born of the marriage are regarded as being a part of the father's kin group rather than that of the mother. On divorce, therefore, the father's family would keep the children. In short it could be said that the bridewealth institution constructs women in two roles—as wives and mothers.

It is worth noting that the rule that the children 'belonged' to the male line was a major cause of friction in colonial times, with colonial officials regarding it as repugnant that a child should be separated from its mother. It was this 'repugnance' that resulted in the introduction of the rule that a child under the age of 7 had to continue living with its mother. Ironically the rule, which is now claimed as part of customary law, was taken from the English Custody of Infant Act (Talfourd's Act) 1839, which was passed in England to overcome the difficulties caused to women by the operation of the presumption that the father of a legitimate child was its natural guardian and had an automatic right to custody.[192] In post-colonial states the presumption has been replaced by the best interests principle articulated in article 3 of the UN Children's Rights Convention 1989 and article 4 of the African Charter on the Rights and Welfare of the Child 1990.[193]

Dower is also an important element in Islamic marriages. The Algerian Code specifies that: 'A marriage contracted without payment of a dowry shall be declared null and void.'[194] Dower in Islamic law is said to act as insurance for the woman in the event of divorce. It is expected to provide security from penury. Unlike bridewealth in patrilineal societies, the dower is a gift from the husband to the wife who is entitled to keep all of it.[195] In Tunisia dower is not a material condition of the marriage, 'but rather a psychological one, a demonstration of a man's love for his wife.'[196] An Na'im notes that in Morocco class is an important factor in whether a woman will receive a dower or not, so that women from wealthy families will, but those from poor ones will not. However, he does note that in one Berber town dower is made a condition of marriage.[197]

---

[192] Custody of Infant Act (Talfourd's Act) 1839 (UK) 2 & 3 Vic c 54. See A Fraser 'Becoming Human: The Origins and Development of Women's Human Rights' (1999) 21 *Human Rights Quarterly* 853 at 866–68.

[193] See also T Bennett 'The Equality Clause and Customary Law' (1994) 10 *South African Journal on Human Rights* 122 at 128.

[194] Algerian Family Code 1984 art 33: Government of Algeria (1998) above n 73 at 10; see also art 9 discussed at 40. An Na'im (ed) *Islamic Family Law* above n 10 at 158. Quassem above n 66 at 23.

[195] Quassem above n 66 at 23; Government of Tunisia (2000) above n 75 para 1050.

[196] Government of Tunisia (2000) above n 75 para 1050.

[197] An Na'im (ed) *Islamic Family Law* above n 10 at 158.

Although seen as the most important part of the 'formalities' of customary marriage, the bridewealth institution is not without its critics.[198] The South African writer Mathabane starts his biography of his mother, grandmother and sister by describing the build-up to the ceremony when bridewealth is given for his sister.[199] He later links the giving of bridewealth to the violent and abusive treatment meted out to his sister by her husband.[200] It is the mistreatment of women in marriage that has led some to question the practice. They link women's subordination and lack of a strong voice within marriage with the payment of bridewealth, which makes both the women and their families of origin dependent on their abusive partners. Sometimes the husband's family is said to be complicit in her mistreatment. Some go so far as to say that the bridewealth institution constructs women as property.[201] Ironically this was also the view of colonial authorities who likened it to purchase.[202] People holding this view argue that to continue with the practice is to perpetuate and encourage the subjugation of women.[203] There is implicit within these criticisms condemnation of the transformation of the institution from being a symbolic transfer of small items to a more commercialised, that is cash-driven, enterprise.[204] In its report to CEDAW, the government of Uganda noted:

> This practice undermines women's dignity and welfare and is prohibited by the Constitution according to Article 33(b) *sic*. Moreover, forcing a woman to live under an intolerable and hostile family environment subjects her to servitude and slave like conditions.[205]

Although the Ugandan government's position may accord with the 1956 Slavery Convention, which seems to outlaw bridewealth-like practices,[206] it is in the

---

[198] WLSA *Lobolo: Its Implications for Women's Reproductive Rights* (Harare, WLSA, 2002).

[199] M Mathabane *African Women; Three Generations* (London, Hamish Hamilton, 1994).

[200] *Ibid*. It is telling that the first chapter on the payment of bridewealth is titled 'Florah: *lobola* Complicates Love' at 3. See also A Shenje-Peyton 'Balancing Gender Equality and Cultural Identity: Marriage Payments in Post-Colonial Zimbabwe' (1996) 9 *Harvard Human Rights Journal* 105.

[201] Southern African Research and Documentation Centre (SARDC) *Beyond Inequalities: Women in Zambia* (SARDC, Harare, 1998) (hereafter SARDC *Zambia*) 41.

[202] E Kisaakye 'Women, Culture and Human Rights: Female Genital Mutilation, Polygamy and Bride Price' in W Benedek, E Kisaakye and G Oberleitner (eds) *Human Rights of Women: International Instruments and African Experiences* (London, Zed Press, 2002) 268 at 281.

[203] *Ibid*.

[204] N Nobhuro 'Aspects of Change in Bridewealth Among the Iteso of Kenya' in D Parkin and D Nyamwaya (eds) *Transformation of African Marriage* (Manchester, Manchester University Press, 1987) 183.

[205] Government of Uganda (2000) above n 133 at 68. Burkina Faso has also formally outlawed the practice under art 244 of the Individual and Family Code. Government of Burkina Faso (1998) above n 11 on art 5 of CEDAW at 6. The Houphouet-Boigny government banned the practice in the Côte d'Ivoire in 1964: Toungara 'Changing the Meaning of Marriage' (2001) above n 12 at 37, 39.

[206] UN Supplementary Convention on the Abolition of Slavery, the Slave Trade, and Institutions and Practices Similar to Slavery, 1956. Adopted by ECOSOC Resolution 608 (XXI) of 30 April 1956, art 1(c)(i).

minority. Indeed the government acknowledges this in the same paragraph, noting that: 'This is a practice prevalent in most districts of Uganda.'[207] Even in Burundi, where it is not recognised as part of the marriage contract, the practice remains tenacious and people continue to pay, highlighting the fact that marriage is seen as a coming together of families and not individuals.[208] Similarly Toungara notes that although abolished in the Côte d'Ivoire, the practice continues.[209] In other states, attempts at setting a limit on the amount of bridewealth payable have not been successful. The colonial authorities in Southern Rhodesia, now Zimbabwe, made several attempts to limit bridewealth, but eventually gave up in 1962 due to the resistance offered by the people.[210]

The Algerian report to CEDAW also reflects widespread support for the practice of dower:

> Because this is a widely accepted and religiously motivated practice, women's movements in Algeria have not challenged it in principle, nor do they claim that it discriminates against women, but they do demand that the value of the dowry be set by law at a symbolic level.[211]

Indeed it appears that the practice has many defenders.[212] These 'traditionalists' hold that the bridewealth institution in this form is unique to the African continent and should be preserved if the African 'culture' is to be preserved.[213] The giving of bridewealth is said to bind families together and to make marriages 'stronger'. This is because both parties to the union are loath to let their families down by dissolving their marriage, and therefore work harder towards making the marriage work.[214] Moreover, it is said that women favour having bridewealth paid for them, as indeed the majority do,[215] because it shows a man's commitment and

---

[207] Government of Uganda (2000) above n 133 at 68.

[208] C Ntampaka 'Reconciling the Sources of Law in the Burundi Code of Persons and of the Family' in A Bainham (ed) *The International Survey of Family Law 1997* (Hague, Kluwer Law International, 1999) 65 at 68.

[209] Toungara 'Changing the Meaning of Marriage' (2001) above n 12 at 36.

[210] F Banda *Women and Law in Zimbabwe: Access to Justice on Divorce* (unpublished Doctoral Thesis, University of Oxford, 1993) 56.

[211] Government of Algeria (1998) above n 73 at 10. Quassem quotes the *hadith* (sayings of the Prophet): 'Women with the least dowry are women with the most blessing' (Quassem above n 66 at 23). See also An Na'im (ed) *Islamic Family Law* above n 10 at 158 on practice in other North African countries.

[212] A Chigwedere *Lobolo: The Pros and Cons* (Gweru, Mambo Press, 1982). By way of contrast see M Chinyenze 'A Critique of Chigwedere's Book *Lobolo: The Pros and Cons* in Relation to the Emancipation of Women in Zimbabwe' (1983–84) 11 *Zimbabwe Law Review* 229.

[213] Chigwedere above n 212.

[214] The obita dicta of Dumbutshena C-J in *Katekwe v Muchabaiwa* 1984 (2) ZLR 112, in which he noted that the payment of bridewealth was at the discretion of the daughter, who could decline to have it paid for her, proved controversial: W Ncube 'Dealing with Inequities in Customary Law: Action, Reaction and Social Change in Zimbabwe' (1991) 5 *International Journal of Law Policy and the Family* 58 at 66–70.

[215] *Ibid* at 68–69.

love, and also because bridewealth is said to act as a guarantee against desertion by the husband, who stands to lose his investment should he abandon the marital home. This is because in many groups customary divorce operates on the fault principle, so that the person deemed to have been the cause of the breakdown forfeits bridewealth. If the woman is deemed the cause of the breakdown, her family may be asked to return a part of the bridewealth, and if the marriage failure is deemed to be because of the husband then he or his family cannot ask for a return of any bridewealth, assuming all had been paid; and indeed if some is outstanding, the woman's family is said to be able to demand that the balance be paid forthwith.[216]

The reality of the situation is that few women and an equally small number of sons-in-law would contemplate marriage without the payment of bridewealth for fear of an ill omen befalling them and their children. Additionally, in patrilineal societies, the woman's position is made perilous by the fact that she knows that it is to her family of origin that she will need to turn should her marriage fail to work, so that it is still in her interests to follow the wishes of the family.[217]

The introduction of *khul'* divorce to Egypt in 2000 has meant that a wife can now ask for a divorce without giving a reason.[218] However, the wife has then to return her dower and forfeit any financial claims that she may have had against the husband. An Na'im notes that this has not acted as a disincentive to wives claiming *khul'* divorces.[219]

The African Protocol on Women's Rights is silent on the issue of bridewealth. However, it could be argued that some of the negative consequences of the practice arising from its abuse are covered in article 3 on the right to dignity, and specifically the injunction contained in article 3(3) to the effect that: 'States parties shall adopt and implement appropriate measures to prohibit any exploitation or degradation of women.'

Relationships in the shadow of law

Although bridewealth is seen as the basis for customary marriage, it is still sometimes difficult to ascertain that a customary marriage has indeed come into being. This is because different groups have different requirements about its delivery. Some expect the entire bridewealth payment to be made before 'transfer' of the woman to her new marital family can take place; others see it as a generational

---

[216] It is difficult to know the extent to which bridewealth transfer occurs post-divorce.
[217] Toungara 'Changing the Meaning of Marriage' (2001) above n 12 at 36
[218] Quassem above n 66 at 26.
[219] An Na'im (ed) *Islamic Family Law* above n 10 at 159.

obligation to be given over time. In yet other cases, the woman's family may give their blessing for the couple to live together on the understanding that the bridewealth will come. Some now wait until the birth of the first child to prove the woman's fertility. It can sometimes be difficult to say that a marriage has indeed occurred.

To overcome this lack of clarity, the Ethiopian Code provides for proof of marriage in default of a marriage certificate.[220] The criteria are: 'A man and a woman are deemed to have the possession of the status of spouses when they mutually consider themselves and live as spouses and when they are considered and treated as such by their family and community.'[221] If satisfied by the proof given of the existence of a marriage, a court may presume that a marriage has been concluded.[222] The Tanzanian statute works on a similar presumption that if a couple have lived together for two or more years and regard themselves as married, and are so regarded by their community, then they will be taken to have a de facto union.[223]

However, in systems where these presumptions do not operate, a woman in a cohabiting relationship can be left vulnerable to desertion without any recourse to law, either customary or statutory. She has what can only be called an irregular/de facto/unrecognised union, defined by Mair as one which has 'received none of the possible forms of legal sanction'.[224] Economically vulnerable women may be particularly affected here. Surveys have revealed that women, sometimes poor, but not always, may prefer to be the 'mistress' of a rich man than the wife of a poor one.[225] Should the woman have children with the man and remain with him for many years, should she not be entitled, on his death or the termination of the relationship, to receive support?

On the other side of the coin, the possibility of 'other unions' may explain both the willingness of Zambian men to contract customary marriages and why 'highly educated women prefer Ordinance marriages', which are technically monogamous.[226] In the Côte d'Ivoire, fear that their husbands may be using family money (community property) to buy gifts for their women friends leads wives to put some of the property out of the 'community reach' by registering the property in the names of their children.[227]

[220] Ethiopian Revised Family Code 2000 art 95.
[221] *Ibid* art 96. See also art 99(2) and art 106 on irregular unions.
[222] *Ibid* art 97(1).
[223] Rwezaura above n 142.
[224] L Mair *African Marriage and Social Change* (London, Frank Cass, 1969) 44.
[225] B Harrell-Bond *Modern Marriage in Sierra Leone: A Study of the Professional Group* (The Hague, Mouton, 1975); Toungara 'Changing the Meaning of Marriage' (2001) above n 12 at 45; W Karanja ' "Outside Wives" and "Inside Wives" in Nigeria A Study of Changing Perceptions in Marriage' in D Parkin and D Nyamwa (eds) *Transformations of African Marriage* (Manchester, Manchester University Press, 1987) 247; Kuenyehia and Ofei-Aboagye above n 114 at 27.
[226] SARDC *Zambia* above n 201 at 42.
[227] Toungara 'Changing the Meaning of Marriage' (2001) above n 12 at 4.

The potential for confusion and lack of clarity may be the reason why the African Protocol on Women's Rights 2003 insists on registration of marriages to evidence legal validity.[228] Although in line with existing human rights law, not least the Convention on Consent to Marriage, Minimum Age of Marriage and Registration of Marriages 1962,[229] and a useful aid in checking both consent and age of potential spouses, this requirement in turn creates its own problems, partly because many legal systems regard unregistered customary law unions as entitled to some legal recognition. It is for this reason that Kenya, Namibia and South Africa objected to the registration provision at the 2003 ministerial meeting considering the draft Protocol. The Namibian objection is particularly interesting in light of the Concluding Observations of CEDAW when considering the Namibian report. There the Committee 'recommended that the Government ensure, as soon as feasible, the registration of all customary marriages, so as to ensure that women could enjoy all rights that accrued as a result of marriage.'[230]

The CEDAW, although also expressing a preference for registration,[231] appears to recognise the difficulties created by pluralism, so that it recognises plural family forms but demands that these should 'accord with principles of equality and justice for all people'.[232] The exclusion of women in de facto unions from accessing property acquired during the partnership is also identified as a problem leading the Committee to note: 'Property laws that discriminate in this way against married or unmarried women with or without children should be revoked or discouraged.'[233] Seen in this light, the African Protocol provision requiring registration appears to show the triumph of hope over experience.

Pluralism and the internal conflicts between marriage systems

The bridewealth issue is not the only one that can, in the words of Mathabane, 'complicate love'.[234] As we have seen, the existence of plural marriage systems creates its own difficulties. This is particularly so in systems that provide for the

---

[228] African Protocol on Women's Rights art 6(d).
[229] Convention on Consent to Marriage, Minimum Age of Marriage and Registration of Marriages 1962.
[230] CEDAW Concluding Comments to the Initial Report of Namibia CEDAW A/52/38/Rev.1 (Part II) para 125. See also para 110, in which the Committee expresses concern about 'the prevalence of polygamous marriages and the non-registration of customary marriages'.
[231] CEDAW General Recommendation No 21 para 39.
[232] *Ibid* para 13; see also para 29.
[233] *Ibid* para 33.
[234] Mathabane above n 199 at 4.

recognition of both monogamous and polygynous marriages. Although men are technically not supposed to marry different women under the two systems, many do. This practice is particularly common with migrant workers, who may have a 'home' wife, that is a rural-based wife, and a 'town' wife.[235] Whilst it is of course possible for one couple to contract a customary union by the payment of bridewealth followed by the registration of their marriage under the monogamous Marriage Act regime, often men marry different women under different marriage systems, creating chaos and confusion.[236] This creates legal uncertainty, which leaves women vulnerable to falling between the cracks of the plural system and being left without legal protection.[237] In its report to CEDAW, Burkina Faso gave the following reason for its attempts to change the law to make all marriages monogamous, unless the parties agreed to polygyny before registration:

> Faced with the current situation in Burkina Faso, with several forms of marriage—polygamy, forced and traditional marriages and so on—which have a tendency to create conflict situations within families and put women in a degrading position of inferiority, the law had to make a political choice by taking steps with the aim of enfranchising women and protecting them against all forms of discrimination in relation to marriage and family relationships.[238]

However, even in countries like the Côte d'Ivoire, which outlawed polygyny in 1964 and recognises only monogamous marriages under the Code, empirical research showed the continuing co-existence of customary, Islamic and secular law, which may conflict with Code provisions.[239] In some states the confusion is further compounded by the legislatures passing conflicting laws. Zimbabwe is an example of this. Marriage under the Marriage Act[240] is monogamous. However, the Administration of Estates Amendment Act[241] provides that if a man who had contracted a Marriage Act marriage, followed by other unions (with different women), dies, then his estate is to be treated as if he were married polygynously.[242] This results in the anomaly that led Gubbay C-J to say that it is 'not possible for a person to be monogamously and polygamously married at one time'.[243]

---

[235] Government of Namibia (1997) above n 151 at 171.

[236] Banda above n 126.

[237] Various State reports to CEDAW identify this as a problem. Government of Nigeria (1997) above n 62 at 63.

[238] Government of Burkina Faso (1998) above n 11 at 25.

[239] Toungara 'Changing the Meaning of Marriage' (2001) above n 12 at 45.

[240] Marriage Act (Cap 5:11).

[241] Administration of Estates Amendment Act 1997 (Cap 6:01).

[242] *Ibid* s 68A(4) discussed in F Banda 'Inheriting Trouble: Changing the Face of the Customary Law of Succession in Zimbabwe' in A Bainham (ed) *International Survey of Family Law 1997* (The Hague, Kluwer International, 1999) 525 at 537.

[243] *Makwiramiti v Fidelity Life Assurance of Zimbabwe (Pvt) Ltd and Anor* 1998 (2) ZLR 471, 474 discussed in Banda above n 126 at 474. See also *Mujawo v Chogugudza* 1992 (2) ZLR 421 (SC) and *Gwatidzo v Gwatidzo* Unreported Judgment HC–H–232-2000.

The Ethiopian Revised Family Code of 2000, which has no hierarchy of marriages and demands monogamy, regardless of the system parties choose, provides simply: 'A person shall not conclude a marriage as long as he is bound by bonds of a preceding marriage.'[244] In the Gambia, if a man married under the technically monogamous Christian Marriages Act marries another person, for example by converting to another religion, he is not prosecuted for bigamy and the two marriages co-exist, unless the woman in the first marriage opts out by way of divorce.[245]

Pluralism and polygyny

> There are men who, for physical reasons cannot satisfy themselves with only one wife . . . In that case they should seek treatment.[246]

Conflicts over whether polygyny constitutes a violation of women's rights or is in fact a 'good' system that protects them, have been on-going for a long period of time. Those who are against polygyny point to the fact that the custom is degrading to women and violates their rights vis-à-vis equality with men.[247] This view finds support within the human rights paradigm, which does not condone polygyny and sees it as not conducive to the continuation of positive gender relations.[248] The Rwandan Constitution appears to outlaw polygyny, providing: 'Only monogamous marriages shall be recognized within the conditions and forms prescribed by law.'[249]

Those who support the continuation of the practice of polygyny argue that rather than violate women's rights, polygyny may facilitate their enjoyment. Nhlapo would argue that a woman may see her human dignity as being enhanced by marriage.[250] In this case, it may be preferable to be the wife of a polygynist than to remain unmarried. This argument is particularly powerful in states that would

---

[244] Revised Family Code 2000 art 11.

[245] Gaye and Njie above n 79 at 4–5.

[246] Exchange between an Islamist Deputy and the Minister of Religious Affairs during the debate to amend the Personal Status Law in Morocco, which law proposed that polygyny should be severely curtailed and permitted only in rare cases with the permission of a judge and the first wife of a man. Tremlett above n 83.

[247] L Tibatemwa-Ekirikubinza above n 138 at 437. Nothing more poignantly captures the emotional trauma brought on by polygyny than Ba's award-winning novel *So Long a Letter* (London, Heinemann, 1989). Twa women living in the Great Lakes region do not appear to like it much either. See D Jackson *Twa Women, Twa Rights in the Great Lakes Region of Africa* (London, Minority Rights Group, 2003) 12.

[248] See for example CEDAW General Recommendation No 21 para 14.

[249] Constitution of Rwanda 1991 Art 25, reproduced in C Heyns (ed) (1996) above n 17, 287 at 289.

[250] T Nhlapo 'African Family Law Under an Undecided Constitution: the Challenge for Law Reform in South Africa' in J Eekelaar and T Nhlapo (eds) *Changing Family* (Oxford, Hart Publishing, 1998) 617 at 628–29.

punish a woman for having a child out of wedlock. If a woman has a desire to be a mother then marriage, including to a polygynist, may be the only avenue open to her.[251] Others take a more pragmatic view, noting that although polygyny may violate a strict reading of equality and non-discrimination provisions based on sex, women's economic vulnerability increases their dependence on men and thus makes polygyny a necessary evil.[252]

The intensity of the debate over polygyny has not lessened with time. This can best be seen in the debates held during the drafting of the African Protocol on Women's Rights, which were discussed in Chapter 3. The upshot of all this heat was the rather mild-mannered compromise, which appeared in the final draft that was adopted by the African Union, to the effect that:

> monogamy is encouraged as the preferred form of marriage and that the rights of women in marriage and family, including in polygynous marital relations, are promoted and protected.[253]

There are several problems with this provision, not least its violation of the Protocol's mission, which is to protect women from discrimination. Although reflecting the compromise put forward by government officials, the provision is not drafted in a way that makes clear the nature of the rights sought to be protected. Moreover, there appears to be an internal conflict with other provisions of the African Protocol on Women's Rights, not least article 8(f), which calls on states to 'reform existing discriminatory laws and practices in order to promote and protect the rights of women'.[254] If one sees the 'object and purpose' of the African Protocol as being the eradication of discrimination against women, then the continued recognition of polygyny is in direct violation of the objects and purpose of the instrument. However, it may well be that some will choose to interpret article 3(2) of the African Protocol on Women's Rights, which provides for a woman's right to 'respect as a person and to the free development of her personality', as meaning that a woman may, as Nhlapo suggests, regard her dignity as being protected by entering into a polygynous relationship, the other guarantees of non-discrimination and freedom from degrading and inhuman treatment notwithstanding.

Polygyny also raises issues that are fundamental to the human rights of young girls who are often coerced into marriage. The clearest is that of consent—if an 11-year-old girl is told by her father that she is to marry one of his friends, or indeed the rich man offering a high bridewealth for her, how is she to resist?[255]

---

[251] A Armstrong *et al* 'Uncovering Reality: Excavating Women's Rights in the African Family' (1993) 7 *International Journal of Law, Policy and the Family* 314.

[252] Government of Namibia (1997) above n 151 at 172. F Kaganas and C Murray 'Law, Women and the Family in the New South Africa' (1991) *Acta Juridica* 116.

[253] African Protocol on Women's Rights art 6(c).

[254] See also *ibid* art 2(1)(d).

[255] Gaye and Njie above n 79 at 9.

Had polygyny not been allowed, she might have been spared. Of course the counter argument to this is to say that by criminalising polygyny we are actually making women more vulnerable to abuse. The 11-year-old might still be 'married off' to the friend, except that the 'marriage' would have no legal recognition and might leave the young woman even more vulnerable to violence and deprivation of access to property and other resources. The problem is exacerbated by the lack of voice and autonomy in decision-making of young girls.

Interestingly, although Islamic countries pushed for a provision recognising polygyny during the drafting of the Protocol on Women's Rights, An Na'im contends that polygyny is not widely practised in north African countries.[256] The Ethiopian government has condemned polygyny as a practice that exacerbates the vulnerability of Ethiopian women. This was said in the context of the increase in the spread of the HIV virus.[257] In other parts of Africa, class and urbanisation seem to have become important intersecting factors in determining prevalence, so that Kuenyehia and Ofei-Aboagye note that in Ghana there is a higher incidence of polygyny in the rural areas (34 per cent of women) compared to the urban areas (28 per cent of women reported that they were in polygynous unions).[258] It is of course entirely possible that all this reflects is the fact that, due to the high cost of living, urban men are no longer formalising their extra-marital relationships. Polygyny has also been said to increase conflict and to lead to competition and violence between wives and children for scarce resources, and to lead to claims of alienation of affection.[259]

It is clear that underpinning the practice of polygyny is women's economic vulnerability. It is probably true to say that it is more often than not poverty and pressure on limited land and other resources that results in the inability to feed and clothe all their children, and hence leads to early marriage and polygyny as a way of solving the immediate problem of limited resources.[260] Are we not better off concentrating on improving women's socio-economic rights with the aim of increasing their agency and turning them from dependent to independent people? This is not to suggest an atomisation of the family framework, which some see as

---

[256] An Na'im (ed) *Islamic Family Law* above n 10 at 160. He identifies Algeria, Libya and Morocco as countries where it is rarely practised. In Egypt it appears to be mainly practised in the 'traditional working class areas of Cairo'. Tunisia outlaws polygyny. Aouij above n 64 at 42–43.

[257] See IRIN news 'Ethiopia: Government Criticizes Attitude towards Women's Rights' Addis Ababa (25 June 2003) downloaded from: http://www.irinnews.org/report.asp?ReportID=34974&SelectRegion=Horn_of_Africa.

[258] Kuenyehia and Ofei-Aboagye above n 114 at 24.

[259] W Wabwile 'Child Support Rights in Kenya and in the United Nations Convention on the Rights of the Child 1989' in A Bainham (ed) *International Survey of Family Law* (Bristol, Jordan Publishing, 2001) 267 at 267 fn 2; Jackson above n 247 at 12; S Oloko and F Saba 'Psychosocial Effects of Reproductive Rights Abuse' in B Owasonoye (ed) *Reproductive Rights of Women in Nigeria: The Legal, Economic and Cultural Dimensions* (Lagos, Human Development Initiatives, 1999) 140 at 148–49.

[260] See the documentary by G Barnes and L Paton *The Child Brides* (London, Umbrella Pictures, 1998).

alien to the African communal worldview. Rather, it is to suggest that familial relationships in the widest sense may still continue, but that within those relationships, women would be able to choose whom they married and when, without the pressure and desperation that so often leads to ruined lives.

Other types of marriage arrangements

In addition to the complications created by men's multiple marriage careers, marriage in Africa also embraces other forms of union. One such is the sororate marriage, whereby the family of a woman who cannot bear children, will allow her sister or other female relative to bear children for the couple. By 'remedying' the 'fault', they save themselves from the possibility of having to return the bridewealth paid. This marriage type reinforces the idea that women are defined by their reproductive capacities—maybe in a way more oppressive than Nnaemeka's unqualified valorisation of motherhood on the African continent recognises.[261] If it is found that it is the husband who is impotent or infertile then his brother may act as a 'substitute', and again any children born of this union will be regarded as those of the couple. It is difficult to ascertain the frequency of arrangements such as these. Kolajo notes that in some parts of Nigeria a barren wife may give bridewealth for a woman to bear children on her behalf. The children from these 'woman to woman marriages' are considered those of the wife who gave the bridewealth.[262]

Levirate unions, where a woman whose husband has died may choose to stay on as the 'wife', often symbolically, of one of his brothers, have also operated in Africa. It is not unknown for a woman to be compelled to marry the brother of the deceased husband. The practice of levirate is also sometimes called widow inheritance. Although not sanctioned by the Shari'a, Gaye and Njie note that in Gambia some women will agree to it, mistakenly believing it to be a religious requirement.[263] Due to abuse of the practice, some states have outlawed it, noting that it violates the dignity of women.[264] Controversially, the Zimbabwean Customary Marriages Act recognises levirate unions as valid marriages if they are solemnised in term of the Act.[265] It is of course true to say that sometimes these levirate unions involve intimate relations taking place. This has also created difficulties, not least because of the spread of HIV through sexual contact. It is for this reason that the

---

[261] Nnaemeka above n 50 at 9.
[262] A Kolajo *Customary Law in Nigeria through the Cases* (Ibadan, Spectrum Books, 2000) at 235.
[263] Gaye and Njie above n 79 at 21.
[264] It is banned in Burkina Faso by art 244 of the Individual and Family Code. See Government of Burkina Faso (1998) above n 11 at 6.
[265] Customary Marriages Act Cap 5:07 s 3(1).

practice, which is outlawed in the 1956 Slavery Convention,[266] is now discouraged, and indeed resisted by women themselves. With HIV on the increase, Mhoja equates 'wife inheritance' as being on par with committing suicide.[267]

Despite its illegality in many states, the practice has been tenacious—largely because of women's economic dependence, which makes them reliant on the continued support of the deceased husband's family, and also because, in patrilineal societies, the women wish to see their children growing up under the umbrella of the father's family, with all the financial and spiritual protections that encompasses. Some women also stay because they fear that the marital family may demand a return of the bridewealth paid for them, which bridewealth may have been dissipated by the family of origin.[268]

Those who cannot afford bridewealth resort to self-help. This may involve kidnapping the woman and taking her to the home of the man.[269] Compensation will then be paid.[270] Discussing Swaziland, Nhlapo notes that the smearing of red ochre on the face of a woman means that she is betrothed to the person, or his representative, doing the smearing. Clearly a woman can be smeared against her will.[271] In Zimbabwe, a woman who finds that she is pregnant can elope (preferably assisted by her paternal aunt) to the home of the man responsible for the pregnancy. He may then accept her and enter into negotiations for the payment of bridewealth and seduction damages, or refuse to marry her and offer, or be asked to pay, seduction damages only. Interestingly, any future husband will be given a 'discount' on the bridewealth payable, because, to put it crudely, the woman is seen as 'damaged goods', and one seldom pays full price for those.

There are of course other types of marriage that are not linked to the bridewealth institution in any way. These include the giving of a woman as 'blood compensation' to the family of a murder victim. The woman is given by the family group of the murderer. Amongst the Shona of Zimbabwe, this practice, which is forbidden by the criminal law, is known as *kuripa ngozi*.[272] The person given is often a young girl. The purpose of giving a female is that she will bear a child to

---

[266] Supplementary Convention on the Abolition of Slavery, the Slave Trade, and Institutions and Practices Similar to Slavery 1956, art 1(c)(iii).

[267] M Mhoja 'Impact of Customary Inheritance Law on the Status of Women in Africa: A Challenge to Human Rights Activists (Tanzanian Case Study)' (1999) 11 *African Society of International and Comparative Law* 285 at 293.

[268] *Ibid* at 289.

[269] S Tamale 'How Old is Old Enough? Defilement Law and the Age of Consent in Uganda' (2001) 7 *East African Journal of Peace & Human Rights* 82 at 86.

[270] L Favali and R Pateman *Blood, Land and Sex: Legal and Political Pluralism in Eritrea* (Indianapolis, Indiana University Press, 2003) 168–69.

[271] T Nhlapo *Marriage and Divorce in Swazi Law and Custom* (Mbabane, Websters, 1992) 47.

[272] M Maboreke 'Understanding Law in Zimbabwe' in A Stewart (ed) *Gender, Law and Social Justice* (Oxford, Blackstone, 2000) 101–16.

replace the person who has been murdered. The practice has also been reported in Eritrea.[273] The practice can be said to be a form of violence against women.[274]

In Ghana the *trokosi* are young girls given to shrine priests in an effort to appease angry spirits or to compensate for a death. The Ghanaian Constitution outlaws the practice of *trokosi*.[275] However, the fact that these practices continue, albeit in a very limited way, highlights the vulnerability of women, indeed girls, who are powerless to decide their own destiny and who are traded like pawns in a game of chess. There seems to be something offensive about asking a young girl, in the colloquial language of criminology, 'to do time for someone else's crime'. Why should she be asked to marry, live and bear children for a stranger? Needless to say, middle class girls and women are not traded in this way. It is poor, illiterate and, more often than not, rural girls who are the subject of these rights abuses.

Early marriage

The issue of early marriage is particularly problematic throughout the continent.[276] There have been several international attempts to tackle the problem, including the 1956 Slavery Convention,[277] the UN Convention on Consent to Marriage, Minimum Age of Marriage and Registration of Marriages 1962[278] and CEDAW 1979,[279] and on the continent the African Charter on the Rights and Welfare of the Child 1990, prohibits early marriage and specifies 18 as the legal age of marriage.[280] Similarly other UN committees have also pointed out the impor-

---

[273] Favali and Pateman above n 270 at 168–69.

[274] Southern African Research and Documentation Centre (SARDC) *Beyond Inequalities: Women in Southern Africa* (Harare, SARDC, 2000) 160.

[275] Constitution of Ghana 1992 art 26(2) on harmful practices and art 28(3) on the right of a child to be free from degrading and inhuman treatment. See also s 314A Criminal Code 1960 (Act 29).

[276] Forum on Marriage above n 149. Appendix 2 of the Report reproduces data on consent to marriage, minimum age for marriage and rights within marriage throughout the world. See 47–50.

[277] The United Nations Supplementary Convention on the Abolition of Slavery, the Slave Trade, and Institutions and Practices Similar to Slavery 1956 art 2. See also Beijing Platform for Action 1995 Strategic Objective L. 274(e).

[278] UN Convention on Consent to Marriage, Minimum Age of Marriage and Registration of Marriages 1962. It did not actually set a minimum age for marriage, preferring to leave it to individual states. However, the 1965 Recommendation on Consent to Marriage, Minimum Age for Marriage and Registration of Marriages sets the relatively low age of 15 as the minimum. General Assembly Resolution Adopting the Recommendation on Consent to Marriage, Minimum Age for Marriage and Registration of Marriages (1 November 1965) A/RES/2018 (XX) Principle II, reproduced in United Nations *The United Nations and the Advancement of Women 1945–1996* (New York, United Nations, 1996) 173–74.

[279] CEDAW 1979 art 16(2). See also CEDAW General Recommendation No 21 paras 36, 38, 39.

[280] ACRWC art 21(2).

tance of ensuring that early marriage does not occur by setting a minimum age of marriage for both sexes.[281]

More recently the Protocol on the Rights of African Women 2003 has also specified a minimum age of marriage of 18 years.[282] This provision was objected to by Tunisia and Sudan at the 2003 ministerial meeting on the draft Protocol to the African Charter on Women's Rights.[283] There is some irony in the fact that these two countries may be the only ones actually reflecting the reality of the situation on the ground and acknowledging that the practice is widespread within their borders. Most other jurisdictions have marriages taking place before the age of 18—whatever the national law may provide. Indeed many national laws appear to allow marriage below the age of 18.[284] Tamale contends that in Uganda it is middle class parents who push for a marriage age of 18 because their children are more likely still to be in higher education. Due to economic pressures, girl children in the rural areas are more likely to finish school at the end of the primary cycle and be married by the age of 18.[285]

The problem of early marriage is compounded by poor record keeping and non-registration of births, thus making it difficult to check on the age of girls who are marrying. Here Chanock's assertion[286] that the rights paradigm is of limited use in trying to stop abuse may indeed be true. However, it may well be that the problem is not with the rights paradigm but with the narrow application thereof. Outlawing child marriage by itself is not enough. In Vienna it was stated that human rights of women and the girl child were to be seen as an 'inalienable, integral and indivisible part of universal human rights'.[287] So while it may be a good starting point to specify a minimum age of marriage, in order to comply with human rights norms listed, this legal sanction must go hand-in-hand with strong social rights provision, including appropriate schooling,[288] health, and access to

---

[281] Committee on Economic Social and Cultural Rights, General Comment No 14 (2000) on The Right to the Highest Attainable Standard of Health (Art 12 of the ICESCR) E/C.12/2000/4,CESCR (11 August 2000) para 22. Human Rights Committee, General Comment No 28 para 23.

[282] African Protocol on Women's Rights art 6(b).

[283] For Tunisia, the objection is in keeping with its Personal Status Code 1956 as amended, which sets the age of marriage at 17 for females (with her consent) and 20 for males. See Government of Tunisia (2000) above n 75 paras 40, 1042, 1052. Marriage before that age is permitted with the consent of both parents. An Na'im (ed) *Islamic Family Law* above n 10 at 183.

[284] A Carbert, J Stanchieri and R Cook *A Handbook for Advocacy in the African Human Rights System Advancing Reproductive and Sexual Health* (Nairobi, IPAS, 2002) 16.

[285] S Tamale 'How Old is Old Enough? Defilement Law and the Age of Consent in Uganda' (2001) 7 *East African Journal of Peace & Human Rights* 82 at 90.

[286] Chanock above n 33 at 63.

[287] World Conference on Human Rights, Vienna Declaration and Programme of Action 1993, (I) para 18. See also African Charter, preamble.

[288] UNICEF has noted that an educated woman has fewer children and that these children are likely to live longer. The benefits of both education and delaying marriage are long term and generational. UNICEF *The State of the World's Children: Education* (New York, UNICEF, 1999) 54–57; UNICEF *The State of the World's Children* (New York, UNICEF, 2004) 1–16, 17–25. See also K Annan 'Foreword' in UNICEF *The State of the World's Children* (2004) vii. See also K Watkins *The OXFAM Education Report*

resources and employment opportunities, including participation in the community and public life.[289] Children also have the right to be heard and to have their opinions respected.[290] It is the failure to provide this comprehensive set of rights that is at the heart of the early marriage conundrum rather than the rights paradigm itself. Put simply, the problem is not with rights, but with commitment to the full implementation of those rights.

To summarise, the complexity of the marriage systems in Africa has led some to advocate that uniform codes of marriage be enacted.[291] These would still allow cultural and religious pluralism, but would have the same basic requirements for the validity of all marriages solemnised within state borders. However, the experience of the Côte d'Ivoire, which enacted a unitary civil code more than 40 years ago but which continues to have plural normative orderings, shows that some cultural practices are immune to top-down legal change. An examination of state reports to CEDAW shows that 'culture', broadly defined, is seen as the chief impediment to the enjoyment of Convention rights by women.[292] Commenting on the initial state report of Algeria, the Committee also noted that it had been concerned:

> by the State party's constant citing of religious principles and cultural specificities to justify why the status of women has not kept up with the overall advances of society.[293]

For its part the Algerian government argued for an evolutionary approach to change. It noted that by taking a long-term view of 'cultural-religious transformation', the gains made would be sustainable and less likely to be resisted:

(Oxford, OXFAM, 2000) 195–98; World Vision *Every Girl Counts: Development Justice and Gender* (Milton Keynes, World Vision, 2001) 66–73; Report of the Special Rapporteur on the Right to Education, Katarina Tomasevski (9 January 2001) E/CN.4/2001/52; Beijing Platform for Action 1995, Strategic Objective L4 paras 279, 280; Norway Ministry of Foreign Affairs *Norway Fighting Poverty: The Norwegian Government's Action Plan for Combating Poverty in the South Towards 2015* (Oslo, Norwegian Ministry of Foreign Affairs, 2002) 32; Orientations Stratégiques 1:2 Education in UEMOA Annexe à la Recommendation No 03/99/CM/UEMOA—Plan d'action communautaire pour le renforcement du rôle de la femme dans l'UEMOA, available from http:www.izf.net/izf/ Documentation/JournalOfficiel/AfriqueOuest/dec99/annex1_REC_03_99.htm.

[289] CEDAW arts 7 and 8. See also CEDAW General Recommendation No 23 Women in Public Life UN Doc A/52/38/Rev.1. See also African Protocol on Women's Rights art 9; Human Rights Committee General Comment No 28 para 29.

[290] CRC art 12; Van Bueren above n 18 at 742–45.

[291] M Chanock 'Law, State and Culture: Thinking About "Customary Law" after Apartheid' (1991) *Acta Juridica* 52 at 64–70.

[292] Government of Algeria (1998) above n 73 at 10, 14, 27; Government of Burkina Faso (1998) above n 11 at 3, 7, 27; Government of Egypt (2000) above n 70 at 90; Government of Namibia (1997) above n 151 at 173; Second and Third Periodic Reports of States Parties: United Republic of Tanzania (1996) (hereafter Government of Tanzania (1996)) CEDAW/C/TZA/2–3 at 2–3, 23; Initial Report of States Parties: South Africa (1998) CEDAW/C/ZAF/1 (hereafter Government of South Africa (1998)) at 7, 34–38. Government of Uganda (2000) above n 133 at 16, 24, 61.

[293] The Committee considered the initial report at its 406th, 407th and 412th meetings on 21 and 26 January 1999 (see CEDAW W/C/SR.406, 407 and 412) para 71. See also paras 75 and 92 asking the state to modify its Family Code. See also para 67 on Algeria's reservations to arts 2, 9(2), 15(4) and 16, which the Committee describe as 'obstacles to the Convention's full implementation'. See also CEDAW General Recommendation No 21 paras 45, 46, 50.

What is required, in effect, is a reinterpretation of the role of religion in society, something that will demand patience and time and that can only be achieved by raising the general cultural level. That is why the Algerian government intends to take a gradual approach to introducing elements of gender non-discrimination and equality, while ensuring that there is no backsliding with respect to the personal status of women.[294]

This in turn suggests that change may be more forthcoming once there has been a levelling off of power imbalances between men and women. When women have greater bargaining power, brought about in part by a strengthening of their economic position together with communal dialogue and education, then we may start to see a marked shift in gender relations and the achievement of equality between men and women.

Having examined the different types of marriage on the African continent, including their formalities, I shall now move on to consider divorce, starting with the grounds for divorce and then moving on to look at proprietary consequences and issues surrounding children. Separation, divorce and annulment of marriage is dealt with in article 7 of the Protocol to the African Charter on Women's Rights 2003.

Divorce

The Shari'a has different grounds for divorce for men and women.[295] Quassem notes that in Egypt divorce is by 'a judge's decision'.[296] A woman can approach the courts for divorce from her husband if she has suffered harm and cannot live with him any longer. The five 'grounds' recognised as evidencing this harm include: a serious or contagious disease or defect that deprives a wife of her conjugal rights; ill treatment by the husband; fear of seduction, usually brought on by an unduly long absence of the husband, for example if he is serving a prison sentence of three years or more; the husband's wilful refusal to meet his wife's expenses; and the case where a husband takes a second wife and the first wife suffers material or moral harm as a result. The second wife is also allowed to seek divorce if the existence of the first wife was not disclosed to her.[297] In 2000 Egypt also recognised the right of

---

[294] Government of Algeria (1998) above n 73 at 10.

[295] An Na'im (ed) *Islamic Family Law* above n 10 at 159. This violates art 7(b) of the African Protocol on Women's Rights. See also J Connors 'The Women's Convention in the Muslim World' in J Gardner (ed) *Human Rights as General Norms and a State's Right to Opt Out* (London, British Institute of International and Comparative Law, 1997) 85 at 102.

[296] Quassem above n 66 at 25. For an account of the history of divorce law in Egypt see L Welchman 'Egypt: New Deal on Divorce' in A Bainham (ed) *International Survey of Family Law 2004* (Bristol, Jordan Publishing, 2004) 123. I am grateful to Dr Lynn Welchman for letting me see an advance copy of this article.

[297] Quassem above n 66 at 25.

wives to seek a *Khul'* divorce.[298] This allows the wife to apply for a divorce on the simple ground that she no longer wishes to continue living with the husband. A three-month period during which mediators are engaged usually follows this type of application. Although giving a wife latitude to exit marriage without having to identify a failing or fault of the husband, there is a penalty to be paid by the wife. That penalty is that she must return her dower and she forfeits any other financial claims.[299] Empirical research shows that the response to this change in the law has been interesting, with more women than men welcoming it. More people disagreed with the law (48.5 per cent) than agreed with it (40.5 per cent). Research also highlighted the fact that knowledge of the change in the law was patchy.[300]

The requirement that separation, divorce or annulment of marriage be 'effected by judicial order', found in the Protocol to the African Charter on Women's Rights 2003,[301] was objected to by Egypt, Libya and Sudan. These objections call to mind reservations made by some Islamic states to parts of article 16 of CEDAW. Egypt's rationale for the differences in grounds for divorce and property entitlements after divorce, expressed in its reservation to CEDAW, is explained by reference to the different obligations imposed upon men and women at the time of entering into marriage.[302] Men have to give dower to their wives. They are also expected to provide for the family during the subsistence of the marriage, whereas women are allowed to retain their money and property without the reciprocal obligation of support. Given these different responsibilities, Egypt argues that it would not be right to grant women the same rights of divorce as men.

Although not an ideal situation, it has to be conceded that the Shari'a does at least give women the opportunity to exit marriage. This is not quite the 'Islam does not allow women to divorce scenario' of popular myth. However, it is equally true that there is more than one interpretation of the Shari'a, leading an Egyptian human rights organisation to note, on the issue of Egypt's reservations:

> Thus the justifications used by the Egyptian government for its reservations can be easily refuted on the basis of the experiences of other Islamic countries. This shows the necessity of studying these experiences; examining the Islamic jurisprudential schools that support women's rights; and drawing upon them to improve women's conditions and to drop the larger part of Egypt's reservations.[303]

---

[298] Welchman above n 296.

[299] Quassem above n 66 at 26. Cf Government of Algeria (1998) above n 73 at 41; World Bank *MENA Development Report: Gender and Development in the Middle East and North Africa* (Washington DC, World Bank, 2004)152.

[300] E Fawzy 'Law No 1 of 2000: A New Personal Status Law and a Limited Step on the Path to Reform' in L Welchman (ed) *Women's Rights & Islamic Family Law* (London, Zed Press, 2004) 58 at 82–83.

[301] African Protocol on Women's Rights art 7(a).

[302] Egypt Reservation to art 16, downloaded from http://www.bayefsky.com/html/egypt_t2_cedaw.php.

[303] Cairo Institute for Human Rights Studies 'Reservation is not a Justification' (1996) *Sawasiah* 8 at 8–9.

The Algerian Family Code is said to provide for divorce 'at the will of the husband, by mutual consent, or on the petition of the wife'.[304] Tunisia provides for judicial divorce and has the same grounds for both men and women.[305]

Elsewhere, in keeping with the different marriage forms, different grounds exist for dissolving the marriage. Where civil or statute marriage is concerned, many systems have moved to a no-fault-based system.[306] Namibia is one country that retains the doctrine of matrimonial fault in its civil divorce law.[307] Tanzania's Law of Marriage Act 1971 recognises irretrievable breakdown as the sole ground for divorce. Regardless of which system of marriage the parties choose, customary, civil or religious, the Act requires them to get a judicial divorce. However, parties are required to go for conciliation to Marriage Conciliatory Boards before they can file for a judicial divorce. Rwezaura and Wanitzek note that this requirement often creates tension, not least because Catholic Marriage Conciliatory Boards not sanctioning divorce are likely to refuse to give the certificate confirming the breakdown of the marriage. By way of contrast, Muslim Boards are unlikely to second guess a husband who has already pronounced the *talaq* thus divorcing his wife in accordance with his personal law.[308]

The Ethiopian Revised Family Code 2000 provides that regardless of marriage type, 'the causes and effects of dissolution of marriage shall be the same'.[309] The Ethiopian Code of 2000 recognises that parties can agree to divorce provided they have been married for more than six months. If divorcing by mutual consent, they do not have to give reasons.[310] Still, the court may counsel the parties and give them a three-month cooling-off period to think through the decision and seek reconciliation.[311] It is also open for one party to ask the court for divorce.[312] Currently in Uganda, divorce follows the marriage system under which the parties contracted their marriage. The Divorce Act, which regulates civil and Hindu marriages, is interesting in that it overtly discriminates against women with regard to the grounds for divorce. Specifically, it allows a husband to divorce his wife on the grounds of her adultery, but a wife would have to couple adultery with another fault ground, such as bigamy, cruelty or desertion, before she could be granted a

---

[304] Algerian Family Code 1984 art 48. Government of Algeria (1998) above n 73 at 40–41.

[305] An Na'im (ed) *Islamic Family Law* above n 10 at 183.

[306] South Africa Divorce Act 1979 (for a discussion of its provisions see J Sinclair and J Heaton *The Law of Marriage* vol 1 (Cape Town, Juta, 1996) 197); Zimbabwe Matrimonial Causes Act 1987 [Cap 5:13]: Ghana Matrimonial Causes Act 1971 (Kuenyehia and Ofei-Aboagye above n 114 at 39–41). Although described as no fault systems, both still require the introduction of facts (often fault based) evidencing the irretrievable breakdown of the marriage.

[307] Government of Namibia (1997) above n 151 at 174.

[308] Rwezaura and Wanitzek above n 141 at 20–21.

[309] Ethiopia Revised Family Code 2000 art 74.

[310] *Ibid* art 77(3).

[311] *Ibid* art 78(1)–(2).

[312] *Ibid* art 76(b).

divorce.[313] To add insult to injury, it seems that the Penal Code gives different definitions of adultery depending on whether a man or a woman is involved. A man can only commit adultery with a married woman, so if he is married and having extra-marital intercourse with an unmarried woman that is acceptable! By way of contrast, a woman commits adultery if she has intercourse with *any* man who is not her husband, so *all* extra-marital activity is proscribed.[314]

With most marriages between black Africans starting off as customary law unions, it is important to consider how these types of marriages are ended. Not being registered, there is often no need to seek judicial intervention from formal or local courts. Rather, the informal dispute-resolving mechanism is used to dissolve the marriage. There are no 'formal grounds' for divorce per se.[315] They vary between groups.[316] Armstrong *et al* note that 'grounds' for divorce at customary law are no more than 'reasons justifying the conclusion by the parties that there is little point in going on'.[317] Given the open-endedness of the 'rules', they go on to identify the chief reasons given by men and women in seeking to convince the family councils that the marriage is no longer practicable. Husbands' complaints against their wives include 'disobedience, a quarrelsome disposition, neglect of household duties and children, disrespect for elders or ancestors, and refusal of conjugal rights'.[318] Wives have complained about their husbands' 'gross ill treatment, failure to provide for the family, neglect of sexual duties and cruelty'.[319] The reasons given throw light on the gendered nature of marriage as requiring obedience and good housekeeping skills from women, and from men that they fulfil their roles as breadwinners. It is a traditional rather than companionate or partnership model of marriage.

In making complaints about the failure of the spouse to live up to their end of the marital bargain, the parties try to legitimate their discontent by highlighting the failure of the spouse whilst minimising their own role in the breakdown of the marriage. The reason for this is not hard to find—it can be traced back to the payment of bridewealth at the start of the marriage. A woman and her family will be anxious to minimise her role in the breakdown, because they do not want to have to return part of the bridewealth. How much is determined by length of marriage and number of children—that is by seeing how much of the bridewealth, in terms of genetrical and labour value, has been enjoyed by them.[320] Similarly the

---

[313] Discussed by Naggita above n 134 at 45. Government of Uganda (2000) above n 133 at 67. This will be changed when the Domestic Relations Bill 2003 is promulgated.

[314] *Ibid.*

[315] Woodman above n 1 at 200.

[316] Kuenyehia and Ofei-Aboagye above n 114 at 38–39.

[317] A Armstrong *et al* 'Uncovering Reality: Excavating Women's Rights in the African Family' (1993) 7 *International Journal of Law, Policy and the Family* 314 at 350.

[318] *Ibid* at 351.

[319] *Ibid.*

[320] In modern times it is unclear that the return of bridewealth is a frequent occurrence.

husband's family are also reluctant to accept the blame for the marriage breaking down, not least because they may forfeit the right to demand a refund of bridewealth, or, as will be more likely, if they had not finished paying all of the bridewealth, they may be asked to hand over the balance under pain of losing (temporarily) rights to the children of the marriage, who will be held as 'security' by the wife's family. This jockeying for position and the desire to see the continuation of the marriage, especially if it remains advantageous to the two families, usually sees the adoption of what Roberts identifies as the deployment of therapeutic mediation whereby:

> [J]oint decision making on specific issues is postponed in favour of an examination of the relationships that have broken down within the family . . . It aims at a break with the original conversation in which the parties were engaged; a new situation is invoked or imposed.[321]

With both parties put under family pressure to sustain the marriage, only those with independent means will be able to make a decision for themselves as to whether they should persevere with the marriage or give up on it. Empirical research from Zimbabwe showed that husbands were more likely to have this autonomy, because they had money and, more often than not, were supporting their wider families, who relied on them and were therefore unlikely to try to force them to stay in unions that they found to be unsatisfactory. Of the women, it was largely women employed in the formal sector who were best able to resist family pressure to stay in unsatisfactory marriages. This is in no way to suggest that other groups of women did not strike out on their own, but realistically those who were self-supporting could go it alone in a way in which women dependent on husbands or their families of origin for financial support could not.[322]

It is telling that state reports to CEDAW indicate low property ownership by women, thus making distribution on divorce that much more important, not least because women help to acquire the property.[323]

---

[321] S Roberts 'Three Models of Family Mediation' in R Dingwall and J Eekelaar (eds) *Divorce Mediation and the Legal Process* (Oxford, Oxford University Press, 1988) 145.

[322] F Banda *Women and Law in Zimbabwe: Access to Justice on Divorce* (unpublished doctoral thesis, University of Oxford, 1993) 217.

[323] Government of Uganda (2000) above n 133 at 63; Government of Nigeria (2003) above n 96 at 49.

Property distribution on divorce

In dividing property, human rights norms enjoin courts to divide it equally.[324] Indeed, the recently adopted African Protocol on the Rights of Women 2003 provides:

> in the case of separation, divorce or annulment of marriage, women and men shall have the right to an equitable sharing of joint property deriving from the marriage.[325]

In plural systems, the division of property on divorce is linked to the marriage system under which a woman married.[326] The entitlements of women with unregistered customary law unions appear in most systems to be meagre.[327] Generally, the statutory redistributive powers of the courts do not apply to unregistered customary law unions due to their non-registration.[328] Under Shona customary law a wife is entitled to two categories of property. The first is her *mavoko* or hands property, which is property that she has acquired by dint of extra work done by her, which work is separate from that done for the family. This may be weaving baskets, or any other skill. The second category of property is the *mombe yeumai*, which is the cow given to her on the occasion of her daughter's marriage, assuming she has a daughter who has married.[329] Although some women do continue to receive the actual cow, for many cash is now substituted. If this is the case, it is likely that the woman will have dissipated the cash during the course of the marriage, usually buying food and other provisions for the family. In practice most rural women with unregistered customary law unions do not consider themselves entitled to anything, and therefore do not put in claims for property.[330]

A major difficulty for women is that property is often seen as belonging to the family. Kolajo lists three characteristics of family property in Nigeria. These are:

---

[324] ICCPR art 23(4); Human Rights Committee General Comment No 28 paras 20, 26; CEDAW art 16(1)(h); CEDAW General Comment No 21 paras 25–33, see in particular paras 30–33; African Charter, art 18(3).

[325] Art 7(d). See also Constitution of Ghana 1992 Art 22(3)(a)(b); Dzidzornu above n 112 at 509; Woodman above n 1 at 201; Constitution of Malawi 1994 s 24(1)(b)(i).

[326] A Paliwala 'Family Transformation and Family Law: Some African Developments in Financial Support on Relationship Breakdown' in S Adelman and A Paliwala (eds) *Law and Crisis in the Third World* (London, Zell, 1993) 270.

[327] E Uzodike 'Women's Rights in Law and Practice: Property Rights' in A Obilade (ed) *Women in Law* (Lagos, Southern University Law Centre and Faculty of Law, 1993) 304 at 304–6; Sinclair and Heaton above n 59 at 176.

[328] W Ncube *Family Law in Zimbabwe* (Harare, Legal Resources Foundation, 1989) at 167. In South Africa customary law applies to marriages contracted before the Act. Recognition of Customary Marriages Act 1998 s 7(1).

[329] Ncube above n 214 at 73.

[330] Government of Uganda (2000) above n 133 at 63.

First, it belongs to the family as a distinct perpetual legal entity. Secondly, members . . . do not possess any separate, disposable, attachable or inheritable interests therein. Thirdly, the fact that this property is vested in a body corporate implies that no transaction affecting interests therein is valid unless done by, or with the consent of the family itself acting through its alter ego which, for some purposes, is the family head and for others, the family council.[331]

In Mozambique, property of people in de facto unions is separate and thus parties may regulate their individual property as they see fit.[332] However, even when individual ownership is recognised, often the property is registered in the name of the man, so that in Kenya, Nyamu-Musembi notes that 95 per cent of land is held in the name of the man and that 'even co-ownership of the matrimonial home is a rarity'.[333]

Looked at objectively, it is difficult to see what property rural women *could* ask for. The 'house' would be part of the compound of the wider family. She could not demand it for herself, nor, in a patrilineal society, could she continue to live in that house after the dissolution of the marriage. Rural houses are not mortgaged to building societies and cannot be sold in the same way that brick-under-tile homes can in the urban and peri-urban areas. This leaves the livestock. Most families own it in common, so that it would be difficult to separate the husband's livestock from that belonging to the wider family. Even if it were possible, the practicalities of moving livestock over considerable geographical distances would preclude her from taking it. Although technically possible, it would be a difficult goal to achieve given the constraints of the rural economy and the quarantine sometimes imposed when there is an outbreak of disease. Selling it is of course a possibility. Needless to say, the woman would need considerable mental and moral stamina to withstand all the obstacles that would no doubt be put in her way.[334] In its 2003 report to CEDAW, the Nigerian government notes that:

Very often women are unable to enforce property rights in a court of law due to ignorance of such rights, lack of financial security and the fear of antagonizing their in-laws.[335]

---

[331] Kolajo above n 262 at 77. See also Nyamu-Musembi above n 120 at 238–39; L Tibatemwa-Ekirikubinza 'Family Relations and the Law in Uganda: Insights into Current Issues' in A Bainham (ed) *International Survey of Family Law 2002* (Bristol, Jordan Publishing, 2002) 433 at 434; Hubbard and Cassidy above n 183 at 268.

[332] Southern African Research and Documentation Centre (SARDC) *Beyond Inequalities: Women in Mozambique* (SARDC, Maputo, 2000) (hereafter SARDC *Mozambique*) at 41.

[333] Nyamu-Musembi above n 120 at 230. The figure of 90 per cent ownership of land and property being in the hands of men is also cited in Nigeria. Government of Nigeria (2003) above n 96 at 49.

[334] Government of Tanzania (1996) above n 292 at 5.

[335] Government of Nigeria (2003) above n 96 at 49. In Uganda it has been noted that women are reluctant to challenge their husbands on property ownership because of a fear of violence. L Tibatemwa-Ekirikubinza *More Sinned Against than Sinning: Women's Violent Crime in Uganda* (Copenhagen, Criminalistisk Institut, 1998) 102.

The attitude of women who have made direct financial contributions to the acquisition of marital property is less compliant. In Kenya and Zimbabwe, women have tried to invoke general law concepts, such as partnership and unjust enrichment, to try to convince the courts to give them more than their customary entitlements.[336]

There has been an effort in some African countries to mitigate the perceived harshness of the customary law by integrating general and customary law, and providing that the redistributive powers of the court using Matrimonial Causes statutes are to apply to all types of marriage. However, for some, this is limited to customary marriages that have been registered.[337] Kenya allows courts to exercise their redistributive powers under the Married Women's Property Act 1882.[338] In other jurisdictions, the parties will have chosen the marital regime to apply to their property in the event of a divorce at the time of contracting the marriage. South Africa is one such. It provides that parties can elect to have a union in community of property, in which case property is divided in half on divorce. If, however, they marry out of community of property, then their property may be divided between them by the court exercising its discretionary powers.[339] South African law provides that for black people who contracted civil marriages prior to the Marriage and Matrimonial Property Laws Amendment Act 3 of 1988, the marriage is out of community.[340]

In the Ethiopian Revised Family Code 2000 parties have a choice of matrimonial regime on entering into the marriage.[341] Parties are able to maintain their personal property separately and so, on divorce, each takes out what each brought in.[342] Any common property or property acquired jointly is shared.[343] If the parties had agreed to pool their property, with one of them being in charge of administering the joint estate, then they are both equally responsible for any debts incurred,[344] although the party responsible for administration may be asked to pay a penalty if he or she was negligent in the management of the

---

[336] See discussion of cases in Banda above n 126 at 479–83. See also Nyamu-Musembi, who discusses the Kenyan case of *Karanja v Karanja* [1976] Kenya Law Reports 307, where the court used the doctrine of presumptive trust to award the wife in a customary marriage one third of the matrimonial property. However, she notes that the continued operation of the separate property based system works against women. Nyamu-Musembi above n 120 at 231 and 237–39.

[337] Zimbabwe is one such country. The Matrimonial Causes Act Cap 5:13 applies to marriages registered under the Marriage Act Cap 5:11 and the Customary Marriages Act Cap 5:7.

[338] Nyamu-Musembi above n 120 at 230.

[339] Government of South Africa above n 292 at 108.

[340] Sinclair and Heaton above n 59 at v, 227; Sinclair 'Embracing New Family Forms' above n 3 at 803 fn 11; J Sonnekus 'Some Reflections on the Position of a Deceived Wife in a Dualistic System of Matrimonial Property Law' in P Lodrup and E Modvar (eds) *Family Life and Human Rights* (Oslo, Gyldendal Akademisk, 2004) 839 at 842–43.

[341] Art 85(1).

[342] Art 86(1).

[343] Arts 90–93.

[344] Art 89, 93(1).

common property.[345] It is more likely than not that the administrator will be the husband. The separate property regime, although seemingly respecting the parties' individuality again ignores the fact that often women enter into marriage with very little. Their home-making role, particularly in poor societies such as Ethiopia, makes it unrealistic to think that they will acquire property in any meaningful way during the course of the marriage. Operating on the principle of 'take what you have paid for' negates a woman's domestic contribution, for all she is able to point to are the clothes on her back and maybe a few pots and pans.[346] Indeed in dividing common property it is provided that: 'The utmost care shall be taken to give each spouse things which are most useful to him.'[347] Moreover, even when women do earn, the bulk of their money goes on the purchase of consumables, again leading to women having nothing to point to as being property that they helped to acquire, thus diminishing their entitlements.[348] It is for this reason that one must read with caution statements such as that contained in the Algerian report to CEDAW, to the effect that 'the wife has the right to full freedom in the disposition of her property'.[349] Freedom to dissipate nothing is no freedom at all.

In Tanzania, the injunction to consider equal division was upheld in the case of *Bi Hawa Mohammed*,[350] where the contribution of the woman to the acquisition of marital property was acknowledged. Similarly, the Zimbabwean cases of *Muchada v Muchada*[351] and *Nyathi v Nyathi*[352] also recognised women's enterprise and commitment to their marriages and their financial contribution to the acquisition of property as entitling them to a half share of matrimonial effects. However, this equal distribution is rare. This is despite courts being asked to take into consideration factors such as:

(a) the income, earning capacity, assets and other financial resources which each spouse has or is likely to have in the foreseeable future;
(b) the financial needs, obligations and responsibilities which each spouse and child has or is likely to have in the foreseeable future;
(c) the standard of living of the family, including the manner in which any children were being educated or trained, or expected to be educated or trained;

---

[345] Art 87.
[346] Cf Government of Uganda (2000) above n 133 at 63.
[347] Ethiopia Revised Family Code 2000 art 91(3).
[348] F Banda 'The Provision of Maintenance for Women and Children in Zimbabwe' (1995) 2 *Cardozo Women's Law Journal* 71 at 78.
[349] Art 38 of the Family Code of Algeria 1984 as cited in Government of Algeria (1998) above n 73 at 43.
[350] *Bi Hawa Mohammed v Ali Sefu* (Unreported), Tanzania Court of Appeal, Civil Appeal No 9/1983 discussed in Paliwala above n 326 at 278.
[351] *Muchada v Muchada* Unreported Judgment HC–H–66–87 discussed in Banda above n 348 at 77.
[352] *Nyathi v Nyathi* Unreported Judgment HC–B–77–89 at 17 discussed in Banda above n 348 at 78. See also Ncube above n 214 at 58–79.

(d) the age, physical and mental condition of each spouse and child;
(e) the direct or indirect contribution made by each spouse of the family, including contributions made by looking after the home, caring for the family and other domestic duties;
(f) the duration of the marriage.[353]

The granting of judicial discretion in the distribution of property is not without its problems.[354] Although homemaking, the main occupation of most married women, is to be taken into account, in reality it is not often given the weight that it deserves. This is partly because judges refuse to see domestic contribution as being on a par with financial contribution.[355] A Kenyan judge observed that a stay-at-home wife/homemaker who was claiming a share of matrimonial property wanted to 'sit on her husband's back with her hands in his pockets', meaning that she wanted to reap that which she had not sown.[356]

It is because of statements like this that the African Protocol on Women's Rights provides that states should 'take measures to recognize the economic value of the work of women in the home'.[357]

Weitzman has noted that often the husband's income, which he is enabled to earn because of the wife's sacrifice and free homemaking activity, is the major asset of the marriage and, in fairness, should be shared equally between the parties.[358] It goes without saying that equality will only be achieved by gender-sensitive judges who see 'women's work' in the home as being on par with 'men's work' outside it. The legal training of judges often leads them to see property as following title, so that the person in whose name the property is registered, more often than not the

---

[353] Zimbabwe Matrimonial Causes Act (Cap 5:13), s 7(3). Compare this to s 25 of the English Matrimonial Causes Act 1973 as amended. See also J Eekelaar *Regulating Divorce* (Oxford, Clarendon Press, 1991).

[354] See Kuenyehia and Ofei-Aboagye above n 114 at 41–45 on case law in Ghana. Like Nigeria, Ghanaian law appears to rely on principles of equity sometimes very narrowly construed. Government of Nigeria (2003) above n 96 at 49.

[355] See for example the English case of *Cowan v Cowan* [2001] 2 FLR 192. But see the earlier case of *White and White* [2000] 2 FLR 981(HL), where it was said that equality of distribution at divorce was desirable and also that there should be no discrimination between the weighting given to contributions made by way of domestic labour and those made by working outside the home. M Freeman 'Exploring the Boundaries of Family Law in England in 2000' in A Bainham (ed) *International Survey of Family Law 2002* (Bristol, Jordan Publishing, 2002) 133 at 133–37. It was not until October 2002 that the Court of Appeal in England gave a woman who had looked after hearth and home half of the matrimonial property for the first time: *Lambert v Lambert* [2003] 1 WLR 926.

[356] Kwacha J in *Tabitha Wangeci Nderitu v Simon Nderitu Kariuki* Civil Appeal No 023 of 1997 as cited in Nyamu-Musembi above n 120 at 236. See too Kuenyehia and Ofei-Aboagye above n 114 at 43.

[357] African Protocol on Women's Rights art 13(h), CEDAW General Recommendation No 21 para 32.

[358] L Weitzman 'Marital Property: Its Transformation and Division in the United States' in L Weitzman and M Maclean (eds) *Economic Consequences of Divorce: The International Perspective* (Oxford, Clarendon Press, 1992) 85 at 97. The Weitzman approach was adopted, to great media outcry, by the Court of Appeal in the English case of *McFarlane v McFarlane and Parlour v Parlour* [2004] EWCA (Civ) 872.

man, is the 'rightful' owner of the property and that is the end of the matter.[359] This narrow legalism is reinforced by their socialisation, whereby they see it as women's role to look after the family home.[360] In fulfilling this obligation, women are only 'doing their jobs'. Indeed, in societies in which customary norms permeate all spheres of life and thinking, is this not why men pay bridewealth for women? An interview with a High Court judge in Zimbabwe yielded the following insight on judicial interpretation of section 7(3) of the Matrimonial Causes Act on property distribution:

> The whole system is a lottery depending on which judge you draw. We have people from a broad spectrum . . . It is a multi-ethnic and cross-cultural judiciary and everybody has their own inherent prejudices. I have been horrified by some of the decisions which have been handed down. I mean recently there was this case of a woman in a 14 year marriage which had broken down because the husband had taken a lover. She had borne six children. She walked out of that marriage with nothing. Not the children. Not the house. No nothing. The judge saw that there was irretrievable breakdown. He said that the children of the marriage could be adequately cared for by the new woman. Yet he forgets—I mean how could he expect her to contribute financially when she was busy having all those babies? So basically all he did was to get rid of the old wife and replace her with the new wife. And he saw nothing wrong with that. I mean absolutely nothing.[361]

In line with its reservation to article 16 of CEDAW on equal distribution of property on divorce, Egypt does not recognise equal sharing of property on divorce for people subject to Muslim personal law. Indeed it appears not to recognise that the wife in an Islamic marriage which ends by divorce is entitled to any of the 'husband's property'. The reason for this is said to lie in the uneven responsibilities and obligations of men and women in the marriage contract. Egypt reasons that since men have to give a dower for the wife and have an obligation to support her during the duration of the marriage, which support obligation is not reciprocal, it would be unfair then to hold that the husband has also to give her a half share of the matrimonial property on divorce. In short, the Egyptian reservation seems to suggest that giving women half would be akin to unjust enrichment of the wife at the expense of the husband. However, what the reservation fails to take into account is that often women do take on the responsibility of supporting the family, either singly or in conjunction with the husband. It also fails to take into account inflation. Factoring this into the equation, it may well be that a woman's dower on divorce is a pittance and insufficient to provide her with enough to live on. Finally the Egyptian reservation fails to recognise that couples may order their lives differently; indeed their marital contracts may not reflect the

---

[359] See African Protocol on Women's Rights art 8(d). See also arts 8(c) and 8(e).
[360] Government of Uganda (2000) above n 133 62. In Egypt, a woman will be 'allowed' to work if it does not interfere with her family responsibilities. An Na'im (ed) _Islamic Family Law_ above n 10 at 171.
[361] Quoted in Banda above n 348 at 76.

marital paradigm on which the reservation appears to be based. In this regard there is some confusion, with the Egyptian report to CEDAW suggesting a view of marriage based on the partnership model:

> Women and men share full responsibility for all matters arising from their marriage, including the maintenance and support of the family unit and decisions about the number and spacing of their children.[362]

The division of property on divorce is of course rendered more complex by the existence of polygynous unions. If a man has several wives—the first of whom he married 40 years ago when he had nothing to his name and the last of whom he married last year when the family had substantial assets—how should the respective contributions be measured and entitlements ascertained? It goes without saying that mixing and mis-matching of marriage forms, and indeed entering into legally polygynous unions, creates difficulties about how the matrimonial property is to be divided on divorce. In the Zimbabwean case of *Jengwa*[363] the judge was faced with a woman who had entered into a customary law union with the defenant in 1972. There had been periods of estrangement during which the husband had relations with at least five other women, some of whom he married, although the exact number was never ascertained. She was awarded a third of the property because consideration had to be given to the other wives. The judge noted that had the marriage been monogamous, then it was more than likely she would have been given a half share, thus highlighting the fact that often it is the first wife who is forced to forfeit her share 'for the common good'. The judge did note that in polygynous cases justice could only be done if the property rights of all concerned parties (that is co-wives) were taken into account.[364] Here it must be noted that the South African legislature has tried to address the issue of property division where the man was married polygynously. The Recognition of Customary Marriages Act 1998 explicitly provides that where a man has more than one spouse, the other spouses must be joined in the action and the interests of any other third parties considered.[365]

The Human Rights Watch report on women's access to property in Kenya captures many of the difficulties experienced by women in trying to get their fair share of marital property.[366] It suggests that barriers include ignorance of the laws complicated by the plethora of marriage statutes; reluctance to demand their entitlement for fear of ostracisation; socialisation of women and pure discrimination. These problems are not unique to Kenya. Indeed the report captures the universal

---

[362] Government of Egypt (2000) above n 70 at 89.
[363] *Jengwa v Jengwa* 1999 (2) ZLR 120.
[364] *Ibid* at 133.
[365] Recognition of Customary Marriages Act 1998 s 7(4)(b).
[366] Human Rights Watch *Double Standards: Women's Property Right Violations in Kenya* (London, Human Rights Watch, 2003) at 32–43.

dilemma of the African woman wanting her share of the property which she has helped, by dint of her labour, to acquire. That so few do acquire property is testament to the resilience of patriarchy, and points to the limitations of relying solely on national and international laws.

Maintenance after divorce

In what appears to be an apparent omission, the African Protocol, in article 7 on divorce, is silent on the issue of maintenance of women after divorce. It focuses on reciprocal obligations to maintain children.[367] All that is guaranteed to women is the right to an equitable share in the property of the marriage.[368] This is in direct contrast to CEDAW, which in article 16(1)(c) provides that men and women shall have: 'The same rights and responsibilities during marriage and at its dissolution.' At the national level, most statutes now provide for a reciprocal obligation to pay maintenance.[369] In reality it is mainly men who pay maintenance to women. However, the assessment as to whether to order payment of maintenance, for how long and how much, is dependent on the proof of reasonable needs that vary across economic brackets. In Commonwealth African states that have adopted the English law on divorce, there has also been a move towards seeing maintenance as a temporary stop-gap measure to enable the woman to get back on her feet. To facilitate this 'clean break' between the partners, rehabilitative maintenance is ordered for a limited time period.[370]

In customary law there have been statutory inroads made into the customary presumption that a man was responsible for supporting his wife only for as long she lived with him.[371] Prior to statutory intervention, the position was that after the marriage ended she became the responsibility of her family to whom she returned. Similarly, if children in customary patrilineal societies 'belonged' to the father's line then it followed that they would be provided for within that family. Amongst the Shona in Zimbabwe, if a man and woman divorced and the child went to live with its mother whilst it was still young, all that was required of the father was that he hand over a beast of thanks to the woman's family when he went

---

[367] African Protocol on Women's Rights art 7(c).

[368] *Ibid* at art 7(d).

[369] Ghana Matrimonial Causes Act 1971 (Act 367) s 16(1). Kuenyehia and Ofei-Aboagye above n 114 at 48. However, as currently drafted the Ugandan law appears to suggest that women have the right to receive maintenance and men the obligation to pay. Penal Code ss 152, 153 and 215. Government of Uganda (2000) above n 133 at 68. However, this could probably be challenged as a violation of equality rights in the Constitution. *Ibid.*

[370] Sinclair and Heaton above n 59 at 150–52.

[371] Cf A Armstrong 'Maintenance Statutes in Six Countries in Southern Africa' (1990) 34 *Journal of African Law* 132. The Constitution of Malawi 1994 s 24(1)(b)(ii).

to collect his child. However, increasingly, even when a customary marriage has existed, the courts are granting custody to the mother. This then requires the father to pay maintenance for the children. This requirement generates a lot of tension amongst men, who feel that the woman has been given a double benefit—the 'wealth' in the form of the children and now the monthly payments from him. That they should now lose the right to live with their children and be asked to pay maintenance monthly, even after they have paid bridewealth, strikes many men as daylight robbery.[372]

The requirement introduced into some legal systems that a man has an obligation to maintain his wife or wives, even those with whom he has unregistered customary law unions, has also led to a great deal of resentment. The payment of bridewealth is premised on her family having the responsibility to look after her should the marriage fail to work. Asking him to pay long after he has ceased to enjoy the benefits of her company again arouses anger. It is of course important to acknowledge that many women are in 'irregular unions' from which no entitlements to maintenance arise after the union has ended.[373]

However, the reality about maintenance in most countries is simply this: few women know that they are entitled to claim maintenance for their children, let alone for themselves; courts are over-crowded; the process is long, cumbersome and costly in terms of both money and time—all of this effort for an uncertain outcome.[374] Enforcement of maintenance orders is notoriously difficult.[375] When the money does come, it comes sporadically. The hyper-inflation in many countries means that the amounts ordered are so miniscule as to make their collection uneconomic for the recipient. Also, maintenance payments and claims work best when the person paying is in regular employment; the salary can be ascertained, and if necessary an order made directing the employer to pay the money into the bank account of the beneficiary—assuming, of course, she has one. The vast majority of people on the continent are not in formal employment; they work in the informal sector and agriculture where the returns fluctuate. It goes without saying that if mothers are the preferred primary care givers, then mothers are the ones burdened with trying to find the resources to look after children. It is the failure to meet this challenge, even in two-parent families, that leads to girls being forced to marry early and sometimes being sent to work for relatives and strangers who can abuse them with impunity.

---

[372] Ncube above n 214 at 71–72.
[373] SARDC *Mozambique* above n 332 at 41.
[374] WLSA Lesotho *In Search of Justice: Where do Women in Lesotho Go?* (Lesotho, WLSA, 2000) 201ff; WLSA Swaziland *Charting the Maze: Women in Pursuit of Justice in Swaziland* (Mbabane, WLSA, 2000) 81–83, 174ff.
[375] Government of South Africa above n 292 at 109; Wabwile above n 259 at 267–84. This is not a uniquely African phenomenon. See M Maclean and J Eekelaar *Maintenance after Divorce* (Oxford, Clarendon Press, 1986).

In Islam, a husband's obligation to support his wife terminates after he gives her the rest of her dower and the expiration of the period of *iddat*, which is said to be three menstrual cycles after the couple separate. This is to ensure that she is not with child by him. If he divorces her without good excuse and without her consent, then he will be required to pay her compensation (*mut'a al-talaq*) of at least two years' maintenance, with no ceiling put on the level of maintenance.[376] There is an obligation to provide her with a home and maintenance for any young children over whom she may have custody.[377] In the case of *Danial Latifi & Another v Union of India*[378] the Indian Supreme Court held that depriving Muslim women of the right to long-term maintenance enjoyed by women from other religions violated Article 14 of the Constitution, mandating equality and equal protection of the law to all persons otherwise similarly circumstanced, and also violated Article 15 of the Constitution, which prohibits any discrimination on the ground of religion, as the Act would obviously apply to Muslim divorced women only and solely on the ground of their belonging to the Muslim religion.[379]

Tunisia not only recognises that men and women have the same right to divorce, but also makes provision for a husband who is at fault to pay maintenance for 'material and emotional damages'.[380]

Children

Joan May once asserted that under (patrilineal) customary law children had few 'rights'.[381] Indeed she asserted that a child's right was limited to 'membership of the patrilineage'.[382] This rather limited view of children's rights under customary law is premised upon the idea that the child's individual rights are subsumed within the collective duties, obligations and responsibilities that are to be borne by all members of the family collective. Within this paradigm, gender relations may dictate that the girl child be responsible for the feeding and caring of other members of the family. It may also require her to give up school in order to fulfil this role.

Arguably the question of whether children have rights has been resolutely answered by the almost universal ratification of the United Nations Convention

---

[376] An Na'im (ed) *Islamic Family Law* above n 10 at 172. The discussion here is on Egypt.

[377] *Ibid*.

[378] *Danial Latifi & Anor v Union of India* Supreme Court of India, Civil Jurisdiction Writ Petition (civil) No 868/1986.

[379] *Ibid* at 15. Cf Coomaraswamy above n 2 at 53–54.

[380] An Na'im (ed) *Islamic Family Law* above n 10 at 159.

[381] J May *Changing People, Changing Laws* (Gweru, Mambo Press, 1987) 75.

[382] *Ibid*.

on the Rights of the Child 1989 (CRC) and the coming into force in 1999 of the African Charter on the Rights and Welfare of the Child 1990 (ACRWC).[383] This is not to suggest that 'culture' no longer plays a role in defining and determining the parameters of childhood. Clearly it does.[384]

Both Conventions have as their starting point the notion of the best interests of the child, with the CRC providing that the best interest of the child 'shall be *a* primary consideration';[385] whilst the ACRWC puts it more forcefully, providing that the child's best interest 'shall be *the* primary consideration',[386] thus making it paramount. Children's rights are to be exercised and enjoyed without discrimination on the basis of sex.[387] Children's rights have received constitutional recognition in some states.[388] Included in the recognition of the notion that children have rights is the understanding that both parents, without discrimination, are under an obligation to provide and care for the children in equal measure.[389]

It seems increasingly true to say that whatever the marital regime of the parties, where the children are young, the maternal preference prevails. This results in women being given custody of children in the majority of cases. It was noted in the earlier discussion on feminist constructions of the family, that some construe this maternal preference as reflecting the uneven burden placed on women, who are given young children (who are more labour intensive than older children) to look

[383] W Ncube (ed) *Law, Culture, Tradition and Children's Rights in Eastern and Southern Africa: Issues in Law and Society* (Aldershot, Dartmouth, 1998); D Chirwa 'The Merits and Demerits of the African Charter on the Rights and Welfare of the Child' (2002) 10 *International Journal of Children's Rights* 157. It is worth remembering that the definition of women in the African Protocol on Women's Rights also includes girls: see art 1(k).
[384] A An Na'im (ed) 'Cultural Transformation and Normative Consensus on the Best Interests of the Child' (1994) 8 *International Journal of Law, Policy and the Family* 62.
[385] CRC art 3(1). J Eekelaar 'Beyond the Welfare Principle' (2002) 14 *Child and Family Law Quarterly* 237.
[386] ACRWC art 4(1).
[387] CRC art 2(1); ACRWC art 3. See also ACRWC art 21(1)(b) which requires states to eliminate: 'those customs and practices discriminatory to the child on the grounds of sex or other status'; ICCPR art 24(1); Human Rights Committee General Comment No 17 on the Rights of the Child. HRI/GEN/1/REV.7. See also Human Rights Committee (2000) General Comment No 28 on Equality Between Men and Women at para 28.
[388] Constitution of the Republic of Namibia 1990 Art 15; Constitution of the Republic of South Africa 1996 s 28; Constitution of the Republic of Ghana 1992 Art 28; Constitution of Malawi 1994 s 23; Constitution of Uganda 1995 Art 34. Uganda is also one of an increasing number of states to pass a Children's Statute 1996. See S Arach-Amoko 'The Rights of the Child: The Case of Uganda' in United Nations (ed) *Bringing International Human Rights Home* (New York, United Nations, 2002) 150; Woodman above n 1 at 199, 203, 204.
[389] CRC art 18(1); ACRWC art 20(1)(a)–(c). African Protocol on Women's Rights arts 6(i), 7(c). Human Rights Committee General Comment 19 on Protection of the Family, the Right to Marriage and Equality of the Spouses paras 8, 9. But see B Rwezaura 'The Value of a Child: Marginal Children and the Law in Contemporary Tanzania' (2000) 14 *International Journal of Law, Policy and the Family* 326; B Kamchedzera 'The Rights of the Child in Malawi: An Agenda for Research on the Impact of the UN Convention in a Poor Country' (1991) 5 *International Journal of Law, Policy and the Family* 24.

after[390] There is also gender stereotyping inherent in the operation of the maternal preference rule, in that it constructs women's role as being to look after children. It is also assumed that women are the primary care givers.[391]

Women's role in child care was acknowledged at the first United Nations conference on human rights held in Teheran in 1968, with the preamble to the Resolution on Women's Rights providing:

> Bearing in mind the great contribution made by women to social, political, economic and cultural life and the part they play in the family, particularly in the rearing of children.[392]

Women's role in child care appears to have been enshrined in the national laws of some states. On the Egyptian law, Quassem notes: 'The mother is *entitled* to custody, even if she is not a Muslim, because she, more than any other, has a right to care for her child and is more capable of doing so' (emphasis added).[393] In Egypt, the mother is awarded custody of boys until the age of 10 and girls until the age of 12. She may ask to be allowed to keep the male child until the age of 15 and the female until marriage, if that would be better for the child.[394] Throughout this period the father is under an obligation to support the children and he may see them regularly.[395] Again, here one can see the gendering of custody decisions. A mother may keep the girl child for longer because she is the best person to socialise her into the ways of good womanhood and ultimately wifehood. Interestingly, it would appear that in both the Islamic and customary systems, custody may be in the hands of the mother but, more often than not, the divorced father retains parental authority over the children.[396]

In Equatorial Guinea, on divorce, 'children under the age of five *traditionally* stayed with their mother and older children were given into the custody of their fathers' (emphasis added).[397] Similarly, in its report to CEDAW, the government of Burkina Faso notes that if the child is under 7, 'custody must preferentially be awarded to the mother unless *force majeure* intervenes or if the interests of the child require otherwise'.[398] As a result of the maternal preference to look after young children 'rule', Rwezaura notes that in Tanzania often women will not con-

---

[390] Delphy above n 37 at 99; C Smart *The Ties That Bind* (London, Routledge, 1984) 122, 178.

[391] Sinclair and Heaton above n 59 at 154–58.

[392] Resolution IX Adopted by the International Conference on Human Rights in Teheran on Measures to Promote Women's Rights in the Modern World and Endorsing the Secretary-General's Proposal for a Unified Long Term United Nations Programme for the Advancement of Women (12 May 1968) A/CONF.32/41 reproduced in United Nations *The United Nations and the Advancement of Women 1945–1996* (New York, United Nations, 1996) 177. See also Smart above n 390 at 122.

[393] Quassem above n 66 at 27; see also Kuenyehia and Ofei-Aboagye above n 114 at 51.

[394] Law No 25 of 1929 as amended by Law No E 100 of 1985 art 20.

[395] Quassem above n 66 at 89.

[396] See for example SARDC *Mozambique* above n 332 at 39.

[397] CEDAW Concluding Observations to the Initial Report of Equatorial Guinea CEDAW A/44/38 (1989) para 168.

[398] Government of Burkina Faso (1998) above n 11 at 27. See also Government of Nigeria (1997) above n 62 at 64; Kuenyehia and Ofei-Aboagye above n 114 at 51.

test custody of any children above the age presumed to favour the mother.[399] Indeed some will voluntarily hand over custody once the child reaches the 'transfer' age (in Tanzania that is 7).[400] This has led to debates about whether the age to which mothers keep children should be raised to 15.[401] By way of contrast, Ncube asserts that, in Zimbabwe, women actively fight for custody of their children, so that research showed that 90 per cent of the civil business of the former Community courts was spent on custody and maintenance claims brought by women.[402]

In the South African case of *Hugo*[403] the maternal presumption worked to deprive a child of being cared for by his father. To mark the start of his Presidency, Mandela had granted amnesties to certain categories of women prisoners who had children under the age of 12. This was to enable the women to look after their children, who, being young, were said to need the care and attention of their mothers. The applicant, Hugo, who was serving a prison term, challenged this single sex amnesty as constituting direct discrimination against him and indirect discrimination against the child, whose mother had died, leaving the child without a parent as primary care giver. Hugo was unsuccessful. The court acknowledged the differential treatment, but noted that it was not unfair and therefore did not violate the equality clause in the Constitution. In a dissenting judgment, Kriegler J warned that this stereotyping of women as nurturers could be counterproductive, particularly since:

> Reliance on the generalization that women are the primary care giver is harmful in its tendency to cramp and stunt the efforts of both men and women to form their identities freely.[404]

This was met by a rejoinder from O'Regan J, to the effect that the judgment of the majority merely reflected the status quo, which it would be inequitable to ignore. It was argued that taking a formalist approach to equality would entrench inequality.[405]

This mother preference is particularly interesting, not least because in its gendered construct of primary carer it seems to go against the provisions of the CRC and the ACRWC, neither of which expresses a parental preference, focusing instead on the outcome of the welfare test (best interests principle). This is reiterated in CEDAW and the Protocol to the African Charter on Women's

---

[399] B Rwezaura 'Gender Justice and Children's Rights: A Banner for Family Law Reform in Tanzania' in A Bainham (ed) *International Survey of Family Law 1997* (The Hague, Kluwer International, 1999) 413 at 418.

[400] *Ibid.*

[401] *Ibid.*

[402] Ncube above n 214 at 71.

[403] *President of the Republic of South Africa v Hugo* 1997(4) SA 1.

[404] *Ibid* at 37.

[405] *Ibid* at 49–50; Sinclair 'Ebb and Flow' above n 3 at 394–97.

Rights.[406] These provisions have been incorporated into a number of domestic laws on children.[407] It could of course be argued that an examination of the facts reveals that the mother is the person best able to provide for the child's best interests. However, some of the presumptions cited suggest that rather than starting from a position of neutrality, judges begin from a position that seriously hampers men's ability to compete on a level playing field with women to obtain custody of their children.[408]

The men most affected by this gender bias are men who have never married the mothers of their children. In some common law systems, their rights are close to non-existent. They need not be consulted over any decisions affecting the child.[409] They may have the obligation to support but no rights of access, custody or guardianship over their children.[410] Discussing Namibia, Hubbard and Cassidy note that the unequal treatment of unmarried fathers violates article 15(1) of the Namibian Constitution, which provides that children have a right to know and to be brought up by their parents.[411] They also note that the Namibian Social Security Act 34 of 1994, which makes provision for maternity but not paternity leave or parental leave, 'reinforces the notion that women bear the primary responsibility for child care'.[412] In South Africa, constitutional challenges based on discrimination on grounds of marital status have given unmarried fathers greater rights.[413]

The gender stereotyping that seems to be prevalent on the African continent constitutes a violation of article 5(a) of CEDAW as it reinforces 'the stereotyped roles for men and women'. It also goes against article 5(b) of CEDAW and article 13(1) of the African Protocol on Women's Rights.

What is interesting about the operation of this maternal preference is that it so clearly goes against customary law, which says that children born of a union for which bridewealth has been given should go to the father's line.[414] Atsenuwa contends that when a mother is given custody, 'she has in fact no more than a day to day care of the child with the father's right merely held in abeyance'.[415] How far is it true to say that the maternal preference, first introduced into customary law by

[406] CEDAW, art 16(1)(d)(f); African Protocol on Women's Rights art 7(c).

[407] Section 71 of the Nigerian Matrimonial Causes Act as cited in A Atsenuwa 'Women's Rights within the Family Context: Law and Practice' in A Obilade (ed) *Women in Law* (Lagos, Southern University Law Centre and Faculty of Law, 1993) 116 at 124.

[408] Sinclair and Heaton above n 59 at 155.

[409] This is not in keeping with CEDAW. CEDAW General Recommendation No 21 paras 19, 20.

[410] It is worth noting at this point that a duty to support exists independently of the privilege of access to that child, with access being seen as the right of the child and not the parent.

[411] Cf Hubbard and Cassidy above n 183 at 271–72.

[412] Hubbard and Cassidy above n 183 at 264 fn.

[413] *Fraser v Children's Court, Pretoria North* 1997 (2) SA 261 (CC).

[414] Ncube above n 328 at 126 fn 82; Ncube above n 214 at 70.

[415] A Atsenuwa 'Women's Rights within the Family Context: Law and Practice' in A Obilade (ed) *Women in Law* (Lagos, Southern University Law Centre and Faculty of Law, 1993) 116 at 125.

way of the repugnance clause during the colonial era, has taken root and usurped the 'paternal family preference rule'?

Research would seem to indicate that the maternal preference rule meets little resistance from men until such time as they are ordered to pay maintenance for their children. It is at this point that they challenge the maternal preference rule, citing their customary entitlements to custody by virtue of their earlier payment of bridewealth.[416] The other time that men ask for custody is if the former wife or partner begins to cohabit with another man. This is seen as not being in the best interests of the children, not least because 'they will be brought up in the ways of another family', or more accurately, the ways of a man who has not given bridewealth for the woman, and who cannot substitute for the father in the same way that a stepmother or female relative is often asked to step into the maternal role.[417] There is here a conflation of a woman who re-partners as being a 'bad wife' and by extension a 'bad mother'. Indeed the fear of losing their children means that sometimes women will remain in unhappy marriages, or, if the marriage ends, they will not re-partner or claim maintenance from the former husband in case that provokes him to ask for custody of 'his' children.[418]

In patrilineal customary law, a man who makes a woman pregnant but does not want to marry her may still establish paternity by acknowledging the child as his, usually by way of payment of 'seduction damages' or a compensatory gift. The child may remain with its mother; and should the father wish to bring the child to live with him, then the custom of the Shona of Zimbabwe would be that he would hand over a beast as *chiredzwa* or the rearing fee, a token of his gratitude to the woman's family. These days he would also have to pay maintenance from the time the woman names him as the father.[419]

Armstrong contends that part of the reason for the tensions which arise from the application of the best interests principle in custody decisions, is its construction of the parents as the only people capable of looking after the children. She argues that this enforced nuclearisation of the African family does not actually reflect the day-to-day reality of many people's lives.[420] Research shows that more often than not, responsibility for child care is shared within the wider family, with the care of the child entrusted to the person best able to provide it with 'school and

---

[416] Zimbabwe Women Resource Centre and Network (ZWRCN) and SARDC-WIDSAA *Beyond Inequalities: Women in Zimbabwe* (Harare, SARDC, 1998) 49; M Maboreke 'The Love of a Mother: Problems of Custody in Zimbabwe' in A Armstrong and W Ncube (eds) *Women and Law in Southern Africa* (Harare, Zimbabwe Publishing House, 1987) 158.

[417] Maboreke above n 416 at 157; F Banda 'Custody and the Best Interests of the Child in Zimbabwe' (1994) 8 *International Journal of Law, Policy and the Family* 191.

[418] F Banda 'The Provision of Maintenance for Women and Children in Zimbabwe' (1995) 2 *Cardozo Women's Law Journal* 71 at 87.

[419] The same principle appears to apply in Ghana. Kuenyehia and Ofei-Aboagye above n 114 at 53.

[420] A Armstrong *A Child Belongs to Everyone: Law, Family and the Construction of the Best Interests of the Child in Zimbabwe*, Innocenti Occasional Papers 11 (Florence, International Child Development Centre, 1995). See also Bonthuys above n 3 at 57–58.

sadza', sadza being the maize meal porridge that is a staple in many southern African states.[421] This builds into the obligations of support said to be part of traditional family. Reality again seems to indicate a breaking down of these wider family ties, with richer relations no longer prepared to take on the children of poorer relatives; or if they do take them on, then expecting them to serve the immediate family in a domestic capacity in return for board, lodging and (sometimes) schooling. Young girls from poor families are the most likely to be sent to relatives 'to assist with the work'.

Sinclair also questions the parental focus in children cases, noting that in middle class families, the children may actually spend more time with the woman who is paid to look after the home and the children than with the parents.[422]

Nationality

Children

The area where father preference remains strong is over nationality of children.

The famous case of *Dow v Attorney General of Botswana* challenged this father presumption.[423] Unity Dow was a Tswana woman who had three children, one born before she met and married an American man named Nathan Dow who fathered the other two children. The law recognised that her first child, who was deemed 'illegitimate', was entitled to Tswana citizenship, because children born out of wedlock are the responsibility of their mother and her kin group. The other two children were said to be American citizens, because they followed their father's citizenship in the same way that the children born to a Tswana man married to an alien woman would be entitled to Tswana citizenship. This was clearly discriminatory on the face of it. The distinction also had practical implications. These included the fact that as non-citizens, the last two children would not be able to access the benefits of citizenship offered, including free education. It goes without saying that it made international travel complicated for the Dow family. Unity Dow challenged the Citizenship Act of 1984, which was the source of the father preference rule, as being unconstitutional in that it was discriminatory on the basis of sex. She also said that it violated international human rights principles, including CEDAW.

---

[421] A Armstrong 'School and Sadza' (1994) 8 *International Journal of Law Policy and the Family* 150; A Belembaogo 'The Best Interests of the Child: The Case of Burkina Faso' (1994) 8 *International Journal of Law Policy and the Family* 202.

[422] J Sinclair 'Ebb and Flow' above n 3 at 397.

[423] *Dow v Attorney-General of Botswana* [1991] LRC (Const) 574.

Interestingly, the Botswana government acknowledged the differential treatment, but defended it on the ground that in patrilineal societies it was 'customary' for a married woman to move to live with her husband, who was the head of the family and whose name and family line the children took and followed. This was a bald acknowledgement on the part of the government that men's rights prevailed, notwithstanding the fact that, as already noted, women tend to bear the disproportionate burden of child rearing. It was also an interesting mixing of normative orders. Specifically the government relied on patrilineal principles grounded in customary law to justify the discrimination, and yet the Citizenship Act was actually based on general law. Further mixing its normative orders, the government sought to defend Dow's point on constitutional discrimination by noting that sex was not included as a proscribed ground in the non-discrimination provision.[424] Moreover, the state argued that aspects of personal law were granted dispensation from the operation of non-discrimination provision.[425] Although the Constitution did ring fence aspects of personal law from the non-discrimination provision, the excluded aspects of personal law did not list citizenship, not least because it is not a concept recognised at customary law in the same manner in which it is constructed under civil or general law. As noted in Chapter 3, it was held, and confirmed on appeal, that Dow had indeed suffered the discrimination complained of.[426] Subsequent to the case, the Citizenship Act was amended and Botswana ratified CEDAW.[427]

This normative pick and mix is not unique to Botswana. The Algerian and Egyptian governments have used similar justifications to those of the Botswana government when making reservations to article 9(2) on nationality of children in CEDAW. They argue that it is 'customary' for children to follow their father's nationality, and thus seek exemption from the provision that the child should be entitled to adopt the nationality of either or both parents.[428] These and other reservations do violence to the object and purpose of the Convention. It is important to note that the multi-cultural CEDAW Committee has also raised its

---

[424] Constitution of Botswana 1966 Art 15(3). Art 15 is the non-discrimination provision. However, Art 3, which is on fundamental rights and freedoms of the individual, does include sex as a ground entitling a person to the enjoyment of his or her 'fundamental rights and freedoms'. Dow relied on this Art 3 in her claim for sex discrimination.

[425] Constitution of Botswana 1966 Art 15(4)(c).

[426] *Attorney General of Botswana v Dow* [1992] LRC (Const) 623. See U Dow 'National Implementation of International Law: The Dow Case' in United Nations (ed) *Bringing International Human Rights Law Home* (New York, United Nations, 2002) 112.

[427] L Stratton 'The Right to Have Rights: Gender Discrimination in National Laws' (1992) 77 *Minnesota Law Review* 195.

[428] President Mubarak is reported to have issued a decree in 2003 providing that children born to Egyptian mothers would be considered Egyptian. J Chu and A Radwan 'Raising Their Voices' *Time Magazine* (London, 23 February 2004) 42 at 44.

concerns about the inability of women to pass on their nationality to their children,[429] and asked for the reservations to be uplifted.[430]

Interestingly, even Tunisia appears to equivocate over nationality rights of children, so that in its report to CEDAW, Tunisia noted that the child of a Tunisian mother and a non-Tunisian father had the right to claim Tunisian citizenship a year before coming of age, or if before her nineteenth birthday her parents made a joint declaration. The CEDAW criticised Tunisia for its reservations, not least its reservation to article 9(2) on nationality of children. It urged the state to take the necessary steps to withdraw these reservations.[431]

The provision on nationality of children also proved controversial during the drafting of the African Protocol on Women's Rights. Problems arose at the 2001 government experts meeting, when attempts were made to expand the article dealing with the right of a married woman to retain or change her nationality to include the right to pass on her nationality to her children by mutual consent/agreement. The following was proposed as a new article 7(g):

> [A] woman shall have the right to keep her nationality, obtain another one or take up the nationality of her husband, or *transfer her nationality to her children by mutual agreement.*

The italicised phrase was challenged by Algeria, Egypt, Libya and Sudan. The proposed article 7(g) mirrored articles 9(1) and 9(2) of CEDAW.[432] By the time of the Meeting of Ministers in March 2003, the provision had been split into two articles, which provided:

> 6(g) a woman shall have the right to retain her nationality or to acquire the nationality of her husband.

> 6(h) a woman and a man shall have equal rights with respect to the nationality of their children except where this is contrary to a provision in national legislation or is contrary to national security interests.

These are the provisions found in the final Protocol on Women's Rights.[433] Interestingly article 6(h) contains a claw-back clause making the child's right to nationality subject to national legislation. The ability of a state to invoke national law in this manner is questionable.[434] At the March 2003 ministerial meeting, South Africa and Zambia objected to this new provision.

---

[429] CEDAW Concluding Observations to the Initial Report of Algeria (1999) para 83.

[430] *Ibid* paras 55, 67.

[431] CEDAW Concluding Observations to the Third and Fourth Periodic Report of Tunisia CEDAW/C/SR. 567 and 568 at paras 188–90.

[432] See also CEDAW General Recommendation No 21 para 6, Human Rights Committee General Comment No 17 para 8 and Human Rights Committee General Comment No 28 para 25.

[433] African Protocol on Women's Rights arts 6(g)–6(h).

[434] Vienna Convention on the Law of Treaties 1969 art 27. See also *Legal Resources Foundation v Zambia* Communication 211/98, Decision of the AfCmHPR, 29th Ordinary Session, April/May 2001 [2001] IIHRL 1 (1 May 2001) (see chapter 3 p. 47 n 51) at para 70. See too the framing of Norway's objection to the Algerian reservation to art 9 of CEDAW. United Nations 'Declarations and Reservations' available from

Women

It is telling that globally, many of the human rights cases brought by or on behalf of women to national and international tribunals are on the issue of nationality of married women and their ability to maintain a nationality or identity of their own, independent of their husbands; or indeed to be able to pass on that nationality and the benefits of citizenship to their husbands if they marry non-nationals, in the same way that citizen men can when they marry non-nationals. The legal 'disowning' of married women persists, despite the fact that one of the earliest instruments passed by the United Nations to correct women's inequality was on the nationality of married women.[435] The number of cases brought by married women highlights the gendered construct that sees women as being like children, who lack capacity and who should follow the line/citizenship of the father/husband.[436]

The cases and some national laws also force us to interrogate the very notion of citizenship and women's exclusion from the benefits emanating therefrom.[437] This is manifested through the denial of women's right to participate meaningfully in the public sphere. It is also made explicit in the denial of their self-determination, not in the formal international law sense denoting states' right to self-determination, but in the equally powerful violations of their rights to decide their own destiny in the most personal matters, such as whether they marry, whom they marry and when they marry; if they work outside the home, for whom they work outside the home and how long they work outside the home; what happens to the money they earn working outside the home; if they have children and, indeed, how many children they have.

It is of course ironic that on marriage women cease to be citizens of their birth families but are never fully recognised as citizens of their marital families. A

http://sim.law.uu.nl/SIM/Library/RATIF.nsf/1b02bda6311c4e2dc12568b8004f23f4/493002d26b4d8b94c1 2568bd003a0efc?OpenDocument.

[435] Convention on the Nationality of Married Women 1957, 309 UNTS 65.

[436] *Abdulaziz Cabales and Balkandi v UK* 28 May 1985 (No 94), 7 EHRR 471 paras 70–85; *Aumeeruddy Cziffra v Mauritius* (2000) AHRLR 3 (HRC 1981), *Proposed Amendments to the Naturalization Provisions of the Political Constitution of Costa Rica*, Inter American Court of Human Rights, Advisory Opinion 0C–4/84 of 19 January 1984, Ser A No 4, 5 HRLJ 161; *Rattigan and Others v Chief Immigration Officer and Others* 1994 (2) ZLR 54 (SC); *Salem v Chief Immigration Officer* 1994 (2) ZLR 287 (SC). Significantly, after the *Rattigan* and *Salem* decisions, the Zimbabwean government amended the constitution by equalising downwards so that neither men nor women had an automatic right to import alien spouses. W Ncube 'Defending and Protecting Gender Under a Decidedly Undecided Constitution in Zimbabwe' in J Eekelaar and T Nhlapo (eds) *Changing Family* (Oxford, Hart Publishing, 1998) 509 at 521; A Gubbay 'The Effect of the Deportation of Alien Husbands Upon the Constitutionally Protected Mobility Rights of Citizen Wives in Zimbabwe' in United Nations (ed) above n 64 at 116. Arguably the *Lovelace v Canada* case was also about 'citizenship' and belonging. See Knop above n 31 at 358–72. Human Rights Committee General Comment No 19 at paras 5, 7. Human Rights Committee General Comment No 28 at para 26.

[437] Tamale above n 42 at 54.

poignant example of this is the Kenyan case of *Virginia Otieno v Joash Ougo*, where a woman lost the right to bury her husband in the city where they had spent most of their married life, in order that the deceased's family of origin could bury him at their 'family' homestead.[438] She was merely a stranger, not entitled to make decisions about her husband's final resting place. Here we can see how in some personal law systems women are seen and treated as 'stateless' persons. The difference is that the woman may never be given full citizenship rights in her marital family in the same way that a stateless person may be given refugee status and the rights which come with that, which may include an option to apply for naturalisation in the receiving country.

It has long been stated that property ownership is a route for women to move from dependence to independence. The chapter now moves on to consider issues of property distribution through death.

Death

The British Broadcasting Corporation's correspondent in Kinshasa recounted a revealing story about the death of his landlord and the fight for the rent that ensued:

> It started the day that he died . . . Even as the rest of the family was wailing or praying by the side of his coffin, a succession of uncles, brothers and sons came to knock on my gate, each one declaring he was now the rightful owner of the house, and demanding the cash.

The report went on:

> The law courts do not count for much here in Kinshasa. Their judges are as underpaid and as easily corrupted as most other civil servants . . . So the dispute over who is the rightful owner of the house, and how the rent money is shared out just rumbles on and on, with no prospect of a just settlement.[439]

Evocative as the story is, a few facts leap out at one. The first is the sheer desperation of the relatives, who could not even wait until the body was laid to rest. The second is the relatives themselves: 'uncles, brothers and sons'. Where were the aunts, sisters and daughters? The third thing which strikes one is the 'dispute over who is the rightful owner of the house'. If there were sons, there must have been a mother, who is mentioned in the dispatch. Why was the house not rightfully hers? Whilst this dispute 'rumbled on', where were the wife and children expected to live? Who would fend for them? Given that the courts were said 'not [to] count for much', to whom could the wife and children turn with their problems? In short,

---

[438] *Virginia Otieno v Joash Ougo* (1982–1988) 1 KAR 1049.
[439] M Dummett 'Inheritance Dispute Kinshasa Style', downloaded from: http://news.bbc.co.uk/1/hi/world/from_our_own_correspondent/29762447.stm 26 April 2003.

this vignette captures with humour and poignancy an everyday occurrence for many women on the African continent today—widowed and without hope.[440] The problem is exacerbated by the fact that people die without leaving wills, which are in any event not part of the 'African way' of doing things. The assumption is that the wider family will work with and provide for the 'immediate' family which remains.[441] However, urbanisation and capitalism have done much to remove this collective accountability. The economic crisis facing Africa means that old customary notions of inheritance 'on behalf of the wider family group' have been replaced by a more individualist sense of entitlement.

Let us start with a discussion of the 'idealised' customary position. There are as many customary laws on inheritance as there are marriage types. What follows is a summary of the commonalities found in some patrilineal societies.[442] On the death of a man, it was said that the eldest male relative inherited the property.[443] This was done in a representative or administrative capacity. The deceased's property was to be used to look after the remaining family, hence the preference for a male heir. The assumption was that women would leave the family of origin to marry. Giving women the property might result in it being passed to a 'foreign family'.[444] If the man had children then it would be the eldest son who would inherit. If the son was a minor then a guardian would be appointed from within the family to administer the property until he reached maturity. The wife was not entitled to inherit from her husband.[445]

It is of course true to say that the system was subject to change and manipulation. There are reports that show that the families did not always select the eldest male relative as the heir, but the person deemed most responsible and likely to fulfil support and proper administrative obligations towards the family.[446] There are also case reports which show that women, and particularly daughters, were prepared to challenge the 'male inherits presumption'.[447] This includes the Nigerian case of *Nzekwu v Nzekwu*, where the judge held that male heir presumption, which

[440] See generally U Ewelukwa 'Post-Colonialism, Gender, Customary Injustice: Widows in African Societies' (2002) 24 *Human Rights Quarterly* 424; Empowering Widows in Development *Widows without Rights: The First International Widow's Conference* (London, Empowering Widows in Development, 2001).

[441] See the opinion of Ngcobo J in the South African Constitutional Court decision in *Bhe v Magistrate Khayelitsha* CCT-49-03.

[442] There have been several studies done on inheritance throughout Africa. J Wengi (ed) *The Law of Succession in Uganda: Women, Inheritance Laws and Practices* (Kampala, Women and Law in East Africa, 1994); W Ncube and J Stewart (eds) *Widowhood and Inheritance Laws, Customs and Practices in Southern Africa* (Harare, Women and Law in Southern Africa, 1995).

[443] Dzidzornu notes that in Ghanaian patrilineal societies the property passed to the man's wider family. Dzidzornu above n 112 at 502.

[444] Naggita above n 134 at 47; Banda above n 242.

[445] Government of South Africa above n 292 at 110.

[446] A Armstrong 'Rethinking Culture and Tradition in Southern Africa. Research from WLSA' in A Stewart (ed) *Gender, Law and Social Justice* (Oxford, Blackstone, 2000) 87.

[447] *Bhe v Magistrate Khayelitsha* above n 441, *Chihowa v Mangwende* 1987 (1) ZLR 228. But see *Vareta v Vareta* SC–126–90 (Unreported), *Magaya v Magaya* 1999 (1) ZLR 100.

allowed the son to alienate property during the lifetime of the widow, was 'barbarous and repugnant to natural-justice, equity and good conscience'.[448]

Despite these random incursions into the customary 'laws' of inheritance, it is true to say that urbanisation, the demands of capitalism and the impact of structural adjustment programmes have all lead to the abandonment of the idea of communal or family responsibility on the part of the person inheriting, with the result that often women have found themselves unsupported and unable to access land and property in their own right.[449] Not able to support themselves or their children, some women resort to sex work (prostitution) or throw themselves at the mercy of employers, who exploit their vulnerability by making them work long hours for little pay.

The last two decades of the twentieth century saw governments in Africa making a concerted effort to introduce legislation regulating intestate succession. They were influenced in part by the development goals that required them to ensure that women could access property and, in particular, land. Inheritance is one of the key ways in which property passes.[450] Governments also came under pressure from lobby groups within their countries and international agencies without.[451] They pointed out the suffering endured by women after the death of a husband, father and breadwinner. The rights culture gaining ground internationally also played its part.[452] The reporting guidelines to CEDAW require states to address the rights and obligations of widows and daughters, including the ability to inherit land, whether these rights and obligations are the same for husbands and brothers, whether there are any mourning rituals and the issue of the levirate.[453] The African Commission has also asked states parties to report on women's access to property, including by way of inheritance.[454]

[448] *Nzekwu v Nzekwu* [1989] 2 NWLR 373 cited by E Nwosu 'The Law and Women: Theory and Practice' in Constitutional Rights Project (ed) *Unequal Rights: Discriminatory Laws and Practices against Women in Nigeria* (Lagos, Constitutional Rights Project, 1995) 18 at 18–19. For other cases see Government of Nigeria (2003) above n 96 at 13; Ewelukwa above n 440 at 462–65.

[449] F Butegwa 'Mediating Culture and Human Rights in Favour of Land Rights for Women in Africa: A Framework for Community Level Action' in A An Na'im (ed) *Cultural Transformation and Human Rights in Africa* (London, Zed Press, 2002) 108 at 111.

[450] Royal Tropical Institute (KIT) and OXFAM *Gender Perspectives on Property and Inheritance* (Amsterdam, KIT and Oxford, OXFAM, 2001).

[451] D Narayan *et al Voices of the Poor. Can Anyone Hear Us?* (Washington DC, World Bank, 2000) at 198–200. World Bank *Engendering Development through Gender Equality in Rights, Resources and Voice* (Washington DC, World Bank, 2001) 121.

[452] See Declaration on the Elimination of All Forms of Discrimination against Women 1967 art 6; CEDAW 1979 art 14, specifically art 14(2)(g), art 16(1)(h); CEDAW General Recommendation No 21 paras 34–35.

[453] United Nations, Commonwealth Secretariat and IWRAW *Assessing the Status of Women: A Guide to Reporting under the Convention on the Elimination of All Forms of Discrimination against Women* (London, Commonwealth Secretariat, 2000) paras 37–39 at 44. See also Human Rights Committee General Comment No 28 para 26.

[454] R Murray *The African Commission on Human Rights and International Law* (Oxford, Hart Publishing, 2000) at 44.

In pushing through legal change despite local resistance, governments can be seen to be attempting to fulfil their obligations under article 2(f) and 5(a) of CEDAW 1979, and article 18(3) of the African Charter, as well as the sub-regional instruments and initiatives on securing women's rights. Most recent, of course, has been the African Protocol on Women's Rights, which has article 20 on widows' rights and article 21 on the right to inheritance. Moreover the AU Declaration on Gender Equality 2004 provides that states have a duty to: 'Actively promote the implementation of legislation to guarantee women's land, property and inheritance rights including their right to housing.'[455]

Countries that introduced legislation included Ghana in the mid-1980s,[456] Zambia[457] in the late 1980s, Zimbabwe[458] and Uganda in the late 1990s.[459] The Constitution of Malawi also protects women from deprivation of property, including that acquired by inheritance.[460] The South African legislature has acted to prohibit gender-based inequalities, which would include any rules that say that women cannot inherit family property.[461]

The statutes tried to lay out a framework for the division of property on death. Not surprisingly, the existence of polygyny and the importance of recognising the expectations of the wider family created some strange hybrids.[462] As a basic minimum, all made provision for the wife, or wives if a polygynous situation pertained. Radically, Burkina Faso changed the law to allow the wife, who used not to be entitled to inherit anything, to be the sole heir.[463] The inheritance law of the Côte d'Ivoire recognises that where the spouses have opted for a matrimonial property regime of community of property, the remaining spouse is automatically entitled to half the total estate. Thereafter the spouse would also be eligible for

---

[455] AU Solemn Declaration on Gender Equality in Africa 2004 art 7.

[456] Intestate Succession Law 1985 (PNDCL 111); G Woodman 'Ghana Reforms the Law of Intestate Succession' (1985) *Journal of African Law* 118; Intestate Succession (Amendment Law 1991) (PNDC Law 264). See an example of the mischief that the amendment was designed to prevent in Dzidzornu above n 112 at 519 fn 69. Woodman above n 1 at 205 fn 34. However, it is worth noting that the Akan, who comprise a large proportion of the population of Ghana, are matrilineal and object to the 'patrilineal' law, thus highlighting the difficulty of trying to impose a 'one size fits all' law on disparate groups.

[457] The Intestate Succession Act 1989 Cap 59 of the Laws of Zambia. SARDC *Zambia* above n 201 at 42–43. C Himonga 'Protecting the Minor Child's Inheritance Rights' in A Bainham (ed) *International Survey of Family Law* (Bristol, Jordan Publishing, 2001) 457; C Himonga 'Inheritance Conflicts over the Matrimonial Home: Safeguarding the Family against Homelessness' in A Bainham (ed) *International Survey of Family Law 2003* (Bristol, Jordan Publishing, 2003) 461.

[458] Administration of Estates Amendment Act 1997. The Act is discussed in Banda above n 242.

[459] Government of Uganda (2000) above n 133 at 17, 69–70. But see Naggita above n 134 at 46–48. See also Constitution of Uganda 1995 Art 31(2).

[460] Constitution of Malawi 1994 s 24(2)(c).

[461] South Africa Equality Act 2000 s 8(c). Sinclair 'Embracing New Family Forms' above n 3 at 824 fn 118; *Juleiga Daniels v Campbell NO* CCT 40/03 at para 23.

[462] The Zambian Intestate Succession Act 1989 s 5 is one such statute. See WLSA Zambia *Inheritance in Zambia: Law and Practice* (Lusaka, WLSA, 1994) 82.

[463] Government of Burkina Faso (1998) above n 11 at 26.

supplementary benefits 'after the children, the brothers and sisters, the father and then the mother of the deceased'.[464] However, where the parties wish to keep their assets separate, then unless the deceased leaves a will, the inheritance 'does not have to be shared with the spouse but is divided among descendants and those cited by the 1964 law'.[465] It goes without saying that these changes have been actively resisted.[466] These conflicts between law and social practice can also be seen in case law, with some judges willing to give women equal inheritance rights to men[467] and others not.[468] Even in countries like Mozambique with a long history of formal gender equality, one finds that discriminatory customary-based practices are tenacious and difficult to change.[469]

Changes in inheritance legislation also made provision for the deceased's children, those born both within the bonds of marriage and outside it. Where they differed was over what role and share was to be played and given to the deceased's wider family.[470]

On their face these laws are progressive. They bind all courts and family councils. Realistically though, if a woman finds herself before the family council at the point of distribution of the estate, it is doubtful that she will feel able to challenge any deviations from the law, or indeed take her grievance on appeal. It could be argued that the individual construction of the human rights language, which formed the impetus for legal change, does not adequately capture the complexity of family relations.

In Islamic countries women inherit proportionately less than men.[471] In Egypt women are supposed to inherit 'half as much as male relatives of the same degree of relation to the deceased'.[472] The assumption is that the daughter will marry and become the responsibility of her husband.[473] An Na'im contends that this presumption has sometimes led to daughters in Egypt not being awarded any property.[474] Part of the justification for the inequality is said to be the fact that men have obligations which women do not. These include giving dower for a wife or wives. The obligations also include the requirement to provide for a wife or wives and any children. Some women have argued that the dower element could be forfeited if their

---

[464] Toungara 'Changing the Meaning of Marriage' (2001) above n 12 at 39.
[465] *Ibid* at 45.
[466] *Ibid.*
[467] Perhaps one of the best examples of this is the Tanzanian case of *Ephraim v Pastory*. See Mhoja above n 267 at 296–97. See also the Zimbabwean decision of *Chihowa v Mangwende* 1987 (1) ZLR 228 (SC), *Mojekwu v Mojekwu* (1997) 7 NWLR (Pt 512) 283. See also Dzidzornu above n 112 at 503–4; *Bhe v The Magistrate Khayelitsha* (CC) above n 441.
[468] *Magaya v Magaya* above n 447; *Mthembu v Letsela and Another* above n 191.
[469] SARDC *Mozambique* above n 332 at 39–41
[470] SARDC *Zambia* above n 201 at 43.
[471] An Na'im (ed) *Islamic Family Law* above n 10 at 161–62.
[472] *Ibid* at 161.
[473] Quassem above n 66 at 29 n 35.
[474] An Na'im (ed) *Islamic Family Law* above n 10 at 161.

inheritance entitlement was raised to half. Sometimes people will transfer property to their female relatives during their lifetimes to avoid the application of the rules.[475]

Changes made to the Tunisian Personal Status Code mean that an only daughter is able to inherit her parent's estate in its entirety through statutory reversion.[476] Moreover, provision is made for a 'mandatory bequest in favour of the daughter's children if she should predecease her father'.[477] However, An Na'im contends that women still inherit half as much as their brothers.[478]

It is noteworthy that few legal systems meet the requirements of article 21 of the African Protocol to the effect that widows are entitled to receive an equitable share in the husband's property[479] and that 'women and men shall have the right to inherit, in equitable shares, their parents' properties'.[480] Egypt entered an objection to this provision during the consideration of the Protocol at the March 2003 ministerial meeting.

The construction, in patrilineal societies, of the woman as an 'outsider' in the marital family always works against her. Widows are often blamed for the deaths of their husbands—even if the husbands die in hospital of medically certified diseases. In situations like this, it becomes difficult for a woman to exercise her 'rights' and demand her share of the property. Many women are afraid that demanding a fair settlement will result in them being labelled witches and accused of having killed their husbands.[481] The accusation can sometimes be used as a tactic for depriving a widow of the marital property. Having been called a witch, it is unlikely she will want to confirm the slur by demanding her full entitlement.[482] Asked why they did not try to persuade their husbands to write wills in order to avoid some of the problems of property grabbing that occur with intestacy, women at a seminar on land in Zimbabwe noted:

> We are afraid of asking our husbands to make wills. He would ask, 'What makes you think I am going to die?' Or he would become suspicious that we want to kill him. His relatives would also be surprised. They would say he is too much ruled by his wife.[483]

This reluctance appears to defy class, so that even urban and middle class women have been reluctant to claim their entitlements.[484] Of course it may well be that

---

[475] 'Out of the Shadows, into the World' *Economist* (London, 19 June 2004) 29.
[476] Government of Tunisia (2000) above n 75 para 1042.
[477] *Ibid.*
[478] An Na'im (ed) *Islamic Family Law* above n 10 at 162.
[479] African Protocol on Women's Rights art 21(1).
[480] *Ibid* art 21(2).
[481] Cf Akande above n 60 at 12. See also Mhoja above n 267 at 291.
[482] World Health Organization *World Report on Violence and Health* (Geneva, WHO, 2002) 128.
[483] M Chenaux-Repond, *Women Farmers' Position: Our Response to the Report of the Land Tenure Commission* (1996) cited in Banda above n 242 at 529.
[484] Dzidzornu above n 112 at 505. D Martin 'Law, Custom and Economic Empowerment of Women in Sub Saharan Africa: A Conceptual Framework' in A Stewart (ed) *Gender, Law and Social Justice* (Oxford, Blackstone, 2000) 71 at 75–77.

with time and greater financial contribution by women to the acquisition of family property, this reluctance will pass.

A related issue is that of guardianship of children. As already noted, in patrilineal societies, once bridewealth has been paid, the children are said to 'belong' to the male line. Algeria has used its Family Code to override the assumption that guardianship of children on the death of their father followed the male line. Instead it is now given to the mother.[485] This is in keeping with the recently adopted African Protocol on Women's Rights, which provides in article 20(b) that:

> a widow shall automatically become the guardian and custodian of her children, after the death of her husband, unless this is contrary to the interests and welfare of the children.

During the March 2003 ministerial meeting finalising the African Protocol, Egypt and Sudan placed on record their objections to this provision. By way of contrast, Tunisia is fully in compliance.[486] However, in both Algeria and other African countries grounded in traditional practice, a woman may see it as being in her children's best interests that they remain within the family unit of the deceased husband. Claiming her rights may bring her into direct conflict with this aim, thus highlighting one of the age-old conundrums about exercising one's rights—they may sometimes lead to a curtailment of the entitlements of others.[487] Here one also sees the clash of individualist principles operating within a cultural milieu that is not grounded in individualism.[488]

The complexity of winding up an estate using the formal institutions and processes makes it likely that few people will bother to use the law. Also, the cost associated with engaging assistance to mediate the labyrinth of rules, alien concepts and languages presupposes that the estate is large and worth a great deal of money. Realistically most people in Africa would be classified as cash-poor, thus making it unlikely that they will actively engage with formal processes.[489] There is of course here the need to understand that judges and other administrators charged with enforcing the law, may themselves not be in agreement with the rights contained in the new inheritance laws, seeing them as reflecting the perspective of the dominant group or an alien ethos. Research from Tanzania shows that the police refuse to assist widows who are being harassed by their dead husbands' relatives, on the grounds that it is a family matter.[490] The principal of the Judicial College in Zimbabwe, who trains magistrates, recounted this experience

---

[485] Government of Algeria (1998) above n 73 at 42.
[486] Government of Tunisia (2000) above n 75 para 1042.
[487] Cf J Eekelaar 'Personal Rights and Human Rights' (2002) 2 *Human Rights Law Review* 181 at 187–91.
[488] Dzidzornu above n 112 at 501.
[489] See Sachs J in *Juleiga Daniels v Campbell NO* CCT 40/03 at para 23.
[490] Mhoja above n 267 at 292.

of a training session on the Administration of Estates Amendment Act 1997 in Bulawayo, the second city and home to the Ndebele people, who have at times experienced brutality at the hands of the Mugabe regime based in the capital Harare:[491]

> I did a group in Matebeleland. There were a few of them who were Ndebele. They said that it (the law) sounded too Shona to them. I explained that we as professionals were there to implement and interpret the law—we weren't there to repeal it. I told them not to be emotional. I urged them to do the right thing.[492]

It has long been clear that the formal framing of rights does not lead to a transformation of gender relations and the equitable redistribution of property. Far from it. There is a vast literature on the reasons for women's continued socioeconomic and cultural subordination.[493] Part of the difficulty of women using the law is that they may not be aware of its provisions. Even when aware of the provisions of the law, there is often great reluctance to utilise it to vindicate their rights. This may be because women do not see themselves as entitled persons.[494] Research in Zambia has linked this to the bridewealth institution, which is said to reduce women to the status of minors, which leaves them without a voice in the management of family resources. Indeed the report goes further to suggest that the bridewealth institution constructs women as property and that this makes it difficult for women to claim their rights on the death of the husband.[495] Dzidzornu argues that education efforts should not only focus on women; he sees it as equally important that men be educated to understand that they can, and should, consider settling the matrimonial property on their wives in preference to the wider family.[496] Given that in many circumstances women do not even know what their husbands earn during life, this idea is radical. It requires a shift from thinking communal to thinking nuclear, and also from seeing the wife as an outsider, even to her husband, to seeing her as truly 'his nearest and dearest'.

It is as well to acknowledge that gendered notions of entitlement are also apparent around men's ability to inherit from their wives. A man who sought to claim his deceased wife's property would have his masculinity questioned. Indeed, he would be mocked.

Linked to the difficulties of using the law are mourning rituals that are unique to women. Again the African Protocol has tried to address these in article 20,

---

[491] J Alexander, J McGregor and T Ranger *Violence and Memory* (Oxford, James Currey, 2000).

[492] As quoted in Banda above n 242 at 548.

[493] An excellent bibliography can be found in KIT (2001) above n 450. See also L Wanyeki (ed) *Women and Land in Africa: Culture, Religion and Realizing Women's Rights* (London, Zed Press, 2002). Margaret Owen founded the Widows in Development Project http://www.widowsrights.org.): M Owen *A World of Widows* (London, Zed Press, 1996).

[494] Banda above n 242 at 548.

[495] SARDC *Zambia* above n 201 at 41.

[496] Dzidzornu above n 112 at 520.

which provides in part that: 'widows are not to be subject to inhuman, humiliating or degrading treatment'.[497] Some of the practices envisaged by these prohibitions include mourning rites in Igbo land, Nigeria, which are said to involve:

> [S]having her hair, sitting on a bare floor besides the husband's corpse, not bathing until the corpse is buried, wailing loudly around the community for three consecutive Ibo market weeks and not remarrying for at least one year after the husband's death. It is of particular interest that men who lose their wives are not expected to go through these customs.[498]

Mhoja notes that in Tanzania women are sometimes subject to 'widow cleansing', which involves being forced to have intercourse with strangers. This exposes them to a high risk of contracting HIV or, if the husband died of AIDS, of passing on the HIV virus. Mhoja also sees the mourning rites as a violation of a woman's right to bodily integrity and as infringing upon her dignity.[499] Amongst the Nnewe of Nigeria there is a custom (*nrachi*) whereby a father may keep one of his daughters with him. She may not marry but can bear children. On his death she is entitled to inherit the same share of his property as if she were a man. Her children are also eligible to inherit. A 'non-*nrachi*' woman and her children would not be so entitled. An inheritance dispute arose when the second cousin of the deceased sought to disinherit the grandchildren and great-grandchildren born of daughters who had not undergone the *nrachi* initiation. It was argued that the grandchildren could not inherit because *nrachi* had not occurred. This custom was held to be a violation of women's rights and repugnant to natural justice and morality by the Court of Appeal in Enugu.[500] Specifically it was noted that:

> The *Nrachi* custom, which is designed to oppress and cheat women, compromises the basic tenets of family life, is inequitable and judicially unenforceable. Accordingly, a female child does not need the performance of *Nrachi* in order to inherit her deceased father's estate.[501]

Citing CEDAW, the judge further noted that the practice of *nrachi* encouraged prostitution and was in violation of article 6 of CEDAW. Furthermore, he cited article 5(a) of CEDAW on cultural stereotyping, and declared the granddaughter to have been a victim of the violation this provision. Finally he noted: 'In view of

---

[497] African Protocol on Women's Rights art 20(a). See also arts 1(g), 2(1)(b), 3, 4(1), 4(2)(c), 5(d). Enugu State in Nigeria has enacted The Prohibition of Infringement of a Widow's and Widower's Fundamental Human Rights Law No 3 of 2001. Government of Nigeria (2003) above n 96 at 15.

[498] F Oyekanmi 'Women and the Law: Historical and Contemporary Perspectives in Nigeria' in A Obilade (ed) *Women in Law* (Lagos, Southern University Law Centre and Faculty of Law, 1993) 28 at 30. See also Ewelukwa above n 440 at 437–39. Government of Nigeria (2003) above n 96 at 9, 49.

[499] Mhoja above n 267 at 292, 300.

[500] *Muojekwo and Others v Ejikeme and Others* [2000] 5 NWLR 402. Head note reproduced in (2000) 3 *Commonwealth Human Rights Law Digest* 116.

[501] *Ibid* at 116.

the fact that Nigeria is a party to the Convention, the courts of law should give or provide teeth to its provisions.'[502]

The unequal inheritance laws and the discriminatory mourning rituals all constitute clear violations of the human rights of women. The strategies for changing the discriminatory practices discussed have included: calls for education, particularly outreach programmes; bringing cases to court; lobbying the government to change the law and incorporate international human rights norms into domestic law; lobbying international agencies to try to persuade the government to implement the law; and finally, networking with other advocates to send information and complaints to the African Commission.[503] Ultimately, though, it seems to come down to one point, and that is:

> [G]ender based discrimination is a cultural product; the culture itself must be changed if we are to achieve a society based on equality. The most viable way . . . is by transforming popular beliefs and attitudes.[504]

Conclusion

This chapter has considered the debates around the construction of family in African societies. Through an examination of the content of some family laws, gender relations have been laid bare. What is clear is that there is a plethora of human rights norms which call for state intervention in the domestic sphere. Moreover, those norms make clear that men and women are to have equal rights within marriage and at its end. States have tried to respond to these demands by changing domestic laws.[505] However, a consideration of state reports to the Women's Committee has shown that there is a wide gap between legal provision and practice on the ground. This suggests a pessimistic assessment of the ability of 'home grown' instruments, such as the African Protocol on Women's Rights, to bring about real and lasting change.

Two issues that are closely related to women's rights in the family are violence against women and reproductive rights. These are considered in the next chapter.

---

[502] As cited in C Odinkalu 'Customary Law and Women's Inheritance Rights in Commonwealth Africa' (2000) 13 *Interights Bulletin* 39 at 40.
[503] Mhoja above n 267 at 301–2.
[504] Mhoja above n 267 at 303. Dzidzornu above n 112 at 520.
[505] CEDAW arts 3, 24. CEDAW General Comment No 21 para 50.

5

Violence against Women and Reproductive Rights

In 2002, the Vice-President of Uganda made public the fact that she had, over a number of years, been subjected to physical violence by her husband.[1] The reaction to this news was revealing. While she received some support, it came mainly from women's groups. The majority of people, men as well as women, said that she had been wrong to make public what had taken place within the privacy of the home. Evidently the 'privacy' argument trumped the woman's right to protection from violence.[2] Reinforced in this way, the Vice-President's husband went on to say publicly that he had 'only' slapped her and that this was to correct her, because he felt she needed to know that her public role ended at the gate. When she entered the home she was his wife and not the Vice-President of Uganda. In her role as wife, she had to submit to him and not be impertinent.

What is interesting to me about this story is the idea of the universal wife: a good wife is one who is obedient and who does not challenge accepted gender roles. Also worthy of note is that the universality of this view of wifehood is reinforced by the Vice-President's status, which does not exempt her from the 'good wife is a silent wife' paradigm, nor does it protect her from violence within the home.[3] The public response to the story is also worth commenting on. If a woman of the Vice-President's stature can be assaulted by her husband, seemingly with impunity, what must it be like for other 'ordinary' women? Indeed what was the effect of the backlash against the Vice-President?[4] No doubt it served to warn women experiencing violence that reporting the violence might result in them being pilloried and their suffering ignored. Why, then, bother engaging publicly with the issue?

---

[1] S Tamale 'Gender Trauma in Africa' (2004) 48 *Journal of African Law* 50 at 55.

[2] An excellent judicial consideration of gender-based violence is Sachs J's judgment in the South African constitutional case of *S v Baloyi* 2000 (2) SA 425. On the results of privileging privacy over protection see 435–37.

[3] Cf *S v Baloyi* above n 2 at 431.

[4] The woman in question is no longer Vice-President, and some have linked her demotion with the making public of her private difficulties.

The issue of violence against women has been with us for centuries. Within marriage women continue to experience violence in silence, unable to speak because of social-cultural constraints and also because they know that they are not always able to count on the support of either family or community. Added to this has been state institutional indifference to their plight. Although all of these constraints still exist today, the degree to which they continue is markedly different from community to community[5] and country to country. In much the same way that the concept of family shifts within and across national boundaries, so too the causes and consequences of violence against women differ from state to state and within states.[6]

This chapter attempts to discuss the issue of violence against women within the family.[7] In doing this it must be conceded from the outset that violence within the family manifests itself in many different ways and cannot be discussed adequately without reference to external factors. The efforts of the international community to address the issue of violence against women are also considered. The discussion then moves on to examine a related issue, that of reproductive rights.

Defining the problem

The United Nations Special Rapporteur on Violence against Women has defined violence within the family as including:

> [W]oman battering, marital rape, incest, forced prostitution, violence against domestic workers, violence against girls, sex selective abortions and female infanticide, traditional violent practices against women including forced marriage, son preference, female genital mutilation and honour crimes.[8]

It is not possible in this section to consider all the forms of violence identified by the Special Rapporteur. This is in no way to suggest that violence between

---

[5] See for example, H Becker 'The Least Sexist Society? Perspectives on Gender, Change and Violence among the Southern African San' (2003) 29 *Journal of Southern African Studies* 1.

[6] Amnesty International *Broken Bodies, Shattered Minds. Torture and Ill-Treatment of Women* (London, Amnesty, 2001); Special Rapporteur on Violence against Women Integrating the Human Rights of Women and the Gender Perspective: Violence against Women in the Family E/CN.4/1999/68 (hereafter cited as Special Rapporteur on Violence against Women in the Family (1999a)) para 8; L Tibatemwa-Ekirikubinza *More Sinned against than Sinning: Women's Violent Crime in Uganda* (Copenhagen, Criminalistisk Institut, 1998).

[7] World Health Organization (WHO) *World Report on Violence and Health* (Geneva, WHO, 2002) 89–103.

[8] Special Rapporteur on Violence against Women (1999a) above n 6 at para 7. See also Report of the Special Rapporteur on Violence against Women, Its Causes and Consequences, 5 February 1996, Ms Radhika Coomaraswamy Submitted in Accordance with Commission on Human Rights Resolution 1995/85 E/CN.4/1996/53 paras 23–28; F Pickup, S Williams and C Sweetman *Ending Violence against Women: A Challenge for Development and Humanitarian* Work (Oxford, OXFAM, 2001).

intimates is the only form of family violence. Indeed the importance of recognising the breadth and scope of violence against women can be seen in the plethora of international instruments and initiatives to tackle violence against women. Moreover, focusing on violence against women is in no way to suggest that men do not experience violence too. Clearly some do.[9] However, here I am focusing on gender-based violence, which is defined in CEDAW General Recommendation 19 as:

> [V]iolence which is directed against a woman because she is a woman or that affects women *disproportionately*.[10] (emphasis added)

International developments around violence against women

Simply and powerfully, the African Charter provides: 'Human beings are inviolable. Every human being shall be entitled to respect for his life and integrity of his person.'[11] This echoes the standard provisions on the right to life, liberty and security of the person,[12] the right to be free from degrading and inhuman treatment,[13] found in international human rights instruments. The Organization of American States (OAS) Convention on the Prevention, Punishment and Eradication of Violence against Women 1994[14] directly addresses the issue of violence against women. It defines violence as:

> [A]ny act or conduct, based on gender, which causes death or physical, sexual or psychological harm or suffering to women, whether in the public or private sphere.[15]

It calls on states parties to 'pursue . . . policies to prevent, punish and eradicate such violence'.[16]

Following on from the Vienna Conference in 1993, the United Nations General Assembly adopted the Declaration on the Elimination of Violence against Women 1993 (DEVAW).[17] It defines violence against women in the family as including:

---

[9] D Narayan, R Chambers, M Shah and P Petesch *Voices of the Poor Crying Out for Change* (Oxford, Oxford University Press, 2000) 122.

[10] CEDAW General Recommendation No 19 on Violence against Women UN Doc A/47/38 para 6.

[11] African Charter art 4.

[12] ICCPR art 9(1); African Charter art 6.

[13] UDHR art 5; ICCPR art 7; African Charter art 5.

[14] OAS Convention on the Prevention, Punishment and Eradication of Violence against Women 1994 reproduced in (1994) 33 *International Legal Materials* 1535.

[15] *Ibid* art 1.

[16] *Ibid* art 7, which then goes on to list activities and initiatives which the state can and should engage in to fulfil its duties. See arts 7(a)–(h).

[17] General Assembly Declaration on the Elimination of Violence against Women 1993 (DEVAW) GA Res 48/104.

> Physical, sexual and psychological violence occurring in the family including battering, sexual abuse of female children in the household, dowry related violence, marital rape, female genital mutilation and other traditional practices harmful to women, non spousal violence and violence related to exploitation.[18]

It is fair to say that the DEVAW built on attempts by the Committee on the Elimination of Discrimination against Women to tackle the silence within the Convention on the Elimination of All Forms of Discrimination against Women 1979 (CEDAW) on the topic of violence against women. The word 'violence' does not appear anywhere in the Convention. The closest that the Convention comes to addressing the issue is in article 6 on exploitation of women, but this article explicitly identifies trafficking and forced prostitution as the 'evils' requiring attention. No other forms of violence are mentioned, even in article 16 on marriage and family relations. The Women's Committee attempted to repair the omission by way of general recommendation. Specifically the Committee made two General Recommendations on violence.[19] Of these, it is General Recommendation No 19 that has had the most far-reaching effect. It is a considered and comprehensive examination of violence that starts with the statement:

> Gender-based violence is a form of discrimination that seriously inhibits women's ability to enjoy rights and freedoms on a basis of equality with men.[20]

The introduction of a gendered construction of violence was an important step. Another important development marked in General Recommendation No 19 is the Committee's adoption of the notion of state responsibility for the actions of non-state actors as enunciated by the Inter American Court on Human Rights in the case of *Velasquez Rodriguez v Honduras*.[21] This was a case concerning the disappearance of a student called Velasquez, by person or persons unknown. His family alleged that the Honduran government had been complicit in his disappearance and, when told about the disappearance, had failed to act to investigate or to provide any other remedy. The Honduran government denied any involvement in the disappearance and argued that it could not be held accountable for violations committed by non-state actors. Finding for the complainant(s), the Inter American Court on Human Rights held that:

> The State has a legal duty to take reasonable steps to prevent human rights violations and to use the means at its disposal to carry out a serious investigation of violations

---

[18] DEVAW art 2(a). The term 'violence against women' is defined in art 1. See too Beijing Platform for Action 1995 s D para 113.

[19] CEDAW General Recommendation No 12 on Violence against Women UN Doc A/44/38; CEDAW General Recommendation No 19 above n 10.

[20] *Ibid* para 1.

[21] *Velasquez Rodriguez v Honduras* (1989) 28 *International Legal Materials* 291. Also reported as *Velasquez Rodriguez Case (Honduras)* 4 Inter Am general recommendation No 19 Ct HR Ser C No 4 1988.

committed within its jurisdiction, to identify those responsible, to impose appropriate punishment and to ensure the victim adequate compensation. This obligation implies the duty of State Parties to organize the governmental apparatus and, in general, all the structures through which public power is exercised, so that they are capable of juridically ensuring the free and full enjoyment of human rights.[22]

This clear articulation of the doctrine of due diligence means that the old police classic 'we do not deal with "domestics"' can no longer be used as an excuse for inaction.[23] That, at least, is the theory. The reality, as reflected by research undertaken by an NGO[24] in Ghana is that:

> Out of the about ten per cent (of complainants) who reported (violence), 68 per cent were dissatisfied with the responses from the agencies.[25] Respondents said that it is possible for the police to make a mockery of you should you report a case of rape by a spouse or tell you to go back to your home to get the issue settled.[26]

At this point, it is also worth noting that violence against women has been addressed at various United Nations Conferences, including Cairo,[27] Vienna, where it was the rallying cry for women from all over the world,[28] and of course Beijing.[29] Indeed the issue has progressed to the stage where the Special Rapporteur on Violence against Women has seen fit to equate violence against women in the private sphere with torture, noting that:

---

[22] *Velasquez Rodriguez case (Honduras)* above n 21 para 174. See also Special Rapporteur on Violence against Women (1999a) above n 6 at para 24. See also CEDAW General Recommendation No 19 para 9; DEVAW art 4(d); CEDAW General Recommendation No 24 para 15; R Cook 'Accountability in International Law for Violations of Women's Rights by Non-State Actors' in D Dallmeyer (ed) *Reconceiving Reality: Women and International Law* (Washington, American Society for International Law, 1993) 93; J Crawford (UN International Law Commission Special Rapporteur on State Responsibility) 'Revising the Draft Article on State Responsibility' (1999)10 *European Journal of International* Law 435 at 440. See also Amnesty International *Broken Bodies, Shattered Minds: Torture and Ill-Treatment of Women* (London, Amnesty International, 2001) 23–40.

[23] Special Rapporteur on Violence against Women, Its Causes and Consequences, above n 8, paras 31–39. H Charlesworth and C Chinkin *Boundaries of International Law* (Manchester, Manchester University Press, 2000) 148–51.

[24] A Tagoe 'Nkyinkyim Violence against Women Project' in Womankind Worldwide (ed) *What Works Where? Successful Strategies to End Violence against Women* (London, Womankind Worldwide, 2002) 12.

[25] *Ibid.* Defined as police, social welfare and hospitals.

[26] *Ibid* at 12. This is in spite of a very progressive constitution. *Ibid.* See also Amnesty International 'Kenya: Rape—The Invisible Crime' AI Index: AFR 32/001/2002 at 16–26, 28–29.

[27] International Conference on Population and Development, Cairo (18 October 1994) UN Doc A/CONF.171/13 para 4.9.

[28] Vienna Declaration and Platform for Action (1993) paras 18, 38. Charlesworth and Chinkin above n 23 at 73.

[29] Beijing Platform for Action 1995 paras D112–23; UN General Assembly Report of the Ad Hoc Committee of the Whole of the Twenty-Third Special Session of the General Assembly. Further Actions and Initiatives to Implement the Beijing Declaration and Platform for Action UN Doc A Res/S-23/3 (hereafter Beijing + 5 Outcome Document (2000)) paras 13, 14.

Depending on its severity and the circumstances giving rise to state responsibility domestic violence can constitute torture or cruel, inhuman and degrading treatment or punishment under the International Covenant on Civil and Political Rights and the Convention against Torture and other Cruel, Inhuman or Degrading Treatment or Punishment. This view challenges the assumption that intimate violence is a less severe or terrible form of violence than that perpetrated directly by the State.[30]

There have also been African initiatives around the issue of violence against women, not least the Addendum to the Southern African Development Community (SADC) Declaration on Gender and Development focusing on the issue of Violence against Women.[31] Using the Vienna Declaration and Programme of Action as the starting point,[32] the SADC document identifies violence as including physical, emotional, economic, sexual and psychological violence.[33] Specific forms of violence identified include economic deprivation, sexual abuse of children, marital rape, trafficking and forced prostitution, and female genital mutilation.[34] Although an important sub-regional initiative, the SADC Declaration binds only the 14 countries belonging to the SADC bloc.

It is the African Protocol on Women's Rights which, when in force, will set the standard for the whole continent, or more accurately, ratifying states. Having the benefit of examining all the initiatives that have so far been made internationally, the African Protocol shows a comprehensive understanding of the problem, and addresses violence as it affects girls and women in their many different guises, as daughters, wives, mothers, widows,[35] the elderly,[36] refugees and during times of armed conflict. The Protocol defines violence against women as meaning:

[A]ll acts perpetrated against women which cause or could cause them physical, sexual, psychological, and economic harm, including the threat to take such acts; or to undertake the imposition of arbitrary restrictions on or deprivation of fundamental freedoms in private or public life in peace time and during situations of armed conflict or of war.[37]

[30] Special Rapporteur on Violence against Women (1996) above n 8 at para 42. She says that this view deserves the attention of 'rapporteurs and treaty bodies that investigate these violations together perhaps with appropriate NGO experts and jurists' (at para 50). See also paras 43–49. Mackinnon has long argued that 'private violence' should be equated with torture. See C Mackinnon 'On Torture: A Feminist Perspective on Human Rights' in K Mahoney and P Mahoney (eds) *Human Rights in the 21st Century: A Global Perspective* (The Hague, Kluwer, 1993) 21. See also R Copelon 'Intimate Terror: Understanding Domestic Violence as Torture' in R Cook (ed) *Human Rights of Women: National and International Perspectives* (Philadelphia, University of Pennsylvania Press, 1994) 116.
[31] The Prevention, Eradication of Violence against Women and Children: An Addendum to the 1997 Declaration on Gender and Development by SADC Heads of State or Government 1998 (hereafter SADC Addendum on Violence 1998). (1999) *SADC Gender Monitor*
[32] SADC Addendum on Violence 1998 above n 31 art 4.
[33] *Ibid* art 5.
[34] *Ibid* art 5(a)(b).
[35] African Protocol on Women's Rights art 20(a).
[36] *Ibid* art 22(b).
[37] *Ibid* art 1(j). See also preamble paras 8, 11, 12.

In line with the DEVAW,[38] the Protocol links issues of violence against women to existing human rights norms.[39] Indeed so comprehensive is the coverage of the Protocol that it even enters headlong into the pornography debate, siding with those who see pornography not as an issue of choice or freedom of expression, but of discrimination and oppression of women.[40]

National developments and constraints

An examination of national laws shows that in recent years African states have been proactive in the formulation of legislation prohibiting violence against women.[41] State reports to the Women's Committee also highlight policy initiatives taken to address the issue of violence against women.[42] However, despite these legal gains, research on the ground[43] shows quite clearly that gender-based violence is a persistent and serious problem that affects women throughout their life cycles.[44] The reasons for this appear to be linked to issues of gender, and specifically the place of women in the home, women's economic dependence and lack of voice.[45] Some commentators have even linked the issue of violence against

---

[38] DEVAW art 3. See also CEDAW General Recommendation No 19 para 7.

[39] African Protocol on Women's Rights art 4 on the right to life, integrity and security of the person.

[40] African Protocol on Women's Rights art 13(m). T Maitse 'Political Change, Rape and Pornography in Post Apartheid South Africa' in C Sweetman (ed) *Violence against Women* (Oxford, OXFAM, 1998) 55. See also Optional Protocol to the Convention on the Rights of the Child on the Sale of Children, Child Prostitution and Child Pornography GA Res 54/263 Annex II.

[41] Tanzania Sexual Offences Special Provisions Act 1998 discussed in L Sheikh 'TAMWA: Levina's Song-Supporting Women in Tanzania' in H Chigudu (ed) *Composing a New Song: Stories of Empowerment from Africa* (London, Commonwealth Secretariat, 2003) 95 at 118–20. On Namibian efforts to enact a Domestic Violence statute see D Hubbard and E Cassidy 'Family Law Reform in Namibia: Work in Progress' in A Bainham (ed) *International Survey of Family Law 2002* (Bristol, Jordan Publishing, 2002) 255 at 266–67; C Edwards 'Law and Non Consensual Sex in Marriage' in NCSM (ed) *Non Consensual Sex in Marriage Project* (London, CHANGE, 2002) 1.

[42] Initial Report of States Parties: South Africa (1998) CEDAW/C/ZAF/1 (hereafter Government of South Africa (1998)) 111–20. See also Constitutional Rights Project 'Seminar on Discriminatory Laws and Practices against Women in Nigeria: Recommendations' in Constitutional Rights Project *Unequal Rights: Discriminatory Laws and Practices against Women in Nigeria* (Lagos, Constitutional Rights Project, 1995) vii–viii.

[43] A Armstrong *Culture and Choice: Lessons from Survivors of Gender Violence in Zimbabwe* (Harare, Violence against Women Research Project, 1998); Tibatemwa-Ekirikubinza above n 6; Human Rights Watch *Just Die Quietly: Domestic Violence and Women's Vulnerability to HIV in Uganda* (London, Human Rights Watch, 2003) (hereinafter cited as Human Rights Watch (2003) Uganda Report).

[44] F Banmeke 'Violence and Sexual Abuse of Women' in B Owasonoye (ed) *Reproductive Rights of Women in Nigeria: The Legal, Economic and Cultural Dimensions* (Lagos, Human Development Initiatives, 1999) 77 at 87; C Sweetman 'Editorial' in C Sweetman (ed) *Gender and Lifecycles* (Oxford, OXFAM, 2000) 2; F Sakala 'Violence against Women in Southern Africa' in P McFadden (ed) *Southern Africa in Transition: A Gendered Perspective* (Harare, SAPES, 1998) 27.

[45] P McFadden 'Sex, Sexuality and The Problems of AIDS in Africa' in R Meena (ed) *Gender in Southern Africa: Conceptual and Theoretical Issues* (Harare, SAPES, 1992) 157.

women to the payment of bridewealth by men for women. They say that the bridewealth institution leads men to treat women as property that they have 'bought'.[46] Seen in this light, a man may feel entitled to 'chastise' his wife if he thinks that she is 'out of line'.[47]

Equally important in understanding violence against women is the socialisation of women, some of whom are brought up to believe that it is the 'right' of the man to beat his wife. Research conducted in Uganda showed that '70 percent of men, and 90 percent of women, believed that it was justifiable, in one or more circumstances, for a man to beat his wife or female partner'.[48] Indeed I have heard it said that some women believe that when a man beats you, it shows that he loves you; he would not bother 'chastising' someone he did not love. This argument is not unlike that made to justify beatings meted out to children. 'Correcting' a child, it is argued, is a way of trying to put the child on to the right path and is for the good of the child. Indeed article 20 of the African Charter on the Rights and Welfare of the Child specifically provides:

> Parents or other persons responsible for the child shall have the primary responsibility for the upbringing and development of the child and shall have the *duty*
>
> (c) to ensure that domestic discipline is administered with humanity and in a manner consistent with the inherent dignity of the child.[49] (emphasis added)

This provision makes it difficult to know what is meant by the phrase 'child abuse',[50] not least because one person's 'abuse' is another's 'reasonable chastisement' or 'domestic discipline'.[51] Read together with article 31 on the duties of a child, and specifically the injunction that a child has a duty to obey her elders at all times,[52] it becomes clear that it is difficult for a child to challenge her elders. This is one of the explanations for early marriage and all the negative consequences resulting therefrom.[53]

---

[46] WLSA *Lobolo: Its Implications for Women's Reproductive Rights* (Harare, WLSA, 2002) at 40–42. CHANGE 'NCSM Marriage, Culture and Violence: Messages from the Survey' CHANGE Non Consensual Sex in Marriage Project 2002 (cyclostyle) (hereafter CHANGE 'Marriage, Culture and Violence') at 2; A Mugisa 'Stop Bride Price Women Demand' *New Vision* (Kampala, 25 July 2002) downloaded from: http://allafrica.com/stories/printable/200207250061.html at 1.

[47] I Ovonji-Odida 'Non Consensual Sex in Marriage and Other Forms of Sexual Abuse: Uganda' in CHANGE (ed) *Non Consensual Sex in Marriage Information Package Number One* (London, CHANGE, 1999): see in particular 4–7.

[48] *Ibid.* See also J Wagman 'Domestic Violence in Rakai Community, Uganda' (2003) 45 *Women's Health News* 7–8 at 8. J Seager *The Atlas of Women* (London, The Women's Press, 2003) 26–27.

[49] ACRWC art 20(1)(c). 'Domestic discipline' is undefined.

[50] Child abuse is prohibited. *Ibid* art 16(1).

[51] WHO *World Report on Violence* (2002) above n 7 at 59–86; S Mayisela 'Working with a Rejected, Emotionally Deprived Child' (2001) 39 *Women's Health Project Review* 6–8.

[52] ACRWC art 31(a).

[53] Forum on Marriage and the Rights of Women and Girls *Early Marriage: Whose Right to Choose?* (London, Forum on Marriage and the Rights of Women and Girls, 2000) (hereafter Forum on Marriage) at 7, 22.

Perhaps one of the most common reasons given by women for not reporting violence is the fear of reprisals, and also the sense that their complaints will not be taken seriously by the police. The Nigerian report to CEDAW confirms this, noting that police treat complaints dismissively, laughing them off as 'two fighting' or as a 'husband and wife problem'.[54] It may well be that the lack of faith in state institutions is well founded. Research in Zambia showed that the courts did not appear to take violence against women very seriously.[55] Courts made outrageous statements, including a case in which a man was alleged to have killed his wife and the judge said 'The deceased was to blame';[56] and in another that:

> The provocation offered by your wife was such that any self respecting person would lose control. The facts reveal that you did not use a lethal weapon; you only used your fists. I feel this case calls for maximum leniency.[57]

This institutional complicity leads to reliance on the informal dispute resolving mechanism of the family, which, as already noted in the discussion on divorce in Chapter 4, is geared towards therapeutic mediation or 'reconciling the parties' so that they can 'go away and live in peace with each other'. The other pervasive influence in the violence conundrum is the increased power of the church. There has been an explosion of the newer Christian churches whose membership comprises mainly women. Religion has always been conservative. Although the various strands of both Islam and Christianity identify different roles for men and women, they ultimately emphasise the importance of mutual respect and tolerance between the sexes.[58] Nevertheless, it is sad, but true, to say that the translation and interpretation of religious texts has often resulted in women being told that it is their duty to submit themselves to their husbands or partners.[59] Occasionally the submission is expected to stretch to sexual harassment and abuse at the hands of church officials.[60] The difficulty with this line of reasoning has been that it has

---

[54] Combined Second and Third Periodic Reports of States Parties: Nigeria CEDAW/C/NGA/2–3 (hereafter Government of Nigeria (1997)) at 23; Human Rights Watch *South Africa Violence against Women and the Medico-Legal System* (London, Human Rights Watch, 1998); Edwards above n 41at 5–6.

[55] In C Watts, O Osman and E Win (eds) *The Private is Public: A Study of Violence against Women in Southern Africa* (Harare, WILDAF, 1995) 41.

[56] *Ibid.*

[57] *Ibid.*

[58] H Mahdi 'The Position of Women in Islam' in A Imam *et al* (eds) *Women and the Family in Nigeria* (Dakar, Codesria, 1989) 59; F Sow 'Fundamentalism, Globalisation, and Women's Human Rights in Senegal' in J Kerr and C Sweetman (eds) *Women Reinventing Globalization* (Oxford, OXFAM, 2003) 69; M Kukah 'Women, the Family and Christianity: Old Testament, New Testament and Contemporary Concepts' in A Imam *et al* (eds) *Women and the Family in Nigeria* (Dakar, Codesria, 1989) 65; S Minkah-Premo *Coping with Violence against Women* (Accra, Asempa Publishers, Christian Council of Ghana, 2001) 61.

[59] S Ahmed 'Islam and Development: Opportunities and Constraints for Somali Women' in C Sweetman (ed) *Gender, Religion and Spirituality* (Oxford, OXFAM, 1998) 69; Beijing Platform for Action 1995 para 24.

[60] S Minkah-Premo above n 58 at 46.

left women in the impossible position of feeling unhappy at being assaulted or emotionally and psychologically abused, but feeling unable to break out of the marriage because of its religious sanctity, and also because the gendered construct of a woman's role in these religions is the foundation of the home, thus adding extra pressure on women to persevere in wholly unacceptable circumstances. It also means that the husband or partner is able to take advantage of the religious beliefs because he knows that the woman will persevere and is unlikely to leave him, thus lessening the chances that he will see any reason to modify his unacceptable behaviour.

All this notwithstanding, the church has been identified as having an important role to play in the reduction of violence against women and in educating the general public about other health-related issues, including HIV.[61] Faith may also offer a solace to women who are HIV positive.[62] Moreover, religion has sometimes played a useful role in court decisions. In the Nigerian case of *Mojekwu v Mojekwu*,[63] the court held in favour of a woman having equal rights of inheritance with a man, reasoning:

> In my humble view, it is the monopoly of God to determine the sex of a baby and not the parents. Although the scientific world disagrees with this divine truth, I believe that God, the creator of human beings, is also the final authority of who should be male and female. Accordingly for a custom or customary law to discriminate against a particular sex is to say the least an affront on the Almighty God himself. Let nobody do such a thing.[64]

---

[61] World Vision 'Mobilise Churches in Fight against AIDS Says World Vision Presenter at Barcelona AIDS Conference' 6 July 2002 downloaded from: http://www.worldvision.org/worldvision/pr/nsf/stable/pr_barcelona_presenter. United Nations Office for the Coordination of Humanitarian Assistance, IRIN (hereafter IRIN)'Swaziland: AIDS Indaba Highlights Conflicting Views' 18 October 2003 downloaded from: http://www.irinnews.org/reports.asp?ReportID=36743&SelectRegion=Southern Africa.

[62] See L Doyal and J Anderson *My Heart is Loaded: African Women with HIV Surviving in London: Report of a Qualitative Study* (London, Terrence Higgins Trust, 2003) 16. However, the authors note that:

> [A]number of women feared rejection by other members of the congregation. Several reported that moral judgments against HIV positive people were especially strong within the church and this made them reluctant to reveal their status . . . Several also reported being afraid that information given in church might get back to their family members.

Ibid.

[63] *Mojekwu v Mojekwu* [1997] 7 NWLR Pt. 512 at 305.

[64] *Ibid* as cited in B Owasonoye 'Right to Family Assets and Succession' in B Owasonoye (ed) *Reproductive Rights of Women in Nigeria: The Legal, Economic and Cultural Dimensions* (Lagos, Human Development Initiatives, 1999) 114 at 134. Churches in Africa have played an important role in both education and development initiatives. B Walker 'Christianity, Development and Women's Liberation' in C Sweetman (ed) *Gender, Religion and Spirituality* (Oxford, OXFAM, 1998) 15.

Economic violence

One of the most pervasive forms of violence against women is economic.[65] Both the SADC Addendum Declaration on Violence[66] and the African Protocol on Women's Rights define violence as including economic harm.[67] Here a man may use the threat of withholding money, or indeed withhold money, for food and other necessities from the woman to keep the wife 'in line', as punishment or simply because he does not feel like fulfilling his obligations of support towards the family. Ekpiken notes an interesting counter to this, where a man with an educated wife refuses to 'let her' work and forces her to stay at home because of his jealousy.[68] Sometimes it is the unemployment of the husband that is the cause of the violence. The reason for spousal violence is that the husband feels emasculated by his inability to fulfil his role as family breadwinner, and therefore takes out his frustration on the wife and children.[69]

Linked to economic violence is the issue of sexual harassment of women within the workplace. A woman trying to earn a living in order to keep her family fed and children in school may be subject to sexual harassment. Although proscribed in the African Protocol,[70] it is clear that the practice known as the 'carpet interview' in Zimbabwe is prevalent. CEDAW General Recommendation No 19 provides that sexual harassment constitutes violence against women.[71] The Indian Supreme Court has made particularly good use of this General Recommendation in the case of *Vishaka & Others v State of Rajasthan & Others*,[72] where the court found that a woman had been sexually harassed (she had actually claimed that she had been raped by work colleagues). It ordered the government to formulate anti-sexual harassment policies and drew up guidelines using CEDAW General

---

[65] Cf Human Rights Watch (2003) Uganda Report above n 43 at 36–39.

[66] SADC Addendum on Violence 1998 above n 31 art 5.

[67] African Protocol on Women's Rights art 1(j).

[68] R Epikene 'Violence against Women: The Case of Cross-River State' in Constitutional Rights Project (ed) *Unequal Rights: Discriminatory Laws and Practices against Women in Nigeria* (Lagos, Constitutional Rights Project, 1995) 63–65.

[69] Narayan *et al* above n 9 at 118–20.

[70] African Protocol on Women's Rights art 13(c). See also Vienna Declaration and Platform for Action 1993 para 18.

[71] CEDAW General Recommendation No 19 para 17. The Côte D'Ivoire is one of the few (African) countries explicitly prohibiting sexual harassment. Côte d'Ivoire, Act No 98–756 of 23 December 1998 cited in chapter on Côte d'Ivoire in Center for Reproductive Rights *Women of the World: Francophone Africa Laws and Policies Affecting Their Reproductive Lives* (New York, Center for Reproductive Rights, 2001)127–28. See also the South African Employment Equity Act No 55 of 1998 s 6(3); *Nstabo v Real Security* Case No C259/2000 Labour Court, South Africa judgment of 14 November 2003; N Naylor 'The Long Walk to Freedom from Sexual Harassment' paper presented at the Advancing Women's Rights Conference, Hosted by the Women's Law Centre, Cape Town, available at http://www.wlce.co.za/conference2003/2003conference_naylor.php.

[72] *Vishaka & Others v The State of Rajistan & Others* 1997 (7) SC 392.

Recommendation No 19 as a model.[73] In another sexual harassment case[74] the Supreme Court of India held that the two most important provisions in the Indian Constitution were the right to life and the right to freedom from discrimination (based on sex).[75] The court also referred to the provisions in the Covenant on Economic, Social and Cultural Rights 1966 on the right to fair conditions of work, to hold that sexual harassment violated women's rights to earn a living and in turn to a right to life and to be free from discrimination based on sex.[76] Finally, the Court noted:

> The message of international instruments such as the Convention on the Elimination of All Forms of Discrimination against Women, 1979 ('CEDAW') and the Beijing Declaration which directs all States Parties to take appropriate measures to prevent discrimination of all forms against women besides taking steps to protect the honour and dignity of women is loud and clear.[77]

Sexual violence against women

Equally important, particularly in light of the HIV/AIDS pandemic engulfing most of Southern Africa[78] and, to a lesser extent, other regions, is the issue of sexual violence against women. Emphasis on the impact of HIV is in no way to suggest that sexual violence would be acceptable if the danger of contracting the HIV virus were not a factor. Rape and violence against women is particularly marked in South Africa.[79] Some have linked the high incidence of rape to the after-effects of apartheid-inspired violence, which so brutalised the black community that aggres-

---

[73] UNIFEM *Bringing Equality Home: Implementing CEDAW* (New York, UNIFEM, 1998) 19.

[74] *Apparel Export Promotion Council v Chopra* (1999) 1 SCJ 265. The case relied heavily on the *Vishaka* case on the issue of sexual harassment of women. See para 20.

[75] *Ibid* at para 22.

[76] *Ibid.*

[77] *Ibid.* See also African Protocol on Women's Rights art 13(d).

[78] O Shisano and M Zungu-Dirwayi 'HIV/AIDS in South Africa: Entitlement and Rights to Health-Implications of the 2002 HIV Survey' in J Murison *et al* (eds) *Remaking Law in Africa: Transnationalism Persons and Rights* (Edinburgh, Centre of African Studies, 2004) 313; J Van Woudenberg *Women Coping wth AIDS. We Take It as It Is* (Amsterdam, Royal Tropical Institute, 1998); Commonwealth Secretariat and Maritime Centre of Excellence for Women's Health *Gender Mainstreaming in HIV/AIDS: Taking a Multi-Sectoral Approach* (London, Commonwealth Secretariat, 2002) 32; M Heywood 'Preventing Mother-to-Child Transmission in South Africa: Background, Strategies and Outcomes of the Treatment Action Campaign Case against the Minister of Health' (2003) 19 *South African Journal on Human Rights* 278.

[79] Research conducted in the Gauteng province of South Africa revealed that a woman was killed by her partner every four days. L Vetten 'Research into Preventing Intimate Femicide in the Gauteng Province' (2003) 45 *Women's Health Project Review* 14 at 14; See also Amnesty International above n 26 at 14–15.

sion became the norm.[80] Elsewhere Mandela has noted: 'Violence thrives in the absence of democracy, respect for human rights and good governance.'[81]

I would like to make clear that in discussing issues of sexual violence against women in South Africa, I do not wish to confirm stereotypes or to engage in the construction of Africa as a disproportionately violent or 'diseased continent'.[82] Commenting on the South African Truth and Reconciliation Commission, Ross notes that the only other time that women's voices were heard in respect to violations which affected them directly rather than indirectly, was when they were questioned about sexual violence against them. Ross cautions against focusing women's experience of violence solely on sex, because it defines the experience of being a woman in very narrow and unsatisfactory terms.[83] These caveats notwithstanding, it is worth noting that in its report to CEDAW, the South African government did concede that 'South Africa has a high incidence of all forms of violent crime, including gender violence'.[84]

Part of the explanation for the high rate of sexual violence is rooted in the gendered construction of men and women's sexuality. Armstrong's research in Zimbabwe throws light on why these perceptions may exist.[85] 'Nice'—for which read 'good'—women do not easily consent to sex, particularly outside marriage. It is a man's job to 'persuade' a woman into having sexual intercourse with him.[86] In this equation it becomes unclear when persuasion tips over into coercion. Moreover, given the fact that 'traditionally' unmarried women remained under the guardianship of their fathers, who could claim 'seduction damages' for the 'deflowering' of an unmarried daughter and the reduction in her bridewealth value, it becomes clear that a woman's sexuality was never hers to make decisions about in the first place, and by definition consent was not hers to give either. Indeed, what sometimes followed (and indeed still follows) was (and is) pressure to marry the man.[87]

---

[80] S Armstrong 'Rape in South Africa: An Invisible Part of Apartheid's Legacy' in C Sweetman and F de Selincourt (eds) *Population and Reproductive Rights* (Oxford, OXFAM, 1994) 35at 36; Shisano and Zungu-Dirwayi previous n 78 at 316.

[81] N Mandela, 'Foreword' in WHO *World Report on Violence and Health* (Geneva, WHO, 2002) ix.

[82] See Arnfred's discussion on South African President Mbeki's claim that Africa is again being portrayed as the 'diseased' (dark) continent. S Arnfred (ed) *Rethinking Sexualities in Africa* (Lund, Nordic Africa Institute, 2004) 10. See too K Jungar and K Olinas 'Preventing HIV? Medical Discourses and Invisible Women' in S Arnfred (ed) *Rethinking Sexualities in Africa* (Lund, Nordic Africa Institute, 2004) 97 at 97–99. But see also E Cameron 'Aids Denial and Holocaust Denial-Aids, Justice and the Courts in South Africa' (2003) 120 *South Africa Law Journal* 525.

[83] F Ross *Bearing Witness: Women and the Truth and Reconciliation Commission in South Africa* (Cambridge, Polity Press, 2002) 19.

[84] Government of South Africa (1998) above n 42 at 111.

[85] Armstrong above n 43 at 76–80.

[86] Cf I Ovonji-Odida above n 47 at 4. See also CHANGE 'Marriage, Culture and Violence' above n 46 at 1.

[87] On the issue of compulsion see Human Rights Committee General Comment No 28 para 24. See also the outcry following the decision of the Supreme Court of Zimbabwe in the case of *Katekwe v*

Minority and indigenous women are another group that experience a high incidence of (sexual) violence against them not only from within the group, but also at the hands of the majority.[88]

Non-consensual sex in marriage

The construct of women as 'sexual property' is most clearly pronounced in the marital relationship.[89] If part of the reason for the payment of bridewealth is that the man is entitled to enjoy exclusive sexual access to the woman, then some might say by way of extension that that includes sex on demand. Here it is important to move away from a definition of rape based solely on penetrative sex. With this in mind, the CHANGE project defines non-consensual sex in marriage thus:

> A woman is subjected to non-consensual sex in marriage by her husband if she is involved in sexual activity either without her consent or where her consent is obtained under coercive conditions.[90]

Armstrong notes that the issue of consent is further complicated by the different perceptions about what constitutes coercion of men and women. In her research she asked men if they had ever forced their wives to have intercourse against their will. The same question was asked of wives: had they ever been forced to have intercourse against their will? The discrepancy in response was wide, with 17 per cent of men saying that they had forced unwilling spouses to have sex, as opposed to 36 per cent of women who reported having been coerced.[91] Research conducted by Human Rights Watch in Uganda showed that: 'Thirty-four out of fifty women expressly confirmed that their husbands physically forced them to have sex against their will.'[92] This shows quite clearly that some men still hold on to the notion that 'when a woman says no, she really means yes, or at least,

---

Muchabaiwa 1984 (2) ZLR 112. The court held that the promulgation of the Legal Age of Majority Act meant that once a woman reached the age of 18, majority, her father/guardian would lose the right to claim seduction damages for her. F Banda 'Inheritance and Marital Rape' in A Bainham (ed) *International Survey of Family Law 2001* (Bristol, Jordan Publishing, 2001) 475 at 478–80; A Tsanga *Taking Law to the People: Gender, Law Reform and Community Legal Education in Zimbabwe* (Harare, Women's Law Centre and Weaver Press, 2003) 60–64.

[88] D Jackson *Twa Women, Twa Rights in the Great Lakes Region of Africa* (London, Minority Rights Group, 2003) 12. See also DEVAW 1993 preamble.

[89] Armstrong above n 43 at 80–83.

[90] CHANGE 'Non Consensual Sex in Marriage: Definitions Related to NCSM' in CHANGE *Non Consensual Sex in Marriage* (London, CHANGE, 2002) 2.

[91] Armstrong above n 43 at 80–81. The women in these relationships also experienced physical assault.

[92] Human Rights Watch (2003) Uganda Report above n 43 at 25.

maybe'.[93] If this is the case, then how can it be possible that a man can rape his own wife? The findings of Human Rights Watch and Armstrong are replicated in Mali:

> Malian populations and communities do not recognize the concept of reproductive and sexual health for women and girls because sexuality is and remains masculine. A husband alone decides whether to have sexual intercourse with his wife. This attitude which concerns both illiterate and highly educated populations seems normal to men and women alike because it has been so deeply engrained over centuries.[94]

Although some states have changed their laws explicitly to prohibit rape within marriage,[95] they are few and far between.[96] Indeed in Malawi there was great resistance to attempts to pass a Bill outlawing rape within marriage.[97] Sometimes change is brought about by judicial intervention.[98] The recognition of the crime of marital rape[99] has always been controversial, not least because it constitutes a 'double' incursion into the private sphere, that is a 'violation' of family privacy and the privacy of the marital relationship.[100] The African Protocol on Women's Rights provides:

> States Parties shall take appropriate and effective measures to enact and enforce laws to prohibit all forms of violence against women including unwanted or forced sex whether the violence takes place in private or public.[101]

The privacy of the marital relationship leads to many women not being able to conceive of forced sex within marriage as constituting rape. A good example of this

---

[93] *Ibid* at 79.

[94] K Maiga 'Legal Tools for the Prevention of Female Genital Mutilation, Case Study: Mali' Afro-Arab Consultation on Legal Tools for the Legal Protection of Female Genital Mutilation, Cairo, 21–23 June 2003 1 at 4; A Diallo 'Paradoxes of Female Sexuality in Mali: On the Practices of *Magonmaka* and *Bolokoli-kela*' in S Arnfred (ed) *Rethinking Sexualities in Africa* (Lund, Nordic Africa Institute, 2004) 173 at 182. Although reinforcing Maiga's view, Diallo does acknowledge that there are some who think that married women 'have the right to request and enjoy sexual intercourse in perfect harmony with religious and customary requirements'. *Ibid* at 182.

[95] Namibia Rape Act 8 of 2000 s 2(3) as cited in D Hubbard and E Cassidy 'Family Law Reform in Namibia: Work in Progress' in A Bainham (ed) *International Survey of Family Law 2002* (Bristol, Jordan Publishing, 2002) 255 at 265. Zimbabwe Sexual Offences Act [Cap 9:21] s 8(1). See Special Rapporteur on Violence in the Family (1999a) above n 6 para 231.

[96] P Sen 'Change Programme on Non Consensual Sex in Marriage: Briefing Paper. Ending the Presumption of Consent' in CHANGE (ed) *Non Consensual Sex in Marriage Project Information Package Number One* (London, CHANGE, 1999)1.

[97] R Tenthani 'Row Over Marital Rape Bill' (2001) downloaded from: http://.news.bbc.co.uk/hi/english/world/africa/newsid_1728000/11728875.stm; Edwards above n 41 at 1. See also V Nkiwane *Marital Rape: What are the Consequences of Removing the Husband's Immunity from Prosecution?* (Dissertation submitted in partial fulfilment of the requirements for the Post Graduate Diploma in Women's Law, Women's Law Centre, University of Zimbabwe, 2000).

[98] *H v H* 1999 (2) ZLR 358. F Banda 'Inheritance and Marital Rape' in A Bainham (ed) *International Survey of Family Law 2001* (Bristol, Jordan Publishing, 2001) 475 at 484–86.

[99] Arguably proscribed by CEDAW art 2(g), which calls on states to: 'repeal all national penal provisions which constitute discrimination against women'.

[100] Cf Special Rapporteur on Violence against Women (1996) above n 6 para 64.

[101] African Protocol on Women's Rights art 4(2)(a). Cf CEDAW art 2(g).

is the group of Sierra Leonean women who were interviewed by Physicians for Human Rights about their experiences of violence during the civil war. Eighty per cent of the women were in favour of the legal protection of women's rights. However, over half of these noted that a husband had a right to beat his wife and that it was the duty of the wife to have intercourse with her husband whenever he demanded it; her own wishes were irrelevant.[102] Within the Sierra Leonean context this may be linked to the brutalisation of women during the civil war, which has led the women to believe that rape only occurs when a stranger forces one to have sex without one's consent. It is not an unusual view though.[103]

Meanwhile in Ghana women reported that refusing to have sexual intercourse with their husbands could result in their being beaten, especially if the husbands were drunk.[104] Indeed there are some national legal systems that define rape as excluding rape within marriage. The Nigerian Criminal Code[105] defines rape as follows:

> Any person who has unlawful carnal knowledge of a woman or girl, without her consent, or with her consent if the consent is obtained by force or by means of threats or intimidation of any kind, or by fear or harm, or means of a false and fraudulent representation as to the nature of the act, *or in the case of a married woman, of impersonating her husband* is guilty of an offence called rape.[106] (emphasis added)

The Nigerian report to CEDAW then goes on to note:

> In a traditional setting, spousal rape is inconceivable. Under Nigerian Laws in both section 357 of the Criminal Code and section 282 of the Penal Code, a husband cannot be charged with marital rape. Once the marriage is subsisting and the wife has attained puberty then any sexual intercourse with her is never rape.[107]

---

[102] Physicians for Human Rights (2002) 'War Related Sexual Violence in Sierra Leone: A Population Based Assessment' (23 January 2002) downloaded from http://www.phrusa.org/research/sierra_leone.report.html at 9.

[103] P McFadden above n 45 at 187–88; Amnesty International above n 26 at 27.

[104] Narayan *et al* above n 9 at 121.

[105] Nigeria Criminal Code (Chapter 77 Laws of Federation 1990) as cited in Government of Nigeria (1997) above n 54 at 22. Cf Botswana Penal Code (Amendment) Act 1998 [Cap 08:01] s 141 cited in WLSA, Botswana *Chasing the Mirage: Women and the Administration of Justice* (Gaberone, WLSA, 1999) 52.

[106] Government of Nigeria (1997) above n 54 at 22. In 1995 the Nigerian Constitutional Rights Project called for the expansion of the definition of rape to include marital rape. Constitutional Rights Project Communiqué 'Seminar on Discriminatory Laws and Practices against Women in Nigeria' in Constitutional Rights Project *Unequal Rights: Discriminatory Laws and Practices against Women in Nigeria* (Lagos, Constitutional Rights Project, 1995) vi at vii. The Kenyan Penal Code is similarly drafted. See s 139 of the Penal Code (Chapter 63) as cited in Amnesty International above n 26 at 7.

[107] *Ibid.* See also the English case of *Knott v Mohamed* [1969] 1 QB 1, where an English court decided on appeal that, although 'distasteful', the practice of early marriage was part of Nigerian 'culture' and had to be respected. In this case a 26-year-old Nigerian man had brought his teenage wife to England. She had gone to the doctor to have a sexual transmitted infection treated and the doctor had called the social services. The issue was whether the girl should be removed into care. The court of first instance said yes, the appeal court said no. See also D Narayan and P Petesch *Voices of the Poor from Many Lands* (Washington DC, World Bank; New York, Oxford University Press, 2002) 41–42.

There are other countries that specifically exclude non-consensual sex in marriage from the definition of rape.[108] For example, the Ethiopian Penal Code defines rape as compelling

> a woman to submit to sexual intercourse *outside wedlock*, whether by the use of violence or grave intimidation, or after having rendered her unconscious or incapable of resistance.[109] (emphasis added)

Here it would appear that right to freedom from degrading and inhuman treatment does not extend to freedom from sexual assault and indeed compulsion within marriage, which seems to be recognised and indeed validated by the law.

The Tanzanian Penal Code is also quite revealing in its construction of rape, providing as it does that a person is guilty of rape if he

> has unlawful carnal knowledge of a woman or a girl, without her consent, or with her consent if the consent is obtained by means of threats or intimidation of any kind, or by fear of bodily harm, or by means of false representations as to the nature of the act, or in *the case of a married woman by impersonating her husband.*[110] (emphasis added)

The Tanzanian position is worth exploring further. The statute appears to be explicit in its exclusion of the notion of marital rape. If anything, it suggests that a married man *could*, if he so wished, use threats or intimidation to induce his wife to have intercourse with him, and this would be within the law. Although section 66 of the Tanzanian Marriage Act 1971 provides that it is illegal to assault one's spouse, the Tanzanian country report to the 4th World Conference for Women in Beijing stated that wife assault was common in Tanzania and that 90 per cent of women had been battered, or had experienced violence in some form.[111] This would seem to suggest that the legal system is ineffective in adequately tackling issues of violence, and also that there appears to be a 'culture' of violence whereby men feel that they are entitled to 'chastise' their wives, or indeed force them to have intercourse, and the wives feel (or are led to believe) that it is the husband's prerogative so to do.

From the foregoing, it would appear that the woman's position in (customary) marriage does not allow for the notion of bodily integrity when it comes to sexual intercourse with her husband; nor do notions of inhuman and degrading treatment apply to involuntary intercourse with the husband. For a wife to complain

---

[108] In the Côte d'Ivoire marital rape is not considered a criminal offence: Center for Reproductive Rights above n 71, chapter on 'Côte d'Ivoire' at 127. The same applies in Benin: Center for Reproductive Rights above n 71, chapter on 'Benin' 24 at 39.

[109] Ethiopia Penal Code art 589.

[110] Tanzania Penal Code Cap 16 s 130. Although the Tanzanian law on violence (against women) was radically overhauled by the Sexual Offences Special Provisions Act 1998, it is telling that the marital rape exemption has been retained. See Sheikh above n 41 at 120.

[111] Center for Reproductive Law and Policy and FIDA Kenya *Women of the World Report: Anglophone Africa* (New York, CRLP, 1997) 125.

about unwanted sexual advances is to lay herself open to divorce. This, for many African women, is the nightmare scenario, not least because they run the risk of losing their children—or think they do. There is also the issue of family pressure to remain in the marriage—that could be for purposes of maintaining family honour, or to avoid her family having to give back some of the bridewealth paid for her, or because they cannot afford to have her back.

The situation is rendered even more difficult by the legal system and the difficulties inherent in bringing a rape prosecution. The non-recognition of the crime of marital rape in most legal systems is a major stumbling block, for one cannot be heard to complain about the violation of a non-existent right. Even if the legal system did recognise the crime of marital rape, the question would still need to be asked—how many members of the public would know about it and, knowing about it, how many would be in a position to prosecute the case to its conclusion? On a continent which does not have social security systems that act as a safety net such as those available to women in the north, albeit that they do not always function adequately, a woman's ability to complain about non-consensual intercourse is somewhat constrained.

Sexual violence against young women and girls

There has also been a marked increase in sexual violence against young girls in Africa.[112] Here it is worth noting that children comprise the majority population on the continent.[113] Of these, young girls are particularly vulnerable to violence, especially sexual assault, not least because there are a few people who still think that intercourse with a virgin will cure HIV/AIDS.[114] Even the majority who do not believe this myth may still see intercourse with a young girl as being 'safer' than intercourse with an older woman, because it is assumed that she will not have had many partners. Moreover, there are instances of girls being sexually abused and harassed by teachers, thus preventing them from finishing school or actively participating in school.[115] This is specifically outlawed by the African Protocol on

---

[112] B Rwezaura 'Protecting the Rights of the Girl Child in Commonwealth Jurisdictions' in A Byrnes *et al* (eds) *Advancing the Human Rights of Women: Using International Human Rights Standards in Domestic Litigation* (London, Commonwealth Secretariat, 1997) 114 at 123–26. Cf CEDAW General Recommendation No 24 para 12(b). Sexual violence violates the CRC art 34, ACRWC arts 16(1), 27.

[113] 'Children and HIV/AIDS' *Observer* (London, 11 July 2004).

[114] Amnesty International above n 26 at 15; Commonwealth Secretariat *Integrated Approaches to Eliminate Gender-Based Violence* (London, Commonwealth Secretariat, 2003) 6. This violates the CRC art 24(1).

[115] World Bank *Education and HIV/AIDS: A Window of Hope* (Washington DC, World Bank, 2002) 22, 23.

Women's Rights.[116] In its report to CEDAW, the Nigerian government undertook to promulgate a law to protect young girls and women from sexual harassment at school and in the workplace.[117] Despite national policies prohibiting discrimination against girls, abuse of girls by their teachers continues, and includes having to cook and clean for the teachers—tasks which are never assigned to boys.[118]

One of the most shocking incidents of the sexual assault of girls of school-going age occurred at a boarding school in Kenya where school boys went on a rampage and raped 71 girls. In the rampage, 19 girls died. The response of the headmaster to the rapes was astonishing. He noted that the boys had 'not meant to cause any harm', they had '*only*' wanted to rape.[119]

Equally shocking is the South African research, which showed that for many young men and women, the use of force in relationships was 'an integral part of a normal love relationship'.[120] This would appear to suggest that a 'boyfriend' or person who is known to the woman 'cannot rape' her.[121] Asked by a researcher if he would force a girl into having sex with him even if she did not want or like it, a boy in the 14- to 19-year-old urban male sample responded: 'There are no negotiations in that issue. If my penis wants it, it must get sex. No other ways about it.'[122]

Sometimes the sexual abuse comes from closer to home, at the hands of relatives, including uncles and stepfathers.[123] Reported in Swaziland is the practice of '*kulamuta*', which allows a man 'access to a wife's sisters, in most cases it is young girls'.[124] Meanwhile in Malawi:

> The culture of *fisi* allows an appointed member of (the) community to have sex with girls at age 12–14 before they can marry; 'the results of this has been girls having unwanted babies and contracted [sic] HIV/AIDS.'[125]

---

[116] African Protocol on Women's Rights art 12(1)(c); T Skard *Continent of Mothers: Understanding and Promoting Development in Africa Today* (London, Zed Press, 2003) 91.

[117] Government of Nigeria (1997) above n 54 at 14. See also M Stephens 'Women Still Living in Fear' (1999) 32 *Women's Health Project* 1 at 1.

[118] This is stereotyping and violates CEDAW art 5(a), 10(c). See also African Protocol on Women's Rights arts 3(3), 12(1)(b). Arguably the girl child's right to leisure, recreation and to participate in cultural activities enshrined in art 12 of the ACRWC is violated.

[119] Cited in O Nwanko 'Violence against Women: An Overview' in Constitutional Rights Project *Unequal Rights: Discriminatory Laws and Practices against Women in Nigeria* (1995) 50.

[120] C Varga 'Links Between Sexual Dynamics and Reproductive Health Behaviour among Kwazulu/Natal Youth' in (1999) *Women's Health News* 21 at 21; Commonwealth Secretariat and Maritime Centre of Excellence for Women's Health above n 78 at 38.

[121] Varga above n 120 at 22.

[122] *Ibid* at 21.

[123] Skard above n 116 at 94–100.

[124] Quoted in CHANGE 'Marriage, Culture and Violence' above n 46 at .3.

[125] Quoted in D Wijeyesekera 'NCSM and Health: A Connection Ignored' in CHANGE (ed) *Non Consensual Sex in Marriage* (London, CHANGE, 2002) 3.

In West Africa, the trafficking of girls for work in the domestic sector[126] opens them up to sexual and economic exploitation.[127] They work long hours and for little or no pay.[128] To address the trafficking problem, the Economic Community of West African States (ECOWAS) adopted a Declaration on the Fight against Trafficking in Persons 2001.[129] The Declaration identifies both regional and international resolutions and human rights instruments addressing the issue of trafficking, and calls on states to take practical measures to address the problem. Measures to be taken include consultation between countries of origin and transit, as well as of the victims,[130] and data gathering on the nature of the problem, particularly as it affects women and children, and on the methods used.[131] In addition to this there are to be educational campaigns using the media,[132] better training of officials,[133] and the creation of specialised anti-trafficking units within law enforcement agencies.[134]

A major difficulty confronting women who have experienced violence is that of access to justice, discussed below.

[126] Combined Fourth and Fifth Periodic Report to CEDAW: Nigeria CEDAW/C/NGA/4–5 (Government of Nigeria (2003)) at 15. Human Rights Watch *Borderline Slavery: Child Trafficking in Togo* (London, Human Rights Watch, 2003) (hereafter Human Rights Watch (2003) Togo Report). Special Rapporteur on Violence against Women (1996) above n 8 paras 77, 81.

[127] This violates CRC arts 19, 32, 34, 35. It also violates ACRWC art 15. See also the ILO Convention No 182 Concerning the Prohibition and Immediate Action for the Elimination of the Worst Forms of Child Labour, reproduced in Human Rights Watch (2003) Togo Report above n 126 at 57–60. See also Special Rapporteur on Violence against Women (1996) above n 8 paras 66–72, 86–90. Optional Protocol to the Convention on the Rights of the Child on the Sale of Children, Child Prostitution and Child Pornography. GA/RES/54/263 of 25 May 2000. See report of the Special Rapporteur on the Sale of Children, Child Prostitution and Child Pornography (4 February 2002) E/CN.4/2002/88 paras 57–59; Protocol to Prevent, Suppress and Punish Trafficking in Persons, Especially Women and Children, Supplementing the United Nations Convention against Transnational Organized Crime 2000, Adopted by UN General Assembly Resolution A/55/25 of 15 November 2000 (Palermo Protocol) available at http://www1.umn.edu/humanrts/instree/trafficking.html. A Gallagher 'Human Rights and the New UN Protocols on Trafficking and Migrant Smuggling: A Preliminary Analysis' (2001) 23 *Human Rights Quarterly* 975.

[128] Skard above n 116 at 100–101. See too an autobiographical account of domestic exploitation of young girls, M Nazer and D Lewis *Slave* (London, Virago Press, 2004).

[129] ECOWAS Declaration A/DC/12/12/01 on the Fight against Trafficking in Persons, Twenty-Fifth Ordinary Session of Authority of Heads of State and Government Dakar, 20–21 December 2001 available from http://www.ecowas.int.

[130] *Ibid* art 6.

[131] *Ibid* art 13.

[132] *Ibid* art 9.

[133] *Ibid* art 10.

[134] *Ibid* art 11.

Issues of access to justice

Johnson has identified three barriers to access to justice.[135] These are geographical, financial and socio-psychological barriers. When courts are situated a long way from where people live, then physical access becomes difficult.[136] Given that most women live in rural areas and most (criminal) courts are based in urban areas, the issue of access becomes an important one. The travel costs are often prohibitive, as are the costs of visiting the police station to give witness statements. The medical evidence necessary to prosecute may have been destroyed by the time a woman reaches a hospital or clinic which has qualified personnel.[137] Indeed the medical or health facilities may not exist at all, or, if they do exist, may be in a parlous state. It is questionable if the police and judiciary will be sympathetic to a complaint about a 'domestic matter'.

The price of justice is not only financial but may lead to the ostracisation of the woman and a difficult life for the children of the marriage. Such socio-psychological factors also militate against women making complaints. For a woman to report her husband for raping or assaulting her is to break what many consider to be the very foundation of marriage. She lays herself open to divorce and social exclusion. There is also the fear that reporting one's husband will result in him being put in prison, and the children will lose their father and the family the main breadwinner.

For some women who are raped or complain of violence, there is the danger that their families will reject them, or in extreme cases murder them to preserve the family from shame or to restore the family's 'honour'.[138] This often results in women experiencing multiple human rights violations, including the ultimate violation of the right to life. A study of violence against women, specifically murder, conducted in Alexandria, Egypt, showed that '47% of the women were killed by a relative after they had been raped'.[139]

---

[135] E Johnson 'Thinking About Access: A Preliminary Typology of Possible Strategies' in M Cappelletti and B Garth (eds) *Access to Justice Volume 3* (Florence, Tipografia,1978) at 8.
[136] See art 8 of the African Protocol on Women's Rights.
[137] Amnesty International above n 26 at 17–21.
[138] Special Rapporteur on Violence against Women in the Family (1999a) above n 6 at para 18; Beijing + 5 Outcome Document (2000) above n 29 at para 69(e).
[139] WHO *World Report on Violence* (2002) above n 7 at 93.

Strategies for combating violence against women

The World Health Organization's report on violence and health notes that although much attention is focused on assisting survivors of sexual violence, greater attention needs to be paid to primary prevention.[140] Suggestions made here include: running programmes in communities, schools and refugee settings; supporting 'culturally sensitive and participatory approaches to changing attitudes and behaviour';[141] the promotion of gender equality; programmes tackling underlying causes of violence, including economic deprivation and lack of education; and programmes reducing the vulnerability of women whilst promoting 'more gender-equitable notions of masculinity'.[142] These strategies reflect the holistic approach taken in international instruments, including DEVAW, which suggests counselling, enforcement of laws[143] and strengthening institutions[144] to ensure that women are protected and their right to be free from violence enforced. Interestingly DEVAW anticipates the active engagement of, and co-operation with, non-governmental[145] and inter-governmental regional organisations[146] in the anti-violence endeavour.[147]

The SADC Addendum on Violence, which was suggested as a template by the East Africa and SADC group during the drafting of the provisions on violence in the African Protocol on Women's Rights, puts forward a five-point plan including:

(a) legal measures,[148]
(b) social, economic, cultural and political measures,[149]
(c) services, which will include providing information on services available to victims of violence,[150]
(d) measures including education, training and awareness building,[151] and

---

[140] *Ibid* at 173.
[141] *Ibid.*
[142] *Ibid.*
[143] DEVAW art 4(f). This includes ensuring that 'the re-victimisation of women does not occur because of gender insensitive laws'. Amnesty International above n 26 at 30–34.
[144] DEVAW art 4(i).
[145] *Ibid* arts 4(e), 4(o), 4(p).
[146] *Ibid* art 4(q). See also art 5 on working with specialised UN agencies and the exchange of information and expertise.
[147] See too Commonwealth Secretariat above n 114 at 17–33.
[148] SADC Addendum on Violence above n 31 1998 arts 8–12. See also African Protocol on Women's Rights arts 4(2)(a)(b), 8(f).
[149] SADC Addendum on Violence 1998 above n 31 arts 13–15. See also African Protocol on Women's Rights arts 4(2)(c), (d).
[150] SADC Addendum on Violence 1998 above n 31 arts 16–19. See also African Protocol on Women's Rights art 4(2)(e),(f).
[151] SADC Addendum on Violence 1998 above n 31 arts 20–22. See also African Protocol on Women's Rights art 4(2)(d).

(e) the requirement that states make adequate provision for these services in their budgets.[152]

Amnesty International builds on these recommendations by suggesting that states be encouraged to ratify the Optional Protocol to CEDAW.[153] The CEDAW General Recommendation No 19 contains many of the recommendations already mentioned.[154] However, of particular note is its focus on rural women:

> States parties should report on the risk to rural women, the extent and nature of violence and abuse to which they are subject, their need for and access to support and other services and the effectiveness of the measures to overcome violence.[155]

I now move on to look at an issue closely related to violence, and that is reproductive rights.[156]

Reproductive rights

When I think about reproductive rights I imagine a maypole,[157] with the ribbons attached to the pole representing the plethora of rights comprising all that is meant by the term 'reproductive rights'. These ribbons or rights include, but are not limited to, the right to life, liberty and security of the person, the right to equality and to be free from all forms of discrimination, the right to information and education, the right to choose whether and when to have children, the right to decide if one should marry, the right to benefit from scientific progress and the right to

[152] SADC Addendum on Violence 1998 above n 31 art 24. Cf African Protocol on Women's Rights art 4(2)(i).

[153] Amnesty International above n 26 at 31.

[154] CEDAW General Recommendation No 19 para 24. CEDAW General Recommendation No 24 on Health UN Doc A/54/38/Rev 1 paras 29, 31(f). Cf Beijing Declaration and Platform for Action 1995 paras 124–29; Beijing + 5 Outcome Document (2000) above n 29 at para 90ff.

[155] CEDAW General Recommendation No 19 para 24(q). See also *ibid* para 21 and DEVAW preamble.

[156] Integration of the Human Rights of Women and the Gender Perspective. Violence against Women. Special Rapporteur on Violence against Women, Policies and Practices That Impact Women's Reproductive Rights and Contribute to, Cause or Constitute Violence against Women E/CN.4/1999/68.Add.4.21 January 1999 (hereafter Special Rapporteur on Violence against Women (1999b)); World Bank *Engendering Development through Gender Equality in Rights, Resources and Voice* (Washington DC, World Bank, 2001) 49–50; R Copelon and B Petchesky 'Toward an Interdependent Approach to Reproductive and Sexual Rights as Human Rights: Reflections on the ICPD and Beyond' in M Schuler (ed) *From Basic Needs to Basic Rights: Women's Claim to Human Rights* (Washington DC, Women Law and Development International, 1995) 343.

[157] In feudal England a maypole was a symbol of fertility.

privacy.[158] This highlights that reproductive rights comprise both civil and political and economic, social and cultural rights.

From population control to reproductive rights

There has over time been a shift from conflating population policy with reproductive rights.[159] For many years the desire to control and contain the rapid global population expansion led to states defining family planning as an essential part of demographic control. In this way issues of reproduction were not seen as individual rights, but rather as part of the state remit to control population growth as a means of facilitating development and ending poverty.[160] The most extreme example of this is China, which has the largest population in the world.[161] However, there has been a shift towards seeing 'family planning' not as the sole preserve of the state, but rather as part of the reproductive health rights of men and women.

It is the Cairo Conference of 1994[162] that has been credited with revolutionising the way we think about reproductive health and reproductive rights. Reproductive health was defined as:

> [A] state of complete physical, mental and social well-being and not merely the absence of disease or infirmity, in all matters relating to the reproductive system and to its functions and processes. Reproductive health therefore implies that people are able to have a safe and satisfying sex life and that they have the capability to reproduce and the freedom to decide if, when, and how often to do so.[163]

---

[158] These are but some of the rights included in the International Planned Parenthood Federation (IPPF) *Charter on Sexual and Reproductive Rights* (London, IPPF, 1998); CEDAW General Recommendation No 24 para 4; Special Rapporteur on Violence against Women (1999b) above n 156 paras 3–14. See also Center for Reproductive Rights (CRR) and International Programme on Reproductive and Sexual Health Law University of Toronto *Bringing Rights to Bear: An Analysis of the Work of the United Nations Treaty Monitoring Bodies on Reproductive and Sexual Rights* (New York, CRR, 2002) 14–15.

[159] J Mozze 'From Family Planning and Maternal Child Health to Reproductive Health' in C Sweetman and F de Selincourt (eds) *Population and Reproductive Rights* (Oxford, OXFAM, 1994) 6.

[160] N Visvanathan 'Introduction to Part 1' in N Visvanathan, L Duggan, L Nisonoff N Wiegersmal (eds) *The Women, Gender and Development Reader* (London, Zed Books, 1997) 20; W Wanzala 'Towards an Epistemological, Methodological Framework of Development' in P McFadden (ed) *Southern Africa in Transition: A Gendered Perspective* (Harare, SAPES, 1998) 1 at 12.

[161] Special Rapporteur on Violence against Women (1996) above n 8 paras 95–97.

[162] International Conference on Population and Development 1994 (ICPD).

[163] *Ibid* para 7.2. See also Beijing Platform for Action 1995 para 94. Holding on to these gains at the Cairo Plus 5 conference held in the Netherlands was a challenge. See Center for Reproductive Law and Policy (CRLP) *ICPD+5 Gains for Women despite Opposition* (New York, CRLP, 2000); Beijing + 5 Outcome Document (2000) above n 29 at para 72(i).

Reproductive rights are said to:

[E]mbrace certain human rights that are already recognized in national laws, international human rights documents and other consensus documents. These rights rest on the recognition of basic rights of all couples and individuals to decide freely and responsibly the number, spacing and timing of their children and to have the information and means to do so, and to attain the highest standard of reproductive and sexual health. It also includes their right to make decisions concerning reproduction free of discrimination, coercion and violence, as expressed in the human rights documents.[164]

This places us firmly within the human rights framework and gives men and women together, or individually, the right to make decisions concerning their reproductive rights with limited state interference.[165] CEDAW provides in article16(e) that men and women have:

The same rights to decide freely and responsibly on the number and spacing of their children and to have access to the information, education and means to enable them to exercise those rights.[166]

The African Protocol takes up much of the Cairo programme, and in article 14(1) on health and reproductive rights provides:

States Parties shall ensure that the right to health of women, including sexual and reproductive health is respected and promoted. This includes:

(a) the right to control their fertility;[167]
(b) the right to decide whether to have children, the number of children and the spacing of children;[168]
(c) the right to choose any method of contraception.[169]

---

[164] ICPD para 7.3. See also Beijing Platform for Action 1995 paras 95, 96, 223. CEDAW, General Recommendation No 24 para 31(e). See too World Health Organization (WHO) *Guidelines to Reporting under CEDAW* (Geneva, WHO, 1998); Beijing + 5 Outcome Document (2000) above n 29 para 72(j).

[165] This is not to say that the de-linking of population concerns and reproductive rights is complete. Rather, population control is seen as part of the development agenda. See UN General Report of the Ad Hoc Committee of the Whole of the Twenty First Session of the General Assembly: Key Actions for the Further Implementation of the Programme of Action of the International Conference on Population and Development (1 July 1999) UN Doc A/S-21/5/Add.1 para 8; see also para 15(a). Cf H Zurayak 'The Meaning of Reproductive Health for Developing Countries: The Case of the Middle East' in C Sweetman (ed) *Gender, Development and Health* (Oxford, OXFAM, 2001) 22. But see also B Harmann 'Population Control in the New World Order' in D Eade (ed) *Development for Health* (Oxford, OXFAM, 1997) 80.

[166] CEDAW art 16(1)(e). See also CEDAW arts 4(2), 5(b), 11(1)(f), 11(2)(b), 11(2)(d), 12(1), 12(2). CEDAW General Recommendation No 24 on Health.

[167] Provision objected to by Sudan at the Meeting of Ministers, Addis Ababa, Ethiopia on 28 March 2003. See Draft Protocol to the African Charter on Human and Peoples' Rights on the Rights of Women in Africa as Adopted by the Meeting of Ministers, Addis Ababa, Ethiopia, 28 March 2003, MIN/W0M/RTS.DRAFT.PROT. (II) Rev. 5.

[168] Provision objected to by Burundi, Senegal and Sudan at Meeting of Ministers, Addis Ababa, Ethiopia on 28 March 2003.

[169] Provision objected to by Sudan at Meeting of Ministers, Addis Ababa, Ethiopia on 28 March 2003.

Also in 2003, African women met at the first conference on sexual and reproductive health producing a statement on further action.[170] Internationally, there have been moves towards drafting a separate instrument on Reproductive and Sexual Health by the women of South and Central America.[171]

Life cycles

Reproductive rights have to be conceived as existing throughout the life cycle of a woman and not just during the reproductive or child-bearing years.[172] This means that we have to look at issues affecting abortion, adolescent sexual health, pregnancy and related issues, the effects of age and, of course, intersectional discrimination faced by, amongst others, disabled, indigenous, minority and refugee women.[173]

Abortion

Abortion has long been controversial[174] and most countries have strictly drawn abortion laws.[175] Zimbabwe's Termination of Pregnancy Act[176] allows termination on limited grounds. These include endangerment of a mother's life or serious risk to her health, a serious risk that the child will be born with physical or mental

---

[170] S Holland-Muter 'First African Sexual and Reproductive Health Rights Conference: An Overview' (2003) 44 *Women's Health News* at 13.

[171] V Pandjiarjian 'A Daring Proposal: Campaigning for an Inter-American Convention on Sexual Rights and Reproductive Rights' in J Kerr and C Sweetman (eds) *Women Reinventing Globalization* (Oxford, OXFAM, 2003) 77.

[172] Vienna Declaration and Programme for Action 1993(II) para 41. Beijing Platform for Action 1995 para 92. CEDAW General Recommendation No 24 paras 2, 7, 29; Special Rapporteur on Violence against Women (1996) above n 8 para 54; CESCR General Comment No 14 on the Highest Attainable Standard of Health E/C/12/2000/4 para 21; Beijing + 5 Outcome Document (2000) above n 29 at para 72(e); Report of the Ad Hoc Committee of the Whole of the Twenty-first Special Session of the General Assembly (1999) para 44; Commonwealth Secretariat above n 114 at 3; UEMOA, 1999 1:1 santé objectifs Annexe A.

[173] Preliminary Report Submitted by the Special Rapporteur on Violence against Women, Its Causes and Consequences, Ms Radhika Coomaraswamy in Accordance with Commission on Human Rights resolution 1994/45. E/CN.4/1995/42, 22 November 1994 (hereafter Special Rapporteur on Violence against Women (1994)) para 56; CEDAW General Recommendation No 24 para 6.

[174] See for example South African case of *Christian Lawyers Association v Minister of Health* 1998 (4) SA 1113 in which the plaintiffs challenged the Choice on Termination of Pregnancy Act 1996 arguing that it violated the constitutionally protected right to life. The case was dismissed, it being held that a foetus was not the bearer of the right to life. See T Naude 'The Value of Life: A Note on *Christian Lawyers Association of South Africa v The Minister of Health*' (1999) 15 *South Africa Journal on Human Rights* 541. See also Beijing + 5 Outcome Document (2000) above n 29 at para 72(o), which, echoing ICPD, makes clear that abortion should not be seen as a form of contraception.

[175] T Bennett 'Abortion and Human Rights in Sub-Saharan Africa' (2000) 3 *Initiatives in Reproductive Health Policy* 1; R Cook and B Dickens 'Human Rights Dynamics of Abortion Law Reform' (2003) 25 *Human Rights Quarterly* 1.

[176] Termination of Pregnancy Act [Cap 15:10].

'problems' and finally where the pregnancy was a result of unlawful intercourse. In the last category would be included rape, statutory rape (that is sex with a young woman under the age of 16) and incest. Permission for a termination must be applied for and certified by a magistrate, unless the woman is claiming endangerment to her life or a serious threat of permanent injury, in which case the medical superintendent can consent, provided that he is acting on the advice of two independent doctors.[177] This cumbersome procedure calls to mind the 'joke' that used to be told about a country where permission to have an abortion took 10 months to obtain. The result of this overly bureaucratised system is that desperate women will have recourse to illegal abortions that have the potential to go disastrously wrong.[178] The Center for Reproductive Rights notes:

> African adolescents are at a high risk of complications from unsafe abortion. In Kenya adolescents make up 60% of cases involving abortion complications. In Ethiopia, the Ministry of Health has called the incidence of teenage unsafe abortion a 'national epidemic'. Ghanaian adolescents have the highest risk of all age groups for illegal and unsafe abortion, due in part to low access and use of contraceptives.[179]

South Africa permits abortion on demand up to 12 weeks.[180] From 13 to 20 weeks an abortion may be obtained with the consent of a doctor.[181] After 20 weeks the consent of two doctors, or a doctor and a registered midwife, is required.[182] However, data from South Africa show that, even in countries with liberal abortion policies, there are difficulties in service delivery,[183] and also issues of staff retention and harassment.[184]

The African Protocol on Women's Rights is the first human rights instrument in the world to contain a provision recognising a woman's right to abortion.[185] It provides that states parties undertake to:

---

[177] WLSA *Zimbabwe Pregnancy and Childbirth: Joy or Despair?* (Harare, WLSA, 2001) 24.

[178] *Ibid* at 41. S Tamale 'How Old is Old Enough? Defilement Law and the Age of Consent in Uganda' (2001) 7 *East African Journal of Peace & Human Rights* 82 at 100; Special Rapporteur on Violence (1999b) above n 156 paras 59–65.

[179] Centre for Reproductive Rights 'Common Reproductive Health Concerns in Anglophone Africa May 2002' at http:///.crlp.org/pub_fac_wowaa.html at 1. The situation for the adult population seems equally dire: *ibid* at 2. See also Bennett (2000) above n 175 at 3.

[180] Choice on Termination of Pregnancy Act. Act No 92 of 1996, s 2(1)(a).

[181] *Ibid* s 2(1)(b). For the conditions see s 2(1)(b)(i)–(iv).

[182] *Ibid* s 2(1)(c). For conditions see s 2(1)(c)(i)–(ii).

[183] M Stephens 'Abortion Reform in South Africa' (2000) 3 *Initiatives in Reproductive Health Policy* 4 at 5.

[184] A television 'exposé' revealed that users of abortion services were sometimes subject to abuse by tired and over-worked staff, who themselves felt unappreciated and indeed condemned by colleagues not doing the same work. See Women's Health Project 'On the Carte Blanche Exposé' (2002) 42 *Women's Health Project Review* 5. On the provision of abortion services see CEDAW General Recommendation No 24 paras 11, 14.

[185] R Mabuwa 'Africa's New Protocol for Women's Rights: An African Agenda for Action' http://www.reproductiverights.org/rfn_03_09_2.html#3.

[P]rotect the reproductive rights of women by authorizing medical abortion in cases of sexual assault, rape, incest, and where the continued pregnancy endangers the mental and physical health of the mother or the life of the mother or the foetus.[186]

Still, it is noteworthy that during the drafting stage of the African Protocol on Women's Rights, three states, Libya, Rwanda and Senegal, strongly objected to the abortion provision.

For states with more liberal abortion laws, such as South Africa, the African Protocol on Women's Rights enjoins them not to downgrade their laws. Specifically, article 31 provides:

None of the provisions of the present Protocol shall affect more favourable provisions for the realization of the rights of women contained in the national legislation of States Parties or in any other regional, continental or international conventions, treaties or agreements applicable in these States Parties.[187]

Although in some jurisdictions there is medical intervention during the pregnancy to ascertain the sex of the foetus with a view to aborting it if it is female,[188] son preference as manifested through the abortion of female fetuses has not been reported in sub-Saharan Africa.[189] This is not to say that it does not happen at all.

It is clear that gender disparities manifest themselves after birth, especially when it is time for the children go to school[190] or they need to access health care.

Reproductive rights for adolescents

Early adolescence is a particularly difficult time for girls.[191] They may be forced to marry early.[192] In her reproductive rights report, the Special Rapporteur on Violence against Women notes that:

---

[186] African Protocol on Women's Rights art 14(2)(c). See also CEDAW General Recommendation No 24 paras 31(c), 14 and para 11, which provides that the state is under an obligation 'to provide legally for the performance of certain reproductive health services for women'. Should there be conscientious objectors, the state is under a duty to 'ensure that women are referred to alternative health providers'. The premise here is that the national legal system permits abortion. See also Report of the Ad Hoc Committee of the Whole of the Twenty-First Special Session of the General Assembly. Addendum. Key Actions for the Future Implementation of the Programme of Action of the International Conference on Population and Development. A/s-21/5/Add.1, 1 July 1999 (ICPD+5) para 63iii.

[187] Cf art 23 of CEDAW.

[188] See Special Rapporteur on Violence against Women (1996) above n 8 at para 98. See also Special Rapporteur against Women (1999b) above n 156 paras 39–43. See also A Sen 'A Hundred Million Women are Missing' *New York Review of Books* reproduced in H Steiner and P Alston *International Human Rights in Context: Law, Politics, Morals* (Oxford, Clarendon Press, 2000) 165.

[189] Skard above n 116 at 70. But figures for North Africa suggest slight male to female gender imbalance. Seager above n 48 at 41.

[190] See also African Protocol on the Rights of Women art 12(1)(a).

[191] CEDAW General Recommendation No 24 para 12(b); Committee on the Rights of the Child General Comment No 4 on Adolescent Health and Development CRC/GC/2003/5.

[192] CEDAW above n 191 para 15(d). M Quattara, P Sen and M Thomson 'Forced Marriage, Forced Sex: The Perils of Childhood for Girls' in C Sweetman (ed) *Violence against Women* (Oxford, OXFAM, 1998) 27.

In Nigeria, a quarter of all women are married by the age of 14, one half by the age of 16 and three quarters by the age of 18. In Botswana, 28 per cent of women who have ever been pregnant were pregnant before reaching the age of 18.[193]

If girls are lucky enough to be attending school, they may be subject to sexual or other abuse at the hands of teachers or classmates.[194] One South African head-master of a farm school noted that the problem of sexual assault of young girls was exacerbated by the long distances the children had to walk to school, and could be improved by providing transport to and from school.[195]

Early marriage leads to early pregnancy,[196] which in turn brings with it a height-ened risk of vesico-vaginal fistula (VVF) or recto-vaginal fistula (RVF)[197] and potential death during childbirth of the mother or the baby, or in some instances both.[198] Reviewing the Ethiopian Report, the United Nations Children's Rights Committee expressed concern at the high incidence of early and forced mar-riage,[199] and 'at the insufficient provision for adolescent health care and at the high incidence of early pregnancy in the State party'.[200] The effects of this could be mitigated by the provision of free universal primary education and basic health services.

There is an important link made between educating girls and the delay in enter-ing marriage, which is in turn linked to women having fewer children, with posi-tive health benefits for both.[201] If money is short then it is likely that the girl child will not go to school or receive medical treatment. Part of the prioritisation of the educational needs of the boy child over the girl is linked to a way of thinking underlined by the saying 'educating a girl is like watering another man's gar-den'.[202] By this is meant that the girl will eventually marry and leave the family,

---

[193] Special Rapporteur on Violence against Women (1999b) above n 156 para 36. See also Skard, who notes that 'About half of African girls are married before the age of 18.' Skard above n 116 at 72; Forum on Marriage above n 53 at 9.

[194] African Protocol on the Rights of Women art 12(1)(c).

[195] Government of South Africa (1998) above n 42 at 119. The government pledges to put systems into place 'to deal with violence against girls and women within the education arena'. At 119.

[196] Egyptian National Council for Childhood and Motherhood *Girls Needs in Upper Egypt, Aswan* (Cairo, Egyptian National Council for Childhood and Motherhood, 2001) 9.

[197] Skard above n 116 at 73. Special Rapporteur on Violence against Women (1999b) above n 156 at para 38. See also W Oloko and S Saba 'Psychosocial Effects of Reproductive Rights Abuse' in B Owasonoye (ed) *Reproductive Rights of Women in Nigeria: The Legal, Economic and Cultural Dimensions* (Lagos, Human Development Initiatives, 1999) 140 at 143; F Tahzib 'Social Factors in the Aetiology of Vesico-Vaginal Fistulae' in A Imam *et al* (eds) *Women and the Family in Nigeria* (Dakar, Codesria, 1989) 75.

[198] See CESCR art 12(2)(a); CESCR General Comment No14 para 14. See also CEDAW General Recommendation No 24 para 27; G Barnes and L Paton *The Child Brides* [documentary film] (London, Umbrella Pictures, 1998).

[199] UN Committee on the Rights of the Child Concluding Observations on the Rights of the Child: Ethiopia_CRC/C/15/Add.144 paras 15, 41, 64.

[200] *Ibid* para 60.

[201] UNICEF *The State of the World's Children: Education* (New York, UNICEF, 1999) 54–57.

[202] Cf Special Rapporteur on Violence against Women (1994) above n 173 at para 156.

and become someone else's responsibility. Also, if she marries, then the benefit of the education will not be enjoyed by the parents but by the family of marriage.

For adolescent girls there is also the issue of pregnancy whilst still at school. Often this leads to the expulsion of the girl from school.[203] Even if the person who impregnated her is also at school, he may be allowed to continue. It is important that provision be made for young women who fall pregnant to continue their schooling.[204] Threats of expulsion may lead to the young woman trying to conceal the pregnancy, or abandoning or 'dumping' the baby out of fear. If death results then in many jurisdictions she will be charged with murder, while the man will go free.[205] It therefore becomes imperative that countries enact infanticide statutes which distinguish between a distressed mother abandoning the baby or ending the life of her child and other forms of violence leading to death. The Zimbabwean Infanticide Act[206] provides that if a woman kills her child within the first six months of its life then she will be charged with infanticide.[207] The maximum sentence is 5 years' imprisonment.[208] The onus is on the state to rebut the presumption that a woman who kills her child within the first six months of its life was disturbed as result of giving birth.[209] The statute then lists factors which need to be taken into account in ascertaining the state of mind of the mother. These are particularly sensitive to the plight of young mothers and include:

(a) the effects which the birth had, or which she believed it would have, on her social, financial or martial situation;
(b) the difficulties which were created, or which she believed would be created, in caring for the child in the social, financial or marital situation in which it was born;
(c) the difficulties which she had, or which she believed she would have, in caring for the child due to her inexperience or inability;

---

[203] See the Botswana case of *Student Representative Council of Molepole College of Education v Attorney-General* Civil Appeal No 13 of 1994, where a policy requiring female students who had fallen pregnant to keep away from college for a year was held to be discriminatory. R Cook and I Merali 'The Interpretation and Application of Human Rights on Reproductive and Sexual Health by Commonwealth Courts' (1999) *Commonwealth Law Bulletin* 109. See also the Zimbabwean case of *Mandizvidza v Morgenster College* discussed in Ch 2.

[204] CEDAW provides for this. See CEDAW art 10(f). CEDAW General Recommendation No 24 para 28. See also ACRWC, art 11(6); CESCR General Comment No 14 para 1. See also African Protocol on Women's Rights art 12(2)(c). But see Women's Health Project 'Schools Kick Out Pregnant Adolescents' (2001) 39 *Women's Health Project Review* at 14.

[205] WLSA, Zimbabwe *Pregnancy and Childbirth: Joy or Despair?* (Harare, WLSA, 2001) at 68, 132–35.

[206] Infanticide Act [Cap 9:12].

[207] *Ibid* s 2(1). However, this does not preclude a charge of murder being brought in certain circumstances. See s 6.

[208] *Ibid* s 2(1).

[209] *Ibid* s 2(2).

(d) any other relevant circumstances or consideration, whether based on the psychological effects of the woman's mind arising from the birth itself, or otherwise.[210]

The issue of school-girl (early) pregnancy is linked to the need to provide adequate education on issues of sexual and reproductive health.[211] 'Sex education' is
a controversial issue, with some arguing that giving children information about
reproductive health[212] is likely to encourage them to have sex, whilst others point
out that the young will continue to have sex and it is better that they practise safe
sex, especially in light of increased HIV infections.[213] Tamale is robust in her pre-
scription for engaging with the issue of adolescent sexuality, noting that we should
aim to:

> [D]emystify(ing) sex, desocializing teenagers from the belief that sex is a taboo activity,
> dissociating sex from procreation and morality; and engaging teenagers in effective sex
> education.[214]

In the English case of *Gillick*,[215] a Catholic mother challenged the decision of a
local health authority to issue guidelines to doctors operating within its area to the
effect that if they were consulted by a minor under the age of 16 who was seeking
contraception/contraceptive advice without the explicit consent of a parent, doctors should provide it. The House of Lords held that the doctor should first try to
persuade the child to include the parent or guardian in the decision. If, however,
it became clear to the doctor that the child would not do so and, in the doctor's
opinion, it seemed likely that the child would go ahead and have intercourse
anyway, and the child understood the consequences of her actions, then the doctor should offer that child such contraceptive advice and assistance as the doctor
deemed appropriate.

Around the world, the church, particularly, but not only, the Roman Catholic
church,[216] is heavily implicated in the denial of the fact that sexual intercourse
often occurs outside the marital relationship. The church preaches abstinence as
the only way forward. The influence of the church can be seen in the position taken

---

[210] Infanticide Act, s 4.
[211] CEDAW art 10(h), art 14(2)(b), art 16(1)(e); CEDAW General Recommendation No 24 paras
18, 31(b).
[212] ICPD (1994) para 7.45 calls on states to 'remove . . . barriers to reproductive health information
and care for adolescents'. Art 11(2)(h) of the ACRWC, 1990 identifies the need for the 'promotion of
the child's understanding of primary health care'.
[213] Committee on the Rights of the Child General Comment No 3 HIV/AIDS and the Rights of the
Child CRC/GC/2003/1.
[214] Tamale above n 178 at 100.
[215] *Gillick v West Norfolk and Wisbech Area Health Authority* [1986] AC 112; [1985] 3 All ER 402.
[216] See for example BBC 1 *Panorama* documentary presented by Steve Bradshaw, entitled 'Sex and
the Holy City', aired on BBC 1 on 12 October 2003. See also http://www.bbc.co.uk/panorama. Excerpts
from the programme reproduced in Index on Censorship 'Sex and the Holy City' (2004) 1 *Index on
Censorship* 84–90; Sow above n 58 at 74.

by the United States regime of George Bush, which has allocated funding for AIDS prevention but has tied this aid by insisting that abstinence should be pushed as the only acceptable form of behaviour, with condom usage being spoken of only to 'high risk' groups such as sex workers/prostitutes. The preference is for the ABC approach.[217] This stance is particularly dangerous in the context of societies with high incidence of sexual violence and AIDS. Rates of HIV are higher among women than men[218] and among teenage girls than boys.[219] The African Protocol on Women's Rights provides that women have the right:

> [T]o self protection and to be protected against sexually transmitted infections, including HIV/AIDS.[220]

It is important that innovative means that extend beyond classroom learning be found of communicating information about contraception and sexual health, including information on HIV.[221] There have been many initiatives in this regard, including use of theatre and music. One of the most well known is a South African programme using the radio.[222] Morrell has also noted the importance of a gendered approach to sex education that engages boys in discussion about the issue of

---

[217] ABC stands for (A) Abstinence, (B) Be faithful, and (C) Condom usage. P Gill 'Experts Attack Bush's Stance in AIDS Battle' *Observer* (London, 11 July 2004).

[218] UNAIDS (2004) 'Fact sheet AIDS Epidemic in Sub-Saharan Africa' from http://www.unaids.org notes that there are 13 HIV positive women for every 10 positive men. Declaration of Commitment of the UN General Assembly Special Session on HIV/AIDS, June 2001 (reproduced in Human Rights Watch (2003) Uganda Report above n 43 at 73–75 para 4); Human Rights Watch 'Women and HIV/AIDS' at http://www.hrw.org.women/aids.html; Women's Health Project 'Women are More at Risk of HIV Infection' (2003) 45 *Women's Health Review* at 13; CEDAW General Recommendation No 24 at para 12(a).

[219] UNAIDS (2004) above n 218 provides that amongst the 15–24 age group in Mali and Kenya the rate is 45 women for every 10 men; Rwezaura 'Protecting the Rights of the Girl Child' above n 112 at 125. Special Rapporteur on Violence against Women (1999b) above n 156 at para 20; C Bayliss 'Safe Motherhood in the Time of AIDS: The Illusion of Reproductive "Choice" ' in C Sweetman (ed) *Gender, Development and Health* (Oxford, OXFAM, 2001) 40 at 46; S Msimang 'HIV/AIDS, Globalisation and the International Women's Movement' in J Kerr and C Sweetman (eds) *Women Reinventing Globalization* (Oxford, OXFAM, 2003) 109 at 111; S Msimang 'Caution! Women Moving: Strategies for Organizing Feminist Visions of the Future' in J Kerr *et al* (eds) *The Future of Women's Rights* (London, Zed Press, 2004) 170 at 176–78; Beijing + 5 Outcome Document (2000) above n 29 at para 72(a); A De Waal 'Apocalypse: The True Story of AIDS' (2004) 1 *Index on Censorship* 25.

[220] African Protocol on Women's Rights art 14(1)(d). See also CEDAW General Recommendation No 24 para 30; CESCR General Comment No 14 at para 20; Beijing + 5 Outcome Document (2000) above n 29 at para 103(b). See also United Nations *HIV/AIDS and Human Rights: International Guidelines* (New York, United Nations, 1998)

[221] See generally papers in A Cornwell and A Wellbourn (eds) *Realizing Rights: Transforming Approaches to Sexual and Reproductive Well-Being* (London, Zed Press, 2002); P Mutungu *Life Skills, Sexual Maturation and Sanitation: What's (Not) Happening in Our Schools. An Exploratory Study from Kenya* (Harare, Weaver Press, 2003).

[222] Z Ibrahim 'Radio HIV HOP in South Africa' in A Cornwell and A Welbourn (eds) above n 221 at 191. See also B Kaim 'Involving Young People in Their Reproductive Health: A Case Study from Zimbabwe' also in A Cornwell and A Welbourn (eds) 181.See the policies of the Egyptian government. Combined Fourth and Fifth Periodic Report of States Parties: Egypt (2000) CEDAW/C/EGY4–5 at 20.

masculinity, and specifically about '*doing* masculinity differently'.[223] He highlights
a programme which facilitates small-group discussion about issues of gender in
high schools. Although targeted at the boys, Morrell notes 'the intervention
impacted most on female learners'.[224] The young women became more assertive
and 'insisted on being respected by boys, friends and teachers'.[225] He suggests that
the programme could be incorporated into the Life Skills Curriculum.[226]

An issue that affects all women from puberty until menopause is that of menstruation, which is sex specific, meaning that it only happens to women. Again
women may not be able to access, in financial terms, sanitary products. Indeed in
Zimbabwe, there has been a shortage of sanitary products for some time, and
when available they are prohibitively priced, meaning that only rich women can
afford to purchase them.[227] This leads to the use of unsuitable alternatives, which
in turn increases the risk of urinary tract infections and results in the need to access
medical treatment at a greater cost to the state, or more accurately the woman,
than if basic sanitary provision had been made available in the first place.

Assuming that a girl survives the adolescent years into adulthood, it is likely that
she will carry many pregnancies, not all of which will go to term, largely due to
poor nutrition and healthcare.[228] Arguably, it is the knowledge that not all their
children will survive that leads people to have many children.

Contraception

Although women have a right to access contraception,[229] the content of this 'right'
may be severely curtailed by cultural considerations which say that a woman who
uses contraception is 'loose'. National budgetary constraints may mean that contraceptive choice is limited. In some countries, the contraceptive of choice (state
choice) is depo provera, which may not suit all women, but which is preferred
because it is dispensed by way of injection and the contraceptive effects last a

[223] R Morrell 'Mobilising Caring in Men' (2002) 42 *Women's Health Project Review* 14. See also
J Bujra 'Targeting Men for a Change: AIDS Discourse and Activism in Africa' in F Cleaver (ed)
Masculinities Matter: Men, Gender and Development (London, Zed Press, 2002) 209. Skard above n 116
at 38.
[224] Morrell above n 223 at 15.
[225] *Ibid.*
[226] *Ibid.* UNAIDS and PANOS *Young Men and HIV: Culture, Poverty and Social Risk* (London,
Panos, 2001). See also CESCR General Comment No 14 para 20. See also paras 22 and 23 on adolescents.
[227] 'Indifference to Women's Cries for Help Deplorable' *Daily News* (Zimbabwe, 5 March 2003)
downloaded from: http://www.dailynews.co.zw/daily/2003/March/March5/10800.html at 2. The
paper noted that International Women's Day (8 March) was to be marked by demonstrations organised by the Zimbabwe Women's Resource Centre over the 'escalating cost of menstruation'.
[228] See also CEDAW General Recommendation No 24 paras 7, 9.
[229] Beijing Declaration 1995 para 17.

number of months making it cheap and convenient.[230] Also some national systems still require the consent of the husband before issuing a woman with contraception.[231] The Special Rapporteur on Violence against Women recounts the story of 'M':

> [A] married Ugandan mother who was beaten by her husband for not producing more children, and further beaten when her husband discovered that she was using contraceptives.[232]

Migrant men have sometimes proved particularly resistant to 'allowing' their wives to use contraception, fearing that they will have intercourse with other men in their absence. Of course, this does not mean that the men are themselves faithful.[233] Indeed the passing of a sexually transmitted infection is often from a married man to his wife. Within the South African context, Msimang links the AIDS problem to apartheid policies that separated families for long periods of time and only provided accommodation for individuals in single sex hostels peopled by men.[234] Rural to urban migration of women may also lead to an increased incidence of sexually transmitted infection as, unable to find any other work, the women are forced into prostitution.[235]

The African Protocol on Women's Rights provides that reproductive rights include:

> [T]he right to be informed on one's health status and on the health status of one's partner, particularly if infected with sexually transmitted infections, including HIV/AIDS, in accordance with internationally recognized standards and best practices.[236]

---

[230] S Ogbuagu 'Depo-Provera: A Choice or an Imposition on the African Woman. A Case Study of Depo Provera Usage in Maiduguri' in A Imam *et al* (eds) *Women and the Family in Nigeria* (Dakar, CODESRIA, 1989) 81.

[231] See CEDAW General Recommendation No 24 paras 14 and 21. See also Special Rapporteur on Violence against Women (1999b) above n 156 at para 73. Southern African Research and Documentation Centre (SARDC) *Beyond Inequalities: Women in Zambia* (Harare, SARDC, 1998) (hereafter SARDC *Zambia*) at 43–44. In Chad a married woman requires the consent of her husband in order for her to be sterilised. See chapter on 'Chad' in Center for Reproductive Rights *Women of the World: Francophone Africa Laws and Policies Affecting Their Reproductive Lives* (New York, Center for Reproductive Rights, 2001) 89 at 100; R Cook and D Maine 'Spousal Veto over Family Planning Services' (1987) 77 *American Journal of Public Health* 339.

[232] Special Rapporteur on Violence against Women (1999b) above n 156 para 2. See also WLSA above n 46 at 40.

[233] H Becker 'The Least Sexist Society? Perspectives on Gender, Change and Violence among the Southern African San' (2003) 29 *Journal of Southern African Studies* 1 at 17; Human Rights Watch (2003) Uganda Report above n 43 at 22. See also ICPD para 7.34 requiring 'mutual respect and willingness to accept responsibility for the consequences of sexual behaviour'.

[234] Msimang 'HIV/AIDS' above n 219 at 110; Shisano and Zungu-Dirwayi above n 78 at 316.

[235] CEDAW General Recommendation No 24 para 21.

[236] African Protocol on Women's Rights art 14(1)(e). There is a delicate balance to be drawn between protecting the right to privacy and confidentiality of a person diagnosed as being HIV positive and those with whom he or she may have (unprotected) sexual intercourse thus opening them up to infection. Shisano and Zungu-Dirwayi above n 78 at 22. It is already a crime to infect another

Although positive and to be welcomed, this provision seems to be premised on a marriage based on equal power between spouses—this is not often the case.[237] Attempts by women to ask their husbands to use condoms can lead to violence. In the course of giving legal advice, a woman informed me that she had a chronic sexually transmitted infection because her husband kept re-infecting her. I asked her why she did not ask him to wear a condom. She said that she had, but he had replied angrily that she was his wife and not his 'prostitute'—only his 'prostitute' could make that demand of him.[238] This highlights the helplessness and powerlessness of many women on the continent in negotiating safe sex with their partners.[239] It was only when I pointed out the dangers of her contracting HIV[240] and the fact that her children would be left without a mother should she die, that she said that she would do something about the situation.

The introduction of the female condom may go some way to mitigating the male resistance to the condom use conundrum.[241] The Center for Reproductive Rights notes that:

> In southern Africa where HIV rates are highest, condom use is lowest. Similarly in Ghana, only 3% of women and 7% of men have ever used a condom to prevent sexually transmitted infection (STI).[242]

It has been said that it is only by empowering African women, the group with the highest infection rate, that the AIDS pandemic can be contained.[243] The dynamics of gender relations mean that when women are infected they may not tell the partner/husband for fear of violence or abandonment.[244] The HIV pandemic leaves children without mothers and, for all the talk of stereotyping, without their primary care givers. This throws the burden of looking after children on

---

person deliberately in Zimbabwe. See Sexual Offences Act s 15. J Csete and J Smith 'Submission to the Parliamentary Portfolio Committee on Justice and Constitutional Development, Parliament of South Africa, on the Draft Criminal Law (Sexual Offences) Amendment Bill, 2003' from Amnesty International and Human Rights Watch, 15 September 2003, AI Index: AFR 53/006/2003, also available at http://www.hrw.org/press/2003/09/sa_drafcrimelaw.htm at 2.

[237] Cf 'Gender Imbalance Contributing to the Spread of AIDS-Legislator' *Herald* (Harare, 14 October 2003) downloaded from http://www/allafrica.com/stories/printable/200310140275.html. Human Rights Watch (2003) Uganda Report above n 43 at 23, 36–37.

[238] Cf SARDC *Zambia* above n 231 at 44.

[239] Bayliss above n 219 at 42–44. Skard above n 116 at 33. See also CEDAW General Recommendation No 24 para 8. Human Rights Watch (2003) Uganda Report above n 43 at 23–24.

[240] WHO *World Report on Violence* (2002) above n 7 at 101.

[241] E Schatz 'Conversations on Sex, Condoms and HIV/AIDS in Rural Malawi' (2003) 45 *Women's Health Project Review* 17. But see Msimang 'Caution' above n 219 at 181.

[242] Center for Reproductive Rights 'Common Reproductive Concerns in Anglophone Africa' May 2002, Item F055. Available http://www.crlp.org/pub_fac_wowaa.html at 2. See also Varga above n 120 at 21.

[243] J Laurence 'Empowering Women is the Way Forward to Saving African Women from AIDS Devastation' *Independent* (London, 17 May 2004).

[244] Amnesty International above n 26 at 15.

any siblings, usually daughters, who, if poor, may in turn be forced to marry early or to engage in prostitution, with the disastrous consequences that entails and which we have already discussed. To reinforce the message, Skard offers this frightening statistic:

> By the end of 2001, the more than seventeen million people who lost their lives to AIDS in sub-Saharan Africa have left behind eleven million orphans, and the numbers are expected to double over the next decade.[245]

Given the gravity of the situation, the AU Gender Equality Declaration 2004 calls on states to set up an AIDS Watch Africa unit within the Office of the Chairperson of the Commission. The unit would then have the responsibility of producing annual reports on the HIV/AIDS situation on the continent and also promoting of the local production of anti-retroviral drugs.[246]

Pregnancy

Pregnancy can be a hazardous time for women. The World Health Organization has identified an increased incidence of violence against women during pregnancy.[247] The situation is exacerbated by the shortage of health personnel to assist women during pregnancy and at delivery.[248] The problem is particularly acute for rural women, who may have to travel long distances to access the most basic medical care. All societies have myths and rituals around pregnancy, some of which may be harmful to the mother.[249] These sometimes include food taboos, which may limit the mother's intake of certain nutritious foods.

Skard notes that the West and Central African regions have the highest maternal morbidity rate of all the regions of the world.[250] In Mali it is estimated that one in every nineteen women loses her life as a result of pregnancy-related complications.[251] In West and Central Africa maternal mortality runs at one in thirteen.[252]

---

[245] Skard above n 116 at 35.

[246] AU Solemn Declaration on Gender Equality in Africa 2004 art 10.

[247] WHO *World Report on Violence* (2002) above n 7 at 101. Special Rapporteur on Violence against Women (1999b) above n 156 at para 24.

[248] See CESCR General Comment No 14 para 14. See also paras 46–52 on violations of state obligations to respect, protect and fulfil Covenant rights on issues of health.

[249] H Usman 'Harmful Traditional Practices and Reproductive Health' in B Owasanoye (ed) *Reproductive Rights of Women in Nigeria: The Legal, Economic and Cultural Dimensions* (Lagos, Human Development Initiatives, 1999) 46 at 53–54.

[250] Skard above n 116 at 72.

[251] Center for Reproductive Rights (CRR) and Association des Juristes Maliennes *Claiming Our Rights: Surviving Pregnancy and Childbirth in Mali* (New York, CRR; Bamako: Association des Juristes Maliennes, 2003) 24.

[252] Skard above n 116 at 72. See Beijing + 5 Outcome Document (2000) above n 29 at para 72(b) on the state's obligation 'to ensure that the reduction of maternal mortality and morbidity is a health sector priority'.

The impact on African women's bodies of carrying many pregnancies, often spaced close together, is severe. Post-partum depression may go undiagnosed and untreated.[253]

Linked to post pregnancy and the HIV pandemic, is the issue of breast-feeding. It used to be that campaigns pronouncing 'breast is best' were used to encourage mothers to breast-feed their children for as long as possible. The message was particularly effective in pointing out the health benefits associated with breast-feeding for mother and child. Indeed the African Charter on the Rights and Welfare of the Child 1990 (ACRWC) provides that the state has an obligation to provide information to the public including 'the advantages of breast feeding'.[254] It is for this reason that the amendment of that message to 'breast is best, *provided the mother is not HIV positive*' has been harder to communicate.[255] HIV positive mothers fear that if they do not breast-feed their babies, this will reveal their status to outsiders. Moreover, in cultures where breast-feeding is the accepted behaviour for a 'good mother', it may be difficult to resist the pressure to breast-feed. Financial constraints also play a part. If one is to accept the message that breast-feeding may increase the likelihood of mother-to-child transmission of the HIV virus, then one has to have credible options. For a newborn baby, formula milk may be the only option, although some have advocated a return to wet-nursing, but this assumes that the HIV status of the wet-nurse is known. However, the use of formula is not without its problems. There is the issue of cost.[256] Formula is expensive relative to the average income of a family in Africa. Even if provided for free, there is the question of a clean water supply[257] and wood or fuel with which to boil the water needed for the preparation of the formula. Moreover, in order to prepare the formula properly, one may need to know how to read the instructions[258] and, of course, to accurately measure out the right amount. Given the frequency with which young infants need feeding, it may well be that many mothers will decide 'breast may not be best, but it is the easiest and most practical avenue open to me'.

Women in formal employment may also suffer prejudice as a result of pregnancy. Indeed it is not unknown for employers to avoid hiring women of reproductive age 'in case they go off and start having babies and costing the company money in maternity benefits and time off to look after "their" children'.[259] This of course assumes that all women of reproductive age *want* to have children. It also

---

[253] CEDAW General Recommendation No 24 para 12(c).

[254] ACRWC art 14(2)(h).

[255] Skard above n 116 at 34–35.

[256] Cf Human Rights Watch (2003) Uganda Report above n 43 at 30.

[257] ACRWC art 14(2)(c).

[258] Cf M Nyirarukundo 'Reproductive Rights in Senegal: Limited by Social Expectations' (2000) 3 *Initiatives in Reproductive Health Policy* 7 at 7.

[259] Cf J Mubangizi 'Too Pregnant to Work: The Dilemma of Economic Rationality versus Equality *Woolworths (Pty) Ltd v Whitehead*' (2000) 16 *South African Journal on Human Rights* 691.

assumes that the mother will be the primary care giver—an assumption which, though reflecting the status quo, challenges the provisions of human rights instruments on both parents being equally responsible for the care and upbringing of their children.[260] Few countries guarantee equal parental leave. Maternity leave is given to women (obviously!), but few companies or countries have enshrined the rights of men to be given paternity leave.

Clearly this reinforces stereotyping and makes clear that the reproductive burden is to be borne solely by women. It could be argued that there is, within the African Protocol on Women's Rights, an over-emphasis on pregnant and lactating women, which leaves the impression that it is only in the state of pregnancy that women are entitled to protection.[261] Special protection suggests that women are in some way vulnerable, but the arena in which they receive this special protection is when doing their 'reproductive work'. Why is this considered outside the norm and thus as requiring special protection? Is it because it has to be distinguished from the normative and 'proper' work carried out by men? Calling the work that women do in the reproductive field deserving of 'special protection' makes it appear abnormal, but that is only if 'normal' is defined from a male perspective.[262] For Otto, maternity provision should be a human right rather than a special measure.[263]

Older women

Continuing through a woman's life cycle, we see that the focus, even if in a limited way, of most health care systems on women within their reproductively productive cycles, leaves those older women who have reached menopause poorly provided for.[264] No longer considered 'useful', their health needs are the most

---

[260] CEDAW; art 5(b) CRC; art 18(1); ACRWC arts 19 and 20, African Protocol on Women's Rights art 6(i). Beijing + 5 Outcome Document (2000) above n 29 at paras 60, 82(d). *President of the Republic of South Africa and Another v Hugo* 1997 (4) SA 1.

[261] See African Protocol on Women's Rights art 24(b)on the right of pregnant or nursing women to an environment suitable to their condition; see also art 14(2)(b) on state responsibility to ensure 'appropriate health care for expectant and nursing mothers'; finally see art 4(2)(j). Beijing +5 Outcome Document (2000) above n 29 at para 11.

[262] C Mackinnon *Towards a Feminist Theory of the State* (Cambridge, Harvard University Press, 1989) 220, 225–26.

[263] D Otto ' "Gender Comment": Why Does the UN Committee on Economic, Social and Cultural Rights Need a General Comment on Women?' (2002) 14 *Canadian Journal of Women and the Law* 1 at 20.

[264] CEDAW General Recommendation No 24 para 12(a); CESCR, General Comment No 6 on The Economic, Social and Cultural Rights of Older Persons, (13th Session, 1995) UN Doc HRI.GEN/1/Rev.5, 26 April 2001; Beijing + 5 Outcome Document (2000) above n 29 at para 3. Kigali Declaration 2003 art 20 calls on states to develop a Protocol to protect the rights of people with disabilities and the elderly. M Gorman 'Older People and Development: The Last Minority' in D Eade (ed) *Development and Social Diversity* (Oxford, OXFAM, 1999) 36.

neglected.[265] Children are immunised for childhood diseases, young women are given limited maternity care, but older women are ignored.[266] Conditions like osteoporosis, exacerbated by years of backbreaking labour and inadequate nutrition, are left untreated. Older women may be seen as a source of wisdom[267] in the romantic view we have of them, but they are also seen as consumers rather than generators of resources, and may be subjected to emotional and psychological violence. Dementia[268] is not taken seriously, or leads to women being ostracised or called witches.[269] The mental health of women exhausted from working innumerable hours and being the primary carers and providers is often ignored. It is however, an important factor in an holistic understanding of an effective right to health.

Although widowhood occurs earlier and earlier in Africa, the fact that women generally outlive men[270] means that women are left without the protection of a powerful male, their husbands. One of the by-products of the HIV/AIDS pandemic has been that the younger generation comprising parents die early, leaving orphans requiring care.[271] Where they are still alive, the burden for caring for AIDS orphans falls on the grandparents, who may not have the physical ability to be running after toddlers and, more importantly, may not have the financial resources necessary to cope, not least because of inequitable inheritance laws.[272] This may lead to children having to leave school. Needless to say, the grandparents may themselves be at the stage in life where they are in need of care.[273]

---

[265] CEDAW General Recommendation No 24 para 24.

[266] WHO *World Report on Violence* (2002) above n 7 at 123–45, see especially 123–32.

[267] Older women and grandmothers can be an important source of information. J Aubel and I Toure 'Strengthening Grandmother Networks to Improve Community Nutrition: Experience from Senegal' in C Sweetman (ed) *Gender, Development and Health* (Oxford, OXFAM, 2001) 62.

[268] Mental health prejudice affects people of all ages. CEDAW General Recommendation No 24 para 5. V Patel, J Mutambirwa and S Nhiwatiwa 'Stressed, Depressed or Bewitched? A Perspective on Mental Health, Culture and Religion' in D Eade (ed) *Development for Health* (Oxford, OXFAM, 1997) 40.

[269] F Pickup, S Williams and C Sweetman above n 8 at 93–94.

[270] World Bank *Engendering Development* above n 156 at 67.

[271] B Rwezaura ' "This is not my Child": The Task of Integrating Orphans into the Mainstream of Society in Tanzania' in A Bainham (ed) *International Survey of Family Law* (Bristol, Jordan Publishing, 2001) 410; Beijing + 5 Outcome Document (2000) above n 29 at para 103(c), which calls in part for the assistance of children orphaned as a result of HIV/AIDS; World Bank *Education and Aids* above n 115 at 16–20.

[272] J Appleton 'At My Age I Should Be Sitting under That Tree: The Impact of AIDS on Tanzania's Lake Shore Communities' in C Sweetman (ed) (2000) *Gender and Lifecycles* 19. See also Commonwealth Secretariat and Maritime Centre of Excellence for Women's Health above n 78 at 38; C Roys 'Widows and Orphans Property Disputes: The Impact of AIDS in Rakai District Uganda' in D Eade (ed) *Development for Health* (Oxford, OXFAM, 1997) 94; Gorman above n 264 at 42.

[273] This is anticipated by art 18(4) of the African Charter. See also African Protocol on Women's Rights art 22. See also CESCR General Comment No 14 para 25.

Disabled women

Disabled women may experience reproductive rights violations disproportion-ately.[274] That they are entitled to enjoy the same human rights as able-bodied people is often ignored.[275] In many African states, governments struggle to meet the basic health needs of the majority of their able-bodied populations. Due to resource constraints and, more importantly, discriminatory attitudes towards dis-abled people, their health needs are often ignored.[276] Moreover there is a link between disability and poverty, so that there is a higher incidence of poverty among the disabled than able-bodied people.[277]

With respect to reproductive rights issues, both young girls and women may be subject to physical violence and sexual abuse. In Zimbabwe, I have heard stories of the rape of blind women, sleeping at the railway station because they are home-less.[278] The men who rape them target them specifically because they know that they cannot be identified, and also because the state system does not stretch to DNA testing. As these women often have to beg to get enough to eat, they are unlikely to be able to access health provision services to seek help with contracep-tion, or indeed pre-natal care.[279]

The Canadian Supreme Court has, in the case of *Eldridge v British Columbia (Attorney-General)*,[280] provided an important lead on the nature of state obliga-tions for people with disabilities. The case involved three deaf people, who sued the Government of British Columbia for failing to provide interpreters for the deaf when they were accessing medical services. The appellants noted that this failure constituted a breach of their constitutional rights to equality. The court held that although the government provided equally for able-bodied and disabled people, the effect of *not* providing interpreters for deaf people constituted discrimination against them. Without interpreters to assist them in communicating with health

[274] CEDAW General Recommendation No18 (1991) on Disabled Women UN, Doc A/46/38, CEDAW General Recommendation No 24 paras 6, 25. CESCR, General Comment No 5 on Persons with Disabilities (11th Session, 1994) Un Doc HRI/GEN/1/Rev.5, 26 April 2001.

[275] C McClain-Nhlapo 'Invisible Women' (2004) 14 *Interights Bulletin* 100. The whole volume of the bulletin covers issues pertaining to human rights and disability.

[276] See CESCR General Comment No 14 para 26, which emphasises the importance to both public and private health providers of the principle of non-discrimination when dealing with the health needs of disabled people.

[277] World Health Organization (WHO) '25 Questions and Answers on Health and Human Rights' (2002) 1 *Health and Human Rights Publication Series* 1 (hereafter WHO '25 Questions') at 23.

[278] Art 23(b) of the African Protocol on Women's Rights explicitly calls for states to 'ensure the right of women with disabilities to freedom from violence, including sexual abuse, discrimination based on disability and the right to be treated with dignity'. See also CEDAW General Recommendation No 24 para 25; CEDAW General Recommendation No 18.

[279] Again the African Charter identifies the disabled as requiring protection in art 18(4). See also the African Protocol on Women's Rights art 23.

[280] *Eldridge v British Columbia (Attorney-General)* [1997] 3 SCR 624.

service providers, their effective access to the free health care services provided by the government was hampered. Specifically, the hard of hearing experienced adverse discrimination because they could not access or enjoy health services in the same way as could the able bodied.[281]

Women refugees[282]

Violations of women's rights during armed conflict are well documented.[283] However, it is worth examining further one of the by-products of war and that is migration.[284] Women and children are the biggest casualties of war, and displacement, so that the Beijing Platform for Action notes that: 'Women and children constitute some 80 per cent of the world's millions of refugees and other displaced persons.'[285] Despite the negative rhetoric on refugees in the north,[286] the reality is that Africa absorbs most of its own refugees. Indeed Africa is the only region to have a Refugee Convention of its own.[287] The African Protocol contains many provisions addressing the needs of refugees, including article 11(3) which demands that states parties protect women 'against all forms of violence, rape and other forms of sexual exploitation, and to ensure that such acts are considered war crimes, genocide and/or crimes against humanity'.[288]

---

[281] See also Montreal Principles (2004). H Dagut and R Morgan 'Barriers to Justice: Violations of the Rights of Deaf and Hard of Hearing People in the South African Justice System' (2003) 19 *South African Journal on Human Rights* 27.

[282] CEDAW General Recommendation No 24 paras 6, 25; WHO *World Report on Violence* (2002) above n 7 at 225. C Beyani 'The Needs of Refugee Women. A Human Rights Perspective' (1995) 3 *Gender and Development* 29.

[283] C Chinkin 'Rape and Sexual Abuse of Women in International Law' (1994) 5 *European Journal of International Law* 326; P Sellars 'The Context of Sex Violence: Violence as Violations of International Humanitarian Law' in K McDonald and G Swaak (eds) *Substantive and Procedural Aspects of International Criminal Law: The Experience of International and National Courts* (The Hague, Kluwer, 2000) 263.

[284] F Butegwa, F Mukasa and S Mozere *Human Rights of African Women in Conflict Situations: The WILDAF Initiative* (Harare, WILDAF, 1995) 13–35. C Beyani *Human Rights Standards and the Movement of People within States* (Oxford, Oxford University Press, 2000).

[285] Beijing Platform for Action 1995 para E136.

[286] Coverage of asylum issues in English newspapers has often been inflammatory. See Article 19 (May 2003) 'What's the Story?'

[287] OAU Convention Governing the Specific Aspects of Refugee Problems in Africa 1969 AHSG, CAB/LEG/24.3. Also available at http://www.africa-union.org; Beyani above n 284 at 119–24. See also African Charter, art 12(3).

[288] See also arts 4(2)(k), 10(2)(c). See the judgment of the United Nations International Criminal Tribunal for Rwanda. *In the case of Akayesu* Case No ICTR-96-4-T. N Pillay 'Violence against Women: State Sponsored Violence' in United Nations (ed) *Bringing International Human Rights Law Home* (New York, United Nations, 2002) 61. See also UNHCR *Sexual Violence against Refugees: Guidelines on Prevention and Responses* (Geneva, UNHCR, 1995); UNHCR *Guidelines on International Protection: Gender Related Persecution within the Context of Article 1A (2) of the 1951 Convention and/or its 1967 Protocol Relating to the Status of Refugees* (7 May 2002) HCR.GIP/02/01.

However, due to shortage of resources, the conditions under which refugees and internally displaced people live is challenging.[289] Women are particularly vulnerable to physical abuse as a result of the frustration of their partners, who beat them; sexual abuse at the hands of aid personnel[290] and those responsible for guarding them;[291] and they may also have to provide 'sexual favours' to access food or protection.[292] Added to this is the likelihood of inadequate health facilities[293] in the camps, making it unlikely that the reproductive health needs of women and adolescents will be met.[294] Should women fall pregnant in the camps, they are without the support networks of family and other women, which may be disconcerting for first-time mothers and disorienting for even the most experienced mother. The break in schooling for children increases pressures on young women to marry early.[295] In poor countries where resources are already stretched, the influx of more people to use up the limited services may create resentment in the local population, who may behave in an abusive way towards the refugees. All of this is alienating and increases the likelihood of depression and suicide.

Health as a human right

The right to health is recognised and guaranteed in both international and regional instruments.[296] However, access to health care in the broadest terms presents a constant challenge to many in Africa.[297] This can be linked in part to the

---

[289] Z Abraham and H Hajiyannis 'The Reproductive Health Needs of Young Refugees in South Africa' (2001) 39 *Women's Health Project Review* at 17; T Mukabideli 'Refugee Health: The Plight of Rwandan Women' (2000) 3 *Initiatives on Reproductive Health Policy* 10.

[290] Human Rights Watch *Refugees Still at Risk: Continuing Refugee Protection Concerns in Guinea* (New York, Human Rights Watch, 2001). See also Human Rights Watch *War within War: Sexual Violence against Women in Eastern Congo* (New York, Human Rights Watch, 2002).

[291] Human Rights Watch *Seeking Refuge, Finding Terror: The Widespread Rape of Somali Women Refugees in North Eastern Kenya* (New York, Human Rights Watch, 1993); Human Rights Watch *Crime or Custom? Violence in Tanzania's Refugee Camps* (New York, Human Rights Watch, 2000).

[292] ICPD para 10.24.

[293] Cf African Protocol on Women's Rights art 10(2)(d).

[294] C Harris and I Smith 'The Reproductive Health of Refugees: Lessons Beyond ICPD' in C Sweetman (ed) (2001) *Gender, Development and Health* (Oxford, OXFAM, 2001) 10; WHO '25 Questions' above n 277 at 27–28.

[295] F Butegwa *et al* above n 284 at 21. See also ICPD para 5.5.

[296] ICESCR art 12, CEDAW art 12; African Charter art 16.

[297] CESCR General Comment No 14 provides an interpretation of the right to health as demanding these essential elements: availability, accessibility defined as physical, economic and information, acceptability and quality. At para 12. See also the list of core obligations at para 43. CEDAW, art 12(1). See also CEDAW General Recommendation No 24 paras 13–15, 29–31; ICPD (1994) paras 7.2, 7.3; Beijing Platform for Action 1995 para 94; B Toebes 'Towards an Improved Understanding of the International Human Right to Health' (1999) 21 *Human Rights Quarterly* 661 at 666–67, 677–78. WHO '25 Questions' above n 277 at 7–15. African Commission 'Summary of the Facts of the Ogoni Case' 1 (27 May 2002) ACHPR/COMM/A044/1 (27 May 2002) 1 at 4.

rolling back of state-provided health care services, due to financial cut-backs brought on by structural adjustment programmes that demanded the abandonment of state subsidies on basic services and led to increased privatisation of services, placing them out of the reach of many.[298] The Zimbabwe office of the Women and Law in Southern Africa Trust reports on a 73 per cent decrease in the use of the family planning services provided by the Harare municipality after charges were introduced for accessing health services, including contraception.[299] In its General Recommendation No 24, the CEDAW makes clear its concerns about privatisation and goes on to note that states parties 'cannot absolve themselves of responsibility in these areas by delegating or transferring these powers to private sector agencies'.[300] The African Protocol is alive to these new challenges and provides that states should:

> ensure that the negative effects of globalisation and any adverse effects of the implementation of trade and economic policies and programmes are reduced to a minimum for women.[301]

Arguably all Africans (both men and women) have been affected negatively by globalisation,[302] so the African Protocol on Women's Rights might have referred to the disproportionate impact on women of these policies rather than simply demanding that they be reduced to a minimum for women.[303]

---

[298] Skard above n 116 at 163. P Maramba, B Olateru-Olagebi and R Webanenou *Structural Adjustment Programmes and the Human Rights of African Women* (Harare, WILDAF, 1995). See in particular 13–18 on the right to health. On p 15 is a diagram with the shocking information that state spending on defence has increased out of all proportion to spending on health and education, no doubt explaining the inclusion in the African Protocol on Women's Rights 2003 of art 10(3), enjoining states 'to take the necessary measures to reduce military expenditure significantly in favour of spending on social development in general and the promotion of women in particular'. See also A Kuenyehia 'The Impact of Structural Adjustment Policies on Women's International Human Rights: The Example of Ghana' in R Cook (ed) *Human Rights of Women: National and International Perspectives* (Philadelphia, University of Pennsylvania Press, 1994) 422.

[299] WLSA, Zimbabwe above n 205 at 41.

[300] CEDAW General Recommendation No 24 para 17.

[301] African Protocol on Women's Rights art 19(f). See also Report by the Independent Expert on Structural Adjustment, Mr Fantu Cheru, Effects of Structural Adjustment Policies on the Full Enjoyment of Human Rights (24 February 1999) UN Doc E/CN.4/1999/50. See also Beijing + 5 Outcome Document (2000) above n 29 para 101(a)–(o); L Tshuma 'The Impact of the IMF/World Bank Dictated Economic Structural Programmes on Human Rights: Erosion of Empowerment Rights' in P Nherere and M d'Engelbronner-Kolf (eds) *The Institutionalisation of Human Rights in Southern Africa* (Oslo, Nordic Human Rights Publications, 1993) 195; WHO '25 Questions' above n 277 at 24.

[302] J Stiglitz *Globalisation and Its Discontents* (London, Penguin, 2002) 9, 24, 49, 247–48. Johannesburg Declaration on Sustainable Development 2002 paras 4, 15, reproduced in N Middleton and P O'Keefe *Rio Plus Ten: Politics, Poverty and the Environment* (London, Pluto Press, 2003) 108–12, also available from http://www.johannesburgsummit.org; Z Randriamoro 'African Women Challenging Neo-Liberal Economic Orthodoxy: The Conception and Mission of the GERA Programme' in J Kerr and C Sweetman (eds) *Women Reinventing Globalization* (Oxford, OXFAM, 2003) 44 at 48; WHO '25 Questions' above n 277 at 25.

[303] R McCorquodale and R Fairbrother 'Globalisation and Human Rights' (1999) 21 *Human Rights Quarterly* 735; B Adeleye-Fayemi 'Creating a New World with New Visions: African Feminism and

A related issue is that of aid policies of northern states. Given that women carry the disproportionate burden of reproductive 'work', international policies such as the United States Mexico City Policy[304] raise concern. Specifically this policy has led to a cut in funding from the United States to organisations that offer abortion services,[305] or information or counselling on abortion.[306] The effects have been catastrophic, not least because both governments and non-governmental organisations involved in reproductive rights work have to agree to the US plan or risk forfeiting all reproductive health funding.[307] The global gag rule is based on the United States government responding not to the needs of 'aid recipients', but rather to domestic pressures brought to bear on it by, amongst others, fundamentalist Christian groups.

It is difficult to see how the global gag rule can be squared with the demands of international human rights. Specifically, the Committee overseeing the Covenant on Economic, Social and Cultural Rights[308] has noted that states have minimum core obligations,[309] which provide that a failure to provide basic essential services, including food, health care, shelter and housing, to a significant number of people in the state constitutes a violation of the Covenant.[310] Although acknowledging resource constraints, the Committee makes clear that 'the obligation remains for a State Party to ensure the widest possible enjoyment of the relevant rights under

Trends in the Global Women's Movement' in J Kerr *et al* (eds) *The Future of Women's Rights* (London, Zed Press, 2004) 38–39.

[304] Commonly known as the global gag rule. See http://www.globalgagrule.org.

[305] Except where there is a threat to the life of a woman, or in cases of rape or incest.

[306] Globalgagrule.org 'Access Denied: US Restrictions on International Family Planning—Introduction' downloaded from http://www.globalgagrule.org at http://64.224.18238/globalgagrule/ at 1. See also Population Action International 'Why the Global Gag Rule Undermines US Foreign Policy and Harms Women's Health' downloaded from: http://www.populationaction.org/resources/factsheets/factsheet_5.htm.

[307] IRIN 'Kenya: US Policy Jeopardizing Women's Health Says Report' downloaded from: http://www.irinnews.org/print.asp?ReportID=36839; IRIN 'Ethiopia: Rapid Birth Rate "Undermining" Economic Recovery' downloaded from: http://www.irinnews.org/print.asp?Report ID=37068. See also Globalgagrule.org 'The Impact of the Global Gag Rule in Ethiopia' from http://www.globalgagrule.org.

[308] The United States has not ratified this Covenant.

[309] CESCR General Comment 3: The Nature of States Parties' Obligations (art 2(1) of the Covenant), (Fifth Session, 1990) UN DOC E/1991/23. Annex III para 10. See also The Maastricht Guidelines on Violations of Economic, Social and Cultural Rights (1998) 20 *Human Rights Quarterly* 69 para 9. These built on the Limburg Principles on the Implementation of the International Covenant on Economic, Social and Cultural Rights UN Doc E/CN.4/1987/17. V Dankwa, C Flinterman and S Leckie 'Commentary on the Maastricht Guidelines on Violations of Economic, Social and Cultural Rights' (1998) 20 *Human Rights Quarterly* 705 at 716–18; 'Montreal Principles on Women's Economic, Social and Cultural Rights' (2004) 26 *Human Rights Quarterly* 760.

[310] CESCR General Comment No 3 at para 10.This has not prevented oil rich Nigeria from failing to provide basic health care services to 49% of its population. M Arigbede 'COPODIN Family: Dare to Be Different' in H Chigudu (ed) *Composing a New Song: Stories of Empowerment from Africa* (London, Commonwealth Secretariat, 2003) 1 at 3.

the prevailing circumstances'.[311] Poverty and other demands on state funds notwithstanding, this requires the protection of vulnerable members of society by means of the state providing 'relatively low cost targeted programmes'.[312] In its General Comment on health,[313] the Committee on Economic, Social and Cultural Rights (CESCR) confirms that the following are 'obligations of comparable priority':

> To ensure reproductive, maternal (pre-natal as well as post-natal) and child health care.[314]

Of obligations under the African Charter, which also provides for a right to health,[315] it is noted:

> The International Covenant on Economic, Social and Cultural Rights is characterized by the terms 'maximum available resources' and 'progressive realisation'. In contrast, the rights contained in the Charter are immediately enforceable and are not subject to resource constraints, although in reality, the availability of resources could potentially play a role in the determination of whether or not a State Party has met its obligations in terms of the Charter.[316]

In the international arena Africa as 'supplicant' finds itself in an invidious position—experiencing extreme hardship but reliant on northern 'generosity' to help meet its needs.[317] There is a here a parallel between women's inability to negotiate safe sex with partners and the inability of southern states to have relationships based on equality of bargaining power with northern states. Nothing more clearly

---

[311] CESCR General Comment No 3 at para 11. See also Maastricht Guidelines 9 and 10. Montreal Principles (2004); WHO '25 Questions' above n 277 at 14–15.

[312] CESCR General Comment No 3 at para 12.

[313] CESCR General Comment No 14 paras 43–45. Special Rapporteur on Violence against Women (1999b) above n 156 at paras 66–78 at 17–20. See South African Case of *Soobramoney v Minister of Health, Kwa Zulu Natal* 1998 (1) SA 765 (CC), where the court held that s 27 of the Constitution on the right to health did not entitle a person to dialysis treatment. Rather, in determining health policy the needs of many had to be factored in when deciding how limited resources should be allocated. Also, the court noted that determination of health care policy should be left to the executive not the judiciary. For a short commentary on the case see R Burchill 'Soobramoney v Minister of Health (Kwa-Zulu Natal) Constitutional Court of South Africa CCT 32/97 (26 November 1997)' (1998) *Human Rights Law Review* 41. But see the cases which followed. *Government of South Africa v Grootboom* 2001 (1) SA 46 (CC). See also the South African case of *Minister of Health and Others v Treatment Action Campaign and Others* 2002 (5) SA 721 (CC); T Magaisa 'Minister of Health and Others v. Treatment Action Campaign and Others' (2003) 47 *Journal of African Law* 117; G Van Bueren 'Including the Excluded: The Case for an Economic, Social and Cultural Human Rights Act' (2002) *Public Law* 456.

[314] CESCR General Comment No 14 para 44. ACRWC, 1990 art 14. Constitution of the Republic of South Africa, 1996 Art 27(1)(a). See also African Protocol on Women's Rights art 14(2)(b).

[315] African Charter art 16.

[316] G Bekker 'The Social and Economic Rights Action Center and the Center for Economic and Social Rights/Nigeria' (2003) 47 *Journal of African Law* 126 at 128. African Commission on Human and Peoples' Rights above n 297 at 3. Cf UN Report of the Ad Hoc Committee of the Twenty-First Special Session of the General Assembly (1999) above n 165 para 11.

[317] Cf S Sinding 'Resist Attempts to Roll Cairo Back' (2003) 44 *Women's Health Project Review* 17.

shows this than the reliance on northern countries for aid in general,[318] but more explicitly for funding to tackle the HIV pandemic.[319] African leaders are reduced to bystanders as they watch, and hope that the Global Fund[320] will be topped up and they will be able to access funding without too many strings being attached.[321]

It says a great deal about the aid situation that one of the main donors in the AIDS field is a private businessman by the name of Gates. Still, it is important to acknowledge initiatives such as that by former United States President Clinton, which involves rolling out country programmes and which works in conjunction with other agencies, including the World Health Organization, to try to stem the spread of HIV and to provide anti-retroviral drugs for those who need them.[322]

Specifically the Clinton Foundation's HIV/AIDS initiative aimed in 2003 to get drugs to people at a cost of 36 cents a day.[323] However, even at that relatively inexpensive price, few people on a continent where an entire family sometimes has to subsist on US$1 a day can afford to pay for drugs. The problem is compounded when more than one family member is affected. According to statistics produced by the United Nations:

> [B]y the end of the year 2000, 36.1 million people worldwide were living with HIV/AIDS, 90 per cent in developing countries and 75 per cent in sub-Saharan Africa.[324]

Although commendable, the Clinton initiative to negotiate cheaper prices for drugs represents but the tip of the iceberg. This links up with the issue of drug patents and intellectual property claims of international pharmaceutical companies, which for a long time resisted demands to allow the production of life-saving anti-retroviral drugs in generic form.[325] Pharmaceutical companies argued that they need to recoup the cost of developing the drugs and to generate enough income for research into drug treatments for the future.

---

[318] Overseas Development Institute (ODI) 'Can We Attain the Millennium Development Goals in Education and Health through Public Expenditure and Aid?' (April 2003) *ODI Briefing Paper*. See UN General Assembly Declaration on the Right to Development adopted by GA Res.41/128, 4 December 1986, art 3; Charter of the UN arts 55, 56 and ICESCR art 23 on international co-operation. WHO '25 Questions' above n 277 at 14–15.

[319] Sustainable Development Plan of Implementation 2002 para 58(b).

[320] See http://www.theglobalfund.org.

[321] Sustainable Development Plan of Implementation 2002 para 48(b). S Boseley 'Show Them the Money' *Guardian* (London, 30 October 2003).

[322] S Boseley 'Clinton's AIDS Deal Snubs Bush Plan' *Guardian* (London, 7 April 2004).

[323] *Ibid.*

[324] United Nations (2001) HIV/AIDS General Assembly Declaration para 3 . See also UNAIDS 'Fact sheet AIDS Epidemic in Sub-Saharan Africa' (2004) downloaded from www.unaids.org.

[325] Stiglitz above n 302 at 7–8, 245–46; Middleton and O'Keefe above n 302 at 45. See also the website of the South African Treatment Action Campaign, headed by the inspirational and incomparable Zachie Achmet, on its success in pressuring the South African government to relent and agree to provide free anti-retrovirals in public health institutions. See http://www.tac.org.za/; S Boseley 'US Firms Try to Block Cheap AIDS Drugs' *Guardian* (London, 20 March 2004); OXFAM *Cut the Cost Campaign* (Oxford, OXFAM, 2002). See http://www.oxfam.org.uk/cutthecost.

In 2003, President Bush announced that he was setting up a $15 billion fund to be disbursed over five years in the fight against AIDS in the developing world. However, it soon became clear that much of the 'aid' was tied. One of the early requirements, since removed due to international lobbying and pressure, was the requirement that anti-retroviral drugs be sourced from US-based pharmaceutical companies, which would supply the more expensive patented drugs.[326] Moreover, a large chunk of the money was to be used on abstinence campaigns.

The last section considers strategies that have been put forward to improve upon women's reproductive rights.

Strategies to protect women's reproductive rights

Seeing women's reproductive rights throughout their life cycle, it becomes clear that at every stage women are vulnerable. To address this vulnerability and to ensure that their rights are adequately protected, the Special Rapporteur on Violence against Women[327] makes 15 recommendations.[328] Her recommendations, echoed in other documents,[329] include ratification of international instruments; exercising due diligence in eliminating violence against women; the elimination of discrimination against women in the provision of health services; provision for training health workers in culturally and linguistically appropriate ways to deal with issues pertaining to reproductive rights;[330] sensitivity when dealing with the health needs of minorities; assistance in setting up refuges[331] and support groups; including the setting up of police stations staffed by women police officers; funding and commissioning research into issues affecting women's health, the provision of financial and institutional support for research on safe and

---

[326] S Boseley 'US Applauded for U-Turn on Cheap AIDS Drugs' *Guardian* (London, 18 May 2004).

[327] Special Rapporteur on Violence against Women (1999b) above n 156. See also B Klugman and J Moorman 'Gender Empowerment Issues within the Health Sector' (2003) 44 *Women's Health Project Review* 3.

[328] Special Rapporteur on Violence against Women (1999b) above n 156 at paras 79–93.

[329] See for example CEDAW General Recommendation No 24 paras 29–31; AU Solemn Declaration on Gender Equality in Africa 2004 preamble, arts 1, 2, 4, 10.

[330] Here it is worth mentioning the Niamey Declaration emanating from a conference on Women, Islam and Family Planning. It called into question the misuse and misinterpretation of religion which resulted in violations of women's rights and to their being denied access to reproductive health services. The conference highlighted too the importance of having culturally appropriate approaches to manage cultural sensitivities around issues pertaining to reproduction and women's rights. See IPPF Africa Region and Family Welfare Association of Niger (ANBEF) *Report of the Regional Conference on Women, Islam and Family Planning, Niamey, Niger 23–25 October 1995* (London, IPPF, 1995). For the text of the Niamey Declaration see 22–23.

[331] Of course one has to assess the milieu to ensure that refuges are socially and culturally appropriate and will not lead to the woman being further ostracised for having gone to seek help from strangers.

effective methods of contraception, and also the treatment for and protection against HIV/AIDS.[332]

Here it is worth reiterating that the high cost of anti-retroviral drugs is a major problem and in itself constitutes a violation of people's right to adequate, affordable and accessible health services as provided for in the CESCR.[333] Although challenges to the use of intellectual property and patent rules to protect the interests of pharmaceutical companies and, by implication, deny the rights of millions of people to available drugs are ongoing, Msimang notes with concern the 'silence from our Northern sisters about the pandemic that is claiming so many lives'.[334]

Conclusion

The chapter has considered issues pertaining to violence against women and reproductive rights. It has highlighted the gender dimensions of violations of women's rights within these two spheres. Specifically it has made explicit that women experience violence in disproportion to men. This reveals that it is their relative powerlessness within society and the marital contract that lays them open to abuse. With regard to reproductive rights issues, women's life experiences are defined in terms of the three roles of daughter, wife/partner and mother.[335] Focusing on intersectional discrimination affecting refugee women, disabled women and elderly women again highlights how the dominant voices drown out the voices of the minority, and also how the majority experience renders invisible the needs of other women.[336] Perhaps the most vulnerable group of all is that comprising young women.[337]

---

[332] Cf CESCR (2000) General Comment No 14. See also Commonwealth Secretariat and Maritime Centre of Excellence for Women's Health above n 78 at 56–57.

[333] CESCR art 12(1) and art 15(1)(b) on the right to benefit from scientific progress. African Charter art 16. Skard above n 116 at 31. Msimang 'HIV/AIDS' above n 219 at 112.

[334] Msimang 'HIV/AIDS' above n 219 at 112; Msimang 'Caution' above n 219 at 182–83.

[335] Beijing +5 Outcome Document (2000) above n 29 at para 60.

[336] CEDAW General Recommendation No 24 para 6.

[337] Beijing + 5 Outcome Document (2000) above n 29 at para 43.

6

Female Genital Cutting, Human Rights and National Legislation

The people who practice FGC are honourable, upright, moral people who love their children and want the best for them.[1]

Introduction

From silence, to female circumcision, to female genital mutilation, to clitoridectomies, back to 'female circumcision' and harmful traditional practices via female genital surgeries, operations and cutting, before resting at female genital mutilation again, this multiple-named practice has become the 'hot-button' issue of recent years.[2] Mirroring its name changes have been the strategies advanced for dealing with the practice—these have varied from a laissez-faire attitude rooted in the belief that 'cultures' should be left to develop and change at their own pace free from external influence, to dealing with it as a health issue, as an issue about children, then to constructing it as a form of gender-based violence. All the approaches have been linked to calls for education as a tool in the struggle to transform attitudes and to bring the practice to an end.[3] Although not mutually exclusive, these approaches reflect the concerns and perspectives of different

---

[1] G Mackie 'Female Genital Cutting: The Beginning of the End' in B Shell-Duncan and Y Hernlund (eds) *Female 'Circumcision in Africa: Culture, Controversy and Change* (Colorado, Lynne Rienner Publishers, 2000) 253 at 280.

[2] The debate about what to call the practice is vociferous and on-going. In recent academic writing the preference has been to use the term Female Genital Cutting (FGC); in international instruments it would appear that increasingly the term used is Female Genital Mutilation (FGM). This chapter uses both terms.

[3] A Spadacini and P Nichols 'Campaigning against Female Genital Mutilation in Ethiopia Using Popular Education' (1998) 6 *Gender and Development* 2.

disciplines—anthropology with its emphasis on the study of culture,[4] the health concerns of the medical profession[5] and the regulatory focus of law.[6]

It is noticeable that the raised profile of the practice of female genital cutting (FGC) has been contemporaneous with the raised profile of human rights in global discourse.[7] The human rights canon encompasses all the perspectives on FGC identified above.[8] It is from the human rights perspective that the chapter explores the issue of female genital cutting and methods of tackling it.

The chapter starts with a consideration of the discourse around the naming of the practice and reasons given for its continuation. Thereafter it examines the debates that have occurred between black and white feminists over the construction of and strategies for dealing with FGC. The chapter then moves on to look at the location of FGC within the human rights framework. Thereafter, it considers the use of law as a tool for the regulation of behaviour and as a means of eradicating the practice. This is followed in the last section by a consideration of the role of civil society organisations in tackling the practice. Initiatives in three countries that are attempting to bring about an end to the practice of FGC are examined.

Constructing an understanding of the practice

In much the same way as the naming of the problem has changed and shifted over time, so too the definition or understanding of what constitutes or falls under the rubric of female genital mutilation has also evolved. The long-standing understanding of the practice has been that it comprises three 'types'. These are:

---

[4] E Gruenbaum *The Female Circumcision Debate: An Anthropological Perspective* (Philadelphia, University of Pennsylvania Press, 2001).

[5] British Medical Council *Female Genital Mutilation: Caring for Parents and Child Protection. Guidance from the British Medical Association* (London, British Medical Association, 2001); British Medical Association *The Medical Profession and Human Rights: Handbook for a Changing Agenda* (London, Zed Books, 2001).

[6] A Rahman and N Toubia (eds) *Female Genital Mutilation: A Guide to Laws and Policies Worldwide* (London, Zed Press, 2000); E Boyle and S Preves 'National Politics as International Process: The Case of Anti-Female Genital Cutting Laws' (2000) 34 *Law and Society Review* 703.

[7] H Lewis 'Between *Irua* and "Female Genital Mutilation": Feminist Human Rights Discourse and the Cultural Divide' (1995) 8 *Harvard Human Rights Journal* 1; F Sow 'Mutilations Génitales Féminines et Droits Humains en Afrique' (1998) 23 *Development* 13.

[8] D Berry 'Conflicts between Minority Women and Traditional Structures: International Law, Rights and Culture' (1998) 7 *Social and Legal Studies* 55; M Foblets 'Salem's Circumcision: The Encounter of Cultures in a Civil Action. A Belgian Case Study' (1991) 1 *Recht der Werkelijkheid* 43; A Slack 'Female Circumcision: A Critical Appraisal' (1988) 10 *Human Rights Quarterly* 43; A Renteln 'Is the Cultural Defense Detrimental to the Health of Children?' (1994) 7 *Law and Anthropology, International Yearbook for Legal Anthropology* 27; A Renteln *The Cultural Defense* (Oxford, Oxford University Press, 2004).

Type I—Excision of the prepuce with or without excision of part or all of the clitoris;
Type II—Excision of the prepuce and clitoris together with partial or total excision of the labia minora;
Type III—Excision of part or all of the external genitalia and stitching/narrowing of the vaginal opening (infibulation).[9]

The World Health Organization has added a fourth category, termed loosely 'unclassified'. In common with the other three, it has within it an element of manipulation of part of the genitalia. However, Type IV goes beyond cutting to include the following practices:

Type IV—Unclassified: Pricking, piercing, or incision of the clitoris and/or labia; Stretching of the clitoris and/or labia; Cauterisation by burning of the clitoris and surrounding tissues; Scraping (angurya cuts) of the vaginal orifice or cutting (gishiri cuts) of the vagina; Introduction of corrosive substances into the vagina to cause bleeding or herbs into the vagina with the aim of tightening or narrowing the vagina; Any other procedure that falls under the definition of female genital mutilation given above.[10]

This redefinition has had the effect of increasing significantly the number of countries where the practice occurs to cover large swathes of the African continent that previously had had no, or low, incidence reported of the 'traditional' FGC. As an example, the dry sex practices found in many southern African communities, which have been implicated in the spread of the HIV virus, must now be considered under the rubric of female genital mutilation as they fit Type IV. A survey undertaken in Lusaka, Zambia, indicated that 86% of sexually active women introduced drying agents into their vaginas to enhance the sexual pleasure of partners. Significantly 60% of women were in salaried employment, thus challenging the notion that these practices are the preserve of the poor or uneducated.[11] Type IV FGC also includes other practices such as 'pulling' of the labia to elongate them, a practice common to some Southern African groups and parts of Uganda.[12] It could also be argued, controversially perhaps, that the virginity tests performed upon Zulu girls in South Africa might fall under the rubric of FGC.[13]

[9] World Health Organization (WHO) *Female Genital Mutilation Programmes: What Works and What Doesn't A Review* WHO/CHS/WMH/99.5 (hereafter WHO *Female Genital Mutilation Programmes*) 3.

[10] *Ibid.*

[11] Southern African Research and Documentation Centre (SARDC) *Beyond Inequalities: Women in Zambia* (Harare, SARDC, 1998) 43.

[12] F Nagubere-Munaaba 'Victims of Protection' (M Phil thesis submitted to the Faculty of Law, University of Zimbabwe, Harare, 2001) 162.

[13] Reuters, Johannesburg 'Virginity Tests on Comeback Trail in South Africa' reproduced in (2001) *Jenda: A Journal of Culture and African Women Studies: 1,* 1 at http://www.jendajournal.com/jenda/vol1.1/virginity.html. S Msimang 'HIV/AIDS, Globalisation and the International Women's Movement' in J Kerr and C Sweetman (eds) *Women Reinventing Globalization* (Oxford, OXFAM, 2003) 109 at 112; S Leclerc-Madlala 'Virginity Testing Diverts Attention from the Lack of Male Sexual Responsibility' (2003) 40 *Women's Health Project Review* 3. South African law bans FGM. See South Africa Equality Act 2000 s 8(b). Virginity testing has also been recorded in Lesotho. Special Rapporteur

Here it is worth noting that a criticism often made of the anti-FGC lobby is that it conflates the types, thus creating the impression that in all places the most severe type is practised. This is said to be a gross distortion of the facts.[14] Abusharaf contends that there can be several types practised in one country.[15] This highlights the importance of careful description and carefully targeted intervention strategies.

Regardless of the type, it seems that commonalities exist in rationales put forward for the continuation of the practice, which are linked to the position of women within society, the valuing of the purity of women together with a need to control their sexuality and the premium put on marriage.[16] The exception is labia pulling, which is said to enhance sexual pleasure.

Reasons given for the practice

In direct contrast to the practice of elongation of the labia identified in certain Southern African countries, in parts of Sierra Leone, one of the reasons advanced for the continuation of the practice includes controlling the growth of the female genitalia so that they do not grow to rival those of the male:

> In short, the clitoris is analogous to a *dysfunctional* penis where women's reproduction and (hetero) sexuality is concerned. Thus, excision can be interpreted metaphorically and physiologically as an eschewal of undeveloped, inhibiting, masculinity.[17]

Ahmadu explains that for the Kono of north-eastern Sierra Leone, the practice was constructed around the societal belief that children are born androgynous. The initiation ritual involving excision denotes the point at which the ambiguity is removed, the sex of the person becomes fixed and the person is ascribed the title man or woman. However, having given this explanation for the cultural under-pinnings of the practice, Ahmadu goes on to note that in modern times this is not the explanation that is given by those who continue the practice.[18] She notes:

on Violence against Women, Its Causes and Consequences, Ms Radhika Coomaraswamy Submitted in Accordance with Commission on Human Rights Resolution 1995/85 (5 February 1996) E/CN.4/1996/53 para 29.

[14] See for example B Shell-Duncan, W Obiero and L Muruli 'Women without Choices: The Debate Over Medicalisation of Female Genital Cutting and Its Impact on a Northern Kenyan Community' in B Shell-Duncan and Y Hernlund (eds) *Female 'Circumcision' in Africa: Culture, Controversy and Change* (Colorado, Lynne Reiner Publishers, 2000) 109 at 109–10.

[15] R Abusharaf 'Revisiting Feminist Discourse on Infibulation: Responses from Sudanese Feminists' in B Duncan and Y Hernlund (eds) above n 14, 151 at 152.

[16] World Vision *Female Genital Mutilation and Early Marriage in Africa* (Milton Keynes, World Vision 2002) 9.

[17] F Ahmadu 'Rites and Wrongs: An Insider/Outsider Reflects on Power and Excision' in B Shell-Duncan and Y Hernlund (eds) above n 14, 283 at 298.

[18] *Ibid* at 296.

[S]uch worldview explanations that justify genital operations could rightly be inter-preted as local ideological rationalizations that ensure the social status quo and the dominance of one group over another.[19]

Within this paradigm, the dominant group includes older women exerting an influence over younger women within the society.[20] Ahmadu herself appears to equivocate over the construct of power that she ascribes to the ritual and training surrounding it. She explains the rationale behind the requirement that young women subvert themselves to both older women and selected men thus:

Secondly, novices are taught the *art* of subservience to some categories of men, that is, their future husbands and other male representatives of those lineages. . . . In the second instance vis à vis their husbands and their male (and female) lineage representatives, young novices are taught to *feign* subservience—in verbal communication, body language and gestures, and the performance of domestic duties—in order to live har-moniously among their affines.[21]

Ahmadu uses seductive words like 'art' and 'feign' to mask the subservience of younger women and to obfuscate gender hierarchies. Although she notes that the initiators' role involves creating a 'dual-natured' woman, at once honed in the art of appearing subservient yet simultaneously strong,[22] the primary goal of the cut-ting appears to be to enable the initiated woman to compete in a strong market for a husband-provider, who will be able to look after her and the children born of the union in return for her subservience. Seen in this way, it becomes difficult to distinguish the socialisation of Kono women in this 'dual-sex' structure from the socialisation of women in patrilineal (more accurately, patriarchal) societies. Moreover, the changes wrought to Sierra Leonean society by colonialism and a long and brutal civil war, accompanied by economic and social transformation and (arguably) collapse, call into question the notion that the society has remained unaffected and continues to operate on the basis of an unmodified dual-sex model.

There are still other reasons put forward to explain the practice of FGC. For example, Babatunde has argued that for the Keti Yoruba of Nigeria, FGC is linked to fertility and is not for 'purposes of control and power'.[23] He notes:

The logic of the practice is couched in the anthropological term of prestation, a gift that you give under pain of sanction, for which you receive a greater gift in return. The logic of clitoridectomy is that by taking a tiny bit of the sacred instrument of fertility as an offering, the god of fertility will bless you with more children and easier childbirth.[24]

---

[19] *Ibid.*
[20] *Ibid.*
[21] *Ibid* at 300.
[22] *Ibid.*
[23] E Babatunde *Women's Rights versus Women's Rites: A Study of Circumcision among the Ketu-Yoruba of South Western Nigeria* (Eritrea, Africa World Press, 1998) 21.
[24] *Ibid* at 181.

Although religion, specifically Islam, used to be put forward as the reason for the practice, this has been challenged. The Special Rapporteur on Violence against Women makes clear that she is 'firmly convinced that neither Islam, nor any other religion, is connected with female genital mutilation.'[25] However, discussing the findings of the Sudan Demographic Health Survey of 1991–92, Abusharaf notes that it is significant that both Muslim and Christian women undergo the practice with 47 per cent of Christian women being 'circumcised', 'whereas among Muslim women in the region of Darfur, 65 per cent have not been "circumcised".'[26]

The often heated debates over the naming of the practice, as well as the meaning to be ascribed to it, have been echoed in the feminist debates. These are worth exploring further.

Feminist contestations over meaning and strategies around FGC

The FGC debate has brought to the fore different feminist perspectives on 'culture', 'sisterhood', and strategies for interpreting and addressing culturally rooted practices. Debates in feminist circles in the 1980s showed that there was tension between northern-based (western) feminists such as Fran Hosken,[27] who called for the abolition of FGC, which she described as gender-based violence and a local manifestation of the operation of patriarchy,[28] and southern (African) feminists, who saw this approach as a new form of cultural imperialism that was to be resisted.[29] The southern women objected to the essentialising of African woman-

---

[25] Special Rapporteur on Violence against Women (1996) above n 13 at para 114. International Women's Rights Action Watch 'FGM in Court and Culture: An Advocacy Lesson from Egyptian Women' (1997) 11 *The Women's Watch* 1; Religious Tolerance Organisation 'Female Genital Mutilation in Africa, the Middle East, and the Far East' at http://www.religioustolerance.org/fem_cirm.htm; Afro-Arab Consultation on 'Legal Tools for the Prevention of Female Genital Mutilation' Cairo, 23 June 2003 (hereafter Cairo Declaration on FGM 2003) preamble available at http://www.aidos.it. See also 'Mrs Mubarak Launches Strong Initiative against FGM' *Egyptian Gazette* (Cairo, 22 June 2003). However, see A Mbye 'We Shall not Ban FGM President Jammeh Tells Religious Elders' (newspaper/magazine report) (Gambia, 15–17 January 1999) (on file with author). See also L Dellenberg 'A Reflection on the Cultural Meanings of Female Circumcision: Experiences from Fieldwork in Casamance, Southern Senegal' in S Arnfred (ed) *Rethinking Sexualities in Africa* (Lund, Nordic Institute, 2004) 79 at 82.

[26] Abusharaf above n 15 at 152.

[27] F Hosken *The Hosken Report: Genital/Sexual Mutilation of Females* (Lexington, Women's International Network, 1994); F Hosken *Stop Female Genital Mutilation: Women Speak Facts and Actions* (Lexington, Women's International Network News, 1995).

[28] J Davison *Gender, Lineage, and Ethnicity in Southern Africa* (Oxford, Westview, 1997) 32–33.

[29] Abusharaf summarises the criticisms of the Hosken report. Abusharef above n 15 at 160–64. See also K Green and H Lim 'What is This Thing about Female Circumcision? Legal Education and Human Rights' (1998) 7 *Social and Legal Studies* 365 at 370.

hood into an homogeneous 'oppressed' group. They resented too the tone used by Hosken and her acolytes, which they denounced as imperious, hectoring and culturally insensitive.[30] They challenged the assertion made that this was a uniquely African/Arab practice and the value judgments that entailed. Interestingly, Gunning's research indicates that far from being a uniquely African practice, FGS (she calls it surgery) was performed on women in both the United States of America and Europe as a means of treating hysteria and controlling nymphomania.[31]

A group of African women researchers were so outraged by what they saw as western misrepresentations of 'African practices' that they put out a statement on genital cutting.[32] In it, they likened the new-found interest in FGC to Christian crusades of old and noted that:

> [T]he new crusaders have fallen back on sensationalism, and have become insensitive to the dignity of the women they want to 'save'. They are totally unconscious of the latent racism that such a campaign evokes in countries where ethnocentric prejudice is so deep-rooted. And in their conviction that this is a 'just cause', they have forgotten that these women from a different race and a different culture are also human beings, and that solidarity can only exist alongside self-affirmation and mutual respect.[33]

The statement went on to note that AAWORD condemned FGC. However, it argued that in working out strategies for the elimination of the practice, attention should be paid not only to the cultural underpinnings and justifications advanced for its continuation, but also to issues of exploitation and poverty that contributed to the perpetuation of the practice. Failure to do this was likened to 'refusing to see the sun in the middle of the day'.[34] It was further noted that westerners who ignored these factors also appeared to ignore the fact that they were beneficiaries of the exploitation of African people including women. Finally, western campaigners were told that:

> They must accept that it is a problem for African women, and that no change is possible without the conscious participation of African women.[35]

---

[30] See also Rahman and Toubia above n 6 at 10.

[31] I Gunning, 'Arrogant Perception, World Travelling and Multi-Cultural Feminism: The Case of Female Genital Surgeries' (1991) 23 *Columbia Human Rights Law Review* 189 at 201, 205–211. See also Boyle and Preves above n 6 at 709; Slack above n 8 at 461; G Greer *The Whole Woman* (London, Doubleday, 1999) 94.

[32] AAWORD (Association of African Women for Research and Development) 'A Statement on Genital Mutilation' reproduced in H Steiner and P Alston *International Human Rights in Context: Law, Politics, Morals* (Oxford, Clarendon Press, 2000) 418–19.

[33] *Ibid* at 419. See also M Mutua 'Savages, Victims, and Saviors: The Metaphor of Human Rights' (2001) 42 *Harvard International Law Journal* 201 at 226–27.

[34] AAWORD as cited in Steiner and Alston above n 32 at 419.

[35] *Ibid.* See also A Diallo 'Paradoxes of Female Sexuality in Mali: On the Practices of *Magonmaka* and *Bolokoli-kela*' in S Arnfred (ed) *Rethinking Sexualities in Africa* (Lund, Nordic Africa Institute, 2004) at 186–88.

This statement set the parameters for the feminist debates that were to follow. Although the heat was taken out of the debate, largely by more careful use of language, recent developments have shown that it is simplistic to see the debate as being purely a black/white one. Indeed not all white women have condemned the practice.[36] After the publication of her book, *The Whole Woman*, Germaine Greer came under a lot of criticism from women of all shades for equivocating over FGC. In the chapter entitled 'Mutilation', Greer admitted to some doubts about condemning the practice.[37] At the reading/discussion that I attended at the Friends House in London, the aforementioned chapter was the one that generated the most heat and argumentation. Greer was lambasted by women from all sides of the racial and cultural divide, both for writing about things that she did not know about or had not herself experienced, and also for not criticising what some saw as a practice that was obviously discriminatory towards women and violated their rights. Admitting to a growing ambivalence, Greer had written:

> Although I was among the feminists at Mexico City in 1985 who first raised the problem of FGM in an international forum, I am loath now to pronounce upon its significance as a cultural phenomenon given the occult attachment to self mutilation that can be discerned in our culture.[38]

Pursuing the theme of self-mutilation in some northern societies, she had gone on to say:

> If an Ohio punk has the right to have her genitalia operated on, why has not the Somali woman the same right? We ought at least to entertain that the African woman is having FGM done for herself and allow her the same access to professional assistance as Jen Angel (the Ohio punk) can expect.[39]

Over time it has come to seem that the majority of African women on the continent who write about FGC are unequivocal about their desire to see the practice ended.[40] However, those in the diaspora, with greater exposure to 'northern' writing and debate, are still fighting a rearguard action to challenge perceptions of

---

[36] M Parker 'Female Circumcision and Cultures of Sexuality' in T Skelton and T Allen (eds) *Culture and Global Change* (London, Routledge, 1998) 201; Dellenberg above n 25 at 88–92.

[37] Greer above n 31 at 94–105.

[38] *Ibid* at 97.

[39] *Ibid* at 99. See also R Howard 'Health Costs of Social Degradation and Female Self-Mutilation in North America' in K Mahoney and P Mahoney (eds) *Human Rights in the Twenty-First Century* (The Hague, Kluwer Publishing, 1993) 503.

[40] See P Akpan 'Health Complications Arising from FGM' The African Women's Development and Communication Network (FEMNET) (2001) *Our Rights*, where she says, at 3: '. . . the consequences of FGM are grave. More effort should be put into eradicating this cruel practice that debases humanity as a whole, particularly women.' Downloaded from http://www.africaonline.co.ke/femnet/ rights2.html. See also the Editorial 'FGM: This Evil Practice Must Stop!' FEMNET (2001) *Our Rights*, downloaded from http://www.africaonline.co.ke/femnet/rights1.html. The editorial ends 'Finally, a deadline must be set for the total elimination of this *evil* from the face of the earth' (emphasis added). At 1. See also S Minkah-Premo *Coping with Violence against Women* (Accra, Asempa Publishers, 2001) 10, 12, 15, 28.

African women as backward and the practice as oppressive. Part of the defence strategy for this group involves noting the increase in the use of plastic surgery by northern women, in itself a 'cultural practice' rooted in socialisation and male oppression, the same reasons said to be given by northern women in condemning FGC. The construction of cosmetic surgery as the northern equivalent of FGC is widespread. To show the hypocrisy of northerners who condemn FGC, the United States-based *JENDA* Journal pieced together articles on a Hollywood surgeon who operated on women to create 'designer vaginas'.[41] The implication was that there was little to distinguish so-called female genital mutilation and the 'designer vagina' surgery. Interestingly, the *Sunday Times* published in London also ran a feature on vaginoplasty in its style section. Discussing the American phenomenon of vaginal plastic surgery, the article noted:

> Actually they seemed to mean the whole thing—vagina, labia majora, labia minora and all . . . Most of them seemed to be worried about the way they look on the outside; it seems most wanted to look like eight year old girls, with innocent, tightly closed outer lips and practically no inner lips or pubic hair.[42]

Seemingly without irony, on the same day, the same newspaper ran an interview with Shukri Harir Ismael, a Somali radio agony aunt and soap opera producer, part of whose remit involves challenging the practice of FGC. Highlighted in the interview are the words: 'I told my mother that female genital mutilation was criminal, not religious. She wouldn't speak to me for weeks.'[43]

The frustration of the diaspora Africans is grounded in a perception that African practices are highlighted to show, in the words of Babatunde, that:

> Africa is the land of torture and mutilation. America is the center of healing. The intermediaries, as usual, are the missionaries. This time however, the missionaries are African-Americans. America is also the land of well-motivated freedom fighters who must take the battle to other lands on behalf of all abused women.[44]

In this mode, Alice Walker has come in for a great deal of criticism for her book *Possessing the Secret of Joy*.[45] She is lambasted for replicating the mistakes of white feminists, who construct(ed) Africa as the 'dark' continent ripe for salvation by

---

[41] 'Genital Landscaping, Labia Remodelling and Vestal Vagina: Female Genital Mutilation or Female Genital Cosmetic Surgery' [Media Articles on Designer Vaginas] (2001) *Jenda: A Journal of Culture and African Women's Studies: 1*, 1 at http://www.jendajournal.com/jenda/vol1.1/Dvagina. html. Interestingly this collection of newspaper and magazine pieces came after two articles arguing against proposals to outlaw FGC in Nigeria. N Omoigu 'Protest against Bill H22 Outlawing "FGM" in Nigeria' (2001) *Jenda: A Journal of Culture and African Women Studies: 1*, 1 downloaded from http://www.jendajournal.com/jenda/vol1.1/omogui.html; S Nwabuzor 'Opposition to Proposed HB22 Bill on Female Genital Mutilation' in (2001) *Jenda: A Journal of Culture and African Women Studies: 1*, 1 downloaded from http:///www.jendajournal.com/jenda/vol1.1/nwaubuzor.html.

[42] 'Vanessa Wilde's Secret Diary' *Sunday Times* (London, 15 September 2002) 39.

[43] 'A Life in the Day' *Sunday Times* (London, 15 September 2002) 66.

[44] Babatunde above n 23 at 18.

[45] A Walker *Possessing the Secret of Joy* (New York, Pocket Books, 1992).

America with its liberal values.[46] Ironically for someone like Walker, who has contributed much to an expanded understanding of feminism and its various constituencies, she finds herself being criticised for assuming that there is a unitary 'African' position, thus homogenising the African experience.[47] Moreover, she is charged with creating African victims to further her own objectives, which are said to be to expose and lobby for the ending of a practice that she so evidently abhors. Her authority to speak on the subject is challenged by Oyewumi, who notes:

> It needs to be understood that representation cannot be on the bases of pigmentation or a common collection of body parts, but on the commonality of interests, recognizing that interests are dynamic and situational. It is a fallacy to think that common interests can be discerned just by colour, and it is a mistake to act as if groups and group interests are cast in stone.[48]

Similarly Nako asserts that Walker's position is dangerous, for:

> In speaking about and for African women Walker does nothing to disrupt the hegemonic hierarchies, but rather reinforces them because she acts as a legitimating presence who facilitates discourse on a taboo subject.[49]

Over time the voices of a range of African women,[50] both diaspora and local, have become more prominent in the FGC debate. Of particular interest is the work of Efua Dorkenoo and Nahid Toubia, who both founded organisations[51] to tackle issues of FGC and women's health, and increasingly human rights, and who have both contributed to the literature on FGC.[52] They have addressed the causes and consequences of the practice and put forward practical suggestions for tackling it.

---

[46] O Oyewumi 'Alice in Motherland: Reading Alice Walker on Africa and Screening the Colour "Black"' (2001) *Jenda: A Journal of Culture and African Women's Studies:* 1, 2 downloaded from http://www.jendajournal.com/jenda/vol1.2/oyewumi.html. See also N Nako 'Possessing the Voice of the Other: African Women and the "Crisis of Representation" in Alice Walker's Possessing the Secret of Joy' (2001) *Jenda: A Journal of Culture and African Women's Studies:* 1, 2 downloaded from http://www.jendajournal.com/jenda/vol1.2/nako.html; Babatunde above n 23 at 17ff. Gunning above n 31 at 199.

[47] Oyewumi above n 46 at 6.

[48] Nako above n 46 at 9. See also Gunning above n 31 at 198.

[49] Nako above n 46 at 5.

[50] A El Dareer *Woman, Why Do You Weep?* (London, Zed Press, 1982); O Koso-Thomas *Circumcision of Women: A Strategy for Eradication* (London, Zed Press, 1987); El Sadaawi's biography and her public stance on the issue have also done much to raise the profile of FGC. N El Sadaawi *The Hidden Face of Eve: Women in the Arab World* (London, Zed Press, 1997). See also Abusharaf on the work of Sudanese feminists and religious leaders. Abusharaf above n 15 at 156ff; L Obiora 'Bridges and Barricades: Rethinking Polemics and Intransigence in the Campaign against Female Circumcision' (1997) 47 *Case Western Reserve Law Review* 275; W Dirie and C Miller *Desert Flower* (London, Virago Press, 1998); F Kassindja and L Bashir *Do They Hear You When You Cry?* (London, Bantam Press, 1998).

[51] Dorkenoo founded The Foundation for the Development for the Health and Welfare of Women (FORWARD). Toubia founded Research Action and Information Network for the Bodily Integrity of Women (RAINBO).

[52] E Dorkenoo *Cutting the Rose: Female Genital Mutilation The Practice and Its Prevention* (London, Minority Rights Publications, 1994); E Dorkenoo and S Elworthy *Female Genital Mutilation: Proposals for Change* (London, Minority Rights Group, 1996); N Toubia *Female Genital Mutilation: A Call for*

Interestingly, in her critique of literature on FGC, Ahmadu notes that Toubia has not been cut and that Dorkenoo comes from an ethnic group that does not practice FGC, thus seeming to question their authority to speak on the issue.[53]

The issue of agency and 'representativity' (or who speaks 'for' or about a particular issue) is clearly an important one when discussing FGC. In this regard, Gunning has developed an interesting and sensitive approach for discussing cultures other than one's own. She models it on the world-travelling approach devised by Lugones.[54] Gunning sees the world-travelling approach as being about recognising 'both independence and interconnectedness'[55] between self and others. She puts forward a three-point methodology for examining the cultural practices of others that one finds challenging. This three-point strategy requires one to '(1) understand one's own historical context, . . . (2) . . . see yourself as the other woman might see you . . . (3) . . . see the other woman, her world, her sense of self through her eyes.'[56]

If one accepts the underlying principle of Gunning's world-travelling method, which is 'walk in my shoes before you judge me', one can see why conflicts have arisen between feminists over the practice of FGC. Those who wish to eradicate it cannot understand how anyone would seek to defend what is clearly, to them, a physically painful and potentially dangerous (life-threatening) practice; whilst those who seek to defend it, do so as much out of outrage at the lack of understanding and patronising condemnation from the 'other' side, as from a perception that the 'other side' should put its own house in order, that is deal with issues such as cosmetic surgery and racism, before criticising others. Arguably both sides have failed to engage in the 'playfulness' that Gunning determines is important in world travelling:

> 'playfulness' is used to describe an openness in traveling, an attitude that rejects rules and structures and a willingness to engage in a reconstruction of self without a concern for competence. . . . Playfulness demands . . . a willingness to explore new behavior or attitudes without determining the 'rightness' or 'wrongness' . . . At the end of a playful journey, one finds that the victims of arrogant perception[57] are really 'subjects, lively beings, resistors,' [and] 'constructors of [their own] visions. One can recognize and respect their independence and yet understand their interconnectedness with oneself.[58]
> (notes omitted)

Global Action (Rainbo, New York, 1995); N Toubia 'Female Genital Mutilation' in J Peters and A Wolpe (eds) *Women's Rights, Human Rights: International Feminist Perspectives* (New York, Routledge, 1995) 224; Rahman and Toubia above n 6.

[53] Ahmadu above n 17 at 283.

[54] M Lugones 'Playfulness, World-Traveling and Loving Perception' (1987) 2 *Hypatia* 3, as cited by Gunning above n 31 at 202.

[55] *Ibid* at 204.

[56] Gunning above n 31 at 194.

[57] Those ordinarily constructed as the deviant other.

[58] Gunning above n 31 at 204.

This chapter now moves on to consider the development of FGC within the human rights discourse.

The human rights framework

Gender is central to the practice of FGC, and also to a study of human rights and their impact on the lives of women and children.[59] An examination of FGC from a human rights perspective reveals that, although at first left untouched because it was a 'cultural issue',[60] over time it has been considered under four rubrics:[61]

(a) health,
(b) violence,
(c) equality/discrimination,
(d) children's rights.

Of the four approaches, health has often been seen as the most culturally neutral and inoffensive. The first United Nations sponsored gathering to address the practice was convened around the issue of female circumcision as a health issue. However, difficulties identified with using the health approach are that it masks the fact that the practice constitutes gender-based violence against women and violates the rights of the girl child. Moreover, focusing on the negative health consequences of FGC leaves open the possibility of the continuation of the practice as long as it is made safer. Medicalisation, although favoured by some,[62] is seen as masking the gendered nature of FGC and impeding efforts to eradicate it.

Overhanging the debate about the most suitable approach has been a consideration of the values underpinning modern human rights and whether these are universally applicable. It is rare to find a discussion around the issue of cultural relativism that does not touch on the issue of FGM as evidencing culturally specific values.[63] It is indeed true that in many university human rights courses, cultural

---

[59] H Crawley *Refugees and Gender: Law and Process* (Bristol, Jordan Publishing, 2001) 185–86, 190.

[60] In response to a request made by the Economic and Social Council (ECOSOC) of the UN to the World Health Organization (WHO) asking it to look into 'customs involving ritual practices on girls and the measures in effect or planned to put an end to those practices'. WHO responded that 'the ritual practices in question resulting from social and cultural conceptions are not within WHO's jurisdiction' (as cited by Religious Tolerance Organisation at http://www.relgioustolerance.org/fem_cirm.htm).

[61] Cairo Declaration for the Elimination of FGM 2003 above n 25 at para 1. For a brief historical survey of the development of FGM as a human rights violation see United Nations 'Traditional Practices Affecting the Health of Women and Girls: A Human Rights Issue' at http:www.unhchr.ch/women/focus-tradpract.html.

[62] Ahmadu above n 17; Greer above n 31.

[63] A James 'Reconciling International Human Rights and Cultural Relativism: The Case of Female Circumcision' (1994) 8 *Bioethics* 1. J Berkey 'Circumcision Circumscribed: Female Excision and Cultural Accommodation in the Medieval Near East' (1996) 28 *International Journal of Middle Eastern Studies* 19.

relativism more often than not entails a discussion of FGC. One of the leading human rights text and materials books, by Steiner and Alston, has a chapter on universalism. The gender section is followed by a discussion headed 'Custom and Culture', which focuses on 'female circumcision/genital mutilation'.[64] Interestingly, even when not discussing FGC, the cases used to illustrate 'culture' are African, thus seeming to suggest that law in western states operates in 'culturally neutral ways' and that women in the north do not experience gender-based discrimination. This is evidently untrue.

To a large extent, the approaches identified in considering FGC can already be found in existing international human rights instruments.[65] The international bill of rights comprising the Universal Declaration of Human Rights 1948 (UDHR), the International Covenant on Civil and Political Rights 1966 (ICCPR) and the International Covenant on Economic Social and Cultural Rights 1966 (ICESCR), contains provisions guaranteeing the right to be free from discrimination based on sex as well as equal protection of the law. The UDHR and ICCPR guarantee the right to life and to liberty and security of the person.[66] Crawley identifies the violation of autonomy and the infringement of the right to 'corporeal non interference' as 'the most important reason' for recognising FGC as a violation of the human rights of women.[67] The right to health is guaranteed in the ICESCR.[68] The UDHR and the ICCPR also provide for freedom from torture or degrading and inhuman treatment, as does the Convention against Torture 1984 (CAT).[69] For Crawley, the breach of the non-derogable article 5 of the UDHR on degrading and inhuman treatment makes FGC an incontrovertible violation of women's fundamental rights.[70] Moreover, the 2002 United Nations High Commission for Refugees Gender Asylum Guidelines appear to suggest that FGC can be construed

---

[64] Steiner and Alston above 32 at 404, 409.

[65] For a compilation of the relevant provisions see Center for Reproductive Rights (CRR) 'International Provisions Guaranteeing Freedom from FC/FGM' (paper submitted to the Afro-Arab Expert Consultation on Legal Tools for the Prevention of Female Genital Mutilation, Cairo, June 2003) 1–6; CRR *Female Genital Mutilation: A Matter of Human Rights* (New York, CRR, 2002); CRR and Toronto Centre for Reproductive Rights *Bringing Rights to Bear: An Analysis of the Work of the United Nations Treaty Monitoring Bodies on Reproductive and Sexual Rights* (New York, CRR, 2002) at 69–80.

[66] UDHR art 3; ICCPR art 6(1).

[67] Crawley above n 59 at 184.

[68] ICESCR art 12. See also UDHR art 25(1). The African Charter 1981 also contains similar provisions. See A Carbert, J Stanchieri and R Cook *A Handbook for Advocacy in the African Human Rights System Advancing Reproductive and Sexual Health* (Nairobi, IPAS, 2002) 30–31, 46.

[69] UDHR art 5; ICCPR art 7. Convention against Torture and Other Cruel, Inhuman or Degrading Treatment or Punishment (10 December 1984) 1465 UNTS 85.

[70] Crawley above n 59 at 186; Special Rapporteur on Torture Mr Peter Kooijmans Torture and Other Cruel, Inhuman or Degrading Treatment or Punishment E/CN.4/1986/15. See also Immigration Appellate Authority *Asylum Gender Guidelines* (London, Immigration Appellate Authority, 2000) 4 fn 7 and 13 fn 31; Lord Rooker, House of Lords Debate on Asylum Seekers: Female Persecution, Hansard HL (10 July 2001) col 1004.

as 'torture'.[71] However, Van Bueren is concerned about the resentment that may arise in labelling as torture what some see as necessary cultural practices.[72] Nevertheless, she does say that if done without the consent of the girl then the cutting can constitute torture.[73] Fleeing FGC has also been construed as entitling a person to protection under the United Nations Refugee Convention 1951.[74]

In 2001, the European Parliament adopted a Resolution on Female Genital Mutilation,[75] which strongly condemns FGM as a violation of fundamental human rights and calls on Member States to work towards its eradication by a variety of means. The right of children to be free from harm is recognised in both the United Nations Convention on the Rights of the Child 1979 (CRC) and the African Charter on the Rights and Welfare of the Child 1990 (ACRWC).

Although CEDAW is silent on the issue of FGC, the Committee has, in a series of General Recommendations, tackled the practice. In the first, General Recommendation 14 on Female Circumcision,[76] the Committee noted its concern about the continuation of the practice sustained by cultural, traditional and economic pressures. Whilst recognising the initiatives taken by women to combat the practice, the Committee made several recommendations, not least that governments should work with NGOs to tackle the practice and also the importance of education, particularly of health officials. The Committee also noted the importance of working with 'politicians, professionals, religious and community leaders at all levels'.[77]

General Recommendation 19 on Violence against Women was the second attempt made by the Women's Committee to consider the issue of FGM.[78] The General Recommendation identified 'traditional attitudes by which women are regarded as subordinate to men or as having stereotyped roles'[79] as the reason for the perpetuation of 'widespread practices involving violence or coercion, such as family violence and abuse, forced marriage . . . and female circumcision'.[80] Again,

---

[71] UNHCR *Guidelines on International Protection: Gender Related Persecution within the Context of Article 1A(2) of the 1951 Convention and/or its 1967 Protocol Relating to the Status of Refugees* (7 May 2002) HCR.GIP/02/01 para 36 (vii).

[72] G Van Bueren *The International Law on the Rights of the Child* (Dordrecht, Martinus Nijhoff, 1995) 308 fn 93.

[73] *Ibid* at 308.

[74] Convention Relating to the Status of Refugees (28 July 1951) 189 UNTS 150; Crawley above n 59 at 175ff, 193–96; UNHCR above n 71 at para 28; European Parliament Resolution on Female Genital Mutilation 2001 2001/2035 (INI) A-5-285-2001 para 14 and M Randall 'Refugee Law and State Accountability for Violence against Women: A Comparative Analysis of Legal Approaches to Recognising Asylum Claims Based on Gender Persecution' (2002) 25 *Harvard Women's Law Journal* 281.

[75] European Parliament Resolution on Female Genital Mutilation 2001 above n 74.

[76] CEDAW General Recommendation No 14 (Ninth Session, 1990): Female Circumcision UN Doc A/45/38.

[77] *Ibid* para (a)(iii).

[78] CEDAW General Recommendation No 19 on Violence Against Women UNDocA/47/38.

[79] *Ibid* para 11.

[80] *Ibid.*

suggestions advanced for dealing with violence included education campaigns, law reform and attempts at cultural change.[81]

In its General Recommendation on Health,[82] the Committee shifts its terminology from circumcision to FGM and links the practice with 'a high risk of death and disability',[83] and thus a threat to the right to life. It also links FGM and other practices identified as harmful, such as polygyny and marital rape, to 'the risk of contracting HIV/AIDS and other sexually transmitted diseases.'[84] In addition to pushing for 'the enactment and effective enforcement of laws that prohibit FGM and marriage of girl children',[85] the General Recommendation also calls for gender sensitivity in the design of health policies and the training of health personnel to include 'comprehensive, mandatory, gender sensitive courses on women's health and human rights, in particular gender based violence'.[86]

State reports to CEDAW also identify FGM as a practice that affects women and girls negatively. They provide information on strategies being used to tackle the problem.[87] CEDAW also questions states parties on steps that are being undertaken to eradicate FGC and other harmful practices.[88]

The issue of FGM as constituting violence against women has also been identified in the United Nations General Assembly Declaration on the Elimination of Violence against Women 1993 (DEVAW).[89] FGM is seen as a violation of fundamental human rights found in the international bill of rights discussed above.[90] Again, the Declaration provides an holistic overview of strategies that should be employed to tackle gender-based violence, which include education, counselling and law reform, coupled with adequate enforcement and co-operative relations between agencies.[91]

The appointment of the Special Rapporteur on Violence against Women in 1994 helped to raise the profile of FGM and to highlight the urgency of working towards its early eradication. Taking up the definition of gender-based violence found in the UN General Assembly Declaration in 1993, the Special Rapporteur

---

[81] *Ibid* para 24.
[82] CEDAW General Recommendation No 24 on Health UN Doc A 54/38/Rev./.
[83] *Ibid* para 12(b).
[84] *Ibid* para 18.
[85] *Ibid* para 15(d).
[86] *Ibid* para 31(f).
[87] Combined Fourth and Fifth Periodic Report to CEDAW: Nigeria (2003) CEDAW/C/NGA/4–5 (hereafter Government of Nigeria (2003)) at 15; Combined Fourth and Fifth Periodic Reports of States Parties: Ethiopia (2002) (hereafter Government of Ethiopia (2002)) CEDAW/C/ETH/4–5 paras 31–36, 67.
[88] CEDAW List of Issues and Questions with Regard to the Consideration of State Reports: Ethiopia CEDAW/PSWG/2004/I/CRP.1/Add.2 paras 22, 23, 25, 26. See also CEDAW Concluding Observations on the Ethiopian Report (2004) CEDAW A/59/38 paras 229, 251, 252. CEDAW Concluding Observations on the Nigerian Report CEDAW A/59/38 part I (2004) paras 288, 299, 300, 307.
[89] DEVAW art 2(a).
[90] *Ibid* art 3.
[91] *Ibid* art 4.

identifies FGM as a manifestation of gender-based violence.[92] Although refusing
to condemn all cultural practices as being negative or harmful, the Special
Rapporteur makes clear that:

> [T]hose practices that constitute definite forms of violence against women cannot be
> overlooked nor justified on the grounds of tradition, culture or social conformity.[93]

The Special Rapporteur on Violence against Women has also identified FGM as
having negative health consequences and as constituting a violation of the reproductive rights of women and girls.[94] She urges governments 'to engage in education and community outreach efforts aimed at addressing the deeply ingrained
cultural attitudes that continue to foster the practice'.[95] The Special Rapporteur
asks governments to address the increasing medicalisation of the practice, and
notes with concern the involvement of health professionals in its perpetuation.[96]

   Although initially reluctant to engage with what were considered 'cultural practices',[97] the World Health Organization has been a major player in the global FGM
debate, furnishing statistics, evaluating strategies for change and generally coordi-
nating the efforts to tackle FGM within the United Nations.[98] In this it has been
assisted by the appointment of a Special Rapporteur on Harmful Traditional
Practices Affecting the Health of Women and Children[99] together with a Special
Working Group on Traditional Practices.[100] These efforts must be seen in light of
other initiatives. Specifically the Cairo Programme of Action urged governments to:

> [P]rohibit female genital mutilation wherever it exists and to give vigorous support to
> efforts among non-governmental and community organisations and religious institu-
> tions to eliminate such practices.[101]

---

[92] Special Rapporteur on Violence against Women (1996) above n 13 at para 54. See also Report of
the Secretary-General on Traditional or Customary Practices Affecting the Health of Women and Girls
(18 July 2003) UN GA A/58/169 paras 22–24.
   [93] Special Rapporteur on Violence against Women above n 13 (1996) para 101.
   [94] Special Rapporteur on Violence against Women Policies and Practices that Impact Women's
Reproductive Rights and Contribute to, or Cause Violence Against Women (21 January 1999)
EICN.4/1999/68. Add.4 paras 32–34.
   [95] *Ibid* para 35.
   [96] *Ibid.*
   [97] H Charlesworth and C Chinkin *Boundaries of International Law* (Manchester, Manchester
University Press, 2000) 226.
   [98] In 1997, the World Health Organization issued a joint statement with UNICEF and UNFPA condemning FGM and pledging to work with NGOs in a joint effort to eliminate it. In CRR *Female Genital
Mutilation: A Matter of Human Rights* (New York, CRR, 2002) 50.
   [99] Eighth Report on the Situation Regarding the Elimination of Traditional Practices Affecting the
Health of Women and Girls, Proposed by Ms Halima Embarek-Warzazi E/CN.4/Sub.2/2004/41.
   [100] Report by the Working Group on Traditional Practices Affecting the Health of Women and
Children UN Doc E/CN 1986/42. See also the Report of the UN Seminar on Traditional Practices
Affecting the Health of Women and Children UN Doc E/CN.4/Sub.2/1991/48 and Report of the
Second Regional Seminar on Traditional Practices Affecting the Health of Women and Children UN
Doc E/CN.4/Sub.2/1994/10. Finally see Report of the Secretary General on Traditional or Customary
Practices Affecting the Health of Women Fifty-Third Session (10 Sept 1998) UN Doc A/53/354.
   [101] Programme of Action of the ICPD 1994 para 4.22.

The Fourth Women's Conference held in Beijing in 1995[102] and its follow-up conference tackled the issue of FGM, identifying it as a violation of the rights of women and the girl child.[103]

In June 2003, an Afro-Arab consultative meeting on FGM and the Law, sponsored by the United Nations, the European Union and others, was held in Cairo.[104] It resulted in the adoption of the Cairo Declaration for the Elimination of FGM 2003. The preamble to the Declaration makes clear that neither Christianity nor Islam sanctions FGM.[105] It also notes that FGM constitutes a violation of the rights of women and girls, and that the practice should be eradicated. It calls on governments, acting in concert with civil society, to lead efforts to end the practice. Although multiple inter-disciplinary strategies are envisaged for tackling FGM, the Declaration calls for 'using legislative measures as a pivotal tool'.[106]

Perhaps the most well-known agency dealing with the issue of FGC is the Inter-African Committee on Traditional Practices Affecting the Health of Women and Children (IAC).[107] Together with the Women's Unit of the (former) OAU, the IAC, drafted a Convention on the Elimination of All Forms of Harmful Practices (HPs) Affecting the Fundamental Human Rights of Women and Girls 2000.[108] Although it was eventually incorporated into the draft of the African Protocol on Women's Rights, it is instructive to see what the co-drafted Convention provided. In common with other human rights instruments, the draft Harmful Practices Convention listed a number of regional and international Conventions and Declarations designed to protect the rights of women and children, but noted that in spite of the instruments:

[102] Beijing Declaration and Platform for Action, Fourth World Conference on Women, Beijing, noted in part: 'Any harmful aspect of certain traditional, customary or modern practices that violates the rights of women should be prohibited and eliminated' (para 224). United Nations *Beijing to Beijing+ 5: Review and Appraisal of the Implementation of the Beijing Platform for Action* (New York, United Nations, 2001) 218, 225.

[103] See too Report of the Secretary-General Traditional or Customary Practices Affecting the Health of Women and Girls 2003 above n 92 paras 11ff.

[104] Afro-Arab Expert Consultation on 'Legal Tools for the Prevention of Female Genital Mutilation' Cairo, June 2003. This was one of many meetings held to discuss how to tackle FGM. The report of the Special Rapporteur on Traditional Practices notes that meetings were also held in Sudan, Sweden, Canada, Belgium and Tanzania. See Special Rapporteur on Traditional Practices (2004) above n 99 at paras 20–34, 65–66, 75.

[105] See too Special Rapporteur on Traditional Practices (2004) above n 99 at para 67.

[106] Cairo Declaration for the Elimination of FGM 2003 above n 25, preamble.

[107] The Inter-African Committee on Traditional Practices Affecting the Health of Women and Children (IAC) was formed by a group of African women meeting in Dakar Senegal. It has 26 chapters. See Rahman and Toubia above n 6 at 10. C Welch *Protecting Human Rights in Africa: Roles and Strategies of Non-Governmental Organisations* (Philadelphia, University of Pennsylvania Press, 1995) 87–106.

[108] This was attached to the Suggestions of the Women's Unit to Improve the Existing Text of the Draft Protocol as Presented to the OAU. Attachment to a Letter from Professor Johnson, Director Education, Science, Culture and Social Affairs Department to Professor Dankwa, Chairman of the African Commission (7 February 2000) File No ES/WU/RW/51.00 (on file with the author).

[T]he health and basic rights of women and girls, such as the right to life, health and bodily integrity, continue to be impinged upon by harmful practices which include widowhood rites, nutritional taboos, female genital mutilation, forced and/or early childhood marriage.[109]

Article 1 of the Convention defined harmful practices, while article 2 called upon states to enact legislation to prohibit harmful practices and to guarantee equality between men and women, as well as demanding that states ratify the relevant human rights instruments. States were also required to run education and information campaigns. State obligations were further developed in article 3, which called on states to work with religious and other social and traditional leaders.[110]

The draft Convention made clear in article 4 that the medicalisation of the practice was not to be permitted. Significantly, article 5 went beyond prevention to consider rehabilitation and the requirement that victims should be provided with social support services, including health services, emotional and psychological counselling, and family reintegration, and finally given skills training to enable them to become self-supporting. The rest of the Convention dealt with monitoring, including the setting up of a five-person Committee to oversee the Convention.

As noted in Chapter 3, the OAU Legal Unit passed the IAC/Women's Unit Draft Convention on Harmful Practices to the Chairperson of the African Commission on Human Rights, with a suggestion that the IAC Convention be incorporated into the Draft Protocol to the African Charter on Human and Peoples' Rights on the Rights of Women in Africa (African Protocol on Women's Rights). This was duly done, and in the final version of the Protocol harmful practices are defined as 'all behaviour, attitudes and/or practices which negatively affect the fundamental rights of women and girls, such as their right to life, health, dignity, education and physical integrity'.[111]

Article 5 of the Protocol embraces the key provisions of the IAC/Women's Unit Convention and, in addition to requiring states to condemn practices that violate norms established in existing international human rights instruments,[112] provides four strategies for dealing with harmful practices:

(a) creating public awareness of the problem and educating all stakeholders;
(b) aiming for the total eradication of the practice by prohibiting its medicalisation;
(c) providing support and rehabilitation services for victims of FGM;
(d) protection of women and girls who have been cut or are at risk of being cut.[113]

---

[109] Draft Convention on the Elimination of Harmful Practices 2000, preamble.
[110] *Ibid* art 3(2).
[111] African Protocol on Women's Rights art 1(g).
[112] *Ibid* art 5. See also Addendum to SADC Declaration on Gender and Development on the Prevention and Eradication of Violence against Women and Children 1997 art 5(a); AU Solemn Declaration on Gender Equality in Africa 2004 preamble.
[113] African Protocol on Women's Rights arts 5 (a)–5(d). Cf the European Parliament Resolution on Female Genital Mutilation 2001 above n 74 paras Z, 3, 4, 7, 11.

It is noteworthy that the Protocol adopts all four human rights approaches identified earlier in this section. FGC and other harmful practices that endanger the health and general well-being of women are proscribed in article 2(1)(b), which further requires the state to enact and implement legislative or regulatory measures to curb discrimination. Article 2 on state obligations also requires states 'to modify social and cultural patterns of conduct of women and men . . . with a view to achieving the elimination of harmful cultural and traditional practices'.[114] In addition to the provision of information and educating the population about the rights of women,[115] the Protocol enjoins states to prohibit 'all forms of exploitation, cruel, inhuman or degrading punishment and treatment'.[116] Given the myriad reasons for the continuation of harmful practices, states are enjoined to 'identify the causes and consequences of violence against women and take appropriate measures to prevent and eliminate such violence'.[117] As already noted, the Protocol defines woman as including the girl child, so that all the Protocol provisions discussed herein are said also to apply to the girl child.[118]

Children's rights

It is in the context of children's rights that the issue of FGC has taken root.[119] This can be attributed to the raised profile of children's rights[120] and the almost universal ratification of the United Nations Children's Rights Convention 1989 (CRC). Constructed around the welfare principle (best interests of the child), the CRC, in addition to guaranteeing right to life,[121] also provides that 'States shall ensure to the maximum extent possible the survival and development of the child.'[122] The CRC also guarantees the child's right to be free from abuse.[123] The article on the right to health[124] goes on to protect against 'traditional practices

---

[114] African Protocol on Women's Rights art 2(2).
[115] *Ibid* art 8(c). See also art 4(2)(d).
[116] *Ibid* art 4(1).
[117] *Ibid* art 4(2)(c).
[118] *Ibid* art 1(k).
[119] Although obviously focusing on the rights of the girl child, it is important to acknowledge, without conflating the two, that there are elements of overlap between circumcision of boys and cutting of girls, particularly when one looks at issues of consent.
[120] Van Bueren above n 72.
[121] CRC art 6(1).
[122] CRC art 6(2). See also Vienna Declaration and Programme of Action World Conference on Human Rights 1993, which states 'The World Conference urges States to repeal existing laws and regulations and remove customs and practices which discriminate against and cause harm to the girl-child.' Vienna Declaration 1993 (II) para 49.
[123] CRC art 19(1).
[124] CRC art 24(1).

which are prejudicial to the health of children'.[125] Arguably FGC would fall under this rubric. It is, however, worth noting that during the drafting of the CRC, there was some controversy over the inclusion of this article and the naming of FGC as a harmful practice, with Senegal noting that there should not be an over-regulation of different cultures. However, Sweden, Canada, Japan and Venezuela took the view that the Working Group on Traditional Practices Affecting Women and Children had defined harmful traditional practices as including female circumcision and this definition had been accepted by the World Health Organization, and argued for its inclusion in the Children's Rights Convention.[126]

The United Nations Declaration on the Elimination of all Forms of Intolerance and Discrimination based on Religion or Belief 1981 also protects children from religious practices or beliefs that are injurious to their physical and mental health or to their full development.[127]

There is an apparent tension in the CRC between a child's autonomy rights (right to make decisions for herself)[128] and issues of legal paternalism (rights of parents/guardians to assist the child in decision making). There is, for example, a potential conflict between a child's wish to assert her autonomy rights by refusing FGC and a parent's construction of a child's best interests as demanding that the child undergo the procedure for 'her own good'. Developing Freeman's[129] theory of liberal paternalism, Eekelaar[130] puts forward a three-point test to determine how much autonomy a child should be allowed:

> [T]he claims revolve around children's 'basic' interests (to physical, emotional and intellectual care); their 'developmental' interests (that their potential should be developed so that they enter adulthood as far as possible without disadvantage) and their 'autonomy' interests (the freedom to choose a life-style of their own). The first of these has preeminent status. The other two can reasonably be compromised. For example, surely no one would have wanted, when very young, to have been left uncontrolled in dangerous situations. But the plausibility of the claim that children would wish to be provided with equal life chances has the potential for considerable social impact.[131]

Clearly here the child's autonomy rights, which are grounded in a wish to uphold both basic and developmental rights, can and should be recognised as 'trumping'

---

[125]   CRC art 24(3).

[126]   Van Bueren above n 72 at 307.

[127]   United Nations Declaration on the Elimination of All Forms of Intolerance and Discrimination Based on Religion or Belief UN GA Res 36/55, adopted 25 January 1981. See also Secretary-General Report on Traditional or Customary Practices Affecting the Health of Women and Girls 2003 para 25; Kigali Declaration 2003 preamble; The European Parliament Resolution on Female Genital Mutilation 2001 para I. See also para H.

[128]   CRC art 12.

[129]   M Freeman *The Rights and Wrongs of Children* (London, Frances Pinter, 1983) 56.

[130]   J Eekelaar 'The Importance of Thinking that Children Have Rights' (1994) 8 *International Journal of Law, Policy and the Family* 221.

[131]   *Ibid* at 231. CRC General Comment No 5 paras 6(b), 6(c).

any conflicting parental views. However, there are the cultural demands of article 5 of the CRC to contend with:

> States Parties shall respect the responsibilities, rights and duties of parents, or, where applicable, the members of the extended family or community as provided for by local custom, legal guardians or other persons legally responsible for the child, to provide, in a manner consistent with the evolving capacities of the child, appropriate direction and guidance in the exercise by the child of the rights recognised in the present Convention.[132]

The answer to the conundrum is that the parents should exercise their responsibilities over the child in a way that is consistent with upholding the child's rights as enunciated in the Convention.[133] The child should not be made to undergo FGC. Technical answers notwithstanding, it has to be a source of concern that for many girl children, their vulnerability is linked to both their minority status and gender, which leave them with little or no bargaining power vis à vis decisions about their lives.[134] This was recognised by the Committee on Children's Rights in its concluding observations on the report submitted by Ethiopia.[135] Moreover, it is worth noting the reservation made by Djibouti to the CRC, that:

> It shall not consider itself bound by any provisions or articles that are incompatible with its religion and traditional values.[136]

The tension between children's rights and parental interests is also reflected in the ACRWC. Mirroring the CRC, the ACRWC also protects a child's rights to life,[137] survival and development,[138] health,[139] and to be free from abuse,[140] and provides that the child has a right to freedom of expression.[141] All of this is

---

[132] See also CRC General Comment No 5 para 9.

[133] J Eekelaar above n 130 at 233. See too Human Rights Committee General Comment No 17 para 6; M Freeman 'Cultural Pluralism and the Rights of the Child' in J Eekelaar and T Nhlapo (eds) *Changing Family* (Oxford, Hart Publishing, 1998) 289. A Renteln *The Cultural Defense* above n 8 at 67–70. But see A An Na'im 'Cultural Transformation and Normative Consensus on the Best Interests of the Child' (1994) 8 *International Journal of Law, Policy and the Family* 62 at 66; M Cottier 'Swiss Local Child Protection and the Challenges of Immigration' (Tesina submitted to the International Institute for the Sociology of Law, Oñati, Spain, 2001) 82–84.

[134] CRC General Comment No 5 at para 6(a); Human Rights Committee General Comment No 17 paras 3, 5. Crawley above n 59 at 184. See also Renteln 'Is the Cultural Defense Detrimental?' above n 8 at 27, 67.

[135] Concluding Observations of the Committee on the Rights of the Child: Ethiopia (21 February 2001) CRC/C/15/Add.144 (Concluding Observations/Comments) paras 36 and 37. See also Secretary-General's Report on Traditional or Customary Practices Affecting the Health of Women and Girls 2003 above n 92 para 35.

[136] Reproduced in C Heyns (ed) *Human Rights Law in Africa* (The Hague, Martinus Nijhoff, 2004) vol 1 at 58.

[137] ACRWC art 5(1).

[138] *Ibid* art 5(2).

[139] *Ibid* art 14.

[140] *Ibid* art 16.

[141] *Ibid* art 7; C Himonga 'The Right of the Child to Participate in Decision Making: A Perspective from Zambia' in W Ncube (ed) *Law, Culture, Tradition and Children's Rights in Eastern and Southern Africa* (Ashgate, Aldershot, 1998) 95.

grounded in the welfare principle.[142] Harmful practices, including FGM and early marriage, are tackled in article 21, which provides:

(1) States Parties . . . shall take all appropriate measures to eliminate harmful social and cultural practices affecting the welfare, dignity, normal growth and development of the child and in particular:
 (a) those customs and practices prejudicial to the health or life of the child; and
 (b) those customs and practices discriminatory to the child on the grounds of sex or other status.
(2) Child marriage and the betrothal of girls and boys shall be prohibited and effective action, including legislation, shall be taken to specify the minimum age of marriage to be eighteen years and make registration of marriages in an official registry compulsory.

However, in common with article 29 of the African Charter, the ACRWC has a provision covering the duties or responsibilities of the child, which include a duty to respect 'his [sic] parents, superiors and elders at all times and to assist them in case of need.'[143] For the girl child, this respect for elders and providing assistance in case of need could include agreeing to marry early to enable her family to get bridewealth for her.[144] To facilitate marriage, she may 'agree' to be cut to make her a more attractive marriage prospect.[145] If the community practices FGC, one cannot separate out the marriage issue. Indeed in societies where marriage remains the sole career choice for a woman, her family may see it as being in her best interests to be cut, for that enhances her marriage prospects.[146] Examining violations of the rights of the girl child, the Beijing Platform for Action noted that girls were:

often subjected to various forms of . . . violence and harmful practices such as female infanticide and prenatal sex selection, incest, female genital mutilation and early marriage, including forced marriage.[147]

[142] ACRWC art 4(1).
[143] ACRWC art 31(a). This obligation to family and others is also found in The League of Arab States Charter on the Rights of the Arab Child 1990 art 3, reproduced in G Alfredson and K Tomasevski (eds) *Thematic Guide to Documents on the Human Rights of Women* (The Hague, Martinus Nijhoff, 1995) 277.
[144] CRC General Comment No 5 at paras 6(d), 6(e), 32(g). Secretary-General's Report on Traditional or Customary Practices Affecting the Health of Women and Girls 2003 above n 92 para 20.
[145] Crawley above n 59 at 179; Gunning above n 31 at 233.
[146] J Kabeberi-Machaira 'Female Genital Mutilation and the Rights of the Girl Child in Kenya' in W Ncube (ed) *Law, Culture, Tradition and Children's Rights in Eastern and Southern Africa: Issues in Law and Society* (Aldershot, Dartmouth, 1998) 249 at 259.
[147] Beijing Declaration and Platform for Action 1995 para 39. See also Programme of Action of the International Conference on Population and Development 1994 para 5.5.

Efficacy of the human rights approach

The discussion has shown that there is a multitude of human instruments and initiatives that exist to tackle FGM and other gender-based human rights violations. The expansion of the human rights canon and its increasing popularity shows that there is a common understanding of the need to set basic minimum standards to which states should subscribe. Rahman and Toubia believe:

> [T]hat framing issues such as FC/FGM as violations of women's rights is not only appropriate, but is an important means by which to raise the political profile of these neglected rights and to generate dialogue on how best to stop them.[148]

What remains to be seen is the effectiveness of both human rights and national legislation in bringing about real change.

The human rights approach has been influential in bringing FGC to international prominence and has influenced the enactment of legislation by national governments. Until fairly recently law does not appear to have been a central part of eradication efforts. This may be because laws have only recently been enacted and have not yet had time to 'bed down'. It may also be because law may not be seen as the most appropriate tool for dealing with a practice that is deeply rooted in cultural and (erroneously) religious justification. Legal change has also come about as a result of pressure from international donors. The European Parliament Resolution on Female Genital Mutilation 2001 makes an explicit connection between aid and the adoption by aid-receiving countries of policies and laws to tackle the practice. Specifically it

> [c]alls on the Council, Commission and Member States to use the human rights clause to make combatting female genital mutilation a priority issue in relations with non-Member States, particularly those States which have preferential relations with the EU under the Cotonou agreement, and to *put pressure* on them to adopt the necessary legislative, administrative, judicial and preventive measures to put an end to these practices.[149] (emphasis added)

The enactment of laws may be seen as an attempt by states to be seen to be 'doing something' about the problem of FGC, but without taking the necessary steps for implementation.

---

[148] Rahman and Toubia above n 6 at xiv.

[149] European Parliamentary Resolution on Female Genital Mutilation 2001 para 26. See also paras 18, 19, 20, 21, 23, 24. A Osborn and S Boseley 'EU States May Ban Aid to States that Allow Female Circumcision' *Guardian* (London, 30 November 2000). Boyle and Preves above n 6 at 714–15, 725. The United States Congress has also passed a law 'requiring the US executive directors of international financial institutions to oppose non-humanitarian loans to countries where FGM is practised but where the government has not "taken steps to implement educational programs designed to prevent the practice".' In Center for Reproductive Law and Policy 'Legislation on Female Genital Mutilation in the United States' (1997) *Reproductive Freedom in Focus* at 4.

National legislation

In discussing the usefulness of law in tackling FGM, the old adage 'changing the law is easier than changing society' is apposite. The regulatory role of law has always been recognised.[150] What is less clear is whether law is an appropriate tool to tackle practices that are rooted in or justified using social, cultural or religious terms? The answer to the question has varied over time. Early colonial initiatives to ban the practice met with local resistance and generally failed to bring about an end to the practice.[151] Post-independence initiatives have met with varied success. The reasons for this will now be explored.

Colonial initiatives

Colonial initiatives in Kenya to ban 'this barbaric practice' included the attempts of missionaries at the turn of the twentieth century and then of local government in the Meru District in 1950s. In 1946, in the Sudan, the British administration decided against an outright ban and outlawed only the most severe form. However, in both instances there was a failure to end the practice. Indeed Sudan currently has one of the highest incidences of FGC (the most severe form). In response to the ban in colonial Kenya, the girls of Meru District cut themselves, and became known as *ngaitana*, meaning 'I will circumcise myself', for that is precisely what they did.[152] In modern times Meru District is also said to have one of the highest incidence of excision within Kenya.[153]

Reasons for this local resistance are not hard to find. The most obvious is the political resistance to a further erosion of local autonomy by the indigenous populations who had already been forced to concede political power to the colonial authorities. Resistance to anti-circumcision laws by women and girls also enabled them to play a part in the anti-colonial struggle. Other reasons for the failure of the ban is that it did not take into account the cultural underpinnings of the practice.[154] For the girls involved, FGC marked the transition from girlhood into

---

[150]   See generally L Katzive 'Using the Law to Promote Women's Rights: Considerations in Drafting and Implementing Legislation to Prevent FC-FGM' (paper presented at the Afro-Arab Expert Consultation on Legal Tools for the Prevention of Female Genital Mutilation, Cairo, 21–23 June 2003) 1.

[151]   L Thomas ' "Ngaitana" (I Will Circumcise Myself): Lessons from Colonial Campaigns to Ban Excision in Meru Kenya' in B Shell-Duncan and Y Yernlund (eds) *Female 'Circumcision' in Africa: Culture, Controversy and Change* (Colorado, Lynne Rienner Publishers, 2000) 129.

[152]   *Ibid* at 130.

[153]   *Ibid* at 146.

[154]   El Dareer above n 50 at 92.

womanhood. The attendant rituals and training also provided them with the social tools to be good daughters and wives.[155] Moreover, in Kenya, the imposition of fines on the fathers of circumcised girls came to be seen as part of a moneymaking exercise for the local elite acting in concert with the colonial authority. This created a great deal of resentment and helped to build up further resistance, it not being clear why people should be punished for an act voluntarily entered into. Modern attempts to ban the practice may be subject to the same constraints.

The use of law to ban the practice of FGM is, in post-colonial societies, a fairly recent development—in fact most of the laws passed in Africa are post-1990.[156] By way of contrast, northern states appear to have begun legislating against FGC earlier. This may be because in northern states only a minority of people practice FGC and thus it is easier to outlaw it.[157] As previously noted, the increase in anti-FGC legislation can be linked to the growing acceptance of human rights norms and aid conditionality.

Post-independence laws on FGM

There has been a radical shift in countries' attitudes towards FGM in post-independent African states. Initially there was a 're-claiming' of African cultural values much denigrated during the colonial period, so that Jomo Kenyatta, the first post-independence President of Kenya, spoke in favour of a return to African values, including 'circumcision'.[158] Yet in December 2001, Kenya legislated against the practice.[159] This shift can be linked to a greater recognition of the rights of women and the girl child, and demands from these two constituencies that the state enforce the law. The commitment to upholding the rights of this group, and in particular girl children, is evidenced by the spate of suits to protect their rights in Kenyan courts.[160]

In addition, the constitutional bills of rights of many countries contain many of the protections found in the international human rights instruments discussed

---

[155] Thomas above n 151 at 145–48.
[156] The exceptions are The Central African Republic's Ordinance of 1966 and Guinea's Criminal Code Provision of 1965. See Rahman and Toubia above n 6 at 61. United Nations *Beijing to Beijing+5* above n 102 at 218. Secretary-General's Report on Traditional or Customary Practices Affecting the Health of Women and Girls 2003 above n 92 para 19. See also paras 4, 5.
[157] Toubia *Female Genital Mutilation* above n 52 at 45. But see Renteln *The Cultural Defense* above n 8 at 53.
[158] J Kenyatta *Facing Mount Kenya: The Tribal Life of the Gikuyu* (New York, Vintage Books, 1965) 125–48.
[159] Children Act 2001. N Rugene 'FGM On Children, Forced Marriages Outlawed' in *Daily Nation* (Nairobi, 11 December 2001) at http://www.nationaudio.com/News/DailyNation/Today/News28.html.
[160] J Wanjiala 'Can the Law Stop Female Circumcision?' (paper presented at the Afro-Arab Consultation on Legal Tools for the Prevention of Female Genital Mutilation, Cairo, 21–23 June 2003) 1.

above. They have provisions covering the right to life, liberty and security of the person, the right to bodily integrity, and the right to be free from discrimination based on sex and to equality before the law. The right to health is also guaranteed in many of the constitutions. Although the constitutions of most countries provide for the right to culture and freedom of religion, some explicitly provide that cultural considerations cannot detract from the centrality of constitutional provisions, which are said to be supreme. The Ugandan Constitution 1995 provides an example of this. Article 2(2) states:

> If any other law or custom is inconsistent with any of the provisions of this Constitution, the Constitution shall prevail, and that other law or custom shall, to the extent of the inconsistency, be void.

Similarly the provision on women's rights makes clear that:

> Laws, cultures, customs or traditions which are against the dignity, welfare or interest of women or which undermine their status, are prohibited by this Constitution.[161]

This is an important legal contribution to the effort to eradicate FGC. Although not explicitly mentioning FGC as being a violation, a few of the newer (post-1990) constitutions also contain provisions dealing with harmful practices. The Constitution of Ghana[162] in Article 26(2) tackles cultural values and practices, providing:

> All customary practices which dehumanize or are injurious to the physical and mental well being of a person are prohibited.

This must be read together with Article 39(2), which provides that as part of the directives of state policy, the government is to:

> [E]nsure that appropriate customary and cultural values are adopted and developed as an integral part of the growing needs of society as a whole: and in particular that traditional practices which are injurious to the health and well-being of the person are abolished.

Arguably this would demand that the Ghanaian state tackle FGC, because it is a practice that is injurious to the rights of women and girls. In recent years African countries have passed separate legislation specifically outlawing FGC. Katzive notes that of the '28 African countries where FC/FGM is prevalent, 15 have at least one specific law or regulation addressing this practice'.[163] The majority of African

---

[161] Constitution of Uganda 1995 Art 33(6). Cf Art 35(4) of the Constitution of the Federal Democratic Republic of Ethiopia 1994. See also Special Rapporteur on Violence against Women (1996) above n 13 at para 109.

[162] Constitution of the Republic of Ghana approved on 28 April 1992. In C Heyns (ed) *Human Rights Law in Africa* (The Hague, Kluwer International, 1996) 140. See also Secretary-General's Report on Traditional or Customary Practices Affecting the Health of Women and Girls 2003 above n 92 paras 4, 5.

[163] Katzive above n 150 at 3.

states that have laws prohibiting FGC have criminal sanctions attached. In countries that do not have laws specifically targeted at dealing with FGC, there are general provisions in the criminal (penal) codes dealing with assault or grievous bodily harm, which can be used to bring a prosecution in the event of FGC.[164] There are also statutes protecting children, such as the Kenyan and Ghanaian Children Acts.

The discussion that follows focuses on the 1998 Togolese law, which combines punishment of offenders and rehabilitation of victims/survivors.[165] Article 1 outlaws FGM 'practiced by any person, whatever his or her position', whilst article 2 defines what is meant by FGM. The section on sanctions is worth reproducing here.

> Art.3. Any person who by traditional or modern methods practices or promotes female genital mutilations or participates in these activities shall be guilty of an act of intentional violence against the person of the excised girl or woman.

> Art.4. Any person who commits the intentional acts of violence defined in Article 3 shall be punished by imprisonment from two months to five years and by a fine of 100, 000 to 1,000,000 francs [approximately US$160–1,600], or by either of these punishments.

> The punishments shall be doubled in case of recidivism.

> Art.5. If the mutilations result in the death of the victim, the penalty will be 5 to 10 years of imprisonment [reclusion].

> Art.6. When by denunciation it might have been possible to prevent one or more perpetrators from committing additional female genital mutilations, anyone having knowledge of an excision already planned, attempted or practiced, who fails to inform immediately the public authorities, shall be punished with one month to one year of imprisonment or with a fine of 20,000 to 500,000 francs [approximately US$32–800].

> Exempt from these provisions are relatives to the fourth degree, by blood or by marriage, of the perpetrator of or accomplice to the prohibited activities.

> Art.7. The directors of both public and private health facilities are required to ensure the most appropriate medical care to the victims of female genital mutilation arriving at their centers or establishments.

> The competent public authorities should be informed without delay in order to permit them to follow the evolving state of the victim and to meet the requirements of this provision.[166]

The Togolese law is interesting on several counts. It does not countenance FGC even when done under medical supervision. The punishment for engaging in or abetting FGC is a fine or imprisonment, which sanctions are to be doubled if the

---

[164] WHO *Female Genital Mutilation Programmes* above n 9 at 14, 168. Rahman and Toubia above n 6. See also Katzive above n 150 at 7–14.
[165] Loi No 98–016 as reproduced in Rahman and Toubia above n 6 at 226.
[166] *Ibid.*

person has engaged in these activities before. No doubt this is aimed at dissuading excisors from continuing the practice. The option of paying a fine is removed should death result from cutting.

In assigning responsibility, the Togolese law moves beyond those directly involved in the cutting to include 'anyone having knowledge of an excision already planned, attempted or practiced'. This is a wide-ranging and far-reaching provision, which draws into its net anyone (excluding relatives in the prohibited degrees) who has had contact with the girl or her family.[167] It seems that it will not be enough to plead ignorance or to say 'I only found out after the event and could do nothing to stop it', for one is still required to report an attempt to cut, whether it has been successfully completed or not. Arguably the provision sets an impossibly high standard. How, for example, is one to judge 'having knowledge of an excision already planned?' Is the fact that people in that family or village have sometimes practised cutting their daughters sufficient? This can lead to rumour-mongering and it may be difficult to prove that a person knew of a planned cutting. Given how widely the net is cast in terms of the people who are under an obligation to report, it may well be that the law makes unjustifiable and unfair demands on people who stand to be severely punished for omissions.[168] Moreover, it is unclear whether threatening parents, guardians or carers with imprisonment can be said to be in the best interests of the child. The imprisoned person is likely to lose his or her job and livelihood, thus exposing the child to the risk of poverty and destitution.[169]

An impressive part of the Togolese law is article 7, which directs public health officials to treat the victims of FGC. This means that unlike many criminal laws, the Togolese law does not stop at the door of the court. It does not see the prosecution of the offenders as bringing the matter to an end. Rather, it is cognisant of the victim and keeps her at the centre by providing that her health needs are to be ministered to by health officials. All that remains to be said is that one would hope that the medical intervention will be holistic, taking care of the physical and psychological needs of the victim.[170]

---

[167] The law in the Côte d'Ivoire is similarly drafted. See art 4 of Loi No 98–757, 23 December 1998, on the Prohibition of Violence against Women. As cited in Rahman and Toubia above n 6 at 131.

[168] The Cairo Declaration for the Elimination of FGM 2003 (above n 25) notes that 'provided sufficient outreach and sensitisation has taken place, members of the community with knowledge of cases of FGM should be held criminally liable for failure to report such cases' (para 11).

[169] It is for this reason that Wanjiala advocates the use of civil law to deal with the practice instead of criminal law. Wanjiala above n 160 at 5. It may well be that civil law is preferable where FGC is threatened but has not yet been carried out. See, for example, the Tanzanian case where a father was reported to the police for wanting to have his daughters cut. By the time the case was heard, the daughters had been cut and had married, and they refused to testify against him. Awaken 'Police Blamed for Lack of Action against Perpetrators of FGM' (2004) *Awaken* at 9.

[170] It is of course imperative that the health provision be available, accessible, acceptable, affordable and of good quality. CESCR General Comment No 14 para 12. See too B Toebes 'Towards an Improved Understanding of the International Human Right to Health' (1999) 21 *Human Rights Quarterly* 661.

It is trite to say that the existence of a law does not necessarily lead to its enforcement. In their 2000 survey on national laws, Rahman and Toubia discussed legal initiatives to tackle the practice, and yet they found that of 28 African countries surveyed, there had been prosecutions in only four.[171] Recently there have been more cases of law being used to tackle the practice with civil suits and prosecutions being brought.[172] Still, there are more countries with laws that are not enforced than there are those which implement the law. There are many reasons for non-enforcement of the law,[173] not least the absence of political will to interfere in what many regard as a private and very personal matter,[174] the shortage of personnel and popular resistance.[175] Ahmadu asserts that (in Sierra Leone and Gambia) politicians' fear of the social power of circumcisors means that there could never be a legal ban.[176] However, in response to the case of a 14-year-old girl who bled to death after being cut in Freetown, the Sierra Leonean Ombudsman is reported to have said that the practice should be banned as: 'This act is a clear violation of the rights of the girl child to which Sierra Leone has agreed as a signatory to the Convention on the Rights of the Child.'[177]

Advantages of using law to tackle FGC

The benefits of having a law and enforcing it include sending out a message to the society as a whole that the practice is a violation of the rights of women and girls that will not be tolerated.[178] This helps to raise the status of girls, leads to their having a greater sense of security, and also validates their sense of human worth and

[171] Burkina Faso, Egypt, Ghana and Senegal. Rahman and Toubia above n 6 at 111ff.

[172] *Awaken* (2004) at 2, 5, and 8. Center for Reproductive Rights 'Using the Law to Protect Kenya's Young Women from FGM' (2002) XI *Reproductive Freedom News* 6.

[173] E Dorkenoo above n 52 at 24–35; K Maiga 'Legal Tools for the Prevention of Female Genital Mutilation, Case Study: Mali' (paper presented at the Afro-Arab Consultation on Legal Tools for the Legal Protection of Female Genital Mutilation, Cairo, 21–23 June 2003) at 3.

[174] For example the Tanzanian Pastor who tried to enlist the help of the police to stop three girls being cut and who alleges that instead of assisting, the police turned on him and beat him. Awaken 'Police Blamed for Lack of Action against Perpetrators of FGM' (May 2004) *Awaken*, at 9.

[175] Awaken 'Elders Vow to Continue with FGM' (May 2004) *Awaken* at 7.

[176] Ahmadu above n 17 at 299 and 311 fn 15.

[177] Centre for Reproductive Law and Policy 'Teenage Girl in Sierra Leone Dies after Female Circumcision' (2002) XI *Reproductive Freedom News* 8. Katzive above n 150 at 6. See also Awaken 'UN Agencies Express Concern about Lack of Political Will to End FGM' (May 2004) *Awaken* 5.

[178] The World Health Organization recommends that governments must enact and use anti-FGM laws to protect girls and to educate communities about FGC (WHO *Female Genital Mutilation Programmes* above n 9 at 14). See also Recommendations Relating to Traditional Practices (United Nations, 1991) as cited in G Alfredson and K Tomasevski (eds) *Thematic Guide to Documents on the Human Rights of Women* (Hague, Martinus Nijhoff, 1995) 309. See European Parliament Resolution on Female Genital Mutilation 2001 paras 11 and 24; Katzive above n 150 at 3–4, Cairo Declaration for the Elimination of FGM 2003 (above n 25) at para 12.

esteem. They are equal citizens and their rights count for as much as those of their fathers, husbands and brothers.[179] It also makes possible a continuation of schooling and may lead to a delay in marriage.[180] Effective enforcement of law protects the most vulnerable members of society. The Special Rapporteur on Violence against Women has noted that state failure to protect the rights of female citizens to physical integrity and life, sends out a message that:

> [S]uch attacks are justified and will not be punished. To avoid such complicity, States must demonstrate due diligence by taking active measures to protect, prosecute and punish private actors who commit abuses.[181]

Having sanctions in place acts as a deterrent to those who may want to continue the practice. The Chief of the Military Police in Ouagadougou, Burkina Faso, noted:

> Only the law can protect girls and clarifies what is wrong from right. The fact that the law can protect girls if properly applied is illustrated in the case of an official in Ouagadougou, who was planning to send his two daughters to their grandparents in the rural areas for excision. The girls informed their friends who in turn notified the National Committee on Excision. The gendarme notified local police and health care providers in the rural village who contacted the grandparents and warned them not to attempt excision. When the girls arrived in the village, the grandparents were asked to present the girls for examination before they returned to their father. They complied and excision was prevented. In this case having the law in place gave the police, committee and health professionals the legitimacy to intervene.[182]

The effectiveness of this robust approach can be seen in the fact that since the passage of the law outlawing FGM in Burkina Faso, there have been '57 trials for cases of excision and . . . 2,632 awareness raising and deterrence patrols by policemen and 488 on-site visits in cases of excision'.[183] One could of course also argue

---

[179] The improvement of women's position in society is seen as crucial to eradication efforts. See Awaken 'Fresh Demands Made on African Governments to end FGM' (May 2004) *Awaken* at 4. Secretary-General's Report on Traditional or Customary Practices Affecting the Health of Women and Girls 2003 at para 21.

[180] Secretary-General Report on Traditional or Customary Practices Affecting the Health of Women and Girls 2003 above n 92 para 20.

[181] Special Rapporteur on Violence against Women (1996) above n 13 at para 33.

[182] Cited in WHO *Female Genital Mutilation Programmes* above n 9 at 16. See also Rahman and Toubia above n 6 at 116. They discuss the work of the National Committee against Excision in Burkina Faso, which has 'established a 24 hour telephone hotline for individuals who wish to report an incident of FC/FGM that has either occurred or is likely to occur'. See also S Robinson 'The Last Rites' *Time* (Europe, 5 December 2001) at http://www.time.com/time/europe/af/printout/0,9869, 1875799,00.html. Robinson quotes Drissa Kone, a community health worker in Northern Ivory Coast, as saying: 'You can talk to these women all you want about the human rights side of it, or the danger to the girls. But it's the threat of being arrested that has an effect . . . Let one woman in this region be arrested for performing excisions, and watch how fast they stop doing it.' Robinson above this n at 2. Wanjiala above n 160 at 4.

[183] G Kambou 'The Law as a Tool for Behavioural Change: The Case of Burkina Faso' (paper presented at the Afro-Arab Expert Consultation on Legal Tools for the Prevention of Female Genital Mutilation, Cairo, 21–23 June 2003) 1 at 4.

that the approach illustrates the importance of inter-agency co-operation as much as it does the importance of having a law in place. This inter-agency approach is also reflected in Ghana's National Reproductive Health Service Policy and Standards, which engage state agents (law, health, education) as well as community and traditional leaders, and those responsible for doing the cutting.[184]

Boyle and Preves see law as crucial to eradication efforts, for not only does it create an international consensus about the need to deal with the problem, but it also reinforces the efforts of advocates working to eliminate the practice as well as sending out a powerful symbolic message that there are consequences to FGC, a lack of prosecutions notwithstanding.[185]

Disadvantages of using law to tackle FGC

The most obvious contra-indication to passing law is that more often than not it can drive the practice underground, leaving victims without access to essential medical services.[186] Banning the practice may actually result in an increase: a 1989 campaign to ban the practice by the government of Uganda, working with the Ugandan chapter of the Inter African Committee, resulted in a dramatic increase in the number of women and girls who underwent FGC in the following season.[187] Additionally, law may result in the lowering of the age at which their practice is carried out. School-going children may be exempt, but babies may not be so lucky.[188] It is also not clear that criminalising a cultural practice, which many perform on their children because they consider it to be in their best interests to be cut, will lead to a decrease in the practice.[189] Mackie notes:

> If some outsider tells you that you are a bad person because of some family tradition you follow, and you follow this tradition because you are a good person, then will you abandon the practice and thereby confirm the outsider's ignorant judgment that you are a bad person? I think not.[190]

[184] Rahman and Toubia above n 6 at 166. This accords with the United Nations Recommendations Relating to Traditional Practices 1991 paras (d)–(m), cited in G Alfredson and K Tomasevski (eds) *Thematic Guide to Documents on the Human Rights of Women* (Hague, Martinus Nijhoff, 1995) 309–10. See also WHO *Female Genital Mutilation Programmes* above n 9 at 29. See also Cairo Declaration for the Elimination of FGM 2003 (above n 25) paras 2, 7, 8.

[185] Boyle and Preves above n 6 at 706–7.

[186] Renteln *The Cultural Defense* above n 8 at 53.

[187] WHO *Female Genital Mutilation Programmes* above n 9 at 117.

[188] Awaken 'Tanzania: Circumcisors Working Quietly to Avoid Law' (2004) *Awaken* at 9.

[189] Gunning above n 31 at 233. N Toubia 'Legislation as a Tool of Behaviour Change' (paper presented at the Afro-Arab Consultation on Legal Tools for the Prevention of Female Genital Mutilation, Cairo, 21–23 June 2003) 1.

[190] Mackie above n 1 at 278. Cf Renteln 'Is the Cultural Defense Detrimental?' above n 8 at 69; Lord Rea, House of Lords Debate on Female Circumcision, Hansard HL (10 November 1998) col 738.

If anything, outlawing the practice, or criminalising those who continue it, will lead to the resentment and resistance identified in the discussion on the colonial era. Moreover, Mackie contends that criminal law is inappropriate because it was only designed to deal with a minority of miscreants and is therefore inappropriate in countries where the majority of the population practice FGC. He argues that a law which does not have popular backing is ineffective and arguably undemocratic.[191]

Rahman and Toubia introduce an interesting dimension to the discussion on the efficacy of using criminal sanctions, observing that if practised by one group, then using criminal law to deal with the practice could lead to inter-ethnic tension.[192] However, they go on to qualify this caveat, noting:

> . . . a well studied and strategically timed introduction of a criminal law prohibiting FC/FGM is a strong political and legal tool. If social change is well underway, with substantial popular backing and approval from the political establishment, the process of introducing, debating and successfully passing a law could itself serve to accelerate change. On the other hand, poorly timed or hastily introduced laws can backfire by truncating an emerging social dialogue, causing social rifts, and driving the practice underground.[193]

This proposition is supported by Rwezaura, who notes that efforts made by the Tanzanian government to educate people about the dangers of FGC have borne fruit. There has been a move towards a symbolic incision, 'drawing just a little blood, without removing anything'. This new, modified form is popularly known as the '*Mkato wa CCM*', is named after the Chama Cha Mapinduzi (CCM) political party, which forms the government of Tanzania.[194]

Toubia regards a purely legal approach as failing to engage with the reasons why women continue the practice. She identifies the erosion of women's social power and their desire to hold on to this power as a reason for the continuation of the practice. Without an engagement with this issue and a comprehensive restructuring of gender relations, law reform may come to naught.[195] Toubia advocates that states consider passing packages of law, which would address women's unequal status in family life and lack of access to resources including land, as essential to 'empowering women to become equal citizens economically and socially'.[196]

It becomes clear from reviewing the literature that irrespective of whether the commentator supports or rejects the use of law to eradicate the practice, all are

[191] Mackie above n 1 at 278. Cf Gunning above n 31 at 193.
[192] Rahman and Toubia above n 6 at 62. The Cairo Declaration for the Elimination of FGM 2003 above n 25 at para 16; Renteln *The Cultural Defense* above n 8 at 53.
[193] *Ibid.*
[194] B Rwezaura 'Competing Images of Childhood in the Social and Legal Systems of Contemporary Sub-Saharan Africa' (1998) 12 *International Journal of Law, Policy and the Family* 253 at at 270 n 54.
[195] Toubia above n 189 at 4.
[196] *Ibid* at 6.

agreed that the effort must be multi-disciplinary and involve many agencies and constituencies.[197]

The role of civil society organisations in eradicating FGC

It is fair to say that, in Africa, civil society in the form of NGOs has been at the forefront of efforts to eradicate the practice.[198] Indeed governments and international agencies now see civil society organisations as central to eradication efforts.[199] Methods used to tackle the practice have varied from peer education, to engagement with state actors (particularly in the health sector) as well as talking to religious and traditional elders, to lobbying for law reform, helping to draft legislation and developing symbolic alternatives. In looking at the work of civil society, Welch has suggested focusing on the three Es: education, empowerment and enforcement.[200]

Select case studies

Given the multiplicity of approaches, it is not possible to cover them all. The chapter considers, in outline, three strategies currently being employed to tackle the practice of FGC and one that deals with its consequences. The most well known, and arguably the one that has been judged the greatest success, is the Senegalese-based TOSTAN project.

TOSTAN

TOSTAN is Wolof for breakthrough.[201] The TOSTAN programme, which was devised by Molly Melching, combines a participatory educational empowerment

---

[197] Secretary-General's Report on Traditional or Customary Practices Affecting the Health of Women and Girls 2003 above n 92 paras 6–8. Cairo Declaration for the Elimination of FGM 2003 above n 25 at para 2. Special Rapporteur on Traditional Practices (2004) above n 99 at para 82.

[198] In particular is the work of the Inter-African Committee on Traditional Practices. See Welch above n 107 at 87.

[199] Secretary-General's Report on Traditional or Customary Practices Affecting the Health of Women and Girls 2003 above n 92 paras 10, 17, 41, 44, 49. Cairo Declaration for the Elimination of FGM 2003 above n 25 at paras 3, 6. Special Rapporteur on Traditional Practices (2004) above n 99 at para 21. CRC General Comment No 5 paras 35, 36. Government of Ethiopia (2002) above n 87 at para 32.

[200] Welch above n 107 at 88. See also Toubia's four hypotheses on the relation between FGC, social change and women's empowerment. Toubia above n 189 at 4.

[201] It is also known as the TOSTAN Village Empowerment Programme (VEP).

approach with the aim of teaching vital skills.[202] Utilising a human rights framework, the programme is constructed around six modules that last for two months each. The main themes covered by the modules include: human rights, to give women the grounding to enable them better to understand and defend their rights; an understanding of problem solving to enable them to identify, analyse and work towards resolving violations of their rights as well as ways of working to end FGC within their communities; a module on basic hygiene and another on women's health, to enable them better to understand the physiology of women's bodies and to help to dispel some of the myths surrounding the health and aesthetic justifications for the practice. Finally women are taught about management skills for income-generating projects. Led by local trainers, the programme is boosted by visits from participants from other villages who have gone through the TOSTAN programme. These visits provide positive reinforcement to those villagers in the process of transformation. The programme also encourages participants to 'adopt' a friend with whom to share knowledge gained from the class, thus leading to widespread dissemination of the programme.

The success of TOSTAN has been linked to the fact that it is said to respect local culture and to honour local/traditional wisdom. It never seeks to tell people what to do, but rather facilitates the learning process. In this way 'ownership' of the process is in the hands of the programme participants, and this is more likely to lead to greater legitimacy and long-term acceptance. One of the main components of the TOSTAN approach has been the collective pledging by the village/community to end the practice. This is done by means of a public declaration.[203] Public declarations have also been adopted in northern Ghana.[204]

Mackie has identified education, social mobilisation using local cultural terms together with the public pledge, as the three inter-dependent elements that are necessary if social transformation is to be achieved.[205] The TOSTAN approach embraces all three. Another reason for the success of the TOSTAN approach is that it is organic. It utilises local experiences and embraces local perspectives rather than being a top-down imposition. In 2004, the 'follow-up committee' of a community that had pledged to stop the practice reported one of their number, who had continued to cut girls, to the police for prosecution, thus showing that a ground-up approach that starts by winning over the people affected is more likely to lead to effective enforcement of the law.[206]

---

[202] M Melching 'You are an African Woman' Lecture Given at the John F Kennedy School of Government, Harvard University, 16 November 2000 at 2. Downloaded from http:www.tostan.org/index1.html.

[203] The first such public affirmation was the Malicounda Declaration 1997. See Mackie above n 1 at 257.

[204] Association of Church Development Projects 'Resolution on Female Genital Mutilation Practice in Ghana and Efforts towards Eradication', October 2000 (on file with author). See also (2000) 2 *FORWARD Newsletter* at 2.

[205] Mackie above n 1 at 259.

[206] Awaken 'The Impact of Community Abandonment of FGC on Circumcisors' (2004) *Awaken* at 8.

Just as important is the communal aspect of the pledging system that binds a community together and lessens the possibility of a person/family being ostracised for being different. Mackie also notes the importance of group consensus, particularly amongst groups which inter-marry.[207] If one group is to give up the practice, then other groups with whom they traditionally inter-marry have also to be prepared to accept un-cut women. Without this mutual understanding, success may be short-lived.

TOSTAN's success can be linked to its thoroughness. It takes a year to complete the modules. It is therefore a programme that demands that both participants and funders have patience and adopt a long-term view of behavioural change. However, the pay off is in its internal legitimacy, which augurs well for long-term eradication. The TOSTAN model is being 'exported' to regional neighbours.[208]

In closing, it is worth noting that following on the widespread domestic and international support of the TOSTAN programme, the government of Senegal enacted, in 1999, a law outlawing the practice.

Alternative coming-of-age programme—Kenya

Some communities in Kenya have been persuaded to adopt alternative rites in place of FGC. The aim of these alternative rites is to maintain the educational and celebratory elements attached to 'coming of age rituals' whilst abandoning the more harmful aspects, which would of course include cutting. One such new rite is known as *ntanira na mugambo* or 'circumcision through words'.[209] It grew out of a joint collaboration between a Kenyan women's NGO called Maendeleo ya Wanawake Organisation (MYWO), the Programme for Appropriate Technology in Health (PATH) and rural families.[210] The first 'circumcision through words' took place in Gatunga in August 1996.

The programme, through a process of dialogue with families, sought to encourage an ending of the practice of FGC without losing the more positive aspects of the culture that underpin it. To do this, the week of seclusion, which would traditionally have been set aside for the healing of cut girls, is used to impart 'family life skills' and 'traditional wisdom' such as respect for elders. The programme has spread to other districts and more alternative rights ceremonies have taken place.[211] To ensure sustainability of the programme people have been trained to

---

[207] Mackie above n 1 at 270, 271 and 280.
[208] Awaken 'Interest Picks Up on Tostan's Strategy to end FGM' (2004) *Awaken* at 8.
[209] M Reaves 'Alternative Rite to Female Circumcision Spreading in Kenya' Africa News Online, 9 November 1997. Downloaded from: http://www.africanews.org/specials/19971119_fgm.html. Secretary-General's Report on Traditional or Customary Practices Affecting the Health of Women and Girls 2003 above n 92 para 10.
[210] Kabeberi-Machaira above n 146 at 249.
[211] WHO *Female Genital Mutilation Programmes* above n 9 at 109.

act as Family Life Education trainers. They are on hand to advise the initiates during the time of seclusion. These trained peer educators are an important reinforcement, training the initiates and supporting the community. Additionally, the young women who have undergone the alternative ritual form support groups that meet regularly.

The most obvious benefit of the programme is that it aims to bring an end to cutting. The programme requires a public commitment to the values of the alternative rites approach, together with a pledge by both parents that they will not have their daughters cut. In this way 'the men, women, girls and community leaders . . . form a core group of anti-FGM support groups and activists'.[212] Another advantage is that in maintaining the traditions around the rites of passage (bar the cutting), it shows a respect for local cultural values.

However, it is as well to acknowledge that the premise upon which the practice was based may no longer obtain. Specifically, it assumes that girls would be cut as part of the rites of passage and seeks to circumvent this, but the reality appears to be that the age at which cutting occurs may be much lower than the age at which girls pass into womanhood. It may thus be counter-productive to link the two practices—cutting and rites of passage.[213] Another difficulty that arose with the project was the disinformation campaigns launched by those opposed to the change. They said that it was an externally (foreign) generated ritual, designed to teach girls about sex and to provide them with contraceptives, resulting in them becoming promiscuous. This disinformation campaign had to be actively tackled, and it was pointed out that the programme was initiated and run by locals and not foreigners. Those young women who had participated in the programme were brought in to testify that they had not been taught immoral things.[214] Finally, the programme requires ongoing communal support so that those 'initiates' not cut in one season will not bow to pressure to be cut in coming seasons. This collective, long-term change may be hard to sustain.

Use of media and other approaches—Ethiopia

Ethiopia, with its diversity of ethnic groups and religions, is an interesting case study. FGC, although widespread in Ethiopia, has regional variations in terms of types practised and the age at which girls are cut. There are, for example, groups that engage in FGC when the girl is a baby, those that wait until she is a little older (say 7 or 8 and those groups that cut 15 days before a woman is due to marry. This demands a nuanced approach which takes into account these regional variations. It may, in the case of the 15 days before marriage group, be better to target the

---

[212] *Ibid.*
[213] Mackie above n 1 at 276.
[214] WHO *Female Genital Mutilation Programmes* above n 9 at 110.

future groom and his family, and persuade him/them of the complications arising out of the practice of FGC and thus persuade him/them to accept an uncut bride. In this way, the woman would be spared being cut, for it would no longer be a pre-condition to marriage. Tackling communities that cut babies is somewhat more problematic because young infants are kept indoors and it is more difficult to penetrate this private sphere. Where school-age children are involved, teachers could be trained to be particularly vigilant and to liaise with a health/community worker if a child disclosed that she was about to be cut. This section focuses on the education efforts of the National Committee for Traditional Practices of Ethiopia (NCPTE).

The popular education campaign devised by the NCPTE uses a variety of media including print (posters, stickers, and books), video and other audio-visual tools. The aim of the campaign is to educate the public about the origins and health consequences of the practice, its prevalence and myths surrounding it. Ultimately it is hoped to engage the public in eradication efforts. The participants are shown videos and then given literature to take away with them. Two story books have been devised around the issue, one showing a positive outcome and the other a negative outcome in that the cut woman loses her child in childbirth.[215] She is later found to be unable to have other children and loses her husband as a result. Language and context are of course key in the presentation of materials. For example, it has been found effective to show men a video of an actual cutting, because this is often the first time they see at first hand what the practice entails.

Another group, the Integrated Community Education Development Association (ICEDA) also uses video as an educational tool in schools. It is important that the content of these videos be both culture- and age-sensitive. Caution must be exercised to avoid (further) traumatising young people, especially girls, by showing them films of young girls being cut.

Radio has also been a powerful tool in the fight to eradicate FGC in Ethiopia.[216] Working with a government media agency, the NCPTE created a series of 28 radio programmes on FGC and early marriage. The programmes, in nine of the local languages, were broadcast to an estimated 96 per cent of the school community. They were supplemented by leaflets in English and Amharic, which were sent out to schools. In addition to the schools programme, there were two further

---

[215] G Metike *Ali's Story* (Addis Ababa, National Committee on Traditional Practices in Ethiopia (NCTPE), undated); G Metike *Yimer's Story* (Addis Ababa, National Committee on Traditional Practices in Ethiopia (NCTPE), undated).

[216] In Mali music has been used to spread the message about FGC being a violation of women's rights. Sahel Initiative Third Millennium 'Stop Excision for the Dignity of Women from Mali' (2001/2) musical compact disk made with the help of Canadian Centre for International Studies and Co-operation (CECI) with financing from the Canadian International Development Agency (CIDA). Longinotto's documentary film has also received positive reviews: K Longinotto *The Day I Will Never Forget* (New York, Women Make Movies, 2002).

ten-minute radio programmes aimed at the general population. These were broadcast on weekends.[217]

It is interesting to note that education has featured in all the approaches. Linked to that has been the importance of community involvement in the programme both as planners and participants.[218] Finally the importance of understanding the cultural grounding of the practice and respecting local wisdom has also been manifest.[219]

Other international initiatives have included declaring 6 February the International Day of Zero Tolerance of FGM, marked in both Africa and other parts of the world.[220] An international petition campaign to stop FGM has been initiated by two Italian NGOs and one from Tanzania.[221] The petition makes clear that it regards FGM as a violation of the human right to respect for physical integrity. It also considers the practice a violation of the right to life and non-discrimination and calls on states to ensure respect for human rights and to enact legislation to outlaw the practice. Additionally there should be education and information campaigns, and co-operation between local, national and international NGOs.

The focus thus far has been on prevention strategies. This section concludes with a brief consideration of a project that assists women who have already been cut, or who have experienced health-related problems.

The Foundation for Research and Development on African Women's Health (FORWARD) Dambatta Project in Nigeria

The FORWARD Nigeria project, whilst working on preventive education, also helps women who have been cut, some of whom suffer from vesico-vaginal fistula (VVF). They may face rejection by their husbands as a result. The Dambatta project seeks to rehabilitate these women.[222] It does this by accessing medical services on the women's behalf, enabling them to receive treatment and to be 'mended'. It also provides literacy classes and trains the women in income-generating projects. As it is a live-in programme, children are welcomed. They are enrolled in local schools if they are of school-going age. A supplementary nutrition programme is

---

[217] F Pickup, S Williams and C Sweetman *Ending Violence against Women: A Challenge for Development and Humanitarian* Work (Oxford, OXFAM, 2001) 246–47.

[218] Secretary-General's Report on Traditional or Customary Practices Affecting the Health of Women and Girls 2003 above n 92 paras 48, 49; Government of Ethiopia (2002) above n 87 at paras 32–35, para 67.

[219] See also WHO *Female Genital Mutilation Programmes* above n 9 at 28 on typology for tackling the practice. Special Rapporteur on Traditional Practices (2004) above n 99 at paras 81–84.

[220] Special Rapporteur on Traditional Practices (2004) above n 99 at paras 35–57.

[221] AIDOS, No Peace without Justice and TAMWA 'Solemn Appeal against Female Genital Mutilation' at www.stopfgm.org.

[222] FORWARD 'Dambatta' in *FORWARD Annual Report 2003–2004* (London, FORWARD, 2004) 14.

also in place to assist the children of these mothers. At the end of the stay at the centre, it is hoped that in addition to the physical healing, the women will experience psychic healing and be empowered to return to their communities to live full lives. The income-generating skills they learn at the centre are designed to enable them to become economically independent and this acts as a boost to their confidence. The project offers small loans as start-up capital, which the women return once their enterprises are up and running. The recruits have spoken positively about the project. Some of the women who had been rejected by their husbands have said that on seeing them healed and economically productive, their husbands have asked them to return. Not all have obliged![223]

The strength of the project lies in its holistic approach. Formal literacy classes are linked to practical skills training to enable a woman to make her own way in the world once she leaves Dambatta. Additionally, there is access to medical facilities and the support of knowing that one is not alone in one's plight. Friendships with similarly situated women are made and act as a positive reinforcement. Finally, the programme is to be commended for its gender sensitivity in recognising the need to provide for childcare to enable women to participate in the project.

Conclusion

The chapter has considered the evolution in understanding of the practice of FGC and feminist responses to it. Although there were differences in approach between northern and southern women, it seems that over time the more sensitive use of language has resulted in the dissipation of tension and the building of coalitions to tackle the practice. The chapter has also considered the efficacy of the human rights and law approach in tackling FGC. It is clear that although useful, law reform alone is inadequate to bring about an end to the practice. If anything, a purely legal approach runs the risk of:

> making a mockery of the law or creating a situation where girls and women are faced with the double jeopardy of suffering FGM to appease an old social order and then get penalized by the modern legal system.[224]

The combination of women's low status in society linked to the impact of custom, culture, tradition and the wrong interpretation of religion means that the potential for transformation is difficult, but not impossible. What is required is an inclusive, inter-agency approach that takes in the best of the cultural values under consideration and rejects, by means of communal dialogue and agreement, the

---

[223] Interview with Project Director Dr Rahmat Mohammed in London, June 2002.
[224] Toubia above n 189 at 6.

more harmful elements.[225] An acknowledgment of, and engagement with, the economic disempowerment of the majority of African women and girls is also crucial.

The next chapter considers the academic debate on reconciling cultural values and human rights norms. It also explores the related issues of development and the participation of women in public life.

---

[225] A An Na'im 'State Responsibility under International Human Rights Law to Change Religious and Customary Laws' in R Cook (ed) *Human Rights of Women: National and International Perspectives* (Philadelphia, University of Pennsylvania Press, 1994) 167.

7

Culture, Development and Participation

When this book was conceived, I thought that I would spend a lot of time analysing the 'culture'/human rights conundrum. However, as time has gone on, I am not so sure that there is much more to be said that has not already been written on the matter. Suffice to say that just as much has been endured by women in the name of the ill-defined 'culture', and some might add religion here as well, so too much has been promised to women in the name of human rights.

This chapter considers briefly, the issue of 'culture' and its relation to human rights norms before moving on to examine what I, and many others before me,[1] now consider to be the chief impediment to the enjoyment of rights by women, and that is the on-going violations of their social and economic rights, and their exclusion from participation in decision making.[2] This suggests for me the need to focus on the pledge made in Vienna, where the rights of women and the girl child were said to be an 'inalienable, integral, indivisible part of universal human rights'.[3] Indeed Tripp notes that: 'It seems incongruous to focus so heavily on cultural dimensions of women's oppression, while disregarding how culture and material conditions interact.'[4]

---

[1] M Nussbaum 'Women and Human Development: The Capabilities Approach' in M Molyneaux and S Razavi (eds) *Gender Justice, Development and Rights* (Oxford, Oxford University Press, 2003) 45 at 54, 56, 62. D Elson 'Gender Justice, Human Rights and Neo-Liberal Economic Policies' in M Molyneaux and S Razavi S (eds) (2003) (above) 78; A Stewart 'The Contribution of Feminist Legal Scholarship to the "Rights Approach to Development"' in A Stewart (ed) *Gender, Law and Social Justice* (Oxford, Blackstone, 2000) 1. See also A Stewart 'Entitlement, Pluralism and Gender Justice in Sub Saharan Africa' in J Murison *et al* (eds) *Remaking Law in Africa: Transnationalism Persons and Rights* (Edinburgh, Centre of African Studies, 2004) 195; World Bank *Sub-Saharan Africa: From Crisis to Sustainable Growth: A Long Term Perspective Study* (Washington DC, World Bank, 1989) 54 as cited in M Chanock 'Human Rights and Cultural Branding: Who Speaks and How?' in A An Na'im (ed) *Cultural Transformation and Human Rights in Africa* (London, Zed Press, 2002) 38 at 59; United Nations *The United Nations and the Advancement of Women 1945–1996* (New York, United Nations, 1996) 7.

[2] AU Solemn Declaration on Gender Equality in Africa 2004 preamble, arts 2, 6–8; UDHR art 22.

[3] Vienna Declaration and Programme for Action 1993 (I) para 18. Beijing Declaration 1995 para 9; Beijing Platform for Action 1995 para 10.

[4] A Tripp 'The Politics of Women's Rights and Cultural Diversity in Uganda' in M Molyneaux and S Razavi (eds) above n 1, 413 at 414.

I begin by considering culture within the human rights field and the culture/human rights debate, and then I look at the issue of development, in particular women's engagement with the development paradigm. My focus then turns to the (special) needs of rural women before considering the issue of political participation of women. Before concluding, I examine the work of non-governmental organisations in the delivery of rights.

The monolith—'culture'

Discussions about 'Culture, custom and tradition',[5] into which is sometimes collapsed religion, have occupied anthropologists, historians, sociologists and more recently lawyers, amongst others, for decades.[6] The United Nations has not been immune. Indeed cursory examination of considerations of 'culture' within the UN system shows that it has occupied a great deal of time and attention.

For women, the focus of the 'culture debate' within the United Nations has largely been on women in the family and the impact of custom on their enjoyment of rights.[7] Even after the adoption of CEDAW, the issue of 'culture' has continued to feature as an impediment to the enjoyment by women of their rights, appearing in conference resolutions and platforms for action such as Nairobi 1985,[8] Vienna 1993,[9] Cairo 1994,[10] Beijing 1995,[11] Copenhagen 1995[12] and Johannesburg 2002.[13]

The Women's Committee has made several General Recommendations[14] explaining provisions in the Convention and making recommendations as to how the rights contained therein could be implemented. Some of these General

[5] Cf A An Na'im and J Hammond in A An'Na'im (ed) *Cultural Transformation and Human Rights in Africa* (London, Zed Press, 2002) 14 at 23.

[6] See the synopsis of discussion on the meaning of 'culture' in A An Na'im and J Hammond *ibid* at 21–27.

[7] United Nations *Advancement of Women* above n 1 at 17, 23.

[8] Forward Looking Strategies for the Advancement of Women to the Year 2000 (1985) UN Doc A/CONF.116/28/Rev. paras 93, 101, 115, 118, 121.

[9] Vienna Declaration and Programme for Action1993 (II) paras 38, 49

[10] ICPD 1994 para 4.4(c).

[11] Beijing Platform Critical Areas of Concern 1995 para 42. See also Beijing + 5 Outcome Document (2000) UN Doc A/S-23/10/Rev.1 para 95(i).

[12] See also Copenhagen Declaration on Social Development, Adopted by the World Summit for Social Development, Held in Copenhagen from 6 to 12 March 1995—Commitment 5, on the Achievement of Equality and Equity Between Women and Men A/CONF.166/9, 1995, 5 para (a).

[13] The Johannesburg Declaration on Sustainable Development 2002 para 20.

[14] 25 General Recommendations to date.

Recommendations have identified 'culture', religion and other practices as being impediments to the enjoyment by women of their rights.[15]

Echoing our earlier discussion in Chapter 2, CEDAW General Recommendations also identify the conflicts between constitutional provisions of equality and customary norms:

> While most countries report that national constitutions and laws comply with the Convention, custom, tradition and failure to enforce those laws in reality contravene the Convention.[16]

In a strongly universalist, some might argue culturally particular, statement, the Committee makes clear that women's rights in the family have to be respected:

> States Parties should resolutely discourage any notions of inequality of women and men which are affirmed by laws, or by religious or private law or by custom, and progress to the state where reservations, particularly to article 16 will be withdrawn.[17]

From the foregoing it would appear that for the Committee, 'culture' represents a major impediment to women's enjoyment of their human rights. This negative construct of culture admits of no possibility that it could to be used to facilitate women's empowerment.[18] The diverse geographical, religious and racial composition of the Committee notwithstanding, the focus of the CEDAW General Recommendations on practices occurring mainly in countries in the south, leaves open the possibility of charges of cultural insensitivity and condescension.[19] The questioning of state representatives presenting country reports before the Committee also shows culture being raised frequently,[20] and being

---

[15] CEDAW General Recommendation No 21 para 3; CEDAW General Recommendation No 19 para 21. See also para 20, which provides 'In some States there are traditional practices perpetuated by culture and tradition that are harmful to the health of women and children.'

[16] CEDAW General Recommendation No 21 para 15.

[17] *Ibid* para 44. See also paras 13, 41, 45, 46, 50.

[18] For an excellent critique of this approach see C Nyamu 'How Should Human Rights and Development Respond to Cultural Legitimization of Gender Hierarchy in Developing Countries?' (2000) 41 *Harvard International Law Journal* 381.

[19] S Wolf 'Culture, Family Law and Women's Rights: Blaming Culture for the Failure to Uphold the Rights of Women' (Essay for the MA in International and Comparative Legal Studies, Department of Law, School of Oriental and African Studies, 2002; on file with the departmental office); N Nzegwu 'Questions of Agency: Development, Donors, and Women of the South' in (2002) *Jenda: A Journal of Culture and African Women's Studies* at http://www.jendajournal.com/jenda/vol1.1/nzegwu.html; M Mutua 'Savages, Victims, and Saviors: The Metaphor of Human Rights' (2001) 42 *Harvard International Law Journal* 201 at 222. But see R Holtmaat *Towards Different Law and Public Policy: The Significance of Article 5(a) CEDAW for the Elimination of Structural Gender Discrimination* (The Hague, Ministry of Social Affairs and Employment, 2004) 36.

[20] CEDAW Concluding Observations Ethiopia CEDAW A/51/38 (1996) para 139; 'CEDAW Concludes Consideration of Morocco's Report' (20 January 1997) UN press release WOM/927 at http://www.un.org/News/Press/docs/1997/19970120.wom937.html at 1; UN/CEDAW 'Need to Modify Cultural Practices Harmful to Women in Democratic Republic of Congo Stressed by Discrimination Committee Experts' UN Press Release WOM/1164 downloaded from: http://www.un.org/News/Press/docs.2000/200001225.wom1164.doc.html.

constructed by the states reporting as an impediment to progress and 'modern-isation'.[21]

The move towards mainstreaming[22] within the work of UN bodies has also resulted in a greater engagement with issues affecting women by non-CEDAW committees. An examination of state reports to CESCR by the International Women's Rights Action Watch yielded the information that 'culture' was seen as a continuing impediment to the enjoyment by women of their rights.[23] General Comments made by the Human Rights Committees also show an appreciation of the impact of culture on the ability of women to enjoy their rights.[24] General Comment 28 reads in part: 'Inequality in the enjoyment of rights by women throughout the world is deeply embedded in tradition, history and culture, including religious attitudes.'[25]

Regional considerations of 'culture'

Having been left out of early UN norm making due to colonialism, African states, far from constructing 'culture' as problematic, chose to present it as a positive in the African Charter of 1981.[26] This may be linked to their anger at the colonisation process, which initially resulted in resistance by post-colonial states to 'inter-ference in their internal affairs', which stance was justified by reference to the self-determination provisions in the UN Charter.[27]

---

[21] Combined Second and Third Periodic Reports of States Parties: Nigeria CEDAW/C/NGA/2–3 at 21; Initial Report of States Party: Algeria (1998) CEDAW/C/DZA/1(hereafter Government of Algeria (1998)) at 4; Combined Fourth and Fifth Periodic Report of States Parties: Egypt (30 March 2000) CEDAW/C/EGY4–5 at 32.

[22] A Gallagher 'Ending the Marginalization: Strategies for Incorporating Women Into the United Nations Human Rights System' (1997) 19 *Human Rights Quarterly* 283 at 284; Report of the Secretary-General on the Question of Integrating the Human Rights of Women throughout the United Nations System (25 March 1998) E/CN.4/1998/49 para 9.

[23] IWRAW 'Equality and Rights: The International Covenant on Economic, Social and Cultural Rights, Art 3. Background Paper for the Proposed General Comment on ICESCR Art 3' (paper presented at Meeting on Art 3 of the International Covenant on Economic, Social and Cultural Rights Held at the University of Toronto, Faculty of Law, 19–20 July 2003) 1 at paras 44–48. The analysis of art 10 of the Covenant on Protection of Marriage and Family Relations shows that discrimination against women in the family was a persistent problem. D Otto ' "Gender Comment": Why Does the UN Committee on Economic, Social and Cultural Rights Need a General Comment on Women?' (2002) 14 *Canadian Journal of Women and the Law* 1 at 41. IWRAW *Equality and Women's Economic, Social and Cultural Rights* (Minnesota, IWRAW, 2004) 40–41.

[24] Human Rights Committee General Comments Nos 19, 24, 28.

[25] Human Rights Committee General Comment No 28 para 5.

[26] African Charter, preamble, arts 17(2), 29(7). See also OAU Cultural Charter for Africa 1976.

[27] UN Charter arts 1(2) and 2(7); OAU Cultural Charter for Africa 1976.

At first glance it would appear that the African Charter seems to construct 'African culture' as an undifferentiated, homogenised whole. Grounded in the African Charter is the assumption that all Africans on the continent will immediately understand what is meant by the term 'African cultural values', but are these values not mediated over time, space and place? Appiah and Tripp both point out that an over-emphasis on 'culture' or difference runs the risk of concealing a basic truth, which is the acceptance of, and demand for, the respect of (individual) human rights the world over.[28] On the notion that there is a distinctly 'African' culture, Appiah has noted:

> If there is a lesson in the broad scope of this circulation of cultures, it is surely that we are all already contaminated by each other; there is no longer a fully autochthonous 'echt' African culture awaiting salvage by our artists. (A)nd there is a clear sense in some post-colonial writing that the postulation of a unitary Africa over and against a monolithic West—the binarism of Self and Other—is the last of the shibboleths of the modernizers that we must learn to live without.[29]

While one cannot deny the potency of 'culture' in political and social discourse, it seems clear that, although not defined in the African Charter, commentators have noted that 'positive African cultural values' have to be read as being compatible with the rest of the Charter, especially its provisions on non-discrimination and, where women are concerned, the injunction in article 18(3) that the state has an obligation to eliminate '*every* discrimination against women' (emphasis added).[30] In *LRF v Zambia*, the African Commission noted that 'The Charter must be interpreted holistically and all clauses must reinforce each other.'[31] Consideration of state reports by the African Commission shows that the Commission is alive to the role that restrictive interpretations/constructions of culture play in limiting and denying women their human rights.[32]

Nevertheless, Chanock highlights the manipulative use made by African and Asian elites acting 'on behalf of' states, of the language of 'culture', noting that they resist moves towards the adoption and enforcement of human rights within

[28] A Appiah 'Citizens of the World' in M Gibney (ed) *Globalizing Rights* (Oxford, Oxford University Press, 2003) 189 at 193, 200, 214–16, 228, 229; Tripp above n 4 at 416–17.

[29] A Appiah *In My Father's House: Africa in the Philosophy of Culture* (New York, Oxford University Press, 1992) as cited in W Wanzala 'Towards an Epistemological and Methodological Framework of Development' in P McFadden (ed) *Southern Africa in Transition: A Gendered Perspective* (Harare, SAPES, 1998) 9 fn 26; A Appiah 'Citizens of the World' above n 28 at 212, 224, 227, 228–31.

[30] C Beyani 'Toward a More Effective Guarantee of Women's Rights in the African Human Rights System' in R Cook (ed) *Human Rights of Women: National and International Perspectives* (Philadelphia, University of Pennsylvania Press, 1994) 285; M Mutua 'Banjul Charter: The Case for an African Cultural Fingerprint' in A An Na'im (ed) *Cultural Transformation and Human Rights in Africa* (London, Zed Press, 2002) 67 at 88–89. See too ACRWC art 21(1)(b).

[31] *Legal Resources Foundation v Zambia*, Communication 211/98, Decision of the AfCmHPR, 29th Ordinary Session, April/May 2001 [2001] IIHRL 1 (1 May 2001) para 70.

[32] R Murray *The African Commission on Human Rights and International Law* (Oxford, Hart Publishing, 2000) 44.

their states by appealing to notions of 'culture' and cultural identity.[33] Specifically he notes how the rulers of some of these states have 'tried to push rights issues out of the realm of both state and society and into that of "culture" '.[34] It is for this reason, he argues, that we need to look at 'culture' at the macro rather than micro level. The deployment, by state elites, of 'culture' as a defence to change, is not because such 'culture' is valued, but rather because it can be used as a bulwark against 'modernity', change and a claim for rights.[35]

> There is typically a wide gap between those who speak for cultures and those who live the culture spoken about. While cultures are complex and multi-vocal, in the representation of cultures the voices of the elites overwhelm others. Assertions about cultures tend to be totalizing and simplifying, privileging some voices and patterns of acts, and ignoring and marginalizing others.[36]

Moreover, one can also pinpoint state complicity in not wishing to upset influential (read male) people by challenging the privileges that unequal 'cultural interpretations' bestow upon them. Governments therefore see adopting a laissez-faire position vis-à-vis 'cultural practices' that may discriminate against women as a price worth paying for maintaining patronage.[37] However, alive to international aid-donor pressures to be seen to be engaging with human rights norms, they play a game of double bluff, telling aid donors and UN institutions that they are keen to bring about change to gender relations, and give as evidence of this the ratification of human rights instruments and the creation of women's departments and ministries, but then go on to note that their backs are against the wall and that they face almost insurmountable resistance from the 'people', whilst at the same time telling the 'folks back home' that they are being pressured into making legal and other changes by outsiders and that their hands are tied because the 'foreigners' will not give them money to develop the country otherwise.

Alive to the misuse of culture to deny women their rights, the African Protocol on Women's Rights contains a provision guaranteeing that women have the right 'to live in a positive cultural context'.[38] States are under an obligation to 'take all appropriate measures to enhance the participation of women in the formulation

---

[33] M Chanock 'Human Rights and Cultural Branding: Who Speaks and How?' in A An Na'im (ed) *Cultural Transformation and Human Rights in Africa* (London, Zed Press, 2002) 38 at 63. See also R Higgins *Problems and Process: International Law and How We Use It* (Oxford, Clarendon Press, 1994) at 96–97; S Goonesekere 'Women's Rights and Children's Rights: The United Nations Conventions as Compatible and Complementary International Treaties' (1992) *1 Innocenti Occasional Papers Child Rights Series* 1 at 25–26.

[34] *Ibid.*

[35] *Ibid.* See also 38–39, 42.

[36] *Ibid* at 39.

[37] L Favali and R Pateman *Blood, Land and Sex: Legal and Political Pluralism in Eritrea* (Indianapolis, Indiana University Press, 2003) 224.

[38] African Protocol on Women's Rights art 17(1).

of cultural policies at all levels'.[39] The preamble to the Protocol makes clear that 'positive African values' have to be based on 'the principles of equality, peace, freedom, dignity, justice, solidarity and democracy'.

The culture v human rights industry[40]

Running parallel to international and regional norm making in the human rights field has been debate about how to reconcile any tensions between culture and human rights principles. This debate has been criticised as being too narrowly constructed.[41] Sousa Santos notes that the framing of debate is in itself problematic because:

> The debate is an inherently false debate, whose polar concepts are both and equally detrimental to an emancipatory conception of human rights. All cultures are relative, but cultural relativism as a philosophical posture is wrong. All cultures aspire to ultimate concerns and values, but cultural universalism as a philosophical posture is wrong.[42]

There has been a great deal written about culture and human rights and how to reconcile the two. Much of the work has focused on 'Africa' and 'Asia', which has helped to suggest that there is a single 'African' or 'Asian' cultural or value system.[43] The focus on these two regions calls into question whether the south has 'problematic cultures' that need to be 'modernized and sorted out', whilst the north is free from 'culture', or at least the negative aspects of it that are ascribed to the south.[44] As an aside, as a black African teacher of human rights living in the north, I have noticed that while students from Africa and Asia always write about their own communities, the vast majority of white students from the north prefer to write about negative cultural practices occurring in the south. The sometimes uncritical sense of entitlement to write about 'other' displayed by some white students, is linked in my view to a lack of reflection about self and community

---

[39] *Ibid* art 17(2). See also SADC Declaration on Gender and Development 1997 art H(iv).

[40] I use the word 'industry' advisedly. Typing in cultural relativism and human rights to http://www.google.com can keep one occupied indefinitely.

[41] Chanock above n 33 at 63. He thinks that 'there are better ways to approach these questions and the clearest is through an attention to the detailed articulation by those affected, of wrongs, and of needs'. *Ibid.*

[42] B Sousa Santos 'Towards a Multicultural Conception of Human Rights' (1997) XXIV *Sociologia del Diritto* 27 at 41.

[43] Cf A Rao 'The Politics of Gender and Culture in International Human Rights Discourse' in J Peters and A Wolper (eds) *Women's Rights, Human Rights: International Feminist Perspectives* (New York, Routledge, 1995) 167 at 168. Rao is also critical of the ahistorical constructions of culture.

[44] *Ibid.* See also K Bhavanani 'Women, Culture, Development: Three Visions' in K Bhavanani *et al* (eds) *Feminist Futures: Re-imagining Women, Culture and Development* (London, Zed Press, 2003) 7, 13; Tripp above n 4 at 414–18.

that is grounded in ongoing northern (academic, media and other) constructions of the south as perpetually in need of salvation and the north as being more progressive.[45]

The human rights/culture story has many protagonists. I have decided to limit the cast of characters to those who hold that delivery of human rights is only possible where states are prepared to act on discriminatory cultural practices by way of prohibition, to those who see culture as not necessarily being an impediment to the enjoyment by women of their rights, and finally to An Na'im who incorporates all these arguments in presenting his methodological model for the mediation of culture and human rights in a transformative process for both.

Tiring of the softly softly approach that has not yielded greater enjoyment of rights by women, Beyani has argued for a more radical approach to the resolution of the 'culture or human rights' conundrum.[46] He proposes that cultural norms be put through the filter of human rights. If they are found to discriminate against women, then the human rights norm has to prevail over the 'culture'. This revolutionary approach, reflected in the 'universalist' constitutions discussed in Chapter 2, has been criticised as being insufficiently sensitive to the needs of people who may value the cultural traditions that do not do well in the human rights test.[47] Enforced change runs the risk of rejection.[48] It also suggests a ranking of systems that always has human rights as superior to culture and custom.[49] Indeed Bennett notes that 'African culture (and customary law) has not shared the prestige enjoyed by human rights'.[50]

At the opposite end of the spectrum and directly contradicting Beyani are the cultural purists or 'traditionalists', who call for a 'return to' the old cultural ways of doing things and also for the preservation of 'culture' from external interference, which would include human rights norms.[51] Commenting on this position in relation to religion on the Indian subcontinent, Mukhopdhyay notes that failing to take a stance on gender is tantamount to:

---

[45] In seven years of teaching only three white students have ever actively critiqued the location of self in writing about other. Similarly, not a single African or Asian student has ever discussed reasons for focusing on self and not other. Mutua is eloquent on this issue. Mutua above n 19.

[46] Beyani above n 30 at 285–92.

[47] T Nhlapo 'Cultural Diversity, Human Rights and the Family in Contemporary Africa: Lessons from the South African Constitutional Debate' (1995) 8 *International Journal of Law, Family and Policy* 208.

[48] A Allott 'Reforming the Law in Africa: Aims, Difficulties and Techniques' in A Sanders (ed) *Southern Africa in Need of Law Reform* (Durban, Butterworths, 1981) 228.

[49] T Nhlapo 'African Family Law under an Undecided Constitution—the Challenge for Law Reform in South Africa' in J Eekelaar and T Nhlapo (eds) *Changing Family* (Oxford, Hart Publishing, 1998) 617 at 618, 624.

[50] T Bennett *Human Rights and African Customary Law under the South African Constitution* (Cape Town, Juta, 1995) 1.

[51] See discussion in Nhlapo above nn 47 and 49.

[T]aking the side of the fundamentalists, who render religion uniform throughout the world by enforcing traditions of hierarchical gender roles and relations, and presenting them as unchanging and authoritative.[52]

From the 'Islamic perspective' Mir-Hosseini sees the clash as between those whom she terms 'secular fundamentalists', who see all things religious and cultural as backward, and 'religious fundamentalists', who hanker for a return to a static 'tradition' and the past.[53]

Trying to accommodate the two views is Donnelly, who prefers a weak cultural relativism, or what he later calls a relatively strong universalism,[54] which acknowledges that culture 'may be an important source of the validity of a moral right or rule'.[55] As a result of this acknowledgement he is prepared 'to defend a weak cultural relativist position that permits deviations from universal human rights standards'.[56] Donnelly's acceptance of minor difference is grounded in his belief that fundamentally there is normative consensus in all societies that human rights are a common good.[57] He argues that exemptions must be very narrowly drawn, and anyone claiming a cultural 'let':

[W]ould have to show that the underlying cultural vision of human nature or society is both morally defensible and incompatible with the implementation of the 'universal' human rights in question.[58]

As he notes, this is not an easy test to satisfy. For Donnelly, some behaviours that may have been tolerated before, including sex and race discrimination, are in modern times indefensible. Donnelly sees principles of non-discrimination as non-derogable and thus non-negotiable.[59]

The methodology of the Dutch Advisory Council on International Affairs[60] for dealing with the plural values/human rights conundrum is that human rights do not have to be applied uniformly throughout the world, especially since they are

---

[52] M Mukhopadhay 'Some Thoughts on Gender and Culture' in D Eade (ed) *Development and Social Diversity* (Oxford, OXFAM, 1999) 93 at 94; U Narayan *Dislocating Cultures: Identities, Traditions, and Third-World Feminism* (New York, Routledge, 1997).

[53] Z Mir-Hosseini 'Islamic Law and Feminism: The Story of a Relationship' Coulson Memorial Lecture, School of Oriental and African Studies, 3 December 2003; A Mayer *Islam and Human Rights* (Boulder, Westview, 1999) 12–17; A An Na'im 'Cultural Transformation and Normative Consensus on the Best Interests of the Child' (1994) 8 *International Journal of Law, Policy and the Family* 62 at 69.

[54] J Donnelly *Universal Human Rights in Theory and Practice* (Ithaca, Cornell University Press, 1989) 116.

[55] *Ibid* at 110.

[56] *Ibid.*

[57] *Ibid* at 113, 121–22, 122.

[58] *Ibid.*

[59] *Ibid* at 121. UNDP *Human Development Report Cultural Liberty in Today's Diverse World* (New York, United Nations, 2004) 58, 89. Human Rights Committee General Comment No 24 para 9.

[60] Advisory Council on International Affairs *Universality of Human Rights and Cultural Diversity* (The Hague, Advisory Council on International Affairs, 1998).

being applied in a diverse range of social, cultural and economic environments. Using this approach states have some latitude. Latitude is determinable by looking at the prevailing circumstances, the right which is said to have been violated, and the specific nature and seriousness of the violation.[61] Latitude as used by the Advisory Council seems to reflect the margin of appreciation doctrine employed by the European Court[62] and, arguably, Sachs.[63] Within this framework it is hoped that violators of the rights of women will be given little, if any, latitude to justify their actions. In Vienna it was agreed:

> The international community must treat human rights globally in a fair and equal manner, on the same footing, and with the same emphasis. While the significance of national and regional particularities and various historical, cultural and religious backgrounds must be borne in mind, it is the duty of States, regardless of their political, economic and cultural systems, to promote and protect *all* human rights and fundamental freedoms.[64] (emphasis added)

Despite this injunction states remain resistant to prompting change. Of course a cynic would argue that states have no problem in imposing change when it suits them, for example in the public/political sphere. Perhaps the circumspection only comes where issues pertaining to women's rights are concerned.

Interestingly, women commentators,[65] such as Nyamu-Musembi[66] and Hellum,[67] seem to argue that 'culture' can be an aid in social transformation rather than the burden and impediment that it has sometimes been constructed as being. Challenging the Beyani approach, Nyamu-Musembi posits: instead of throwing out the baby with the bath water or 'abolishing' customs and culture that appear to be inimical to women's rights, we should look closely at local cultures and see which aspects we can best use to achieve the aspirations of human rights.[68] Rather than seeing customs and 'culture' as 'fences', she points out that some have used

---

[61] Compare Donnelly above n 54 at 115–16, 118, in which he talks about the need 'to combine the universality of human rights and their particularity, and thus accept a certain limited relativity for even universal human rights'.

[62] *Marcx v Belgium* (1979) 2 EHRR 330.

[63] A Sachs 'Introduction' in J Eekelaar and T Nhlapo (eds) *Changing Family* (Oxford, Hart Publishing, 1998) xi. Sachs advocates what he terms proportionality.

[64] Vienna Declaration and Programme of Action 1993 (I) para 5. This accords with the Vienna Convention on the Law of Treaties 1969 art 27.

[65] This is not an attempt to collapse all 'women' into one homogeneous category. Women commentators can be located along the entire spectrum of the human rights/culture/religion debate. See Goonesekere above n 33 at 25–26; Rao above n 43.

[66] C Nyamu-Musembi 'Are Local Norms and Practices Fences or Pathways? The Example of Women's Property Rights' in A An Na'im (ed) *Cultural Transformation and Human Rights in Africa* (London, Zed Press, 2002) 126. See also Nyamu above n 18.

[67] A Hellum *Women's Human Rights and Legal Pluralism in Africa: Mixed Norms and Identities in Infertility Management in Zimbabwe* (Oslo, Mond Books, 1999).

[68] Nyamu-Musembi above n 66 at 126–32. Cf Nhlapo above n 49 at 624. See also M Mutua 'Banjul Charter: The Case for an African Cultural Fingerprint' in A An Na'im (ed) *Cultural Transformation and Human Rights in Africa* (London, Zed Press, 2002) 67 at 80.

them as 'pathways', a means to challenge discriminatory practices.[69] She argues that the abolitionist approach to culture fails to see that there is normative movement between the state system and local system with one influencing the other. On the role of the state, she notes that the 'apparatus (of the state) plays an active role in shaping cultural norms at the local level'.[70] The assumption that local practices do not embrace women's rights ignores the dynamism of local cultures, and also minimises and ignores the impact of human agency in bringing about change.[71] She argues that a view of culture or local norms as fixed and immutable means that one enters the debate with a mind closed to the possibility of the transformative potential of the local/human rights interaction.[72]

> A genuine engagement with practice at the local level is powerful in dislodging both the abolitionist imagination of the local as the repository of unchanging patriarchal values and the defensive relativist portrayal of local norms as bounded, immutable and well settled.[73]

Furthermore, she notes that one cannot bring about real and lasting change by ignoring what goes on at the local level, for changes to the law will not work. Her solutions involve engaging in empirical work to test out human rights norms on the ground, with the aim of showing that local cultures can evolve to reflect human rights norms.[74] Finally she highlights the importance of engaging non-state institutions because of their role in 'articulating cultural norms which impact directly at the grassroots level'.[75]

Nyamu-Musembi tests her own hypotheses by way of fieldwork in a Kenyan community, focusing on property rights of women and specifically access to land. Although her data on community-generated change on the ground and on the ability of women to challenge unfair norms within the framework of informal institutions are ambiguous, she highlights the fact that there are people, albeit few, challenging the prevailing pro-male norms as pointing to the possibility of changes being wrought in the local sphere and thus to the transformative potential of human rights norms on local practices.[76]

However, it is clear that the problem for women is that they are excluded from participating in local institutions and thus influencing the operating norms.[77] It is

---

[69] Nyamu-Musembi above n 66 at 141. Cf A Rao 'The Politics of Gender and Culture in International Human Rights Discourse' in J Peters and A Wolper (eds) *Women's Rights, Human Rights: International Feminist Perspectives* (New York, Routledge, 1995) 167 at 173–74.

[70] Nyamu-Musembi above n 66 at 126.

[71] *Ibid* at 127.

[72] *Ibid.*

[73] *Ibid* at145. See also Nyamu where she suggests an approach based on 'critical pragmatism': Nyamu above n 66 at 416–18.

[74] Cf Elson above n 1 at 91.

[75] Nyamu-Musembi above n 66 at 147. See also United Nations Development Project (UNDP) *Human Development Report 2000* (New York, UN, 2000) 7.

[76] Nyamu-Musembi above n 66 at 143.

[77] *Ibid* at 142.

telling that in Nyamu-Musembi's research, when women do finally participate it is as a result of donor and state pressure being applied to local groups, thus highlighting the dangers of both an evolutionary approach, which waits for change to be community generated, and the top-down approach, which leads to the imposition of solutions on groups that may be unwilling to be bound by such new norms and resentful of outside 'meddling'.

Hellum appears to share the scepticism of Nyamu-Musembi on the abolitionist stance to dealing with clashes between cultures and human rights.[78] She is of the view that the all-or-nothing approach to human rights is singularly unhelpful. Rather, she argues for a pluralist understanding of human rights as operating in different socio-cultural contexts; in this way the multiplicity of human experience can be accommodated without everyone being shoe-horned into one model or understanding of 'human rights'.[79]

This call for a pluralist or a differentiated understanding of human rights as they operate in different cultures calls to mind An Na'im's enthusiasm for the Sach's 'doctrine' of human rights as encompassing not only the right to be the same, but also the right to be different.[80] But how much difference is to be allowed and who is to decide? What do we mean by same? Men and women being different, is it illogical to seek equality (sameness) of treatment? Given the discussion on equality in Chapter 2, does sameness have the same meaning in all societies? Clearly not. As we have seen in Chapters 3 and 4, during the drafting of the African Protocol on Women's Rights, states with Islam as the dominant religion resisted the use of the word 'same', arguing that men and women inhabited different spheres in which their responsibilities were different.

If a gendered cultural concept of 'same' leads to women being awarded fewer entitlements, should we accept this as a part of respecting difference and let it be? Is it to be sameness as between men and women in a country, or between men and women belonging to the same group, or indeed sameness as between women within a country? In the Indian case of *Danial Latifi v Union of India*,[81] the Supreme Court refused to uphold different treatment of Muslim women in the allocation of post-divorce maintenance on the basis that one group of women in a state could not be deprived of rights enjoyed by other, different groups of women.[82] Moreover, far from being unfettered, sameness and difference within the South African Constitution, which is the basis of Sach's framework, both come

---

[78] Hellum above n 67.
[79] *Ibid* at 421ff. M Pieterse 'The Promotion of Equality and Prevention of Unfair Discrimination Act 4 of 2000: Final Nail in the Customary Law Coffin?'(2000) 117 *South Africa Law Journal* 627 at 627.
[80] A An Na'im 'Introduction' in A An Na'im (ed) *Cultural Transformation and Human Rights in Africa* (London, Zed Press, 2002) 11 at 1.
[81] *Danial Latifi & Another v Union of India* Supreme Court of India Civil Original Jurisdiction Written Petition (civil) No 868/1986.
[82] *Ibid* at 15 of cyclostyle judgment.

hedged with the proviso that the fundamental principles of equality and non-discrimination found in the bill of rights cannot be derogated from, whatever one's 'culture'. If this is indeed the case, we seem to come back to a position of seeing certain rights, for example non-discrimination on grounds of sex, as being non-derogable.

Echoing Howard,[83] the Women and Law in Southern Africa (WLSA) research group[84] would see the issue as being about choice, so that people are to be allowed to choose for themselves the normative order and framework that they wish to have applying to their inter-personal dealings. However, these choices in the WLSA outlook are not without boundaries; they are subject to human rights norms, thus calling into question the level of 'choice' involved. If anything, the WLSA 'solution' is not far removed from the repugnance clause of old, meaning that the choice is that which is acceptable to those in charge of determining 'acceptable mores'. Moreover, the concept of choice is itself problematic.[85] It suggests a level playing field and equality of bargaining power with the other party or community involved in determining jointly the parameters of cultural frameworks and 'acceptable' derogations therefrom. With so much stacked against them, not all women are in a position to negotiate their own self-constructed value system.[86]

The joys of listening and talking to each other— obtaining normative consensus through cross-cultural dialogue

An Na'im is the person who has best engaged with the culture/human rights conundrum, fashioning a methodology to try to reach normative consensus.[87] In

---

[83] R Howard 'Women's Rights in English-Speaking Sub-Saharan Africa' in C Welch and R Meltzer (eds) *Human Rights and Development in Africa* (New York, State University of New York Press, 1984) as cited in Donnelly above n 54 at 124.

[84] Women and Law in Southern Africa Trust (WLSA) *Standing at the Cross-Roads: WLSA and the Rights Dilemma Which Way to Go?* (Harare, WLSA, 1998) 40.

[85] A Armstrong 'Internalising International Women's Rights Norms' in P Nherere and M d'Engelbronner-Kolf (eds) *The Institutionalisation of Human Rights in Southern Africa* (Oslo, Nordic Human Rights Publications, 1993) 55 at 63–65.

[86] See Nussbaum above n 1 at 51–54, 64–65, 71.

[87] A An Na'im (ed) *Human Rights in Cross-Cultural Perspectives* (Philadelphia, University of Pennsylvania Press, 1992); A An Na'im 'State Responsibility under International Human Rights Law to Change Religious and Customary Laws' in R Cook (ed) *Human Rights of Women: National and International Perspectives* (Philadelphia, University of Pennsylvania Press, 1994) 167; An Na'im 'Introduction' above n 80.

essence he acknowledges that all the commentators considered make valid points. However, he asks how we are going to go about accommodating the need to respect experiences rooted in culture and religion with the guarantees of human rights? For An Na'im, it is not a question of either human rights or culture, but rather of creating a positive relationship based on interaction and engagement between the two. To achieve this he proposes that there be discussions within the fora (global and local—recognising of course that neither is an homogeneous monolith) followed by a discussion inter-partes—that is global with local. This approach he calls internal discourse followed by cross-cultural dialogue with the aim of transforming both.[88] The relationship is symbiotic:

> While human rights regimes in and of themselves provide no panacea for all the problems of any society, or those of the world at large, they are a critical part of any solution. On the other hand, while religions are not easy allies to engage, the struggle for human rights cannot be won without them, particularly in the African context.[89]

A cautionary note to An Na'im's methodology is linked to the need to factor in power, class and gender considerations when working out who is involved in the process of dialogue at both the local and global levels, not least because for true normative consensus to be reached, all voices and perspectives must be heard.[90] This calls, in Chanock's words, for resisting the 'essentializing (of) cultures and quieting the diversity of voices so that only the dominant are heard'.[91] On the resistance of the local to change, Chanock further notes: 'It is internal conflicts about ways of doing things far more than any conflict with outsiders that has led to the essentializing of cultures.'[92] Here one could add the essentialising of women's role in upholding 'culture' has increased resistance to change.

The main criticism of An Na'im comes from Sousa Santos,[93] who argues that An Na'im is too deferential to the international human rights framework. Sousa Santos claims that An Na'im does not challenge the 'universality' of the so-called universal but takes it as a given, and a positive one at that. Using the An Na'im methodology, he states:

> Against universalism, we must propose cross-cultural dialogues on isomorphic concerns. Against relativism, we must develop cross-cultural procedural criteria to distinguish progressive politics from regressive politics, empowerment from disempow-

---

[88] An Na'im 'State Responsibility' above n 87 at 167. Ngubane calls this process 'holding conversations of minds': J Ngubane *Conflict of Minds* (New York, Books in Focus, 1979) as cited in A Belden Fields *Re-Thinking Human Rights for the New Millennium* (New York, Palgrave, 2003) 98.

[89] A An Na'im (ed) *Cultural Transformation and Human Rights in Africa* (London, Zed Press, 2002) at 54. See also Nyamu above n 66 at 393–95.

[90] He acknowledges this. *Ibid.*

[91] Chanock above n 33 at 41.

[92] *Ibid* at 45.

[93] Sousa Santos above n 42 at 41.

erment, emancipation from regulation. To the extent that the debate sparked by human rights might evolve into a competitive dialogue among different cultures on principles of human dignity, it is imperative that such competition induce the transnational coalitions to race to the top rather than to the bottom (what are the absolute minimum standards? the most basic human rights? the lowest common denominators?).[94]

Together with An Na'im's methodology, Nyamu-Musembi's solution to the culture/human rights conundrum can be summed up in the diagram below.

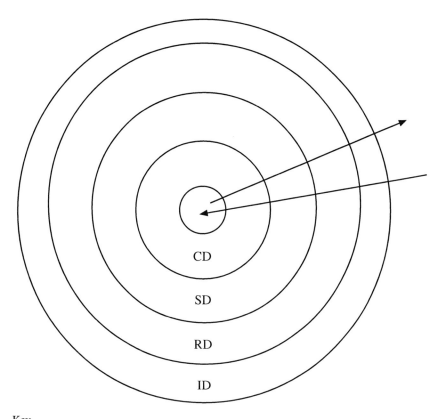

Key

Centre circle represents the individual,
CD represents community
SD represents public domain or state
RD represents regional domain
ID represents international domain

---

[94] *Ibid* at 35.

There is movement indicated by the arrows between all the circles, with norms and values flowing in both directions. There is interaction between the two farthest points, so that international norms of human rights are designed to benefit the individual, or the centre circle. We have seen how at the individual level the language of entitlement and rights has permeated so that, for example, in inheritance claims, women are prepared to invoke human rights principles to justify their demands. In reverse, we have seen how what constitutes family or community values (CD) has an impact on the pace of change in state policy, particularly in consultation before changes to the law are made. Community values also influence the relationship between the state (SD) and the regional (RD) and international domains (ID), for while states are responsible for implementing human rights norms, when reporting to international or regional human rights bodies, states often say that they are not able to, due to local resistance. Similarly at the international level, the recognition of local/community resistance to cultural change is seen by the constant references to culture in international conference documents.

Normatively, the regional is influenced by the international, as we have seen when considering articles 18(3) and 60 of the African Charter. Moreover, the acceptance of socio-economic and cultural rights as justiciable and central to the human rights discourse, is an example of the triumph of southern/regional concerns at the international level.[95] It goes without saying that the walls of these circles are permeable, allowing free movement/osmosis between them. It should also be remembered that there may be many more circles, or semi-autonomous social fields or normative orders, than those represented in the diagram.

As noted in the introduction to this chapter, culture is clearly not the only factor worth considering when discussing women's empowerment. Arguably what is needed in order for there to be a radical improvement in the lives of women is greater participation of women not only in the formulation of cultural and national policies and law, but also in the enjoyment of socio-economic rights and the benefits of development. But what is development? The understanding of the realisation of the concept has changed over time.[96]

---

[95] Grand Bay (Mauritius) Declaration and Plan of Action 1999; Kigali Declaration 2003 art 4; C Odinkalu 'Back to the Future: the Imperative of Prioritizing for the Protection of Human Rights in Africa' (2003) 47 *Journal of African Law* 1 at 3.

[96] H Slim 'What is Development?' in D Eade (ed) *Development and Social Diversity* (Oxford, OXFAM, 1999) 63; J Stiglitz *Globalisation and Its Discontents* (London, Penguin, 2002) 252.

Development

The United Nations Declaration on the Right to Development 1986, whilst constructing development as 'an inalienable human right',[97] describes development as:

> [A] comprehensive economic, social and cultural and political process, which aims at the constant improvement of the well-being of the entire population and of all individuals on the basis of their active, free and meaningful participation in development and in the fair distribution of benefits resulting there from.[98]

The responsibility for delivering on development goals is said to lie primarily with states.[99] However, it is also said that 'all human beings' are to be responsible for development.[100] Drafted during the Cold War and at the height of the fight to end apartheid in Namibia and South Africa, the Declaration is strongly anti-colonial and pro self-determination.[101] There is also a strong focus on fairness and equality on the international playing field.[102] The demand for a new international economic order[103] is in itself a recognition of the inequality of economic bargaining counters between the old west and third world, and of the need to redress that imbalance.[104]

So how has development been constructed on the African continent? Here again one must be careful not to homogenise.[105] There are many different perspectives. I examine only a few of the dominant trends.

Development as a human right is recognised in the African Charter.[106] There appears to be some resentment on the continent of the model of development that is seen as linked to a move towards an imposition of neo-liberal economies. Specifically the focus of the criticism coming from Africa has been on the inequity and suffering created by this neo-liberal model, which initially imposed structural adjustment programmes on states that were required to uplift subsidies on basic

---

[97] General Assembly Declaration on the Right to Development adopted by GA Res.41/128, 4 December 1986, art 1(1).

[98] *Ibid* preamble, para 2. See also arts 1 and 2. I Shivji *The Concept of Human Rights in Africa* (Dakar, Codesria, 1989) 29–33.

[99] General Assembly Declaration on the Right to Development 1986 art 3(1). See Shivji above n 98 at 83–84.

[100] General Assembly Declaration on the Right to Development 1986 art 2(2).

[101] *Ibid* preamble and art 1(2). C Chinkin and S Wright 'The Hunger Trap: Women, Food and Self-Determination' (1993) 4 *Michigan Journal of International Law* 262 at 299–300.

[102] Declaration on the Right to Development 1986 art 3(3).

[103] *Ibid* art 3(3). See also UDHR art 28.

[104] Slim above n 96 at 65. Chinkin and Wright above n 101 at 306. See also H Charlesworth, C Chinkin and S Wright 'Feminist Approaches to International Law' (1991) 85 *American Journal of International Law* 613 at 614ff.

[105] Wanzala above n 29 at 9.

[106] African Charter art 22.

goods and services, which were also to be privatised,[107] to the detriment of the ordinary people, especially women.[108] From the donor perspective, the principle seems to be 'less government is better government'.[109]

African states are also pressured to move towards a policy of trade liberalisation, by which is meant that they are required to 'open up' their economies and markets to foreign goods and services. Interestingly, the same demands are not made of northern economies—these are allowed to maintain trade barriers and domestic subsidies.[110] The Norwegian government is one of the few northern governments to acknowledge this as a problem that needs to be addressed.[111]

In addition to critiquing the neo-liberal model of development, there has also been a call for a model of development that focuses less on economic growth and more on people as agents of change,[112] capable of using indigenous knowledge and working within their communities to bring about sustainable development.[113] Dube criticises the northern model of development for failing to take into account the African experience and in particular the importance of culture for African people.[114] Although attached to the idea that 'culture' is an important element in development initiatives on the continent, Dube never explicitly tells us his understanding of the concept. From a gender perspective Bhavanani argues for a

[107] G Monbiot 'On the Edge of Lunacy' *Guardian* (London, 6 January 2004) 23. Discussing the privatising initiatives of DFID (The British Development Agency) he notes that while £56 million has been spent privatising copper mines in Zambia, this has to be contrasted with the £700,000 spent on improving nutrition.

[108] Elson above n 1 at 91–92, 94–99.

[109] World Bank *Engendering Development through Gender Equality in Rights, Resources and Voice* (Washington DC, World Bank, 2001) 89–90; Executive Summary of the 1994 World Survey on the Role of Women in Development (extract) ST/ESA/241, 1995 reproduced as Document No 109 in United Nations *Advancement of Women* above n 1, 481 at 482 para 8. But see Nussbaum above n 1 at 71. See also Elson above n 1 at 80–81, 83–84. Chinkin and Wright above n 101 at 290, 296, 304, 316.

[110] Action for Southern Africa (ACTSA) *Freedom to Grow: Bringing down the Barriers to Southern Africa's Trade with Europe* (London, ACTSA, 2001). See also N Kachingwe *Between a Rock and a Hard Place: Africa Faces No Win Situation in Trade Deal with Europe* (Harare, Mwengo and East and Southern Africa Civil Society Economic Policy Project, 2003); N Middleton and P O'Keefe *Rio Plus Ten: Politics, Poverty and the Environment* (London, Pluto Press, 2003) 74–75; Stiglitz above n 96 at 268–69; World Summit on Sustainable Development Plan of Implementation 2002 para 61(c).

[111] Norway, Ministry of Foreign Affairs *Fighting Poverty: The Norwegian Government's Action Plan for Combating Poverty in the South Towards 2015* (Oslo, Norwegian Ministry of Foreign Affairs, 2002) at 27–28, 55.

[112] Slim above n 96 at 66; Beijing Declaration 1995 para 16; Cotonou Agreement between the European Union and the African, Caribbean and Pacific Group of States art 9(1), reproduced in C Heyns (ed) *Human Rights Law in Africa* (The Hague, Martinus Nijhoff, 2004) vol 1 at 721.

[113] See for example T Dube 'ORAP and the Spirit of Zenzele' in H Chigudu (ed) *Composing a New Song: Stories of Empowerment from Africa* (London, Commonwealth Secretariat, 2003) 67; E Sikazwe 'Women for Change and its Work with Rural Communities' *ibid* at 129, 140 fn 175; Beijing Platform for Action 1995 para 14, which calls for 'an holistic approach to all aspects of development'.

[114] Dube above n 113 at 9. See also Wanzala above n 29 at 21. But see Slim above n 96 at 65; Norway, Ministry of Foreign Affairs above n 111 at 27–28, 46–54, 55; O Anacleti 'Research into Local Culture: Implications for Participatory Development' in D Eade (ed) *Development and Social Diversity* (Oxford, OXFAM, 1999) 69.

women, development and culture approach that tries to ensure that 'political economy is not privileged above culture, but, rather, that the two are seen as operating simultaneously and in synchrony'.[115] Her view finds support in the 2004 UNDP Human Development Report, which focuses on issues of culture and identity and notes that development cannot be divorced from the social-cultural milieu of the country under consideration.[116] However, for Chiriga, Africa's underdevelopment is in large measure because of poverty, conflict and the high expenditure on military hardware and unemployment.[117]

The New Partnership for Africa's Development (NEPAD) is an attempt by African states to set the framework for development on the continent and for rene-gotiating the terms of the conversation on development with the north.[118] However, it too has been criticised for the lack of transparency and consultation in its negotiation, for adopting a top-down approach to development, for being overly influenced by neo-liberal policies of the north, for inadequately addressing the inequality of bargaining power that has existed between north and south for centuries,[119] and, by feminists, for treating gender issues as an afterthought.[120] The inability of African leaders to engage with the intransigent Zimbabwean regime of Robert Mugabe has also led to questions being asked about its commit-ment to human rights and the effectiveness of the peer review mechanism built into NEPAD.[121] It is here worth noting that Zimbabwe has not agreed to submit itself to the peer review mechanism so the criticism may be premature.

These developments notwithstanding, there has not been a radical rebalancing of bargaining counters between north and south. Globalisation has heightened

[115] K Bhavanani above n 44 at 13. See also collection of papers in E Chiwone and Z Gambahaya (eds) *Culture and Development* (Harare, Mond Books, 1998).

[116] UNDP *Human Development* above n 59 at 38–45. For a summary of the report see UNDP 'Cultural Liberty Essential for Human Development Argues 2004 Report' Press Release, Brussels, 15 July 2004 available from http://www.undp.org; M Malloch Brown 'Foreword' in UNDP *Human Development* above n 59 at v.

[117] S Chiriga 'Perspectives on the Beijing Policy Process in the SADC Region' in P McFadden (ed) *Southern Africa in Transition: A Gendered Perspective* (Harare, SAPES, 1998) 105 at 111. See also M Arigbede 'COPODIN Family: Dare to Be Different' in H Chigudu (ed) *Composing a New Song: Stories of Empowerment from Africa* (London, Commonwealth Secretariat, 2003) 1 at 25.

[118] For NEPAD see http://www.iss.co.za/nepad. T Maluwa 'The Constitutive Act of the African Union and Institution Building in Postcolonial Africa' (2003) 16 *Leiden Journal of International Law* 157 at 164. See also World Summit on Sustainable Development Plan of Implementation 2002 paras 56 and 56(b).

[119] ACTSA (2001) above n 110. Cf Elson above n 1 at 108–9.

[120] S Tamale 'Gender Trauma in Africa: Enhancing Women's Access to Resources' (2004) 48 *Journal of African Law* 50 at 51. But see NEPAD, 2001 paras 49, 45, 67, 68, 118, 120, 166. See also AU Durban Declaration on Mainstreaming Gender and Women's Participation in the African Union 2002; R Murray *Human Rights in Africa* (Cambridge, Cambridge University Press, 2004) at 142–43.

[121] NEPAD The African Peer Review Mechanism, downloaded from: http://iss.co.za/nepad; T Maluwa above n 118 at 165–66; J Cilliers *NEPAD's Peer Review Mechanism* Institute for Security Studies. Occasional Paper No 64, November 2002 at 1–8.

rather than lessened global inequalities of bargaining power.[122] For An Na'im and Hammond, globalisation is 'the means by which developed countries sustain their economic and political hegemony over developing countries'.[123] From a gender perspective Kerr and Sweetman have argued that it is not globalisation per se that is the problem, but rather globalisation of the 'wrong things'. They argue that there should be a reinvention of globalisation to deliver rights for all.[124]

Northern economic dominance, together with on-going (civil, political, economic and health) crises in most African economies,[125] means that although southern states remain most in need of 'development', the engine for change is not located in the south but in the north, which determines both the nature and pace of development in the south. This is ironic, especially when seen in light of article 20(3) of the African Charter, which provides that all people are entitled to receive assistance from states parties for liberation struggles 'against foreign domination, be it political, economic or cultural'. Arguably development as dependency has become even more entrenched as time has passed.[126] This last point can best be seen in the use of development 'aid' by northern states after the attacks on the United States mainland of 11 September 2001.[127] The aim of international aid has often been said to be about the creation of democratic states that respect human rights,[128] not least those of women.[129] Linked to this is a belief that democratic states create the conditions for economic success.[130] Economic prosperity is then

[122] Action for Southern Africa (ACTSA) 'Africa: What the G8 Must Deliver: A Briefing by Action for Southern Africa and World Development Movement' (London, ACTSA, 2002) 1 at 1; Stewart 'Entitlement' above n 1 at 195, 198. See The Johannesburg Declaration on Sustainable Development 2002 paras 14, 15.

[123] An Na'im and Hammond above n 5 at 32. See also S Msimang 'Caution! Women Moving: Strategies for Organizing Feminist Visions of the Future' in J Kerr *et al* (eds) *The Future of Women's Rights* (London, Zed Press, 2004) 170 at 173–74.

[124] J Kerr and C Sweetman 'Editorial' in J Kerr and C Sweetman (eds) *Women Reinventing Globalization* (Oxford, OXFAM, 2003) 3. See also A Giddens *Runaway World: How Globalisation is Reshaping Our Lives* (London, Profile Books, 2002) 3, 6–19; UNDP *Human Development* above n 59 at 85ff.

[125] UNDP '2003 Human Development Index Reveals Development Crisis and Human Development Report 2003 Charts Decade-Long Income Drop in 54 Countries' press releases from http://www.undp/hdr2003. *The World in 2004* (London, The Economist, 2003) 97. See also D Mason 'Africa's Extremes' *The World in 2004* at 86.

[126] W Rodney *How Europe Underdeveloped Africa* (London, Bogle L'Overture, 1972). See also H Chigudu, 'Conclusion' in H Chigudu (ed) *Composing a New Song: Stories of Empowerment from Africa* (London, Commonwealth Secretariat, 2003) 161 at 164.

[127] See transcript for BBC Radio 4 Analysis programme 'Development on the Frontline' Broadcast on 27 November 2003 available at: http://newsvote.bbc.co.uk/nol/shared/spl/hi/programmes/analysis/transcripts/27_11_03.txt 1–9.

[128] This can clearly be seen in the Cotonou Agreement between the European Union and the African, Caribbean and Pacific Group of States. See J Akandji-Kombe 'Introduction to the Cotonou Agreement' in C Heyns (ed) *Human Rights Law in Africa* (The Hague, Martinus Nijhoff, 2004) vol 1, 703 at 709–13. See also Cotonou Agreement 2000, preamble, arts 1 and 9.

[129] Akandji-Kombe above n 128 at 714. Cotonou Agreement 2000 arts 1, 9(2).

[130] Giddens above n 124 at 65; T Manana 'Conventional Economic Theories and Gender Analysis' in R Meena (ed) *Gender in Southern Africa* (Harare, SAPES, 1992) 126; The World Bank *Assessing*

supposed to rid the world of the deprivation and related unhappiness that create the conditions that allow terrorism to flourish, or so the theory goes.

International aid policy

Although the United Nations had in 2000 agreed the Millennium Development Goals,[131] with poverty eradication and the halving of poverty by the year 2015 as a key goal,[132] the emphasis of major donors can be seen to have shifted since 11 September 2001.[133] Specifically there has been a shift in aid budgets from poverty reduction/alleviation to combating 'terror'.[134] The United States has added to the existing aid determination criteria of good governance, human rights and democracy, a 'new' criterion, based not on need but on whether the aid-requesting country is seen to 'be with us or against us'. Pakistan having passed the 'with us' test has had massive debt write offs, a huge influx in aid and the acceptance of a President who came to power by way of military coup, without the application of the 'human rights, good governance and democracy' test.

Similarly, in December 2003 it was announced by the United States that Ethiopia, Uganda and Rwanda, all of which had supported the United States in its Iraqi adventure, would be 'allowed' to bid for contracts for the post-conflict reconstruction of Iraq. More recently, states wishing to receive aid from the US have been told that first they have to agree that they will not extradite any United States soldiers in their jurisdiction to be tried at the International Criminal Court.[135] Evidently human rights concerns can take a back seat to the anti-terror focus and the national interests of the United States.[136]

The *explicit* politicisation of aid (aid has always been politicised) can be seen in the shifting priorities of donor countries, so that the Policy Director of OXFAM, a leading international development agency, notes:

Aid: What Works, What Doesn't and Why (Washington DC, The World Bank, 1998) 87 on the link between effectiveness of investment with the enjoyment of civil liberties by the populace.

[131] United Nations Millennium Declaration (8 September 2000) GA Res.55/2 also available at http://www.developmentgoals.org.

[132] See also World Summit Sustainable Development Plan of Implementation 2002 para 6(a).

[133] With a few notable exceptions, aid to the south from the north has been in steady decline for some time. UNDP 'Human Development Report 2003' above n 125 at 31. United Nations *Capacity Building in Africa: Effective Aid and Human Capital* (New York, United Nations, 2002) says that the drop in aid has been precipitous since the beginning of the 1990s (at 21). The report cites the AIDS crisis and conflict situation as requiring the building of a 'new constituency for African development assistance.' *Ibid.*

[134] BBC Radio 4 Analysis Programme above n 127 at 6.

[135] D Rennie 'Republicans in Threat to Block Overseas Aid' *Daily Telegraph* (London, 27 November 2004); 'Don't Sign Anything' (2004) 45 No 25 *Africa Confidential*.

[136] BBC Radio 4 Analysis Programme above n 127 at 7.

[W]hat we're seeing is very little money going to places in Africa like the Democratic Republic of Congo, like Liberia, like some of the big emergencies in the Horn of Africa, and a lot of money going to places like Iraq and Afghanistan, and I think there's just a huge amount of political will to really prioritise Iraq and Afghanistan and very little political will to prioritise some of the most neediest places in the world like the Congo.'[137]

He notes that whilst US$74 is mobilised per person in Iraq, in the Congo the sum is $17 per person.[138] Similarly, President Bush's initial plan to establish a Millennium Challenge Corporation to tackle poverty with an investment of $1.7 billion in the 2003 fiscal year was downgraded to $1.3 billion, 'partly because on the minds of the budgeters was the war on Iraq and the unknown cost'.[139] Ultimately the sum was further reduced and a request was being made for $800 million.[140]

However, on the other side of the aid coin is the view of an anonymous commentator who, following the Johannesburg Sustainable Development Summit 2002, noted:

The West are now the social workers of Africa, looking after its starving children while those children's elders and 'betters' junket on power and plunder and credit cards. The West receives no thanks in return, just abuse and hatred. We have the likes of Mugabe to thank for that.[141]

These are some of the international considerations underpinning aid and, with it, development. The chapter has not dealt with the equally contentious issue of debt relief or repayment. Vaughan uses the analogy of vampires sucking blood to explain the understanding of ordinary Malawians of debt and its repayment.[142]

The chapter now moves on to consider the inclusion of women within development discourse. The theorising of women's participation in the development process is now well established, with Boserup's work in 1970[143] being credited with kicking off the movement.[144]

---

[137] *Ibid* at 5.

[138] *Ibid.*

[139] Patrick Cronin, Senior Vice President at the Centre for Strategic and International Studies, Washington. *Ibid* at 5.

[140] *Ibid.*

[141] ZWNews 'Comment' (9 September 2002) downloaded from http://www/zwnews.com/issuefull.cfm?ArtID=5116; C McGreal 'How African Leaders Scored an Own Goal by Attacking Their Best Friend in the West' *Guardian* (London, 3 September 2003).

[142] M Vaughan 'Vampires in Malawi' *London Review of Books* (20 March 2003) 34.

[143] E Boserup *Women's Role in Economic Development* (New York, St Martins Press, 1970).

[144] The view of Boserup as women's development pioneer is contested. See N Visvanathan 'Introduction to Part 1' in N Visvanathan, L Duggan, N Nisonoff and N Wiegersmal (eds) *The Women, Gender and Development Reader* (London, Zed Books, 1997) 17 at 27. See also Nzegwu 'Questions of Agency' above n 19 at 5–6; Chiriga above n 117 at 113; M Snyder and M Tadesse 'Introduction' in M Snyder and M Tadesse (eds) *African Women and Development* (London, Zed Books, 1995) 1 at 1.

Women in the development process: transformations

The engagement of feminist theorists with the development process has yielded three broadly defined movements or phases that form part of a continuum.[145] These are the Women in Development (WID), Women and Development (WAD), and Gender and Development (GAD) approaches. Part of the last is linked to what lawyers like to think of as the Gender, Law and Development approach (or GLAD) and the move towards a human rights approach to development. WID, WAD and GAD have also been called the welfare, equity, anti-poverty, efficiency and empowerment approaches.[146]

Women in Development (WID)

Historically, 'development' tended to focus on a top-down approach, which assumed that all people would benefit from initiatives that were geared towards modernising what were seen as economically 'backward' societies. Initially there was no attempt to locate development initiatives within gender or cultural frameworks. However, over time it became clear that women were not benefiting from this model of development, which was technically gender neutral in its approach. Specifically, development initiatives ignored existing socio-structural inequalities and, in particular, inequality between the sexes. These critiques led to a challenging of the dominant development model and the emergence of the Women in Development school, which dominated the UN Decade for Women from 1975–85.[147]

Grounded within the WID paradigm is article 14 of CEDAW on rural women. It concentrates on adding women[148] to the development initiative by providing them with better access to health care,[149] allowing them to participate in development planning[150] and policy making at all levels, organising self-help groups and

---

[145] E Rathgeber 'WID, WAD, GAD: Trends in Research and Practice' (1990) 24 *The Journal of Developing Areas* 489. See also summary of J Hunt 'Situating Women's Development Needs within the Human Rights Framework' in G Moon (ed) *Making Her Rights a Reality: Women's Human Rights and Development* (Victoria, Community Aid Abroad, 1995) 24. See also C Moser *Gender, Planning and Development* (New York, Routledge, 1993); Visvanathan above n 144.

[146] Hunt above n 145 at 28–30; Visvanathan above n 144 (citing Moser (previous n) at 20; Chiriga above n 117 at 111; J Rowlands 'Empowerment Examined' in D Eade (ed) *Development and Social Diversity* (Oxford, OXFAM, 1999) 86 at 89–90; Snyder and Tadesse above n 144 at 5–18; Nyamu above n 66 at 383–90.

[147] United Nations *1999 World Survey on the Role of Women in Development: Globalization, Gender and Work* (New York, United Nations, 1999) vii–viii.

[148] See CEDAW art 14(1)(2).

[149] CEDAW art 14 (2)(b).

[150] *Ibid* art 14(2)(a).

co-operatives,[151] granting them access to credit,[152] and allowing them to enjoy adequate living conditions by accessing adequate housing, sanitation, electricity and water supplies.[153] Rural women are also to benefit directly from social security programmes.[154] This of course assumes that such programmes exist. It goes without saying that education is mentioned in a broad framework that includes both formal and informal education, which will lead to an 'increase in their technical proficiency'.[155]

However, there were many criticisms of the WID model. WID is loosely associated with the phrase 'add women and stir', meaning that there was an inadequate engagement with the realities of women's lives, and indeed total ignorance about gender relations and the way that they impacted upon women's ability both to participate in and to benefit from development initiatives. The focus of this development model on work done outside the home ignored women's unpaid domestic labour and also their reproductive roles. Moreover, WID collapsed all women into one category, ignoring differences between the sexes and also between women themselves.[156] Moreover WID was criticised for adopting a non-participatory approach, with women being seen as passive recipients and beneficiaries of development initiatives.[157] WID was also criticised for being based on a narrow understanding of local conditions by donors.[158]

Women and Development (WAD)

Given the critiques of the WID approach, there was a shift in theoretical perspective to embrace the Women and Development (WAD) model. There was from the outset a questioning of the starting point of the WID approach as putting women into development, it being argued that women had always been a part of the development process.[159] WAD honed in on global inequality as it affected both men and women in the developing world.[160] The assumption here was that an equitable international economic order would lead to an improvement of the lives of the world's poor and, within this, the improvement in women's position.[161] However, like WID, WAD was criticised for uncritically accepting gender roles and not

---

[151] CEDAW art 14 (2)(e).
[152] *Ibid* art 14(2)(g).
[153] *Ibid* art 14(2)(h).
[154] *Ibid* art 14 (2)(c).
[155] *Ibid* art 14 (2)(d); United Nations '1994/5' paras 15 and 39 in United Nations *Advancement of Women* above n 1 at 483 and 485.
[156] Chiriga above n 117 at 113.
[157] Snyder and Tadesse above n 144 at 9.
[158] Chiriga above n 117 at 113.
[159] Nzegwu 'Questions of Agency' above n 19 at 6.
[160] UN Declaration on Development 1986 art 8 reads in part: 'Effective measures should be undertaken to ensure that women have an active role in the development process.'
[161] United Nations above n 147 at ix.

adequately addressing the different burdens placed on men and women in the family and society, and in particular for ignoring women's reproductive work.[162] This critique opened the way for the Gender and Development (GAD) approach, which addressed the lack of focus on the private sphere work done by women, including reproduction.[163]

Gender and Development (GAD)

By focusing on gender rather than women, the GAD approach is said to be an acknowledgement of the fact that the transformation of society and the move towards development for all requires the engagement and commitment of both men and women, and the transformation of gender relations.[164] The GAD approach also acknowledges differences between women and the fact that 'culture' operates in different ways in different places.[165] GAD is also said to see people as agents for change and not as mere ciphers.[166] However, there is some controversy as to whether the removal of the spotlight from women to gender will lead to women's issues and concerns being rendered invisible.[167]

Nevertheless the GAD approach has been widely accepted. Internationally the view has taken root that without a radical transformation in gender relations, and specifically the improvement of women's lot, there will not be a material improvement in livelihoods in the south. In a foreword to a report entitled 'Engendering Development', the World Bank President notes:

> While disparities in basic rights; in schooling, credit and jobs; or in the ability to participate in public life take their most direct toll on women and girls, the full costs of gender inequality ultimately harm everyone . . . Ignoring gender disparities comes at great cost—to peoples' well-being and to countries' abilities to grow sustainably, to govern effectively, and thus to reduce poverty.[168]

[162] Rathgeber above n 145 at 493.

[163] United Nations above n 147 at ix–x.

[164] *Ibid.*

[165] J Mosse *Half the World, Half a Chance: An Introduction to Gender and Development* (Oxford, OXFAM, 1993) 7–8. However, Nyamu contends that GAD 'continues to portray women as victims of culture': Nyamu above n 18 at 388.

[166] Rathgeber above n 145 at 494.

[167] See C Sweetman 'Introduction' in C Sweetman (ed) *Beyond Men's Involvement in Gender and Development: Policy and Practice* (Oxford, OXFAM, 2001) 1; F Cleaver 'Men and Masculinities: New Directions in Gender and Development' in F Cleaver (ed) *Masculinities Matter: Men, Gender and Development* (London, Zed Press, 2002) 1; Beijing + 5 Outcome Document (2000) above n 11 at paras 51, 52, 53. On religious considerations in implementing GAD in a largely Muslim society see F Adamu 'A Double Edged Sword: Challenging Women's Oppression within Muslim Societies in Northern Nigeria' in C Sweetman (ed) *Gender, Religion and Spirituality* (Oxford, OXFAM, 1998) 56 at 58–59. B Adeleye-Fayemi 'Creating a New World with New Visions: African Feminism and Trends in the Global Women's Movement' in J Kerr *et al* (eds) *The Future of Women's Rights* (London, Zed Press, 2004) 38 at 45.

[168] J Wolfensohn 'Foreword' in World Bank above n 109 at xi. See Elson's critique of the World Bank report: Elson above n 1 at 88–91, 93, 97–98. Norway, Ministry of Foreign Affairs above n 111 at 24.

This explains the (re)new(ed) focus on gender in development aid. The third UN Millennium Development Goal calls for the promotion of gender equality and the empowerment of women. This follows hard upon the second goal, which is the achievement of universal primary education by the year 2015.[169] Education is seen as one of the key ways of ending poverty and uplifting women.[170] The goals set for states parties are:

> By the year 2000, provide universal access to basic education and ensure completion of primary education by at least 80 per cent of primary school-age children; close the gender gap in primary and secondary school education by the year 2005; provide universal primary education in all countries before the year 2015.[171]

It goes without saying that these goals are not even close to realisation in Africa.[172]

Although theoretically sound, one of the challenges of the GAD approach is its 'deliverability'.[173] While the transformation of gender relations in society requires the engagement of both men and women, often gender is taken to mean exclusively 'women's issues', with the implication that women should be the ones to address them.[174] Can real transformation of gender roles occur without the willingness of men to change? As the beneficiaries of privilege, why would they change? As was noted by the judge in the Zimbabwean case of *Magaya,* changing the customary law of inheritance to allow women to share in property would be unpopular with male elders who provide the bulwark for resisting socio-cultural change in the name of culture.[175] Datta's research in Botswana suggests that men are reluctant to change, and women-focused NGOs are sceptical about the feasibility of a truly gendered approach succeeding, not least because of the perceived intransigence of men and the backlash against gender equality.[176]

---

[169] See World Bank *2003 World Bank Atlas* (Washington DC, World Bank, 2003) 72–73.

[170] K Watkins *The OXFAM Education Report* (Oxford, OXFAM, 2000) 18, 35–38. See also World Bank above n 109 at 42–43, 168, 199; World Bank *2003 World Bank Atlas* above n 169 at 18–19; Beijing Platform for Action 1995 paras 69–88; Beijing + 5 Outcome Document (2000) above n 11 at para 67; Nussbaum above n 1 at 63; Forum on Marriage and the Rights of Women and Girls *Early Marriage: Whose Right to Choose?* (London, Forum on Marriage and the Rights of Women and Girls, 2000) 12–14; UNESCO *Dakar Framework for Action, Education for All: Meeting our Collective Commitments* (Paris, UNESCO, 2000) at http://www.unesco.org/education.

[171] Beijing Platform for Action 1995 Strategic Objective B1 para 80(b). See K Watkins previous n at 18ff; UNICEF *The State of the World's Children* (New York, UNICEF, 2004) 6.

[172] The World Bank notes: 'Sub-Saharan Africa made no real progress in closing the gender gap in average years of schooling between 1970–1990'. The World Bank above n 109 at 44. See also K Watkins above n 170; UNICEF above n 171; World Bank *2003 World Bank Atlas* above n 169 at 16.

[173] But see N Kabeer 'Gender, Development, and Training: Raising Awareness in the Planning Process' in D Eade (ed) *Development and Social Diversity* (Oxford, OXFAM, 1999) 16.

[174] A Gallagher above n 22 at 304; Stewart 'Entitlement' above n 1 at 197.

[175] *Magaya v Magaya* 1999 (1) ZLR 100 at 113; Rathgeber above n 145 at 495. But see the efforts of the Zambian Women for Change Programme discussed in E Sikazwe 'Women for Change and its Work with Rural Communities' in H Chigudu (ed) *Composing a New Song: Stories of Empowerment from Africa* (London, Commonwealth Secretariat, 2003) 129 at 150, 158.

[176] K Datta 'A Coming of Age? Re-Conceptualising Gender and Development in Urban Botswana' (2004) 30 *Journal of Southern African Studies* 251 at 261ff.

Moreover, as Hunt notes, 'trying to slot women into a development approach which is still fundamentally structured in a gender biased way is a major difficulty we face'.[177]

Gender, Law and Development (GLAD)

One of the ways of starting to address the structural impediments to women's access to the benefits of development has been by way of lobbying for legal change in a bid to strengthen women's rights and improve their access to resources.[178] This may be termed the Gender, Law and Development (GLAD) approach.[179] The focus has been on changing laws on inheritance and property rights, particularly as they pertain to land. This has involved challenging the restrictive interpretation of customary and religious laws and lobbying for change where necessary.[180]

The GLAD approach highlights a shift from seeing lawyers as concerned solely with issues of human rights, and economists and other social scientists as concerned with issues of development.[181] The coming together of law/human rights and development concerns has yielded what is now known as the rights-based approach to development.[182] This approach flows from the work of Amartya Sen.[183] Specifically, a rights-based approach to development recognises that:

> Human rights and human development are both about securing basic freedoms. Human rights express the bold ideas that all people have claims to social arrangements that protect them from the worst abuses and deprivations—and that secure the freedom for a life

[177] Hunt above n 145 at 30. See also R Cook 'Preface' in Royal Tropical Institute (KIT) and OXFAM (eds) *Gender Perspectives on Property and Inheritance* (Amsterdam, KIT and Oxford, OXFAM, 2001) 9 at 10.

[178] Rathgeber above n 145 at 494–95. See also R Howard 'Women's Rights and the Right to Development' in J Peters and A Wolper (eds) *Women's Rights, Human Rights: International Feminist Perspectives* (New York, Routledge, 1995) 301; A Stewart 'Juridifying Gender Justice: From Global Rights to Local Justice' in J Hatchard and A Perry-Kessaris (eds) *Law and Development: Facing Complexity in the 21st Century* (London, Cavendish Press, 2003) 37 at 47–49.

[179] Cf World Bank above n 109 at 4, 115. But see A Stewart 'The Dilemmas of Law in Women's Development' in S Adelman and A Paliwala (eds) *Law and Crisis in the Third World* (London, Zell, 1993) 219.

[180] Stewart 'Entitlement' above n 1 at 203–4.

[181] UNDP above n 75 at 2.

[182] H Charlesworth 'Women's Human Rights Defined' in G Moon (ed) *Making Her Rights a Reality: Women's Human Rights and Development* (Victoria, Community Aid Abroad, 1995) 44; Hunt above n 145 at 30–34; World Bank above n 109 at 36–41. See also UNDP *Integrating Human Rights with Sustainable Development* (New York, UNDP, 1998) 1. See K Watkins *The OXFAM Poverty Report* (Oxford, OXFAM, 1995) 1. See also Stewart 'Entitlement' above n 1 at 196; Nussbaum above n 1 at 71, 72–73; Chinkin and Wright above n 101 at 313–15; UNICEF above n 171 at 91–93; UDHR arts 22, 25(1); Kigali Declaration 2003 art 4; AU Solemn Declaration on Gender Equality in Africa 2004 art 6. Finally see CESCR General Comment No 2 International Technical Assistance (art 22) 1990 EC/1990/23 at paras 5, 6.

[183] A Sen *Development as Freedom* (Oxford, Oxford University Press, 1999); Nussbaum above n 1 at 59; Norway, Ministry of Foreign Affairs above n 111 at 24. See also 'Preface by the Prime Minister' in Norway, Ministry of Foreign Affairs above n 111 at 3.

of dignity. Human development, in turn, is a process of enhancing human capabilities—to expand choices and opportunities so that each person can lead a life of respect and value. When human development and human rights advance together, they reinforce one another—expanding people's capabilities and protecting their rights and fundamental freedoms.[184]

In short, human rights provide sanction, enforceability, targeted goals and structure.[185] They act as the buttress and framework for people as they seek to have their capabilities recognised and affirmed.[186] Within the capabilities framework, poverty is no longer treated as a 'moral' problem;[187] rather the relief from poverty is an entitlement, part of a series of (human rights) freedoms that include freedom from the indignity associated with being poor.[188] Chinkin notes that the 'Denial of human rights is both a cause and a consequence of being poor.'[189]

Gender and poverty[190]

Nussbaum has adopted Sen's capabilities approach and expanded on the gender dimensions.[191] She notes that there is a strong correlation between gender inequality and poverty which leads to an 'acute failure of central human capabilities'.[192] A gendered approach to poverty requires one to consider the concepts of entitlements and endowments:[193]

---

[184] UNDP above n 75 at 2.

[185] *Ibid.* But see C Chinkin 'The United Nations Decade for the Elimination of Poverty: What Role for International Law?' in M Freeman (ed) *Current Legal Problems* (Oxford, Oxford University Press, 2001) 553 at 566–71.

[186] Overseas Development Institute (ODI) 'What Can We Do with a Rights Based Approach to Development?' (1999) 3 *Briefing Paper*; H Kennedy *Just Law* (London, Chatto & Windus, 2004) 3–9; S Goonesekere 'A Rights Based Approach to Realising Gender Equality' at: http://www.un.org/womenwatch/daw/news/savitri.htm.

[187] Cf Charlesworth above n 182 at 44; J Kerr 'From "Opposing" to "Proposing" Finding Proactive Global Strategies for Feminist Futures' in J Kerr *et al* (eds) *The Future of Women's Rights* (London, Zed Press, 2004) 14 at 24–25. But see also 25–26.

[188] United Nations Secretary-General, Kofi Annan in WHO '25 Questions and Answers on Health and Human Rights' (2002) 1 *Health and Human Rights Publication Series* 1 at 26.

[189] Chinkin above n 185 at 556.

[190] Intra household poverty has been defined as 'the condition of deprivation, not having enough food, shelter and other essentials to meet basic needs'. Executive Summary of the 1994 World Survey on the Role of Women in Development at para 34, reproduced in UN *Advancement of Women* above n 1 at 485. See also Vienna Declaration and Programme of Action 1993 (I) para 25.

[191] See also Norway, Ministry of Foreign Affairs above n 111 at 24, 61, 74; Stewart above n 178 at 39–40.

[192] Nussbaum above n 1 at 58. See also 69.

[193] See Beijing Platform for Action 1995 Strategic Objective A on Women and Poverty paras 47–67; Beijing + 5 Outcome Document (2000) above n 11 paras 7–8; Forum on Marriage above n 170 at 28–30.

An entitlement is a right to command resources. An endowment consists of the skills, access and other resources that make it possible to exercise an entitlement. In that sense, poverty is a failure to ensure entitlements because of inadequate endowments. In gender terms, this can be seen in terms of asymmetries between women and men in their entitlements and endowments. Taken together, these asymmetries reproduce the vicious cycle of poverty and explain why men and women experience it differently.[194]

So what are the rights or entitlements that need to be implemented before women can be said to be truly human?[195] Elson points out that:

> To have an entitlement implies access to an accountable process in which the discretion of the decision maker is limited. If my access to a resource is at the arbitrary discretion of a public official or dependent on . . . the goodwill of a husband . . . then I do not get that resource as of right.[196]

Those most likely to experience resource deprivation are rural women.

The rural/urban divide

Compared with urban women, rural women have lower levels of education, marry earlier, have more children closer together but ironically have the worst access to health care facilities, and have fewer employment opportunities, in fact their work is often not even counted as work.[197] Nyamu notes that even when poverty is generalised, rural women experience poverty disproportionately.[198] Not only do they suffer sex discrimination, but their social, economic and political power, relative to their urban counterparts, is diminished.[199] Here nothing more clearly illustrates the dominance of the urban woman's voice than the debate that ensued over the identification of 'salaried women' as requiring special protection during the drafting of the African Protocol on Women's Rights. The Kigali draft of 1999, which was adopted by the African Commission, provided that States Parties committed themselves to:

[194] Executive Summary of the 1994 World Survey on the Role of Women in Development para 35 in UN *Advancement of Women* above n 1 at 485. See also World Bank above n 109 at 61–72. See also Sen above n 183 at 20 and Nussbaum above n 1.Elson above n 1 at 100–2; CESCR *Substantive Issues Arising in the Implementation of the International Covenant on Economic, Social and Cultural Rights: Poverty and the International Covenant on Economic, Social and Cultural Rights* E/C/12/2001/10 para 14; Stewart above n 178 at 39–40.
[195] Stewart above n 178 at 39–40, 47.
[196] Elson above n 1 at 102–3.
[197] Secretary-General, United Nations Improvement of the Situation of Women in Rural Areas (7 June 1999) UN Doc GA54/123; Beijing Declaration 1995 para 26.
[198] C Nyamu 'The International Human Rights Regime and Rural Women in Kenya' (2000) 6 *East African Journal of Peace and Human Rights* 1at 2; Wanzala warns against homogenising rural women and not factoring in 'differential status within kinship and family systems, age differences and other factors which disaggregate women': Wanzala above n 29 at 12, 13.
[199] Nyamu above n 198 at 1.

Recognize the right of salaried women to be responsible for their spouse and children.[200]

The Women's Unit[201] of the former Organisation for African Unity questioned the focus on salaried women and noted that all women contributed to looking after their children, and that there was therefore not any need for salaried women to receive special attention.[202] As originally drafted, article 15(k) highlighted the way in which the professional women comprising the working group viewed themselves as requiring special attention, thus again highlighting the distance between the African woman of the Draft Protocol and the 'ordinary' women of Africa, many of whom are engaged in subsistence agriculture work in the informal economy, and who experience greater levels of inequality and discrimination.[203] This view is supported by research which shows that more women are employed in the informal sector than are employed in the formal sector.[204] Elson also notes that there are more informal than formal jobs in Africa, and that of the new jobs created 93 per cent are informal.[205]

The special needs of rural women were acknowledged by the inclusion within CEDAW of a separate article (14) focusing specifically on rural women. An examination of CEDAW reports sent in by African states shows that all identify rural women as being disproportionately disadvantaged when compared to both men and to their urban sisters.[206] The Women's Committee has acknowledged, in two General Recommendations, the work done by women in the informal sector.[207]

Although the African Protocol on Women's Rights does not have a specific provision on rural women as does CEDAW,[208] it does cover a lot of the issues that concern them, not least the right to food security,[209] the right to adequate

[200] Kigali draft 1999 art 15(k).

[201] Suggestions of the Women's Unit to Improve the Existing Text of the Draft Protocol as Presented to the OAU. Attachment to the letter from Professor T Maluwa, OUA Legal Counsel to Professor Dankwa, Chairman of the African Commission on Human and Peoples' Rights, 7 March 2000, CAB/LEG/72.20/27/Vol.II.

[202] *Ibid.*

[203] Elson above n 1 at 93.

[204] *Ibid* at 94.

[205] *Ibid.* See African Protocol on Women's Rights art 13(e)(f). Cf art 13(k).

[206] Government of Algeria (1998) above n 21 at 37. Third Periodic Report of States Parties: Uganda (2000) CEDAW/C/UGA/3 (hereafter Government of Uganda (2000)) at 57; Combined Fourth and Fifth Periodic Report to CEDAW: Nigeria (2003) CEDAW/C/NGA/4–5 at 52; Second Periodic Report of States Parties: Morocco CEDAW/C/MOR/2 at 51.

[207] CEDAW General Recommendation No 16 (Tenth Session, 1991) on Unpaid Women Workers in Rural and Urban Family Enterprises UN Doc A/46/38, General Recommendation No 17 (Tenth Session, 1991) on Measurement and Quantification of the Unremunerated Domestic Activities of Women and Their Recognition in the Gross National Product UN Doc A/44.38; Beijing + 5 Outcome Document (2000) above n 11 at paras 47, 85(b), 94(e). Cf Wanzala above n 29 at 10.

[208] The East Africa and SADC group did, during the drafting of the African Protocol on Women's Rights, suggest that there was a need for a separate article on rural women. East Africa and SADC Group 'Comments on the Draft Protocol to the African Charter on Human and Peoples' Rights on the Rights of Women in Africa' (2001) (unpublished, on file with author).

[209] African Protocol on Women's Rights art 15.

housing,[210] the right to live in a positive cultural context,[211] the right to a healthy and sustainable environment,[212] and the right to sustainable development,[213] which article mirrors CEDAW article 14 but adopts the GAD approach. Also protected are property rights, including the right to inherit[214] and to be free from inhuman and degrading treatment,[215] the right to education (although surprisingly there is no mention of the special needs of rural women),[216] the right to access to justice,[217] the right to be free from violence[218] and harmful practices,[219] and of course the right to peace.[220] An interesting innovation is the recognition of indigenous knowledge systems,[221] which goes some way to challenge the dominance of northern-inspired epistemologies as being the only acceptable ones.[222]

The drafting of article 13 on economic and social welfare rights is important in that it constructs these rights as justiciable and as requiring state commitment to respect, protect and fulfil them.[223] Before listing the specific rights to be protected it is provided:

> States parties shall adopt and *enforce legislative* and other measures to guarantee women equal opportunities in work and career advancement and other economic opportunities.[224]

[210] *Ibid* art 16. See also CESCR General Comment No 4 on the Right to Housing UN Doc E/1992/23. See also L Farha 'Is There a Woman in the House? Re/Conceiving the Human Right to Housing' (2002) 14 *Canadian Journal of Women and Law* 118; see Communication 155/96 *The Social and Economic Rights Action Center and the Center for Economic and Social Rights v Nigeria*, Fifteenth Annual Activity Report of the African Commission, 2001–2002, Annex V (The *Ogoni* case). It is worth remembering that in the *Ogoni* case the African Commission adopted the violations approach to economic, social and welfare rights, which augurs well for the African Protocol on Women's Rights.

[211] African Protocol on Women's Rights art 17.

[212] *Ibid* art 18; Beijing Declaration 1995 para 36; World Summit on Sustainable Development Plan of Implementation 2002 paras 56(h), 56(j)(ii), 60(a).

[213] African Protocol on Women's Rights art 19. Cf Chinkin and Wright above n 101 at 287, 292, 307, 320.

[214] African Protocol on Women's Rights art 21.

[215] *Ibid* art 20(a) (within the context of widows' rights). See also arts 3(3), 4(1).

[216] *Ibid* art 12.

[217] *Ibid* art 8.

[218] *Ibid* art 4.

[219] *Ibid* art 5.

[220] *Ibid* art 10.

[221] *Ibid* art 18(2)(c); World Conference on Sustainable Development Plan of Implementation 2002 paras 47(h), 64(c).

[222] Cf Visvanathan above n 144 at 25; Wanzala above n 29 at 21.

[223] The Maastricht Guidelines on Violations of Economic Social and Cultural Rights 1997 guideline 6, reproduced in (1998) 20 *Human Rights Quarterly* 69. See V Dankwa, C Flinterman and S Leckie 'Commentary on the Maastricht Guidelines on Violations of Economic, Social and Cultural Rights' (1998) 20 *Human Rights Quarterly* 705 at 711–12; Montreal Principles 2004; J Ngwake 'Realizing Women's Economic, Social and Cultural Rights: Challenges and Strategies in Nigeria' in (2002) 14 *Canadian Journal of Women and Law* 142.

[224] African Protocol on Women's Rights art 13. See also the Preamble which reaffirms:

> [T]he principle of promoting gender equality as enshrined in the Constitutive Act of the African Union as well as the New Partnership for Africa's Development, relevant Declarations, Resolutions and Decisions, which underline the commitment of the African States to ensure the full participation of African women as equal partners in Africa's development.

Moreover, see art 9(1)(c). Finally see art 2(1)(c).

It is around the issue of women's access to land that (rural) women's participation in community life can be seen to be particularly important.[225] Specifically, the focus on women in rural areas[226] has been around issue of land ownership and issues of inheritance.[227] For the World Bank, women's land ownership is a crucial part of its 'engendering development' approach, not least because ownership of land enables women to access credit and loans more easily.[228] It also enables them to access education for their children and leads to an improvement in their socio-economic status.[229] Whilst recognising the importance of working with customary land tenure systems, the World Bank seems to adopt an uncritical stance in its acceptance of the work of the 'local community' and land management committees in the allocation of land.[230] Specifically the World Bank fails to factor in considerations of gender and, importantly, the absence of women's voice in the allocation of land.[231] Nyamu-Musembi's[232] work reveals how women's participation in local institution decision-making processes is limited. Examining the work of land adjudication committees in Kenya, she notes that these committees are run by men.[233] Specifically, these men all tend to be older than

---

[225] African Protocol on Women's Rights 2003 art 9(1)(c). See also arts 7(d), 15(a), 19(c), 21(1), 21(2); CEDAW art 14(2)(g); SADC Declaration 1997 art H(iii); L Wanyeki (ed) *Women and Land in Africa: Culture, Religion and Realizing Women's Rights* (London, Zed Press, 2002); Copenhagen Declaration on Social Development 1995 Commitment 5 para(e), reproduced in United Nations *Advancement of Women* above n 1 at 611; A Manji 'Gender and the Politics of the Land Reform Process in Tanzania' (1998) 36 *Journal of Modern African Studies* 645.

[226] E Sikazwe 'Women for Change and its Work with Rural Communities' in H Chigudu (ed) *Composing a New Song: Stories of Empowerment from Africa* (London, Commonwealth Secretariat, 2003) 129; H Chigudu 'Conclusion' in H Chigudu (ed) *ibid* at 166.

[227] World Summit on Sustainable Development Plan of Implementation 2002 para 61(b). See also *Ephraim v Pastory* [1990] LRC 757; United Nations Executive Summary of the 1994 World Survey on the Role of Women in Development (extract) ST/ESA.241, 1995, reproduced as document 109 in United Nations *The United Nations and the Advancement of Women 1945–1996* (New York, UN, 1996) 481 para 43; World Bank *Land Policies for Growth and Poverty Reduction* (Washington DC, World Bank, 2003) 60; Beijing Platform for Action 1995 para 51. See also Tripp for a discussion of the controversy surrounding the Ugandan Land Bill and the omission of a clause giving women co-ownership of land: Tripp above n 4 at 420–27.

[228] World Bank above n 109 at 37, 51–53, 120–23; World Bank above n 227 at 57–62. But see A Manji 'Capital, Labour and Land Relations in Africa: A Gender Analysis of the World Bank's Policy Research Report on Land Institutions and Land Policy' (2003) 24 *Third World Quarterly* 97.

[229] World Bank above n 227 at 58. But see Chinkin above n 185 at 585–86.

[230] World Bank above n 227 at 64. But see WLSA *A Critical Analysis of Women's Access to Land in the WLSA Countries* (Harare, WLSA, 2001) 22–24.

[231] On the implications of customary law land tenure for women see A Whitehead and D Tsikata 'Policy Discourses Women's Land Rights in Sub-Saharan Africa: The Implications of the Re-turn to the Customary' (2003) 3 *Journal of Agrarian Change* 67.

[232] Nyamu-Musembi above n 66. Cf H Odame 'Men in Women's Groups: A Gender and Agency Analysis of Local Institutions' in F Cleaver (ed) *Masculinities Matter: Men, Gender and Development* (London, Zed Press, 2002) 138.

[233] Nyamu-Musembi above n 66 at 142. See also A Nzioki 'The Effects of Land Tenure on Women's Access and Control of Land in Kenya' in A An Na'im (ed) *Cultural Transformation and Human Rights in Africa* (London, Zed Press, 2002) 218 at 256.

50.[234] She goes on to note that the technical criteria for membership of the committee is long-term knowledge of the history of land ownership in the area, in which case (older) women who manage family land holdings would be uniquely qualified to be committee members. That they are not leads Nyamu-Musembi to note: 'It is about perceptions of authority and power. Not all knowledge matters.'[235] In an attempt to circumvent some of the problems identified in Kenya, South Africa has passed the Communal Land Rights Act, which provides that women should form at least one third of the membership of land committees.[236] Moreover, the statute makes clear that:

> A woman is entitled to the same legally secure tenure rights in or to land and benefits from land as a man, and no law, community or other rule, practice or usage may discriminate against any person on the ground of gender of such person.[237]

A consideration of women's participation in politics and decision making follows.

Political participation

Of increasing importance has been women's right to participate in politics and decision making. Indeed one of the first treaties put forward by the United Nations Commission on the Status of Women was the Convention on the Political Rights of Women 1952.[238] It provided that women had the right to participate in the political life of their countries, including the right to vote.[239]

The importance of women's political participation was recognised in DEDAW (Declaration on the Elimination of all Forms of Discrimination Against Women) 1967[240] and then later CEDAW, which demands of states parties that women be allowed to participate at the national level[241] and also that they be put forward for service at the international level.[242] The continuing gender disparity at the higher levels of the United Nations and other regional bodies[243] suggests that this remains an on-going challenge.[244]

---

[234] Nyamu-Musembi above n 66 at 142.

[235] *Ibid.*

[236] Communal Land Rights Act No 11 of 2004 ss 22(3), 22(4).

[237] *Ibid* s 4(3).

[238] Convention on the Political Rights of Women 1952 193 UNTS 135.

[239] *Ibid* art 1. See also ICCPR art 25; UDHR art 21; African Charter art 13, but see proviso that participation is to be in accordance with the law.

[240] DEDAW art 4.

[241] CEDAW art 7. See also CEDAW General Recommendation No 23 on Women in Public Life UN Doc. A/52/38/Rev.1 para 4 .

[242] CEDAW art 8. See CEDAW General Recommendation No 23 paras 35–40.

[243] On the participation of women in the bodies of the African Union see Murray above n 120 at 136–38.

[244] CEDAW General Recommendation No 23 para 39; Vienna Declaration and Platform for Action 1993 (II) para 43.

The African Protocol on Women's Rights, in article 9, also focuses on the right of women to participate in the political and decision-making processes of their countries,[245] while article 8(e) provides that states should ensure that 'women are represented equally in the judiciary and law enforcement organs'. Finally article 9(1)(c) provides for the equal participation of men and women in development.

Increasingly the participation of women in public life has even been recognised by institutions such as the World Bank, which talks of the need for women to have 'voice'.[246] The World Bank also sees positive benefits in the involvement of women in national political life, not least because it asserts that studies have shown that the greater participation of women in public life leads to a decrease in the levels of corruption.[247] The Commonwealth Secretariat goes so far as to argue that 'without gender parity in politics there is no democracy'.[248] Nevertheless, there remain large gender disparities in political participation and representation at all levels of government—from local councils to national assemblies and cabinets.[249] Indeed the World Bank notes:

> In no developing region did women make up more than 8 per cent of cabinet ministers in 1998. In Middle East and North Africa women held only two per cent of cabinet positions . . . and in Sub-Saharan Africa, roughly 6 percent.[250]

The report goes on to note that even when elected to hold cabinet positions, women tend to be in 'women's ministries' and those dealing with social welfare or 'soft/female' issues. They are not likely to be found in the 'big decision making or spending departments' such as finance, or indeed defence.[251] Minority and indigenous women experience further exclusion. Often they are not consulted about projects and programmes, including those designed to be for 'their' benefit.[252]

---

[245] See too AU Solemn Declaration on Gender Equality in Africa 2004 preamble, arts 2, 5, 12.

[246] World Bank above n 109 at 57–59. See also Commonwealth Secretariat *Gender Mainstreaming: Commonwealth Strategies on Politics, Macroeconomics and Human Rights* (London, Commonwealth Secretariat, 1998) 8–25; J Foster, S Makanya and G Mutukwa (eds) *Women in Politics and Decision Making in Southern Africa* (Harare, WILDAF, 1999).

[247] World Bank above n 109 at 12. See also 94–95.

[248] Commonwealth Secretariat above n 246 at 10. See also the International Parliamentary 'Universal Declaration on Democracy and the New Delhi Declaration' (1997) at http://www.ipu.org/wmn-e/approach.htm at 1.

[249] R Meena 'Conceptual Issues-Gender in Southern Africa' in I Mandaza (ed) *Governance and Human Development in Southern Africa* (Harare, SAPES, 1998) 119 at 131–33.

[250] World Bank above n 109 at 58. However, it is worth noting that Rwanda has now outstripped Sweden as the country with the highest number of women in its legislature. Rwandan women now hold 48.8% of the seats, with Sweden having 45.3% women in its parliament. See 'Rwanda Has the Most Women MPs' *The Guardian* (London, 23 October 2003). For a full list of countries, see International Parliamentary Union (2003) 'Women in National Parliaments' at http://www.ipu.org.wmn-e/classif.htm 1. For regional breakdowns see http://www.ipu.org.wmn-e/world.htm 1–2; World Bank MENA Development Report (2004) 132.

[251] World Bank above n 109 at 58.

[252] D Jackson *Twa Women, Twa Rights in the Great Lakes Region of Africa* (London, Minority Rights Group, 2003) 16–17.

Women's participation in both national and local institutions is also constrained by the requirement that candidates have attained a minimum level of education, which may exclude women.[253] Tamale's research indicates that in national politics women are subject to a great deal of harassment and are denigrated by both members of the public and their parliamentary peers.[254] Other constraints may include family responsibilities that preclude women having 'extra time' for politics.[255] Added to this is the fact that sometimes a woman may require the consent of her husband to work, or to participate in activities occurring outside the home.[256]

The main method adopted to increase the participation of women in politics has been by way of quota or reservation.[257] Change can come about through constitutional or legal intervention, as in the case of Uganda, or else through the initiatives of political parties.[258] The SADC Gender and Development Declaration 1997 'encourages' states parties to aim for 'the achievement of at least 30 per cent target of women in political and decision making structures by year 2005'.[259] The

---

[253] L Mwenda 'Review of the Political Situation of Women in Malawi' in J Foster *et al* (eds) *Women in Politics and Decision Making in Southern Africa* (Harare, WILDAF, 1999) 22 at 36; CEDAW General Recommendation No 23 para 23.

[254] See for example her discussion on sexual harassment of female parliamentarians. S Tamale *When Hens Begin to Crow: Gender and Parliamentary Politics in Uganda* (Boulder, Westview Press, 1999) at 131–38. See also A Tripp *Women and Politics in Uganda* (Oxford, James Currey, 2000) 223–26, 230. L Frank 'Historical and Current Context of the Participation of Women in Politics and Decision Making in Namibia' in J Foster *et al* (eds) above n 253, 64 at 86; D Shabangu 'Review of the Political Situation of Women in Swaziland' in J Foster *et al* (eds) above n 253, 96 at 102–4, 111–12. See also J Foster *et al* 'Introduction' in *ibid* at 9–14. In Kenya a male Member of Parliament was censured for saying that women judges were divorcees or likely to divorce their husbands once elected. L Nduta 'Leaders Condemn MP Sifuna as Unfit for 21st Century Parliament' *Daily Nation* (Nairobi, 22 March 2002) downloaded from http://www.nationaudio.com/News/DailyNation/Today/News49.html 1–2.

[255] Cf CEDAW General Recommendation No 21 paras 11, 12.

[256] *Ibid* para 17. Combined Second, Third, Fourth and Fifth Periodic Reports of States Parties: Gabon CEDAW/C/GAB/2–5 at 25, 27.

[257] The Constitution of Uganda 1995 has an affirmative action provision calling for inclusion of marginalised groups: Art 32. See also Arts 33(5) and 78. It also has as a principle of state policy the requirement that the state ensures gender balance and fair representation of marginalised groups (see Principle VI). Women in Uganda are guaranteed one third of all local government seats and a woman representative from each district to sit in parliament. Tripp above n 254 at 230–33. Commonwealth Secretariat above n 246 at 15. See also S Tamale 'Towards Legitimate Governance in Africa: The Case of Affirmative Action and Parliamentary Politics in Uganda' in E Quashigah and O Okafor (eds) *Legitimate Governance in Africa* (Hague, Kluwer International, 1999) 235; B Odongo-Mwaka 'Women in the Democratic Process in Uganda: Gender and Justice' in J Hatchard and A Perry-Kessaris (eds) *Law and Development: Facing Complexity in the 21st Century* (London, Cavendish Press, 2003) 246 at 253.

[258] Commonwealth Secretariat above n 246 at 15–17; CEDAW General Recommendation No 23 para 33; A Goetz and S Hassim 'In and against the Party: Women's Representation and Constituency Building in Uganda and South Africa' in M Molyneaux and S Razavi (eds) *Gender Justice, Development and Rights* (Oxford, Oxford University Press, 2003) 306; A de Abreu 'Background to the Participation of Women in Politics in Mozambique' in J Foster *et al* above n 253, 42 at 43–46.

[259] SADC Gender and Development Declaration 1997 art H(ii); CEDAW General Recommendation No 23 para 16; Commonwealth Secretariat above n 246 at 8. See also Beijing + 5 Outcome Document (2000) above n 11 at paras 22, 23 and 81; de Abreu above n 258 at 43.

figure of 30 per cent is taken to be the 'critical mass'. With women comprising 30 per cent or more of the parliamentary members, the assumption is that they will be able to make a difference. The quota of 30 per cent of seats to be held by women set by the African National Congress at the time of the 1994 elections has been credited with making South Africa one of the countries with the highest number of women representatives.[260] The CEDAW has suggested the use of temporary special measures to redress the gender imbalance in public participation.[261] The African Union has gone further and prescribed that all its institutions must ensure that women comprise 50 per cent of staff.[262]

The use of temporary special measures is an important tool that can help to address gender imbalance in decision-making processes at a faster rate than if left unregulated.[263] However, there are some potential downsides, not least the fact that the setting aside of a specific number of seats for women may actually lead to stasis, with it being felt that the 'gender question' does not need to be addressed because 'women already have their share of seats in parliament'. With regard to women's participation on land committees, Nyamu-Musembi has noted that when women have been elected to leadership positions at the local level it has been at the insistence of foreign donors working with the government, leading her to ask whether external imposition of women participants is the only way to bring about change.[264] There is of course the danger in holding seats 'for women' of backlash, resistance or plain intransigence in seeing that the quotas are filled.[265] The reluctance of former President Moi of Kenya to fill the Kenyan quota of women in the East African Assembly is an example.[266]

Is representation sufficient?[267] Once in parliament, can women transform the

---

[260] Commonwealth Secretariat above n 246 at 16. A similar result was achieved by FRELIMO in Mozambique, *ibid.*

[261] CEDAW General Recommendation No 5 (Seventh Session, 1988)'Temporary Special Measures' UN Doc A/43/38; CEDAW General Recommendation No 23 para 15, 43; CEDAW General Recommendation No 25 on Temporary Special Measures para 22; Beijing + 5 Outcome Document (2000) above n 11 at para 81(b). See also the African Protocol on Women's Rights art 9(1).

[262] AU Durban Declaration on Mainstreaming Gender and Women's Effective Participation in the African Union, 2002. See also AU Declaration on Gender 2004 preamble.

[263] Commonwealth Secretariat above n 246 at 14–16; *Guido Jacobs v Belgium* Communication No 943/2000. CCPR/C/81/D/943/2000 paras 9:4, 9:5; World Bank MENA Development Report (2004) 138–39.

[264] Nyamu-Musembi above n 66 at 142.

[265] See for example the contention of the author in *Guido Jacobs v Belgium* above n 263 para 7:2.

[266] M Munene 'Will the Law Review Process Give Women a Voice?' *Daily Nation* (Nairobi, 12 December 2001) downloaded from: http://www.nationaudio.com/News/Daily/Nation/Today/News/News31html 1–4; 'Outrage Over Moi Order to Ministers' *Daily Nation* (Nairobi, 28 November 2001) http://www.nationaudio.com/News/Daily/Nation/Today/News/News31html.

[267] S Longwe 'Towards Realistic Strategies for Women's Political Empowerment in Africa' in C Sweetman (ed) *Women and Leadership* (Oxford, OXFAM, 2000) 24; A Rao and M Friedman 'Transforming Institutions: History and Challenges: An International Perspective' in Royal Tropical Institute (KIT) and OXFAM (eds) *Institutionalizing Gender Equality: Commitment, Policy and Practice* (Oxford, OXFAM, KIT, 2000) 67; Odongo-Mwaka above n 257 at 251; Goetz and Hassim above n 258.

tenor and focus of the conversation to be more inclusive of gender concerns?[268] The conflation of gender and women is a longstanding one. Having got in on 'quotas', should women parliamentarians and leaders be asked to 'look out for their sisters' and fight the 'women's corner' at every turn? After all, men are allowed to choose the interest groups with which they align themselves.[269]

One suggested solution to this conundrum has been to have women elected only by women within a district. In this way women would be given a direct mandate to work towards the attainment of equal opportunity for everyone.[270] Can women resist being co-opted into the masculine way of 'doing government'?[271] In an interesting study of household leadership styles of female-headed households in Botswana, Datta and McIlwaine identify that female-headed households are not necessarily more egalitarian than male-headed households. In fact, a significant proportion of Batswana women emulated 'male models of leadership when they headed households'.[272]

High expectations of the effectiveness of women's participation in institutional politics may be exaggerated. The focus on largely urban public institutions[273] ignores the plight of rural people, and particularly of rural women. For them, greater powers of decision-making may rest with the family patriarch or local chief than rest with 'state' institutions. How can women gain an effective voice and participate meaningfully in land, education and health dispute-processing structures within their locales?[274]

Issues of citizenship and participation at the domestic level reflect the gendered construct of women's domain or space, including the areas they are allowed to inhabit and the activities in which they are permitted to participate. Specifically their freedom of movement within the public space may be curtailed. An example

---

[268] Tripp above n 254 at xvii, 219–20; Adeleye-Fayemi above n 167 at 41–42, 47–48, 51–52.

[269] Tripp above n 254 at xviii. Tripp offers an interesting insight into the pressures brought to bear on female members of parliament and cabinet officials in Uganda over the decision by the government to abandon a clause in the Land Bill which would have given women co-ownership of land. Party loyalty seems to have trumped over 'sisterhood' in many high-profile cases. Tripp above n 4 at 425. But see the responses of the 'women's movement' which met leaders and expressed its disappointment. Tripp above n 4 at 426–27.

[270] Tripp above n 254 at 232. See also Tamale, who observes that women politicians, whether elected on the open roll or by way of affirmative action, tend to spend time lobbying on women's issues. Tamale above n 257 at 260.

[271] Shabangu above n 254 at 119, 121; Tripp above n 254 at 225.

[272] K Datta and C McIlwaine ' "Empowered Leaders" Perspectives on Women Heading Households in Latin America and Southern Africa' in C Sweetman (ed) *Women and Leadership* (Oxford, OXFAM, 2000) 40 at 44. But see Commonwealth Secretariat above n 246 at 11.

[273] Admittedly there is increasing provision for women's participation in 'local authorities' but the extent of women's participation at this level remains to be seen. Tripp above n 254 at 223–24.

[274] T Skard *Continent of Mothers: Understanding and Promoting Development in Africa Today* (London, Zed Press, 2003) 61; Odongo-Mwaka above n 257 at 252; CEDAW General Recommendation No 23 para 5. See also SADC Declaration 1997 art C(i); Beijing + 5 Outcome Document (2000) above n 11 at para 86(b); Government of Uganda (2000) above n 206 at 56.

of this is the *Longwe* case.[275] A Zambian woman, Sarah Longwe, was denied entry
to an international hotel in Lusaka on the ground that unaccompanied women
were not allowed into the hotel because the hotel residents and male patrons did
not want to be disturbed. Apparently this ban on *all* unaccompanied women
entering the hotel bar had been implemented because 'women not accompanied
by a male . . . used to fight amongst themselves for men'.[276] The assumption here
was that Longwe had violated male space and, more importantly, that all women
on their own were potentially prostitutes. No evidence was ever produced to prove
this.[277]

Sued for sex discrimination, the defendant hotel contended that the barring of
Longwe had nothing to do with the fact that she was a woman, rather it was
because she was unaccompanied by a man![278] The defendant then went on to
contend that, as a hotel, it was a private enterprise not subject to constitutional
provisions, including those guaranteeing freedom of movement, freedom of
association and proscribing discrimination including that based on sex.

The court rejected the argument that as a private company the hotel was above
national law, noting that the constitution was the supreme law of the country
governing both public and private enterprises.[279] The court ruled that Longwe's
freedom of movement guaranteed by the Zambian Constitution had been violated.[280] The judge further ruled that Longwe had been discriminated against
because of her sex:

> The reason for the discrimination was because she was a female who did not have male
> company at the material times. Now if that is not discrimination on the basis of sex or gen-
> der, what else is it, looking at the matter in a reasonable, ordinary person's perspective? I
> have not been able to find any reasonable argument to persuade me into holding that this
> was not based on the fact that at the material time this female (the petitioner) because she
> was female, and nothing else, was commanded by the hotel to be accompanied by another
> human being, but who must be a male in order for her to be allowed by the hotel to patron-
> ize this bar. On the other hand, an unaccompanied male who is not in the company of a
> female, was free to patronize the same bar. This was very naked discrimination against the
> females on the basis of their gender or sex, by the respondent hotel.'[281]

This judgment is remarkable for its invocation of international human rights
norms, including CEDAW, to highlight the point that, unless a country has
entered reservations, ratification of international human rights instruments is to

---

[275] *Longwe v Intercontinental Hotels* [1993] 4 LRC 221. See also the later case of *Mwanza v Holiday Inn*. Discussed in UNIFEM *Bringing Equality Home: Implementing CEDAW* (New York, UNIFEM, 1998) 24.

[276] Defendant's sole witness—[1993] 4 LRC 221 at 223.

[277] *Ibid.*

[278] *Ibid* at 224.

[279] *Ibid* at 230–31. See also CEDAW art 2(e).

[280] See also CEDAW art 15(4).

[281] [1993] 4 LRC 221 at 232.

be seen as 'a clear testimony of the willingness [of a state] to be bound by provisions of such a document'.[282] Zambia was just such a state.

Needless to say, there have been many recommendations made to improve the participation of women in decision making.[283] Suggestions have included legislating to ensure that women will be allowed to participate and putting in place temporary special measures, making more 'women-friendly environments' in the public sphere, educating the populace about the importance of the participation of all people (including women) in national life, and changing the way in which politics is conducted, for example by putting in place more family-friendly parliamentary sitting times. However, what comes through most clearly from the research conducted in Uganda by Goetz and Hassim, Odongo-Mwaka, Tamale and Tripp, is that, in Tamale's words, when hens begin to crow,[284] resistance to allocating them 'crowing rights' (voice) increases, so what is needed is a transformation of gender relations on the ground, which will see women as equal partners with men, working towards uplifting all members of society.

'Civil society' and non-governmental organisations

Human rights, good governance and democracy, like the three wise men in the biblical Christmas story, are seen by many as the bearers of good will.[285] Over the years the role of broadly defined 'civil society', and specifically non-governmental organisations (NGOs), in helping to guide states towards the three wise men has grown.[286] Although the duty to enforce and protect human rights is said to lie with

---

[282] *Ibid* at 233. See also CEDAW art 24.

[283] See for example CEDAW General Recommendation No 23 paras 41–50. Commonwealth Secretariat *Gender Mainstreaming: Commonwealth Strategies on Politics, Macroeconomics and Human Rights* (London, Commonwealth Secretariat, 1998) 18–25; de Abreu above n 258 at 62–63; Shabangu above n 254 at 123–24; L Mwenda 'Review of the Political Situation of Women in Malawi' in J Foster *et al* (eds) *Women in Politics and Decision Making in Southern Africa* (Harare, WILDAF, 1999) 22 at 38–39.

[284] Of course the reference here is to the fact that hens (women) do not crow. Only cockerels (men) do. Tamale above n 254 at 1.

[285] See J Donnelly 'Human Rights, Democracy and Development' (1999) 21 *Human Rights Quarterly* 608. The concept of good governance is not without its problems, meaning different things to different constituencies. Watkins above n 182 at 197–98; Chinkin and Wright above n 101 at 314.

[286] Tripp warns against homogenising civil society which has multiple manifestations particularly in its relations with the state: Tripp above n 254 at 21. C Welch *Protecting Human Rights in Africa: Roles and Strategies of Non-Governmental Organizations* (Philadelphia, University of Pennsylvania Press, 1995); M Chanock 'Human Rights and Cultural Branding: Who Speaks and How?' in A An Na'im (ed) *Cultural Transformation and Human Rights in Africa* (London, Zed Press, 2002) 38 at 60; World Bank above n 109 at 103–4; O Okafor 'Modest Harvests: on the Significant (but Limited) Impact of Human Rights NGOs on Legislative and Executive Behaviour in Nigeria' (2004) 48 *Journal of African Law* 23; World Bank MENA Development Report (2004) 140.

states, increasingly NGOs have been engaged in the task.[287] Sometimes aid donors prefer to work directly with NGOs, bypassing governments, or to funnel aid through International NGOs (INGOs).[288] However, aid transfer is again shifting back to government to government co-operation, with the exception of southern governments not seen to be human rights, good governance and democracy compliant, in which case they may be denied aid altogether (for example Zimbabwe), or it may continue to be funneled through the non-state sector.[289]

The work of NGOs

There are many different kinds of NGOs. Shivji identifies five types: the INGOS (International NGOs), LONGOS (Local-Based NGOs), FONGOS (Foreign NGOs), GONGOS (Government NGOs),[290] FFUNGOS (Foreign-Funded NGOs).[291] There are of course other transnational organisations that coalesce around a specific topic or issue.[292]

Law and human rights organisations are found within all these forms of NGOs.[293] Subsumed within these are 'women-oriented' NGOs. Here one can see how the public/private divide exists even at the NGO level. 'Women's groups' tend to focus on women's disadvantage as experienced within the home and community. By way of contrast, 'malestream', as opposed to mainstream, human rights organisations concern themselves with public sphere—for which read 'serious'—

---

[287] The Kigali Declaration 2003 not only recognises civil society organisations, but also calls upon states to protect them as they do their work: art 28; Grand Bay Declaration 1999 arts 17–19; Vienna Declaration and Programme of Action 1993 (I) para 38.

[288] C Pippan 'A Donor View: The EU, Development, Co-operation and the Non State Sector' in G Hollands and G Ansell (eds) *Winds of Small Change. Civil Society Interaction with the African State* (Vienna, Austrian Development Institute, 1998) 140 at 140; Watkins above n 182 at 207.

[289] See for example the discussion of the Maastricht Treaty provisions on the issue of EU foreign and security policy aims, in Pippan above n 288 at 150. Beijing + 5 Outcome Document (2000) above n 11 at para 102(d).

[290] Oloka-Onyango identifies a sub-species of GONGOs which, within the East African context, he calls MUNGOs (named after the respective Presidents in the region—Museveni, Moi or Mkapa-organised NGOs.) The removal of Moi from power has changed the alliteration! J Oloka-Onyango 'Modern Day Missionaries or Misguided Miscreants? NGOs, the Women's Movement and the Promotion of Human Rights in Africa' in W Benedek and G Oberleitner (eds) *Human Rights of Women: International Instruments and African Experiences* (London, Zed Press, 2002) 286. Linked to the Oloka-Onyango typology are the 'First Lady' or wifeist inspired movements discussed by H Abdullah 'Religious Revivalism, Human Rights Activism and the Struggle for Women's Rights in Nigeria' in A An Na'im (ed) *Cultural Transformation and Human Rights in Africa* (London, Zed Press, 2002) 151 at 171.

[291] Shivji above n 98 at 34–35, 61.

[292] M Keck and K Sikkink *Activists Beyond Borders* (Ithaca, Cornell University Press, 1998) 10–34.

[293] Both Shivji and Oloka-Onyango criticise what they see as an over-emphasis by these organisations on civil and political rights in preference to socio-economic and cultural rights which are important on the continent. Shivji above n 98 at 61; Oloka-Onyango above n 290 at 290.

violations of rights by state actors. The lack of mainstreaming of women's rights within the work of local human rights agencies means that until a proper programme of mainstreaming is undertaken, women's agencies will have to continue to exist independent of male dominated ones.[294]

FFUNGOS, and indeed even LONGOs, tend to use as the model of human rights work that emanating from the dominant INGOs, such as Amnesty International and Human Rights Watch, who see it as their role to expose and shame states by recording human rights violations and calling for the state to desist. Issues of gender-based discrimination have not featured prominently in the work of Amnesty International. Indeed for Amnesty, the foray into the arena of women's rights, and specifically a focus on violence against women, is, within the context of its long engagement with human rights issues, fairly recent.[295] Although sometimes criticised as being too 'American', Human Rights Watch has more to celebrate. It has an established women's rights section and also engages with gender-based violations in the context of its other regional work.

Generally human rights NGOs on the continent have done good work. This has included representing victims of human rights violations before the African Commission.[296] A regional women's NGO, WILDAF, was the driving force in lobbying for an instrument on Women's Rights on the continent.[297] The depth and reach of the African Protocol on Women's Rights, and arguably its radical vision, can be said to be the result of NGO input. The drafting and coming into force of the SADC Declaration on Gender and Development 1997 and the Addendum on Violence the following year, can be attributed to lobbying by the vibrant and strong women's movement in the southern African region. NGOs are also acknowledged in the SADC Declaration on Gender and Development 1997.[298]

---

[294] Oloka-Onyango above n 290 at 291.

[295] Recent efforts are, however, impressive—see Amnesty International (2004) *Sudan, Darfur: Rape as a Weapon of War* AI Index: AFR 54/076/2004, 19 July 2004.

[296] Murray above n 32 at 87–102; A Motala 'Non-Governmental Organizations in the African System' in M Evans and R Murray (eds) *The African Charter on Human and Peoples' Rights: The System in Practice 1986–2000* (Cambridge, Cambridge University Press, 2002) 246. Most of the cases brought before the African Commission on Human Rights are brought by NGOs. Indeed almost each chapter in Evans and Murray highlights the contribution of NGOs to the work of the African Commission.

[297] Murray above n 32 at 96 fn. NGOs and other non-state actors were also influential in the drafting of the Optional Protocol to CEDAW. A Byrnes and J Connors 'Enforcing the Human Rights of Women: A Complaints Procedure for the Convention on the Elimination of All Forms of Discrimination against Women' (1996) 21 *Brooklyn Journal of International Law* 679.

[298] SADC Declaration 1997 art F(iv). NGOs seem to have played a major role in post-Beijing national action plans, often working together with governments to meet the Beijing challenges. See Chiriga above n 117 at 118–20, 128,130.

Women's NGOs have also been involved in lobbying for changes in the law, helping to draft legislation[299] and training government personnel.[300] Where the relationship with the government is co-operative, NGOs are able to assist with providing human rights education.[301] Although co-operation between the state and local NGOs can be useful, Abdullah notes that sometimes the closeness of the relationship between state and NGO has led to organisations becoming co-opted by the state machinery, which in turn makes it difficult for NGOs to propose a radical agenda.[302]

The case of *Unity Dow* in Botswana, which was discussed in Chapters 3 and 4, is an excellent example of the coming together of local, regional and international NGOs to challenge discriminatory laws by bringing a test case. In *Dow*, the Minnesota-based International Women's Rights Action Watch, assisted by Urban Morgan Institute for Human Rights, filed an *amicus curiae* brief. Research for the case and lobbying was undertaken by a regional NGO, the Women and Law in Southern Africa group working with the locally-based Emang Basadi. They were funded by the Swedish Development Agency SIDA.[303]

At the international level, the human rights committees have benefited enormously from the shadow reports produced by NGOs. Indeed the Committee on Economic, Social and Cultural Rights sometimes proceeds even when a state has not turned in its report, relying on any shadow reports produced by NGOs.[304] The

---

[299] The Tanzania Media Women's Association (TAMWA) lobbied for a statute outlawing violence against women. The TAMWA draft was accepted in large measure and resulted in the passing of the Sexual Offences Special Provisions Act 1998. The NGO is also involved in education campaigns on the provisions of the Act. L Sheikh 'TAMWA: Levina's Song-Supporting Women in Tanzania' in H Chigudu (ed) *Composing a New Song: Stories of Empowerment from Africa* (2003) 95 at 168–69; R Chitiga *Civil Society Guide to Law Making Process in SADC Countries* (Harare, Development Innovations and Networks East and Southern Africa Office (IRED), 1998); L Zulu 'Institutionalizing Changes: South African Women's Participation in the Transition to Democracy' in S Rai (ed) *International Perspectives on Gender and Democratization* (New York, Macmillan, 2000) 166; J Beall 'Doing Gender from Top to Bottom? The South African Case' (2001) 12 *Women: A Cultural Review* 135 at 140.

[300] Cf Odongo-Mwaka above n 257 at 252. See also the contributions in J Foster, S Makanya and G Mutukwa (eds) *Women in Politics and Decision Making in Southern Africa* (Harare, WILDAF, 1999), all of which deal with the NGO role lobbying for greater political participation of women, and also of encouraging and supporting women politicians in whatever forum they find themselves.

[301] African Protocol on Women's Rights art 12(1)(e); P Kiirya 'LABE: Beating the Community Drums' in H Chigudu (ed) *Composing a New Song: Stories of Empowerment from Africa* (London, Commonwealth Secretariat, 2003) 35 at 63–64; Sheikh above n 299 at 115. H Chigudu 'Conclusion' in H Chigudu (ed) (2003) at 169; A Chanda *Informal Education for Human Rights in Zambia* (Harare, SAPES, 1997); M d'Engelbronner-Kolff *The Provision of Non-Formal Education for Human Rights in Zimbabwe* (Harare, SAPES, 1997); MENA Development Report (2004) 140–41.

[302] Abdullah above n 290 at 171. Cf P Kiirya above n 301 at 60, 63; Chigudu above n 226 at 168–69.

[303] A Molokomme 'Discriminatory Citizenship Laws in Botswana: Emang Basadi' in Women, Law and Development: International and Human Rights Watch Women's Rights Project (ed) *Women's Human Rights Step by Step* (Washington DC, Women, Law and Development International, 1997) 133.

[304] Report of the Fifth Meeting of Persons Chairing the Human Rights Treaty Bodies— Recommendations (1994) UN Doc A/49/537 reproduced in H Steiner and P Alston *International Human Rights in Context: Law, Politics, Morals* (Oxford, Clarendon Press, 2000) 981.

role of NGOs in service delivery[305] has been recognised in the United Nations Declaration on the Elimination of Violence against Women 1993, which calls on states parties to:

> Facilitate and enhance the work of the women's movement and non governmental organizations and cooperate with them at the local, national and regional levels.[306]

These are all important contributions made by the human rights NGO lobby and, specifically, women's groups within that lobby. However, collapsing all women's rights organisations into one group as though women were homogeneous ignores the intersections of class and, in some areas, religion in the construction of the agenda of the organisation. The issue of religion and religious difference is more marked in some regions than in others. Nigeria is a case in point.[307] Abdullah notes how organisations in Nigeria are sometimes divided by religion. An example of conflict came when a 'Christian' organisation proposed that the divorce law be changed so that if a couple divorced after 10 years of marriage, the woman would be automatically granted one half of the marital assets. The 'Muslim' women's organisation objected strongly, noting that it would prejudice women in polygynous unions.[308] Interestingly, Abdullah notes how, despite their apparent differences, the two organisations are united by their conservatism and their willingness to subscribe to gender roles that see women as located largely within the family. Moreover, neither organisation presses for a model of equality which demands that women be treated the same as men.[309] These religious differences can sometimes feed into the political divisions[310] that are now manifesting themselves in Nigerian politics.[311]

The issue of class is one that cannot be avoided when discussing NGOs on the continent.[312] By the nature of their work, law and human rights NGOs are led and staffed in large part by those with university education, that is the professional

---

[305] See also World Bank above n 109 at 104. But see P Daley 'Start with the Destitute: Refugees and NGO Recolonization of Africa' (1994) *Africa World Review* 24.

[306] DEVAW art 4(p). See also art 4(e). Interestingly the role of NGOs in advocacy was recognised as far back as 1967 in DEDAW art 11(2). Vienna Declaration and Programme of Action 1993 (I) para 38. Beijing Platform for Action 1995 para 26.

[307] Adamu above n 167 at 56.

[308] Abdullah above n 290 at 170. Cf Oloka-Onyango above n 290 at 290. For disagreements between women's groups at the international level see Otto's account of the Beijing Conference: D Otto 'Holding Up Half the Sky But for Whose Benefit?' (1996) 6 *Australian Feminist Law Journal* 7.

[309] Abdullah above n 290 at 171. However, it is fair to say that she does acknowledge the work of the Federation of Muslim Women's Associations in Nigeria (FOMWAN) in challenging the unilateral repudiation of women, forced and early marriage. Abdullah above n 290 at 169. Cf F Sow 'Fundamentalism, Globalisation, and Women's Human Rights in Senegal' in J Kerr and C Sweetman (eds) *Women Reinventing Globalization* (Oxford, OXFAM, 2003) 69 at 74.

[310] Cf Tripp above n 4 at 436. Tripp notes that in Uganda the effects of the 'war on terror' have been to marginalise Muslim communities, who now feel further alienated and 'attacked' by the attempts of the women's lobby to have polygyny abolished via the Domestic Relations Bill 2003.

[311] Adamu above n 167 at 59–60.

[312] Wanzala above n 29 at 4, 8.

classes. Indeed Odinkalu has noted that human rights activism is a badge of privilege.[313] Still, class privilege can be used to good effect, so that Toungara notes that
in the Côte d'Ivoire elite women lobbied against retrogressive changes in the Civil
Code.[314] Nevertheless it is true to say that women's NGOs tend to be dominated
by elite women who drive four-by-fours (also called Range Rovers, Pajeros or
SUVs (sports utility vehicles))—vehicles that generally never see the terrain for
which they were designed. It is said that urban-based NGO women have an aver-
sion to spending longer than a day out of the city,[315] unless of course the night is
to be spent in a well-appointed hotel with a *per diem* (daily allowance)[316] in United
States dollars. The hierarchies within these organisations are no different than one
would find in any government organisation, with the spoils (foreign trips, consul-
tancies and US dollars) being largely enjoyed by those at the top.[317] I appreciate
that this statement reinforces the view of NGO women as pampered, but they are
not alone—politicians are often more avaricious and have access to state funds
with which to indulge their avarice. To conclude my tirade, a Namibian student
on a human rights programme on which I taught, spoke, to much nodding and
acknowledgement from her peers, of 'briefcase NGOs'. I had no idea what she
meant, until she explained that these were one or two person NGOs set up with the
express purpose of accessing hard currency.[318]

My rather uncharitable characterisation of the NGO movement as somehow US
dollar driven reveals one of the enduring conundrums about NGOs in Africa;
most are actually FFUNGOs (Foreign-Funded NGOs). The 'foreign' is mainly
northern. This northern funding brings with it dilemmas for southern NGOs.[319]
The clearest dilemma is of course that around the issue of voice and bargaining
power.[320] Although often constructed (by northerners) as relationships based on
the principle of partnership, in reality the recipient is working to an agenda set by

---

[313] C Odinkalu 'Why More Africans Don't Use Human Rights Language' (2000) *Human Rights
Dialogue* 3 reproduced in H Steiner and P Alston *International Human Rights in Context: Law, Politics,
Morals* (Oxford, Clarendon Press, 2000) 946. Cf Shivji above n 98 at 61.

[314] J Toungara 'Changing the Meaning of Marriage: Women and Family Law in Cote d'Ivoire' in
Royal Tropical Institute (KIT) and OXFAM (eds) *Gender Perspectives on Property and Inheritance*
(Amsterdam, KIT and Oxford, OXFAM, 2001) 33 at 46.

[315] Shivji bemoans the lack of critical engagement by NGOs at the grassroots (rural) level: Shivji
above n 98 at 61. See also Chigudu above n 226 at 164–65. For some, the middle class lifestyle is seen
to be a necessary reflection of the sacrifices made to send the person to University. Cf M Arigbede above
n 117 at 4, 10–11. But in the Zambian Women for Change programme 'animators' (facilitators) live in
the rural areas with the community for extended periods of time: Sikazwe above n 226 at 134.

[316] The issue of per diem is, in relation to African (women's) NGOs, deserving of an entire chapter
of its own!

[317] Cf Wanzala above n 29 at 9–10. See in particular the poem 'The Development Set' quoted in full
by W Wanzala at 10 fn 29.

[318] Cf Shivji above n 98 at 61. Tripp above n 254 at 198.

[319] Chigudu above n 226 at 163–64.

[320] See generally the papers in D Eade *Development and Patronage* (Oxford, OXFAM, 1997). The
COPODIN project in Nigeria has refused to accept donor funding for all the reasons identified:
Arigbede above n 117 at 7, 29, 30.

the donor. Of the inequitable model of partnership used in development funding Nzegwu has noted:

> The history of NGOs in the South shows that donors do not readily accept that economically disadvantaged peoples and groups can be equals. They are not seen as having agency. They are treated as if they lack intelligence, and their opinions are often ignored.[321]

This means that sometimes the aid recipient has to abandon what the organisation sees as a local priority in favour of the donor's perception of need or priority. Shivji notes that international human rights organisations often share the values and perspectives of their governments about what is 'best for Africa', and push a similar uncritical line to their governments on the issue of human rights.[322] Some might argue that the renewed focus on the issue of female genital cutting is just such a case.[323]

Equally problematic is the linking of aid to agreeing with the global political agenda of certain northern states. The flurry of activity in early 2003 that saw non-permanent members of the Security Council, in particular those from the south,[324] being lobbied and offered 'inducements' to vote in favour of the second resolution agreeing to the invasion of Iraq by Britain and the United States, which was in the event never tabled, is eloquent testament to this phenomenon. Linked to this was the row that ensued within the INGO Save the Children, with the United States chapter castigating the British chapter for having come out against the Iraqi (second Gulf) War. The United States chapter pointed out that it received a considerable amount of funding from the government and that an anti-war stance would not be 'helpful' when it next went cap in hand to ask for funding.[325] These are not the only examples. During the crisis, again in 2003, over the ordination as Archbishop of a homosexual bishop from the United States in the Anglican Church, southern churches were 'warned' that if they continued to oppose the ordination, they could expect a cut in funding, leading the Archbishop of Central Africa to retort that he was a man of principle who would not compromise on biblical teaching.[326]

---

[321] Nzegwu 'Questions of Agency' above n 19 at 2. But see C Pippan, who claims that the European Union has opted for 'a bottom-up approach to development and democracy, which influences both its general development cooperation policy and its specific strategy on democratization in third countries': Pippan above n 288 at 150.

[322] Shivji above n 98 at 59; Daley above n 305 at 25.

[323] See the European Parliamentary Resolution on Female Genital Mutilation 2001 discussed in Ch 6.

[324] Guinea and Angola received visits from high-ranking American and British envoys.

[325] K Maguire 'How British Charity was Silenced on Iraq' *Guardian* (London, 28 November 2003). The British Director General of Save the Children UK responded that the organisation would never be silenced.

[326] C Morgan 'Anglicans Say US Church is Taking Aid Revenge in Gay Row' *Sunday Times* (London, 19 October 2003) 3. See also J Humphrys 'A Split Church Can Be Reborn' *Sunday Times* (London, 19 October 2003) 21.

Given the relationship of dependence, which appears to get worse rather than better as the years pass,[327] Shivji notes that African NGOs have not addressed the imperialist or negative policies of northern funders.[328] Linked in with aid is the issue of accountability for the funds. This in turn results in constant demands for auditing to check, legitimately some might argue in the light of past experience, that donor funds are not being misused. To this end there is a demand for the production of a seemingly endless stream of reports. This generation of applications and reports has sometimes been said to require hiring a person or persons to work on report writing as their main activity. The former UNICEF representative to the West and Central Africa region notes:

> It is estimated that an African country with considerable donor aid could receive a thousand delegations and send nearly ten thousand reports every year.[329]

It has been argued that often 'aid' is a job creation scheme for northern NGOS or governments to keep their own populations in work.[330] As part of the 'aid package', a donor can demand the use of the 'expertise' of a donor national.[331] Sometimes this may be strategic, for example in parts of the former Eastern bloc and Central Asia, there was a rush to provide 'technical assistance', which may just have been a cover for states to gain commercial advantage over rivals by recommending the 'incorporation' of the donor's laws on tax or commerce.[332] In such a case, how does one measure a 'successful outcome', from the perspective of the donor or the recipient?[333]

The issue of the appropriateness and acceptability of the solutions proposed is particularly acute where women's rights are concerned. In a now notorious newspaper article, Rod Liddle, an English journalist, recounted his visit to a Swedish sponsored UNICEF project in Uganda.[334] He said that as part of the aid package, cultural norms were to change. This he referred to as the 'Swedenisation of Uganda'. In a process of 'ruthlessly extracting cultural concessions for hard cash', Ugandans were to be 'allowed' to keep their singing and dancing, but were to be

---

[327] Dependence on donor funding is not a uniquely southern NGO problem. Increasingly INGOs have also to 'chase' donor funding, which sometimes means responding to donor led intervention. Pippan above n 288 at 144–46.

[328] Shivji above n 98 at 61.

[329] Skard above n 274 at 162.

[330] Wanzala above n 29 at 14.

[331] Cf M Zamboni '*Rechtsstaat*: Just What is Being Exported by Swedish Development Assistance Organisations?' (2001) 2 *Law, Social Justice and Global Development* http://elj.warwick.ac.uk/global/issue/2001–2/zamboni.html at 7. Shivji above n 98 at 50 n 22.

[332] S Newton 'Post-Communist Legal Reform: The Elision of the Political' in J Hatchard and A Perry-Kessaris (eds) *Law and Development: Facing Complexity in the 21st Century* (London, Cavendish Press, 2003) 161 at 163, 176, 177.

[333] Zamboni above n 331 at 9.

[334] Cf R Liddle 'On Why Africa Must Take Responsibility for its Own Problems' *Guardian* (London, 7 February 2002). Cf Zamboni above n 331 at 9.

encouraged to relinquish more 'questionable' practices such as polygyny, female genital cutting, large families and 'brides for sale'.[335] One might think this smacks of imposing, in the words of Burman, 'first world solutions for third world problems'.[336]

Interestingly, it would appear that the problem of donor agenda setting and demand may not be only north to south. Writing about the Swedish development process, Zamboni[337] identifies how the Swedish agencies that deliver assistance to southern states are themselves dependent on the goodwill and agenda of SIDA, the Swedish Development Agency, which, being government funded, is in itself dependent on the agenda of the politicians.[338]

Perhaps one of the greatest obstacles faced by NGOs is at the national level. Some governments are wary of NGOs, seeing them as threatening and 'subversive'.[339] Because of this, there is an attempt to gag them. Tripp notes how sometimes NGOs can be accused of lobbying for foreign interests by a government resistant to the agenda being put forward by NGOs.[340] The Zimbabwean way is by requiring registration before one can set up an NGO. What this means in practice is that those whose mandates are not considered to be compatible with 'national policy or development goals' are refused registration, which means in turn that they cannot set up or, if already in existence, continue to exist. Moreover, human rights organisations are to be prohibited from receiving foreign funding, making it impossible for them to carry out their work.[341] This is clearly a violation of the United Nations Declaration on Human Rights Defenders 1998.[342]

Also, and this is by way of mitigation to the picture painted of the avarice of people working in the NGO sector, it is as well to remember that even if the state does not harass them, they may still experience difficulties within the communities or societies in which they work. This is particularly true of women's rights NGO

---

[335] Liddle above n 334.

[336] S Burman 'First World Solutions for Third World Problems' in L Weitzman and M Maclean (eds) *Economic Consequences of Divorce: The International Perspective* (Oxford, Clarendon Press, 1992) 367. See also B Andreassen 'Democratization and Human Rights Beyond Borders: On the Donor-Recipient Connection' in P Nherere and M d'Engelbronner-Kolf (eds) *The Institutionalisation of Human Rights in Southern Africa* (Oslo, Nordic Human Rights Publications, 1993) 195; E McAllister 'Aid Conditionality as a Lever for Women's Equality: Help or Hindrance?' in J Kerr (ed) *Ours By Right* (London, Zed Books, 1993) 106.

[337] Zamboni above n 331; Middleton and O'Keefe above n 110 at 95.

[338] Zamboni above n 331 at 6.

[339] Dube above n 113 at 76.

[340] Tripp above n 4 at 424.

[341] S Dorman 'NGOs and the Constitutional Debate in Zimbabwe: From Inclusion to Exclusion' (2003) 29 *Journal of Southern African Studies* 845; B Zulu 'First the Media, Now the NGOs' *Mail and Guardian* (Johannesburg, 11 October 2002) downloaded from http://www.zwnews.com/issueful.cfm?ArtID=5308.

[342] Declaration on the Right and Responsibility of Individuals, Groups and Organs of Society to Promote and Protect Universally Recognized Human Rights and Fundamental Freedoms. GA Res. 53/144 adopted 9 December 1998. See also Beijing Platform for Action 1995 para 228.

activists, who are accused variously of being 'single/divorced, frustrated, can't
keep a man, home-wreckers and prostitutes', and those are just some of the print-
able epithets.[343] Even if these epithets are not used, their motivation is questioned,
with Mutua describing women working to eradicate female genital cutting in
Africa as 'Western inspired'.[344] There is a double insult within that: first, it
removes the agency of African women committed to working towards an eradication of the practice within their communities; and, second, it suggests that the
women would not have got to that point of their own volition. Although I did earlier say that female genital cutting (FGC) had been taken up as a cause célèbre by
some northern donors, this should not detract from the fact that African women
have always been in conversation on the issue—indeed, as noted in Chapter 6 on
FGC, the first international conference sponsored by the UN was held in Sudan in
1981 and was attended by many activists from the continent. The point of difference between northern and southern women has been over the use of language
and the strategies to tackle the practice, and not whether the practice should continue without comment.[345]

The explosion of NGOs in Africa and indeed internationally, raises questions of
accountability. Technically states are accountable to their citizens and the international community. To whom are NGOs accountable?[346] One could argue
donors, but are donors the focus of the work of NGOs or the facilitators?
Alternatively one could suggest that NGOs are responsible to their constituents.
However, it is possible that the constituents, due to ignorance or vulnerability,
may feel unable to challenge NGOs that make promises but do not deliver.
Outside of the threat of a cut to funding, there is little sanction that can be imposed
on NGOs which are not performing. It is undoubtedly true that for all their
shortcomings, they are better at, and more committed to, delivering goods, services and hope to the people than are many governments.

Conclusion

This chapter started by looking at the age-old debate about how human rights
norms could be reconciled with 'local' 'cultural' or religious values. The perspectives of a range of commentators were considered to show that the resolution of
the problem is not simple; indeed there are as many answers as there are questions.
The chapter then considered the issue of development, how the understanding of

[343] Cf Sheikh above n 299 at 96, 106.
[344] Mutua above n 68 at 82.
[345] J Oloka-Onyango above n 290 at 289.
[346] Daley above n 305 at 29.

the concept has changed over time and its gendered dimensions. The chapter looked at the impact of poverty on women and focused on the lives of rural women. Given the centrality of participation in policy and decision making, the inclusion of women in their national parliaments and other organs for decision making was examined. The woman's voice was found to be, if not entirely absent, certainly not well represented. Strategies for addressing this problem through the use of temporary special measures were considered. With the increased rolling back of the state, the chapter closed by examining the work done by NGOs. Although increasing in number as well as influence, NGOs are not without their critics. Chief among these is the increasing gap between the lives of relatively wealthy NGO workers and their poorer constituents. Moreover there is the age-old problem of dependency on northern funders for project finance and all that entails. This seems to be a problem affecting all NGOs in the world and not just southern ones.

The conclusion now follows. It considers the efficacy of using law and human rights to improve the lives of women on the African continent.

8

Conclusion

It was Week 6 in my law and society class on gender and human rights. We had looked at the content of family laws in Africa, the meaning of non-discrimination, including intersectional discrimination, examined human rights instruments on the issue and were now in the final stretch—how to reconcile the substantive content of family and personal laws, particularly those based on custom and religion, with human rights norms. That is when a voice piped up: 'Fareda, all this human rights business that you have been teaching us is foolishness.' Augustine, the Nigerian student whose peers were now looking at him as if he wanted to test the validity of his right to life, continued: 'To say that women in Africa have rights and are equal to men is an abomination.' His peers clearly thought him the foolish one for risking so much on a Monday morning. Surely his weekend could not have been that bad. I have to confess to suppressing a giggle and for admiring him for saying what I had heard so many times before, albeit framed differently. The word 'abomination' is not one that trips lightly off the tongue. When I think of how far we as women worldwide have yet to go to have our humanity recognised, I sometimes think he has a point.

This book has tried to provide a broad overview of the development of women's rights internationally, with a focus on women's rights on the African continent. That there have been great strides in the development of international and regional instruments pertaining to the rights of women is not in doubt. What remains unclear is whether there has been any material change to women's lives as a result of these instruments, and indeed, whether the proliferation of human rights instruments is the solution or part of the problem. Does the existence of a now almost comprehensive body of law indicate progress, or merely create a false sense of achievement? Kennedy notes: 'people inside the (human rights) movement can mistake reform of their world for reform of the world.'[1] Another question that needs to be asked is has law, broadly constructed to include international human rights law, state laws including personal laws and the 'living law', brought liberation to African women, or has it proved to be yet another irrelevance to their

---

[1] D Kennedy 'The International Human Rights Movement: Part of the Problem?' (2002) 15 *Harvard Human Rights Journal* 101 at 118.

lives? Indeed, of what use is law to a continent riven by internal conflicts and which has by and large seen a drop in standards of living almost across the board?

This chapter starts with a consideration of the legal gains made by women at the international level before moving on to look at the impediments that have been identified as inhibiting women from enjoyment of their rights. The last section considers the expansion of the feminist project on the African continent to embrace groups whose concerns are not always addressed.

Overview of the development of human rights

Given its focus, CEDAW is the best known of the human rights instruments pertaining to women. There has within the UN system been an attempt at main-streaming women's rights[2] to reflect the injunction of the UN Secretary-General that for 'every human rights violation, there is a gender dimension'.[3]

At the regional level[4] there is the African Charter. There has also been the development of a regional instrument on children's rights that builds on the UN Children's Rights Convention. Moreover, there are sub-regional initiatives of groups of states, including those of SADC and l'UEMOA. These instruments have built upon gains made at conferences such as the Beijing Conference 1995. Another development has been the formation of the African Union whose Constitutive Act 2000 claims a commitment to gender equality.

The adoption of the African Protocol on Women's Rights in 2003 put women's rights on the continent centre stage. However, the radicalism of the document is not reflected in state enthusiasm to ratify it or to incorporate its vision into national policy, hence, one year after adoption, it is yet to come into force. The apparently slow ratification of the African Protocol on Women's Rights[5] is indicative of the more general problem that has been manifest throughout our discussions, namely that legal change may be easy, but implementation and commitment to long-term change is less so. This begs the question, what good is a visionary document without visionary leaders prepared to commit themselves and

---

[2] J Connors 'Mainstreaming Gender within the International Framework' in A Stewart (ed) *Gender, Law and Social Justice* (Oxford, Blackstone, 2000) 19; Human Rights Committee, General Comments No 18 and 28; Committee on the Elimination of Race Discrimination General Comment No 25. The Committee on Economic Social and Cultural Rights has adopted General Comment No 16.

[3] Report of the Secretary-General on the Question of Integrating the Human Rights of Women throughout the United Nations System (25 March 1998) E/CN.4/1998/49 (25 March 1998) para 9.

[4] G Naldi 'Future Trends in Human Rights in Africa: The Increased Role of the OAU' in M Evans and R Murray (eds) *The African Charter on Human and Peoples' Rights: The System in Practice, 1986–2000* (Cambridge, Cambridge University Press, 2002) 17–31.

[5] It is worth remembering that the ACRWC took nine years to come into force, so the pace of ratification may not be as slow as appears to those keen to get the instrument up and running.

their governments to improving the lives of women and girl children within their societies?

Normative developments at the international and regional level have fed into national policy planning. On the legal front has been a rush to amend or re-draft constitutions. The new constitutions take on board issues previously not covered, including children's rights, more comprehensive non-discrimination provisions that cover gender-based discrimination and, in one radical example, South Africa, sexuality as well. Moreover, increasingly included within constitutional frameworks have been socio-economic and cultural rights. Arguably the inclusion of the latter group of rights shows a greater awareness on the part of states of the problems that most affect their populations. The full belly thesis, which says that one cannot worry about a right to vote or other civil and political rights on an empty stomach, may be discredited, but that does not mean that its central claim, that without socio-economic rights there can be no development of African society, can be discarded too.[6]

This leads into the next question—how much autonomy does the African state enjoy? Is it in a position to deliver rights to its citizens?

The weak African state

Globalisation may have turned the world into a village, but for the average African, this village has feudal conditions in which the African takes on the role of serf. Murray adopts the feminist analysis of international law to argue that Africa, like women in both international and national law, is the excluded continent, with little access to power or influence in decision making.[7] African governments may wield power within the more limited 'domestic' sphere, but in reality, their economies are not within their control. If their economies are not within their control, it begs the question: how far are they able to deliver socio-economic rights to their people? How can a government promise to alleviate the poverty of its people when the mechanisms for doing so are within the gift and control of outsiders?[8] Indeed Bruce argues that the rise of so-called Islamic fundamentalism is:

---

[6] D Martin 'Law, Custom and Economic Empowerment of Women in Sub-Saharan Africa: A Conceptual Framework' in A Stewart (ed) *Gender, Law and Social Justice* (Oxford, Blackstone, 2000) 71.

[7] R Murray *The African Commission on Human Rights and International Law* (Oxford, Hart Publishing, 2000) at 199.

[8] Non-governmental organisations in Britain have claimed that the money spent fighting the war in Iraq could have permanently lifted 2.7 million people out of poverty. M Woolf '60% Believe Billions Spent on War Should Have Gone to the Poor' *Independent* (London, 8 June 2004).

Fuelled by the failure of various forms of the secular nationalist project to improve greatly life for the mass of people in traditionally religious countries.[9]

Bruce also argues that the resistance of some Muslims to granting women autonomy is linked to the fact that if freed from domestic sphere responsibility and enabled to participate in public sphere work, women will dislodge (young) men from jobs that are already in short supply, thus creating the potential for social and political upheaval.[10]

Most African women are three times removed from the levers of the international framework and two times removed from the state framework. It is for this reason that Manji asks of what use the state is to African women.[11] More specifically, she asks how relevant state-generated law is to the majority of African women. Critiquing the legal centralist paradigm on which much law reform and discussion of law in Africa is founded, Manji notes that for many women not only is state law an alien concept, but their experiences of both the law and the state have been as tools not of liberation but of coercion.[12] Tamale links women's isolation from the state with their compromised citizenship rights, which alienation is exacerbated by 'the underdevelopment of democratic institutions on the continent.'[13]

Manji's questioning of state-generated law feeds into a wider and more long-standing debate about the usefulness of law to women and in improving their lives. This is a debate that has international dimensions.[14] Although weak and often not implemented, law remains important, for 'unless a woman's claim to equal

---

[9] S Bruce *Politics and Religion* (Cambridge, Polity Press, 2003). 89 F Mernissi *Beyond the Veil: Male Female Dynamics in Muslim Society* (London, Saqi Books, 2003) 11. Chanock highlights the attractiveness of a culturalist discourse for people faced with rapid change and social and economic dislocation: 'Human Rights and Cultural Branding: Who Speaks and How?' in A An Na'im (ed) *Cultural Transformation and Human Rights in Africa* (London, Zed Press, 2002) 38 at 62.

[10] Bruce above n 9 at 88–89.

[11] A Manji 'Imagining Women's "Legal World": Towards a Feminist Theory of Legal Pluralism in Africa' (1994) 8 *Social and Legal Studies* 434. See also A Stewart 'Should Women Give Up on the State? The African Experience' in S Rai and G Lievesley (eds) *Women and the State: International Perspectives* (London, Taylor Francis, 1996) 23.

[12] Manji above n 11 at 451. Cf A Fellmeth 'Feminism and International Law: Theory, Methodology, and Substantive Reform' (2000) 22 *Human Rights Quarterly* 658 at 661.

[13] S Tamale 'Gender Trauma in Africa: Enhancing Women's Access to Resources' (2004) 48 *Journal of African Law* 50 at 60.

[14] C Smart *Feminism and the Power of Law* (London, Routledge, 1989); R Kapur and B Cossman *Subversive Sites: Feminist Engagement with Law in India* (London, Sage, 1996); P Williams *The Alchemy of Race and Rights* (Cambridge, Harvard University Press, 1991) 146–65; J Conaghan 'Reassessing the Feminist Theoretical Project in Law' (2000) 27 *Journal of Law and Society* 351; B Cossman 'Feminists Engaging with the Law: The Use And Limitations of Rights Discourse in Women's Struggles for Social Change' in B Cossman (ed) *Feminist Legal Theory* (Colombo, International Centre for Ethnic Studies, 1999). A Stewart 'The Contribution of Feminist Legal Scholarship to the "Rights Approach to Development"' in A Stewart (ed) *Gender, Law and Social Justice* (Oxford, Blackstone, 2000) 1; H Charlesworth and C Chinkin *Boundaries of International Law* (Manchester, Manchester University Press, 2000) at 210–12.

treatment is legally recognized, she cannot demand a remedy against discrimination.'[15]

Indeed sometimes legal change has resulted in social change, or in a different way of seeing the problem. Before sexual harassment was defined as such, it was constructed as 'just one of those things that happen when men and women mix'. That it has been named as problem of violence against women, for which international human rights law provides a sanction[16] and some national systems provide remedies,[17] is but one example of how the re-naming of a 'social' problem using the language of law, can begin the social and cultural debate that may bring about gradual change in gender relations. The sanction of law can help to bring about enforced change in behaviour in the workplace. But can law bring about change in the harder to regulate private sphere? The chapter on female genital cutting identified the fact that this was the area in which a great amount of legislative work had been done, and yet the problem continues. What is it that makes some legal change have almost immediate effect on certain behaviours but not on others?

Maboreke identifies several difficulties with relying on law, and in particular when trying to regulate family relations. Law's failings include its lack of legitimacy, which is tied to the fact that for many people state law is peripheral to their lives and is used only by a minority of the population, as well as the social and economic costs associated with using the law.[18] Surveying the legislative and judicial interventions in South Africa, Himonga urges caution, noting that all that may be achieved by a raft of legal change are paper gains rather than substantive change on the ground. She identifies three risk factors in the implementation of new laws.[19] First is the traditional factor, not least the resistance to top-down imposed change by the traditional authorities and other groups who may feel that their values and perspectives are disrespected and ignored, and who may in turn pose a barrier to change by offering implacable resistance.[20] The next risk identified by Himonga is the historical factor rooted in an understanding of the denigration of African values in the past. This rapid legal change, which seems premised on repeating that denigration and disregard for all things African by seemingly

---

[15] UNDP *Human Development Report 2000* (New York, UN, 2000) 7.
[16] CEDAW General Recommendation No 19 para 17. DEVAW art 2(b); African Protocol on Women's Rights art 13(c).
[17] For example South Africa Employment and Equity Act No 55 of 1998 s 6(3).
[18] M Maboreke 'Understanding Law in Zimbabwe' in A Stewart (ed) *Gender, Law and Social Justice* (Oxford, Blackstone, 2000) 101 at 102. See also Martin above n 6 at 81.
[19] C Himonga 'Legislative and Judicial Approaches to the Reform of the Customary Law of Marriage and Succession in South Africa: Implications for the Advancement of Women's Rights' (paper presented at the Conference on Advancing Women's Rights Hosted by the Women's Legal Centre, Cape Town, 30–31 October 2003) available at http://www.wlce.co.za/conference2003/2003conference_himonga.php at 7.
[20] *Ibid.*

overthrowing cultural norms in favour of new western-modelled constitutional norms, may again lead to alienation and a sense of betrayal.[21] Finally Himonga identifies the complexity factor, which involves the passing of very complicated and difficult-to-understand legislation, and notes that such complexity will more likely than not again lead to people ignoring the law.[22]

It seems clear, therefore, that the 'naming' of the problem as one requiring a 'legal', or more accurately state-imposed, solution may not meet with universal approval. Without internal legitimacy, or the support or approval of those who are to be governed by the law, the law will remain ignored and unused. This explains in part the resilience to change of personal laws that may seem, and indeed often are, discriminatory to women. One may argue that reasons for this are not difficult to fathom. The content of personal laws are more often than not determined with reference to religious or social norms, drafted at a more conservative time in history and by those in a position of power and influence.

With regard to the private sphere where state regulation/intervention may be minimal, one may argue that although time has moved on, the people in charge of implementing the laws have continued to come from the same dominant group, largely men.[23] But how, then, do we explain the place of women not only in the construction and perpetuation of cultural norms, but also in the upholding of some of these discriminatory practices? This is not to 'blame the victim' for her plight, but it is to ask what it is about personal laws that still exerts such pull over people, especially in light of the existence of alternative normative orders provided by both state law and international human rights norms. One answer would be to say that women may not be aware of these norms and may therefore not be in a position to exercise the cultural exit option. It may well be, as Maboreke contends, that while law grants women rights and legal capacity, it does not address the issue of women's social dependency.[24]

Another perspective is to say that far from constructing personal laws as negative or oppressive, women see them as providing cultural signifiers of identity—

---

[21] *Ibid* at 8–9.
[22] *Ibid* at 10.
[23] Judges in Commonwealth states have been given training on human rights issues. Victoria Falls Declaration of Principles for Promoting the Human Rights of Women 1994. See also V Dankwa 'The Promotional Role of the African Commission' in M Evans and R Murray (eds) *The African Charter on Human and Peoples' Rights: The System in Practice, 1986–2000* (Cambridge, Cambridge University Press, 2002) 335 at 348; African Charter art 25; African Protocol on Women's Rights art 8. Cf A Tsanga *Taking Law to the People: Gender, Law Reform and Community Legal Education in Zimbabwe* (Harare, Women's Law Centre and Weaver Press, 2003) and A Griffiths *In the Shadow of Marriage: Gender and Justice in an African Community* (Chicago, University of Chicago Press, 1997); U Wanitzek 'The Power of Language in the Discourse on Women's Rights: Some Examples from Tanzania' (2002) 49 *Africa Today* 3 at 8; A Stewart 'Juridifying Gender Justice: From Global Rights to Local Justice' in J Hatchard and A Perry-Kessaris (eds) *Law and Development: Facing Complexity in the 21st Century* (London, Cavendish Press, 2003) 37 at 43.
[24] Maboreke above n 18 at 116.

a way of distinguishing oneself from others not of 'your group'.[25] Personal laws may also provide fluidity and continuity, and be perceived as offering protection and support—not to be scoffed at in this fast-changing world, where few people feel in control of their lives. Armstrong notes:

> Rethinking tradition means uncovering the ways in which it has both good and bad elements for women, accepting this contradiction and using this contradiction to benefit women.[26]

It has of course been meticulously documented that what passes for personal or customary law in state courts bears no relation to what takes place at the local level.[27] It may well be that the way forward is, as Manji suggests, to embrace other normative orderings. By engaging with pluralism as manifested in non-state normative orders, space may be created for renewed debates and contestations over the content of law.[28] It is said that the living law may be more dynamic and adaptable to changing conditions than is generally acknowledged.

The question remains, should there be conditions attached to this re-engagement with pluralism? Specifically, should pluralism be 'permitted' as long as the laws or norms are in line with the criteria found in CEDAW, the African Protocol on Women's Rights 2003 and other human rights instruments? But is this solution not unnecessarily directive and, indeed, undemocratic? Indeed, is this not just another way of calling for the re-introduction of the colonial repugnancy clause, with customary law being made subject to human rights norms and if found to be 'repugnant', having to yield to human rights principles and be 'repealed'. How realistic is that scenario?

The South African scholar Sinclair pronounces herself worried by pluralism, manifested by the expanded recognition of personal status laws in South Africa as a result of constitutional principles of non-discrimination and respect for all. For Sinclair there is a risk of reinforcing 'racial, cultural and religious discreteness'; in short, the 'divisions and dilemma' of the apartheid era. She seems to indicate a preference for a unitary family law.[29]

---

[25] A Armstrong 'Rethinking Culture and Tradition in Southern Africa: Research from WLSA' in A Stewart (ed) *Gender, Law and Social Justice* (Oxford, Blackstone, 2000) 87 at 93–95. Maboreke above n 18 at 108.

[26] Armstrong above n 25 at 93. She suggests that in real life women adopt a pick and mix stance with relation to legal systems taking from both customary and state law (at 99). Armstrong's interpretation is to be preferred to that of Bonthuys, who seems to see black African women as caught between binaries of state law and custom, seemingly ignoring the fact that they are capable of assuming multiple identities and inhabiting different 'cultural spheres' simultaneously and without contradiction. E Bonthuys 'Accommodating Gender, Race, Culture and Religion: Outside Legal Subjectivity' (2002) 18 *South African Journal on Human Rights* 41 at 58.

[27] M Chanock *Law, Custom and Social Order: The Colonial Experience in Malawi and Zambia* (Cambridge, Cambridge University Press, 1985).

[28] A Manji above n 11 at 437. See also Stewart above n 14 at 11–13. Maboreke above n 18.

[29] J Sinclair 'Embracing New Family Forms, Entrenching Outmoded Stereotypes' in P Lodrup and E Modvar (eds) *Family Life and Human Rights* (Oslo, Gyldendal Akademisk, 2004) 801 at 820, 837.

It is as well to acknowledge here that 'law' does not always yield the desired or equitable result.[30] Law can be used by retrogressive forces, which can include a judiciary that is conservative in its interpretation of both customary and human rights law, as seen in the Zimbabwean Supreme Court in the *Magaya*[31] case. Even when the judiciary does act in a progressive way, there are no guarantees that its judgments will be respected, so that the state can curtail legal gains made. This happened again following the decision of the Zimbabwean Supreme Court in *Rattigan*,[32] in which case the decision of the court to give women the same rights as men to 'import' alien spouses, was curtailed by the Zimbabwean government, which passed a constitutional amendment providing that men were to be put on the same footing as women—that is an equalisation downwards, removing the automatic right to family reunion given to men. The plethora of retrogressive laws passed by the Zimbabwean regime controlling freedom of association and the press, all indicate that law can be used as a tool of oppression. Women's experiences of a repressive state either as direct victims of violence or socio-economic deprivation, or indirectly through family, make them reluctant to engage with the state machinery, of which law is seen as a central tool of oppression. However, the laws that women—and indeed all people—want, are laws that respect the tenets of human rights principles of freedom, democracy, human dignity and equality.[33]

The one constant throughout the book has been the long shadow that has been cast by the catch-all phrase 'culture'.

Culture

Constructed by commentators, UN committees and states in their reports to these committees as the great impediment to women's rights, we have seen little of the positive uses to which culture—or more accurately the plural 'cultures' that exist in any one society—can be put. Article 2(f) of CEDAW admits of and anticipates the possibility of internal reform of cultural norms, providing as it does for the *modification* of customs and practices as well as the abolition of discriminatory ones. Martin and Armstrong[34] both identify the need to work within cultural

---

[30] Martin above n 6 at 76; Kennedy above n 1 at 116–17.
[31] *Magaya v Magaya* 1999 (1) ZLR 100.
[32] *Rattigan v Chief Immigration Officer* 1994 (2) ZLR 54.
[33] These principles are enshrined in the Constitutive Act of the African Union. See B Pityana 'The Challenge of Culture for Human Rights in Africa: The African Charter in Comparative Context' in M Evans and R Murray (eds) *The African Charter on Human and Peoples' Rights: The System in Practice, 1986–2000* (Cambridge, Cambridge University Press, 2002) 219 at 245. See also the preamble to the African Protocol on Women's Rights.
[34] Martin above n 6 at 75–77; Armstrong above n 25 at 96–97.

frameworks to bring about internal transition, which they argue is more likely to bring about long-term change than the top-down approach. That internal legitimacy is important is self-evident. However, so is resistance to change by those who enjoy the benefits of a privileged cultural position. What is difficult is balancing the two—the necessity and urgency for the transformation of gender relations, which self-evidently involves transformation of social-cultural attitudes, and the need to take the current rights holders along on that journey.[35]

It is here worth noting that resistance to change is linked specifically to issues that affect women disproportionately. Women often joke that if men had periods then sanitary provision would be made free. On a serious note, if men experienced illogical deprivations of their rights, as women do, it is unlikely that they would tolerate the defence of 'tradition' or 'that is the way we have always done things' being applied to them. The pan-African challenge to colonial notions of white supremacy is testament to that assertion—inherent characteristics such as race and sex have no place in defining entitlement to being seen as a human being and to the enjoyment of human rights. This should come as a birth right.

In the book we have seen examples of women who challenged socio-cultural norms to seek justice. The picture that emerges is of 'culture' as a contested and shifting terrain. The very existence of case law makes clear that views of custom, culture or religion are not fixed—there is no one cultural truth but multiple versions thereof. Indeed some of the 'customs' that we cling to as being uniquely African are not so. For example, we were not the first or only people to give bridewealth as a precursor to marriage—other cultures have done it, not least the Germans.[36] In 1998, the Southern African San passed a resolution calling for a return to positive cultural values, noting:

> Our communities must address the present inequality between men and women in society. Inequality does not honour our traditions and culture. Strategies to rectify gender inequality must be developed by each community.[37]

It may be trite, but it is true that change is an inevitable part of life. It is not sustainable to seek to defend a cultural practice, whatever its provenance, if it relies for its continuation on the denial or forfeiture by another person of their humanity. It may well be that the continued insistence that what are after all positive values—including the excluded, equal resource distribution—are 'Western', is in itself a form of African self-denigration. It is clearly nonsensical to argue that these positive values could only be Western in origin.[38] A feeling that injustice has been

---

[35] Martin above n 6 at 83.

[36] J May *Changing People, Changing Laws* (Gweru, Mambo Press, 1987) 41.

[37] Indigenous People's Consultation (Shakawe, Botswana, 1998) *Principles Adopted by an Indigenous People's Consultation. Held in Shakawe, Botswana from 6–9 September 1998* (D'Kar and Windhoek, Kuru Development Trust and WIMSA, 1999) [cited in H Becker (2003) at 21 fn].

[38] Pityana above n 33 at 222, 225, 227, 245.

perpetrated upon one is not culture- or nation-specific. We all know when we feel discriminated against or unfairly treated, and we all know that the remedy we would like is that which will remove that discrimination or remedy the unfairness. To seek that is not to crave a 'Western' standard, nor is it a sign that one has 'forgotten one's culture'. An internal revolution of negative cultural constructs is not just possible, it is necessary.

Trickier perhaps is the issue of religion, which is sometimes put forward as the reason for the non-implementation of human rights.[39] The difficulty of reconciling human rights norms and religious principles has been exhaustively dealt with by An Na'im.[40]

Morocco is an interesting example of an Islamic state[41] where change has been imposed by way of parliamentary, some say monarchical, diktat. The 2003 revised family law in Morocco is arguably more woman friendly, providing greater rights and protection to women than its predecessor.[42] However, the manner of its enactment, that is by top-down imposition, has been criticised by those in favour of 'upholding pure Islamic principles' as un-Islamic and therefore to be resisted, and viewed with some equivocation by those who favour the changes wrought but who are not necessarily comfortable with the manner in which change has emerged. This returns us to the problem already aired—how can legal change, which honours principles of equality and other human rights norms of dignity, and which has the potential to bring about widespread social change, be managed without creating resistance? Moreover, how can those committed to democratic principles argue against the imposition of repressive laws in undemocratic states, while at the same time welcoming progressive change brought about by top-down legal change by the self-same repressive governments?

It is perhaps in examining the changing nature of the African family that the future development of women's rights lies.

Democratising the family

The abiding stereotype of Africa and Africans is a love of family. Family is widely constructed as extending beyond the immediate marital unit of a woman, man

[39] S Ali 'Development of the International Norm of Non-Discrimination on the Basis of Sex: An Evaluation of Women's Human Rights in Islam and International Law' in A Stewart (ed) *Gender, Law and Social Justice* (Oxford, Blackstone, 2000) 45 at 63.

[40] A An Na'im 'State Responsibility under International Human Rights Law to Change Religious and Customary Laws' in R Cook (ed) *Human Rights of Women: National and International Perspectives* (Philadelphia, University of Pennsylvania Press, 1994) 167. See also A Mayer *Islam and Human Rights* (Boulder, Westview, 1999).

[41] F Mernissi above n 9 at 17.

[42] G Tremlett 'Morocco Boosts Women's Rights' *Guardian* (London, 21 January 2004).

and their children, to embrace the wider kin group, which may even include non-blood relations. Within this family, whether matrilineal or patrilineal, is a strict hierarchy that determines the flow of obligations and responsibilities. This is clearly laid out in the African Charter and the ACRWC, which both provide that the individual has obligations to the wider family and a child has obligations to obey his or her elders at all times.[43] However, it is this very hierarchical construction of the family that has been criticised as leading to the oppression of the less powerful members of the group—usually women and children. Of this, Coomeraswamy has noted:

> Without equity in the family, it is argued there will be no equity in society. Without mutual respect in the family, we can be sure that there will be no respect for the rights of others in society.[44]

This calls for the democratising of the family. This idea was first mooted by O'Donovan[45] and was more recently advocated by Giddens,[46] who contends that in democratic societies,[47] family relations are more egalitarian.[48] But what is it about the wider concept of democracy at both the micro and macro levels that brings about these changes? The answer may have to do with participation in decision making. Simply put, if one participates in the decision-making process, there is a greater likelihood that one will take ownership of the decisions made and become, to resort to cliché, a stake-holder. The input of more members of the family may in turn influence the path that is taken. It is, for example, doubtful that if consulted about the division of property on death of a husband or father, women would choose the 'brothers and men take all' model that is said to be the hallmark of the primogeniture principle in customary laws of patrilineal societies.

This in turn throws up another challenge. Without financial and other non-tangible resources, women do not come to the table with sufficient bargaining counters with which to engage in a meaningful debate with their male peers.[49] As

---

[43] African Charter art 27(1) and art 29(1) ACRWC art 31(a). Pityana above n 33 at 229–31.

[44] R Coomaraswamy 'To Bellow Like a Cow: Women, Ethnicity and the Discourse of Rights' in R Cook (ed) *Human Rights of Women: National and International Perspectives* (Philadelphia, University of Pennsylvania Press, 1994) 39 at 56. See also H Chekir 'Women, the Law and the Family in Tunisia' (1996) 4 *Gender and Development* 43 at 46.

[45] K O'Donovan *Sexual Divisions in Law* (London, Weidenfeld & Nicolson, 1985); K O'Donovan *Family Law Matters* (London, Pluto Press, 1993).

[46] A Giddens *Runaway World: How Globalisation is Reshaping Our Lives* (London, Profile Books, 2002) 65.

[47] The concept of (what constitutes) democracy is, like the conceptualisation of the state in Africa, heavily contested and has been the subject of many treatises: M Salih *African Democracies and African Politics* (London, Pluto Press, 2001) 3; Bruce above n 9 at 209; P Schraeder (ed) *Exporting Democracy Rhetoric v. Reality* (Boulder, Lynne Rienner Publishers, 2002); J Lane and J Ersson *Democracy: A Comparative Approach* (London, Routledge, 2003).

[48] Cf CEDAW General Recommendation No 21 para 42.

[49] E Frazer 'Democracy, Citizenship and Gender' in A Carter and G Stokes (eds) *Democratic Theory Today* (London, Polity Press, 2002) 73. CEDAW General Recommendation No 21 para 26.

long as the men have primary control over the resources such as land, the women will never be able to overcome the socio-structural inequalities that make proper engagement and negotiation as equals feasible.[50] This is not to say that solving the resource problem will automatically lead to change; much work will need to be done with women to shift the psychological damage and sense of unworthiness that comes from being told that one is not deserving of goods, services and (indeed) having one's humanity honoured.

In line with prevailing policy, not least the United Nation's rights-based approach to development, there has been a general move by agencies and groups towards making greater use of the rights-based framework.[51] However, if a rights-based approach is to mean anything then the World Bank and other international agencies will have to prioritise women's concerns and the effective enjoyment of economic, social and cultural rights by this group. Stewart cautions that poor and disadvantaged women may be left out of the law and development framework. [52]

Although comprising the majority, women's inequality of bargaining power at the domestic level is magnified at the state level. Despite paying lip service to women's rights, most states show little real commitment to delivering substantive change to women's lives. For example, it is doubtful that high-sounding statements such as that contained in the African Protocol on Women's Rights, to the effect that less should be spent on defence and more on social development and the promotion of women,[53] will actually be heeded. Instead, the old pattern of overspending on defence, linked up with corruption, will continue without any positive material change to women's lives occurring.

Women are seen as economically weak, not least because of the way national statistics are produced. These often leave out of the calculation of 'work generated value' the work done by women in subsistence agriculture and in private family enterprises.[54] This in turn reinforces the idea of women as economically unproductive and renders them socially powerless. The only time that women are acknowledged by politicians is at election time, when they are courted for their vote. Some have argued that it is the fault of women for not using their vote to demand of politicians that they address women's issues under pain of not being re-elected at future elections. However, this threat only really has force in states with properly run elections and democratically accountable governments, which definition excludes more African countries than it includes, although this is

---

[50] CEDAW General Recommendation No 21 para 27.
[51] Stewart above n 14 at16. The Commonwealth Secretariat *The Harare Commonwealth Declaration* (London, Commonwealth Secretariat, 2002) para 9.
[52] Stewart above n 14 at 5, 18.
[53] African Protocol on Women's Rights art 10(3).
[54] CEDAW General Recommendation No 16; CEDAW General Recommendation No 17.

changing. Still, democracy or consultation in decision making and true personal and political choice may deliver more than written declarations of formal equality.

Expanding the feminist project in Africa

Increasingly, African feminists have begun to engage with the impact of globalisation on local conditions, and in particular on the exclusion of Africa from effective participation in the world economy and in international decision making.[55] In so doing, African women have expanded the analysis of their own disenfranchisement beyond the northern feminist project. Although African women's rights advocates have grown more conscious of the urban/rural divide and the privileges of class, they have remained, consciously or otherwise, blind to other forms of intersectional discrimination, including disability,[56] issues affecting minority and indigenous women, refugee women and the elderly.

If African women are to escape the same charge of elitism or exclusion of diverse voices from our feminist project(s) that northern women have had thrust upon them, then we have to confront the exclusion of these disenfranchised groups within our work.[57] Specifically, in seeking the expansion of the legal domain to include our concerns, we cannot afford to omit the concerns of others who may have issues that are different to our own. Failure to engage with discrimination faced by different groups within our societies is in itself to reinforce the acceptability of gender-based prejudice. As Williams notes:

> For the historically disempowered, the conferring of rights is symbolic of the denied aspects of their humanity: rights imply a respect that places one in the referential range of self and others that elevates one's status from human body to social being.[58]

In conclusion, it goes without saying that human rights cannot conjure up resources that do not exist. It cannot make rich states give to poor ones.[59]

---

[55] J Oloka-Onyango and S Tamale 'The Personal is Political, or Why Women's Rights are Indeed Human Rights: An African Perspective on International Feminism' (1995) 17 *Human Rights Quarterly* 691 at 703–5.
[56] C McClain-Nhlapo 'Invisible Women' (2004) 14 *Interights Bulletin* 100. See Kennedy above n 1 at 113.
[57] Williams above n 14 at 165.
[58] *Ibid* at 53. See also M Minow 'Interpreting Rights: an Essay for Robert Cover' (1987) 96 *Yale Law Journal* 1860 at 1910, as cited in H Charlesworth and C Chinkin *Boundaries of International Law* (Manchester, Manchester University Press, 2000) at 210.
[59] This is clearly evidenced by the difficulty of meeting targets such as those contained in the Millennium Development Goals, and in the frequent challenges to rich countries to allocate larger shares of their budgets to development aid.

However, the growing jurisprudence on socio-economic rights shows that in some instances it can force states to re-think the internal and international distribution of resources. It can also provide a framework within which the nations of the world can agree on baseline standards.[60] For women, that means having our humanity recognised legally, socially and politically. I can do no better than to finish with the words of John Eekelaar:

> [T]o recognise people as having rights from the moment of their birth continuously into adulthood could turn out, politically to be the most radical step of all.[61]

---

[60] This is one of the criticisms of human rights. As we have seen, states cannot agree on the interpretation of human rights norms, nor can they agree on what constitutes a minimum standard.

[61] J Eekelaar 'The Importance of Thinking that Children Have Rights' (1992) 6 *International Journal of Law, Policy and the Family* 221 at 234.

APPENDIX A

Protocol to the African Charter on Human and Peoples' Rights on the Rights of Women in Africa

The States Parties to this Protocol,

CONSIDERING that Article 66 of the African Charter on Human and Peoples' Rights provides for special protocols or agreements, if necessary, to supplement the provisions of the African Charter, and that the Assembly of Heads of State and Government of the Organization of African Unity meeting in its Thirty-first Ordinary Session in Addis Ababa, Ethiopia, in June 1995, endorsed by resolution AHG/Res.240 (XXXI) the recommendation of the African Commission on Human and Peoples' Rights to elaborate a Protocol on the Rights of Women in Africa;

CONSIDERING that Article 2 of the African Charter on Human and Peoples' Rights enshrines the principle of non-discrimination on the grounds of race, ethnic group, colour, sex, language, religion, political or any other opinion, national and social origin, fortune, birth or other status;

FURTHER CONSIDERING that Article 18 of the African Charter on Human and Peoples' Rights calls on all States Parties to eliminate every discrimination against women and to ensure the protection of the rights of women as stipulated in international declarations and conventions;

NOTING that Articles 60 and 61 of the African Charter on Human and Peoples' Rights recognise regional and international human rights instruments and African practices consistent with international norms on human and peoples' rights as being important reference points for the application and interpretation of the African Charter;

RECALLING that women's rights have been recognised and guaranteed in all international human rights instruments, notably the Universal Declaration of Human Rights, the International Covenant on Civil and Political Rights, the International Covenant on Economic, Social and Cultural Rights, the Convention on the Elimination of All Forms of Discrimination Against Women and its Optional Protocol, the African Charter on the Rights and Welfare of the Child, and all other international and regional conventions and covenants relating to the rights of women as being inalienable, interdependent and indivisible human rights;

NOTING that women's rights and women's essential role in development, have been reaffirmed in the United Nations Plans of Action on the Environment and Development in 1992, on Human Rights in 1993, on Population and Development in 1994 and on Social Development in 1995; RECALLING ALSO United Nations Security Council's Resolution 1325 (2000) on the role of Women in promoting peace and security;

REAFFIRMING the principle of promoting gender equality as enshrined in the Constitutive Act of the African Union as well as the New Partnership for Africa's Development, relevant Declarations, Resolutions and Decisions, which underline the commitment of the African States to ensure the full participation of African women as equal partners in Africa's development;

FURTHER NOTING that the African Platform for Action and the Dakar Declaration of 1994 and the Beijing Platform for Action of 1995 call on all Member States of the United Nations, which have made a solemn commitment to implement them, to take concrete steps to give greater attention to the human rights of women in order to eliminate all forms of discrimination and of gender-based violence against women;

RECOGNISING the crucial role of women in the preservation of African values based on the principles of equality, peace, freedom, dignity, justice, solidarity and democracy;

BEARING IN MIND related Resolutions, Declarations, Recommendations, Decisions, Conventions and other Regional and Sub-Regional Instruments aimed at eliminating all forms of discrimination and at promoting equality between women and men;

CONCERNED that despite the ratification of the African Charter on Human and Peoples' Rights and other international human rights instruments by the majority of States Parties, and their solemn commitment to eliminate all forms of discrimination and harmful practices against women, women in Africa still continue to be victims of discrimination and harmful practices;

FIRMLY CONVINCED that any practice that hinders or endangers the normal growth and affects the physical and psychological development of women and girls should be condemned and eliminated;

DETERMINED to ensure that the rights of women are promoted, realised and protected in order to enable them to enjoy fully all their human rights;

HAVE AGREED AS FOLLOWS:

Article 1: Definitions

For the purpose of the present Protocol:

a. "African Charter" means the African Charter on Human and Peoples' Rights;
b. "African Commission" means the African Commission on Human and Peoples' Rights;
c. "Assembly" means the Assembly of Heads of State and Government of the African Union;
d. "AU" means the African Union;
e. "Constitutive Act" means the Constitutive Act of the African Union;
f. "Discrimination against women" means any distinction, exclusion or restriction or any differential treatment based on sex and whose objectives or effects compromise or destroy the recognition, enjoyment or the exercise by women, regardless of their marital status, of human rights and fundamental freedoms in all spheres of life;

g. "Harmful Practices" means all behaviour, attitudes and/or practices which negatively affect the fundamental rights of women and girls, such as their right to life, health, dignity, education and physical integrity;

h. "NEPAD" means the New Partnership for Africa's Development established by the Assembly;

i. "States Parties" means the States Parties to this Protocol;

j. "Violence against women" means all acts perpetrated against women which cause or could cause them physical, sexual, psychological, and economic harm, including the threat to take such acts; or to undertake the imposition of arbitrary restrictions on or deprivation of fundamental freedoms in private or public life in peace time and during situations of armed conflicts or of war;

k. "Women" means persons of female gender, including girls.

Article 2: Elimination of Discrimination Against Women

1. States Parties shall combat all forms of discrimination against women through appropriate legislative, institutional and other measures. In this regard they shall:

   a. include in their national constitutions and other legislative instruments, if not already done, the principle of equality between women and men and ensure its effective application;

   b. enact and effectively implement appropriate legislative or regulatory measures, including those prohibiting and curbing all forms of discrimination particularly those harmful practices which endanger the health and general well-being of women;

   c. integrate a gender perspective in their policy decisions, legislation, development plans, programmes and activities and in all other spheres of life;

   d. take corrective and positive action in those areas where discrimination against women in law and in fact continues to exist;

   e. support the local, national, regional and continental initiatives directed at eradicating all forms of discrimination against women.

2. States Parties shall commit themselves to modify the social and cultural patterns of conduct of women and men through public education, information, education and communication strategies, with a view to achieving the elimination of harmful cultural and traditional practices and all other practices which are based on the idea of the inferiority or the superiority of either of the sexes, or on stereotyped roles for women and men.

Article 3: Right to Dignity

1. Every woman shall have the right to dignity inherent in a human being and to the recognition and protection of her human and legal rights;

2. Every woman shall have the right to respect as a person and to the free development of her personality;

3. States Parties shall adopt and implement appropriate measures to prohibit any exploitation or degradation of women;

4. States Parties shall adopt and implement appropriate measures to ensure the protection of every woman's right to respect for her dignity and protection of women from all forms of violence, particularly sexual and verbal violence.

Article 4: The Rights to Life, Integrity and Security of the Person

1. Every woman shall be entitled to respect for her life and the integrity and security of her person. All forms of exploitation, cruel, inhuman or degrading punishment and treatment shall be prohibited.
2. States Parties shall take appropriate and effective measures to:

   a. enact and enforce laws to prohibit all forms of violence against women including unwanted or forced sex whether the violence takes place in private or public;
   b. adopt such other legislative, administrative, social and economic measures as may be necessary to ensure the prevention, punishment and eradication of all forms of violence against women;
   c. identify the causes and consequences of violence against women and take appropriate measures to prevent and eliminate such violence;
   d. actively promote peace education through curricula and social communication in order to eradicate elements in traditional and cultural beliefs, practices and stereotypes which legitimise and exacerbate the persistence and tolerance of violence against women;
   e. punish the perpetrators of violence against women and implement programmes for the rehabilitation of women victims;
   f. establish mechanisms and accessible services for effective information, rehabilitation and reparation for victims of violence against women;
   g. prevent and condemn trafficking in women, prosecute the perpetrators of such trafficking and protect those women most at risk;
   h. prohibit all medical or scientific experiments on women without their informed consent;
   i. provide adequate budgetary and other resources for the implementation and monitoring of actions aimed at preventing and eradicating violence against women;
   j. ensure that, in those countries where the death penalty still exists, not to carry out death sentences on pregnant or nursing women.
   k. ensure that women and men enjoy equal rights in terms of access to refugee status, determination procedures and that women refugees are accorded the full protection and benefits guaranteed under international refugee law, including their own identity and other documents.

Article 5: Elimination of Harmful Practices

States Parties shall prohibit and condemn all forms of harmful practices which negatively affect the human rights of women and which are contrary to recognised international standards. States Parties shall take all necessary legislative and other measures to eliminate such practices, including:

a. creation of public awareness in all sectors of society regarding harmful practices through information, formal and informal education and outreach programmes;
b. prohibition, through legislative measures backed by sanctions, of all forms of female genital mutilation, scarification, medicalisation and para-medicalisation of female genital mutilation and all other practices in order to eradicate them;
c. provision of necessary support to victims of harmful practices through basic services such as health services, legal and judicial support, emotional and psychological counselling as well as vocational training to make them self-supporting;
d. protection of women who are at risk of being subjected to harmful practices or all other forms of violence, abuse and intolerance.

Article 6: Marriage

States Parties shall ensure that women and men enjoy equal rights and are regarded as equal partners in marriage. They shall enact appropriate national legislative measures to guarantee that:

a. no marriage shall take place without the free and full consent of both parties;
b. the minimum age of marriage for women shall be 18 years;
c. monogamy is encouraged as the preferred form of marriage and that the rights of women in marriage and family, including in polygamous marital relationships are promoted and protected;
d. every marriage shall be recorded in writing and registered in accordance with national laws, in order to be legally recognised;
e. the husband and wife shall, by mutual agreement, choose their matrimonial regime and place of residence;
f. a married woman shall have the right to retain her maiden name, to use it as she pleases, jointly or separately with her husband's surname;
g. a woman shall have the right to retain her nationality or to acquire the nationality of her husband;
h. a woman and a man shall have equal rights, with respect to the nationality of their children except where this is contrary to a provision in national legislation or is contrary to national security interests;
i. a woman and a man shall jointly contribute to safeguarding the interests of the family, protecting and educating their children;
j. during her marriage, a woman shall have the right to acquire her own property and to administer and manage it freely.

Article 7: Separation, Divorce and Annulment of Marriage

States Parties shall enact appropriate legislation to ensure that women and men enjoy the same rights in case of separation, divorce or annulment of marriage. In this regard, they shall ensure that:

a. separation, divorce or annulment of a marriage shall be effected by judicial order;

b. women and men shall have the same rights to seek separation, divorce or annulment of a marriage;
c. in case of separation, divorce or annulment of marriage, women and men shall have reciprocal rights and responsibilities towards their children. In any case, the interests of the children shall be given paramount importance;
d. in case of separation, divorce or annulment of marriage, women and men shall have the right to an equitable sharing of the joint property deriving from the marriage.

Article 8: Access to Justice and Equal Protection before the Law

Women and men are equal before the law and shall have the right to equal protection and benefit of the law. States Parties shall take all appropriate measures to ensure:

a. effective access by women to judicial and legal services, including legal aid;
b. support to local, national, regional and continental initiatives directed at providing women access to legal services, including legal aid;
c. the establishment of adequate educational and other appropriate structures with particular attention to women and to sensitise everyone to the rights of women;
d. that law enforcement organs at all levels are equipped to effectively interpret and enforce gender equality rights;
e. that women are represented equally in the judiciary and law enforcement organs;
f. reform of existing discriminatory laws and practices in order to promote and protect the rights of women.

Article 9: Right to Participation in the Political and Decision-Making Process

1. States Parties shall take specific positive action to promote participative governance and the equal participation of women in the political life of their countries through affirmative action, enabling national legislation and other measures to ensure that:

a. women participate without any discrimination in all elections;
b. women are represented equally at all levels with men in all electoral processes;
c. women are equal partners with men at all levels of development and implementation of State policies and development programmes.

2. States Parties shall ensure increased and effective representation and participation of women at all levels of decision-making.

Article 10: Right to Peace

1. Women have the right to a peaceful existence and the right to participate in the promotion and maintenance of peace.
2. States Parties shall take all appropriate measures to ensure the increased participation of women:

a. in programmes of education for peace and a culture of peace;

b. in the structures and processes for conflict prevention, management and resolution at local, national, regional, continental and international levels;

c. in the local, national, regional, continental and international decision making structures to ensure physical, psychological, social and legal protection of asylum seekers, refugees, returnees and displaced persons, in particular women;

d. in all levels of the structures established for the management of camps and settlements for asylum seekers, refugees, returnees and displaced persons, in particular, women;

e. in all aspects of planning, formulation and implementation of post conflict reconstruction and rehabilitation.

3. States Parties shall take the necessary measures to reduce military expenditure significantly in favour of spending on social development in general, and the promotion of women in particular.

Article 11: Protection of Women in Armed Conflicts

1. States Parties undertake to respect and ensure respect for the rules of international humanitarian law applicable in armed conflict situations which affect the population, particularly women.

2. States Parties shall, in accordance with the obligations incumbent upon them under the international humanitarian law, protect civilians including women, irrespective of the population to which they belong, in the event of armed conflict.

3. States Parties undertake to protect asylum seeking women, refugees, returnees and internally displaced persons, against all forms of violence, rape and other forms of sexual exploitation, and to ensure that such acts are considered war crimes, genocide and/or crimes against humanity and that their perpetrators are brought to justice before a competent criminal jurisdiction.

4. States Parties shall take all necessary measures to ensure that no child, especially girls under 18 years of age, take a direct part in hostilities and that no child is recruited as a soldier.

Article 12: Right to Education and Training

1. States Parties shall take all appropriate measures to:

a. eliminate all forms of discrimination against women and guarantee equal opportunity and access in the sphere of education and training;

b. eliminate all stereotypes in textbooks, syllabuses and the media, that perpetuate such discrimination;

c. protect women, especially the girl-child from all forms of abuse, including sexual harassment in schools and other educational institutions and provide for sanctions against the perpetrators of such practices;

d. provide access to counselling and rehabilitation services to women who suffer abuses and sexual harassment;

e. integrate gender sensitisation and human rights education at all levels of education curricula including teacher training.

2. States Parties shall take specific positive action to:

 f. promote literacy among women;

 g. promote education and training for women at all levels and in all disciplines, particularly in the fields of science and technology;

 h. promote the enrolment and retention of girls in schools and other training institutions and the organisation of programmes for women who leave school prematurely.

Article 13: Economic and Social Welfare Rights

States Parties shall adopt and enforce legislative and other measures to guarantee women equal opportunities in work and career advancement and other economic opportunities. In this respect, they shall:

 a. promote equality of access to employment;

 b. promote the right to equal remuneration for jobs of equal value for women and men;

 c. ensure transparency in recruitment, promotion and dismissal of women and combat and punish sexual harassment in the workplace;

 d. guarantee women the freedom to choose their occupation, and protect them from exploitation by their employers violating and exploiting their fundamental rights as recognised and guaranteed by conventions, laws and regulations in force;

 e. create conditions to promote and support the occupations and economic activities of women, in particular, within the informal sector;

 f. establish a system of protection and social insurance for women working in the informal sector and sensitise them to adhere to it;

 g. introduce a minimum age for work and prohibit the employment of children below that age, and prohibit, combat and punish all forms of exploitation of children, especially the girl-child;

 h. take the necessary measures to recognise the economic value of the work of women in the home;

 i. guarantee adequate and paid pre and post-natal maternity leave in both the private and public sectors;

 j. ensure the equal application of taxation laws to women and men;

 k. recognise and enforce the right of salaried women to the same allowances and entitlements as those granted to salaried men for their spouses and children;

 l. recognise that both parents bear the primary responsibility for the upbringing and development of children and that this is a social function for which the State and the private sector have secondary responsibility;

 m. take effective legislative and administrative measures to prevent the exploitation and abuse of women in advertising and pornography.

Article 14: Health and Reproductive Rights

1. States Parties shall ensure that the right to health of women, including sexual and reproductive health is respected and promoted. This includes:

 a. the right to control their fertility;

b. the right to decide whether to have children, the number of children and the spacing of children;

c. the right to choose any method of contraception;

d. the right to self protection and to be protected against sexually transmitted infections, including HIV/AIDS;

e. the right to be informed on one's health status and on the health status of one's partner, particularly if affected with sexually transmitted infections, including HIV/AIDS, in accordance with internationally recognised standards and best practices;

f. the right to have family planning education.

2. States Parties shall take all appropriate measures to:

g. provide adequate, affordable and accessible health services, including information, education and communication programmes to women especially those in rural areas;

h. establish and strengthen existing pre-natal, delivery and post-natal health and nutritional services for women during pregnancy and while they are breast-feeding;

i. protect the reproductive rights of women by authorising medical abortion in cases of sexual assault, rape, incest, and where the continued pregnancy endangers the mental and physical health of the mother or the life of the mother or the foetus.

Article 15: Right to Food Security

States Parties shall ensure that women have the right to nutritious and adequate food. In this regard, they shall take appropriate measures to:

a. provide women with access to clean drinking water, sources of domestic fuel, land, and the means of producing nutritious food;

b. establish adequate systems of supply and storage to ensure food security.

Article 16: Right to Adequate Housing

Women shall have the right to equal access to housing and to acceptable living conditions in a healthy environment. To ensure this right, States Parties shall grant to women, whatever their marital status, access to adequate housing.

Article 17: Right to Positive Cultural Context

1. Women shall have the right to live in a positive cultural context and to participate at all levels in the determination of cultural policies.

2. States Parties shall take all appropriate measures to enhance the participation of women in the formulation of cultural policies at all levels.

Article 18: Right to a Healthy and Sustainable Environment

1. Women shall have the right to live in a healthy and sustainable environment.

2. States Parties shall take all appropriate measures to:

a. ensure greater participation of women in the planning, management and preservation of the environment and the sustainable use of natural resources at all levels;
b. promote research and investment in new and renewable energy sources and appropriate technologies, including information technologies and facilitate women's access to, and participation in their control;
c. protect and enable the development of women's indigenous knowledge systems;
d. (c. sic.) regulate the management, processing, storage and disposal of domestic waste;
e. (d. sic.) ensure that proper standards are followed for the storage, transportation and disposal of toxic waste.

Article 19: Right to Sustainable Development

Women shall have the right to fully enjoy their right to sustainable development. In this connection, the States Parties shall take all appropriate measures to:

a. introduce the gender perspective in the national development planning procedures;
b. ensure participation of women at all levels in the conceptualisation, decision-making, implementation and evaluation of development policies and programmes;
c. promote women's access to and control over productive resources such as land and guarantee their right to property;
d. promote women's access to credit, training, skills development and extension services at rural and urban levels in order to provide women with a higher quality of life and reduce the level of poverty among women;
e. take into account indicators of human development specifically relating to women in the elaboration of development policies and programmes; and
f. ensure that the negative effects of globalisation and any adverse effects of the implementation of trade and economic policies and programmes are reduced to the minimum for women.

Article 20: Widows' Rights

States Parties shall take appropriate legal measures to ensure that widows enjoy all human rights through the implementation of the following provisions:

a. that widows are not subjected to inhuman, humiliating or degrading treatment;
b. a widow shall automatically become the guardian and custodian of her children, after the death of her husband, unless this is contrary to the interests and the welfare of the children;
c. a widow shall have the right to remarry, and in that event, to marry the person of her choice.

Article 21: Right to Inheritance

1. A widow shall have the right to an equitable share in the inheritance of the property of her husband. A widow shall have the right to continue to live in the matrimonial house. In case of remarriage, she shall retain this right if the house belongs to her or she has inherited it.

2. Women and men shall have the right to inherit, in equitable shares, their parents' properties.

Article 22: Special Protection of Elderly Women

The States Parties undertake to:

a. provide protection to elderly women and take specific measures commensurate with their physical, economic and social needs as well as their access to employment and professional training;
b. ensure the right of elderly women to freedom from violence, including sexual abuse, discrimination based on age and the right to be treated with dignity.

Article 23: Special Protection of Women with Disabilities

The States Parties undertake to:

a. ensure the protection of women with disabilities and take specific measures commensurate with their physical, economic and social needs to facilitate their access to employment, professional and vocational training as well as their participation in decision-making;
b. ensure the right of women with disabilities to freedom from violence, including sexual abuse, discrimination based on disability and the right to be treated with dignity.

Article 24: Special Protection of Women in Distress

The States Parties undertake to:

a. ensure the protection of poor women and women heads of families including women from marginalized population groups and provide the an environment suitable to their condition and their special physical, economic and social needs;
b. ensure the right of pregnant or nursing women or women in detention by providing them with an environment which is suitable to their condition and the right to be treated with dignity.

Article 25: Remedies

States Parties shall undertake to:

a. provide for appropriate remedies to any woman whose rights or freedoms, as herein recognised, have been violated;
b. ensure that such remedies are determined by competent judicial, administrative or legislative authorities, or by any other competent authority provided for by law.

Article 26: Implementation and Monitoring

1. States Parties shall ensure the implementation of this Protocol at national level, and in their periodic reports submitted in accordance with Article 62 of the African Charter, indicate the legislative and other measures undertaken for the full realisation of the rights herein recognised.
2. States Parties undertake to adopt all necessary measures and in particular shall provide budgetary and other resources for the full and effective implementation of the rights herein recognised.

Article 27: Interpretation

The African Court on Human and Peoples' Rights shall be seized with matters of interpretation arising from the application or implementation of this Protocol.

Article 28: Signature, Ratification and Accession

1. This Protocol shall be open for signature, ratification and accession by the States Parties, in accordance with their respective constitutional procedures.
2. The instruments of ratification or accession shall be deposited with the Chairperson of the Commission of the AU.

Article 29: Entry into Force

1. This Protocol shall enter into force thirty (30) days after the deposit of the fifteenth (15) instrument of ratification.
2. For each State Party that accedes to this Protocol after its coming into force, the Protocol shall come into force on the date of deposit of the instrument of accession.
3. The Chairperson of the Commission of the AU shall notify all Member States of the coming into force of this Protocol.

Article 30: Amendment and Revision

1. Any State Party may submit proposals for the amendment or revision of this Protocol.
2. Proposals for amendment or revision shall be submitted, in writing, to the Chairperson of the Commission of the AU who shall transmit the same to the States Parties within thirty (30) days of receipt thereof.
3. The Assembly, upon advice of the African Commission, shall examine these proposals within a period of one (1) year following notification of States Parties, in accordance with the provisions of paragraph 2 of this article.
4. Amendments or revision shall be adopted by the Assembly by a simple majority.
5. The amendment shall come into force for each State Party, which has accepted it thirty (30) days after the Chairperson of the Commission of the AU has received notice of the acceptance.

Article 31: Status of the Present Protocol

None of the provisions of the present Protocol shall affect more favourable provisions for the realisation of the rights of women contained in the national legislation of States Parties or in any other regional, continental or international conventions, treaties or agreements applicable in these States Parties.

Article 32: Transitional Provisions

Pending the establishment of the African Court on Human and Peoples' Rights, the African Commission on Human and Peoples' Rights shall be the seized with matters of interpretation arising from the application and implementation of this Protocol.

Adopted by the 2nd Ordinary Session
of the Assembly of the Union

Maputo, 11 July 2003

APPENDIX B

Convention on the Elimination of All Forms of Discrimination Against Women 1979

The States Parties to the present Convention,

Noting that the Charter of the United Nations reaffirms faith in fundamental human rights, in the dignity and worth of the human person and in the equal rights of men and women,

Noting that the Universal Declaration of Human Rights affirms the principle of the inadmissibility of discrimination and proclaims that all human beings are born free and equal in dignity and rights and that everyone is entitled to all the rights and freedoms set forth therein, without distinction of any kind, including distinction based on sex,

Noting that the States Parties to the International Covenants on Human Rights have the obligation to ensure the equal rights of men and women to enjoy all economic, social, cultural, civil and political rights,

Considering the international conventions concluded under the auspices of the United Nations and the specialized agencies promoting equality of rights of men and women,

Noting also the resolutions, declarations and recommendations adopted by the United Nations and the specialized agencies promoting equality of rights of men and women,

Concerned, however, that despite these various instruments extensive discrimination against women continues to exist,

Recalling that discrimination against women violates the principles of equality of rights and respect for human dignity, is an obstacle to the participation of women, on equal terms with men, in the political, social, economic and cultural life of their countries, hampers the growth of the prosperity of society and the family and makes more difficult the full development of the potentialities of women in the service of their countries and of humanity,

Concerned that in situations of poverty women have the least access to food, health, education, training and opportunities for employment and other needs,

Convinced that the establishment of the new international economic order based on equity and justice will contribute significantly towards the promotion of equality between men and women,

Emphasizing that the eradication of apartheid, all forms of racism, racial discrimination, colonialism, neo-colonialism, aggression, foreign occupation and domination and interference in the internal affairs of States is essential to the full enjoyment of the rights of men and women,

Affirming that the strengthening of international peace and security, the relaxation of international tension, mutual co-operation among all States irrespective of their social and economic systems, general and complete disarmament, in particular nuclear disarmament under strict and effective international control, the affirmation of the principles of justice, equality and mutual benefit in relations among countries and the realization of the right of peoples under alien and colonial domination and foreign occupation to self-determination and independence, as well as respect for national sovereignty and territorial integrity, will promote social progress and development and as a consequence will contribute to the attainment of full equality between men and women,

Convinced that the full and complete development of a country, the welfare of the world and the cause of peace require the maximum participation of women on equal terms with men in all fields,

Bearing in mind the great contribution of women to the welfare of the family and to the development of society, so far not fully recognized, the social significance of maternity and the role of both parents in the family and in the upbringing of children, and aware that the role of women in procreation should not be a basis for discrimination but that the upbringing of children requires a sharing of responsibility between men and women and society as a whole,

Aware that a change in the traditional role of men as well as the role of women in society and in the family is needed to achieve full equality between men and women,

Determined to implement the principles set forth in the Declaration on the Elimination of Discrimination against Women and, for that purpose, to adopt the measures required for the elimination of such discrimination in all its forms and manifestations,

Have agreed on the following:

PART I

Article I

For the purposes of the present Convention, the term "discrimination against women" shall mean any distinction, exclusion or restriction made on the basis of sex which has the effect or purpose of impairing or nullifying the recognition, enjoyment or exercise by women, irrespective of their marital status, on a basis of equality of men and women, of human rights and fundamental freedoms in the political, economic, social, cultural, civil or any other field.

Article 2

States Parties condemn discrimination against women in all its forms, agree to pursue by all appropriate means and without delay a policy of eliminating discrimination against women and, to this end, undertake:

(a) To embody the principle of the equality of men and women in their national constitutions or other appropriate legislation if not yet incorporated therein and to ensure, through law and other appropriate means, the practical realization of this principle;

(b) To adopt appropriate legislative and other measures, including sanctions where appropriate, prohibiting all discrimination against women;

(c) To establish legal protection of the rights of women on an equal basis with men and to ensure through competent national tribunals and other public institutions the effective protection of women against any act of discrimination;

(d) To refrain from engaging in any act or practice of discrimination against women and to ensure that public authorities and institutions shall act in conformity with this obligation;

(e) To take all appropriate measures to eliminate discrimination against women by any person, organization or enterprise;

(f) To take all appropriate measures, including legislation, to modify or abolish existing laws, regulations, customs and practices which constitute discrimination against women;

(g) To repeal all national penal provisions which constitute discrimination against women.

Article 3

States Parties shall take in all fields, in particular in the political, social, economic and cultural fields, all appropriate measures, including legislation, to en sure the full development and advancement of women , for the purpose of guaranteeing them the exercise and enjoyment of human rights and fundamental freedoms on a basis of equality with men.

Article 4

1. Adoption by States Parties of temporary special measures aimed at accelerating de facto equality between men and women shall not be considered discrimination as defined in the present Convention, but shall in no way entail as a consequence the maintenance of unequal or separate standards; these measures shall be discontinued when the objectives of equality of opportunity and treatment have been achieved.

2. Adoption by States Parties of special measures, including those measures contained in the present Convention, aimed at protecting maternity shall not be considered discriminatory.

Article 5

States Parties shall take all appropriate measures:

(a) To modify the social and cultural patterns of conduct of men and women, with a view to achieving the elimination of prejudices and customary and all other practices which are based on the idea of the inferiority or the superiority of either of the sexes or on stereotyped roles for men and women;

(b) To ensure that family education includes a proper understanding of maternity as a social function and the recognition of the common responsibility of men and women in the upbringing and development of their children, it being understood that the interest of the children is the primordial consideration in all cases.

Article 6

States Parties shall take all appropriate measures, including legislation, to suppress all forms of traffic in women and exploitation of prostitution of women.

PART II

Article 7

States Parties shall take all appropriate measures to eliminate discrimination against women in the political and public life of the country and, in particular, shall ensure to women, on equal terms with men, the right:

(a) To vote in all elections and public referenda and to be eligible for election to all publicly elected bodies;

(b) To participate in the formulation of government policy and the implementation thereof and to hold public office and perform all public functions at all levels of government;

(c) To participate in non-governmental organizations and associations concerned with the public and political life of the country.

Article 8

States Parties shall take all appropriate measures to ensure to women, on equal terms with men and without any discrimination, the opportunity to represent their Governments at the international level and to participate in the work of international organizations.

Article 9

1. States Parties shall grant women equal rights with men to acquire, change or retain their nationality. They shall ensure in particular that neither marriage to an alien nor change of nationality by the husband during marriage shall automatically change the nationality of the wife, render her stateless or force upon her the nationality of the husband.

2. States Parties shall grant women equal rights with men with respect to the nationality of their children.

PART III

Article 10

States Parties shall take all appropriate measures to eliminate discrimination against women in order to ensure to them equal rights with men in the field of education and in particular to ensure, on a basis of equality of men and women:

(a) The same conditions for career and vocational guidance, for access to studies and for the achievement of diplomas in educational establishments of all categories in rural as well as in urban areas; this equality shall be ensured in pre-school, general, technical, professional and higher technical education, as well as in all types of vocational training;

(b) Access to the same curricula, the same examinations, teaching staff with qualifications of the same standard and school premises and equipment of the same quality;

(c) The elimination of any stereotyped concept of the roles of men and women at all levels and in all forms of education by encouraging coeducation and other types of education which will help to achieve this aim and, in particular, by the revision of textbooks and school programmes and the adaptation of teaching methods;

(d) The same opportunities to benefit from scholarships and other study grants;

(e) The same opportunities for access to programmes of continuing education, including adult and functional literacy programmes, particulary those aimed at reducing, at the earliest possible time, any gap in education existing between men and women;

(f) The reduction of female student drop-out rates and the organization of programmes for girls and women who have left school prematurely;

(g) The same Opportunities to participate actively in sports and physical education;

(h) Access to specific educational information to help to ensure the health and well-being of families, including information and advice on family planning.

Article 11

1. States Parties shall take all appropriate measures to eliminate discrimination against women in the field of employment in order to ensure, on a basis of equality of men and women, the same rights, in particular:

(a) The right to work as an inalienable right of all human beings;

(b) The right to the same employment opportunities, including the application of the same criteria for selection in matters of employment;

(c) The right to free choice of profession and employment, the right to promotion, job security and all benefits and conditions of service and the right to receive vocational training and retraining, including apprenticeships, advanced vocational training and recurrent training;

(d) The right to equal remuneration, including benefits, and to equal treatment in respect of work of equal value, as well as equality of treatment in the evaluation of the quality of work;

(e) The right to social security, particularly in cases of retirement, unemployment, sickness, invalidity and old age and other incapacity to work, as well as the right to paid leave;

(f) The right to protection of health and to safety in working conditions, including the safeguarding of the function of reproduction.

2. In order to prevent discrimination against women on the grounds of marriage or maternity and to ensure their effective right to work, States Parties shall take appropriate measures:

(a) To prohibit, subject to the imposition of sanctions, dismissal on the grounds of pregnancy or of maternity leave and discrimination in dismissals on the basis of marital status;

(b) To introduce maternity leave with pay or with comparable social benefits without loss of former employment, seniority or social allowances;

(c) To encourage the provision of the necessary supporting social services to enable parents to combine family obligations with work responsibilities and participation in public life, in particular through promoting the establishment and development of a network of child-care facilities;

(d) To provide special protection to women during pregnancy in types of work proved to be harmful to them.

3. Protective legislation relating to matters covered in this article shall be reviewed periodically in the light of scientific and technological knowledge and shall be revised, repealed or extended as necessary.

Article 12

1. States Parties shall take all appropriate measures to eliminate discrimination against women in the field of health care in order to ensure, on a basis of equality of men and women, access to health care services, including those related to family planning.

2. Notwithstanding the provisions of paragraph I of this article, States Parties shall ensure to women appropriate services in connection with pregnancy, confinement and the post-natal period, granting free services where necessary, as well as adequate nutrition during pregnancy and lactation.

Article 13

States Parties shall take all appropriate measures to eliminate discrimination against women in other areas of economic and social life in order to ensure, on a basis of equality of men and women, the same rights, in particular:

(a) The right to family benefits;

(b) The right to bank loans, mortgages and other forms of financial credit;

(c) The right to participate in recreational activities, sports and all aspects of cultural life.

Article 14

1. States Parties shall take into account the particular problems faced by rural women and the significant roles which rural women play in the economic survival of their families, including their work in the non-monetized sectors of the economy, and shall take all appropriate measures to ensure the application of the provisions of the present Convention to women in rural areas.

2. States Parties shall take all appropriate measures to eliminate discrimination against women in rural areas in order to ensure, on a basis of equality of men and women, that they participate in and benefit from rural development and, in particular, shall ensure to such women the right:

(a) To participate in the elaboration and implementation of development planning at all levels;

(b) To have access to adequate health care facilities, including information, counselling and services in family planning;

(c) To benefit directly from social security programmes;

(d) To obtain all types of training and education, formal and non-formal, including that relating to functional literacy, as well as, inter alia, the benefit of all community and extension services, in order to increase their technical proficiency;

(e) To organize self-help groups and co-operatives in order to obtain equal access to economic opportunities through employment or self employment;

(f) To participate in all community activities;

(g) To have access to agricultural credit and loans, marketing facilities, appropriate technology and equal treatment in land and agrarian reform as well as in land resettlement schemes;

(h) To enjoy adequate living conditions, particularly in relation to housing, sanitation, electricity and water supply, transport and communications.

PART IV

Article 15

1. States Parties shall accord to women equality with men before the law.

2. States Parties shall accord to women, in civil matters, a legal capacity identical to that of men and the same opportunities to exercise that capacity. In particular, they shall give women equal rights to conclude contracts and to administer property and shall treat them equally in all stages of procedure in courts and tribunals.

3. States Parties agree that all contracts and all other private instruments of any kind with a legal effect which is directed at restricting the legal capacity of women shall be deemed null and void.

4. States Parties shall accord to men and women the same rights with regard to the law relating to the movement of persons and the freedom to choose their residence and domicile.

Article 16

1. States Parties shall take all appropriate measures to eliminate discrimination against women in all matters relating to marriage and family relations and in particular shall ensure, on a basis of equality of men and women:

(a) The same right to enter into marriage;

(b) The same right freely to choose a spouse and to enter into marriage only with their free and full consent;

(c) The same rights and responsibilities during marriage and at its dissolution;

(d) The same rights and responsibilities as parents, irrespective of their marital status, in matters relating to their children; in all cases the interests of the children shall be paramount;

(e) The same rights to decide freely and responsibly on the number and spacing of their children and to have access to the information, education and means to enable them to exercise these rights;

(f) The same rights and responsibilities with regard to guardianship, wardship, trusteeship and adoption of children, or similar institutions where these concepts exist in national legislation; in all cases the interests of the children shall be paramount;

(g) The same personal rights as husband and wife, including the right to choose a family name, a profession and an occupation;

(h) The same rights for both spouses in respect of the ownership, acquisition, management, administration, enjoyment and disposition of property, whether free of charge or for a valuable consideration.

2. The betrothal and the marriage of a child shall have no legal effect, and all necessary action, including legislation, shall be taken to specify a minimum age for marriage and to make the registration of marriages in an official registry compulsory.

PART V

Article 17

1. For the purpose of considering the progress made in the implementation of the present Convention, there shall be established a Committee on the Elimination of Discrimination against Women (hereinafter referred to as the Committee) consisting, at the time of entry into force of the Convention, of eighteen and, after ratification of or accession to the Convention by the thirty-fifth State Party, of twenty-three experts of high moral standing and competence in the field covered by the Convention. The experts shall be elected by States Parties from among their nationals and shall serve in their personal capacity, consideration being given to equitable geographical distribution and to the representation of the different forms of civilization as well as the principal legal systems.

2. The members of the Committee shall be elected by secret ballot from a list of persons nominated by States Parties. Each State Party may nominate one person from among its own nationals.

3. The initial election shall be held six months after the date of the entry into force of the present Convention. At least three months before the date of each election the Secretary-General of the United Nations shall address a letter to the States Parties inviting them to submit their nominations within two months. The Secretary-General shall prepare a list

in alphabetical order of all persons thus nominated, indicating the States Parties which have nominated them, and shall submit it to the States Parties.

4. Elections of the members of the Committee shall be held at a meeting of States Parties convened by the Secretary-General at United Nations Headquarters. At that meeting, for which two thirds of the States Parties shall constitute a quorum, the persons elected to the Committee shall be those nominees who obtain the largest number of votes and an absolute majority of the votes of the representatives of States Parties present and voting.

5. The members of the Committee shall be elected for a term of four years. However, the terms of nine of the members elected at the first election shall expire at the end of two years; immediately after the first election the names of these nine members shall be chosen by lot by the Chairman of the Committee.

6. The election of the five additional members of the Committee shall be held in accordance with the provisions of paragraphs 2, 3 and 4 of this article, following the thirty-fifth ratification or accession. The terms of two of the additional members elected on this occasion shall expire at the end of two years, the names of these two members having been chosen by lot by the Chairman of the Committee.

7. For the filling of casual vacancies, the State Party whose expert has ceased to function as a member of the Committee shall appoint another expert from among its nationals, subject to the approval of the Committee.

8. The members of the Committee shall, with the approval of the General Assembly, receive emoluments from United Nations resources on such terms and conditions as the Assembly may decide, having regard to the importance of the Committee's responsibilities.

9. The Secretary-General of the United Nations shall provide the necessary staff and facilities for the effective performance of the functions of the Committee under the present Convention.

Article 18

1. States Parties undertake to submit to the Secretary-General of the United Nations, for consideration by the Committee, a report on the legislative, judicial, administrative or other measures which they have adopted to give effect to the provisions of the present Convention and on the progress made in this respect:

(a) Within one year after the entry into force for the State concerned;

(b) Thereafter at least every four years and further whenever the Committee so requests.

2. Reports may indicate factors and difficulties affecting the degree of fulfilment of obligations under the present Convention.

Article 19

1. The Committee shall adopt its own rules of procedure.

2. The Committee shall elect its officers for a term of two years.

Article 20

1. The Committee shall normally meet for a period of not more than two weeks annually in order to consider the reports submitted in accordance with article 18 of the present Convention.

2. The meetings of the Committee shall normally be held at United Nations Headquarters or at any other convenient place as determined by the Committee.

Article 21

1. The Committee shall, through the Economic and Social Council, report annually to the General Assembly of the United Nations on its activities and may make suggestions and general recommendations based on the examination of reports and information received from the States Parties. Such suggestions and general recommendations shall be included in the report of the Committee together with comments, if any, from States Parties.

2. The Secretary-General of the United Nations shall transmit the reports of the Committee to the Commission on the Status of Women for its information.

Article 22

The specialized agencies shall be entitled to be represented at the consideration of the implementation of such provisions of the present Convention as fall within the scope of their activities. The Committee may invite the specialized agencies to submit reports on the implementation of the Convention in areas falling within the scope of their activities.

PART VI

Article 23

Nothing in the present Convention shall affect any provisions that are more conducive to the achievement of equality between men and women which may be contained:

    (a) In the legislation of a State Party; or

    (b) In any other international convention, treaty or agreement in force for that State.

Article 24

States Parties undertake to adopt all necessary measures at the national level aimed at achieving the full realization of the rights recognized in the present Convention.

Article 25

1. The present Convention shall be open for signature by all States.

2. The Secretary-General of the United Nations is designated as the depositary of the present Convention.

3. The present Convention is subject to ratification. Instruments of ratification shall be deposited with the Secretary-General of the United Nations.

4. The present Convention shall be open to accession by all States. Accession shall be effected by the deposit of an instrument of accession with the Secretary-General of the United Nations.

Article 26

1. A request for the revision of the present Convention may be made at any time by any State Party by means of a notification in writing addressed to the Secretary-General of the United Nations.

2. The General Assembly of the United Nations shall decide upon the steps, if any, to be taken in respect of such a request.

Article 27

1. The present Convention shall enter into force on the thirtieth day after the date of deposit with the Secretary-General of the United Nations of the twentieth instrument of ratification or accession.

2. For each State ratifying the present Convention or acceding to it after the deposit of the twentieth instrument of ratification or accession, the Convention shall enter into force on the thirtieth day after the date of the deposit of its own instrument of ratification or accession.

Article 28

1. The Secretary-General of the United Nations shall receive and circulate to all States the text of reservations made by States at the time of ratification or accession.

2. A reservation incompatible with the object and purpose of the present Convention shall not be permitted.

3. Reservations may be withdrawn at any time by notification to this effect addressed to the Secretary-General of the United Nations, who shall then inform all States thereof. Such notification shall take effect on the date on which it is received.

Article 29

1. Any dispute between two or more States Parties concerning the interpretation or application of the present Convention which is not settled by negotiation shall, at the request of one of them, be submitted to arbitration. If within six months from the date of the request for arbitration the parties are unable to agree on the organization of the arbitration, any one of those parties may refer the dispute to the International Court of Justice by request in conformity with the Statute of the Court.

2. Each State Party may at the time of signature or ratification of the present Convention or accession thereto declare that it does not consider itself bound by paragraph I of this article. The other States Parties shall not be bound by that paragraph with respect to any State Party which has made such a reservation.

3. Any State Party which has made a reservation in accordance with paragraph 2 of this article may at any time withdraw that reservation by notification to the Secretary-General of the United Nations.

Article 30

The present Convention, the Arabic, Chinese, English, French, Russian and Spanish texts of which are equally authentic, shall be deposited with the Secretary-General of the United Nations.

IN WITNESS WHEREOF the undersigned, duly authorized, have signed the present Convention.

BIBLIOGRAPHY

—— 'Children and HIV/AIDS' *Observer* (London, 11 July 2004).

—— 'Don't Sign Anything' *Africa Confidential* (2004) 45 No 25.

—— 'Gay Marriage Heads to South African Appeals Court' in http://www.365.gay.com.

—— 'Gender Imbalance Contributing to the Spread of AIDS-Legislator' *Herald* (Harare, 14 October 2003) downloaded from http://www.allafrica.com/stories/printable/200310140275.html.

—— 'Genital Landscaping, Labia Remodelling and Vestal Vagina: Female Genital Mutilation or Female Genital Cosmetic Surgery' [Media Articles on Designer Vaginas] (2001) *Jenda: A Journal of Culture and African Women's Studies* at http://www.jendajournal.com/jenda/vol1.1/Dvagina.html.

—— 'Indifference to Women's Cries for Help Deplorable' *Daily News* (Zimbabwe, 5 March 2003) downloaded from: http://www.dailynews.co.zw/daily/2003/March/March5/10800.html.

—— 'Lesbian Marriage Gets the Nod' at http://www.news24.com/News24/South_Africa/News, 2-7-1442_1628956,000.html.

—— 'A Life in the Day' *Sunday Times* (magazine) (London, 15 September 2002) 66.

—— 'Mrs Mubarak Launches Strong Initiative against FGM' *Egyptian Gazette* (Cairo, 22 June 2003).

—— 'Out of the Shadows, into the World' *Economist* (London, 19 June 2004) 29.

—— 'Outrage over Moi Order to Ministers' *Daily Nation* (Nairobi, 28 November 2001) at http://www.nationaudio.com/News/Daily/Nation/Today/News/News31html.

—— 'Rwanda Has the Most Women MPs' *Guardian* (London, 23 October 2003).

—— 'Saving Amina Lawal: Human Rights Symbolism and the Dangers of Colonialism' (2004) 117 (7) *Harvard Law Review* 2365.

—— 'Sylvia Tamale Attacked for Supporting Non-discrimination on Basis of Sexual Orientation' at www.gwsafrica.org/news/tamale2.htm.

—— 'Vanessa Wilde's Secret Diary' *Sunday Times* (London, 15 September 2002) 39.

—— 'The World's Most Popular Man Reaches 80 and Ponders Buying a Wife in Exchange for 60 Cows' *Guardian* (London, 17 July 1998).

A

AAWORD (Association of African Women for Research and Development) 'A Statement on Genital Mutilation' reproduced in H Steiner and P Alston *International Human Rights in Context: Law, Politics, Morals* (Oxford, Clarendon Press, 2000) 418.

Abdullah, H 'Religious Revivalism, Human Rights Activism and the Struggle for Women's Rights in Nigeria' in A An Na'im (ed) *Cultural Transformation and Human Rights in Africa* (London, Zed Press, 2002) 151.

Abraham, Z and Hajiyannis, H 'The Reproductive Health Needs of Young Refugees in South Africa' (2001) 39 *Women's Health Project Review* 17.

Abusharaf, R 'Revisiting Feminist Discourse on Infibulation: Responses from Sudanese Feminists' in B Shell-Duncan and Y Hernlund (eds) *Female 'Circumcision' in Africa: Culture, Controversy and Change* (Colorado, Lynne Rienner Publishers, 2000) 151.

Action for Southern Africa (ACTSA) *Freedom to Grow: Bringing down the Barriers to Southern Africa's Trade with Europe* (London, ACTSA, 2001).

Action for Southern Africa (ACTSA) 'Africa: What the G8 Must Deliver: A Briefing by Action for Southern Africa and World Development Movement' (London, ACTSA, 2002).

Adamu, F 'A Double Edged Sword: Challenging Women's Oppression within Muslim Societies in Northern Nigeria' in C Sweetman (ed) *Gender, Religion and Spirituality* (Oxford, OXFAM, 1998) 56.

Adeleye Fayemi, B 'Creating a New World with New Visions: African Feminism and Trends in the Global Women's Movement' in J Kerr *et al* (eds) *The Future of Women's Rights* (London, Zed Press, 2004) 38.

Adelman, S 'Constitutionalism, Pluralism and Democracy in Africa' (1998) 42 *Journal of Legal Pluralism* 73.

Adelman, S and Paliwala, A (eds) *Law and Crisis in the Third World* (London, Zell, 1993) 243.

Adinkrah, K 'Ghana's Marriage Ordinance: An Inquiry into a Legal Transplant for Social Change' (1980) 18 *African Law Studies* 1.

Advisory Council on International Affairs *Universality of Human Rights and Cultural Diversity* (The Hague, Advisory Council on International Affairs, 1998).

Afro-Arab Consultation on 'Legal Tools for the Prevention of Female Genital Mutilation' Cairo, 23 June 2003 (Cairo Declaration on FGM 2003) available at http://www.aidos.it.

Afshar, H *Islam and Feminisms: An Iranian Case Study* (Basingstoke, Palgrave, 1998).

Ahmadu, F 'Rites and Wrongs: An Insider/Outsider Reflects on Power and Excision' in B Shell-Duncan and Y Hernlund (eds) *Female'Circumcision' in Africa: Culture, Controversy and Change* (Colorado, Lynne Rienner Publishers, 2000) 283.

Ahmed, S 'Islam and Development: Opportunities and Constraints for Somali Women' in C Sweetman (ed) *Gender, Religion and Spirituality* (Oxford, OXFAM, 1998) 69.

AIDOS, No Peace without Justice and TAMWA 'Solemn Appeal against Female Genital Mutilation' at www.stopfgm.org.

Akande, J 'Women and the Law' in A Obilade (ed) *Women in Law* (Lagos, Southern University Law Centre and Faculty of Law, 1993) 6.

Akandji-Kombe, J 'Introduction to the Cotonou Agreement' in C Heyns (ed) *Human Rights Law in Africa* (The Hague, Martinus Nijhoff, 2004) vol 1 at 703.

P Akpan 'Health Complications Arising from FGM' in The African Women's Development and Communication Network (FEMNET) (2001) *Our Rights*, downloaded from http://www.africaonline.co.ke/femnet/rights2.html.

Albertyn, C and Goldblaat, B 'Facing the Challenge of Transformation: Difficulties in the Development of an Indigenous Jurisprudence of Equality' (1998) 14 *South African Journal on Human Rights* 248.

Alexander, J, McGregor, J and Ranger, T *Violence and Memory* (Oxford, James Currey, 2000).

Alfredson, G and Tomasevski, K (eds) *Thematic Guide to Documents on the Human Rights of Women* (Hague, Martinus Nijhoff, 1995).

Ali, S 'Development of the International Norm of Non-Discrimination on the Basis of Sex: An Evaluation of Women's Human Rights in Islam and International Law' in A Stewart (ed) *Gender, Law and Social Justice* (Oxford, Blackstone, 2000) 45.

Allain, J and O'Shea, A 'African Disunity: Comparing Human Rights Law and Practice of North and South African States' (2002) 24(2) *Human Rights Quarterly* 86.

Allott, A 'Reforming the Law in Africa: Aims, Difficulties and Techniques' in A Sanders (ed) *Southern Africa in Need of Law Reform* (Durban, Butterworths, 1981) 228.

Alston, P and Crawford, J (eds) *The Future of UN Human Rights Treaty Monitoring* (Cambridge, Cambridge University Press, 2000).

Amadiume, I *Male Daughters, Female Husbands: Gender and Sex in an African Society* (London, Zed Press, 1987).

Amnesty International *Broken Bodies, Shattered Minds: Torture and Ill-Treatment of Women* (London, Amnesty International, 2001).

Amnesty International 'Kenya: Rape—The Invisible Crime' (2002) AI-Index: AFR 32/001/2002.

Amnesty International 'The Protocol on the Rights of Women in Africa: Strengthening the Promotion and Protection of Women's Human Rights in Africa' (June 2004) AI-Index: IOR 63/005/2004.

Amnesty International 'Open Letter to the Chairman of the African Union (AU) Seeking Clarification and Assurances that the Establishment of an Effective Court on Human and Peoples' Rights Will Not Be Delayed or Undermined' (9 August 2004) AI-Index: IOR 63/008/2004downloaded from http://web.amnesty.org/library/index/engior630082004.

Amnesty International *Sudan, Darfur: Rape as a Weapon of War* (19 July 2004) AI-Index: AFR 54/076/2004.

An Na'im, A *Human Rights in Cross-Cultural Perspectives* (Philadelphia, University of Pennsylvania Press, 1992).

An Na'im, A 'Cultural Transformation and Normative Consensus on the Best Interests of the Child' (1994) 8 *International Journal of Law, Policy and the Family* 62.

An Na'im, A 'State Responsibility under International Human Rights Law to Change Religious and Customary Laws' in R Cook (ed) *Human Rights of Women: National and International Perspectives* (Philadelphia, University of Pennsylvania Press, 1994) 167.

An Na'im, A (ed) *Cultural Transformation and Human Rights in Africa* (London, Zed Press, 2002).

An Na'im, A 'Introduction' in A An Na'im (ed) *Cultural Transformation and Human Rights in Africa* (London, Zed Press, 2002) 1.

An Na'im, A (ed) *Islamic Family Law in a Changing World: A Global Resource Book* (London, Zed Press, 2002).

An Na'im, A and Deng, F (eds) *Human Rights in Africa: Cross-Cultural Perspectives* (Washington DC, The Brookings Institution, 1990).

An Na'im, A and Hammond, J 'Cultural Transformation and Human Rights' in A An Na'im (ed) *Cultural Transformation and Human Rights* (London, Zed Press, 2002) 14.

Anacleti, O 'Research into Local Culture: Implications for Participatory Development' in D Eade (ed) *Development and Social Diversity* (Oxford, OXFAM, 1999) 69.

Andreassen, B 'Democratization and Human Rights beyond Borders: on the Donor–Recipient Connection' in P Nherere and M d'Engelbronner-Kolf (eds) *The Institutionalisation of Human Rights in Southern Africa* (Oslo, Nordic Human Rights Publications, 1993) 195.

Angelou, M *The Heart of a Woman* (London, Virago, 1986).

Annan, K 'Foreword' in UNICEF *The State of the World's Children 2004* (New York, UNICEF, 2004).

Aouij, E 'Marriage and Family Relations' in United Nations (ed) *Bringing International Human Rights Law Home* (New York, United Nations, 2002).

Appiah, A *In My Father's House: Africa in the Philosophy of Culture* (New York, Oxford University Press, 1992).

Appiah, A 'Citizens of the World' in M Gibney (ed) *Globalizing Rights* (Oxford, Oxford University Press, 2003) 189.

Appleton, J 'At My Age I Should be Sitting under That Tree: The Impact of AIDS on Tanzania's Lake Shore Communities' in C Sweetman (ed) *Gender and Lifecycles* (Oxford, OXFAM, 2000) 19.

Arach-Amoko, S 'The Rights of the Child: The Case of Uganda' in United Nations (ed) *Bringing International Human Rights Home* (New York, United Nations, 2002) 150.

Arigbede, M 'COPODIN Family: Dare to Be Different' in H Chigudu (ed) *Composing a New Song: Stories of Empowerment from Africa* (London, Commonwealth Secretariat, 2003) 1.

Armstrong, A 'Maintenance Statutes in Six Countries in Southern Africa' (1990) 34 *Journal of African Law* 132.

Armstrong, A 'Internalising International Women's Rights Norms' in P Nherere and M d'Engelbronner-Kolf (eds) *The Institutionalisation of Human Rights in Southern Africa* (Oslo, Nordic Human Rights Publications, 1993) 55.

Armstrong, A 'School and Sadza' (1994) 8 *International Journal of Law Policy and the Family* 150.

Armstrong, A *A Child Belongs to Everyone: Law, Family and the Construction of the Best Interests of the Child in Zimbabwe*, Innocenti Occasional Papers 11 (Florence, International Child Development Centre, 1995).

Armstrong, A *Culture and Choice: Lessons from Survivors of Gender Violence in Zimbabwe* (Harare, Violence against Women Research Project, 1998).

Armstrong, A 'Rethinking Culture and Tradition in Southern Africa: Research from WLSA' in A Stewart (ed) *Gender, Law and Social Justice* (Oxford, Blackstone, 2000) 87.

Armstrong, A and Ncube, W (eds) *Women and Law in Southern Africa* (Harare, Zimbabwe Publishing House, 1987).

Armstrong, A and Stewart, J (eds) *The Legal Situation of Women in Southern Africa*, (Harare, University of Zimbabwe Publications, 1990).

Armstrong, A *et al* 'Uncovering Reality: Excavating Women's Rights in the African Family' (1993) 7 *International Journal of Law, Policy and the Family* 314.

Armstrong, S 'Rape in South Africa: An Invisible Part of Apartheid's Legacy' in C Sweetman and F de Selincourt (eds) *Population and Reproductive Rights* (Oxford, OXFAM, 1994) 35.

Article 19 *What's the Story? Results from Research into Media Coverage of Refugees and Asylum Seekers in the UK* (London, Article 19, 2003) available at http://www.article19.org.

Arnfred, S (ed) *Rethinking Sexualities in Africa* (Lund, Nordic Africa Institute, 2004).

Arnfred, S 'Re-thinking Sexualities in Africa: Introduction' in S Arnfred (ed) *Rethinking Sexualities in Africa* (Lund, Nordic Africa Institute, 2004) 7.

Arroba, A 'A Voice of Alarm: A Historian's View of the Family' (1996) 4 *Gender and Development* 8.

Arthur, M 'Mozambique: Women in the Armed Struggle' in P McFadden (ed) *Southern Africa in Transition: A Gendered Perspective* (Harare, SAPES, 1998) 67.

Association of Church Development Projects, *Resolution on Female Genital Mutilation Practice in Ghana and Efforts towards Eradication* (October 2000), on file with author.

Atsenuwa, A 'Women's Rights within the Family Context: Law and Practice' in A Obilade (ed) *Women in Law* (Lagos, Southern University Law Centre and Faculty of Law, 1993) 116.

Aubel, J and Toure, I 'Strengthening Grandmother Networks to Improve Community Nutrition: Experience from Senegal' in C Sweetman (ed) *Gender, Development and Health* (Oxford, OXFAM, 2001) 62.

Awaken 'Fresh Demands Made on African Governments to end FGM' (May 2004) *Awaken* 4.

Awaken 'UN Agencies Express Concern about Lack of Political Will to End FGM' (May 2004) *Awaken* 5.

Awaken 'Elders Vow to Continue with FGM' (May 2004) *Awaken* 7.

Awaken 'The Impact of Community Abandonment of FGC on Circumcisors' (May 2004) *Awaken* 8.

Awaken 'Interest Picks Up on Tostan's Strategy to End FGM' (May 2004) *Awaken* 8.

Awaken 'Police Blamed for Lack of Action against Perpetrators of FGM' (May 2004) *Awaken* 9.

Awaken 'Tanzania: Circumcisors Working Quietly to Avoid Law' (May 2004) *Awaken* 9.

B

Ba, M *So Long a Letter* (London, Heinemann, 1989).

Babatunde, E *Women's Rights versus Women's Rites* (Eritrea, Africa World Press, 1998).

Bainham, A (ed) *The International Survey of Family Law 1997* (The Hague, Kluwer International, 1999).

Bainham, A (ed) *International Survey of Family Law 2001* (Bristol, Jordan Publishing, 2001).

Bainham, A (ed) *International Survey of Family Law 2002* (Bristol, Jordan Publishing, 2002).

Baird, V *Sex, Love and Homophobia* (London, Amnesty International, 2004).

Banda, F *Women and Law in Zimbabwe: Access to Justice on Divorce* (unpublished doctoral thesis, University of Oxford, 1993).

Banda, F 'Custody and the Best Interests of the Child in Zimbabwe' (1994) 8 *International Journal of Law, Policy and the Family* 191.

Banda, F 'The Provision of Maintenance for Women and Children in Zimbabwe' (1995) 2 *Cardozo Women's Law Journal* 71.

Banda, F 'Inheriting Trouble: Changing the Face of the Customary Law of Succession in Zimbabwe' in A Bainham (ed) *International Survey of Family Law 1997* (The Hague, Kluwer International, 1999) 525.

Banda, F 'Inheritance and Marital Rape' in A Bainham (ed) *International Survey of Family Law 2001* (Bristol, Jordan Publishing, 2001) 475.

Banda, F 'Between a Rock and a Hard Place: Courts and Customary Law in Zimbabwe' in A Bainham (ed) *International Survey of Family Law 2002* (Bristol, Jordan Publishing, 2002) 471.

Banda, F 'Global Standards: Local Values' (2003) 17 *International Journal of Law, Policy and the Family* 1.

Banda, F 'The Protection of Women's Rights in Africa' (2004) 14 *Interights Bulletin* 147.

Banda, F and Chinkin, C *Gender, Minorities and Indigenous Peoples* (London, Minority Rights Group, 2004).

Banmeke, F 'Violence and Sexual Abuse of Women' in B Owasonoye (ed) *Reproductive Rights of Women in Nigeria: The Legal, Economic and Cultural* Dimensions (Lagos, Human Development Initiatives, 1999) 77.

Baratta, R 'Should Invalid Reservations to Human Rights Treaties be Disregarded?' (2000) 11 *European Journal of International Law* 413.

Barnes, G and Paton, L *The Child Brides* [documentary film] (London, Umbrella Pictures, 1998).

Bayliss, C 'Safe Motherhood in the Time of AIDS: The Illusion of Reproductive "Choice" ' in C Sweetman (ed) *Gender, Development and Health* (Oxford, OXFAM, 2001) 40.

BBC 1 'Sex and the Holy City' *Panorama* documentary presented by S Bradshaw (12 October 2003) http://www.bbc.co.uk/panorama. Excerpts from the programme reproduced in 'Sex and the Holy City' (2004) 1 *Index on Censorship* 84.

BBC Radio 4 'Development on the Frontline' *Analysis* programme (27 November, 2003) available at: http://newsvote.bbc.co.uk/nol/shared/spl/hi/programmes/analysis/transcripts/27_11_03.txt

Beall, J 'Doing Gender from Top to Bottom? The South African Case' (2001) 12 *Women: A Cultural Review* 135.

Becker, H 'The Least Sexist Society? Perspectives on Gender, Change and Violence among the Southern African San' (2003) 29 *Journal of Southern African Studies* 1.

Bekker, G 'The Social and Economic Rights Action Center and the Center for Economic and Social Rights/Nigeria' (2003) 47 *Journal of African Law* 126.

Belden Fields, A *Re-Thinking Human Rights for the New Millennium* (New York, Palgrave, 2003).

Belembaogo, A 'The Best Interests of the Child: The Case of Burkina Faso' (1994) 8 *International Journal of Law Policy and the Family* 202.

Benedek, W Kisaakye, E and Oberleitner, G *Human Rights of Women: International Instruments and African Experiences* (London, Zed Press, 2002).

Bennett, T 'Conflict of Laws: The Application of Customary Law in Zimbabwe' (1981) 30 *International and Comparative Law Quarterly* 59.

Bennett, T 'The Equality Clause and Customary Law' (1994) 10 *South African Journal on Human Rights* 122.

Bennett, T *Human Rights and African Customary Law under the South African Constitution* (Cape Town, Juta, 1995).

Bennett, T 'Abortion and Human Rights in Sub-Saharan Africa' (2000) 3 *Initiatives in Reproductive Health Policy* 1.

Bennett, T *Customary Law in South Africa* (Cape Town, Juta, 2004).

Berkey, J 'Circumcision Circumscribed: Female Excision and Cultural Accommodation in the Medieval Near East' (1996) 28 *International Journal of Middle Eastern Studies* 19.

Berry, D 'Conflicts between Minority Women and Traditional Structures: International Law, Rights and Culture' (1998) 7 *Social and Legal Studies* 55.

Beyani, C 'Toward a More Effective Guarantee of Women's Rights in the African Human Rights System' in R Cook (ed) *Human Rights of Women: National and International Perspectives* (Philadelphia, University of Pennsylvania Press, 1994) 285.

Beyani, C 'The Needs of Refugee Women: A Human Rights Perspective' (1995) 3 *Gender and Development* 29.

Beyani, C *Human Rights Standards and the Movement of People within States* (Oxford, Oxford University Press, 2000).

Bhavanani, K (ed) *Feminism and Race* (Oxford, Oxford University Press, 2001).

Bhavanani, K 'Women, Culture, Development: Three Visions' in K Bhavanani *et al* (eds) *Feminist Futures: Re-imagining Women, Culture and Development* (London, Zed Press, 2003) 7.

Bhavanani, K, Froan, J and Kurian, P (eds) *Feminist Futures: Re-imagining Women, Culture and Development* (London, Zed Press, 2003).

Bhebe, N and Ranger, T (eds) *The Historical Dimensions of Democracy and Human Rights in Zimbabwe* Volume 1 (Harare, Zimbabwe Publishing House, 2001).

Bhebe, N and Ranger, T 'Introduction' in N Bhebe and T Ranger (eds) *The Historical Dimensions of Democracy and Human Rights in Zimbabwe* (Harare, Zimbabwe Publishing House, 2001) xxi.

Bonthuys, E 'Accommodating Gender, Race, Culture and Religion: Outside Legal Subjectivity' (2002) 18 *South African Journal on Human Rights* 41.

Boseley, S 'Show Them the Money' *Guardian* (London, 30 October 2003).

Boseley, S 'US Firms Try to Block Cheap AIDS Drugs' *Guardian* (London, 20 March 2004).

Boseley, S 'Clinton's AIDS Deal Snubs Bush Plan' *Guardian* (London, 7 April 2004).

Boseley, S 'US Applauded for U-Turn on Cheap AIDS Drugs' *Guardian* (London, 18 May 2004).

Boserup, E *Women's Role in Economic Development* (New York, St Martins Press, 1970).

Bowman, C and Kuenyehia, A (eds) *Women and Law in Sub-Saharan Africa* (Accra, SEDCO Publishing, 2003).

Boyle, E and Preves, S 'National Politics as International Process: The Case of Anti-Female Genital Cutting Laws' (2000) 34 *Law and Society Review* 703.

British Medical Association *The Medical Profession and Human Rights: Handbook for a Changing Agenda* (London, Zed Books, 2001).

British Medical Council *Female Genital Mutilation: Caring for Parents and Child Protection. Guidance from the British Medical Association* (London, British Medical Association, 2001).

Bruce, S *Politics and Religion* (Cambridge, Polity Press, 2003).

Bujra, J 'Targeting Men for a Change: AIDS Discourse and Activism in Africa' in F Cleaver (ed) *Masculinities Matter: Men, Gender and Development* (London, Zed Press, 2002) 209.

Burchill, R '*Soobramoney v Minister of Health (Kwa-Zulu Natal)* Constitutional Court of South Africa CCT 32/97 (26 November 1997)' (1998) *Human Rights Law Review* 41.

Burman, S 'First World Solutions for Third World Problems' in L Weitzman and M Maclean (eds) *Economic Consequences of Divorce: The International Perspective* (Oxford, Clarendon Press, 1992) 367.

Burrows, N 'The 1979 Convention on the Elimination of All Forms of Discrimination against Women' (1985) 32 *Netherlands International Law Review* 419.

Buss, D 'Robes, Relics and Rights: The Vatican and the Beijing Conference on Women' (1998) 7 *Social and Legal Studies* 339.

Butegwa, F 'Using the African Charter on Human and Peoples' Rights to Secure Women's Access to Land in Africa' in R Cook (ed) *Human Rights of Women: National and International Perspectives* (Philadelphia, University of Pennsylvania Pres, 1994) 495.

Butegwa, F 'Mediating Culture and Human Rights in Favour of Land Rights for Women in Africa: A Framework for Community Level Action' in A An Na'im (ed) *Cultural Transformation and Human Rights in Africa* (London, Zed Press, 2002) 108.

Butegwa, F, Mukasa, F and Mozere, S *Human Rights of African Women in Conflict Situations: The WILDAF Initiative* (Harare, WILDAF, 1995).

Byrnes, A and Connors, J 'Enforcing the Human Rights of Women: A Complaints Procedure for the Convention on the Elimination of All Forms of Discrimination against Women' (1996) 21 *Brooklyn Journal of International Law* 679.

Byrnes, A, Connors, J and Bik, L (eds) *Advancing the Human Rights of Women: Using International Human Rights Standards in Domestic Litigation* (London, Commonwealth Secretariat, 1994).

C

Cairo Declaration on FGM, 2003 available at http://www.aidos.it.

Cairo Institute for Human Rights Studies 'In the Name of Shariah' (1996) *Sawasiah* 12.

Cairo Institute for Human Rights Studies 'Reservation is not a Justification' (1996) *Sawasiah* 8.

Cameron, E 'Aids Denial and Holocaust Denial—Aids, Justice and the Courts in South Africa' (2003) 120 *South Africa Law Journal* 525.

Cappelletti, M and Garth, B (eds) *Access to Justice Volume 3* (Florence, Tipografia, 1978).

Carbert, A, Stanchieri, J and Cook, R *A Handbook for Advocacy in the African Human Rights System Advancing Reproductive and Sexual Health* (Nairobi, IPAS, 2002).

Carter, A and Stokes, G (eds) *Democratic Theory Today* (Cambridge, Polity Press, 2002).

Center for Reproductive Law and Policy (CRLP) and FIDA Kenya *Women of the World Report: Anglophone Africa* (New York, CRLP, 1997).

Center for Reproductive Law and Policy (CLRP) 'Legislation on Female Genital Mutilation in the United States' (1997) *Reproductive Freedom in Focus* 4.

Center for Reproductive Law and Policy (CRLP) *ICPD+5 Gains for Women despite Opposition* (New York, CRLP, 2000).

Center for Reproductive Law and Policy *Women of the World: Francophone Africa Laws and Policies Affecting Their Reproductive Lives* (New York, Center for Reproductive Rights, 2001).

Center for Reproductive Law and Policy (CRLP) 'Teenage Girl in Sierra Leone Dies after Female Circumcision' (2002) XI *Reproductive Freedom News* 8.

Center for Reproductive Rights (CRR) 'Common Reproductive Health Concerns in Anglophone Africa May 2002' at http:///.crlp.org/pub_fac_wowaa.html.

Center for Reproductive Rights (CRR) 'Using the Law to Protect Kenya's Young Women from FGM' (2002) XI *Reproductive Freedom News* 6.

Center for Reproductive Rights (CRR) *Female Genital Mutilation: A Matter of Human Rights* (New York, CRR, 2002).

Center for Reproductive Rights (CRR) 'International Provisions Guaranteeing Freedom from FCFGM' (paper submitted to the Afro-Arab Expert Consultation on Legal Tools for the Prevention of Female Genital Mutilation, Cairo, June 2003).

Center for Reproductive Rights (CRR) and Association des Juristes Maliennes *Claiming Our Rights: Surviving Pregnancy and Childbirth in Mali* (New York, CRR; Bamako, Association des Juristes Maliennes, 2003).

Center for Reproductive Rights (CRR) and Toronto Centre for Reproductive Rights *Bringing Rights to Bear: An Analysis of the Work of the United Nations Treaty Monitoring Bodies on Reproductive and Sexual Rights* (New York, CRR, 2002).

Chanda, A *Informal Education for Human Rights in Zambia* (Harare, SAPES, 1997).

Chandler, J *Women without Husbands: An Exploration of the Margins of Marriage* (London, Macmillan, 1991).

CHANGE *Non Consensual Sex in Marriage Information Package Number One* (London, CHANGE, 1999) (cyclostyle).

CHANGE *Non Consensual Sex in Marriage Project* (London, CHANGE, 2002) (cyclostyle).

CHANGE 'NCSM Marriage, Culture and Violence: Messages from the Survey' in *Non Consensual Sex in Marriage Project* (London, CHANGE, 2002).

CHANGE 'Non Consensual Sex in Marriage: Definitions Related to NCSM' in CHANGE *Non Consensual Sex in Marriage* (London, CHANGE, 2002).

Chanock, M 'Neo-Traditionalism and the Customary Law in Malawi' in M Hay and M Wright (eds) *African Women and the Law: Historical Perspectives* (Boston, Boston University Press, 1980) 80.

Chanock, M *Law, Custom and Social Order: The Colonial Experience in Malawi and Zambia* (Cambridge, Cambridge University Press, 1985).

Chanock, M 'Neither Customary nor Legal: African Customary Law in an Era of Family Law Reform' (1989) 3 *International Journal of Law and Family* 72.

Chanock, M 'Law, State and Culture: Thinking about "Customary Law" after Apartheid' (1991) *Acta Juridica* 52.

Chanock, M *The Making of the South African Legal Culture 1902–1936* (Cambridge, Cambridge University Press, 2001).

Chanock, M 'Human Rights and Cultural Branding: Who Speaks and How?' in A An Na'im (ed) *Cultural Transformation and Human Rights in Africa* (London, Zed Press, 2002) 38.

Charlesworth, H 'Human Rights as Men's Rights' in J Peters and A Wolper (eds) *Women's Rights, Human Rights: International Feminist Perspectives* (New York, Routledge, 1995) 103.

Charlesworth., H 'Women's Human Rights Defined' in G Moon (ed) *Making Her Rights a Reality: Women's Human Rights and Development* (Victoria, Community Aid Abroad, 1995) 35.

Charlesworth, H 'Author! Author! A Response to David Kennedy' (2002) 15 *Harvard Human Rights Journal* 127.

Charlesworth, H and Chinkin, C *Boundaries of International Law* (Manchester, Manchester University Press, 2000).

Charlesworth, H, Chinkin, C and Wright, S 'Feminist Approaches to International Law' (1991) 85 *American Journal of International Law* 613.

Cheater, A 'The Role and Position of Women in Pre-Colonial and Colonial Zimbabwe' (1986) XIII *Zambezia*.

Chekir, H 'Women, the Law and the Family in Tunisia' (1996) 4 *Gender and Development* 43.

Chenaux-Repond, M *Women Farmers' Position: Our Response to the Report of the Land Tenure Commission* (1996).

Chiba, M (ed) *Asian Indigenous Laws in Interaction with Received Laws* (New York, KPI, 1986).

Chigudu, H (ed) *Composing a New Song: Stories of Empowerment from Africa* (London, Commonwealth Secretariat, 2003).

Chigudu, H 'Conclusion' in H Chigudu (ed) *Composing a New Song: Stories of Empowerment from Africa* (London, Commonwealth Secretariat, 2003) 161.

Chigwedere, A *Lobolo: The Pros and Cons* (Gweru, Mambo Press, 1982).

Chinkin, C 'Rape and Sexual Abuse of Women in International Law' (1994) 5 *European Journal of International Law* 326.

Chinkin, C 'Reservations and Objections to the Convention on the Elimination of All Forms of Discrimination against Women' in J Gardner (ed) *Human Rights as General Norms and a State's Right to Opt Out* (London, British Institute of International and Comparative Law, 1997) 64.

Chinkin, C 'Gender Inequality and Human Rights Law' in A Hurrell and N Woods (eds) *Inequality, Globalization and World Politics* (Oxford, Oxford University Press, 1999) 95.

Chinkin, C 'The United Nations Decade for the Elimination of Poverty: What Role for International Law?' in M Freeman (ed) *Current Legal Problems* (Oxford, Oxford University Press, 2001) 553.

Chinkin, C and Wright, S 'The Hunger Trap: Women, Food and Self-Determination' (1993) 4 *Michigan Journal of International Law* 262.

Chinyenze, M 'A Critique of Chigwedere's Book *Lobolo: The Pros and Cons* in Relation to the Emancipation of Women in Zimbabwe' (1983–84) 11 *Zimbabwe Law Review* 229.

Chiriga, S 'Perspectives on the Post-Beijing Policy Progress in the SADC Region' in P McFadden (ed) *Southern Africa in Transition: A Gendered Perspective* (Harare, SAPES Trust, 1998) 103.

Chirwa, D 'The Merits and Demerits of the African Charter on the Rights and Welfare of the Child' (2002) 10 *International Journal of Children's Rights* 157.

Chitiga, R *Civil Society Guide to Law Making Process in SADC Countries* (Harare, Development Innovations and Networks East and Southern Africa Office (IRED) 1998).

Chiwone, E and Gambahaya, Z (eds) *Culture and Development* (Harare, Mond Books, 1998).

Chu, J and Radwan, A 'Raising Their Voices' *Time Magazine* (London, 23 February 2004) 42.

Cilliers, J *NEPAD's Peer Review Mechanism* Institute for Security Studies, Occasional Paper 64 (2002).

Clark, B 'The Vienna Convention Reservations Regime and the Convention on Discrimination against Women' (1991) 85 *American Journal of International Law* 281.

Cleaver, F (ed) *Masculinities Matter: Men, Gender and Development* (London, Zed Press, 2002).

Cleaver, F 'Men and Masculinities: New Directions in Gender and Development' in F Cleaver (ed) *Masculinities Matter: Men, Gender and Development* (London, Zed Press, 2002) 1.

Commonwealth Secretariat *Gender Mainstreaming: Commonwealth Strategies on Politics, Macroeconomics and Human Rights* (London, Commonwealth Secretariat, 1998).

Commonwealth Secretariat and Maritime Centre of Excellence for Women's Health *Gender Mainstreaming in HIV/AIDS: Taking a Multi-Sectoral Approach* (London, Commonwealth Secretariat, 2002).

Commonwealth Secretariat *Integrated Approaches to Eliminate Gender-based Violence* (London, Commonwealth Secretariat, 2003).

Conaghan, J 'Reassessing the Feminist Theoretical Project in Law' (2000) 27 *Journal of Law and Society* 351.

Connors, J 'The Women's Convention in the Muslim World' in J Gardner (ed) *Human Rights as General Norms and a State's Right to Opt Out* (London, British Institute of International and Comparative Law, 1997) 85.

Connors, J 'Mainstreaming Gender within the International Framework' in A Stewart (ed) *Gender, Law and Social Justice* (Oxford, Blackstone, 2000) 19.

Constantine-Sims, D *The Greatest Taboo: Homosexuality and the Black Community* (Los Angeles, Alyson Press, 2000).

Constitutional Rights Project *Unequal Rights: Discriminatory Laws and Practices against Women in Nigeria* (Lagos, Constitutional Rights Project, 1995).

Constitutional Rights Project 'Seminar on Discriminatory Laws and Practices against Women in Nigeria: Recommendations' in Constitutional Rights Project *Unequal Rights: Discriminatory Laws and Practices against Women in Nigeria* (Lagos, Constitutional Rights Project, 1995) i.

Constitutional Rights Project Communiqué 'Seminar on Discriminatory Laws and Practices against Women in Nigeria' in Constitutional Rights Project *Unequal Rights: Discriminatory Laws and Practices against Women in Nigeria* (Lagos, Constitutional Rights Project, 1995) vi.

Cook, R 'Reservations to the Convention on the Elimination of All Forms of Discrimination against Women' (1990) 30 *Virginia Journal of International Law* 643.

Cook, R 'Accountability in International Law for Violations of Women's Rights by Non-State Actors' in D Dallmeyer (ed) *Preconceiving Reality: Women and International Law* (Washington, American Society for International Law, 1993) 93.

Cook, R (ed) *Human Rights of Women: National and International Perspectives* (Philadelphia, University of Pennsylvania Press, 1994).

Cook, R 'Preface' in Royal Tropical Institute (KIT) and OXFAM *Gender Perspectives on Property and Inheritance* (Amsterdam, KIT and Oxford, OXFAM, 2001) 9.

Cook, R and Dickens, B 'Human Rights Dynamics of Abortion Law Reform' (2003) 25 *Human Rights Quarterly* 1.

Cook, R and Maine, D 'Spousal Veto over Family Planning Services' (1987) 77 *American Journal of Public Health* 339.

Cook, R and Merali, I 'The Interpretation and Application of Human Rights on Reproductive and Sexual Health by Commonwealth Courts' (1999) *Commonwealth Law Bulletin* 109.

Coomaraswamy, R 'To Bellow Like a Cow: Women, Ethnicity and the Discourse of Rights' in R Cook (ed) *Human Rights of Women: National and International Perspectives* (Philadelphia, University of Pennsylvania Press, 1994) 39.

Cornwell, A and Wellbourn, A (eds) *Realizing Rights: Transforming Approaches to Sexual and Reproductive Well-Being* (London, Zed Press, 2002).

Copelon, R 'Intimate Terror: Understanding Domestic Violence as Torture' in R Cook (ed) *Human Rights of Women: National and International Perspectives* (Philadelphia, University of Pennsylvania Press, 1994) 116.

Copelon, R and Petchesky, B 'Toward an Interdependent Approach to Reproductive and Sexual Rights as Human Rights: Reflections on the ICPD and Beyond' in M Schuler (ed) *From Basic Needs to Basic Rights: Women's Claim to Human Rights* (Washington DC, Women Law and Development International, 1995) 343.

Cossman, B *Feminist Legal Theory* (Colombo, International Centre for Ethnic Studies, 1999).

Cossman, B 'Feminists Engaging with the Law: The Use and Limitations of Rights Discourse in Women's Struggles for Social Change' in B Cossman (ed) *Feminist Legal Theory* (Colombo, International Centre for Ethnic Studies, 1999).

Costa, A 'The Myth of Customary Law' (1998) 14 *South African Journal on Human Rights* 525.

Cottier, M 'Swiss Local Child Protection and the Challenges of Immigration' (Tesina submitted to the International Institute for the Sociology of Law, Oñati, Spain, 2001).

Cottrell, D (ed) *Revisiting Children's Rights* (Leiden, Kluwer, 2001).

Cowen, S 'Can "Dignity" Guide South Africa's Equality Jurisprudence' (2001) 17 *South African Journal on Human Rights* 34.

Crawford, J (UN International Law Commission Special Rapporteur on State Responsibility) 'Revising the Draft Article on State Responsibility' (1999)10 *European Journal of International* Law 435.

Crawley, H *Refugees and Gender: Law and Process* (Bristol, Jordan Publishing, 2001).

Crenshaw, K 'Mapping the Margins: Intersectionality, Identity Politics and Violence against Women of Colour' (1991) 43 *Stanford Law Journal* 1241.

Csete, J and Smith, J 'Submission to the Parliamentary Portfolio Committee on Justice and Constitutional Development, Parliament of South Africa, on the Draft Criminal Law (Sexual Offences) Amendment Bill, 2003, from Amnesty International and Human Rights Watch' (15 September 2003) AI-Index: AFR 53/006/2003.

D

Dagut, H and Morgan, R 'Barriers to Justice: Violations of the Rights of Deaf and Hard of Hearing People in the South African Justice System' (2003) 19 *South African Journal on Human Rights* 27.

Dahl, T *Women's Law: An Introduction to Feminist Jurisprudence* (Oslo, Norwegian University Press, 1987).

Daley, P 'Start with the Destitute: Refugees and NGO Recolonization of Africa' (1994) *Africa World Review* 24.

Dallmeyer, D (ed) *Reconceiving Reality: Women and International Law* (Washington, American Society for International Law, 1993).

Dankwa, V 'The Promotional Role of the African Commission' in M Evans and R Murray (eds) *The African Charter on Human and Peoples' Rights: The System in Practice, 1986–2000* (Cambridge, Cambridge University Press, 2002) 335.

Dankwa, V, Flinterman, C and Leckie, S 'Commentary on the Guidelines on Violations of Economic, Social and Cultural Rights' (1998) 20 *Human Rights Quarterly* 705.

Datta, K 'A Coming of Age? Re-Conceptualising Gender and Development in Urban Botswana' (2004) 30 *Journal of Southern African Studies* 251.

Datta, K and McIlwaine, C ' "Empowered Leaders" Perspectives on Women Heading Households in Latin America and Southern Africa' in C Sweetman (ed) *Women and Leadership* (Oxford, OXFAM, 2000) 40.

Davison, J *Gender, Lineage, and Ethnicity in Southern Africa* (Oxford, Westview, 1997).

de Abreu, A 'Background to the Participation of Women in Politics in Mozambique' in J Foster *et al* (eds) *Women in Politics and Decision Making in Southern Africa* (Harare, WILDAF, 1999) 42.

De Waal, A 'Apocalypse: The True Story of AIDS' (2004) 1 *Index on Censorship* 25.

Dellenberg, L 'A Reflection on the Cultural Meanings of Female Circumcision: Experiences from Fieldwork in Casamance, Southern Senegal' in S Arnfred (ed) *Rethinking Sexualities in Africa* (Lund, Nordic Institute, 2004) 79.

Delphy, C *Close to Home: A Materialist Analysis of Women's Oppression* (London, Hutchinson, 1984).

d'Engelbronner-Kolf, M *The Provision of Non-Formal Education for Human Rights in Zimbabwe* (Harare, SAPES, 1997).

d'Engelbronner-Kolf, M *A Web of Legal Cultures: Dispute Resolution Processes amongst the Sambyu of Northern Namibia* (Maastricht, Shaker Publishing, 2001).

Diallo, A 'Paradoxes of Female Sexuality in Mali: On the Practices of *Magonmaka* and *Bolokoli-kela*' in S Arnfred (ed) *Rethinking Sexualities in Africa* (Lund, Nordic Africa Institute, 2004) 173.

Diduck, A and Kaganas, F *Family Law Gender and the State* (Oxford, Hart Publishing, 1999).

Dingwall, R and Eekelaar, J (eds) *Divorce Mediation and the Legal Process* (Oxford, Oxford University Press, 1988).

Dirie, W and Miller, C *Desert Flower* (London, Virago Press, 1998).

Donnelly, J *Universal Human Rights in Theory and Practice* (Ithaca, Cornell University Press, 1989).

Donnelly, J 'Human Rights, Democracy and Development' (1999) 21 *Human Rights Quarterly* 608.

Dorkenoo, E *Cutting the Rose: Female Genital Mutilation The Practice and Its Prevention*, (London, Minority Rights Publications, 1994).

Dorkenoo, E and Elworthy, S *Female Genital Mutilation: Proposals for Change* (London, Minority Rights 1996).

Dorman, S 'NGOs and the Constitutional Debate in Zimbabwe: From Inclusion to Exclusion' (2003) 29 *Journal of Southern African Studies* 845.

Dow, U 'National Implementation of International Law: The Dow Case' in United Nations (ed) *Bringing International Human Rights Home?* (New York, United Nations, 2002) 112.

Doyal, L and Anderson, J *My Heart is Loaded: African Women with HIV Surviving in London: Report of a Qualitative Study* (London, Terrence Higgins Trust, 2003).

Dube, T 'ORAP and the Spirit of Zenzele' in H Chigudu (ed) *Composing a New Song: Stories of Empowerment from Africa* (London, Commonwealth Secretariat, 2003) 67.

Dugard, J 'The Role of Human Rights Treaty Standards in Domestic Law: the Southern African Experience' in P Alston and J Crawford (eds) *The Future of UN Human Rights Treaty Monitoring* (Cambridge, Cambridge University Press, 2000) 269.

Dummett, M 'Inheritance Dispute Kinshasa Style' downloaded from: http://news.bbc.co.uk/1/hi/world/from_our_own_correspondent/29762447.stm 26 April 2003.

Dzidzornu, D 'Human Rights and Widow's Material Security: The Case of the "Intestate" Ghanaian Widow' (1995) 4 *Law and Politics in Asia, Africa, Asia and Latin America* 489.

E

Eade, D (ed) *Development for Health* (Oxford, OXFAM, 1997).

Eade, D *Development and Patronage* (Oxford, OXFAM, 1997).

Eade, D (ed) *Development and Social Diversity* (Oxford, OXFAM, 1999).

East Africa and SADC Group 'Comments on the Draft Protocol to the African Charter on Human and Peoples' Rights on the Rights of Women in Africa (2001) (Unpublished on file with author).

Economist *The World in 2004* (London, The Economist, 2003).

Edwards, C 'Law and Non Consensual Sex in Marriage' in NCSM (ed) *Non Consensual Sex in Marriage Project* (London, CHANGE, 2002) 1.

Eekelaar, J *Regulating Divorce* (Oxford, Clarendon Press, 1991).

Eekelaar, J 'The Importance of Thinking That Children Have Rights' (1994) 8 *International Journal of Law, Policy and the Family* 221.

Eekelaar, J 'Beyond the Welfare Principle' (2002) 14 *Child and Family Law Quarterly* 237.

Eekelaar, J 'Personal Rights and Human Rights' (2002) 2 *Human Rights Law Review* 181.

Eekelaar, J and Nhlapo, T (eds) *The Changing Family* (Oxford, Hart Publishing, 1998).

Egyptian National Council for Childhood and Motherhood *Girls Needs in Upper Egypt, Aswan* (Cairo, Egyptian National Council for Childhood and Motherhood, 2001).

El Dareer, A *Woman, Why Do You Weep?* (London, Zed Press, 1982).

El-Nimr, R 'Women in Islamic Law' in M Yamani and A Allen (eds) *Feminism and Islam: Legal and Literary Perspectives* (New York, New York University Press, 1996) 87.

El Sadaawi, N *The Hidden Face of Eve: Women in the Arab World* (London, Zed Press, 1997).

Elson, D 'Gender Justice, Human Rights and Neo-Liberal Economic Policies' in M Molyneaux and S Razavi (eds) *Gender Justice, Development and Rights* (Oxford, Oxford University Press, 2003) 78.

Empowering Widows in Development *Widows without Rights The First International Widows' Conference* (London, Empowering Widows in Development, 2001).

Engelke, M 'The Book, the Church and the "Incomprehensible Paradox": Christianity in African History' (2003) 29 *Journal of Southern African Studies* 297.

Epikene, R 'Violence against Women: The Case of Cross-River State' in Constitutional Rights Project *Unequal Rights: Discriminatory Laws and Practices against Women in Nigeria* (Lagos, Constitutional Rights Project, 1995) 63.

Evans, M and Murray, R (eds) *The African Charter on Human and Peoples' Rights: The System in Practice, 1986–2000* (Cambridge, Cambridge University Press, 2002).

Evans, M and Murray, R 'The Special Rapporteurs in the African System' in M Evans and R Murray (eds) *The African Charter on Human and Peoples' Rights: The System in Practice, 1986–2000* (Cambridge, Cambridge University Press, 2002) 280.

Evans, M, Ige, T and Murray, R 'The Reporting Mechanism of the African Charter on Human and Peoples' Rights in M Evans and R Murray (eds) *The African Charter on Human and Peoples' Rights: The System in Practice, 1986–2000* (Cambridge, Cambridge University Press, 2002) 36.

Ewelukwa, U 'Post-Colonialism, Gender, Customary Injustice: Widows in African Societies' (2002) 24 *Human Rights Quarterly* 424.

F

Farha, L 'Is There a Woman in the House? Re/Conceiving the Human Right to Housing' (2002) 14 *Canadian Journal of Women and Law* 118.

Favali, L and Pateman, R *Blood, Land and Sex: Legal and Political Pluralism in Eritrea* (Indianapolis, Indiana University Press, 2003).

Fawzy, E 'Law No. 1 of 2000: A New Personal Status Law and a Limited Step on the Path to Reform' in L Welchman (ed) *Women's Rights and Islamic Family Law* (London, Zed Press, 2004) 58.

Fellmeth, X 'Feminism and International Law: Theory, Methodology, and Substantive Reform' (2000) 22 *Human Rights Quarterly* 658.

FEMNET Editorial 'FGM: This Evil Practice Must Stop!' FEMNET (2001) *Our Rights* downloaded from http://www.africaonline.co.ke/femnet/rights1.html.

Fishbayn, L 'Litigating the Right to Culture: Family Law in the New South Africa' (1999) 13 *International Journal of Law, Policy and the Family* 147.

Foblets, M 'Salem's Circumcision: The Encounter of Cultures in a Civil Action. A Belgian Case Study' (1991) 1 *Recht der Werkelijkheid* 43.

Forum on Marriage and the Rights of Women and Girls *Early Marriage: Whose Right to Choose?* (London, Forum on Marriage and the Rights of Women and Girls, 2000).

FORWARD 'Dambatta' in FORWARD *Annual Report 2003–2004* (London, FORWARD, 2004) 14.

Foster, J, Makanya, S and Mutukwa, G (eds) *Women in Politics and Decision Making in Southern Africa* (Harare, WILDAF, 1999).

Foster, J, Makanya, S and Mutukwa, G 'Introduction' in J Foster *et al* (eds) *Women in Politics and Decision Making in Southern Africa* (Harare, WILDAF, 1999) 9.

Foster, J, Makanya, S and Mutukwa, G (eds) *Women in Politics and Decision Making in Southern Africa* (Harare, WILDAF, 1999).

Frank, L 'Historical and Current Context of the Participation of Women in Politics and Decision Making in Namibia' in J Foster *et al* (eds) *Women in Politics and Decision Making in Southern Africa* (Harare, WILDAF, 1999) 64.

Fraser, A 'Becoming Human: The Origins and Development of Women's Human Rights' (1999) 21 *Human Rights Quarterly* 853.

Frazer, E 'Democracy, Citizenship and Gender' in A Carter and G Stokes (eds) *Democratic Theory Today* (Cambridge, Polity Press, 2002) 73.

Fredman, S 'A Difference with Distinction: Pregnancy and Parenthood Reassessed' [1994] 110 *Law Quarterly Review* 106.

Fredman, S 'Less Equal than Others—Equality and Women's Rights' in C Gearty and A Tomkins (eds) *Understanding Human Rights* (London, Pinter, 1999) 197.

Freeman, M *The Rights and Wrongs of Children* (London, Frances Pinter, 1983).

Freeman, M 'Cultural Pluralism and the Rights of the Child' in J Eekelaar and T Nhlapo (eds) *Changing Family* (Oxford, Hart Publishing, 1998) 289.

Freeman, M (ed) *Current Legal Problems* (Oxford, Oxford University Press, 2001).

Freeman, M 'Exploring the Boundaries of Family Law in England in 2000' in A Bainham (ed) *International Survey of Family Law 2002* (Bristol, Jordan Publishing, 2002) 133.

G

Gaidzanwa, R 'Bourgeois Theories of Gender and Feminism and Their Shortcomings with Reference to Southern African Countries' in R Meena (ed) *Gender in Southern Africa: Conceptual and Theoretical Issues* (Harare, SAPES, 1992) 92.

Gallagher, A 'Ending the Marginalization: Strategies For Incorporating Women into the United Nations Human Rights System' (1997) 19 *Human Rights Quarterly* 283.

Gallagher, A 'Human Rights and the New UN Protocols on Trafficking and Migrant Smuggling: A Preliminary Analysis' (2001) 23 *Human Rights Quarterly* 975.

Gardner, J (ed) *Human Rights as General Norms and a State's Right to Opt Out* (London, British Institute of International and Comparative Law, 1997).

Gaye, A and Njie, M 'Family Law in the Gambia' in A Kuenyehia (ed) *Women and Law in West Africa* (Accra, Women and Law in West Africa, 1998) 2.

Gearty, C and Tomkins, A (eds) *Understanding Human Rights* (London, Pinter, 1999).

Gibney, M (ed) *Globalizing Rights* (Oxford, Oxford University Press, 2003).

Giddens, A *Runaway World: How Globalisation is Reshaping Our Lives* (London, Profile Books, 2002).

Gill, P 'Experts Attack Bush's Stance in AIDS Battle' *Observer* (London, 11 July 2004).

Gilligan, C *In a Different Voice: Psychological Theory and Women's Development* (Cambridge, Harvard University Press, 1982).

Global Fund for AIDS, *Tuberculosis and Malaria* www.theglobalfund.org.

Globalgagrule.org 'Access Denied: US Restrictions on International Family Planning — Introduction' downloaded from www.globalgagrule.org.

Globalgagrule.org 'The Impact of the Global Gag Rule in Ethiopia' from www.globalgagrule.org.

Goetz, A and Hassim, S 'In and against the Party: Women's Representation and Constituency Building in Uganda and South Africa' in M Molyneaux and S Razavi (eds) *Gender Justice, Development and Rights* (Oxford, Oxford University Press, 2003) 306.

Gorman, M 'Older People and Development: The Last Minority' in A Eade (ed) *Development and Social Diversity* (Oxford, OXFAM, 1999) 36.

Goonesekere, S 'Women's Rights and Children's Rights: The United Nations Conventions as Compatible and Complementary International Treaties' (1992) 1 *Innocenti Occasional Papers Child Rights Series* 1.

Goonesekere, S 'A Rights Based Approach to Realising Gender Equality' at http://www.un.org/womenwatch/daw/news/savitri.htm.

Green, K and Lim, H 'What is This Thing about Female Circumcision? Legal Education and Human Rights' (1998) 7 *Social and Legal Studies* 365.

Greer, G *The Whole Woman* (London, Doubleday, 1999).

Griffiths, A *In the Shadow of Marriage: Gender and Justice in an African Community* (Chicago, University of Chicago Press, 1997).

Griffiths, J 'What is Legal Pluralism?' (1986) 24 *Journal of Legal Pluralism* 24.

Gruenbaum, E *The Female Circumcision Controversy: An Anthropological Perspective* (Philadelphia, University of Pennsylvania Press, 2001).

Gubbay, A 'The Effect of the Deportation of Alien Husbands upon the Constitutionally Protected Mobility Rights of Citizen Wives in Zimbabwe' in United Nations (ed) *Bringing International Human Rights Law Home?* (New York, United Nations, 2002) 116.

Gunning, I 'Arrogant Perception, World Travelling and Multi-Cultural Feminism: The Case of Female Genital Surgeries' (1991) 23 *Columbia Human Rights Law Review* 189.

Gutto, S 'Legal Status and Implications of the Decision by the Assembly of Heads of States and Government to Integrate the African Court of Justice and the African Court of Human and Peoples' Rights into One Court' Centre for African Renaissance Studies, University of South Africa, Pretoria (8 August 2004) (on file with author).

H

Hallaq, W *The Origins and Evolution of Islamic Law* (Cambridge, Cambridge University Press, 2004).

Hames, M (2004) 'The Women's Movement and Lesbian and Gay Struggles in South Africa' *Feminist Africa* at http://www.feministafrica.org/2level.html.

Harding, S *The Science Question in Feminism* (Milton Keynes, Open University Press, 1986).

Harmann, B 'Population Control in the New World Order' in D Eade (ed) *Development for Health* (Oxford, OXFAM, 1997) 80.

Harrell-Bond, B *Modern Marriage in Sierra Leone: A Study of the Professional Group* (The Hague, Mouton, 1975).

Harrington, J and Manji, A 'The Emergence of African Law as an Academic Discipline in Britain' (2003) 102 *African Affairs* 109.

Harris, C and Smith, I 'The Reproductive Health of Refugees: Lessons beyond ICPD' in C Sweetman (ed) *Gender, Development and Health* (Oxford, OXFAM, 2001) 10.

Hassim, S 'Nationalism, Feminism and Autonomy: The ANC in Exile and the Question of Women' (2004) 30 *Journal of Southern African Studies* 433.

Hatchard, J and Perry-Kessaris, A (eds) Law *and Development: Facing Complexity in the 21st Century* (London, Cavendish Press, 2003).

Hellum, A 'Gender and Legal Change in Zimbabwe: Childless Women and Divorce from a Socio-Cultural and Historic Perspective' in S Adelman and A Paliwala (eds) *Law and Crisis in the Third World* (London, Zell, 1993) 243.

Hellum, A *Birth Law* (Oslo, Scandinavian University Press, 1993).

Hellum, A *Women's Human Rights and Legal Pluralism in Africa: Mixed Norms and Identities in Infertility Management in Zimbabwe* (Oslo, Mond Books, 1999).

Henrard, K 'From the Constitutional Drawing Board to the Challenges of Implementation: Equality and Population Diversity' in J Murison *et al* (eds) *Remaking Law in Africa: Transnationalism Persons and Rights* (Edinburgh, Centre of African Studies, 2004) 71.

Hevener, N 'An Analysis of Gender-Based Treaty Law: Contemporary Developments in Historical Perspective'(1986) 8 *Human Rights Quarterly* 70.

Heyns, C (ed) *Human Rights Law in Africa* (The Hague, Kluwer International, 1996).

Heyns, C 'Civil and Political Rights in the African Charter' in M Evans and R Murray (eds) *The African Charter on Human and Peoples' Rights: The System in Practice, 1986–2000* (Cambridge, Cambridge University Press, 2002) 137.

Heyns, C (ed) *Human Rights Law in Africa* (The Hague, Martinus Nijhoff, 2004).

Heywood, M 'Preventing Mother-to-Child Transmission in South Africa: Background, Strategies and Outcomes of the Treatment Action Campaign Case against the Minister of Health' (2003) 19 *South African Journal on Human Rights* 278.

Hewlett, S *Baby Hunger: The New Battle for Motherhood* (Charleston, Atlantic Books, 2002).

Higgins, R *Problems and Process: International Law and How We Use It* (Oxford, Clarendon Press, 1994).

Himonga, C 'The Right of the Child to Participate in Decision Making: A Perspective from Zambia' in W Ncube (ed) *Law, Culture, Tradition and Children's Rights in Eastern and Southern Africa* (Ashgate, Aldershot, 1998) 95.

Himonga, C 'Protecting the Minor Child's Inheritance Rights' in A Bainham (ed) *International Survey of Family Law* (Bristol, Jordan Publishing, 2001) 457.

Himonga, C 'Inheritance Conflicts over the Matrimonial Home: Safeguarding the Family against Homelessness' in A Bainham (ed) *International Survey of Family Law 2003* (Bristol, Jordan Publishing, 2003) 461.

Himonga, C 'Legislative and Judicial Approaches to the Reform of the Customary Law of Marriage and Succession in South Africa: Implications for the Advancement of Women's Rights' (paper presented at the Conference on Advancing Women's Rights Hosted by the Women's Legal Centre, Cape Town, 30–31 October 2003) available at http://www.wlce.co.za/conference2003/2003conference_himonga.php.

Himonga, C and Bosch, C 'The Application of Customary Law under the Constitution of South Africa: Problem Solved or Just Beginning?' (2000) 17 *South Africa Law Journal* 306.

Hinz, M 'Family Law in Namibia: The Challenge of Customary and Constitutional Law' in J Eekelaar and T Nhlapo (eds) *Changing Family* (Oxford, Hart Publishing, 1998) 139.

Holland-Muter, S 'First African Sexual and Reproductive Health Rights Conference: An Overview' (2003) 44 *Women's Health News* 13.

Hollands, G and Ansell, G (eds) *Winds of Small Change. Civil Society Interaction with the African State* (Vienna, Austrian Development Institute, 1998).

Holtmaat, R *Towards Different Law and Public Policy: The Significance of Article 5(a) CEDAW for the Elimination of Structural Gender Discrimination* (The Hague, Ministry of Social Affairs and Employment, 2004).

hooks, b *Feminist Theory: From Margin to Centre* (Boston, Southend Press, 1984).

Hosken, F *The Hosken Report: Genital/Sexual Mutilation of Females* (Lexington, Women's International Network, 1994).

Hosken, F *Stop Female Genital Mutilation Women Speak Facts and Actions* (Lexington, Women's International Network News, 1995).

Hossain, S 'Equality in the Home: Women's Rights and Personal Laws in South Asia' in R Cook (ed) *Human Rights of Women: National and International Perspectives* (Philadelphia, University of Pennsylvania Press, 1994) 466.

Howard, R 'Women's Rights in English-Speaking Sub-Saharan Africa' in C Welch and R Meltzer (eds) *Human Rights and Development in Africa* (New York, State University of New York Press, 1984) 124.

Howard, R 'Women's Rights and the Right to Development' in J Peters and A Wolper (eds) *Women's Rights, Human Rights: International Feminist Perspectives* (New York, Routledge, 1995) 301.

Howard, R and Donnelly, J 'Human Dignity, Human Rights and Political Regimes' in J Donnelly (ed) *Universal Human Rights in Theory and Practice* (Ithaca, Cornell University Press, 1989) 66.

Howard, R 'Health Costs of Social Degradation and Female Self-Mutilation in North America' in K Mahoney and P Mahoney (eds) *Human Rights in the Twenty-First Century* (The Hague, Kluwer Publishing, 1993) 503.

Hubbard, D and Cassidy, E 'Family Law Reform in Namibia: Work in Progress' in A Bainham (ed) *International Survey of Family Law 2002* (Bristol, Jordan Publishing, 2002) 255.

Human Rights Watch *Seeking Refuge, Finding Terror: The Widespread Rape of Somali Women Refugees in North Eastern Kenya* (New York, Human Rights Watch, 1993).

Human Rights Watch *South Africa Violence against Women and the Medico-Legal System* (London, Human Rights Watch, 1998).

Human Rights Watch *Crime or Custom? Violence in Tanzania's Refugee Camps* (New York, Human Rights Watch, 2000).

Human Rights Watch *Refugees Still at Risk: Continuing Refugee Protection Concerns in Guinea* (New York, Human Rights Watch, 2001).

Human Rights Watch *War within War: Sexual Violence against Women in Eastern Congo* (New York, Human Rights Watch, 2002).

Human Rights Watch *Just Die Quietly: Domestic Violence and Women's Vulnerability to HIV in Uganda* (London, Human Rights Watch, 2003).

Human Rights Watch *Borderline Slavery: Child Trafficking in Togo* (London, Human Rights Watch, 2003).

Human Rights Watch 'Women and HIV/AIDS' at http://www.hrw.org.women/aids.html.

Human Rights Watch *Double Standards: Women's Property Right Violations in Kenya* (London, Human Rights Watch, 2003).

Human Rights Watch and International Gay and Lesbian Human Rights Commission (IGLHRC) *More Than a Name: State Sponsored Homophobia and Its Consequences in Southern Africa* (New York, Human Rights Watch, 2003).

Humphrys, J 'A Split Church Can Be Reborn' *Sunday Times* (London, 19 October, 2003).

Hunt, J 'Situating Women's Development Needs within the Human Rights Framework' in G Moon (ed) *Making Her Rights a Reality: Women's Human Rights and Development* (Victoria, Community Aid Abroad, 1995).

Hurrell, A and Woods, N (eds) *Inequality, Globalization and World Politics* (Oxford, Oxford University Press, 1999).

I

Ibhawoh, B 'Between Culture and Constitution: Evaluating the Cultural Legitimacy of Human Rights in the African State' (2000) 22 *Human Rights Quarterly* 836.

Ibrahim, Z 'Radio HIV HOP in South Africa' in A Cornwell and A Welbourn (eds) *Realizing Rights: Transforming Approaches to Sexual and Reproductive Well-Being* (London, Zed Press, 2002) 191.

Illumoka, A 'African Women's Economic, Social and Cultural Right: Toward a Relevant Theory and Practice' in R Cook (ed) *Human Rights of Women: National and International Perspectives* (Philadelphia, University of Pennsylvania Press, 1994) 307.

Imam, A, Pittin, R and Omole, H (eds) *Women and the Family in Nigeria* (Dakar, Codesria, 1989).

Immigration Appellate Authority *Asylum Gender Guidelines* (London, Immigration Appellate Authority, 2000).

Indigenous People's Consultation (Shakawe, Botswana, 1998) *Principles Adopted by an Indigenous People's Consultation. Held in Shakawe, Botswana from 6–9 September 1998.* (D'Kar and Windhoek, Kuru Development Trust and WIMSA, 1999).

International Parliamentary Union 'Universal Declaration on Democracy and the New Delhi Declaration' (1997) at http://www.ipu.org/wmn-e/approach.htm.

International Parliamentary Union (2003) 'Women in National Parliaments' at http://www.ipu.org/wmn-e/classif.htm.

International Planned Parenthood Federation (IPPF) *Charter on Sexual and Reproductive Rights* (London, IPPF, 1998).

International Planned Parenthood Federation (IPPF) Africa Region and Family Welfare Association of Niger (ANBEF) *Report of the Regional Conference on Women, Islam and Family Planning, Niamey, Niger, 23–25 October 1995* (London, IPPF, 1995).

International Women's Rights Action Watch (IWRAW) 'FGM in Court and Culture: An Advocacy Lesson from Egyptian Women' (1997) 11 *The Women's Watch* 1.

International Women's Rights Action Watch (IWRAW) 'Equality and Rights: The International Covenant on Economic, Social and Cultural Rights, Article 3. Background Paper for the Proposed General Comment on ICESCR Article 3' (paper presented at Meeting on Article 3 of the International Covenant on Economic, Social and Cultural Rights Held at the University of Toronto, Faculty of Law 19–20 July 2003).

International Women's Rights Action Watch (IWRAW) *Equality and Women's Economic, Social and Cultural Rights* (Minnesota, IWRAW, 2004).

IRIN 'Ethiopia: Government Criticizes Attitude Towards Women's Rights' Addis Ababa (25 June2003) downloaded from: http://www.irinnews.org/report.asp?ReportID=34974 &SelectRegion=Horn_of_Africa.

IRIN 'Ethiopia: Rapid Birth Rate 'Undermining' Economic Recovery' Downloaded from: http://www.irinnews.org/print.asp?ReportID=37068.

IRIN 'Kenya: US Policy Jeopardizing Women's Health Says Report' Downloaded from: http://www.irinnews.org/print.asp?ReportID=36839.

IRIN 'Swaziland: AIDS Indaba Highlights Conflicting Views' 18 October 2003, downloaded from: http://www.irinnews.org/reports.asp?Report ID=36743&SelectRegion=Southern Africa.

Iwobi, A 'Tiptoeing through a Constitutional Minefield: The Great Sharia Controversy in Nigeria' (2004) 48 *Journal of African Law* 111.

J

Jackson, D *Twa Women, Twa Rights in the Great Lakes Region of Africa* (London, Minority Rights Group, 2003).

Jacobsen, M and Bruun, O (eds) *Human Rights and Asian Values: Contesting National Identities and Cultural Representations in Asia* (London, Curzon Press, 2000).

James, A 'Reconciling International Human Rights and Cultural Relativism: The Case of Female Circumcision' (1994) 8 *Bioethics* 1.

Jayawardena, K *Feminism and Nationalism in the Third World* (London, Zed Press, 1986).

Jeater, D *Marriage, Perversion and Power: The Construction of Moral Discourse in Southern Rhodesia 1894–1930* (Oxford, Oxford University Press, 1993).

Johnson, E 'Thinking about Access: A Preliminary Typology of Possible Strategies' in M Cappelletti and B Garth (eds) *Access to Justice, Vol 3* (Florence, Tipografia, 1978) 8.

Jungar, J and Olinas, K 'Preventing HIV? Medical Discourses and Invisible Women' in S Arnfred (ed) *Re-Thinking Sexualities in Africa* (Lund, Africa Institute, 2004) 97.

K

Kabeberi-Machaira, J 'Female Genital Mutilation and the Rights of the Girl Child in Kenya' in W Ncube (ed) *Law, Culture, Tradition and Children's Rights in Eastern and Southern Africa: Issues in Law and Society* (Aldershot, Dartmouth, 1998) 249.

Kabeberi-Machaira, J and Nyamu, C 'Marriage by Affidavit: Developing Alternative Laws on Cohabitation in Kenya' in J Eekelaar and T Nhlapo (eds) *Changing Family* (Oxford, Hart Publishing, 1998) 197.

Kabeer, N 'Gender, Development, and Training: Raising Awareness in the Planning Process' in D Eade (ed) *Development and Social Diversity* (Oxford, OXFAM, 1999) 16.

Kachingwe, N *Between a Rock and a Hard Place: Africa Faces No Win Situation in Trade Deal with Europe* (Harare, Mwengo and East and Southern Africa Civil Society Economic Policy Project, 2003).

Kaganas, F and Murray, C 'Law, Women and the Family in the New South Africa' 1991 *Acta Juridica* 116.

Kaim, B 'Involving Young People in Their Reproductive Health: A Case Study from Zimbabwe' in A Cornwell and A Welbourn (eds) *Realizing Rights: Transforming Approaches to Sexual and Reproductive Well-Being* (London, Zed Press, 2002) 181.

Kambou, G 'The Law as a Tool for Behavioural Change: The Case of Burkina Faso' (paper presented at the Afro-Arab Expert Consultation on Legal Tools for the Prevention of Female Genital Mutilation, Cairo, 21–23 June 2003).

Kamchedzera, B 'The Rights of the Child in Malawi: An Agenda for Research on the Impact of the UN Convention in a Poor Country' (1991) 5 *International Journal of Law, Policy and the Family* 24.

Kapur, R and Cossman, B *Subversive Sites: Feminist Engagement with Law in India* (London, Sage, 1996).

Karanja, W ' "Outside Wives" and "Inside Wives" in Nigeria: A Study of Changing Perceptions in Marriage' in D Parkin and D Nyamwa (eds) *Transformation of African Marriage* (Manchester, Manchester University Press, 1987) 247.

Kassindja, F and Bashir, L *Do They Hear You When You Cry?* (London, Bantam Press, 1998).

Katzive, L 'Using the Law to Promote Women's Rights: Consideration in Drafting and Implementing Legislation to Prevent FC-FGM' (paper presented at the Afro-Arab Expert Consultation on Legal Tools for the Prevention of Female Genital Mutilation, Cairo, 21–23 June 2003).

Keck, M and Sikkink, K *Activists beyond Borders* (Ithaca, Cornell University Press, 1998)

Kennedy, D 'The International Human Rights Movement: Part of the Problem?' (2002) 15 *Harvard Human Rights Journal* 101.

Kennedy, H *Just Law* (London, Chatto & Windus, 2004).

Kenyatta, J *Facing Mount Kenya: The Tribal Life of the Gikuyu* (New York, Vintage Books, 1965).

Kerr, J (ed) *Ours By Right* (London, Zed Books, 1993) 106.

Kerr, J 'From "Opposing" to "Proposing" Finding Proactive Global Strategies for Feminist Futures' in J Kerr *et al* (eds) *The Future of Women's Rights* (London, Zed Press, 2004) 14.

Kerr, J and C Sweetman *Women Reinventing Globalization* (Oxford, OXFAM, 2003).

Kerr, J and C Sweetman 'Editorial' in J Kerr and C Sweetman (eds) *Women Reinventing Globalization* (Oxford, OXFAM, 2003) 3.

Kerr, J, Sprenger, E and Symington, A (eds) *The Future of Women's Rights* (London, Zed Press, 2004).

Kibwana, K (ed) *Law and the Status of Women in Kenya* (Nairobi, Women and Law in East Africa, 1995).

Kiirya, P 'LABE: Beating the Community Drums' in H Chigudu (ed) *Composing a New Song: Stories of Empowerment* (London, Commonwealth Secretariat, 2003) 35.

Kioko, W 'Reforming Family Law in Kenya: The Place of the Repealed Affiliation Act' in Kibwana, K (ed) *Law and the Status of Women in Kenya* (Nairobi, Women and Law in East Africa, 1995) 182.

Kisaakye, E 'Women, Culture and Human Rights: Female Genital Mutilation, Polygamy and Bride Price' in W Benedek, E Kisaakye and G Oberleitner *Human Rights of Women: International Instruments and African Experiences* (London, Zed Press, 2002) 268.

Klugman, B and Moorman, J 'Gender Empowerment Issues within the Health Sector' (2003) 44 *Women's Health Project Review* 3.

Knop, K (ed) *Gender and Human Rights* (Oxford, Oxford University Press, 2003).

Knop, K *Diversity and Self Determination in International Law* (Cambridge, Cambridge University Press, 2002.

Kolajo, A *Customary Law in Nigeria through the Cases* (Ibadan, Spectrum Books, 2000).

Koso-Thomas, O *Circumcision of Women: A Strategy for Eradication,* (London, Zed Press, 1987).

Kowalowol, M 'Re-Conceptualizing African Gender Theory: Feminism, Womanism and the *Arere* Metaphor' in S Arnfred (ed) *Rethinking Sexualities in Africa* (Lund, Nordic Africa Institute, 2004) 251.

Kuenyehia, A 'The Impact of Structural Adjustment Policies on Women's International Human Rights: The Example of Ghana' in R Cook (ed) *Human Rights of Women: National and International Perspectives* (Philadelphia, University of Pennsylvania Press, 1994) 422.

Kuenyehia, A (ed) *Women and Law in West Africa* (Accra, Women and Law in West Africa, 1998).

Kuenyehia, A and Ofei-Aboagye, E 'Family Law in Ghana and its Implications for Women' in A Kuenyehia (ed) *Women and Law in West Africa* (Accra, Women and Law in West Africa, 1998) 23.

Kukah, M 'Women, the Family and Christianity: Old Testament, New Testament and Contemporary Concepts' in A Imam *et al* (eds) *Women and the Family in Nigeria* (Dakar, Codesria, 1989) 65.

Kukah, M 'Shariah, Justice and Constitutionalism in Nigeria' in J Murison *et al* (eds) *Remaking Law in Africa: Transnationalism Persons and Rights* (Edinburgh, Centre of African Studies, 2004) 173.

L

Lacey, N 'Legislation against Sex Discrimination: Questions from a Feminist Perspective' *Journal of Law and Society* (1987) 411.

Lacey, N 'Feminist Legal Theory and the Rights of Women' in Knop, K (ed) *Gender and Human Rights* (Oxford, Oxford University Press, 2003) 13.

Lane, J and Ersson, J *Democracy: A Comparative Approach* (London, Routledge, 2003).

Laurence, J 'Empowering Women is the Way Forward to Saving African Women from AIDS Devastation' *Independent* (London, 17 May 2004).

Leclerc-Madlala, S 'Virginity Testing Diverts Attention from the Lack of Male Sexual Responsibility' (2003) 40 *Women's Health Project Review* 3.

Lewis, H 'Between *Irua* and "Female Genital Mutilation": Feminist Human Rights Discourse and the Cultural Divide' (1995) 8 *Harvard Human Rights Journal* 1.

Liddle, R 'On Why Africa Must Take Responsibility for its Own Problems' *Guardian* (London, 7 February 2002).

Lim, H and Roche, J 'Feminism and Children's Rights: The Politics of Voice' in D Cottrell (ed) *Revisiting Children's Rights* (Leiden, Kluwer, 2001)51.

Linzaad, E *Reservations to UN Human Rights Treaties* (Dordrecht, Martinus Nijhoff, 1995).

Lloyd, A and Murray, R 'Institutions with Responsibility for Human Rights Protection under the African Union' (2004) 48 *Journal of African Law* 165.

Lodrup, P and Modvar, E (eds) *Family Life and Human Rights* (Oslo, Gyldendal Akademisk, 2004).

Longinotto, K *The Day I will Never Forget* [film] (New York, Women Make Movies, 2002).

Longwe, S 'Towards Realistic Strategies for Women's Political Empowerment in Africa' in C Sweetman (ed) *Women and Leadership* (Oxford, OXFAM, 2000) 24.

Lorde, A *Sister Outsider: Essays and Speeches* (New York, Crossing Press, 1984).

Louw, R 'Gay and Lesbian Partner Immigration and the Redefining of Family: *National Coalition for Gay and Lesbian Equality v Minister of Home Affairs (National Coalition)*' (2000) 16 *South Africa Journal on Human Rights* 313.

Lugard, F *The Dual Mandate in British Tropical Africa* (London, William Blackwood, 1922).

Lugones, M 'Playfulness, World-Traveling and Loving Perception' (1987) 2 *Hypatia* 3.

M

Maboreke, M 'The Love of a Mother: Problems of Custody in Zimbabwe' in A Armstrong and W Ncube (eds) *Women and Law in Southern Africa* (Harare, Zimbabwe Publishing House, 1987) 158.

Maboreke, M 'Understanding Law in Zimbabwe' in A Stewart (ed) *Gender, Law and Social Justice* (Oxford, Blackstone, 2000) 101.

Mabuwa, R 'Africa's New Protocol for Women's Rights: An African Agenda for Action' http://www.reproductiverights.org/rfn_03_09_2.html#3.

Machera, M 'Opening a Can of Worms: A Debate on Female Sexuality in the Lecture Theatre' in S Arnfred (ed) *Rethinking Sexualities in Africa* (Lund, Nordic Africa Institute, 2004) 157.

Mackie. G 'Female Genital Cutting: The Beginning of the End' in B Shell-Duncan and Y Hernlund (eds) *Female 'Circumcision' in Africa: Culture, Controversy and Change* (Colorado, Lynne Rienner Publishers, 2000) 253.

Mackinnon, C *Towards a Feminist Theory of the State* (Cambridge, Harvard University Press, 1989).

Mackinnon, C 'On Torture: A Feminist Perspective on Human Rights' in K Mahoney, and P Mahoney (eds) *Human Rights in the 21st Century: A Global Perspective* (The Hague, Kluwer, 1993) 21.

Maclean, M and Eekelaar, J *Maintenance after Divorce* (Oxford, Clarendon Press, 1986).

Magaisa, T '*Minister of Health and Others v Treatment Action Campaign and Others*' (2003) 47 *Journal of African Law* 117.

Maguire, K 'How British Charity was Silenced on Iraq' *Guardian* (London, 28 November 2003).

Mahdi, H 'The Position of Women in Islam' in A Imam *et al* (eds) *Women and the Family in Nigeria* (Dakar, Codesria, 1989) 59.

Mahoney, K and Mahoney, P (eds) *Human Rights in the 21st Century: A Global Perspective* (The Hague, Kluwer, 1993).

Maiga, K 'Legal Tools for the Prevention of Female Genital Mutilation, Case Study: Mali' (paper presented at the Afro-Arab Consultation on Legal Tools for the Legal Protection of Female Genital Mutilation, Cairo, 21–23 June 2003).

Mair, L *African Marriage and Social Change* (London, Frank Cass, 1969).

Maitse, T 'Political Change, Rape and Pornography in Post Apartheid South Africa' in C Sweetman (ed) *Violence against Women* (Oxford: OXFAM, 1998) 55.

Malloch Brown, M 'Foreword' in UNDP *Human Development Report: Cultural Liberty in Today's Diverse World* (New York, United Nations, 2004) v.

Maluwa, T 'The Constitutive Act of the African Union and Institution Building in Postcolonial Africa' (2003) 16 *Leiden Journal of International Law* 157.

Mamashela, M 'Legal Dualism in Lesotho (with Particular Reference to Marriage and Succession)' (1989) 4 *Law and Anthropology* 59.

Manana, T 'Conventional Economic Theories and Gender Analysis' in R Meena (ed) *Gender in Southern Africa* (Harare, SAPES, 1992) 126.

Mandaza, I (ed) *Governance and Human Development in Southern Africa* (Harare, SAPES, 1998).

Mandela, N 'Foreword' in WHO *World Report on Violence and Health* (Geneva, WHO, 2002) i.

Mandela, N 'Special Contribution' in UNDP *Human Development Report Cultural Liberty in Today's Diverse World* (New York, United Nations, 2004) 43.

Manji, A 'Imagining Women's "Legal World": Towards a Feminist Theory of Legal Pluralism in Africa' (1994) 8 *Social and Legal Studies* 434.

Manji, A 'Gender and the Politics of the Land Reform Process in Tanzania' (1998) 36 *Journal of Modern African Studies* 645.

Manji, A 'Capital, Labour and Land Relations in Africa: A Gender Analysis of the World Bank's Policy Research Report on Land Institutions and Land Policy' (2003) 24 *Third World Quarterly* 97.

Mann, K and Roberts, V *Law in Colonial Africa* (London, James Currey, 1991).

Mannathoko, C 'Feminist Theories and the Study of Gender Issues in Southern Africa' in P McFadden (ed) *Southern Africa in Transition: A Gendered Perspective* (Harare, SAPES, 1998) 71.

Maramba, P, Olateru-Olagebi, B and Webanenou, R *Structural Adjustment Programmes and the Human Rights of African Women* (Harare, WILDAF, 1995).

Martin, D 'Law, Custom and Economic Empowerment of Women in Sub Saharan Africa: A Conceptual Framework' in A Stewart (ed) *Gender, Law and Social Justice* (Oxford, Blackstone, 2000) 71.

Mason, D 'Africa's Extremes' *The World in 2004* (London, The Economist, 2003) 86.

Mathabane, M *African Women: Three Generations* (London, Hamish Hamilton, 1994).

Maushart, S *Wifework: What Marriage Really Means for Women* (London, Bloomsbury Publishing, 2002).

May, J *Changing People, Changing Laws* (Gweru, Mambo Press, 1987).

Mayer, A *Islam and Human Rights* (Boulder, Westview, 1999).

Mayer, A 'A Benign Apartheid: How Gender Apartheid has Been Rationalized' (2000) 5 *UCLA Journal of International Law and Foreign Affairs* 237.

Mayisela, S 'Working with a Rejected, Emotionally Deprived Child' (2001) 39 *Women's Health Project Review* 6.

Mbye, A 'We Shall Not Ban FGM President Jammeh Tells Religious Elders' (newspaper/ magazine report) Gambia, 15–17 January 1999 (on file with author).

McAllister, E 'Aid Conditionality as a Lever for Women's Equality: Help or Hindrance?' in J Kerr (ed) *Ours By Right* (London, Zed Books, 1993) 106.

McDonald, K and Swaak, G (eds) *Substantive and Procedural Aspects of International Criminal Law: The Experience of International and National Courts* (The Hague, Kluwer, 2000).

McFadden, P 'Sex, Sexuality and The Problems of AIDS in Africa' in R Meena (ed) *Gender in Southern Africa: Conceptual and Theoretical Issues* (Harare, SAPES, 1992) 157.

McFadden, P (ed) *Southern Africa in Transition: A Gendered Perspective* (Harare, SAPES, 1998).

McFadden, P 'Sexual Pleasure as Feminist Choice' in (2004) *Feminist Africa* at http://www.feministafrica.org/2level.html.

McClain-Nhlapo, C 'Invisible Women' (2004) 14 *Interights Bulletin* 100.

McCorquodale, R and Fairbrother, R 'Globalization and Human Rights' (1999) 21 *Human Rights Quarterly* 735.

McGreal, C 'How African Leaders Scored an Own Goal by Attacking Their Best Friend in the West' *Guardian* (London, 3 September 2003).

Melching, M 'You Are an African Woman' Lecture Given at the John F Kennedy School of Government, Harvard University, 16 November 2000, downloaded from http:www.tostan.org/index1.html.

Meena, R (ed) *Gender in Southern Africa: Conceptual and Theoretical Issues* (Harare, SAPES, 1992).

Meena, R 'Conceptual Issues—Gender in Southern Africa' in I Mandaza (ed) *Governance and Human Development in Southern Africa* (Harare, SAPES,.1998) 119.

Mernissi, F 'Muslim Women and Fundamentalism' in S Sabbagh (ed) *Arab Women: Between Defiance and Restraint* (New York, Olive Branch Press, 1996)162.

Mernissi, F *Beyond the Veil: Male Female Dynamics in Muslim Society* (London, Saqi Books, 2003).

Metike, G *Ali's Story* (Addis Ababa, National Committee on Traditional Practices in Ethiopia (NCTPE), undated).

Metike, G *Yimer's Story* (Addis Ababa, National Committee on Traditional Practices in Ethiopia (NCTPE), undated).

Mhoja, M 'Impact of Customary Inheritance Law on the Status of Women in Africa: A Challenge to Human Rights Activists (Tanzanian Case Study)' (1999) 11 *African Society of International and Comparative Law* 285.

Middleton, N and O'Keefe, P *Rio Plus Ten: Politics, Poverty and the Environment* (London, Pluto Press, 2003).

Mikell, G (ed) *African Feminism: The Politics of Survival in Sub-Saharan Africa* (Philadelphia, University of Pennsylvania Press, 1997).

Mikell, G 'Introduction' in Mikell, G (ed) *African Feminism: The Politics of Survival in Sub-Saharan Africa* (Philadelphia, University of Pennsylvania Press, 1997) 1.

Mills, C *The Racial Contract* (Ithaca, Cornell University Press, 1997).

Minkah-Premo, S *Coping with Violence against Women* (Accra, Asempa Publishers, 2001).

Minow, M 'Interpreting Rights: An Essay for Robert Cover' (1987) 96 *Yale Law Journal* 1860.

Mir-Hosseini, Z 'Islamic Law and Feminism: The Story of a Relationship' Coulson Memorial Lecture, School of Oriental and African Studies, 3 December 2003.

Moghissi, H *Feminism and Islamic Fundamentalism* (London, Zed Press, 1999).

Mohanty a Russo, M and Torres, L (eds) *Third World Women and the Politics of Feminism* (Indianapolis, Indiana University Press, 1991).

Molokomme, A 'Discriminatory Citizenship Laws in Botswana: Emang Basadi' in Women, Law and Development International and Human Rights Watch Women's Rights Project (eds) *Women's Human Rights Step by Step* (Washington DC, Women, Law and Development International, 1997) 133.

Molyneaux, M and Razavi, S (eds) *Gender, Justice, Development and Rights* (Oxford, Clarendon Press, 2003).

Monbiot, G 'On the Edge of Lunacy' *Guardian* (London, 6 January 2004) 23.

Montreal Principles on Women's Economic Social and Cultural Rights, reproduced in (2004) *Human Rights Quarterly* 760, also available from http://cescr.org/node/view/697.

Morolong, S 'Overview of Recent Developments in the Law of Marriage in Botswana' in A Bainham (ed) *International Survey of Family Law 2002* (Bristol, Jordan Publishing, 2002) 67.

Moon, G (ed) *Making Her Rights a Reality: Women's Human Rights and Development* (Victoria, Community Aid Abroad, 1995).

Moore, SF 'Law and Change: The Semi-Autonomous Social Field as an Appropriate Area of Study' (1973) 7 *Law and Society Review* 719.

Moore, SF *Law as Process* (Oxford, James Currey, 1978).

Moore, SF *Social Facts and Fabrications: 'Customary' Law on Kilimanjaro, 1880–1980* (New York, Cambridge University Press, 1986).

Morgan, C 'Anglicans Say US Church is Taking Aid Revenge in Gay Row' *Sunday Times* (London, 19 October 2003).

Morrell, R 'Mobilising Caring in Men (2002) 42 *Women's Health Project Review* 14.

Moser, C *Gender, Planning and Development* (New York, Routledge, 1993).

Moser, R 'Transformation of Southern Tanzania Marriages' in D Parkin and D Nyamwaya (eds) *Transformation of African Marriage* (Manchester, Manchester University Press, 1987) 323.

Mosse, J *Half the World, Half a Chance: An Introduction to Gender and Development* (Oxford, OXFAM, 1993).

Motala, A 'Non-Governmental Organizations in the African System' in M Evans and R Murray (eds) *The African Charter on Human and Peoples' Rights: The System in Practice 1986–2000* (Cambridge, Cambridge University Press, 2002) 246.

Mozze, J 'From Family Planning and Maternal Child Health to Reproductive Health' in C Sweetman and F de Selincourt (eds) *Population and Reproductive Rights* (Oxford, OXFAM, 1994) 6.

Msimang, S 'HIV/AIDS, Globalisation and the International Women's Movement' in J Kerr and C Sweetman (eds) *Women Reinventing Globalization* (Oxford, OXFAM, 2003) 109.

Msimang, S 'Caution! Women Moving: Strategies for Organizing Feminist Visions of the Future' in J Kerr *et al* (eds) *The Future of Women's Rights* (London, Zed Press, 2004) 170.

Mubangizi, J 'Too Pregnant to Work: The Dilemma of Economic Rationality versus Equality *Woolworths (Pty) Ltd v Whitehead*' (2000) 16 *South African Journal on Human Rights* 691.

Mugisa, A 'Stop Bride Price Women Demand' *New Vision* (Kampala, 25 July 2002) downloaded from: http://allafrica.com/stories/printable/200207250061.html.

Mukabideli, T 'Refugee Health: The Plight of Rwandan Women' (2000) 3 *Initiatives on Reproductive Health Policy* 10.

Mukhopadhay, M 'Some Thoughts on Gender and Culture' in D Eade (ed) *Development and Social Diversity* (Oxford, OXFAM, 1999) 93.

Munene, M 'Will the Law Review Process Give Women a Voice?' *Daily Nation* (Nairobi, 12 December 2001) downloaded from: http://www.nationaudio.com/news/DailyNation/Today/News/News3.html.

Murray, R *The African Commission on Human Rights and International Law* (Oxford, Hart Publishing, 2000).

Murray, R 'A Feminist Perspective on Reform of the African Human Rights System' (2001) 1 *African Human Rights Law Journal* 205.

Murray, R *Human Rights in Africa* (Cambridge, Cambridge University Press, 2004).

Murison, J, Griffiths, A and King, K (eds) *Remaking Law in Africa: Transnationalism Persons and Rights* (Edinburgh, Centre of African Studies, 2004).

Mutua, M 'The Banjul Charter and the African Cultural Fingerprint: An Evaluation of the Language of Duties' (1995) 35 *Virginia Journal of International Law* 339.

Mutua, M 'Savages, Victims, and Saviors: The Metaphor of Human Rights' (2001) 42 *Harvard International Law Journal* 201.

Mutua, M 'Banjul Charter: The Case for an African Cultural Fingerprint' in A An Na'im (ed) *Cultural Transformation and Human Rights* (London, Zed Press, 2002) 67.

Mutungu, P *Life Skills, Sexual Maturation and Sanitation: What's (Not) Happening in Our Schools. An Exploratory Study from Kenya* (Harare, Weaver Press, 2003).

Mvududu, S and McFadden, P (eds) *Reconceptualizing the Family* (Harare, WLSA, 2001).

Mwenda, L 'Review of the Political Situation of Women in Malawi' in J Foster *et al* (eds) *Women in Politics and Decision Making in Southern Africa* (Harare, WILDAF, 1999) 22.

N

Naggita, E 'Why Men Come Out Ahead: The Legal Regime and the Protection and Realization of Women's Rights in Uganda' (2000) 6 *East African Journal of Peace* 34.

Nagubere-Munaaba, F 'Victims of Protection' (M Phil thesis submitted to the Faculty of Law, University of Zimbabwe, Harare, 2001).

Nako, N 'Possessing the Voice of the Other: African Women and the "Crisis of Representation" in Alice Walker's *Possessing the Secret of Joy*' (2001) *Jenda: A Journal of Culture and African Women's Studies*: 1, 2, downloaded from http://www.jendajournal.com/jenda/vol1.2/nako.html.

Naldi, G 'Future Trends in Human Rights in Africa: The Increased Role of the OAU' in M Evans and R Murray (eds) *The African Charter on Human and Peoples' Rights: The System in Practice, 1986–2000* (Cambridge, Cambridge University Press, 2002) 1.

Narayan, D, Chambers, R, Shah, M and Petesch, P *Voices of the Poor Crying Out for Change* (Oxford, Oxford University Press, 2000).

Narayan, D, Patel, R, Schaft, K, Rademacher, A and Koch-Schulte, S *Voices of the Poor: Can Anyone Hear Us?* (Washington DC, World Bank, 2000).

Narayan, D and Petesch, P *Voices of the Poor from Many Lands* (Washington DC, World Bank; New York, Oxford University Press, 2002).

Narayan, U *Dislocating Cultures: Identities, Traditions, and Third-World Feminism* (New York, Routledge, 1997).

Naude, T 'The Value of Life: A Note on *Christian Lawyers Association of South Africa v The Minster of Health*' (1999) 15 *South Africa Journal on Human Rights* 541.

Naylor, N 'The Long Walk to Freedom from Sexual Harassment' (paper presented at the Advancing Women's Rights Conference, Hosted by the Women's Law Centre, Cape Town, 30–31 October 2003) available at http://www.wlce.co.za/conference2003/2003conference_naylor.php.

Nazer, M and Lewis, D *Slave* (London, Virago Press, 2004).

Ncube, W *Family Law in Zimbabwe* (Harare, Legal Resources Foundation, 1989).

Ncube, W 'Dealing with Inequities in Customary Law: Action, Reaction and Social Change in Zimbabwe' (1991) 5 *International Journal of Law Policy and the Family* 58.

Ncube, W (ed) *Law, Culture, Tradition and Children's Rights in Eastern and Southern Africa: Issues in Law and Society* (Aldershot, Dartmouth, 1998).

Ncube, W 'Defending and Protecting Gender under a Decidedly Undecided Constitution in Zimbabwe' in J Eekelaar and T Nhlapo (eds) *Changing Family* (Oxford, Hart Publishing, 1998) 509.

Ncube, W and Stewart, J (eds) *Widowhood and Inheritance Laws, Customs and Practices in Southern Africa* (Harare, Women and Law in Southern Africa, 1995).

Ndebele, N *The Cry of Winnie Mandela: A Novel* (London, Ayebia Clarke Publishing, 2003).

Nduta, L 'Leaders Condemn MP Sifuna as Unfit for 21st Century Parliament' *Daily Nation* (Nairobi, 22 March 2002) downloaded from: http://www.nationaudio.com/News/DailyNation/Today/News49.html.

NEPAD see www.iss.co.za/nepad.

Newton, S 'Post-Communist Legal Reform: The Elision of the Political' in J Hatchard and A Perry-Kessaris (eds) Law *and Development: Facing Complexity in the 21st Century* (London, Cavendish Press, 2003) 161.

Ngubane, J *Conflict of Minds* (New York, Books in Focus, 1979).

Ngwake, J 'Realizing Women's Economic, Social and Cultural Rights: Challenges and Strategies in Nigeria' (2002) 14 *Canadian Journal of Women and Law* 142.

Ngwala, A 'The New Land Acts in Tanzania and Women's Access to Land Rights' (paper presented at WLSA Colloquium, Kariba, Zimbabwe, 1999; on file with the author).

Nhlapo, T 'International Protection of Human Rights and the Family: African Variations on a Common Theme' (1989) 3 *International Journal of Law, Policy and the Family* 1.

Nhlapo, T *Marriage and Divorce in Swazi Law and Custom* (Mbabane, Websters, 1992).

Nhlapo, T 'Cultural Diversity, Human Rights and the Family in Contemporary Africa: Lessons from the South African Constitutional Debate' (1995) 8 *International Journal of Law, Family and Policy* 208.

Nhlapo, T 'African Family Law under an Undecided Constitution—the Challenge for Law Reform in South Africa' in J Eekelaar and T Nhlapo (eds) *Changing Family* (Oxford, Hart Publishing, 1998) 617.

Nherere, P and d'Engelbronner-Kolf, M (eds) *The Institutionalisation of Human Rights in Southern Africa* (Oslo, Nordic Human Rights Publications, 1993).

Nkiwane, V *Marital Rape: What are the Consequences of Removing the Husband's Immunity from Prosecution?* (Dissertation submitted in partial fulfilment of the requirements for the Post Graduate Diploma in Women's Law, Women's Law Centre, University of Zimbabwe, 2000).

Nnaemeka, O 'Development, Cultural Forces, and Women's Achievement in Africa' (1996) 18 *Law and Policy* 251.

Nnaemeka, O (ed) *Sisterhood Feminisms and Power* (Asmara, Africa World Press, 1998).

Nnaemeka, O 'Introduction: Reading the Rainbow' in O Nnaemeka (ed) *Sisterhood: Feminisms and Power from Africa to the Diaspora* (Asmara, Africa World Press, 1998).

Nobhuro, N 'Aspects of Change in Bridewealth among the Iteso of Kenya' in D Parkin and D Nyamwaya (eds) *Transformation of African Marriage* (Manchester, Manchester University Press, 1987) 183.

Norway Ministry of Foreign Affairs *Fighting Poverty: The Norwegian Government's Action Plan for Combating Poverty in the South Towards 2015* (Oslo, Norwegian Ministry of Foreign Affairs, 2002).

Ntampaka, C 'Reconciling the Sources of Law in the Burundi Code of Persons and of the Family' in A Bainham (ed) *The International Survey of Family Law 1997* (Hague, Kluwer Law International, 1999) 65.

Nussbaum, M 'Women and Human Development: The Capabilities Approach' in M Molyneaux and S Razavi (eds) *Gender, Justice, Development and Rights* (Oxford, Clarendon Press, 2003) 45.

Nwabuzor, S 'Opposition to Proposed HB22 Bill on Female Genital Mutilation' (2001) 1 *Jenda: A Journal of Culture and African Women Studies:* 1, downloaded from http:///www.jendajournal.com/jenda/vol1.1/nwaubuzor.html.

Nwanko, O 'Violence against Women: An Overview' in Constitutional Rights Project (ed) *Unequal Rights: Discriminatory Laws and Practices against Women in Nigeria* (Lagos, Constitutional Rights Project, 1995) 50.

Nwosu, E 'The Law and Women: Theory and Practice' in Constitutional Rights Project (ed) *Unequal Rights: Discriminatory Laws and Practices against Women in Nigeria* (Lagos, Constitutional Rights Project, 1995) 18.

Nyamu, C 'How Should Human Rights and Development Respond to Cultural Legitimization of Gender Hierarchy in Developing Countries?' (2000) 41 *Harvard International Law Journal* 381.

Nyamu, C 'The International Human Rights Regime and Rural Women in Kenya' (2000) 6 *East African Journal of Peace and Human Rights* 1.

Nyamu-Musembi, C ' "Sitting on her Husband's Back with her Hands in his Pockets": Commentary on Judicial Decision Making in Marital Property Cases in Kenya' in A Bainham (ed) *International Survey of Family Law 2002* (Bristol, Jordan Publishing, 2002) 229.

Nyamu-Musembi, C 'Are Local Norms and Practices Fences or Pathways? The Example of Women's Property Rights' in A An Na'im (ed) *Cultural Transformation and Human Rights in Africa* (London, Zed Press, 2002) 126.

Nyirarukundo, M 'Reproductive Rights in Senegal: Limited by Social Expectations' (2000) 3 *Initiatives in Reproductive Health Policy* 7.

Nzegwu, N 'Gender Equality in Dual-Sex System: The Case of Onitsha' (2001) *Jenda: A Journal of Culture and African Women's Studies* at http://www.jendajournal.com/jenda/vol1.1/nzegwu.html.

Nzegwu, N 'Questions of Agency: Development, Donors, and Women of the South' (2002) *Jenda: A Journal of Culture and African Women's Studies* http://www.jendajournal.com/jenda/vol2.1/nzegwu.html.

Nzioki, A 'The Effects of Land Tenure on Women's Access and Control of Land in Kenya' in A An Na'im (ed) *Cultural Transformation and Human Rights in Africa* (London, Zed Press, 2002) 218.

Nzunda, M 'Criminal Law in Internal Conflict of Laws in Malawi' (1985) 29 *Journal of African Law* 129.

O

Obilade, A (ed) *Women In Law* (Lagos, Southern University Law Centre and Faculty of Law, Lagos, 1993).

Obiora, L 'Bridges and Barricades: Rethinking Polemics and Intransigence in the Campaign against Female Circumcision' (1997) 47 *Case Western Reserve Law Review* 275.

Odame, H 'Men in Women's Groups: A Gender and Agency Analysis of Local Institutions' in Cleaver, F (ed) *Masculinities Matter: Men, Gender and Development* (London, Zed Press, 2002) 138.

Odinkalu, C 'Customary Law and Women's Inheritance Rights in Commonwealth Africa' (2000) 13 *Interights Bulletin* 39.

Odinkalu, C 'Why More Africans Don't Use Human Rights Language' (2000) *Human Rights Dialogue* 3.

Odinkalu, C 'Back to the Future: the Imperative of Prioritizing for the Protection of Human Rights in Africa' (2003) 47 *Journal of African* Law 1.

Odongo-Mwaka, B 'Women in the Democratic Process in Uganda: Gender and Justice' in Hatchard, J and Perry-Kessaris, A (eds) *Law and Development: Facing Complexity in the 21st Century* (London, Cavendish Press, 2003) 246.

O'Donovan, K *Sexual Divisions in Law* (London, Weidenfeld & Nicholson, 1985).

O'Donovan, *Family Law Matters* (London, Pluto Press, 1993).

Ogbuagu, S 'Depo-Provera: A Choice or an Imposition on the African Woman. A Case Study of Depo Provera Usage in Maiduguri' in A Imam *et al* (eds) *Women and the Family in Nigeria* (Dakar, CODESRIA, 1989) 81.

Okafor, O 'Modest Harvests: on the Significant (but Limited) Impact of Human Rights NGOs on Legislative and Executive Behaviour in Nigeria' (2004) 48 *Journal of African Law* 23.

Oloka-Onyango, J 'Modern Day Missionaries or Misguided Miscreants? NGOs, the Women's Movement and the Promotion of Human Rights in Africa' in W Benedek,

E Kisaakye and G Oberleitner (eds) *Human Rights of Women: International Instruments and African Experiences* (London, Zed Press, 2002) 286.

Oloka-Onyango, J and Tamale, S 'The Personal is Political, or Why Women's Rights are Indeed Human Rights: An African Perspective on International Feminism' (1995) 17 *Human Rights Quarterly* 691.

Oloko, S and Saba, F 'Psychosocial Effects of Reproductive Rights Abuse' in B Owasonoye (ed) *Reproductive Rights of Women in Nigeria: The Legal, Economic and Cultural Dimensions* (Lagos, Human Development Initiatives, 1999) 140.

Omoigu, N 'Protest against Bill H22 Outlawing "FGM" in Nigeria' (2001) *Jenda: A Journal of Culture and African Women Studies* 1, 1, downloaded from http://www.jendajournal.com/jenda/vol1.1/omogui.html.

Osborn, A and Boseley, S 'EU States May Ban Aid to States that Allow Female Circumcision' *Guardian* (London, 30 November, 2000).

Otto, D 'Holding Up Half the Sky But for Whose Benefit?' (1996) 6 *Australian Feminist Law Journal* 7.

Otto, D ' "Gender Comment": Why Does the UN Committee on Economic, Social and Cultural Rights Need a General Comment on Women?' (2002) 14 *Canadian Journal of Women and the Law* 1.

Ouguergouz, F *The African Charter on Human and Peoples' Rights* (Leiden, Brill Publishers, 2003).

Overseas Development Institute (ODI) 'Can We Attain the Millennium Development Goals in Education and Health through Public Expenditure and Aid?' (April 2003) *ODI Briefing Paper*.

Overseas Development Institute (ODI) 'What Can We Do with a Rights Based Approach to Development?' (1999) 3 *Briefing Paper*.

Ovonji-Odida, I 'Non Consensual Sex in Marriage and Other Forms of Sexual Abuse: Uganda' in CHANGE *Non Consensual Sex in Marriage Information Package Number One* (London, CHANGE, 1999) 1.

Owasonoye, B (ed) *Reproductive Rights of Women in Nigeria: The Legal, Economic and Cultural Dimensions* (Lagos, Human Development Initiatives, 1999).

Owasonoye, B 'Right to Family Assets and Succession' in Owasonoye, B (ed) *Reproductive Rights of Women in Nigeria: The Legal, Economic and Cultural Dimensions* (Lagos, Human Development Initiatives, 1999) 114.

Oyekanmi, F 'Women and the Law: Historical and Contemporary Perspectives in Nigeria' in A Obilade (ed) *Women in Law* (Lagos, Southern University Law Centre and Faculty of Law, 1993) 28.

Oyewumi, O *The Invention of Women: Making and African Sense of Western Gender Discourse* (Minneapolis, University of Minnesota Press, 1997).

Oyewumi, O 'Ties That Bind: Feminism, Sisterhood and Other Foreign Relations' (2001) *Jenda: A Journal of Culture and African Women Studies* at http://www.jendajournal.com/jenda/vol1.1/oyewumi.html.

Oyewumi, O 'Alice in Motherland: Reading Alice Walker on Africa and Screening the Colour "Black" ' (2001) *Jenda: A Journal of Culture and African Women's Studies;* 1, 2, downloaded from http://www.jendajournal.com/jenda/vol1.2/oyewumi.html.

Owen, M *A World of Widows* (London, Zed Press, 1996).

OXFAM *Cut the Cost Campaign* (Oxford, OXFAM, 2002) See www.oxfam.org.uk/cutthecost.

P

Paliwala, A 'Family Transformation and Family Law: Some African Developments in Financial Support on Relationship Breakdown' in S Adelman and A Paliwala (eds) *Law and Crisis in the Third World* (London, Zell, 1993) 270.

Palley, C *The Constitutional History and Law of Southern Rhodesia 1888–1965* (London, Oxford University Press, 1966).

Pandjiarjian, V 'A Daring Proposal: Campaigning for an Inter-American Convention on Sexual Rights and Reproductive Rights' in J Kerr and C Sweetman (eds) *Women Reinventing Globalization* (Oxford, OXFAM, 2003) 77.

Parker, M 'Female Circumcision and Cultures of Sexuality' in T Skelton and T Allen (eds) 'Culture and Global Change' (London, Routledge, 1998) 201.

Parkin, D and Nyamwaya, D (eds) *Transformations of African Marriage* (Manchester, Manchester University Press, 1987).

Parkin, D and Nyamwaya, D 'Introduction. Transformations of African Marriage: Change and Choice' in D Parkin and D Nyamwaya (eds) *Transformations of African Marriage* (Manchester, Manchester University Press, 1987) 1.

Patel, V, Mutambirwa, J and Nhiwatiwa, S 'Stressed, Depressed or Bewitched? A Perspective on Mental Health, Culture and Religion' in D Eade (ed) *Development for Health* (Oxford, OXFAM, 1997) 40.

Peter, C *Human Rights in Tanzania: Selected Cases and Materials* (Cologne, Rudiger Koppe Verlag, 1997).

Peters, J and Wolper, A (eds) *Women's Rights, Human Rights: International Feminist Perspectives* (New York, Routledge, 1995).

Phillips, A and Morris, H *Marriage Laws in Africa* (London, Oxford University Press, 1971).

Physicians for Human Rights 'War Related Sexual Violence in Sierra Leone: A Population Based Assessment' (23 January 2002) downloaded from http://www.phrusa.org/research/sierra_leone.report.html.

Pickup, F, Williams, S and Sweetman, C *Ending Violence against Women: A Challenge for Development and Humanitarian* Work (Oxford, OXFAM, 2001).

Pieterse, M 'The Promotion of Equality and Prevention of Unfair Discrimination Act 4 of 2000: Final Nail in the Customary Law Coffin?'(2000) 117 *South Africa Law Journal* 627.

Pillay, N 'Violence against Women: State Sponsored Violence' in United Nations (ed) *Bringing International Human Rights Law Home* (New York, United Nations, 2002) 61.

Pippan, C 'A Donor View: The EU, Development, Co-operation and the Non State Sector' in G Hollands and G Ansell (eds) *Winds of Small Change: Civil Society Interaction with the African State* (Vienna, Austrian Development Institute, 1998) 140.

Pityana, B 'The Challenge of Culture for Human Rights in Africa: The African Charter in Comparative Context' in M Evans and R Murray (eds) *The African Charter on Human and Peoples' Rights: The System in Practice, 1986–2000* (Cambridge, Cambridge University Press, 2002) 219.

Population Action International 'Why the Global Gag Rule Undermines US Foreign Policy and Harms Women's Health' downloaded from: http://www.populationaction.org/resources/factsheets/factsheet_5.htm.

Q

Quansah, E 'Is the Right to get Pregnant a Fundamental Human Right in Botswana?' (1995) 39 *Journal of African Law* 97.
Quashigah, E and Okafor, O (eds) *Legitimate Governance in Africa* (Hague, Kluwer International, 1999).
Quassem, Y 'Law of the Family (Personal Status Law)' in N Bernard-Maugiron and B Dupret (eds) *Egypt and Its Laws* (The Hague, Kluwer Law International, 2002) 19.
Quattara, M, Sen, P and Thomson, M 'Forced Marriage, Forced Sex: The Perils of Childhood for Girls' in C Sweetman (ed) *Violence against Women* (Oxford, OXFAM, 1998) 27.

R

Rahman, A and Toubia, N *Female Genital Mutilation: A Guide to Laws and Practices Worldwide* (London, Zed Press, 2000).
Rahmatian, A 'Termination of Marriage in Nigerian Family Laws: The Need for Reform and the Relevance of the Tanzanian Experience' (1996) 10 *International Journal of Law, Policy and the Family* 281.
Rai, S (ed) *International Perspectives on Gender and Democratization* (New York, Macmillan, 2000).
Randall, M 'Refugee Law and State Accountability for Violence against Women: A Comparative Analysis of Legal Approaches to Recognizing Asylum Claims Based on Gender Persecution' (2002) 25 *Harvard Women's Law Journal* 281.
Randriamoro, Z 'African Women Challenging Neo-Liberal Economic Orthodoxy: The Conception and Mission of the GERA Programme' in J Kerr and C Sweetman (eds) *Women Reinventing Globalization* (Oxford, OXFAM, 2003) 44.
Ranger, T 'The Invention of Tradition' in T Ranger and E Hobsbawm (eds) *The Invention of Tradition* (Cambridge, Cambridge University Press, 1983) 211.
Rao, A 'The Politics of Gender and Culture in International Human Rights Discourse' in J Peters and A Wolper (eds) *Women's Rights, Human Rights: International Feminist Perspectives* (New York, Routledge, 1995) 167.
Rao, A and Friedman, M 'Transforming Institutions: History and Challenges: An International Perspective' in Royal Tropical Institute (KIT) and OXFAM (eds) *Institutionalizing Gender Equality: Commitment, Policy and Practice* (Amsterdam, KIT; Oxford, OXFAM, 2000) 67.
Rathgeber, E 'WID, WAD, GAD: Trends and Research in Practice' 1990 (24) *Journal of Developing Areas* 489.
Rea (Lord) House of Lords Debate on Female Circumcision Hansard HL (10 November 1998) col 738.
Read, J and Morris, HF *Indirect Rule and the Search for Justice* (Oxford, Clarendon Press, 1972).

Reaves, M 'Alternative Rite to Female Circumcision Spreading in Kenya' Africa News Online, 9 November 1997, downloaded from: http://www.africanews.org/specials/19971119_fgm.html.

Rehof, L *Guide to the Travaux Préparatoires of the United Nations Convention on the Elimination of All Forms of Discrimination against Women* (Dordrecht, Martinus Nijhoff, 1993).

Religious Tolerance Organization 'Female Genital Mutilation in Africa, the Middle East, and the Far East' at http://www.religioustolerance.org/fem_cirm.htm.

Rennie, D 'Republicans in Threat to Block Overseas Aid' *Daily Telegraph* (London, 27 November 2004).

Renteln, A 'Is the Cultural Defense Detrimental to the Health of Children?' (1994) 7 *Law and Anthropology International Yearbook for Legal Anthropology* 27.

Renteln, A *The Cultural Defense* (Oxford, Oxford University Press, 2004).

Reuters, Johannesburg 'Virginity Tests on Comeback Trail in South Africa' reproduced in (2001) *Jenda: A Journal of Culture and African Women Studies* at http://www.jendajournal.com/jenda/vol1.1/virginity.html.

Reynolds, P 'Transitional Perspectives in Women's Rights' (2004) 14 *Interights Bulletin* 143.

Rhodesia Legislative Assembly Debates 1969, Minster of Internal Affairs, col 629.

Roberts, S 'Some Notes on "African Customary Law" ' (1984) 28 *Journal of African Law* 1.

Roberts, S 'Three Models of Family Mediation' in R Dingwall and J Eekelaar (eds) *Divorce Mediation and the Legal Process* (Oxford, Oxford University Press, 1988) 145.

Robinson, S 'The Last Rites' *Time* (London, 5 December 2001) at http://www.time.com/time/europe/af/printout/0,9869,1875799,00.html.

Rodney, W *How Europe Underdeveloped Africa* (London, Bogle L'Overture, 1972).

Rooker (Lord) House of Lords Debate on Asylum Seekers: Female Persecution, Hansard HL (10 July 2001) col 1004.

Ross, F *Bearing Witness: Women and the Truth and Reconciliation Commission in South Africa* (Cambridge, Polity Press, 2002).

Rowlands, J 'Empowerment Examined' in D Eade (ed) *Development and Social Diversity* (Oxford, OXFAM, 1999) 86.

Royal Tropical Institute (KIT) and OXFAM *Institutionalizing Gender Equality: Commitment, Policy and Practice* (Oxford, OXFAM and Amsterdam, KIT, 2000).

Royal Tropical Institute (KIT) and OXFAM *Gender Perspectives on Property and Inheritance* (Amsterdam, KIT and Oxford, OXFAM, 2001).

Roys, C 'Widows and Orphans Property Disputes: The Impact of AIDS in Rakai District Uganda' in D Eade (ed) *Development for Health* (Oxford, OXFAM, 1997) 94.

Rugene, N 'FGM on Children, Forced Marriages Outlawed' *Daily Nation* (Nairobi, 11 December 2001) at http://www.nationaudio.com/News/DailyNation/Today/News28.html.

Rwezaura, B and Wanitzek, U 'Family Law Reform in Tanzania: A Socio-Legal Report' (1988) 2 *International Journal of Law, Policy and the Family* 1.

Rwezaura, B 'Parting the Long Grass: Revealing and Reconceptualising the African Family' (1995) 35 *Journal of Legal Pluralism and Unofficial Law* 25.

Rwezaura, B 'Protecting the Rights of the Girl Child in Commonwealth Jurisdictions' in A Byrnes *et al* (eds) *Advancing the Human Rights of Women: Using International Human Rights Standards in Domestic Litigation* (London, Commonwealth Secretariat, 1997) 114.

Rwezaura, B 'Competing Images of Childhood in the Social and Legal Systems of Contemporary Sub-Saharan Africa' (1998) 12 *International Journal of Law, Policy and the Family* 253.

Rwezaura, B 'The Proposed Abolition of *De Facto* Unions in Tanzania: A Case of Sailing against the Social Current' in J Eekelaar and T Nhlapo (eds) *Changing Family* (Oxford, Hart Publishing, 1998) 175.

Rwezaura, B 'Gender Justice and Children's Rights: A Banner for Family Law Reform in Tanzania' in A Bainham (ed) *International Survey of Family Law 1997* (The Hague, Kluwer International, 1999) 413.

Rwezaura, B 'The Value of a Child: Marginal Children and the Law in Contemporary Tanzania' (2000) 14 *International Journal of Law, Policy and the Family* 326.

Rwezaura, B ' "This is not my Child": The Task of Integrating Orphans into the Mainstream of Society in Tanzania' in A Bainham (ed) *International Survey of Family Law* (Bristol, Jordan Publishing, 2001) 410.

S

Sabbagh, S (ed) *Arab Women: Between Defiance and Restraint* (New York, Olive Branch Press, 1996).

Sachs, A 'Introduction' in J Eekelaar and T Nhlapo (eds) *Changing Family* (Oxford, Hart Publishing, 1998) xi.

Sahel Initiative Third Millennium 'Stop Excision for the Dignity of Women from Mali' (2001/2) [musical CD].

Salih, M *African Democracies and African Politics* (London, Pluto Press, 2001).

Sakala, F 'Violence against Women in Southern Africa' in P McFadden (ed) *Southern Africa in Transition: A Gendered Perspective* (Harare, SAPES, 1998) 27.

Samuels, S 'Hong-Kong on Women, Asian Values and the Law' (1999) *Human Rights Quarterly* 707.

SARDC *see* Southern African Research and Development Centre.

Schatz, E 'Conversations on Sex, Condoms and HIV/AIDS in Rural Malawi' (2003) 45 *Women's Health Project Review* 17.

Schmidt, E *Peasants, Traders and Wives: Shona Women in the History of Zimbabwe 1870–1939* (Oxford, James Currey, 1992).

Schraeder, P (ed) *Exporting Democracy Rhetoric v Reality* (Boulder, Lynne Rienner Publishers, 2002).

Schuler, M (ed) *From Basic Needs to Basic Rights: Women's Claim to Human Rights* (Washington DC, Women Law and Development International, 1995).

Seager, J *The Atlas of Women* (London, The Women's Press, 2003).

Sellars, P 'The Context of Sex Violence: Violence as Violations of International Humanitarian Law' in K McDonald and G Swaak (eds) *Substantive and Procedural Aspects of International Criminal Law: The Experience of International and National Courts* (The Hague, Kluwer, 2000) 263.

Sewell, T 'It Takes a Race Case for Firms to Listen' *Voice* (London, 4 June 2004).

Sen, A *Development as Freedom* (Oxford, Oxford University Press, 1999).

Sen, A 'A Hundred Million Women are Missing' *New York Review of Books*, reproduced in

H Steiner and P Alston (eds) *International Human Rights in Context: Law, Politics, Morals* (Oxford, Clarendon Press, 2000) 165.

Sen, P 'Change Programme on Non Consensual Sex in Marriage: Briefing Paper. Ending the Presumption of Consent' in CHANGE *Non Consensual Sex in Marriage Project Information Package Number One* (London, CHANGE, 1999).

Shabangu, D 'Review of the Political Situation of Women in Swaziland' in J Foster *et al* (eds) *Women in Politics and Decision Making in Southern Africa* (Harare, WILDAF, 1999) 96.

Sheikh, L 'TAMWA: Levina's Song—Supporting Women in Tanzania' in H Chigudu (ed) *Composing a New Song: Stories of Empowerment from Africa* (London, Commonwealth Secretariat, 2003) 95.

Shell-Duncan, B and Hernlund, Y (eds) *Female 'Circumcision' in Africa: Culture, Controversy and Change* (Colorado, Lynne Rienner Publishers, 2000).

Shell-Duncan, B, Obiero, W and Muruli, L 'Women without Choices: The Debate over Medicalization of Female Genital Cutting and Its Impact on a Northern Kenyan Community' in B Shell-Duncan and Y Hernlund (eds) *Female 'Circumcision' in Africa: Culture, Controversy and Change* (Colorado, Lynne Rienner Publishers, 2000) 109.

Shenje-Peyton, A 'Balancing Gender Equality and Cultural Identity: Marriage Payments in Post-Colonial Zimbabwe' (1996) 9 *Harvard Human Rights Journal* 105.

Shisano, O and Zungu-Dirwayi, M 'HIV/AIDS in South Africa: Entitlement and Rights to Health—Implications of the 2002 HIV Survey' in J Murison *et al* (eds) *Remaking Law in Africa: Transnationalism Persons and Rights* (Edinburgh, Centre of African Studies, 2004) 313.

Shivji, I *The Concept of Human Rights in Africa* (Dakar, CODESRIA, 1989).

Sikazwe, E 'Women for Change and its Work with Rural Communities' in H Chigudu (ed) *Composing a New Song: Stories of Empowerment from Africa* (London, Commonwealth Secretariat, 2003) 129.

Simons, H *African Women: Their Legal Status in South Africa* (London, Hurst and Co, 1968).

Sinclair, J 'Ebb and Flow: The Retreat of the Legislature and the Development of a Constitutional Jurisprudence to Reshape Family' in A Bainham (ed) *International Survey of Family Law* (Bristol, Jordan Publishing, 2002) 393.

Sinclair, J 'Embracing New Family Forms, Entrenching Outmoded Stereotypes' in P Lodrup and E Modvar (eds) *Family Life and Human Rights* (Oslo, Gyldendal Akademisk, 2004) 801.

Sinclair, J and Heaton, J *The Law of Marriage* vol 1 (Cape Town, Juta, 1996).

Sinding, S 'Resist Attempts to Roll Cairo Back' (2003) 44 *Women's Health Project Review* 17.

Sivaramakrishnan, A 'An Under-Caste in Britain?' *Hindu* (24 May 2004).

Skard, T *Continent of Mothers: Understanding and Promoting Development in Africa Today* (London, Zed Press, 2003).

Skelton, T and Allen, T (eds) *Culture and Global Change* (London, Routledge, 1998).

Slack, A 'Female Circumcision: A Critical Appraisal' (1988) 10 *Human Rights Quarterly* 43.

Slim, H 'What is Development?' in D Eade (ed) *Development and Social Diversity* (Oxford, OXFAM, 1999) 63.

Smart, C *The Ties That Bind* (London, Routledge, 1984).

Smart, C *Feminism and the Power of Law* (London, Routledge, 1989).

Smith, J 'Ignore the Fertility Industry's Zealots: You can be Childless and a *Real* Woman' *The Times* (London, 27 August 2003).

Snyder, F 'Colonialism and the Legal Form: The Creation of Customary Law in Senegal' (1981) 19 *Journal of Legal Pluralism* 49.

Snyder, M and Tadesse, M (eds) *African Women and Development* (London, Zed Books, 1995).

Snyder, M and Tadesse, M 'Introduction' in Snyder, M and Tadesse, M (eds) *African Women and Development* (London, Zed Books, 1995) 1.

Sonnekus, J 'Some Reflections on the Position of a Deceived Wife in a Dualistic System of Matrimonial Property Law' in P Lodrup and E Modvar (eds) *Family Life and Human Rights* (Oslo, Gyldendal Akademisk, 2004) 839.

Soundararajan, S 'Adequately Addressed' *Hindu* (27 May 2004).

Sousa Santos, B 'Towards a Multicultural Conception of Human Rights' (1997) XXIV *Sociolgia del Diritto* 27.

Southern African Research and Documentation Centre (SARDC) *Beyond Inequalities: Women in Zambia* (Harare, SARDC, 1998).

Southern African Research and Documentation Centre (SARDC) *Beyond Inequalities: Women in Mozambique* (Maputo, SARDC, 2000).

Southern African Research and Documentation Centre (SARDC) *Beyond Inequalities: Women in Southern Africa* (Harare, SARDC, 2000).

Sow, F 'Mutilations Génitales Féminines et Droits Humains en Afrique' (1998) 23 *Development* 13.

Sow, F 'Fundamentalism, Globalisation, and Women's Human Rights in Senegal' in J Kerr and C Sweetman (eds) *Women Reinventing Globalization* (Oxford, OXFAM, 2003) 69.

Spadacini, A and Nichols, P 'Campaigning against Female Genital Mutilation in Ethiopia Using Popular Education' (1998) 6 *Gender and Development* 2.

Spelman, E *Inessential Woman: Problems of Exclusion in Feminist Thought* (London, Women's Press, 1990).

Steiner, H and Alston, P *International Human Rights in Context: Law, Politics, Morals* (Oxford, Clarendon Press, 2000).

Stephens, M 'Women Still Living in Fear' (1999) 32 *Women's Health Project* 1.

Stephens, M 'Abortion Reform in South Africa' (2000) 3 *Initiatives in Reproductive Health Policy* 4.

Stewart, A 'The Dilemmas of Law in Women's Development' in S Adelman and A Paliwala (eds) *Law and Crisis in the Third World* (London, Zell, 1993) 219.

Stewart, A 'Should Women Give Up on the State? The African Experience' in S Rai and G Lievesley (eds) *Women and the State: International Perspectives* (London, Taylor Francis, 1996) 23.

Stewart, A (ed) *Gender, Law and Social Justice* (Oxford, Blackstone, 2000).

Stewart, A 'The Contribution of Feminist Legal Scholarship to the "Rights Approach to Development"' in A Stewart (ed) *Gender, Law and Social Justice* (Oxford, Blackstone, 2000) 1.

Stewart, A 'Juridifying Gender Justice: From Global Rights to Local Justice' in J Hatchard and A Perry-Kessaris (eds) Law *and Development: Facing Complexity in the 21st Century* (London, Cavendish Press, 2003) 37.

Stewart, A 'Entitlement, Pluralism and Gender Justice in Sub Saharan Africa' in J Murison *et al* (eds) *Remaking Law in Africa: Transnationalism Persons and Rights* (Edinburgh, Centre of African Studies, 2004) 195.

Stewart, J 'Why I Can't Teach Customary Law' in J Eekelaar and T Nhlapo (eds) *Changing Family* (Oxford, Hart Publishing, 1998) 217.

Stiglitz, J *Globalisation and Its Discontents* (London, Penguin, 2002).

Stratton, L 'The Right to Have Rights: Gender Discrimination in National Laws' 77 (1992) *Minnesota Law Review* 195.

Sullivan, D 'The Public/Private Distinction in International Human Rights Law' in J Peters and A Wolper (eds) *Women's Rights, Human Rights: International Feminist Perspectives* (New York, Routledge, 1995)126.

Suzman, J *Minorities in Independent Namibia* (London, Minority Rights Group, 2002).

Sweetman C, 'Editorial' (1996) 4 *Gender and Development* 2.

Sweetman, C (ed) *Women and the Family* (Oxford, OXFAM, 1996).

Sweetman, C (ed) *Violence against Women* (Oxford, OXFAM, 1998).

Sweetman, C (ed) *Gender, Religion and Spirituality* (Oxford, OXFAM, 1998).

Sweetman, C (ed) *Gender and Lifecyles* (Oxford, OXFAM, 2000).

Sweetman, C 'Editorial' in C Sweetman (ed) *Gender and Lifecycles* (Oxford, OXFAM, 2000) 2.

Sweetman, C (ed) *Women and Leadership* (Oxford, OXFAM, 2000).

Sweetman, C (ed) *Gender, Development and Health* (Oxford, OXFAM, 2001).

Sweetman, C (ed) *Beyond Men's Involvement in Gender and Development: Policy and Practice* (Oxford, OXFAM, 2001).

Sweetman, C 'Introduction' in C Sweetman (ed) *Beyond Men's Involvement in Gender and Development: Policy and Practice* (Oxford, OXFAM, 2001) 1.

Sweetman, C and F de Selincourt (eds) *Population and Reproductive Rights* (Oxford, OXFAM, 1994).

T

Tagoe A 'Nkyinkyim, A Violence against Women Project' in Womankind Worldwide (ed) *What Works Where? Successful Strategies to End Violence against Women* (London, Womankind Worldwide, 2002) 12.

Tamale, S *When Hens Begin to Crow: Gender and Parliamentary Politics in Uganda* (Boulder, Westview Press, 1999).

Tamale, S 'Towards Legitimate Governance in Africa: The Case of Affirmative Action and Parliamentary Politics in Uganda' in E Quashigah, O Okafor (eds) *Legitimate Governance in Africa* (Hague, Kluwer International, 1999) 235.

Tamale, S 'How Old is Old Enough? Defilement Law and the Age of Consent in Uganda' (2001) 7 *East African Journal of Peace & Human Rights* 82.

Tamale, S 'Gender Trauma in Africa: Enhancing Women's Access to Resources' (2004) 48 *Journal of African Law* 50.

Tamale, S 'Out of the Closet: Unveiling Sexuality Discourse in Uganda' at http://www.feministafrica.org/2level.html.

Tahzib, F 'Social Factors in the Aetiology of Vesico-Vaginal Fistulae' in A Imam *et al* (ed) *Women and the Family in Nigeria* (Dakar, Codesria, 1989) 75.

Tenthani, R 'Row over Marital Rape Bill' downloaded from: http://.news.bbc.co.uk/hi/english/world/africa/newsid_1728000/11728875.stm.

Teshome, T 'Reflections on the Revised Family Code of 2000' in A Bainham (ed) *International Survey of Family Law 2002* (Bristol, Jordan Publishing, 2002) 153.

Thomas, L ' "*Ngaitana*" (I Will Circumcise Myself): Lessons from Colonial Campaigns to Ban Excision in Meru Kenya' in B Shell-Duncan and Y Yernlund (eds) *Female 'Circumcision' in Africa: Culture, Controversy and Change* (Colorado, Lynne Rienner Publishers, 2000) 129.

Tibatemwa-Ekirikubinza, L *More Sinned against than Sinning: Women's Violent Crime in Uganda* (Copenhagen, Criminalistisk Institut, 1998).

Tibatemwa-Ekirikubinza, L 'Family Relations and the Law in Uganda: Insights into Current Issues' in A Bainham (ed) *International Survey of Family Law 2002* (Bristol, Jordan Publishing, 2002) 433.

Toebes, B 'Towards an Improved Understanding of the International Human Right to Health' (1999) 21 *Human Rights Quarterly* 661.

Toubia, N *Female Genital Mutilation: A Call for Global Action* (New York, Rainbo, 1995).

Toubia, N 'Female Genital Mutilation' in J Peters and A Wolper (eds) *Women's Rights, Human Rights: International Feminist Perspectives* (New York, Routledge, 1995) 224.

Toubia, N 'Legislation as a Tool of Behaviour Change' (paper presented at the Afro-Arab Consultation on Legal Tools for the Prevention of Female Genital Mutilation, Cairo, 21–23 June 2003).

Toungara, J 'Changing the Meaning of Marriage: Women and Family Law in Cote d'Ivoire' in G Mikell (ed) *African Feminism: The Politics of Survival in Sub-Saharan Africa* (Philadelphia, University of Pennsylvania Press, 1997) 53.

Toungara, J 'Changing the Meaning of Marriage: Women and Family Law in Cote d'Ivoire' in Royal Tropical Institute (KIT) and OXFAM (eds) *Gender Perspectives on Property and Inheritance* (Amsterdam, KIT and Oxford, OXFAM, 2001) 33.

Treatment Action Campaign *see* http://www.tac.org.za/.

Tremlett, G 'Morocco Boosts Women's Rights' *Guardian* (London, 21 January 2004).

Tripp, A *Women and Politics in Uganda* (Oxford, James Currey, 2000).

Tripp, A 'The Politics of Women's Rights and Cultural Diversity in Uganda' in M Molyneaux and S Razavi (eds) *Gender Justice, Development and Rights* (Oxford, Oxford University Press, 2003) 413.

Tsanga, A *Taking Law to the People: Gender, Law Reform and Community Legal Education in Zimbabwe* (Harare, Women's Law Centre and Weaver Press, 2003).

Tshuma, L 'The Impact of the IMF/World Bank Dictated Economic Structural Programmes on Human Rights: Erosion of Empowerment Rights' in P Nherere and M d'Engelbronner-Kolf (eds) *The Institutionalisation of Human Rights in Southern Africa* (Oslo, Nordic Human Rights Publications, 1993) 195.

U

UN *see* United Nations.
UNAIDS 'Fact sheet AIDS Epidemic in Sub-Saharan Africa' (2004) from www.unaids.org.
UNAIDS and PANOS *Young Men and HIV: Culture, Poverty and Social Risk* (London, Panos, 2001).
UNDP *Integrating Human Rights with Sustainable Development* (New York, UNDP, 1998).
UNDP *Human Development Report 2000* (New York, UN, 2000).
UNDP *Human Development Report 2003* (New York, United Nations, 2003).
UNDP *Human Development Report: Cultural Liberty in Today's Diverse World* (New York, United Nations, 2004).
UNESCO *Dakar Framework for Action, Education for All: Meeting our Collective Commitments* (UNESCO, Paris 2000) at www.unesco.org/education.
UNHCR *Guidelines on International Protection: Gender Related Persecution within the Context of Article 1A (2) of the 1951 Convention and/or its 1967 Protocol Relating to the Status of Refugees* (7 May 2002) HCR.GIP/02/01.
UNHCR *Sexual Violence against Refugees: Guidelines on Prevention and Responses* (Geneva, UNHCR, 1995).
UNICEF *The State of the World's Children: Education* (New York, UNICEF, 1999).
UNICEF *The State of the World's Children* (New York, UNICEF, 2004).
UNIFEM *Bringing Equality Home: Implementing CEDAW* (New York, UNIFEM, 1998).
United Nations 'Declarations and Reservations' available from http://sim.law.uu.nl/SIM/Library/?RATIF.nsf/1b02bda6311c4e2dc12568b8004f23f4/493002d26b4d8b94c12568bd003a0efc?OpenDocument.
United Nations *The United Nations and the Advancement of Women 1945–1996* (New York, United Nations, 1996).
United Nations *HIV/AIDS and Human Rights: International Guidelines* (New York, United Nations, 1998).
United Nations *1999 World Survey on the Role of Women in Development: Globalization, Gender and Work* (New York, United Nations, 1999).
United Nations 'Traditional Practices Affecting the Health of Women and Girls: A Human Rights Issue' at http:www.unhchr.ch/women/focus-tradpract.html.
United Nations *The Optional Protocol: Texts and Materials* (New York, United Nations, 2000).
United Nations *Beijing to Beijing +5: Review and Appraisal of the Implementation of the Beijing Platform for Action* (New York, United Nations, 2001).
United Nations *Capacity Building in Africa: Effective Aid and Human Capital* (New York, United Nations, 2002).
United Nations *Bringing International Human Rights Law Home* (New York, United Nations, 2002).
United Nations, IWRAW, Commonwealth Secretariat *Assessing the Status of Women: A Guide to Reporting under the Convention on the Elimination of All Forms of Discrimination against Women* (London, Commonwealth Secretariat, 2000).
United Nations, Office for the Coordination of Humanitarian Assistance, IRIN *see* IRIN.

Usman, H 'Harmful Traditional Practices and Reproductive Health' in B Owasanoye (ed) *Reproductive Rights of Women in Nigeria: The Legal, Economic and Cultural Dimensions* (Lagos, Human Development Initiatives, 1999) 46.

Uzodike E 'Women's Rights in Law and Practice: Property Rights' in A Obilade (ed) *Women in Law* (Lagos, Southern University Law Centre and Faculty of Law, 1993) 304.

V

Van Bueren, G *The International Law on the Rights of the Child* (Dordrecht, Martinus Nijhoff, 1995).

Van Bueren, G 'The International Protection of Family Members' Rights as the 21st Century Approaches' (1995) 17 *Human Rights Quarterly* 732.

Van Bueren, G 'Including the Excluded: The Case for an Economic, Social and Cultural Human Rights Act' (2002) *Public Law* 456.

Van Woudenberg, J *Women Coping with AIDS: We Take It as It Is* (Amsterdam, Royal Tropical Institute, 1998).

Varga, C 'Links Between Sexual Dynamics and Reproductive Health Behaviour Among Kwazulu/Natal Youth' (1999) *Women's Health News* 21.

Vaughan, M 'Vampires in Malawi' *London Review of Books* (London, 20 March 2003) 34.

Verkaik, R 'A Lesson in Racism' *Independent* (London, 17 May 2004), available at: http://news.independent.co.uk/uk/legal/story.jsp?story=522155; also at http://www.africaspeaks.com/weblog/archives/00000201.htm.

Vetten, L 'Research into Preventing Intimate Femicide in the Gauteng Province' (2003) 45 *Women's Health Project Review* 14.

Victoria Falls Declaration of Principles for Promoting the Human Rights of Women as Agreed by Senior Judges at the African Regional Judicial Colloquium Zimbabwe, 19–20 August 1994 in A Byrnes *et al* (eds) *Advancing the Human Rights of Women: Using International Human Rights Standards in Domestic Litigation* (London, Commonwealth Secretariat, 1994) 3.

Viljoen, F 'The African Commission on Human and Peoples' Rights: Introduction to the African Commission and the Regional Human Rights System' in C Heyns (ed) *Human Rights Law in Africa* (The Hague, Martinus Nijhoff, 2004) vol 1 385.

Visvanathan, N 'Introduction to Part 1' in N Visvanathan, L Duggan, N Nisonoff and N Wiegersmal (eds) *The Women, Gender and Development Reader* (London, Zed Books, 1997) 17.

Visvanathan, N, Duggan, L, Nisonoff, N and Wiegersmal N (eds) *The Women, Gender and Development Reader* (London, Zed Books, 1997).

W

Wabwile, W 'Child Support Rights in Kenya and in the United Nations Convention on the Rights of the Child 1989' in A Bainham (ed) *International Survey of Family Law* (Bristol, Jordan Publishing, 2001) 267.

Wagman, J 'Domestic Violence in Rakai Community, Uganda' (2003) 45 *Women's Health News* 7.

Walker, A *Possessing the Secret of Joy* (New York, Pocket Books, 1992).

Walker, B 'Christianity, Development and Women's Liberation' in C Sweetman (ed) *Gender, Religion and* Spirituality (Oxford, OXFAM, 1998) 15.

Walker, C 'Women, Tradition and Reconstruction' (1994) *Review of African Political Economy* 347.

Walker, C *Women and Resistance in South Africa* (London, Onyx Press, 1982).

Wanjiala, J 'Can the Law Stop Female Circumcision?' (paper presented at the Afro-Arab Consultation on Legal Tools for the Prevention of Female Genital Mutilation, Cairo, 21–23 June 2003).

Wanitzek, U 'The Power of Language in the Discourse on Women's Rights: Some Examples from Tanzania' (2002) 49 *Africa Today* 3.

Wanyeki, L (ed) *Women and Land in Africa: Culture, Religion and Realizing Women's Rights* (London, Zed Press, 2002).

Wanzala, W 'Towards an Epistemological and Methodological Framework of Development' in P McFadden (ed) *Southern Africa in Transition: A Gendered Perspective* (Harare, SAPES, 1998) 1.

Warioba, C 'Mission Report on Draft Protocol to the African Charter on The Human and Peoples' Rights on the Rights of Women in Africa' Held in Bamako, Mali, 12–16 February 2001 (unpublished—on file with the author).

Warnock, M *Making Babies: Is There a Right to Have Children?* (Oxford, Oxford University Press, 2002).

Watkins, K *The OXFAM Poverty Report* (Oxford, OXFAM, 1995).

Watkins, K *The OXFAM Education Report* (Oxford, OXFAM, 2000).

Watts, C, Osman, O and Win, E (eds) *The Private is Public: A Study of Violence against Women in Southern Africa* (Harare, WILDAF, 1995).

Weitzman, L 'Marital Property: Its Transformation and Division in the United States' in L Weitzman and M Maclean (eds) *Economic Consequences of Divorce: The International Perspective* (Oxford, Clarendon Press, 1992) 85.

Weitzman, L and Maclean, M (eds) *Economic Consequences of Divorce: The International Perspective* (Oxford, Clarendon Press, 1992).

Welch, C *Protecting Human Rights in Africa: Roles and Strategies of Non-Governmental Organizations* (Philadelphia, University of Pennsylvania Press, 1995).

Welchman, L (ed) *Women's Rights & Islamic Family Law* (London, Zed Press, 2004).

Welchman, L 'Introduction' in L Welchman (ed) *Women's Rights & Islamic Family Law* (London, Zed Press, 2004) 1.

Welchman, L 'Egypt: New Deal on Divorce' in A Bainham (ed) *International Survey of Family Law 2004* (Bristol, Jordan Publishing, 2004) 123.

Wengi, J (ed) *The Law of Succession in Uganda: Women, Inheritance Laws and Practices* (Kampala, Women and Law in East Africa, 1994).

Whitehead, A and Tsikata, D 'Policy Discourses on Women's Land Rights in Sub-Saharan Africa: The Implications of the Re-turn to the Customary' (2003) 3 *Journal of Agrarian Change* 67.

WHO *see* World Health Organization.

Wijeyesekera, D 'NCSM and Health: A Connection Ignored' in CHANGE (ed) *Non Consensual Sex in Marriage* (London, CHANGE, 2002).

WILDAF Maputo Declaration on Mainstreaming and the Effective Participation of Women in the African Union, 24 June 2003, available at http://www.wildaf-ao.org.

WILDAF 'The African Charter on Human and Peoples' Rights and the Additional Protocol on Women's Rights' (1999) *WILDAF News* 18.

WILDAF 'Who is the Special Rapporteur on the Rights of Women?' (1999) *WILDAF News* 5.

Williams, P *The Alchemy of Race and Rights* (Cambridge, Harvard University Press, 1991).

WLSA *Standing at the Cross-Roads: WLSA and the Rights Dilemma Which Way to Go?* (Harare, WLSA, 1998).

WLSA *A Critical Analysis of Women's Access to Land in the WLSA Countries* (Harare, WLSA, 2001).

WLSA *Lobolo: Its Implications for Women's Reproductive Rights* (Harare, WLSA, 2002).

WLSA, Botswana *Chasing the Mirage: Women and the Administration of Justice* (Gaberone, WLSA, 1999).

WLSA Lesotho *In Search of Justice: Where do Women in Lesotho Go?* (Lesotho, WLSA, 2000).

WLSA Swaziland *Charting the Maze: Women in Pursuit of Justice in Swaziland* (Mbabane, WLSA, 2000).

WLSA Zambia *Inheritance in Zambia: Law and Practice* (Lusaka, WLSA, 1994).

WLSA Zimbabwe *Pregnancy and Childbirth: Joy or Despair?* (Harare, WLSA, 2001).

Wolf, S 'Culture, Family Law and Women's Rights: Blaming Culture for the Failure to Uphold the Rights of Women' (Essay for the MA in International and Comparative Legal Studies, Department of Law, School of Oriental and African Studies, 2002; on file with the departmental office).

Wolfensohn, J 'Foreword' in World Bank *Engendering Development through Gender Equality in Rights, Resources and Voice* (Washington DC, World Bank, 2001) xi.

Womankind Worldwide *What Works Where? Successful Strategies to End Violence against Women* (London, Womankind Worldwide, 2002).

Women's Health Project 'Schools Kick Out Pregnant Adolescents' (2001) 39 *Women's Health Project Review* 14.

Women's Health Project 'On the Carte Blanche Expose' (2002) 42 *Women's Health Project Review* 5.

Women's Health Project 'Women are More at Risk of HIV Infection' (2003) 45 *Women's Health Review* 13.

Women's Rights Project in Women, Law and Development International and Human Rights Watch Women's Rights Project *Women's Human Rights Step by Step* (Washington DC, Women, Law and Development International, 1997).

Woodman, G 'Ghana Reforms the Law of Intestate Succession' (1985) *Journal of African Law* 118.

Woodman, G 'Family Law in Ghana under the Constitution 1992' in A Bainham (ed) *International Survey of Family Law 2003* (Bristol, Jordan Publishing, 2003) 195.

Woolf, M '60% Believe Billions Spent on War Should Have Gone to the Poor' *Independent* (London, 8 June 2004).

World Bank *Sub-Saharan Africa: From Crisis to Sustainable Growth: A Long Term Perspective Study* (Washington DC, World Bank, 1989).

World Bank *Assessing Aid: What Works, What Doesn't and Why* (Washington DC, The World Bank, 1998).

World Bank *Engendering Development through Gender Equality in Rights, Resources and Voice* (Washington DC, World Bank, 2001).

World Bank *Education and HIV/AIDS: A Window of Hope* (Washington DC, World Bank, 2002).

World Bank *2003 World Bank Atlas* (Washington DC, World Bank, 2003).

World Bank *Land Policies for Growth and Poverty Reduction* (Washington DC, World Bank, 2003).

World Bank *MENA Development Report: Gender and Development in the Middle East and North Africa* (Washington DC, World Bank, 2004).

World Health Organization (WHO) *Guidelines to Reporting under CEDAW* (Geneva, WHO, 1998).

World Health Organization (WHO) *Female Genital Mutilation Programmes: What Works and What Doesn't. A Review* WHO/CHS/WMH/99.5.

World Health Organization (WHO) '25 Questions and Answers on Health and Human Rights' (2002) 1 *Health and Human Rights Publication Series* 1.

World Health Organization (WHO) *World Report on Violence and Health* (Geneva, WHO, 2002).

World Vision *Every Girl Counts: Development Justice and Gender* (Milton Keynes, World Vision, 2001).

World Vision 'Mobilise Churches in Fight against AIDS Says World Vision Presenter at Barcelona AIDS Conference' 6 July 2002 downloaded from: http://www.worldvision.org/worldvision/pr/nsf/stable/pr_barcelona_presenter.

World Vision *Female Genital Mutilation and Early Marriage in Africa*, (Milton Keynes, World Vision 2002).

Z

Zamboni, M '*Rechtsstaat*: Just What is Being Exported by Swedish Development Assistance Organisations?' (2001) 2 *Law, Social Justice and Global Development* at http://elj.warwick.ac.uk/global/issue/2001-2/zamboni.html.

Zimbabwe Women Resource Centre and Network (ZWRCN) and SARDC-WIDSAA *Beyond Inequalities: Women in Zimbabwe* (Harare, SARDC, 1998).

Zulu, L 'Institutionalizing Changes: South African Women's Participation in the Transition to Democracy' in S Rai (ed) *International Perspectives on Gender and Democratization* (New York, Macmillan, 2000) 166.

Zulu, B 'First the Media, Now the NGOs' *Mail and Guardian* (Johannesburg, 11 October 2002) downloaded from http://www.zwnews.com/issueful.cfm?ArticleID=5308.

Zurayak, H 'The Meaning of Reproductive Health for Developing Countries: The Case of the Middle East' in C Sweetman (ed) *Gender, Development and Health* (Oxford, OXFAM, 2001) 22.

ZWNews 'Comment' (9 September 2002) downloaded from http://www/zwnews.com/issuefull.cfm?ArticleID=5116.

DOCUMENTS FROM INTERNATIONAL BODIES

AFRICA

OAU

OAU Protocols / OAU Conventions

OAU Convention Governing the Specific Aspects of Refugee Problems in Africa 1969 AHSG,CAB/LEG/24.3.

African Charter on Human and Peoples' Rights (26 June 1981) OAU Doc CAB/LEG/67/ 3 REV. 5 reprinted in (1982) 21 *International Legal Materials* 59 (African Charter).

African Charter on the Rights and Welfare of the Child 1990 (ACRWC) available from www.africa-union.org.

Protocol to the African Charter on Human and Peoples' Rights on the Establishment of an African Court on Human Rights 1998 OAU/LEG/AFCHPR/PROT (III), adopted by the Assembly of Heads of State and Government, 34th Session, Burkina Faso, 8–10 June 1998.

Protocol to the African Charter on Human and Peoples' Rights on the Rights of Women in Africa 2003. Assembly/AU/Dec.14 (II), Draft Decision on the Draft.

Protocol to the African Charter on Human and Peoples' Rights Relating to the Rights of Women (African Protocol on Women's Rights 2003).

Other OAU documents

OAU Cultural Charter for Africa 1976 available at www.africa-union.org.

Resolution of the OAU Assembly of Heads of State and Government, 31st Ordinary Session, Addis Ababa, June 1995, AHG/Res.240(XXXI).

Draft Terms of Reference for the Special Rapporteur on the Rights of Women in Africa DOC/OS/34c (XXIII) Annex 11, 1996.

Grand Bay (Mauritius) Declaration and Plan of Action (12–16 April 1999) Grand Bay, Mauritius, CONF/HRA/DECL.(I) (1).

Draft Protocol to the African Charter on Human and Peoples' Rights on the Rights of Women DOC/OS/34c (XXIII).

Draft Protocol to the African Charter on Human and Peoples' Rights on the Rights of Women in Africa (Kigali, 15 November 1999) DOC/OS (XXVII)/159b (Kigali Draft).

Drafting Process of the Draft Protocol on Human and Peoples' Rights on the Rights of Women in Africa (Item 8(e)) DOC/OS/ (XXVII)/159b.

Draft Protocol to the African Charter on Human and Peoples' Rights on the Rights of African Women in Africa (13 September 2000). CAB/LEG/66.6

Draft Protocol to the African Charter on Human and Peoples' Rights on the Rights of Women in Africa (as adopted by the Meeting of Government Experts in Addis Ababa on 16 November 2001) 22 November 2001 CAB/LEG/66/6/Rev.1.

Draft Protocol to the African Charter on Human and Peoples' Rights on the Rights of Women in Africa (as adopted by the Meeting of Ministers, Addis Ababa, Ethiopia on 28 March 2003) MIN/WOM.RTS/DRAFT.PROT.(II)Rev.5.

OAU correspondence

Professor **V Dankwa**, Chairman of the African Commission to Dr S Salim, Secretary General of the OAU, 15 November 1999 ACHPR/OS/26.

Professor **T Maluwa**, OAU Legal Counsel to Professor Dankwa, Chairman of the African Commission on Human and Peoples' Rights, 7 March 2000, CAB/LEG/72.20/27/Vol II.

Suggestions of the Women's Unit to Improve the Existing Text of the Draft Protocol as Presented to the OAU. Attachment to letter from Professor **T Maluwa**, OAU Legal Counsel to Professor Dankwa 7 March 2000, CAB/LEG/72.20/27/Vol II.

Prof **L Johnson**, Director, Education, Science, Culture and Social Affairs Department, to Professor V Dankwa, Chairman of the African Commission, 25 February 2000, File No ES/WU/RW/51.00

African Union (AU)

Constitutive Act of the African Union 2000, available at http://www.african,union.org.

AU declarations/initiatives

Durban Declaration on Mainstreaming Gender and Women's Effective Participation in the African Union, 2002 at www.africa-union.org

The First AU Ministerial Conference on Human Rights in Africa 8 May 2003, Kigali, Rwanda, Kigali Declaration MIN/CONF/HRA/Decl.1 (I).

Assembly of Heads of State and Government, Third Ordinary Session, 6–8 July 2004, Addis Ababa, Solemn Declaration on Gender Equality in Africa Assembly/AU/Decl.12 (III) Rev.1.

Sub-regional bodies

Arab states

Cairo Declaration on Human Rights in Islam (5 August 1990) UN GAOR, World Conf on Hum Rts, 4th Sess, Agenda Item 5, UN Doc A/CONF.157/PC/62/Add.18 (1993) (English translation).

League of Arab States Charter on the Rights of the Arab Child 1990 in G Alfredson, and K Tomaseveksi *Thematic Guide to Documents on the Human Rights of Women* (The Hague, Martinus Nijhoff, 1995).

Arab Charter on Human Right 1994 reprinted in (1997) 18 *Human Rights Law Journal* 151, also available from: http://www1.umn.edu/humanrts/instree/arabhrcharter.html.

EAC (East African Community)

Treaty Establishing the East African Community 1999, reproduced in part in Heyns, C (ed) *Human Rights Law in Africa* (The Hague, Martinus Nijhoff, 2004) vol 1 634.

ECOWAS

Treaty of the Economic Community of West African States (ECOWAS) (Revised) 1993, at http:www.ecowas.int.

ECOWAS Declaration A/DC/12/12/01 on the Fight against Trafficking in Persons, Twenty-
Fifth Ordinary Session of Authority of Heads of State and Government Dakar, 20–21
December 2001, available from www.ecowas.int.

SADC (Southern African Development Community)

Treaty of the Southern African Development Community (SADC), 17 July 1992, available
from: http://www.iss.co.za/AF/RegOrg/unity_to_union/pdfs/sadc/8SADC_Treaty.pdf.
Gender and Development: A Declaration by Heads of State or Government of the Southern
African Development Community (SADC), 1997 *SADC Gender Monitor* (1999).
The Prevention and Eradication of Violence against Women and Children, An Addendum to
the 1997 Declaration on Gender and Development by SADC Heads of State or Government
1998 *SADC Gender Monitor* (1999) (cited as SADC Addendum on Violence 1998).

UEMOA

UEMOA Annexe à la Recommendation No 03/99/CM/UEMOA—Plan d'action communautaire pour le renforcement du rôle de la femme dans l'UEMOA available from
http:www.izf.net/izf/Documentation/JournalOfficiel/AfriqueOuest/dec99/annex1_REC
_03_99.htm.
Recommendation No 03/00/CM/UEMOA Relative à la mise en oeuvre d'actions communes en matière de promotion et de renforcement du rôle de la femme dans l'UEMOA,
Dakar, 21 December 1999, available from http://www.izf.net/isf/Documentation/
JournalOfficiel/AfriqueOuest/dec99/REC_03_99.htm.

Commonwealth States

Victoria Falls Declaration of Principles for Promoting the Human Rights of Women as
Agreed by Senior Judges at the African Regional Judicial Colloquium Zimbabwe, 19–20
August 1994 in A Byrnes *et al* (eds) *Advancing the Human Rights of Women: Using
International Human Rights Standards in Domestic Litigation* (London, Commonwealth
Secretariat, 1994) 3.

EUROPE

European Convention on Human Rights 1950, 213 UNTS 221.
Protocol 12 to the Convention for the Protection of Human Rights and Fundamental
Freedoms, Rome, 4.XI.2000, European Treaty Series—No 177.
European Parliament Resolution on Female Genital Mutilation 2001/2035 (INI) A5-285/2001.
Cotonou Agreement between the European Union and the African, Caribbean and Pacific
Group of States Reproduced in C Heyns (ed) (2004) vol 1 721.

OAS (ORGANIZATION OF AMERICAN STATES)

American Convention on Human Rights 1969, 1114 UNTS 123.
OAS Convention on the Prevention, Punishment and Eradication of Violence against
Women 1994 reproduced in (1994) 33 *International Legal Materials* 1535.

UNITED NATIONS

International human rights instruments

Universal Declaration of Human Rights adopted by the UN General Assembly Resolution 217A (III) of 10 December 1948 (UDHR).

Convention Relating to the Status of Refugees, 28 July 1951, 189 UNTS 150.

Convention on the Political Rights of Women 1952 193 UNTS 135.

UN Supplementary Convention on the Abolition of Slavery, the Slave Trade, and Institutions and Practices Similar to Slavery 1956. Adopted by ECOSOC Resolution 608 (XXI) of 30 April 1956.

Convention on the Nationality of Married Women 1957 309 UNTS 65.

Convention on Consent to Marriage, Minimum Age of Marriage and Registration of Marriage. Opened for Signature and Ratification by General Assembly Resolution 1763A (XVIII) of 7 November 1962.

General Assembly Resolution Adopting the Recommendation on Consent to Marriage, Minimum Age for Marriage and Registration of Marriages A/RES/2018 (XX), 1 November 1965, Principle II.

International Covenant on Civil and Political Rights. Adopted by General Assembly Resolution 2200A (XXI) of 16 December 1966. Entered into force 23 March 1976.

International Covenant on Economic, Social and Cultural Rights. Adopted by General Assembly Resolution 2200A (XXI) of 16 December 1966.

Optional Protocol to the International Covenant on Civil and Political Rights, 999 UNTS 171, reprinted in (1967) 6 *International Legal Materials* 383 (ICCPR).

Convention on the Rights of the Child. Adopted by General Assembly Resolution 44/25 of 20 November 1989. Entered into force 2 September 1990 (CRC).

General Assembly Resolution Adopting the Declaration on the Elimination of All Forms of Discrimination against Women (7 November 1967) A/RES/2263 (XXII) (DEDAW).

Vienna Convention on the Law of Treaties 1969. 1155.UNTS 331.

Convention on the Elimination of All Forms of Discrimination against Women 1979 124a UNTS 13 (CEDAW).

United Nations Declaration on the Elimination of All Forms of Intolerance and Discrimination Based on Religion or Belief, UN GA Res. 36/55 adopted 25 January 1981.

Convention against Torture and Other Cruel, Inhuman or Degrading Treatment or Punishment, 10 December 1984, 1465 UNTS 85.

General Assembly Declaration on the Right to Development adopted by GA Res.41/128, 4 December 1986.

General Assembly Declaration on the Elimination of All Forms of Violence against Women, (20 December 1993) GA Res. 48/104 (DEVAW).

Rome Statute of the International Criminal Court 1998 UN Doc CONF.183/9.

Declaration on the Right and Responsibility of Individuals, Groups and Organs of Society to Promote and Protect Universally Recognized Human Rights and Fundamental Freedoms. GA Res. 53/144 adopted 9 December 1998.

Optional Protocol to the Convention on the Elimination of All Forms of Discrimination against Women, adopted and opened for signature, ratification and accession by GA Res.

54/4, 6 October 1999 / Optional Protocol to CEDAW, Adopted by General Assembly Resolution A/54/4 on 6 October 1999.

Optional Protocol to the Convention on the Rights of the Child on the Sale of Children, Child Prostitution and Child Pornography. A/RES/54/263 of 25 May 2000.

Protocol to Prevent, Suppress and Punish Trafficking in Persons, Especially Women and Children, Supplementing the United Nations Convention against Transnational Organized Crime 2000, Adopted by UN General Assembly Resolution A/55/25 of 15 November 2000 (Palermo Protocol) available at http://www1.umn.edu/humanrts/ instree/trafficking.html.

ILO Convention No 182 Concerning the Prohibition and Immediate Action for the Elimination of the Worst Forms of Child Labour, Geneva, 17 June 1999 reprinted in (1999) 38 *International Legal Materials* 1207.

UN conferences

Resolution IX Adopted by the International Conference on Human Rights in Teheran on Measures to Promote Women's Rights in the Modern World and Endorsing the Secretary-General's Proposal for a Unified Long Term United Nations Programme for the Advancement of Women A/CONF.32/41, 12 May 1968.

Report of the World Conference to Review and Appraise the Achievements of the United Nations Decade for Women: Equality, Development and Peace, held in Nairobi from 15 to 26 July 1985; including the Agenda of the Nairobi Forward-Looking Strategies for the Advancement of Women (1986) A/CONF.116/28/Rev.1.

United Nations World Conference on Human Rights: Vienna Declaration and Programme of Action reproduced in (1993) 32 *International Legal Materials* 1661.

International Conference on Population and Development, Cairo (18 October 1994) UN Doc A/CONF. 171/13.

Beijing Declaration and Platform for Action (15 September 1995) reproduced in (1996) 35 *International Legal Materials* 404.

World Summit on Sustainable Development Plan of Implementation 2002, para.6(d). See also Copenhagen Declaration on Social Development, Adopted by the World Summit for Social Development, Held in Copenhagen from 6 to 12 March 1995 A/CONF.166/9, 1995.

United Nations Millennium Declaration (8 September 2000) GA Res.55/2 also available at: http://www.developmentgoals.org.

UN 'Report of the World Conference against Racism, Racial Discrimination and Related Intolerance' (2001) UN Doc A/CONF.189/12.

Johannesburg Declaration on Sustainable Development 2002 downloaded from www.johannesburgsummit.org.

Other UN documents/reports

Report by the Working Group on Traditional Practices Affecting the Health of Women and Children UN Doc E/CN 1986/42.

Limburg Principles on the Implementation of the International Covenant on Economic, Social and Cultural Rights UN Doc E/CN.4/1987/17.

Report of the UN Seminar on Traditional Practices Affecting the Health of Women and Children UN Doc E/CN.4/Sub.2/1991/48.

Report of the Second Regional Seminar on Traditional Practices Affecting the Health of Women and Children UN Doc E/CN.4/Sub.2/1994/10.

Report of the Fifth Meeting of Persons Chairing the Human Rights Treaty Bodies—Recommendations UN. Doc A/49/537 (1994).

Executive Summary of the 1994 World Survey on the Role of Women in Development (extract) ST/ESA/241, 1995 reproduced as Document No 109 in United Nations *The United Nations and the Advancement of Women 1945–1996* (New York, United Nations, 1996) 481.

Report of the Secretary General on Traditional or Customary Practices Affecting the Health of Women Fifty Third Session (10 Sept 1998) UN Doc A/53/354.

Report of the Secretary General on the Question of Integrating the Human Rights of Women throughout the United Nations System (25 March 1998) E/CN.4/1998/49.

Trends Regarding the Integration of a Gender Perspective into the Work of the United Nations Human Rights Treaty Bodies, report by the Secretary-General, submitted to the 10th Meeting of Persons Chairing Human Rights Treaty Bodies (3 September 1998).UN Doc HRI/MC/1998/6.

Report by the Independent Expert on Structural Adjustment, Mr Fantu Cheru, Effects of Structural Adjustment Policies on the Full Enjoyment of Human Rights (24 February 1999)UN Doc E/CN.4/1999/50.

UN General Assembly Report of the Ad Hoc Committee of the Whole of the Twenty First Session of the General Assembly Key Actions for the Further Implementation of the Programme of Action of the International Conference on Population and Development (1 July 1999) UN Doc A/S-21/5/Add.1.

Secretary General, United Nations Improvement of the Situation of Women in Rural Areas (7 June 1999) UN Doc GA54/123.

UN General Assembly Report of the Ad Hoc Committee of the Whole of the Twenty-Third Special Session of the General Assembly. Further actions and initiatives to implement the Beijing Declaration and Platform for Action UN Doc A Res/S–23/3 [cited as Beijing + 5 Outcome Document (2000)].

UN Division for the Advancement of Women, Office of the High Commissioner for Human Rights and United Nations Development Fund for Women *Report of the Expert Group Meeting, Gender and Racial Discrimination* (Croatia 2000), available at http://www.un.org/womenwatch/daw/csw/genrac/report.htm.

Declaration of Commitment of the UN General Assembly Special Session on HIV/AIDS (June 2001) UN Doc A/RES/S-26/2 [reproduced in Human Rights Watch (2003) Uganda Report at 73–75].

Report of the Secretary General on Traditional or Customary Practices Affecting the Health of Women and Girls (18 July 2003) UNGA A/58/169.

Eighth Report on the Situation Regarding the Elimination of Traditional Practices Affecting the Health of Women and Girls, Proposed by Ms Halima Embarek-Warzazi E/CN.4/Sub.2/2004/41.

ECOSOC Specific Human Rights Issues: Note by the Secretary-General (22 June 2004) E/CN.4/Sub.2/2004/33 (22 June 2004).

Specific Human Rights Issues Reservations to Human Rights Treaties Final Working Paper Submitted by Françoise Hampson (19 July 2004) 4 E/CN.4/Sub.2/2004/42.

UN Committees General Comments

CRC (Committee on the Rights of the Child)

Committee on the Rights of the Child General Comment No 3 HIV/AIDS and the Rights of the Child CRC/GC/2003/1.

Committee on the Rights of the Child General Comment No 4 on Adolescent Health and Development CRC/GC/2003/5.

CERD (Committee on the Elimination of Racial Discrimination)

CERD General Comment No 14 on Definition of Discrimination HRI/GEN/1Rev.3.

CERD General Comment No 25 on Gender Related Dimensions of Racial Discrimination (20 March 2000) UN Doc A/55/18.

CESCR (Committee on Economic Social and Cultural Rights)

CESCR General Comment No 2 International Technical Assistance, (article 22) 1990UN Doc EC/1990/23.

CESCR General Comment 3: The Nature of States Parties' Obligations (article 2(1) of the Covenant), (Fifth Session, 1990) UN DOC E/1991/23. Annex III.

CESCR General Comment No 4 on the Right to Housing UN Doc E/1992/23.

CESCR,General Comment No 5 on Persons with Disabilities (11th Session, 1994) (26 April 2001) UN Doc HRI/GEN/1/Rev.5.

General Comment 6 on the Economic, Social and Cultural Rights of Older Persons, (13th Session, 1995) (26 April 2001) UN Doc HRI.GEN/1/Rev.5.

CESCR General Comment No 14 (2000) on The Right to the Highest Attainable Standard of Health (Article 12 of the ICESCR) (11 August 2000) E/C12/2000/4.

CESCR *Substantive Issues Arising in the Implementation of the International Covenant on Economic, Social and Cultural Rights: Poverty and the International Covenant on Economic, Social and Cultural Right*s UN DocE/C/12/2001/10.

Human Rights Committee

Human Rights Committee General Comment No 17 on the Rights of the Child HRI/GEN/1/REV.7

Human Rights Committee General Comment No 18 On Non-Discrimination (21 November 1989) CCPR/C/21/Rev.1.Add.1.

Human Rights Committee General Comment No 19 on Protection of the Family, the Right to Marriage and Equality of the Spouses (Article 23) 27/07/90 (Thirty-ninth session 1990) HRI/GEN/1/Rev.7.

Human Rights Committee General Comment No 24 on Issues Relating to Reservations Made upon Ratification or Accession to the Covenant or the Optional Protocols Thereto, or in Relation to Declarations under Article 41 of the Covenant (2 Nov 1994) CCPR/C/21/Rev.1/Add 6.

Human Right Committee General Comment No 28 on Equality of Rights between Men and Women (article 3) (29/03/2000) CCPR/C/21/Rev.1Add.10, CCPR General Comment 28.

CEDAW General Comments

General Recommendation No 4, On Reservations, UN Doc A/42/38.

CEDAW General Recommendation No 5 (Seventh Session, 1988) Temporary Special Measures UN Doc A/43/38.

CEDAW General Recommendation No 12 on Violence against Women UN Doc A/44/38.

CEDAW (1990) General Recommendation No 14 (Ninth Session, 1990) On Female Circumcision UN Doc A/45/38.

CEDAW General Recommendation No 16 (Tenth Session, 1991) on Unpaid Women Workers in Rural and Urban Family Enterprises UN Doc A/46/38.

CEDAW General Recommendation No 17 (Tenth Session, 1991) on Measurement and Quantification of the Unremunerated Domestic Activities of Women and Their Recognition in the Gross National Product UN Doc A/44.38.

CEDAW General Recommendation No 18 (1991) on Disabled Women UN Doc A/46/38.

CEDAW General Recommendation No 19 on Violence against Women UN Doc A/47/38.

General Recommendation No 20, Reservations to the Convention, UN Doc A/47/38.

CEDAW General Recommendation No 21 Equality in Marriage and Family Relations UN Doc A/49/38.

CEDAW General Recommendation No 23 Women in Public Life UN Doc A/52/38/Rev.1.

CEDAW General Recommendation No 24 on Health UN Doc A/54/38/Rev. 1.

CEDAW General Recommendation No 25 Temporary Special Measures CEDAW/C/2004/WP.1/Rev.1.

CEDAW 'Statement on Reservations to the Convention on the Elimination of All Forms of Discrimination against Women Adopted by the Committee on the Elimination of Discrimination against Women' reproduced in UN, IWRAW, Commonwealth *Assessing the Status of Women: A Guide to Reporting under the Convention on the Elimination of all Forms of Discrimination against Women* (London, Commonwealth Secretariat, 2000) 90.

CEDAW State Reports

CEDAW List of Issues and Questions with Regard to the Consideration of State Reports: CEDAW/PSWG/2004/I/CRP.1/Add.2.

Initial Report of States Party: **Algeria (1998)** CEDAW/C/DZA/1 (Government of Algeria).

Combined Second and Third Periodic Reports of States Parties: **Burkina Faso (1998)** CEDAW/C/BFA//2–3 (Government of Burkina Faso).

Combined Fourth and Fifth Periodic Report of States Parties: **Egypt (2000)** CEDAW/C/EGY4–5 (Government of Egypt).

Combined Fourth and Fifth Periodic Reports of States Parties: **Ethiopia (2002)** CEDAW/C/ETH/4–5 (Government of Ethiopia).

Combined Second, Third, Fourth and Fifth Periodic Reports of States Parties: **Gabon** CEDAW/C/GAB/2–5.

Second Periodic Report of States Parties: **Morocco** CEDAW/C/MOR/2.

Initial Report of States Parties: **Namibia (1997)** CEDAW/C/Nam/1 (Government of Namibia.

Combined Second and Third Periodic Reports of States Parties: **Nigeria (1997)** CEDAW/C/NGA/2–3 (Government of Nigeria).

Combined Fourth and Fifth Periodic Report to CEDAW: **Nigeria (2003)** CEDAW/C/ NGA/4–5 (Government of Nigeria).
Initial Report of States Parties: **South Africa (1998)** CEDAW/C/ZAF/1.
Second and Third Periodic Reports of States Parties: United Republic of **Tanzania (1996)** CEDAW/C/TZA/2–3 (Government of Tanzania).
Combined Second and Third Report of States Parties: **Tunisia (2000)** CEDAW/C/TUN 3–4 (Government of Tunisia).
Third Periodic Report of States Parties: **Uganda (2000)** CEDAW/C/UGA/3 (Government of Uganda).

CEDAW Concluding Observations

CEDAW Concluding Observations to the initial report of **Algeria** (see CEDAW W/C/SR.406, 407 and 412) (1999).
CEDAW Concluding Observations to the Initial Report of **Equatorial Guinea** CEDAW A/44/38 (1989).
CEDAW Concluding Comments **Ethiopia** CEDAW A/51/38 (1996) downloaded from http://www.bayefsky.com./html/ethiopia_t4_cedaw.php.
CEDAW Concluding Comments **Ethiopia** CEDAW/C/SR.646 and 647 also cited as CEDAW A/59/38 (Part 1) paras 226–73 (2004).
CEDAW Concluding Comments to the Initial Report of **Namibia** CEDAW A/52/38/Rev.1 (Part II).
CEDAW Concluding Comments **Nigeria** CEDAW/C/2004/1/CRP.3/Add.2/Rev.1 also cited as CEDAW Concluding Observations on the **Nigerian** Report, CEDAW A/59/38 part I (2004).
CEDAW Concluding Observations to the Third and Fourth Periodic Report of **Tunisia** CEDAW/C/SR 567 and 568.

CRC Concluding Observations

Concluding Observations of the Committee on the Rights of the Child: Ethiopia (21 February 2001) CRC/C/15/Add.144.

UN Press Releases

'CEDAW Concludes Consideration of **Morocco**'s Report' (20 January 1997) UN Press Release, WOM/937 at http://www.un.org/News/Press/docs/1997/19970120.wom937.html.
UN/CEDAW 'Need to Modify Cultural Practices Harmful to Women in Democratic Republic of Congo Stressed by Discrimination Committee Experts' UN Press Release WOM/1164, downloaded from http://www.un.org/News/Press/docs.2000/200001225. wom1164.doc.html.
UNDP '2003 Human Development Index Reveals Development Crisis and Human Development Report 2003 Charts Decade-Long Income Drop in 54 Countries' press releases from http://www.undp/hdr2003.
UNDP 'Cultural Liberty Essential for Human Development Argues 2004 Report' Press Release, Brussels, 15 July 2004, downloaded from www.undp.org.
General Assembly Meetings Coverage 'Women's Anti-Discrimination Committee Considers Report of **Algeria**. Committee Members Call for Further Action by Government to Achieve Gender Equality' Press Release WOM/1475.

General Assembly Meetings Coverage 'Women's Anti-Discrimination Committee Considers Situation of Women in **Gabon.**' Press Release WOM/1476.

UN Reports by Special Rapporteurs

Special Rapporteur on the Right to Education, Katarina Tomasevski (9 January 2001) E/CN.4/2001/52.

Special Rapporteur on Harmful Traditional Practices Affecting the Health of Women and Children Eighth Report on the Situation Regarding the Elimination of Traditional Practices Affecting the Health of Women and Girls, Proposed by Ms Halima Embarek-Warzazi E/CN.4/Sub.2/2004/41.

Special Rapporteur on the Sale of Children, Child Prostitution and Child Pornography (4 February 2002) E/CN.4/2002/88.

Special Rapporteur on Torture Kooijmans, P. Torture and Other Cruel, Inhuman or Degrading Treatment or Punishment E/CN.4/1986/15.

Special Rapporteur on Violence against Women, Preliminary Report Submitted by the Special Rapporteur on Violence Against Women, Its Causes and Consequences in Accordance with Commission on Human Rights Resolution 1994/45, E/CN.4/1995/42, 22 November 1994.

Special Rapporteur on Violence against Women, Its Causes and Consequences, Ms Radhika Coomaraswamy Submitted in Accordance with Commission on Human Rights Resolution 1995/85 (5 February 1996) E/CN.4/1996/53.

Special Rapporteur on Violence against Women Integrating the Human Rights of Women and the Gender Perspective: Violence against Women in the Family (10 March 1999) E/CN.4/1999/68.

Special Rapporteur on Violence against Women, Policies and Practices that Impact Women's Reproductive Rights and Contribute to, Cause or Constitute Violence against Women (21 January 1999) E/CN.4/1999/68.Add.4.

INDEX

Printed in the United Kingdom
by Lightning Source UK Ltd.
123150UK00002B/49/A